Everyman, I will go with thee,
and be thy guide

Percy Bysshe Shelley

POEMS AND PROSE

Edited by
TIMOTHY WEBB
University of Bristol

Critical selection by
GEORGE E. DONALDSON
University of Bristol

EVERYMAN
J. M. DENT · LONDON
CHARLES E. TUTTLE
VERMONT

Selected Poems of Shelley first published in Everyman in 1977
This edition first published in Everyman in 1995

J. M. Dent
Orion Publishing Group
Orion House
5 Upper St Martin's Lane
London WC2H 9EA
and
Charles E. Tuttle Co. Inc.
28 South Main Street
Rutland, Vermont 05701, USA

Typeset in Sabon by CentraCet Limited, Cambridge
Printed in Great Britain by
The Guernsey Press Co. Ltd, Guernsey, C. I.

British Library Cataloguing-in-Publication Data
is available upon request.

ISBN 0 460 87449 7

CONTENTS

NOTE ON THE EDITOR

PERCY BYSSHE SHELLEY – see Chronology of Shelley's Life and Times pp. xi–xiv.

TIMOTHY WEBB is Professor and Head of the Department of English at the University of Bristol. His books include *The Violet in the Crucible: Shelley and Translation* (1976), *Shelley: A Voice Not Understood* (1977), *English Romantic Hellenism* (1982), *Shelley* (with David Pirie, 1984) and *Shelley's 'Devils' Notebook* (with P. M. S. Dawson, 1993). He has recently completed an edition of Leigh Hunt's *Autobiography* and he is working on an edition of Shelley's prose, on a collaborative volume entitled *The Romantic Defence of Poetry*, on travel in the Romantic period, on Ireland and the English Romantics, and on Anglo-Irish literature. He is the General Editor of the Penguin Yeats and has edited a selection of Yeats for the Penguin Poetry Library. For fourteen years he was editor of the *Keats-Shelley Review* and is now one of the founding editors of *Romanticism*.

CHRONOLOGY OF SHELLEY'S LIFE
AND TIMES

1792 Born 4 Aug. at Field Place, Horsham, Sussex; eldest child of Timothy Shelley, landowning Whig MP, later a Baronet.

1802–4 At Syon House Academy, Isleworth, near London.

1804–10 At Eton where he is bullied, develops scientific interests and writes two Gothic novels, *Zastrozzi* and *St Irvyne* (both published 1810). With his sister writes and publishes *Original Poetry by Victor and Cazire* (published and withdrawn 1810).

1810 University College, Oxford (Oct.). *Posthumous Fragments of Margaret Nicholson* published (Nov.).

1811 Meets 16-year-old Harriet Westbrook, whose father is the proprietor of a London coffee-house (Jan.). Expelled from his college (25 Mar.) with his friend Thomas Jefferson Hogg for refusing to answer questions concerning their pamphlet *The Necessity of Atheism* (published Feb.). Begins intellectual friendship with Elizabeth Hitchener, a schoolteacher at Hurstpierpoint. Elopes with Harriet and marries her in Edinburgh (29 Aug.). Visits Keswick (Nov.–Jan.) and meets Robert Southey, whom he later suspects (incorrectly) of writing hostile reviews in the *Quarterly*.

1812 Unexplained nocturnal intruder at Keswick (19 Jan.). Working on lost novel *Hubert Cauvin*. Visits Dublin; speaks, writes and distributes pamphlets on behalf of Catholic emancipation and Repeal of the Union (Feb.–Mar.). *Address to the Irish People* and *Proposals for an Association of . . . Philanthropists* published (Feb.). *Declaration of Rights* printed. Becomes a vegetarian (Mar.). Lives in Wales, then Lynmouth, Devon, where he is watched by government spies and his servant is imprisoned for distributing *Declaration of Rights*. 950 copies out of 1,000 of *Letter to Lord Ellenborough* burnt by printer. Moves to Tremadoc (North Wales) in September; assists in creation of model village and embankment. Meets Thomas Love Peacock and William Godwin. Writing *Queen Mab*.

1813 Unexplained nocturnal incident, possibly designed to scare Shelley away (26 Feb.). Visits Dublin and Killarney, returning to London early in April. *Queen Mab* privately issued (May). Daughter Ianthe born to Harriet (23 June). Settles at Bracknell (July), where he sees much of Peacock.

1814   *A Refutation of Deism* printed. Ferdinand of Spain annuls
Constitution of the Cortes (4 May). Elopes with Mary Godwin
(27 July); together with Claire Clairmont they tour Continent,
newly opened after end of war in April and return on 13 Sept.
Congress of Vienna opens (1 Nov.). Son Charles born to
Harriet (30 Nov.). Financial difficulties.

1815   Mary's first child born (22 Feb.); dies two weeks later. Battle of
Waterloo (18 June). Receives annual income of £1,000 on
death of grandfather (June). Moves to Bishopsgate near
Windsor (Aug.), where he writes *Alastor*.

1816   Son William born to Mary (24 Jan.). *Alastor* published (Feb.).
Summer tour brings him together with recently exiled Byron at
Lake of Geneva, where he writes 'Hymn to Intellectual Beauty'
(late June) and 'Mont Blanc' (late July) and Mary is inspired to
begin *Frankenstein* (published 1818). Returns to England (8
Sept.) and settles at Marlow (autumn); becomes friendly with
Leigh Hunt. Suicide of Mary's half-sister Fanny Imlay (9 Oct.).
Suicide of Harriet (9 Nov.; discovered 10 Dec.). Spa Fields
Riots in London (2 Dec.). Marries Mary (30 Dec.).

1817   Birth of Allegra, Byron's daughter by Claire (12 Jan.). Meets
Keats (Feb.). Habeas Corpus suspended (17 Mar.–31 Jan.
1818); various measures against sedition. Loses Ianthe and
Charles through judgement of Lord Eldon (27 Mar.). Settles at
Marlow (Mar.), where he remains friendly with Peacock, the
Hunts and Hogg and gives help to distressed lace-workers. *A
Proposal for Putting Reform to the Vote* published (Mar.).
Finishes *Laon and Cythna* and begins *Rosalind and Helen*
(Sept.). Daughter Clara born (2 Sept.). *History of a Six Weeks'
Tour* published. In bad health. *An Address to the People on the
Death of the Princess Charlotte* published (written 11–12
Nov.); this concerns the fate of the Derby rioters (executed 7
Nov. through the offices of an *agent provocateur*). *Laon and
Cythna* published and withdrawn (Dec.).

1818   A more discreet version of *Laon and Cythna* published as *The
Revolt of Islam* (Jan.). Departs for Italy (11 Mar.), intending
perhaps to return, but never does so. Sends Allegra to Byron
(28 Apr.). At Leghorn (from 9 May) where he meets John and
Maria Gisborne and Maria's son Henry Reveley; at Bagni di
Lucca (from 11 June), where he completes *Rosalind and Helen*,
translates Plato's *Symposium* (July) and begins essay on the
manners of the Greeks (Aug.). Burdett's motion for
parliamentary reform heavily defeated (2 June). Visits Byron in
Venice to discuss Allegra's future (late Aug.), the inspiration for
Julian and Maddalo; settles at nearby Este till 5 Nov. Clara dies
(24 Sept.). Begins *Prometheus Unbound, Julian and Maddalo*

and 'Lines Written among the Euganean Hills' (autumn). Visits Ferrara, Bologna, Rome (20–7 Nov.) and settles in Naples (11 Dec.). Visits Vesuvius, Bay of Baiae and writes 'Stanzas Written in Dejection' (Dec.).

1819   Visits Paestum and Pompeii (24–5 Feb.). Leaves Naples (28 Feb.). Settles at Rome (5 Mar.), where he finishes Acts II and III of *Prometheus Unbound* (Mar.–Apr.) and perhaps *Julian and Maddalo*. *Rosalind and Helen* published (spring). William dies (7 June). Leaves Rome (10 June) and settles at Leghorn (17 June), where he works on *The Cenci*. 'Peterloo' Massacre in Manchester (16 Aug.); writes *The Mask of Anarchy* (Sept.; not published till 1832). Moves to Florence (2 Oct.); reads hostile review of *The Revolt of Islam* in the *Quarterly* (*c*. 15 Oct.); writes *Peter Bell the Third*, 'Ode to the West Wind' (late Oct.) and long public letter on trial of radical printer Richard Carlile (early Nov.); expands Preface to *Prometheus Unbound*. Begins *A Philosophical View of Reform* (unfinished; not published till 1920). Son Percy Florence born (12 Nov.). 'England in 1819' (Dec.). The 'Six Acts', a series of strongly repressive measures, passed in England (Dec.). Birth (27 Dec.) of 'Elena Adelaide Shelley', Shelley's 'Neapolitan charge', registered as his own child by Mary but of uncertain parentage, and the cause of rumour and blackmail (died 9 June 1820).

1820   Beginnings of Revolution in Spain (1 Jan.). Moves to Pisa (26 Jan.). Death of George III (29 Jan.). Discovery of 'Cato Street Conspiracy' (23 Feb.). *The Cenci* published (spring). Ferdinand VII restores Spanish Constitution and abolishes Inquisition (7 Mar.). Moves to Leghorn (15 June–4 Aug.). Writes 'The Sensitive-plant', 'Ode to Liberty' and 'The Cloud' (possibly at Pisa), 'To a Sky-lark' (probably June), *Letter to Maria Gisborne* (second half of June); translates Homeric *Hymn to Mercury* (early July). Revolt in Naples and promise of Constitution (2–7 July). Bill of Pains and Penalties against Princess Caroline, whom George IV wishes to divorce, introduced in Parliament (5 July) but dropped together with inquiry into her conduct (10 Nov.). At Baths of San Giuliano, near Pisa (Aug.–Oct.). Writes *The Witch of Atlas* (14–16 Aug.) and 'Ode to Naples' (17–25 Aug.). *Promethus Unbound* published (Aug.). Writes *Swellfoot the Tyrant* on the Caroline affair (Aug.–Sept.; published and suppressed in Dec.). Conference at Troppau to discuss policy against revolutionary tendencies in Europe (23 Oct.–17 Dec.; 12 Jan.–12 May 1821 at Laibach). Returns to Pisa (31 Oct.). Friendship with Emilia Viviani (Dec.).

1821 Pirated edition of *Queen Mab* published in London by William Clarke; it is seized and he is later imprisoned because of the contents. Arrival of Edward and Jane Williams (13 Jan.). Working on *Epipsychidion* (finished 16 Feb.). Begins *A Defence of Poetry* in response to Peacock (Feb.–Mar.; not published till 1840). Greek War of Independence begins (6 Mar.; Shelley hears news 1 Apr.). Neapolitan rising crushed by Austrians, and Ferdinand IV restored (7–23 Mar.). Hears of Keats's death in Rome on 23 Feb. (11 Apr.); writes *Adonais* (finished June; printed July). Death of Napoleon (5 May). Rejection of Lord John Russell's motion for parliamentary reform (9 May). Anonymous publication of *Epipsychidion* (May). Coronation of George IV (19 July); death of Queen Caroline (7 Aug.). Visits Byron at Ravenna (Aug.). Writes *Hellas* (Oct.). Byron arrives at Pisa (Nov.).

1822 Working on *Charles the First*. Trelawny arrives (14 Jan.). Greek independence proclaimed (27 Jan.). *Hellas* published (Feb.). Writes poems to Jane; translates scenes from Goethe's *Faust* and Calderón (spring). Allegra Byron dies (20 Apr.). With the Williamses moves to Casa Magni at San Terenzo near Lerici (30 Apr.). Sailing on the *Don Juan* (delivered 12 May). Writing *The Triumph of Life* (? late May–June; unfinished). Drowned with Williams when sailing back from Leghorn to Lerici after welcoming the Hunts (8 July).

1824 *Posthumous Poems* (collected by Mary from Shelley's papers).

INTRODUCTION

I

On 16 August 1822 the body of Percy Bysshe Shelley was cremated on a funeral pyre: the chosen spot was a beach not far from Via Reggio in Italy, where his boat had gone down in a storm. Frankincense and salt were thrown into the furnace, wine and oil over the body; Shelley's friends desired that at the last he should be honoured like a Greek hero. Symbolically, or so it seemed, his heart was not consumed by the flames, so that Edward Trelawny was able to rescue it at the last moment. Later, it became the object of an unseemly squabble between the poet's widow and Leigh Hunt; when she was finally granted custody, Mary Shelley secreted it in a copy of *Adonais*, which she kept inside her pillow. Medical evidence suggests that her affections may have been misplaced; in all probability, the organ which survived the fiery furnace was not Shelley's heart but his liver.

The whole episode is highly instructive not only for Shelley's biographers but for those who are concerned with the value of his poetry. It was Shelley's misfortune that he lived (and died) in dramatic and often exotic circumstances which have attracted more interest than his genuine poetic achievements and which have influenced the responses even of critics who claim an antiseptic indifference to the facts of biography. Even more damaging is the fact that the popular version of Shelley's life presents an idealized and seriously distorted picture of a personality which was richly complex. It is difficult to escape from the legend so potently created by Trelawny, Hogg, Peacock, Mary Shelley and the other early biographers, all of whom had personal reasons for exaggerating Shelley's ethereality, his effeminacy, his weakness, his ignorance of the facts of life, his being a Poet with a capital P. It is also difficult not to make a simple equation between the poetry and the life, not to assume that the poet-hero of *Alastor* is Shelley himself or that *Julian and Maddalo* is a direct transcription from the life. Yet, although many of Shelley's poems do relate very closely to his own experience, Shelley took great care to alchemize them, to purify them of the dross of what was merely personal. He insisted that the limited facts of personal biography should always be avoided or transcended: 'A story of particular facts is as a mirror which obscures and distorts that which should be beautiful: poetry is a mirror which makes beautiful that which is distorted.' Or, to approach it from a different angle: 'The poet and the man are two different natures.'[1]

Shelley had a sense of poetic decorum which would not have been out of place in the eighteenth century. In 'To a Sky-lark' he speaks of the poet 'hidden / In the light of thought', his identity subsumed in the radiance of inspiration. The majority of his most personal poems, notably his lyrics, were not published during his lifetime: some (such as 'To Edward Williams') were sent to friends with strict instructions that they were to be kept private, while others (such as 'To the Moon') were left unfinished and might have had a rather different bearing had they been completed. Some of Shelley's most celebrated and seemingly personal lyrics were intended in all probability as songs for plays such as *Hellas* and *Charles the First*. Of course, these poems are informed by Shelley's own experiences and fuelled by his own emotions but they are not mere spontaneous effusions or overflowings of the heart: instead they offer what T. S. Eliot described as '*significant* emotion, emotion which has its life in the poem and not in the history of the poet'.[2] To interpret them biographically is as crude and pointless as to equate Shakespeare's 'Mistress mine' with Anne Hathaway.

It is also important to recognize the shaping influence of genre and convention. 'The Indian Serenade' (not included here) was regularly interpreted as a directly autobiographical piece until recent researches showed that it was also called 'The Indian Girl's Song', was intended to be sung by a woman and belongs to the tradition of the oriental lyric which typically relies on a certain emotional extravagance.[3] Again, many of what Cleanth Brooks once described as 'Shelley's sometimes embarrassing declarations'[4] can now be traced to the tradition of prophetic poetry, as found for example in the Psalms. Thus, the exaltations and despairs of poems like 'Ode to the West Wind' should be approached in the context of religious experience and the conventions of religious literature rather than with reference to Shelley's habit of dining on bread and raisins.[5] Again, the poetic collapses of poems like *Epipsychidion* are highly stylized and carefully staged developments of the prophetic tradition for which Pindar, Dante and the Bible provide many of the clues.[6] Shelley insists on the evanescence of inspiration and the inadequacy of language; the profuse similes of 'To a Sky-lark' arise from a deep sense of this inadequacy, while *Epipsychidion* very boldly attempts to enact the kindlings and dwindlings of the poetic process. Some may consider these emphases debilitating or unhealthy; nobody should continue to claim that Shelley was simply indulging in 'self-expression'. All of these poems are characterized by extreme artistic self-consciousness.

Shelley had strict notions about the need for the poet to transcend the temptations to self-indulgence and emotional exhibitionism. In *The Triumph of Life* he makes an important distinction between those poets who achieved this moral equilibrium and Rousseau who, by his own admission, did not:

> See the great bards of old, who inly quelled
>
> The passions which they sung, as by their strain
>   May well be known: their living melody
> Tempers its own contagion to the vein
>
>   Of those who are infected with it – I
> Have suffered what I wrote, or viler pain! –
>
>   And so my words were seeds of misery,
> Even as the deeds of others.
>
>   (274–81).

The manuscript reveals that Rousseau is pointing here to 'Homer and his brethren', who may be identified as the Greek tragedians, and Lucretius, Virgil, Dante, Petrarch, Chaucer, Shakespeare, Calderón and Milton, all of whom attained the self-control which is necessary for great artistic achievement.[7] If their poetry has had unfortunate effects, that may be attributed not to any weakness which is inherent in the poetry but to the weakness of their readers, since 'of such truths / Each to itself must be the oracle' (*PU*, II. iv.122–3). If the *Iliad* encourages the wrong kind of militaristic valour, or *Paradise Lost* seems to sanction a vindictive dispensation of justice, it is not because

Homer thirsted for blood or Milton for vengeance but because we impose our own selfishness and our own limitations on what they have written. Homer and his brethren provide the potentially dangerous emotions of their poetry with the antidote of moral and artistic control (they temper their own contagion). Rousseau, on the other hand, did not succeed in mastering his own emotions: he was not able to repress 'the mutiny within' and did not transform 'to potable gold the poisonous waters which flow from death through life'.[8] For all his greatness, Rousseau was not able to achieve the desired internal equilibrium, as his *Confessions* had demonstrated: they were, said Shelley, 'either a disgrace to the confessor or a string of falsehoods'. To make such inadequacies public was a dangerous proceeding: in spite of his humanitarian intentions, 'Rousseau gave license by his writings to passions that only incapacitate and contract the human heart.' In one sense, then, he was as much a tyrant as the French monarchs, whom he despised, or as Napoleon, for whom he paved the way: his words were 'seeds of misery' and 'he prepared the necks of his fellow-beings for that galling and dishonourable servitude which at this moment it bears'.[9] As *Prometheus Unbound* so forcefully asserts, man cannot be free until he dethrones the tyrants of his own soul, a process which involves self-knowledge, self-control and self-reliance. To concentrate, as Rousseau does, on one's own weakness, gloatingly as it seems, is to subject oneself to a despotic control as ruthless and as destructive as any which is exercised from the customary seats of power.

The sense of moral responsibility which informs this passage is characteristic of Shelley, whose conception of poetry had little to do with what was merely fashionable or charming. Though he valued increasingly the aesthetic virtues of poetry, he habitually approached it in terms of its relations to society. A passage in the draft of *Prometheus Unbound* reveals how conscientiously Shelley responded to these claims. Mercury is cataloguing a variety of monsters who can deputize for the Furies in their efforts to overcome the heroic resolve of Prometheus. One of these is the Sphinx, 'subtlest of fiends, / Who ministered to Thebes Heaven's poisoned wine – / Unnatural love, and more unnatural hate' (*PU*, I.347–9), a reference to the story of how Oedipus solved the riddle of the Sphinx, thus making possible his incestuous marriage and the fatal curse which he invoked on his sons. Shelley was exercised by the formulation of the last line and reflected in a note: 'The contrast would have been [more complete] if the sentiment had been transposed: but wherefore sacrifice the philosophical truth, that love however, monstrous in its expression is still less worthy of horror than hatred.'[10] Here Shelley prefers moral truth to a rhetorical contrast which is more satisfying in terms of aesthetics.

As a rule Shelley manages to satisfy both his conscience and his artistic sensibility; nonetheless, it is ironic that a man of such moral tenacity should have been misrepresented for so long as primarily a lyrical poet with little or nothing to say. Critics who have questioned his ultimate stature have always been ready to acknowledge that he had a rare lyrical faculty (or facility, as they might prefer to put it). Indeed, this lyrical ease has often been related to their own critical attitudes, since it was Shelley's fluency, his apparently uncontrolled emotionalism, his habit of going on 'till I am stopped', that produced those results which they found so irritating. 'The effect of Shelley's eloquence is to hand poetry over to a sensibility that has no more dealings with intelligence than it can help', wrote Dr Leavis, notoriously. For Shelley's admirers the poems often provided a similar experience, but their conclusions were exactly the opposite – for them the lack of 'meaning' was a positive virtue, a sign of the highest poetic achievement. For critics such as these, Shelley (like Blake) moved in a world of pure poetry, uncontaminated by realities, insulated from the harsh necessities of meaning. The main result of this unholy alliance between those who despised Shelley and those who adored him was that, between the two extremes, the real Shelley was persistently neglected. To concentrate on Shelley's lyrical poetry was to ignore the poetry by which he would have wished to be judged and remembered, the long and complex poems which grapple with the problems of politics, society, philosophy, love, art and religion. To assess Shelley's achievement on the basis of 'The Indian Serenade' or 'When the lamp is shattered' was to exhibit a seriously distorted perspective, as if one were to base a final judgement of Shakespeare on the songs from the plays. It is true that recent critical trends have enabled us to recognize new virtues in these poems.[11] We can now see that many of Shelley's lyrics belong to identifiable poetic traditions rather than to the pathology of Romantic narcissism or to the poetry of the higher nonsense. It is now evident that many of Shelley's shorter poems address themselves to moral or metaphysical problems of some complexity with great intellectual rigour and precision of inquiry. 'When passion's trance is overpast' explores the decline of love from its first intensity with unsentimental directness; 'Mutability' is also a tightly controlled sequence of logic; more extensive lyrics like 'Lines Written in the Bay of Lerici' and 'To Jane: The Recollection' combine a delicate sense of atmosphere with painful but incisive psychological probings. Beneath these graceful surfaces there is a bony framework, a careful formal patterning which binds all together. Yet, in spite of their excellence, Shelley regarded these poems as the marginalia to far greater enterprises. Critics have persisted in thinking otherwise; perhaps Mrs Shelley was not alone in confusing the heart and the liver.

2

Politics were probably the dominating concern of Shelley's intellectual life. His earliest poetry is an unhappy mixture of Gothic melodramatics and political invective. Throughout his brief life, Shelley was never entirely free from the temptation to blend the two worlds, to turn Lord Castlereagh and Lord Sidmouth, king, priest and politician, into ghouls and vampires, evil monsters from the novels of 'Monk' Lewis and Mrs Radcliffe (Shelley himself had successfully published a Gothic novel while still at school). Yet this fierce indignation, this painful awareness of man's inhumanity to man, was the directing force behind much of his greatest poetry and a number of his most trenchant essays. Shelley was one of those (in Keats' words) 'to whom the miseries of the world / Are misery, and will not let them rest'.[12]

He had been born (in 1792) into a family with political connections. His father, Sir Timothy, was a Sussex landowner, a Whig MP attached to the liberal faction of the Duke of Norfolk; his liberalism did not extend to the behaviour of his own son, with whom he was permanently at odds after Shelley was sent down from Oxford in 1811 for refusing to acknowledge his authorship of an inquiring pamphlet called *The Necessity of Atheism*. Shelley had been intended to succeed his father in the House when he came of age; from his early years he was politically conscious, and his whole career was marked by an unswerving adherence to the principles of political reform and a firm belief in the rightness of his own convictions. Thus, though Shelley was always in opposition and generally derided or ignored, he characteristically expresses himself with an impressive air of authority.

He grew up in that grim period sometimes known at the Bleak Age, the period of profound moral unrest and increasing political agitation which marked the years between the failure of the French Revolution and the passing of the Reform Bill in 1832. The first and perhaps the greatest influence on his political thinking was William Godwin, who later became his father-in-law. In 1812 Shelley described to its author how *An Enquiry Concerning Political Justice* (1793) had 'materially influenced my character':

> I was no longer the votary of Romance; till then I had existed in an ideal world; now I found that in this universe of ours was enough to excite the interest of the heart, enough to employ the discussions of Reason. I beheld in short that I had duties to perform. (*Letters*, I, 227–8)

Godwin had imagined a utopian society in which there would be no need for government; much of Shelley's poetry, early and late, delights in presenting visions of a free and regenerated society, yet a growing sense of what was politically possible and a deeper understanding of human nature soon modified his belief in perfectibility.[13] Equality was 'unattainable except by a parcel of peas or beans' and so was perfection, yet 'my principles incite me to take all the good I can get in politics, for ever aspiring to something more'.[14] Shelley's main aim was to abolish the inequalities in society, to undermine the system of power and privilege on which they were based. In particular, this involved a reform of the electoral system, which currently excluded the vast majority of the population from the right to vote. The unfinished *A Philosophical View of Reform* (1819–? early 1820), intended to be 'an instructive and readable book, appealing from the passions to the reason of men',[15] attracted no publisher but it is a shrewd and comprehensive account which places its subject in the context of European history. Shelley also attacked the unequal distribution of property; paper currency, the 'Ghost of Gold', whose consequences 'have been the establishment of a new aristocracy, which has its basis in fraud as the old one has its basis in force'; the operation of the National Debt; the use of the standing army; the legal system, including the barbaric Game Laws; and the rigid marriage laws which underestimated both the rights of women and the holiness of the heart's affections.[16] Binding together all these abuses were the Church and the monarchy ('the only string which ties the robber's bundle'),[17] who had combined themselves for their own benefit and to 'the destruction of the real interest of all'. Shelley crusaded with great energy: this infuses *Queen Mab* (1813) and its supporting array of essays on social and political problems. It also took Shelley to Dublin, where he addressed public meetings, distributed pamphlets and wrote his *Address to the Irish People*. Yet, most of his activity was closer to home and aligned him with those moderate radicals who were working for reform by peaceful means. Among these was Leigh Hunt, editor of the *Examiner* and later a close and supportive friend, for whose paper he produced a public letter on the trial of the radical printer Richard Carlile, and two notable poems on political subjects ('England in 1819' and *The Mask of Anarchy*), which were not published for discretionary reasons. (Hunt had already spent two years in prison for criticizing the Prince Regent.)[18]

Shelley became increasingly disillusioned both with direct political activity and with poetry which was bluntly didactic. Yet, when the situation demanded it, he could still produce popular verse such as *The Mask of Anarchy*, which was specifically intended for a wide reading public. Poems like these were classed as *exoteric*; in his later years, Shelley preferred to concentrate on poetry of the *esoteric* species, aimed at the 'more select classes of poetical readers'. The aim was no longer simply didactic, but the predominating concerns were still moral and political. In *A Defence of Poetry* (1821) Shelley argues eloquently that poetry has an important social function; history shows that it is closely related to moral and social progress. In his own age the failure of the Industrial Revolution to increase the sum of human happiness could be attributed, along with the other excesses and imbalances of a capitalist economy, to a failure to 'imagine that which we know'. If man 'having enslaved the elements, remains himself a slave', it is because of 'an excess of the selfish and calculating principle' at the expense of imagination and its vehicle, poetry. The battle-lines are clearly drawn: 'Poetry and the principle of Self, of which money is the visible incarnation, are the God and Mammon of the world.'[19]

Poetry is an act of hope; 'it is ever still the light of life; the source of whatever of beautiful or generous or true can have place in an evil time'.[20] Shelley argues for the necessity of hope in the preface to *Laon and Cythna; or, The Revolution of the Golden City: A Vision of the Nineteenth Century* (1817) (published for reasons of discretion under the title *The Revolt of Islam*). There he claims that 'gloom and misanthropy have become the characteristics of the age in which we live, the solace of a disappointment that unconsciously finds relief only in the wilful exaggeration of its own despair'. Yet the signs are that England has survived and that 'a slow, gradual silent change' is beginning to take place. Shelley dedicated his talents to the service of that change. *Laon and Cythna* describes the efforts of two revolutionary leaders, brother and sister, who briefly achieve the overthrow of the Ottoman empire but are finally defeated and subsumed into a mysterious Valhalla of fame after their death. This immensely ambitious epic poem (which has not yet received the full and sustained critical analysis it deserves) is not totally successful in fusing its narrative structure with its philosophical concerns; yet it is a serious and original achievement which attempts to explore the moral and political implications of a revolutionary situation. Some of Shelley's critics pretended that they saw nothing of interest in the Ottoman empire but most of his readers must have recognized that he was attempting to analyse the reasons for the ultimate failure of the French Revolution and that his conclusions were not unconnected with politics in England. Though he allowed his heroes to be executed, Shelley intended his poem both as a primer in moral and political education and as a contribution to hope: it was written 'in the view of kindling within the bosoms of my readers a virtuous enthusiasm for those doctrines of liberty and justice, that faith and hope in something good, which neither violence nor misrepresentation nor prejudice can ever totally extinguish among mankind'.

Laon and Cythna was soon followed by *Prometheus Unbound* (1818–19), a mythological drama which is perhaps Shelley's greatest achievement. The *Prometheus Bound* of Aeschylus had shown the archetypal revolutionary hero at odds with a tyrannical father–god; here Shelley provides a highly personal revisionary version and brings it to a conclusion which elicits its full potential for hope. In rewriting Aeschylus Shelley seems to have discovered new uses for Greek, Christian and Oriental mythology;[21] the psychological profundity of his conception and the brilliantly daring imagery give to this play a satisfying complexity which raises it far above the level of *Laon and Cythna*. Shelley's gift was not for narrative but for psychological and moral explanation and for evoking states of mind; *Prometheus Unbound* is successful because, as Northrop Frye put it, 'it has attained the plotless or actionless narrative which seems to be characteristic of the mythopoeic genre'.[22] Shelley himself declared his intention of familiarizing his readers with 'beautiful idealisms of moral excellence': *Prometheus Unbound* is not didactic, nor does it give in to despair. It is an attempt to show what man might achieve if he devoted himself to the principles of reform, abolished those false constraints which he has permitted to exert their tyranny over him, and reclaimed the human condition from the moral ice and snow which binds us in shivering isolation, each on our barren mountain peak. Shelley emphasizes the necessity for resisting both force from without and the insinuating pressure of our own weakness from within. The play's vocabulary insists on potential; many of the negatives (*unpastured*, *unreclaiming*) imply that if the present situation is not satisfactory it is because man himself has failed to take the necessary action. Yet, although *Prometheus Unbound* is quite deliberately an idealism, much of it deals with the unreclaimed human condition and the insidious and recurrent temptations to despair and apathy. Shelley insists on the necessity of a continuous effort; unlike Godwin, he also recognizes that should man achieve his utopian society on earth he will still be merely man, still subject to many limitations and always in danger of sliding back into an unregenerated state.

Thus, even in his most optimistic works, Shelley's idealism does not preclude some salutary examples of psychological realism; his hope was never naive or simple-minded. In other works, he argued against his own best inclinations; *Julian and Maddalo* presents a disillusioning reply to Julian's question 'if we were not weak / Should we be less in deed than in desire?', while *The Cenci* portrays in Beatrice a character of Promethean potential who does not possess Prometheus' moral self-restraint, gives in to revenge and murders her father: 'all best things are thus confused to ill.' *Hellas*, which anticipates the success of the Greek War of Independence, begins its final chorus on a note of joyful celebration. Yet, before the chorus has ended, the joy has modulated into doubt: 'O cease! must hate and death return? / Cease! must men kill and die? / Cease! drain not to its dregs the urn / Of bitter prophecy.' Shelley delineated with grim precision the *danse macabre* of *The Triumph of Life* yet he also wrote that 'Poetry is the record of the best and happiest moments of the happiest and best minds' and believed that 'Hope ... is a solemn duty which we owe alike to ourselves & to the world'.[23] A number of Shelley's shorter poems obviously follow a dialectical pattern (e.g. 'Ode to Heaven', 'The Two Spirits' and the songs of Apollo and Pan, which contrast with and balance each other). It is part of Shelley's particular subtlety that he argues against himself within the confines of individual poems and that he also sets up poem against poem. The result is a continuous and fruitful dialectic, an energizing tension which gives force to most of his poetry. Perhaps not a little of Shelley's famous 'ungraspability' might be traced to this constant shifting of the terms of reference. What has often been interpreted as mere incoherence or self-contradiction should be acknowledged as a never-ending process of intellectual adjustment, a perpetual balancing of hypothesis against hypothesis, a guarded series of approaches to the ultimately unknowable truth. Sometimes the poem will finish nearer to hope (*Adonais*, 'The Sensitive-plant') sometimes nearer despair (*The Cenci*); mostly the endings are ambivalent, the final assertions tentative and qualified. Sometimes the aspiring flight towards hope and vision is wrecked in a carefully calculated collapse of poetic inspiration (*Epipsychidion*). Shelley's supposedly contradictory endings can thus be seen not as literary failures but as paradoxes justified and even predestined by the very nature of the poems out of which they emerge.[24]

Behind this shifting dialectic we can detect the influence of Shelley's own temperament, given to violent oscillations of mood. But the changes of mood were conditioned not only by Shelley's own variations of health and of happiness but by a much more profound inquisition into the facts of existence. From an early age Shelley was fascinated by both science and philosophy. Although his scientific sophistication has sometimes been exaggerated (according to A. N. Whitehead he would have been 'a Newton among chemists' if he had been born a hundred years later)[25] Shelley once possessed a microscope and conducted scientific experiments; he also took the trouble to read and take notes from recent books such as Humphry Davy's *Elements of Agricultural Chemistry* and he was well informed on theories of light, electricity, the nature of matter and the behaviour of volcanoes. His letters from Italy also show that he was a meticulous observer of cloud formations (an obvious influence both on 'Ode to the West Wind' and 'The Cloud').[26] Many passages in his poetry which were once dismissed as charming but meaningless are now known to be closely related to his philosophical investigations; both were directed towards the discovery of the secret principle of life. Shelley's nature had a strong leavening of scepticism which checks even his most enthusiastic assertions: the skylark is located in 'Heaven, or near it' while his passionate affirmation of the immortality of Keats/ Adonais is fastidiously explicated – 'He wakes or sleeps with the enduring dead' (336). This tendency was strengthened by his reading of the eighteenth-century sceptics and perhaps also of Plato, two of whose dialogues he translated and whose view of the world as 'but a spume that plays / Upon a ghostly paradigm of things' (Yeats) was undoubtedly an influence on his own more melancholy musings.[27] Yet he also possessed a capacity for a very personal kind of religious faith, not related to any institutionalized church, placing a considerable emphasis on man's own potential divinity, but acknowledging the existence of a Power in the universe; this Power he defined as the 'over-ruling Spirit of the collective energy of the moral and material world',[28] the plastic (shaping) stress which he celebrates in *Adonais*. This feeling influences even heterodox poems like 'Hymn to Intellectual Beauty' and apparently secular poems such as 'Ode to the West Wind'. It appears that Shelley also experienced direct and vivid intimations of immortality, through the almost mystical process of poetic inspiration so magnificently analysed in *A Defence of Poetry*.

3

Shelley provided a shrewd analysis of his own abilities in a letter of 1817 to William Godwin:

I am formed, – if for any thing not in common with the herd of mankind – to apprehend minute & remote distinctions of feeling whether relative to external nature, or the living beings which surround us, & to communicate the conceptions which result from considering either the moral or the material universe as a whole.   (*Letters*, I, 577)

The ability to concentrate on the whole rather than on the details is certainly a feature of his work. The attention to minute and remote distinctions of feeling is also characteristic both of his best lyrics and of more detailed explorations such as 'Mont Blanc', *Prometheus Unbound*, *Epipsychidion* and *The Triumph of Life*. Shelley had a highly attuned moral sense; he was also gifted with a delicate insight into the operations of mind, which is the distinguishing feature of many of his greatest poems. Learning from the Greek tragedians and Dante and profiting from the recent example of Wordsworth, Shelley developed a subtle poetry of mind which demands vigilant attention from the reader. Take for example these lines from *Prometheus Unbound*:

> . . . terror, madness, crime, remorse,
> Which from the links of the great chain of things
> To every thought within the mind of man
> Sway and drag heavily, and each one reels
> Under the load towards the pit of death. (II.iv.19–23)

This pessimistic image of the human condition is derived from the sight of fettered convicts hoeing the weeds of St Peter's Square in Rome. There are suggestions here of the great chain of being and of the iron chain of necessity which links cause to effect with inexorable consequence, together with strong resonances of those Roman triumphal processions with chained captives which later provided the framework for *The Triumph of Life*. This image also looks towards the end of the play where 'the tools / And emblems of its last captivity', the signs of man's subjection to a tyranny which is at least partly self-imposed, are transformed into positives: 'Man, oh, not men! a chain of linkèd thought / Of love and might to be divided not' (IV.394–5). As a whole, the passage illustrates Shelley's ability to give concrete form to the most abstract activities of mind and to invest them with a directing emotional intensity. The strength of *Prometheus Unbound* is largely derived from the skill with which Shelley

relates the outer world of politics to the inner world of mind; it
is implied that the repressive systems of politics and religion
represented by Jupiter are intimately related to the psychological
and moral weaknesses of those who tolerate them. Shelley does
not deny the political realities of Regency England – indeed, he
details them with brutal immediacy in 'England in 1819' and
The Mask of Anarchy, not to mention political essays such as
An Address to the People on the Death of the Princess Charlotte
and parts of *A Philosophical View of Reform* – but he insists on
exploring the interior complexities of evil. *The Triumph of Life*
investigates the ways in which even those with the best inten-
tions and the most humane aspirations may be defeated by the
process of life. *Julian and Maddalo* challenges the optimistic
utopianism of Julian (who is obviously a figuring of Shelley
himself), and its curiously open-ended narrative withholds any
resolution which might afford ultimate consolation or confirm
that theory 'Which seeks "a soul of goodness in things ill"'. In
these explorations Shelley discovers important connections
between politics and religion; 'Mont Blanc' and *Prometheus
Unbound* both trace a link between the false divinities which
man has imposed on himself and his acquiescence in the
prevailing political system.

Yet if Shelley's most distinctive literary achievement is his
development of the richly symbolic poetry of mind, he was
highly accomplished in many other areas. No poet of his period,
and few in the history of English literature, can rival the scope
and range of his poetic activities. Contrary to popular opinion,
he was a poet not of one style (the impassioned and lyrical) but
of many. He could produce with equal skill and technical
dexterity the learned formal ode in the high style (*Ode to
Liberty*), the familiar verse epistle (*Letter to Maria Gisborne*),
the satire (fiercely animated as in *The Mask of Anarchy* or more
jocular as in *Peter Bell the Third*), the relaxed conversation
poem (*Julian and Maddalo*), the Dantean history of love (*Epip-
sychidion*), the carefully wrought classical elegy (*Adonais*), the
extended exploratory lyric ('Lines Written in the Bay of Lerici',
'To Edward Williams'), the flyting ('To the Lord Chancellor'),
the delighted celebration of natural energies ('The Cloud'). Even
within his slighter lyrics there is a rich variety ranging from the
simple cry of 'O World, O Life, O Time' to the elegant self-
translation of 'Goodnight'. His descriptions of nature can range

from the metaphysical analogies of 'Mont Blanc' to the precise but densely symbolic imagery of 'Ode to the West Wind' to the simple clarities with which *Julian and Maddalo* begins. His voice can encompass the charming domestic detail ('We sate there, rolling billiard balls about'), the compressed and paradoxical ('It is the unpastured Sea hungering for calm'), the profoundly philosophical ('The One remains, the many change and pass; / Heaven's light forever shines, Earth's shadows fly; / Life, like a dome of many-coloured glass, / Stains the white radiance of Eternity'), the bluntly comic ('He touched the hem of Nature's shift, / Felt faint – and never dared uplift / The closest, all-concealing tunic'), the grotesque ('His big tears, for he wept well, / Turned to millstones as they fell'), the drily witty ('Now he obliquely through the keyhole passed, / Like a thin mist or an autumnal blast'), the morally incisive ('The good want power, but to weep barren tears. / The powerful goodness want: worse need for them. / The wise want love; and those who love want wisdom; / And all best things are thus confused to ill.').[29] There is the ruthlessly unsentimental portrayal of sexual attraction in *The Triumph of Life*, the urbane conclusion to 'The Sensitive-plant', the joyful dance of the universe in Act IV of *Prometheus Unbound*, the Byronic poise of Mephistopheles in the Goethe translation, the gently chiding satire of 'An Exhortation', the pungently unsparing social and political analysis of 'England in 1819'. Shelley was also a fertile and intuitive translator who achieved particular success with the untranslatable *Prologue in Heaven* from Goethe's *Faust* and the light-hearted Homeric *Hymn to Mercury* and in scenes from Calderón's *El mágico prodigioso*. Such versatility makes Shelley not only one of the most European of English poets between Dryden and Eliot but goes a long way towards justifying Wordsworth's statement that 'Shelley is one of the best *artists* of us all: I mean in workmanship of style'.[30]

Though he could assume so many voices, there are three qualities which link all his best poems together. First, there is a general fluency, a controlling impetus which derives both from Shelley's habit of reading aloud and from the urgency of his conviction. Shelley's voice is always assured even when he is expressing his doubts. Secondly, many of his poems, particularly those which deal with the world of nature, exhibit what Shelley once called 'the animation of delight'.[31] The operations of the west wind, the dance of matter in *Prometheus Unbound*, the onset of spring in *Adonais*, the fresh morning setting of *The Triumph of Life* are all given life by an informing source of energy, a vitality which cannot be ignored. Thirdly, the best of Shelley's poetry is born from a fusing of passion and precision which is achieved at a very high level of intensity. Admittedly, the pressure is sometimes too great (Shelley himself once lamented the absence of 'that tranquillity which is the attribute & the accompaniment of power'):[32] both *Prometheus Unbound* and *Epipsychidion* are overheated in places. Much more frequently, however, Shelley achieves a highly impressive blend of imaginative intensity with precise philosophical definition. This is very similar to the balance which Shelley had detected in the 'intense but regulated passion' of a painting by Correggio, and in that 'calm & sustained energy without which true greatness cannot be' which he identified in Dante and in the masterpieces of Greek sculpture.[33] Shelley's own miraculous equilibrium received its most perceptive tribute from Walter Bagehot:

> The peculiarity of his style is its intellectuality; and this strikes us the more from its contrast with his impulsiveness ... So in his writings; over the most intense excitement, the grandest objects, the keenest agony, the most buoyant joy, he throws an air of subtle mind. His language is minutely and acutely searching; at the dizziest height of meaning the keenness of the word is greatest ... In the wildest of ecstasies his self-anatomising intellect is equal to itself.[34]

Few critics have come closer to defining the secret of Shelley's particular excellence.

TIMOTHY WEBB

References

Full details of works cited here can be found in the Select Bibliography. Prose is cited from the edition by D. L. Clark (Albuquerque, NM, 1966), corrected where necessary and possible.

1   *Prose*, 281; *Letters*, II, 310.
2   'Tradition and the Individual Talent', *Selected Essays*, 3rd edn (London, 1951), 22.
3   Discussed in detail by Matthews, 'Shelley's Lyrics', Levin and Chernaik.

4 *Modern Poetry and the Tradition* (Chapel Hill, NC, 1939; new edn, 1965), 237.
5 See Pottle, 'The Case of Shelley', and Bloom, *Shelley's Mythmaking*.
6 See Hughes, 'Kindling and Dwindling: The Poetic Process in Shelley', and 'Coherence and Collapse in Shelley'; Webb, *Shelley: A Voice Not Understood*.
7 Based on Oxford, Bodleian Library, MS Shelley adds e. 9, 24, which reads 'Aeschylus' rather than 'Greek tragedians' and does not include Chaucer; these additions are based on Shelley's statements elsewhere.
8 *Prose*, 295.
9 On Rousseau, see *Letters*, I, 84; *Prose*, 67, 209.
10 Cited in Zillman. Cf. 'I have confidence in my moral sense alone; but that is a kind of originality' (*Letters*, II, 153).
11 For an excellent critical account, see Chernaik; for a collection of essays, see Swinden.
12 *The Fall of Hyperion*, I. 148–9.
13 See Cameron (*passim*) and McNiece.
14 *Letters*, I, 127; II, 153.
15 Ibid., II, 164.
16 Most of these topics are extensively discussed in the Notes to *Queen Mab* or in *A Philosophical View of Reform* (*Prose*, 229–61; quotation from 244).
17 *Prose*, 243.
18 Hunt's letters to and critical appraisals of Shelley can be found in Brimley Johnson; see also Hunt's *Autobiography*.
19 All quotations from *Prose*, 293.
20 *Prose*, 286.
21 For Greek and Christian, see Bloom, *Shelley's Mythmaking*; Wasserman, *Shelley: A Critical Reading*; Webb, *Shelley: A Voice Not Understood*. For Oriental, see Curran, *Shelley's Annus Mirabilis*.
22 *A Study of English Romanticism* (New York, 1968), 110.
23 *Prose*, p. 294; *Letters*, II, 125.
24 Analysed brilliantly by Wasserman, *Shelley: A Critical Reading*.
25 *Science and the Modern World* (Harmondsworth, 1938), 103.
26 For Davy, see Webb, *Shelley: A Voice Not Understood*. For light, electricity and matter, see Grabo and Butter. For volcanoes, see Matthews, 'A Volcano's Voice in Shelley'. For clouds, see Kinghele and Ludlam.
27 W. B. Yeats, 'Among School Children'. For scepticism, see Pulos and Wasserman, *Shelley: A Critical Reading*. For Platonism, see Notopoulos, and Rogers, *Shelley at Work*.
28 *Prose*, 202.

29 *Julian and Maddalo*, 157; *Prometheus Unbound*, III, ii. 49;
    Adonais, 460–3; *Peter Bell the Third*, 313–17, here 167–71; *The
    Mask of Anarchy*, 16–17; *Hymn to Mercury*, 188–9; *Prometheus
    Unbound*, I. 625–8.

30 An oral judgement recorded by Christopher Wordsworth in 1827:
    see *The Critical Opinions of William Wordsworth*, ed. M. L.
    Peacock, Jr., (Baltimore, Md, 1950).

31 *Prometheus Unbound*, IV.322.

32 *Letters*, I, 578.

33 Ibid., II, 50, 20.

34 'Percy Bysshe Shelley' (1856), in *Literary Studies*, Everyman edn
    (London, 1911; repr. 1951), I, 110–11.

NOTE ON THE TEXT

The textual history of Shelley's poetry has been highly unfortunate. Many of the poems by which he is best known were published after his death and without his final authority. Some of these poems (e.g. *The Mask of Anarchy*) had not been published because his publishers feared prosecution; others were less dangerous but had not yet found an appropriate home. Yet others, such as *Letter to Maria Gisborne*, were essentially private, were not intended for immediate publication and had not been prepared for the printer. A significant number of fragments and lyrics were discovered among the manuscript drafts; these were often rough, sparsely punctuated, and sometimes illegible. Nearly all of these poems, representing so many different stages of authorial intention, were published but with little indication of the significant variations in their status. Although his widow and the later nineteenth-century editors deserve great credit for their dedication to an extremely difficult undertaking, they must also take the blame for distorting and sometimes misrepresenting Shelley's achievement. Not infrequently they misread his handwriting, misunderstood his intentions, published lines and even stanzas in the wrong order (as in 'The Boat on the Serchio', and 'Rose leaves, when the rose is dead'), tidied up his grammar and occasionally rewrote his poems according to their own notions of how Shelley might or ought to have written them.

The present edition attempts to be as faithful as possible to Shelley's texts and his intentions, while keeping in mind the claims of legibility. I have modernized spellings where there seemed little point in retaining the old form (e.g. *thro'*) but I have retained any spellings which might have special significance either for sound or meaning (e.g. *sate, leapt*). Shelley's frequent misspellings have been corrected and his ampersands amplified to *and*. In his drafts and fair copies Shelley was liberal and often erratic in his use of capitals; many of these did not appear in the printed versions. I have on occasions ignored Shelley's capitals where they seem unduly obtrusive and where it seems unlikely that he would have retained them in a printed version; in these cases the editions of Mary Shelley have provided an invaluable guide. Conversely, there have been a number of cases where Shelley did not see his own work through the press and the capitalization of the printed version has had to be checked against the remaining drafts and fair copies.

Where possible I have followed first editions or fair copies, though in both cases I have found it necessary to emend both substantively and in matters of punctuation. Notoriously, Shelley was displeased with the *Prometheus Unbound* collection (1820), published in England while he was in Italy. In this instance particularly, I have made use of his own fair copies to correct the first edition. Fair copies by Mary have been checked against manuscript drafts where these are available; fair copies by Shelley have been followed as meticulously as possible in every detail, though it has sometimes been necessary to add punctuation, usually at line endings, if the poem is to make any sense. Such additions have been made with great caution and, where possible, after a consultation of the manuscript draft. *Julian and Maddalo* is a good example: Shelley sent it to Hunt with instructions that it was to be published as it stood, yet even here a few extra commas have proved absolutely necessary. Here as elsewhere, I have followed Shelley's idiosyncratic system of dashes and dots and his characteristic use of the semicolon. In the case of rough drafts such as *The Triumph of Life* I have followed the same principle of minimum intervention: Shelley, of course, would have improved these poems had he lived. The notes indicate whether a poem was published before or after Shelley's death; an attempt has been made to indicate the general context of publication.

The publication history of Shelley's prose is similar to that of the poetry, and equally troubled. Shelley published novels, reviews, philosophical essays and political pamphlets as well as significant prefaces and notes to his poems, but he also left a considerable body of unpublished prose writing (including several translations), most of it unfinished and certainly not ready for the printer. In preparing these unpublished materials, I have followed the editorial principles that I first evolved in editing the poetry. On occasion, the resulting texts may seem to be under-punctuated by the standards of the early nineteenth century. However, I have preferred to pursue the joint editorial objectives of intelligibility and minimum editorial intervention rather than attempting to reconstruct on a comprehensive but speculative basis the text which might have appeared if Shelley's own work had been printed during his lifetime.

POEMS AND PROSE

1 *From* QUEEN MAB;
A PHILOSOPHICAL POEM WITH NOTES

A strange and woe-worn wight
Arose beside the battlement,
   And stood unmoving there.   70
His inessential figure cast no shade
   Upon the golden floor;
His port and mien bore mark of many years,
And chronicles of untold ancientness
Were legible within his beamless eye: 75
   Yet his cheek bore the mark of youth;
Freshness and vigour knit his manly frame;
The wisdom of old age was mingled there
   With youth's primaeval dauntlessness;
     And inexpressible woe,   80
Chastened by fearless resignation, gave
An awful grace to his all-speaking brow.

Spirit. 'Is there a God?'

Ahasuerus. 'Is there a God! – aye, an almighty God,
And vengeful as almighty! Once his voice   85
Was heard on earth: earth shuddered at the sound;
The fiery-visaged firmament expressed
Abhorrence, and the grave of nature yawned
To swallow all the dauntless and the good
That dared to hurl defiance at his throne,   90
Girt as it was with power. None but slaves
Survived, – cold-blooded slaves, who did the work
Of tyrannous omnipotence; whose souls
No honest indignation ever urged
To elevated daring, to one deed   95
Which gross and sensual self did not pollute.
These slaves built temples for the omnipotent fiend,
Gorgeous and vast: the costly altars smoked
With human blood, and hideous paeans rung
Through all the long-drawn aisles. A murderer heard 100
His voice in Egypt, one whose gifts and arts
Had raised him to his eminence in power,

Accomplice of omnipotence in crime,
And confidant of the all-knowing one.
    These were Jehovah's words: –   105

'From an eternity of idleness
I, God, awoke; in seven days' toil made earth
From nothing; rested, and created man:
I placed him in a paradise, and there
Planted the tree of evil, so that he   110
Might eat and perish, and my soul procure
Wherewith to sate its malice, and to turn,
Even like a heartless conqueror of the earth,
All misery to my fame. The race of men
Chosen to my honour, with impunity   115
May sate the lusts I planted in their heart.
Here I command thee hence to lead them on,
Until, with hardened feet, their conquering troops
Wade on the promised soil through woman's blood,
And make my name be dreaded through the land.   120
Yet ever-burning flame and ceaseless woe
Shall be the doom of their eternal souls,
With every soul on this ungrateful earth,
Virtuous or vicious, weak or strong, – even all
Shall perish, to fulfil the blind revenge   125
(Which you, to men, call justice) of their God.'
                    The murderer's brow
Quivered with horror.
                        'God omnipotent,
Is there no mercy? must our punishment
Be endless? will long ages roll away,   130
And see no term? Oh! wherefore hast thou made
In mockery and wrath this evil earth?
Mercy becomes the powerful – be but just:
O God! repent and save.'

                        'One way remains:
I will beget a son, and he shall bear   135
The sins of all the world; he shall arise
In an unnoticed corner of the earth,
And there shall die upon a cross, and purge
The universal crime; so that the few

On whom my grace descends, those who are marked   140
As vessels to the honour of their God,
May credit this strange sacrifice, and save
Their souls alive: millions shall live and die,
Who ne'er shall call upon their Saviour's name,
But, unredeemed, go to the gaping grave.   145
Thousands shall deem it an old woman's tale,
Such as the nurses frighten babes withal:
These in a gulf of anguish and of flame
Shall curse their reprobation endlessly,
Yet tenfold pangs shall force them to avow,   150
Even on their beds of torment, where they howl,
My honour, and the justice of their doom.
What then avail their virtuous deeds, their thoughts
Of purity, with radiant genius bright,
Or lit with human reason's earthly ray?   155
Many are called, but few will I elect.
Do thou my bidding, Moses!'
                     Even the murderer's cheek
Was blanched with horror, and his quivering lips
Scarce faintly uttered – 'O almighty one,
I tremble and obey!'   160

'O Spirit! centuries have set their seal
On this heart of many wounds, and loaded brain,
Since the Incarnate came: humbly he came,
Veiling his horrible Godhead in the shape
Of man, scorned by the world, his name unheard,   165
Save by the rabble of his native town,
Even as a parish demagogue. He led
The crowd; he taught them justice, truth, and peace,
In semblance; but he lit within their souls
The quenchless flames of zeal, and blessed the sword   170
He brought on earth to satiate with the blood
Of truth and freedom his malignant soul.
At length his mortal frame was led to death.
I stood beside him: on the torturing cross
No pain assailed his unterrestrial sense;   175
And yet he groaned. Indignantly I summed
The massacres and miseries which his name
Had sanctioned in my country, and I cried,

"Go! Go!" in mockery.
A smile of godlike malice reillumed   180
His fading lineaments. – "I go," he cried,
"But thou shalt wander o'er the unquiet earth
Eternally." – The dampness of the grave
Bathed my imperishable front. I fell,
And long lay tranced upon the charmèd soil.   185
When I awoke Hell burned within my brain,
Which staggered on its seat; for all around
The mouldering relics of my kindred lay,
Even as the Almighty's ire arrested them,
And in their various attitudes of death   190
My murdered children's mute and eyeless skulls
Glared ghastily upon me.
                          But my soul,
From sight and sense of the polluting woe
Of tyranny, had long learned to prefer
Hell's freedom to the servitude of Heaven.   195
Therefore I rose, and dauntlessly began
My lonely and unending pilgrimage,
Resolved to wage unweariable war
With my almighty tyrant, and to hurl
Defiance at his impotence to harm   200
Beyond the curse I bore.'

Even love is sold

Not even the intercourse of the sexes is exempt from the
despotism of positive institution. Law pretends even to
govern the indisciplinable wanderings of passion, to put
fetters on the clearest deductions of reason, and, by appeals
to the will, to subdue the involuntary affections of our   5
nature. Love is inevitably consequent upon the perception of
loveliness. Love withers under constraint: its very essence is
liberty: it is compatible neither with obedience, jealousy, nor
fear: it is there most pure, perfect, and unlimited, where its
votaries live in confidence, equality, and unreserve.   10
     How long then ought the sexual connection to last? what
law ought to specify the extent of the grievances which
should limit its duration? A husband and wife ought to
continue so long united as they love each other: any law

which should bind them to cohabitation for one moment 15
after the decay of their affection would be a most intolerable
tyranny, and the most unworthy of toleration. How odious
an usurpation of the right of private judgement should that
law be considered which should make the ties of friendship
indissoluble, in spite of the caprices, the inconstancy, the 20
fallibility, and capacity for improvement of the human
mind. And by so much would the fetters of love be heavier
and more unendurable than those of friendship, as love is
more vehement and capricious, more dependent on those
delicate peculiarities of imagination, and less capable of 25
reduction to the ostensible merits of the object.

The state of society in which we exist is a mixture of
feudal savageness and imperfect civilization. The narrow
and unenlightened morality of the Christian religion is an
aggravation of these evils. It is not even until lately that 30
mankind have admitted that happiness is the sole end of the
science of ethics, as of all other sciences; and that the
fanatical idea of mortifying the flesh for the love of God has
been discarded. I have heard, indeed, an ignorant collegian
adduce, in favour of Christianity, its hostility to every 35
worldly feeling![1]

But if happiness be the object of morality, of all human
unions and disunions; if the worthiness of every action is to
be estimated by the quantity of pleasurable sensation it is
calculated to produce, then the connection of the sexes is so 40
long sacred as it contributes to the comfort of the parties,
and is naturally dissolved when its evils are greater than its
benefits. There is nothing immoral in this separation. Con-
stancy has nothing virtuous in itself, independently of the
pleasure it confers, and partakes of the temporizing spirit of 45
vice in proportion as it endures tamely moral defects of
magnitude in the object of its indiscreet choice. Love is free:

---

[1] The first Christian emperor made a law by which seduction was punished
with death; if the female pleaded her own consent, she also was punished with
death: if the parents endeavoured to screen the criminals, they were banished
and their estates were confiscated; the slaves who might be accessory were
burned alive, or forced to swallow melted lead. The very offspring of an illegal
love were involved in the consequences of the sentence. – Gibbon's *Decline and
Fall*, etc., vol. ii, p. 210. See also, for the hatred of the primitive Christians to
love and even marriage, p. 269.

to promise for ever to love the same woman is not less absurd than to promise to believe the same creed: such a vow, in both cases, excludes us from all enquiry. The language of the votarist is this: The woman I now love may be infinitely inferior to many others; the creed I now profess may be a mass of errors and absurdities; but I exclude myself from all future information as to the amiability of the one and the truth of the other, resolving blindly, and in spite of conviction, to adhere to them. Is this the language of delicacy and reason? Is the love of such a frigid heart of more worth than its belief?

The present system of constraint does no more, in the majority of instances, than make hypocrites or open enemies. Persons of delicacy and virtue, unhappily united to one whom they find it impossible to love, spend the loveliest season of their life in unproductive efforts to appear otherwise than they are, for the sake of the feelings of their partner or the welfare of their mutual offspring: those of less generosity and refinement openly avow their disappointment, and linger out the remnant of that union, which only death can dissolve, in a state of incurable bickering and hostility. The early education of their children takes its colour from the squabbles of the parents; they are nursed in a systematic school of ill-humour, violence, and falsehood. Had they been suffered to part at the moment when indifference rendered their union irksome, they would have been spared many years of misery: they would have connected themselves more suitably, and would have found that happiness in the society of more congenial partners which is for ever denied them by the despotism of marriage. They would have been separately useful and happy members of society, who, whilst united, were miserable, and rendered misanthropical by misery. The conviction that wedlock is indissoluble holds out the strongest of all temptations to the perverse: they indulge without restraint in acrimony, and all the little tyrannies of domestic life, when they know that their victim is without appeal. If this connection were put on a rational basis, each would be assured that habitual ill-temper would terminate in separation, and would check this vicious and dangerous propensity.

Prostitution is the legitimate offspring of marriage and its accompanying errors. Women, for no other crime than having followed the dictates of a natural appetite, are driven 90 with fury from the comforts and sympathies of society. It is less venial than murder; and the punishment which is inflicted on her who destroys her child to escape reproach is lighter than the life of agony and disease to which the prostitute is irrecoverably doomed. Has a woman obeyed the 95 impulse of unerring nature; – society declares war against her, pitiless and eternal war: she must be the tame slave, she must make no reprisals; theirs is the right of persecution, hers the duty of endurance. She lives a life of infamy: the loud and bitter laugh of scorn scares her from all return. She 100 dies of long and lingering disease: yet *she* is in fault, *she* is the criminal, *she* the froward and untameable child, – and society, forsooth, the pure and virtuous matron, who casts her as an abortion from her undefiled bosom! Society avenges herself on the criminals of her own creation; she is employed 105 in anathematizing the vice today, which yesterday she was the most zealous to teach. Thus is formed one-tenth of the population of London: meanwhile the evil is twofold. Young men, excluded by the fanatical idea of chastity from the society of modest and accomplished women, associate with 110 these vicious and miserable beings, destroying thereby all those exquisite and delicate sensibilities whose existence cold-hearted worldlings have denied; annihilating all genuine passion, and debasing that to a selfish feeling which is the excess of generosity and devotedness. Their body and mind 115 alike crumble into a hideous wreck of humanity; idiocy and disease become perpetuated in their miserable offspring, and distant generations suffer for the bigoted morality of their forefathers. Chastity is a monkish and evangelical superstition, a greater foe to natural temperance even than 120 unintellectual sensuality; it strikes at the root of all domestic happiness, and consigns more than half of the human race to misery, that some few may monopolize according to law. A system could not well have been devised more studiously hostile to human happiness than marriage.   125

I conceive that, from the abolition of marriage, the fit and natural arrangement of sexual connection would result. I by no means assert that the intercourse would be promiscuous: on the contrary, it appears, from the relation of parent to

child, that this union is generally of long duration, and 130
marked above all others with generosity and self-devotion.
But this is a subject which it is perhaps premature to discuss.
That which will result from the abolition of marriage will
be natural and right, because choice and change will be
exempted from restraint.   135

In fact, religion and morality, as they now stand, compose
a practical code of misery and servitude: the genius of
human happiness must tear every leaf from the accursed
book of God, ere man can read the inscription on his heart.
How would morality, dressed up in stiff stays and finery,   140
start from her own disgusting image, should she look in the
mirror of nature!

From   *No longer now he slays the lamb*
That looks him in the face.

Crime is madness. Madness is disease. Whenever the cause
of disease shall be discovered, the root, from which all vice
and misery have so long overshadowed the globe, will lie
bare to the axe. All the exertions of man, from that moment,
may be considered as tending to the clear profit of his species.   5
No sane mind in a sane body resolves upon a real crime. It is a
man of violent passions, blood-shot eyes, and swollen veins,
that alone can grasp the knife of murder. The system of a
simple diet promises no Utopian advantages. It is no mere
reform of legislation, whilst the furious passions and evil   10
propensities of the human heart, in which it had its origin,
are still unassuaged. It strikes at the root of all evil, and is an
experiment which may be tried with success, not alone by
nations, but by small societies, families, and even individ-
uals. In no cases has a return to vegetable diet produced the   15
slightest injury; in most it has been attended with changes
undeniably beneficial. Should ever a physician be born with
the genius of Locke, I am persuaded that he might trace all
bodily and mental derangements to our unnatural habits, as
clearly as that philosopher has traced all knowledge to sen-   20
sation. What prolific sources of disease are not those mineral
and vegetable poisons that have been introduced for its
extirpation! How many thousands have become murderers
and robbers, bigots and domestic tyrants, dissolute and

abandoned adventurers, from the use of fermented liquors; 25
who, had they slaked their thirst only with pure water, would
have lived but to diffuse the happiness of their own unperv-
erted feelings! How many groundless opinions and absurd
institutions have not received a general sanction from the
sottishness and intemperance of individuals! Who will assert 30
that, had the populace of Paris satisfied their hunger at the
ever-furnished table of vegetable nature, they would have lent
their brutal suffrage to the proscription-list of Robespierre?
Could a set of men, whose passions were not perverted by
unnatural stimuli, look with coolness on an *auto da fé* 35
Is it to be believed that a being of gentle feelings, rising from
his meal of roots, would take delight in sports of blood? Was
Nero a man of temperate life? could you read calm health in
his cheek, flushed with ungovernable propensities of hatred
for the human race? Did Muley Ismael's pulse beat evenly, 40
was his skin transparent, did his eyes beam with healthful-
ness, and its invariable concomitants, cheerfulness and
benignity? Though history has decided none of these ques-
tions, a child could not hesitate to answer in the negative.
Surely the bile-suffused cheek of Buonaparte, his wrinkled 45
brow, and yellow eye, the ceaseless inquietude of his nervous
system, speak no less plainly the character of his unresting
ambition than his murders and his victories. It is impossible,
had Buonaparte descended from a race of vegetable feeders,
that he could have had either the inclination or the power to 50
ascend the throne of the Bourbons. The desire of tyranny
could scarcely be excited in the individual, the power to
tyrannize would certainly not be delegated by a society neither
frenzied by inebriation nor rendered impotent and irrational
by disease. Pregnant indeed with inexhaustible calamity is the 55
renunciation of instinct, as it concerns our physical nature;
arithmetic cannot enumerate, nor reason perhaps suspect,
the multitudinous sources of disease in civilized life. Even
common water, that apparently innoxious pabulum, when
corrupted by the filth of populous cities, is a deadly and 60
insidious destroyer.[1] Who can wonder that all the induce-
ments held out by God himself in the Bible to virtue should
have been vainer than a nurse's tale; and that those dogmas,

---

[1] Lambe, *Reports on Cancer*

by which he has there excited and justified the most ferocious propensities, should have alone been deemed essential; 65 whilst Christians are in the daily practice of all those habits which have infected with disease and crime, not only the reprobate sons, but these favoured children of the common Father's love? Omnipotence itself could not save them from the consequences of this original and universal sin . . . 70

The change which would be produced by simpler habits on political economy is sufficiently remarkable. The monopolizing eater of animal flesh would no longer destroy his constitution by devouring an acre at a meal, and many loaves of bread would cease to contribute to gout, madness and 75 apoplexy, in the shape of a pint of porter, or a dram of gin, when appeasing the long-protracted famine of the hardworking peasant's hungry babes. The quantity of nutritious vegetable matter, consumed in fattening the carcase of an ox, would afford ten times the sustenance, undepraving indeed, 80 and incapable of generating disease, if gathered immediately from the bosom of the earth. The most fertile districts of the habitable globe are now actually cultivated by men for animals, at a delay and waste of aliment absolutely incapable of calculation. It is only the wealthy that can, to any great 85 degree, even now, indulge the unnatural craving for dead flesh, and they pay for the greater licence of the privilege by subjection to supernumerary diseases. Again, the spirit of the nation that should take the lead in this great reform, would insensibly become agricultural; commerce, with all its vice, 90 selfishness and corruption, would gradually decline; more natural habits would produce gentler manners, and the excessive complication of political relations would be so far simplified that every individual might feel and understand why he loved his country, and took a personal interest in its 95 welfare. How would England, for example, depend on the caprices of foreign rulers, if she contained within herself all the necessaries, and despised whatever they possessed of the luxuries of life? How could they starve her into compliance with their views? Of what consequence would it be that they 100 refused to take her woollen manufactures, when large and fertile tracts of the island ceased to be allotted to the waste of pasturage? On a natural system of diet, we should require no spices from India; no wines from Portugal, Spain, France,

or Madeira; none of those multitudinous articles of luxury, 105
for which every corner of the globe is rifled, and which are
the causes of so much individual rivalship, such calamitous
and sanguinary national disputes. In the history of modern
times, the avarice of commercial monopoly, no less than the
ambition of weak and wicked chiefs, seems to have fomented 110
the universal discord, to have added stubbornness to the
mistakes of cabinets, and indocility to the infatuation of the
people. Let it ever be remembered, that it is the direct influ-
ence of commerce to make the interval between the richest
and the poorest man wider and more unconquerable. Let it 115
be remembered that it is a foe to every thing of real worth
and excellence in the human character. The odious and dis-
gusting aristocracy of wealth is built upon the ruins of all that
is good in chivalry or republicanism; and luxury is the fore-
runner of a barbarism scarce capable of cure. Is it impossible 120
to realize a state of society, where all the energies of man shall
be directed to the production of his solid happiness? Cer-
tainly, if this advantage (the object of all political speculation)
be in any degree attainable, it is attainable only by a com-
munity, which holds out no factitious incentives to the avarice 125
and ambition of the few, and which is internally organized
for the liberty, security and comfort of the many. None must
be entrusted with power (and money is the completest species
of power) who do not stand pledged to use it exclusively for
the general benefit. But the use of animal flesh and fermented 130
liquors directly militates with this equality of the rights of
man. The peasant cannot gratify these fashionable cravings
without leaving his family to starve. Without disease and
war, those sweeping curtailers of population, pasturage
would include a waste too great to be afforded. The labour 135
requisite to support a family is far lighter[1] than is usually
supposed. The peasantry work, not only for themselves, but
for the aristocracy, the army, and the manufacturers.   140

---

[1] It has come under the author's experience, that some of the workmen on an
embankment in North Wales, who, in consequence of the inability of the
proprietor to pay them, seldom received their wages, have supported large
families by cultivating small spots of sterile ground by moonlight. In the notes
to Pratt's poem, *Bread, or the Poor*, is an account of an industrious labourer,
who, by working in a small garden before and after his day's task, attained to
an enviable state of independence.

The advantage of a reform in diet is obviously greater than that of any other. It strikes at the root of the evil. To remedy the abuses of legislation, before we annihilate the propensities by which they are produced, is to suppose, that by taking away the effect, the cause will cease to operate. But the efficacy of this system depends entirely on the proselytism of individuals, and grounds its merits, as a 145 benefit to the community, upon the total change of the dietetic habits in its members. It proceeds securely from a number of particular cases to one that is universal, and has this advantage over the contrary mode, that one error does not invalidate all that has gone before.   150

Let not too much, however, be expected from this system. The healthiest among us is not exempt from hereditary disease. The most symmetrical, athletic, and longlived is a being inexpressibly inferior to what he would have been, had not the unnatural habits of his ancestors accumulated 155 for him a certain portion of malady and deformity. In the most perfect specimen of civilized man, something is still found wanting by the physiological critic. Can a return to nature, then, instantaneously eradicate predispositions that 160 have been slowly taking root in the silence of innumerable ages? – Indubitably not. All that I contend for is, that from the moment of the relinquishing all unnatural habits no new disease is generated; and that the predisposition to hereditary maladies gradually perishes, for want of its accustomed supply. In cases of consumption, cancer, gout, asthma, and 165 scrofula, such is the invariable tendency of a diet of vegetables and pure water.

2   TO WORDSWORTH

Poet of Nature, thou hast wept to know
That things depart which never may return:
Childhood and youth, friendship and love's first glow,
Have fled like sweet dreams, leaving thee to mourn.
These common woes I feel. One loss is mine   5
Which thou too feel'st, yet I alone deplore.
Thou wert as a lone star, whose light did shine

On some frail bark in winter's midnight roar:
Thou hast like to a rock-built refuge stood
Above the blind and battling multitude: 10
In honoured poverty thy voice did weave
Songs consecrate to truth and liberty, –
Deserting these, thou leavest me to grieve,
Thus having been, that thou shouldst cease to be.

3   ALASTOR; OR, THE SPIRIT OF SOLITUDE

Preface

The poem entitled *Alastor*, may be considered as allegorical
of one of the most interesting situations of the human mind.
It represents a youth of uncorrupted feelings and adventur-
ous genius led forth by an imagination inflamed and purified
through familiarity with all that is excellent and majestic, to   5
the contemplation of the universe. He drinks deep of the
fountains of knowledge, and is still insatiate. The magnifi-
cence and beauty of the external world sinks profoundly
into the frame of his conceptions, and affords to their
modifications a variety not to be exhausted. So long as it is   10
possible for his desires to point towards objects thus infinite
and unmeasured, he is joyous, and tranquil, and self-
possessed. But the period arrives when these objects cease
to suffice. His mind is at length suddenly awakened and
thirsts for intercourse with an intelligence similar to itself.   15
He images to himself the Being whom he loves. Conversant
with speculations of the sublimest and most perfect natures,
the vision in which he embodies his own imaginations unites
all of wonderful, or wise, or beautiful, which the poet, the
philosopher, or the lover could depicture. The intellectual   20
faculties, the imagination, the functions of sense, have their
respective requisitions on the sympathy of corresponding
powers in other human beings. The Poet is represented as
uniting these requisitions, and attaching them to a single
image. He seeks in vain for a prototype of his conception.   25
Blasted by his disappointment, he descends to an untimely
grave.

The picture is not barren of instruction to actual men. The Poet's self-centred seclusion was avenged by the furies of an irresistible passion pursuing him to speedy ruin. But 30 that Power which strikes the luminaries of the world with sudden darkness and extinction, by awakening them to too exquisite a perception of its influences, dooms to a slow and poisonous decay those meaner spirits that dare to abjure its dominion. Their destiny is more abject and inglorious as 35 their delinquency is more contemptible and pernicious. They who, deluded by no generous error, instigated by no sacred thirst of doubtful knowledge, duped by no illustrious superstition, loving nothing on this earth, and cherishing no hopes beyond, yet keep aloof from sympathies with their 40 kind, rejoicing neither in human joy nor mourning with human grief; these, and such as they, have their apportioned curse. They languish, because none feel with them their common nature. They are morally dead. They are neither friends, nor lovers, nor fathers, nor citizens of the world, nor 45 benefactors of their country. Among those who attempt to exist without human sympathy, the pure and tender-hearted perish through the intensity and passion of their search after its communities, when the vacancy of their spirit suddenly makes itself felt. All else, selfish, blind, and torpid, are those 50 unforeseeing multitudes who constitute, together with their own, the lasting misery and loneliness of the world. Those who love not their fellow-beings live unfruitful lives, and prepare for their old age a miserable grave.

> The good die first, 55
> And those whose hearts are dry as summer dust,
> Burn to the socket!
> *December* 14, 1815.

Nondum amabam, et amare amabam, quærebam quid amarem, amans amare. – *Confess. St. August.*

Earth, ocean, air, belovèd brotherhood!
If our great Mother has imbued my soul
With aught of natural piety to feel
Your love, and recompense the boon with mine,
If dewy morn, and odorous noon, and even,   5

With sunset and its gorgeous ministers,
And solemn midnight's tingling silentness;
If autumn's hollow sighs in the sere wood,
And winter robing with pure snow and crowns
Of starry ice the grey grass and bare boughs;   10
If spring's voluptuous pantings when she breathes
Her first sweet kisses, have been dear to me;
If no bright bird, insect, or gentle beast
I consciously have injured, but still loved
And cherished these my kindred; then forgive   15
This boast, belovèd brethren, and withdraw
No portion of your wonted favour now!

    Mother of this unfathomable world!
Favour my solemn song, for I have loved
Thee ever, and thee only; I have watched   20
Thy shadow, and the darkness of thy steps,
And my heart ever gazes on the depth
Of thy deep mysteries. I have made my bed
In charnels and on coffins, where black death
Keeps record of the trophies won from thee,   25
Hoping to still these obstinate questionings
Of thee and thine, by forcing some lone ghost,
Thy messenger, to render up the tale
Of what we are. In lone and silent hours,
When night makes a weird sound of its own stillness,   30
Like an inspired and desperate alchemist
Staking his very life on some dark hope,
Have I mixed awful talk and asking looks
With my most innocent love, until strange tears
Uniting with those breathless kisses, made   35
Such magic as compels the charmèd night
To render up thy charge: . . . and, though ne'er yet
Thou hast unveil'd thy inmost sanctuary;
Enough from incommunicable dream,
And twilight phantasms, and deep noonday thought,   40
Has shone within me, that serenely now
And moveless, as a long-forgotten lyre
Suspended in the solitary dome
Of some mysterious and deserted fane,
I wait thy breath, Great Parent, that my strain   45

May modulate with murmurs of the air,
And motions of the forests and the sea,
And voice of living beings, and woven hymns
Of night and day, and the deep heart of man.

There was a Poet whose untimely tomb   50
No human hands with pious reverence reared,
But the charmed eddies of autumnal winds
Built o'er his mouldering bones a pyramid
Of mouldering leaves in the waste wilderness: –
A lovely youth, – no mourning maiden decked   55
With weeping flowers, or votive cypress wreath,
The lone couch of his everlasting sleep: –
Gentle, and brave, and generous, – no lorn bard
Breathed o'er his dark fate one melodious sigh:
He lived, he died, he sung, in solitude.   60
Strangers have wept to hear his passionate notes,
And virgins, as unknown he past, have pined
And wasted for fond love of his wild eyes.
The fire of those soft orbs has ceased to burn,
And Silence, too enamoured of that voice,   65
Locks its mute music in her rugged cell.

By solemn vision, and bright silver dream,
His infancy was nutured. Every sight
And sound from the vast earth and ambient air,
Sent to his heart its choicest impulses.   70
The fountains of divine philosophy
Fled not his thirsting lips, and all of great
Or good, or lovely, which the sacred past
In truth or fable consecrates, he felt
And knew. When early youth had past, he left   75
His cold fireside and alienated home
To seek strange truths in undiscovered lands.
Many a wide waste and tangled wilderness
Has lured his fearless steps; and he has bought
With his sweet voice and eyes, from savage men,   80
His rest and food. Nature's most secret steps
He like her shadow has pursued, where'er
The red volcano overcanopies
Its fields of snow and pinnacles of ice

With burning smoke, or where bitumen lakes   85
On black bare pointed islets ever beat
With sluggish surge, or where the secret caves
Rugged and dark, winding among the springs
Of fire and poison, inaccessible
To avarice or pride, their starry domes   90
Of diamond and of gold expand above
Numberless and immeasurable halls,
Frequent with crystal column, and clear shrines
Of pearl, and thrones radiant with chrysolite.
Nor had that scene of ampler majesty   95
Than gems or gold, the varying roof of heaven
And the green earth lost in his heart its claims
To love and wonder; he would linger long
In lonesome vales, making the wild his home,
Until the doves and squirrels would partake   100
From his innocuous hand his bloodless food,
Lured by the gentle meaning of his looks,
And the wild antelope, that starts whene'er
The dry leaf rustles in the brake, suspend
Her timid steps to gaze upon a form   105
More graceful than her own.

                              His wandering step
Obedient to high thoughts, has visited
The awful ruins of the days of old:
Athens, and Tyre, and Balbec, and the waste
Where stood Jerusalem, the fallen towers   110
Of Babylon, the eternal pyramids,
Memphis and Thebes, and whatsoe'er of strange
Sculptured on alabaster obelisk,
Or jasper tomb, or mutilated sphinx,
Dark Aethiopia in her desert hills   115
Conceals. Among the ruined temples there,
Stupendous columns, and wild images
Of more than man, where marble daemons watch
The Zodiac's brazen mystery, and dead men
Hang their mute thoughts on the mute walls around,   120
He lingered, poring on memorials
Of the world's youth, through the long burning day
Gazed on those speechless shapes, nor, when the moon

Filled the mysterious halls with floating shades
Suspended he that task, but ever gazed   125
And gazed, till meaning on his vacant mind
Flashed like strong inspiration, and he saw
The thrilling secrets of the birth of time.

    Meanwhile an Arab maiden brought his food,
Her daily portion, from her father's tent,   130
And spread her matting for his couch, and stole
From duties and repose to tend his steps: –
Enamoured, yet not daring for deep awe
To speak her love: – and watched his nightly sleep,
Sleepless herself, to gaze upon his lips   135
Parted in slumber, whence the regular breath
Of innocent dreams arose: then, when red morn
Made paler the pale moon, to her cold home
Wildered, and wan, and panting, she returned.

    The Poet wandering on, through Arabie   140
And Persia, and the wild Carmanian waste,
And o'er the aërial mountains which pour down
Indus and Oxus from their icy caves,
In joy and exultation held his way,
Till in the vale of Cashmire, far within   145
Its loneliest dell, where odorous plants entwine
Beneath the hollow rocks a natural bower,
Beside a sparkling rivulet he stretched
His languid limbs. A vision on his sleep
There came, a dream of hopes that never yet   150
Had flushed his cheek. He dreamed a veilèd maid
Sate near him, talking in low solemn tones.
Her voice was like the voice of his own soul
Heard in the calm of thought; its music long,
Like woven sounds of streams and breezes, held   155
His inmost sense suspended in its web
Of many-coloured woof and shifting hues.
Knowledge and truth and virtue were her theme,
And lofty hopes of divine liberty,
Thoughts the most dear to him, and poesy,   160
Herself a poet. Soon the solemn mood
Of her pure mind kindled through all her frame

A permeating fire: wild numbers then
She raised, with voice stifled in tremulous sobs
Subdued by its own pathos: her fair hands   165
Were bare alone, sweeping from some strange harp
Strange symphony, and in their branching veins
The eloquent blood told an ineffable tale.
The beating of her heart was heard to fill
The pauses of her music, and her breath   170
Tumultuously accorded with those fits
Of intermitted song. Sudden she rose,
As if her heart impatiently endured
Its bursting burthen: at the sound he turned,
And saw by the warm light of their own life   175
Her glowing limbs beneath the sinuous veil
Of woven wind, her outspread arms now bare,
Her dark locks floating in the breath of night,
Her beamy bending eyes, her parted lips
Outstretched, and pale, and quivering eagerly.   180
His strong heart sunk and sickened with excess
Of love. He reared his shuddering limbs and quelled
His gasping breath, and spread his arms to meet
Her panting bosom: . . . she drew back a while,
Then, yielding to the irresistible joy,   185
With frantic gesture and short breathless cry
Folded his frame in her dissolving arms.
Now blackness veiled his dizzy eyes, and night
Involved and swallowed up the vision; sleep,
Like a dark flood suspended in its course,   190
Rolled back its impulse on his vacant brain.

    Roused by the shock he started from his trance –
The cold white light of morning, the blue moon
Low in the west, the clear and garish hills,
The distinct valley and the vacant woods,   195
Spread round him where he stood. Whither have fled
The hues of heaven that canopied his bower
Of yesternight? The sounds that soothed his sleep,
The mystery and the majesty of Earth,
The joy, the exultation? His wan eyes   200
Gaze on the empty scene as vacantly
As ocean's moon looks on the moon in heaven.

The spirit of sweet human love has sent
A vision to the sleep of him who spurned
Her choicest gifts. He eagerly pursues   205
Beyond the realms of dream that fleeting shade;
He overleaps the bounds. Alas! alas!
Were limbs, and breath, and being intertwined
Thus treacherously? Lost, lost, for ever lost,
In the wide pathless desert of dim sleep,   210
That beautiful shape! Does the dark gate of death
Conduct to thy mysterious paradise,
O Sleep? Does the bright arch of rainbow clouds,
And pendent mountains seen in the calm lake,
Lead only to a black and watery depth,   215
While death's blue vault, with loathliest vapours hung,
Where every shade which the foul grave exhales
Hides its dead eye from the detested day,
Conduct, O Sleep, to thy delightful realms?
This doubt with sudden tide flowed on his heart,   220
The insatiate hope which it awakened, stung
His brain even like despair.

                      While daylight held
The sky, the Poet kept mute conference
With his still soul. At night the passion came,
Like the fierce fiend of a distempered dream,   225
And shook him from his rest, and led him forth
Into the darkness. – As an eagle grasped
In folds of the green serpent, feels her breast
Burn with the poison, and precipitates
Through night and day, tempest, and calm, and cloud, 230
Frantic with dizzying anguish, her blind flight
O'er the wide aëry wilderness: thus driven
By the bright shadow of that lovely dream,
Beneath the cold glare of the desolate night,
Through tangled swamps and deep precipitous dells, 235
Startling with careless step the moon-light snake,
He fled. Red morning dawned upon his flight,
Shedding the mockery of its vital hues
Upon his cheek of death. He wandered on
Till vast Aornos seen from Petra's steep   240
Hung o'er the low horizon like a cloud;

Through Balk, and where the desolated tombs
Of Parthian kings scatter to every wind
Their wasting dust, wildly he wandered on,
Day after day, a weary waste of hours,   245
Bearing within his life the brooding care
That ever fed on its decaying flame.
And now his limbs were lean; his scattered hair
Sered by the autumn of strange suffering
Sung dirges in the wind; his listless hand   250
Hung like dead bone within its withered skin;
Life, and the lustre that consumed it, shone
As in a furnace burning secretly
From his dark eyes alone. The cottagers,
Who ministered with human charity   255
His human wants, beheld with wondering awe
Their fleeting visitant. The mountaineer,
Encountering on some dizzy precipice
That spectral form, deemed that the Spirit of wind
With lightning eyes, and eager breath, and feet   260
Disturbing not the drifted snow, had paused
In its career: the infant would conceal
His troubled visage in his mother's robe
In terror at the glare of those wild eyes,
To remember their strange light in many a dream   265
Of after-times; but youthful maidens, taught
By nature, would interpret half the woe
That wasted him, would call him with false names
Brother, and friend, would press his pallid hand
At parting, and watch, dim through tears, the path   270
Of his departure from their father's door.

    At length upon the lone Chorasmian shore
He paused, a wide and melancholy waste
Of putrid marshes. A strong impulse urged
His steps to the sea-shore. A swan was there,   275
Beside a sluggish stream among the reeds.
It rose as he approached, and with strong wings
Scaling the upward sky, bent its bright course
High over the immeasurable main.
His eyes pursued its flight. – Thou hast a home,   280
Beautiful bird; thou voyagest to thine home,

Where thy sweet mate will twine her downy neck
With thine, and welcome thy return with eyes
Bright in the lustre of their own fond joy.
And what am I that I should linger here,   285
With voice far sweeter than thy dying notes,
Spirit more vast than thine, frame more attuned
To beauty, wasting these surpassing powers
In the deaf air, to the blind earth, and heaven
That echoes not my thoughts? A gloomy smile   290
Of desperate hope wrinkled his quivering lips.
For sleep, he knew, kept most relentlessly
Its precious charge, and silent death exposed,
Faithless perhaps as sleep, a shadowy lure,
With doubtful smile mocking its own strange charms.   295

    Startled by his own thoughts he looked around.
There was no fair fiend near him, not a sight
Or sound of awe but in his own deep mind.
A little shallop floating near the shore
Caught the impatient wandering of his gaze.   300
It had been long abandoned, for its sides
Gaped wide with many a rift, and its frail joints
Swayed with the undulations of the tide.
A restless impulse urged him to embark
And meet lone Death on the drear ocean's waste;   305
For well he knew that mighty Shadow loves
The slimy caverns of the populous deep.

    The day was fair and sunny; sea and sky
Drank its inspiring radiance, and the wind
Swept strongly from the shore, blackening the waves.   310
Following his eager soul, the wanderer
Leaped in the boat, he spread his cloak aloft
On the bare mast, and took his lonely seat,
And felt the boat speed o'er the tranquil sea
Like a torn cloud before the hurricane.   315

    As one that in a silver vision floats
Obedient to the sweep of odorous winds
Upon resplendent clouds, so rapidly
Along the dark and ruffled waters fled

The straining boat. – A whirlwind swept it on,   320
With fierce gusts and precipitating force,
Through the white ridges of the chafèd sea.
The waves arose. Higher and higher still
Their fierce necks writhed beneath the tempest's scourge
Like serpents struggling in a vulture's grasp.   325
Calm and rejoicing in the fearful war
Of wave running on wave, and blast on blast
Descending, and black flood on whirlpool driven
With dark obliterating course, he sate:
As if their genii were the ministers   330
Appointed to conduct him to the light
Of those belovèd eyes, the Poet sate
Holding the steady helm. Evening came on,
The beams of sunset hung their rainbow hues
High 'mid the shifting domes of sheeted spray   335
That canopied his path o'er the waste deep;
Twilight, ascending slowly from the east,
Entwin'd in duskier wreaths her braided locks
O'er the fair front and radiant eyes of day;
Night followed, clad with stars. On every side   340
More horribly the multitudinous streams
Of ocean's mountainous waste to mutual war
Rushed in dark tumult thundering, as to mock
The calm and spangled sky. The little boat
Still fled before the storm; still fled, like foam   345
Down the steep cataract of a wintry river;
Now pausing on the edge of the riven wave;
Now leaving far behind the bursting mass
That fell, convulsing ocean. Safely fled –
As if that frail and wasted human form,   350
Had been an elemental god.
              At midnight
The moon arose: and lo! the etherial cliffs
Of Caucasus, whose icy summits shone
Among the stars like sunlight, and around
Whose cavern'd base the whirlpools and the waves   355
Bursting and eddying irresistibly
Rage and resound for ever. – Who shall save? –
The boat fled on, – the boiling torrent drove, –
The crags closed round with black and jagged arms,

The shattered mountain overhung the sea,   360
And faster still, beyond all human speed,
Suspended on the sweep of the smooth wave,
The little boat was driven. A cavern there
Yawned, and amid its slant and winding depths
Ingulfed the rushing sea. The boat fled on   365
With unrelaxing speed. – 'Vision and Love!'
The Poet cried aloud, 'I have beheld
The path of thy departure. Sleep and death
Shall not divide us long!'

               The boat pursued
The winding of the cavern. Daylight shone   370
At length upon that gloomy river's flow;
Now, where the fiercest war among the waves
Is calm, on the unfathomable stream
The boat moved slowly. Where the mountain, riven,
Exposed those black depths to the azure sky,   375
Ere yet the flood's enormous volume fell
Even to the base of Caucasus, with sound
That shook the everlasting rocks, the mass
Filled with one whirlpool all that ample chasm;
Stair above stair the eddying waters rose,   380
Circling immeasurably fast, and laved
With alternating dash the gnarlèd roots
Of mighty trees, that stretched their giant arms
In darkness over it. I' the midst was left,
Reflecting, yet distorting every cloud,   385
A pool of treacherous and tremendous calm.
Seized by the sway of the ascending stream,
With dizzy swiftness, round, and round, and round,
Ridge after ridge the straining boat arose,
Till on the verge of the extremest curve,   390
Where, through an opening of the rocky bank,
The waters overflow, and a smooth spot
Of glassy quiet mid those battling tides
Is left, the boat paused shuddering. – Shall it sink
Down the abyss? Shall the reverting stress   395
Of that resistless gulf embosom it?
Now shall it fall? – A wandering stream of wind,
Breathed from the west, has caught the expanded sail,

And lo! with gentle motion, between banks
Of mossy slope, and on a placid stream,   400
Beneath a woven grove it sails, and hark!
The ghastly torrent mingles its far roar,
With the breeze murmuring in the musical woods.
Where the embowering trees recede, and leave
A little space of green expanse, the cove   405
Is closed by meeting banks, whose yellow flowers
For ever gaze on their own drooping eyes,
Reflected in the crystal calm. The wave
Of the boat's motion marred their pensive task,
Which nought but vagrant bird, or wanton wind,   410
Or falling spear-grass, or their own decay
Had e'er disturbed before. The Poet longed
To deck with their bright hues his withered hair,
But on his heart its solitude returned,
And he forbore. Not the strong impulse hid   415
In those flushed cheeks, bent eyes, and shadowy frame,
Had yet performed its ministry: it hung
Upon his life, as lightning in a cloud
Gleams, hovering ere it vanish, ere the floods
Of night close over it.
                    The noonday sun   420
Now shone upon the forest, one vast mass
Of mingling shade, whose brown magnificence
A narrow vale embosoms. There, huge caves,
Scooped in the dark base of their aëry rocks
Mocking its moans, respond and roar for ever.   425
The meeting boughs and implicated leaves
Wove twilight o'er the Poet's path, as led
By love, or dream, or god, or mightier Death,
He sought in Nature's dearest haunt, some bank,
Her cradle, and his sepulchre. More dark   430
And dark the shades accumulate. The oak,
Expanding its immense and knotty arms,
Embraces the light beech. The pyramids
Of the tall cedar overarching, frame
Most solemn domes within, and far below,   435
Like clouds suspended in an emerald sky,
The ash and the acacia floating hang
Tremulous and pale. Like restless serpents, clothed

In rainbow and in fire, the parasites,
Starred with ten thousand blossoms, flow around   440
The grey trunks, and, as gamesome infants' eyes,
With gentle meanings, and most innocent wiles,
Fold their beams round the hearts of those that love,
These twine their tendrils with the wedded boughs
Uniting their close union; the woven leaves   445
Make net-work of the dark blue light of day,
And the night's noontide clearness, mutable
As shapes in the weird clouds. Soft mossy lawns
Beneath these canopies extend their swells,
Fragrant with perfumed herbs, and eyed with blooms   450
Minute yet beautiful. One darkest glen
Sends from its woods of musk-rose, twined with jasmine,
A soul-dissolving odour, to invite
To some more lovely mystery. Through the dell,
Silence and Twilight here, twin-sisters, keep   455
Their noonday watch, and sail among the shades,
Like vaporous shapes half seen; beyond, a well,
Dark, gleaming, and of most translucent wave,
Images all the woven boughs above,
And each depending leaf, and every speck   460
Of azure sky, darting between their chasms;
Nor aught else in the liquid mirror laves
Its portraiture, but some inconstant star
Between one foliaged lattice twinkling fair,
Or painted bird, sleeping beneath the moon,   465
Or gorgeous insect floating motionless,
Unconscious of the day, ere yet his wings
Have spread their glories to the gaze of noon.

    Hither the Poet came. His eyes beheld
Their own wan light through the reflected lines   470
Of his thin hair, distinct in the dark depth
Of that still fountain; as the human heart,
Gazing in dreams over the gloomy grave,
Sees its own treacherous likeness there. He heard
The motion of the leaves, the grass that sprung   475
Startled and glanced and trembled even to feel
An unaccustomed presence, and the sound
Of the sweet brook that from the secret springs

Of that dark fountain rose. A Spirit seemed
To stand beside him – clothed in no bright robes   480
Of shadowy silver or enshrining light,
Borrowed from aught the visible world affords
Of grace, or majesty, or mystery; –
But, undulating woods, and silent well,
And leaping rivulet, and evening gloom   485
Now deepening the dark shades, for speech assuming
Held commune with him, as if he and it
Were all that was, – only . . . when his regard
Was raised by intense pensiveness, . . . two eyes,
Two starry eyes, hung in the gloom of thought,   490
And seemed with their serene and azure smiles
To beckon him.

           Obedient to the light
That shone within his soul, he went, pursuing
The windings of the dell. – The rivulet
Wanton and wild, through many a green ravine   495
Beneath the forest flowed. Sometimes it fell
Among the moss with hollow harmony
Dark and profound. Now on the polished stones
It danced; like childhood laughing as it went:
Then, through the plain in tranquil wanderings crept,   500
Reflecting every herb and drooping bud
That overhung its quietness. – 'O stream!
Whose source is inaccessibly profound,
Whither do thy mysterious waters tend?
Thou imagest my life. Thy darksome stillness,   505
Thy dazzling waves, thy loud and hollow gulfs,
Thy searchless fountain, and invisible course
Have each their type in me: and the wide sky,
And measureless ocean may declare as soon
What oozy cavern or what wandering cloud   510
Contains thy waters, as the universe
Tell where these living thoughts reside, when stretched
Upon thy flowers my bloodless limbs shall waste
I' the passing wind!'

           Beside the grassy shore
Of the small stream he went; he did impress   515

On the green moss his tremulous step, that caught
Strong shuddering from his burning limbs. As one
Roused by some joyous madness from the couch
Of fever, he did move; yet, not like him,
Forgetful of the grave, where, when the flame   520
Of his frail exultation shall be spent,
He must descend. With rapid steps he went
Beneath the shade of trees, beside the flow
Of the wild babbling rivulet; and now
The forest's solemn canopies were changed   525
For the uniform and lightsome evening sky.
Grey rocks did peep from the spare moss, and stemmed
The struggling brook: tall spires of windlestrae
Threw their thin shadows down the rugged slope,
And nought but gnarlèd roots of ancient pines   530
Branchless and blasted, clenched with grasping roots
The unwilling soil. A gradual change was here,
Yet ghastly. For, as fast years flow away,
The smooth brow gathers, and the hair grows thin
And white, and where irradiate dewy eyes   535
Had shone, gleam stony orbs: – so from his steps
Bright flowers departed, and the beautiful shade
Of the green groves, with all their odorous winds
And musical motions. Calm, he still pursued
The stream, that with a larger volume now   540
Rolled through the labyrinthine dell; and there
Fretted a path through its descending curves
With its wintry speed. On every side now rose
Rocks, which, in unimaginable forms,
Lifted their black and barren pinnacles   545
In the light of evening, and its precipice
Obscuring the ravine, disclosed above,
Mid toppling stones, black gulfs and yawning caves,
Whose windings gave ten thousand various tongues
To the loud stream. Lo! where the pass expands   550
Its stony jaws, the abrupt mountain breaks,
And seems, with its accumulated crags,
To overhang the world: for wide expand
Beneath the wan stars and descending moon
Islanded seas, blue mountains, mighty streams,   555
Dim tracts and vast, robed in the lustrous gloom

Of leaden-coloured even, and fiery hills
Mingling their flames with twilight, on the verge
Of the remote horizon. The near scene,
In naked and severe simplicity,   560
Made contrast with the universe. A pine,
Rock-rooted, stretched athwart the vacancy
Its swinging boughs, to each inconstant blast
Yielding one only response, at each pause
In most familiar cadence, with the howl   565
The thunder and the hiss of homeless streams
Mingling its solemn song, whilst the broad river,
Foaming and hurrying o'er its rugged path,
Fell into that immeasurable void
Scattering its waters to the passing winds.   570

   Yet the grey precipice and solemn pine
And torrent, were not all; – one silent nook
Was there. Even on the edge of that vast mountain,
Upheld by knotty roots and fallen rocks,
It overlooked in its serenity   575
The dark earth, and the bending vault of stars.
It was a tranquil spot, that seemed to smile
Even in the lap of horror. Ivy clasped
The fissured stones with its entwining arms,
And did embower with leaves for ever green,   580
And berries dark, the smooth and even space
Of its inviolated floor, and here
The children of the autumnal whirlwind bore,
In wanton sport, those bright leaves, whose decay,
Red, yellow, or ethereally pale,   585
Rivals the pride of summer. 'Tis the haunt
Of every gentle wind, whose breath can teach
The wilds to love tranquillity. One step,
One human step alone, has ever broken
The stillness of its solitude: – one voice   590
Alone inspired its echoes, – even that voice
Which hither came, floating among the winds,
And led the loveliest among human forms
To make their wild haunts the depository
Of all the grace and beauty that endued   595
Its motions, render up its majesty,

Scatter its music on the unfeeling storm,
And to the damp leaves and blue cavern mould,
Nurses of rainbow flowers and branching moss,
Commit the colours of that varying cheek,   600
That snowy breast, those dark and drooping eyes.

    The dim and hornèd moon hung low, and poured
A sea of lustre on the horizon's verge
That overflowed its mountains. Yellow mist
Filled the unbounded atmosphere, and drank   605
Wan moonlight even to fullness: not a star
Shone, not a sound was heard; the very winds,
Danger's grim playmates, on that precipice
Slept, clasped in his embrace. – O, storm of death!
Whose sightless speed divides this sullen night: 610
And thou, colossal Skeleton, that, still
Guiding its irresistible career
In thy devastating omnipotence,
Art king of this frail world, from the red field
Of slaughter, from the reeking hospital,   615
The patriot's sacred couch, the snowy bed
Of innocence, the scaffold and the throne,
A mighty voice invokes thee. Ruin calls
His brother Death. A rare and regal prey
He hath prepared, prowling around the world;   620
Glutted with which thou mayst repose, and men
Go to their graves like flowers or creeping worms,
Nor ever more offer at thy dark shrine
The unheeded tribute of a broken heart.

    When on the threshold of the green recess   625
The wanderer's footsteps fell, he knew that death
Was on him. Yet a little, ere it fled,
Did he resign his high and holy soul
To images of the majestic past,
That paused within his passive being now,   630
Like winds that bear sweet music, when they breathe
Through some dim latticed chamber. He did place
His pale lean hand upon the rugged trunk
Of the old pine. Upon an ivied stone
Reclined his languid head, his limbs did rest,   635

Diffused and motionless, on the smooth brink
Of that obscurest chasm; – and thus he lay,
Surrendering to their final impulses
The hovering powers of life. Hope and despair,
The torturers, slept; no mortal pain or fear   640
Marred his repose, the influxes of sense,
And his own being unalloyed by pain,
Yet feebler and more feeble, calmly fed
The stream of thought, till he lay breathing there
At peace, and faintly smiling: – his last sight   645
Was the great moon, which o'er the western line
Of the wide world her mighty horn suspended,
With whose dun beams inwoven darkness seemed
To mingle. Now upon the jagged hills
It rests, and still as the divided frame   650
Of the vast meteor sunk, the Poet's blood,
That ever beat in mystic sympathy
With nature's ebb and flow, grew feebler still:
And when two lessening points of light alone
Gleamed through the darkness, the alternate gasp   655
Of his faint respiration scarce did stir
The stagnate night: – till the minutest ray
Was quenched, the pulse yet lingered in his heart.
It paused – it fluttered. But when heaven remained
Utterly black, the murky shades involved   660
An image, silent, cold, and motionless,
As their own voiceless earth and vacant air.
Even as a vapour fed with golden beams
That ministered on sunlight, ere the west
Eclipses it, was now that wondrous frame –   665
No sense, no motion, no divinity –
A fragile lute, on whose harmonious strings
The breath of heaven did wander – a bright stream
Once fed with many-voicèd waves – a dream
Of youth, which night and time have quenched for ever, 670
Still, dark, and dry, and unremembered now.

O, for Medea's wondrous alchemy,
Which whereso'er it fell made the earth gleam
With bright flowers, and the wintry boughs exhale
From vernal blooms fresh fragrance! O, that God,   675

Profuse of poisons, would concede the chalice
Which but one living man has drained, who now,
Vessel of deathless wrath, a slave that feels
No proud exemption in the blighting curse
He bears, over the world wanders for ever,   680
Lone as incarnate death! O, that the dream
Of dark magician in his visioned cave,
Raking the cinders of a crucible
For life and power, even when his feeble hand
Shakes in its last decay, were the true law   685
Of this so lovely world! But thou art fled
Like some frail exhalation; which the dawn
Robes in its golden beams, – ah! thou hast fled!
The brave, the gentle, and the beautiful,
The child of grace and genius. Heartless things   690
Are done and said i' the world, and many worms
And beasts and men live on, and mighty Earth
From sea and mountain, city and wilderness,
In vesper low or joyous orison,
Lifts still its solemn voice; – but thou art fled –   695
Thou canst no longer know or love the shapes
Of this phantasmal scene, who have to thee
Been purest ministers, who are, alas!
Now thou art not. Upon those pallid lips
So sweet even in their silence, on those eyes   700
That image sleep in death, upon that form
Yet safe from the worm's outrage, let no tear
Be shed – not even in thought. Nor, when those hues
Are gone, and those divinest lineaments,
Worn by the senseless wind, shall live alone   705
In the frail pauses of this simple strain,
Let not high verse, mourning the memory
Of that which is no more, or painting's woe
Or sculpture, speak in feeble imagery
Their own cold powers. Art and eloquence,   710
And all the shows o' the world are frail and vain
To weep a loss that turns their lights to shade.
It is a woe too 'deep for tears', when all
Is reft at once, when some surpassing Spirit,
Whose light adorned the world around it, leaves   715
Those who remain behind, not sobs or groans,

The passionate tumult of a clinging hope;
But pale despair and cold tranquillity,
Nature's vast frame, the web of human things,
Birth and the grave, that are not as they were.   720

4A   HYMN TO INTELLECTUAL BEAUTY:
FIRST VERSION

1

The lovely shadow of some awful Power
  Walks though unseen amongst us, visiting
  This peopled world with as inconstant wing
As summer winds that creep from flower to flower,
Like moonbeams that behind some piny mountain shower 5
  It visits with a wavering glance
  Each human heart and countenance; –
Like hues and harmonies of evening –
  Like clouds in starlight widely spread
  Like memory of music fled   10
Like aught that for its grace might be
Dear, and yet dearer for its mystery.

2

Shadow of Beauty! – that doth consecrate
  With thine own hues all thou dost fall upon
  Of human thought or form, where art thou gone   15
Why dost thou pass away and leave our state
A dark deep vale of tears, vacant and desolate?
  Ask why the sun light not forever
  Weaves rainbows o'er yon mountain river
Ask why aught fades away that once is shewn   20
  Ask wherefore dream and death and birth
  Cast on the daylight of this earth
Such gloom, – why man has such a scope
For love and joy despondency and hope.

3

No voice from some sublimer world hath ever   25
  To wisest poets these responses given
  Therefore the name of God and Ghosts and Heaven

Remain yet records of their vain Endeavour –
Frail spells, whose uttered charm might not avail to sever
 From what we feel and what we see   30
 Doubt, Chance and mutability.
Thy shade alone like mists o'er mountains driven
 Or music by the night-wind sent
 Thro' strings of some mute instrument
Or moonlight on a forest stream   35
Gives truth and grace to life's tumultuous dream

4

Love, hope and Self-esteem like clouds depart –
 And come, for some uncertain moments lent. –
 Man were immortal and omnipotent
Didst thou, unknown and awful as thou art   40
Keep with this glorious train firm state within his heart.
 Thou messenger of sympathies
 That wax and wane in lover's eyes
Thou that to the poets thought art nourishment
 As darkness to a dying flame   45
 Depart not as thy shadow came!
Depart not! – Lest the grave should be
Like life and fear a dark reality

5

While yet a boy I sought for ghosts, and sped
 Thro' many a lonely chamber, vault and ruin 50
 And starlight wood, with fearful step pursuing
Hopes of strange converse with the storied dead
I called on that false name with which our youth is fed
 He heard me not – I saw them not –
 When musing deeply on the lot
Of Life, at that sweet time when winds are wooing 55
 All vocal things that live to bring
 News of buds and blossoming –
Sudden thy shadow fell on me
I shrieked and clasped my hands in extasy. 60

6

I vowed that I would dedicate my powers
 To thee and thine – have I not kept the vow?

With streaming eyes and panting heart even now
I call the spectres of a thousand hours
Each from his voiceless grave, who have in visioned
                                          bowers   65
    Of studious zeal or love's delight
    Outwatched with me the waning night
To tell that never joy illumed my brow
    Unlinked with hope that thou wouldst free
    This world from its dark slavery   70
That thou, o, awful Loveliness!
Would give whate'er these words cannot express.

                            7
The day becomes more solemn and serene
    When Noon is past – there is a harmony
    In Autumn and a lustre in the sky   75
Which thro' the summer is not heard or seen
As if it could not be – as if it had not been –
    Thus let thy shade – which like the truth
    Of Nature on my passive youth
Descended, to my onward life supply   80
    Its hues, to one that worships thee
    And every form containing thee
Whom, fleeting power! thy spells did bind
To fear himself and love all human Kind.

4B   HYMN TO INTELLECTUAL BEAUTY:
SECOND VERSION

                            I
The awful shadow of some unseen Power
    Floats though unseen amongst us, – visiting
    This various world with as inconstant wing
As summer winds that creep from flower to flower. –
Like moonbeams that behind some piny mountain shower, 5
        It visits with inconstant glance
        Each human heart and countenance;
Like hues and harmonies of evening, –
        Like clouds in starlight widely spread, –

Like memory of music fled, –   10
Like aught that for its grace may be
Dear, and yet dearer for its mystery.

2

Spirit of BEAUTY, that doth consecrate
   With thine own hues all thou doest shine upon
   Of human thought or form, – where art thou gone?   15
Why dost thou pass away and leave our state,
This dim vast vale of tears, vacant and desolate?
      Ask why the sunlight not forever
      Weaves rainbows o'er yon mountain river,
Why aught should fail and fade that once is shown,   20
      Why fear and dream and death and birth
      Cast on the daylight of this earth
      Such gloom, – why man has such a scope
For love and hate, despondency and hope?

3

No voice from some sublimer world hath ever   25
   To sage or poet these responses given –
   Therefore the name of God and ghosts and Heaven,
Remain the records of their vain endeavour,
Frail spells – whose uttered charm might not avail to sever
      From all we hear and all we see,   30
      Doubt, chance and mutability.
Thy light alone – like mist o'er mountains driven,
      Or music by the night wind sent
      Through strings of some still instrument,
      Or moonlight on a midnight stream,   35
Gives grace and truth to life's unquiet dream.

4

Love, Hope, and Self-esteem, like clouds depart
   And come, for some uncertain moments lent.
   Man were immortal, and omnipotent,
Didst thou, unknown and awful as thou art,   40
Keep with thy glorious train firm state within his heart.
      Thou messenger of sympathies,
      That wax and wane in lovers' eyes –
Thou – that to human thought art nourishment,

Like darkness to a dying flame!   45
Depart not as thy shadow came,
Depart not – lest the grave should be,
Like life and fear, a dark reality.

                    5
While yet a boy I sought for ghosts, and sped
    Through many a listening chamber, cave and ruin,   50
    And starlight wood, with fearful steps pursuing
Hopes of high talk with the departed dead.
I called on poisonous names with which our youth is fed,
        I was not heard – I saw them not –
        When musing deeply on the lot   55
Of life, at that sweet time when winds are wooing
        All vital things that wake to bring
        News of buds and blossoming, –
        Sudden, thy shadow fell on me;
I shrieked, and clasped my hands in ecstasy!   60

                    6
I vowed that I would dedicate my powers
    To thee and thine – have I not kept the vow?
    With beating heart and streaming eyes, even now
I call the phantoms of a thousand hours
Each from his voiceless grave: they have in visioned bowers
        Of studious zeal or love's delight   65
        Outwatched with me the envious night –
They know that never joy illumed my brow
        Unlinked with hope that thou wouldst free
        This world from its dark slavery,   70
        That thou – O awful LOVELINESS,
Wouldst give whate'er these words cannot express.

                    7
The day becomes more solemn and serene
    When noon is past – there is a harmony
    In autumn, and a lustre in its sky,   75
Which through the summer is not heard or seen,
As if it could not be, as if it had not been!
        Thus let thy power, which like the truth
        Of nature on my passive youth

Descended, to my onward life supply   80
    Its calm – to one who worships thee,
    And every form containing thee,
     Whom, SPIRIT fair, thy spells did bind
To fear himself, and love all human kind.

5   VERSES WRITTEN ON RECEIVING A CELANDINE
IN A LETTER FROM ENGLAND

I thought of thee, fair Celandine,
    As of a flower aery blue
Yet small – thy leaves methought were wet
    With the light of morning dew;
In the same glen thy star did shine   5
As the primrose and the violet,
And the wild briar bent over thee
And the woodland brook danced under thee.

Lovely thou wert in thine own glen
    Ere thou didst dwell in song or story,   10
Ere the moonlight of a Poet's mind
    Had arrayed thee with the glory
Whose fountains are the hearts of men –
Many a thing of vital kind
Had fed and sheltered under thee,   15
Had nourished their thoughts near to thee.

Yes, gentle flower, in thy recess
    None might a sweeter aspect wear,
Thy young bud drooped so gracefully,
    Thou wert so very fair –   20
Among the fairest, ere the stress
Of exile, death and injury
Thus withering and deforming thee
Had made a mournful type of thee,

A type of that whence I and thou   25
    Are thus familiar, Celandine –
A deathless Poet whose young prime

Was as serene as thine;
But he is changed and withered now,
Fallen on a cold and evil time;   30
His heart is gone – his fame is dim,
And Infamy sits mocking him.

Celandine! Thou art pale and dead,
    Changed from thy fresh and woodland state.
Oh! that thy bard were cold, but he   35
    Has lived too long and late.
Would he were in an honoured grave;
But that, men say, now must not be
Since he for impious gold could sell
The love of those who loved him well.   40

That he, with all hope else of good
    Should be thus transitory
I marvel not – but that his lays
    Have spared not their own glory,
That blood, even the foul god of blood   45
With most inexpiable praise,
Freedom and truth left desolate,
He has been bought to celebrate!

They were his hopes which he doth scorn,
    They were his foes the fight that won;   50
That sanction and that condemnation
    Are now forever gone.
They need them not! Truth may not mourn
That with a liar's inspiration
Her majesty he did disown
Ere he could overlive his own.   55

They need them not, for Liberty,
    Justice and philosophic truth
From his divine and simple song
    Shall draw immortal youth   60
When he and thou shall cease to be
Or be some other thing, so long
As men may breathe or flowers may blossom
O'er the wide Earth's maternal bosom.

The stem whence thou wert disunited   65
   Since thy poor self was banished hither,
Now by that priest of Nature's care
   Who sent thee forth to wither
His window with its blooms has lighted,
And I shall see thy brethren there,   70
And each, like thee, will aye betoken
Love sold, hope dead, and honour broken.

6A   MONT BLANC: FIRST VERSION

Scene – Pont Pellisier in the vale of Servox

In day the eternal universe of things
Flows through the mind, and rolls its rapid waves
Now dark, now glittering; now reflecting gloom
Now lending splendour, where, from secret caves
The source of human thought its tribute brings   5
Of waters, with a sound not all its' own:
Such as a feeble brook will oft assume
In the wild woods among the mountains lone
Where waterfalls around it leap forever
Where winds and woods contend, and a vast river   10
Over its rocks ceaselessly bursts and raves

Thus thou Ravine of Arve, dark deep ravine,
Thou many coloured, many voiced vale!
Over whose rocks and pines and caverns sail
Fast cloud shadows and sunbeams – awful scene,   15
Where Power in likeness of the Arve comes down
From the ice gulphs that gird his secret throne
Bursting thro these dark mountains like the flame
Of lightning thro the tempest – thou dost lie
Thy giant brood of pines around thee clinging   20
Children of elder time, in whose devotion
The charmed winds still come, and ever came
To drink their odours, and their mighty swinging

6B MONT BLANC: SECOND VERSION

Lines Written in the Vale of Chamouni

1

The everlasting universe of things
Flows through the mind, and rolls its rapid waves,
Now dark – now glittering – now reflecting gloom –
Now lending splendour, where from secret springs
The source of human thought its tribute brings   5
Of waters, – with a sound but half its own,
Such as a feeble brook will oft assume
In the wild woods, among the mountains lone,
Where waterfalls around it leap forever,
Where woods and winds contend, and a vast river   10
Over its rocks ceaselessly bursts and raves.

2

Thus thou, Ravine of Arve – dark, deep Ravine –
Thou many-coloured, many-voicèd vale,
Over whose pines, and crags, and caverns sail
Fast cloud-shadows and sunbeams: awful scene,   15
Where Power in likeness of the Arve comes down
From the ice gulfs that gird his secret throne,
Bursting through these dark mountains like the flame
Of lightning through the tempest; – thou dost lie,
Thy giant brood of pines around thee clinging,   20
Children of elder time, in whose devotion
The chainless winds still come and ever came
To drink their odours, and their mighty swinging

To hear, an old and solemn harmony;
Thine earthly rainbows stretched across the sweep   25
Of the aerial waterfall, whose veil
Robes some unsculptured image; even the sleep
The sudden pause that does inhabit thee
Which when the voices of the desart fail
And its hues wane, doth blend them all and steep   30
Their periods in its own eternity;
Thy caverns echoing to the Arve's commotion
A loud lone sound no other sound can tame:
Thou art pervaded with such ceaseless motion
Thou art the path of that unresting sound   35
Ravine of Arve! and when I gaze on thee
I seem as in a vision deep and strange
To muse on my own various phantasy
My own, my human mind . . which passively
Now renders and receives fast influencings   40
Holding an unforeseeing interchange
With the clear universe of things around:
A legion of swift thoughts, whose wandering wings
Now float above thy darkness, and now rest
Near the still cave of the witch Poesy   45
Seeking among the shadows that pass by,
Ghosts of the things that are, some form like thee,
Some spectre, some faint image; till the breast
From which they fled recalls them – thou art there

Some say that gleams of a remoter world   50
Visit the soul in sleep – that death is slumber
And that its shapes the busy thoughts outnumber
Of those who wake and live. I look on high
Has some unknown omnipotence unfurled
The vail of life and death? or do I lie   55
In dream, and does the mightier world of sleep
Spread far around, and inaccessibly
Its circles? – for the very spirit fails
Driven like a homeless cloud from steep to steep
That vanishes among the viewless gales. –   60
Far, far above, piercing the infinite sky
Mont Blanc appears, still, snowy and serene,

To hear – an old and solemn harmony;
Thine earthly rainbows stretched across the sweep   25
Of the aethereal waterfall, whose veil
Robes some unsculptured image; the strange sleep
Which when the voices of the desert fail
Wraps all in its own deep eternity; –
Thy caverns echoing to the Arve's commotion,   30
A loud, lone sound no other sound can tame;
Thou art pervaded with that ceaseless motion,
Thou art the path of that unresting sound –
Dizzy Ravine! – and when I gaze on thee
I seem as in a trance sublime and strange   35
To muse on my own separate fantasy,
My own, my human mind, which passively
Now renders and receives fast influencings,
Holding an unremitting interchange
With the clear universe of things around;   40
One legion of wild thoughts, whose wandering wings
Now float above thy darkness, and now rest
Where that or thou art no unbidden guest,
In the still cave of the witch Poesy,
Seeking among the shadows that pass by,   45
Ghosts of all things that are, some shade of thee,
Some phantom, some faint image; till the breast
From which they fled recalls them, thou art there!

3

Some say that gleams of a remoter world
Visit the soul in sleep, – that death is slumber,   50
And that its shapes the busy thoughts outnumber
Of those who wake and live. – I look on high: –
Has some unknown omnipotence unfurled
The veil of life and death? or do I lie
In dream, and does the mightier world of sleep   55
Spread far around and inaccessibly
Its circles? For the very spirit fails,
Driven like a homeless cloud from steep to steep
That vanishes among the viewless gales!
Far, far above, piercing the infinite sky,   60
Mont Blanc appears, – still, snowy, and serene;

Its subject mountains their unearthly forms
Pile round it – ice and rock – broad chasms between
Of frozen waves, unfathomable deeps   65
Blue as the overhanging Heaven, that spread
And wind among the accumulated steeps,
Vast desarts, peopled by the storms alone
Save when the eagle brings some hunter's bone
And the wolf watches her – how hideously   70
Its rocks are heaped around, rude bare and high
Ghastly and scarred and riven! – is this the scene
Where the old Earthquake demon taught her young
Ruin? were these their toys? or did a sea
Of fire envelope once this silent snow?   75
None can reply – all seems eternal now.
This wilderness has a mysterious tongue
Which teaches awful doubt, or faith so mild
So simple, so serene that man may be
In such a faith with Nature reconciled.   80
Ye have a doctrine Mountains to repeal
Large codes of fraud and woe – not understood
By all, but which the wise and great and good
Interpret, or make felt, or deeply feel.

The fields, the lakes, the forests and the streams   85
Ocean, and all the living things that dwell
Within the daedal Earth, lightning and rain,
Earthquake, and lava flood and hurricane –
The torpor of the year, when feeble dreams
Visit the hidden buds, or dreamless sleep   90
Holds every future leaf and flower – the bound
With which from that detested trance they leap;
The works and ways of man, their death and birth
And that of him, and all that his may be,
All things that move and breathe with toil and sound   95
Are born and die, revolve subside and swell –
Power dwells apart in deep tranquillity,
Remote, sublime, and inaccessible
And this, the naked countenance of Earth
On which I gaze – even these primaeval mountains   100
Teach the adverting mind. – the Glaciers creep

Its subject mountains their unearthly forms
Pile round it, ice and rock; broad vales between
Of frozen floods, unfathomable deeps,
Blue as the overhanging heaven, that spread   65
And wind among the accumulated steeps: –
A desert peopled by the storms alone,
Save when the eagle brings some hunter's bone,
And the wolf tracks her there – how hideously
Its shapes are heaped around! rude, bare, and high,   70
Ghastly, and scarred, and riven. – Is this the scene
Where the old Earthquake-daemon taught her young
Ruin? Were these their toys? or did a sea
Of fire envelop once this silent snow?
None can reply – all seems eternal now.   75
The wilderness has a mysterious tongue
Which teaches awful doubt, or faith so mild,
So solemn, so serene, that man may be
But for such faith with nature reconciled;
Thou hast a voice, great Mountain, to repeal   80
Large codes of fraud and woe; not understood
By all, but which the wise, and great, and good
Interpret, or make felt, or deeply feel.

4

The fields, the lakes, the forests, and the streams,
Ocean, and all the living things that dwell   85
Within the daedal earth; lightning, and rain,
Earthquake, and fiery flood, and hurricane,
The torpor of the year when feeble dreams
Visit the hidden buds, or dreamless sleep
Holds every future leaf and flower; – the bound   90
With which from that detested trance they leap;
The works and ways of man, their death and birth,
And that of him and all that his may be;
All things that move and breathe with toil and sound
Are born and die; revolve, subside and swell.   95
Power dwells apart in its tranquillity
Remote, serene, and inaccessible:
And *this*, the naked countenance of earth,
On which I gaze, even these primæval mountains
Teach the adverting mind. The glaciers creep   100

Like snakes that watch their prey, from their far fountains
Slow rolling on: – there, many a precipice
Frost and the Sun in scorn of human power
Have piled: dome, pyramid and pinnacle   105
A city of death, distinct with many a tower
And wall impregnable of shining ice . . . .
A city's phantom . . but a flood of ruin
Is there that from the boundaries of the sky
Rolls its eternal stream . . vast pines are strewing   110
Its destined path, or in the mangled soil
Branchless and shattered stand – the rocks drawn down
From yon remotest waste have overthrown
The limits of the dead and living world
Never to be reclaimed – the dwelling place   115
Of insects, beasts and birds becomes its spoil,
Their food and their retreat for ever gone
So much of life and joy is lost – the race
Of man flies far in dread his work and dwelling
Vanish like smoke before the tempests stream   120
And their place is not known: – below, vast caves
Shine in the gushing torrents' restless gleam
Which from those secret chasms in tumult welling
Meet in the vale – and one majestic river
The breath and blood of distant lands, forever   125
Rolls its loud waters to the Ocean waves
Breathes its swift vapours to the circling air.

Mont Blanc yet gleams on high – the Power is there
The still and solemn Power of many sights
And many sounds, and much of life and death.   130
In the calm darkness of the moonless nights
Or the lone light of day the snows descend
Upon that mountain – none beholds them there
Nor when the sunset wraps their flakes in fire
Or the starbeams dart thro' them – winds contend   135
Silently there, and heap the snows, with breath
Blasting and swift – but silently – its home
The voiceless lightning in these solitudes
Keeps innocently, and like vapour broods
Over the snow. The secret strength of things   140

Like snakes that watch their prey, from their far fountains
Slow rolling on; there, many a precipice,
Frost and the Sun in scorn of mortal power
Have piled: dome, pyramid, and pinnacle,
A city of death, distinct with many a tower   105
And wall impregnable of beaming ice.
Yet not a city, but a flood of ruin
Is there, that from the boundaries of the sky
Rolls its perpetual stream; vast pines are strewing
Its destined path, or in the mangled soil   110
Branchless and shattered stand; the rocks, drawn down
From yon remotest waste, have overthrown
The limits of the dead and living world,
Never to be reclaimed. The dwelling-place
Of insects, beasts, and birds becomes its spoil;   115
Their food and their retreat forever gone,
So much of life and joy is lost. The race
Of man flies far in dread; his work and dwelling
Vanish, like smoke before the tempest's stream,
And their place is not known. Below, vast caves   120
Shine in the rushing torrents' restless gleam,
Which from those secret chasms in tumult welling
Meet in the vale, and one majestic River,
The breath and blood of distant lands, forever
Rolls its loud waters to the ocean waves,   125
Breathes its swift vapours to the circling air.

5

Mont Blanc yet gleams on high: – the power is there,
The still and solemn power of many sights,
And many sounds, and much of life and death.
In the calm darkness of the moonless nights,   130
In the lone glare of day, the snows descend
Upon that Mountain; none beholds them there,
Nor when the flakes burn in the sinking sun,
Or the star-beams dart through them. – Winds contend
Silently there, and heap the snow with breath   135
Rapid and strong, but silently! Its home
The voiceless lightning in these solitudes
Keeps innocently, and like vapour broods
Over the snow. The secret strength of things

Which governs thought, and to the infinite dome
Of Heaven is as a column, rests on thee,
And what were thou and Earth and Stars and Sea
If to the human minds imaginings
Silence and solitude were Vacancy.   145

Which governs thought, and to the infinite dome   140
Of heaven is as a law, inhabits thee!
And what were thou, and earth, and stars, and sea,
If to the human mind's imaginings
Silence and solitude were vacancy?

7 *From* LAON AND CYTHNA; OR, THE REVOLUTION OF THE GOLDEN CITY: A VISION OF THE NINETEENTH CENTURY. IN THE STANZA OF SPENSER

Preface

The Poem which I now present to the world, is an attempt from which I scarcely dare to expect success, and in which a writer of established fame might fail without disgrace. It is an experiment on the temper of the public mind, as to how far a thirst for a happier condition of moral and political society survives, among the enlightened and refined, the tempests which have shaken the age in which we live. I have sought to enlist the harmony of metrical language, the etherial combinations of the fancy, the rapid and subtle transitions of human passion, all those elements which essentially compose a Poem, in the cause of a liberal and comprehensive morality, and in the view of kindling within the bosoms of my readers, a virtuous enthusiasm for those doctrines of liberty and justice, that faith and hope in something good, which neither violence, nor misrepresentation, nor prejudice, can ever totally extinguish among mankind.

For this purpose I have chosen a story of human passion in its most universal character, diversified with moving and romantic adventures, and appealing, in contempt of all artifical opinions or institutions, to the common sympathies of every human breast. I have made no attempt to recommend the motives which I would substitute for those at present governing mankind by methodical and systematic argument. I would only awaken the feelings, so that the reader should see the beauty of true virtue, and be incited to those enquiries which have led to my moral and political creed, and that of some of the sublimest intellects in the world. The Poem therefore, (with the exception of the first Canto, which is purely introductory), is narrative, not didactic. It is a succession of pictures illustrating the growth and progress of individual mind aspiring after excellence, and devoted to the love of mankind; its influence in refining

and making pure the most daring and uncommon impulses
of the imagination, the understanding, and the senses; its   35
impatience at 'all the oppressions which are done under the
sun'; its tendency to awaken public hope and to enlighten
and improve mankind; the rapid effects of the application
of that tendency; the awakening of an immense nation from
their slavery and degradation to a true sense of moral   40
dignity and freedom; the bloodless dethronement of their
oppressors, and the unveiling of the religious frauds by
which they have been deluded into submission; the tranquill-
ity of successful patriotism, and the universal toleration and
benevolence of true philanthropy; the treachery and   45
barbarity of hired soldiers; vice not the object of punishment
and hatred, but kindness and pity; the faithlessness of
tyrants; the confederacy of the Rulers of the World, and the
restoration of the expelled Dynasty by foreign arms; the
massacre and extermination of the Patriots, and the victory   50
of established power; the consequences of legitimate despot-
ism, civil war, famine, plague, superstition, and an utter
extinction of the domestic affections; the judicial murder of
the advocates of Liberty; the temporary triumph of oppres-
sion, that secure earnest of its final and inevitable fall; the   55
transient nature of ignorance and error, and the eternity of
genius and virtue. Such is the series of delineations of which
the Poem consists. And if the lofty passions with which it
has been my scope to distinguish this story, shall not excite
in the reader a generous impulse, an ardent thirst for   60
excellence, an interest profound and strong, such as belongs
to no meaner desires – let not the failure be imputed to a
natural unfitness for human sympathy in these sublime and
animating themes. It is the business of the Poet to commu-
nicate to others the pleasure and the enthusiasm arising out   65
of those images and feelings, in the vivid presence of which
within his own mind, consists at once his inspiration and
his reward.

   The panic which, like an epidemic transport, seized upon
all classes of men during the excesses consequent upon the   70
French Revolution, is gradually giving place to sanity. It has
ceased to be believed, that whole generations of mankind
ought to consign themselves to a hopeless inheritance of
ignorance and misery, because a nation of men who had

been dupes and slaves for centuries, were incapable of 75
conducting themselves with the wisdom and tranquillity of
freemen so soon as some of their fetters were partially
loosened. That their conduct could not have been marked
by any other characters than ferocity and thoughtlessness,
is the historical fact from which liberty derives all its 80
recommendations, and falsehood the worst features of its
deformity. There is a reflux in the tide of human things
which bears the shipwrecked hopes of men into a secure
haven, after the storms are past. Methinks, those who now
live have survived an age of despair. 85

   The French Revolution may be considered as one of those
manifestations of a general state of feeling among civilized
mankind, produced by a defect of correspondence between
the knowledge existing in society and the improvement, or
gradual abolition of political institutions. The year 1788 90
may be assumed as the epoch of one of the most important
crises produced by this feeling. The sympathies connected
with that event extended to every bosom. The most generous
and amiable natures were those which participated the most
extensively in these sympathies. But such a degree of unmin- 95
gled good was expected, as it was impossible to realize. If
the Revolution had been in every respect prosperous, then
misrule and superstition would lose half their claims to our
abhorrence, as fetters which the captive can unlock with the
slightest motion of his fingers, and which do not eat with 100
poisonous rust into the soul. The revulsion occasioned by
the atrocities of the demagogues and the re-establishment of
sucessive tyrannies in France was terrible, and felt in the
remotest corner of the civilized world. Could they listen to
the plea of reason who had groaned under the calamities of 105
a social state, according to the provisions of which, one man
riots in luxury whilst another famishes for want of bread?
Can he who the day before was a trampled slave, suddenly
become liberal-minded, forbearing, and independent? This
is the consequence of the habits of a state of society to be 110
produced by resolute perseverance and indefatigable hope,
and long-suffering and long-believing courage, and the
systematic efforts of generations of men of intellect and
virtue. Such is the lesson which experience teaches now. But
on the first reverses of hope in the progress of French liberty, 115

the sanguine eagerness for good overleapt the solution of
these questions, and for a time extinguished itself in the
unexpectedness of their result. Thus many of the most
ardent and tender-hearted of the worshippers of public
good, have been morally ruined by what a partial glimpse   120
of the events they deplored, appeared to show as the
melancholy desolation of all their cherished hopes. Hence
gloom and misanthropy have become the characteristics of
the age in which we live, the solace of a disappointment
that unconsciously finds relief only in the wilful exaggera-   125
tion of its own despair. This influence has tainted the
literature of the age with the hopelessness of the minds
from which it flows. Metaphysics[1] and enquiries into moral
and political science, have become little else than vain
attempts to revive exploded superstitions, or sophisms like   130
those[2] of Mr Malthus, calculated to lull the oppressors of
mankind into a security of everlasting triumph. Our works
of fiction and poetry have been overshadowed by the same
infectious gloom. But mankind appear to me to be emerging
from their trance. I am aware, methinks, of a slow, gradual,   135
silent change. In that belief I have composed the following
Poem.

I do not presume to enter into competition with our
greatest contemporary Poets. Yet I am unwilling to tread in
the footsteps of any who have preceded me. I have sought   140
to avoid the imitation of any style of language or versifica-
tion peculiar to the original minds of which it is the
character, designing that even if what I have produced be
worthless, it should still be properly my own. Nor have I
permitted any system relating to mere words, to divert the   145
attention of the reader from whatever interest I may have
succeeded in creating, to my own ingenuity in contriving to
disgust them according to the rules of criticism. I have

[1] I ought to except Sir W. Drummond's *Academical Questions*; a volume of
very acute and powerful metaphysical criticism.

[2] It is remarkable, as a symptom of the revival of public hope, that Mr
Malthus has assigned, in the later editions of his work, an indefinite dominion
to moral restraint over the principle of population. This concession answers all
the inferences from his doctrine unfavourable to human improvement, and
reduces the *Essay on Population* to a commentary illustrative of the unanswer-
ableness of *Political Justice*.

simply clothed my thoughts in what appeared to me the most obvious and appropriate language. A person familiar 150 with nature, and with the most celebrated productions of the human mind, can scarcely err in following the instinct, with respect to selection of language, produced by that familiarity.

There is an education peculiarly fitted for a Poet, without 155 which, genius and sensibility can hardly fill the circle of their capacities. No education indeed can entitle to this appellation a dull and unobservant mind, or one, though neither dull nor unobservant, in which the channels of communication between thought and expression have been 160 obstructed or closed. How far it is my fortune to belong to either of the latter classes, I cannot know. I aspire to be something better. The circumstances of my accidental education have been favourable to this ambition. I have been familiar from boyhood with mountains and lakes, and the 165 sea, and the solitude of forests: Danger which sports upon the brink of precipices, has been my playmate. I have trodden the glaciers of the Alps, and lived under the eye of Mont Blanc. I have been a wanderer among distant fields. I have sailed down mighty rivers, and seen the sun rise and 170 set, and the stars come forth, whilst I have sailed night and day down a rapid stream among mountains. I have seen populous cities, and have watched the passions which rise and spread, and sink and change amongst assembled multitudes of men. I have seen the theatre of the more visible 175 ravages of tyranny and war, cities and villages reduced to scattered groups of black and roofless houses, and the naked inhabitants sitting famished upon their desolated thresholds. I have conversed with living men of genius. The poetry of ancient Greece and Rome, and modern Italy, and our own 180 country, has been to me like external nature, a passion and an enjoyment. Such are the sources from which the materials for the imagery of my Poem have been drawn. I have considered Poetry in its most comprehensive sense, and have read the Poets and the Historians, and the Metaphysicians[3] 185

---

[3] In this sense there may be such a thing as perfectibility in works of fiction, notwithstanding the concession often made by the advocates of human improvement, that perfectibility is a term applicable only to science.

whose writings have been accessible to me, and have looked
upon the beautiful and majestic scenery of the earth as
common sources of those elements which it is the province
of the Poet to embody and combine. Yet the experience and
the feelings to which I refer, do not in themselves constitute 190
men Poets, but only prepares them to be the auditors of
those who are. How far I shall be found to possess that
more essential attribute of Poetry, the power of awakening
in others sensations like those which animate my own
bosom, is that which, to speak sincerely, I know not; and 195
which with an acquiescent and contented spirit, I expect to
be taught by the effect which I shall produce upon those
whom I now address.

I have avoided, as I have said before, the imitation of any
contemporary style. But there must be a resemblance which 200
does not depend upon their own will, between all the writers
of any particular age. They cannot escape from subjection
to a common influence which arises out of an infinite
combination of circumstances belonging to the times in
which they live, though each is in a degree the author of the 205
very influence by which his being is thus pervaded. Thus,
the tragic Poets of the age of Pericles; the Italian revivers of
ancient learning; those mighty intellects of our own country
that succeeded the Reformation, the translators of the Bible,
Shakespeare, Spenser, the Dramatists of the reign of Eliza- 210
beth, and Lord Bacon;[4] the colder spirits of the interval that
succeeded; – all, resemble each other, and differ from every
other in their several classes. In this view of things, Ford can
no more be called the imitator of Shakespeare, than Shake-
speare the imitator of Ford. There were perhaps few other 215
points of resemblance between these two men, than that
which the universal and inevitable influence of their age
produced. And this is an influence which neither the meanest
scribbler, nor the sublimest genius of any era can escape;
and which I have not attempted to escape. 220

I have adopted the stanza of Spenser (a measure inexpress-
ibly beautiful), not because I consider it a finer model of
poetical harmony than the blank verse of Shakespeare and
Milton, but because in the latter there is no shelter for

---

[4] Milton stands alone in the age which he illumined.

mediocrity: you must either succeed or fail. This perhaps an 225
aspiring spirit should desire. But I was enticed also, by the
brilliancy and magnificence of sound which a mind that has
been nourished upon musical thoughts, can produce by a
just and harmonious arrangement of the pauses of this
measure. Yet there will be found some instances where I 230
have completely failed in this attempt, and one, which I here
request the reader to consider as an erratum, where there is
left most inadvertently an alexandrine in the middle of a
stanza.

But in this, as in every other respect, I have written 235
fearlessly. It is the misfortune of this age that its Writers,
too thoughtless of immortality, are exquisitely sensible to
temporary praise or blame. They write with the fear of
Reviews before their eyes. This system of criticism sprang
up in that torpid interval when Poetry was not. Poetry, and 240
the art which professes to regulate and limit its powers,
cannot subsist together. Longinus could not have been the
contemporary of Homer, nor Boileau of Horace. Yet this
species of criticism never presumed to assert an understand-
ing of its own: it has always, unlike true science, followed, 245
not preceded the opinion of mankind, and would even now
bribe with worthless adulation some of our greatest Poets
to impose gratuitous fetters on their own imaginations, and
become unconscious accomplices in the daily murder of all
genius either not so aspiring or not so fortunate as their 250
own. I have sought therefore to write, as I believe that
Homer, Shakespeare, and Milton wrote, with an utter
disregard of anonymous censure. I am certain that calumny
and misrepresentation, though it may move me to compas-
sion, cannot disturb my peace. I shall understand the 255
expressive silence of those sagacious enemies who dare not
trust themselves to speak. I shall endeavour to extract from
the midst of insult, and contempt, and maledictions, those
admonitions which may tend to correct whatever imperfec-
tions such censurers may discover in this my first serious 260
appeal to the Public. If certain Critics were as clear-sighted
as they are malignant, how great would be the benefit to be
derived from their virulent writings! As it is, I fear I shall be
malicious enough to be amused with their paltry tricks and
lame invectives. Should the Public judge that my composi- 265

tion is worthless, I shall indeed bow before the tribunal
from which Milton received his crown of immortality, and
shall seek to gather, if I live, strength from that defeat,
which may nerve me to some new enterprise of thought
which may *not* be worthless. I cannot conceive that Lucre- 270
tius, when he meditated that poem whose doctrines are yet
the basis of our metaphysical knowledge, and whose elo-
quence has been the wonder of mankind, wrote in awe of
such censure as the hired sophists of the impure and
superstitious noblemen of Rome might affix to what he 275
should produce. It was at the period when Greece was led
captive, and Asia made tributary to the Republic, fast
verging itself to slavery and ruin, that a multitude of Syrian
captives, bigoted to the worship of their obscene Ashtaroth,
and the unworthy successors of Socrates and Zeno, found 280
there a precarious subsistence by administering, under the
name of freedmen, to the vices and vanities of the great.
These wretched men were skilled to plead, with a superficial
but plausible set of sophisms, in favour of that contempt for
virtue which is the portion of slaves, and that faith in 285
portents, the most fatal substitute for benevolence in the
imaginations of men, which arising from the enslaved
communities of the East, then first began to overwhelm the
western nations in its stream. Were these the kind of men
whose disapprobation the wise and lofty-minded Lucretius 290
should have regarded with a salutary awe? The latest and
perhaps the meanest of those who follow in his footsteps,
would disdain to hold life on such conditions.

The Poem now presented to the Public occupied little
more than six months in the composition. That period has 295
been devoted to the task with unremitting ardour and
enthusiasm. I have exercised a watchful and earnest criticism
on my work as it grew under my hands. I would willingly
have sent it forth to the world with that perfection which
long labour and revision is said to bestow. But I found that 300
if I should gain something in exactness by this method, I
might lose much of the newness and energy of imagery and
language as it flowed fresh from my mind. And although
the mere composition occupied no more than six months,
the thoughts thus arranged were slowly gathered in as many 305
years.

I trust that the reader will carefully distinguish between those opinions which have a dramatic propriety in reference to the characters which they are designed to elucidate, and such as are properly my own. The erroneous and degrading 310 idea which men have conceived of a Supreme Being, for instance, is spoken against, but not the Supreme Being itself. The belief which some superstitious persons whom I have brought upon the stage, entertain of the Deity, as injurious to the character of his benevolence, is widely different from 315 my own. In recommending also a great and important change in the spirit which animates the social institutions of mankind, I have avoided all flattery to those violent and malignant passions of our nature which are ever on the watch to mingle with and to alloy the most beneficial 320 innovations. There is no quarter given to Revenge, or Envy, or Prejudice. Love is celebrated every where as the sole law which should govern the moral world.

In the personal conduct of my Hero and Heroine, there is one circumstance which was intended to startle the reader 325 from the trance of ordinary life. It was my object to break through the crust of those outworn opinions on which established institutions depend. I have appealed therefore to the most universal of all feelings, and have endeavoured to strengthen the moral sense, by forbidding it to waste its 330 energies in seeking to avoid actions which are only crimes of convention. It is because there is so great a multitude of artificial vices, that there are so few real virtues. Those feelings alone which are benevolent or malevolent, are essentially good or bad. The circumstance of which I speak, 335 was introduced, however, merely to accustom men to that charity and toleration which the exhibition of a practice widely differing from their own, has a tendency to promote. Nothing indeed can be more mischievous, than many actions innocent in themselves, which might bring down 340 upon individuals the bigoted contempt and rage of the multitude.

Dedication to Mary

1

So now my summer task is ended, Mary,
    And I return to thee, mine own heart's home;
As to his Queen some victor Knight of Faëry,
    Earning bright spoils for her enchanted dome;
    Nor thou disdain, that ere my fame become   5
A star among the stars of mortal night,
    If it indeed may cleave its natal gloom,
Its doubtful promise thus I would unite
With thy belovèd name, thou Child of love and light.

2

The toil which stole from thee so many an hour,   10
    Is ended, – and the fruit is at thy feet!
No longer where the woods to frame a bower
    With interlacèd branches mix and meet,
    Or where with sound like many voices sweet,
Waterfalls leap among wild islands green,   15
    Which framed for my lone boat a lone retreat
Of moss-grown trees and weeds, shall I be seen:
But beside thee, where still my heart has ever been.

3

Thoughts of great deeds were mine, dear Friend, when first
    The clouds which wrap this world from youth did pass. 20
I do remember well the hour which burst
    My spirit's sleep: a fresh May-dawn it was,
    When I walked forth upon the glittering grass,
And wept, I knew not why; until there rose
    From the near schoolroom, voices, that alas!   25
Were but one echo from a world of woes –
The harsh and grating strife of tyrants and of foes.

4

And then I clasped my hands and looked around –
    – But none was near to mock my streaming eyes,
Which poured their warm drops on the sunny ground – 30
    So without shame, I spake: – 'I will be wise,
    And just, and free, and mild, if in me lies

Such power, for I grow weary to behold
   The selfish and the strong still tyrannise
Without reproach or check.' I then controlled   35
My tears, my heart grew calm, and I was meek and bold.

5

And from that hour did I with earnest thought
   Heap knowledge from forbidden mines of lore,
Yet nothing that my tyrants knew or taught
   I cared to learn, but from that secret store   40
   Wrought linkèd armour for my soul, before
It might walk forth to war among mankind;
   Thus power and hope were strengthened more and more
Within me, till there came upon my mind
A sense of loneliness, a thirst with which I pined.   45

6

Alas, that love should be a blight and snare
   To those who seek all sympathies in one! –
Such once I sought in vain; then black despair,
   The shadow of a starless night, was thrown
   Over the world in which I moved alone: –   50
Yet never found I one not false to me,
   Hard hearts, and cold, like weights of icy stone
Which crushed and withered mine, that could not be
Aught but a lifeless clod, until revived by thee.

7

Thou Friend, whose presence on my wintry heart   55
   Fell, like bright Spring upon some herbless plain;
How beautiful and calm and free thou wert
   In thy young wisdom, when the mortal chain
   Of Custom thou didst burst and rend in twain,
And walked as free as light the clouds among,   60
   Which many an envious slave then breathed in vain
From his dim dungeon, and my spirit sprung
To meet thee from the woes which had begirt it long!

8

No more alone through the world's wilderness,
   Although I trod the paths of high intent,   65

I journeyed now: no more companionless,
  Where solitude is like despair, I went. –
  There is the wisdom of a stern content
When Poverty can blight the just and good,
  When Infamy dares mock the innocent,   70
And cherished friends turn with the multitude
To trample: this was ours, and we unshaken stood!

9

Now has descended a serener hour,
  And with inconstant fortune, friends return;
Though suffering leaves the knowledge and the power   75
  Which says: – Let scorn be not repaid with scorn.
  And from thy side two gentle babes are born
To fill our home with smiles, and thus are we
  Most fortunate beneath life's beaming morn;
And these delights, and thou, have been to me   80
The parents of the Song I consecrate to thee.

10

Is it, that now my inexperienced fingers
  But strike the prelude of a loftier strain?
Or, must the lyre on which my spirit lingers
  Soon pause in silence, ne'er to sound again,   85
  Though it might shake the Anarch Custom's reign,
And charm the minds of men to Truth's own sway
  Holier than was Amphion's? I would fain
Reply in hope – but I am worn away,
And Death and Love are yet contending for their prey.   90

11

And what art thou? I know, but dare not speak:
  Time may interpret to his silent years.
Yet in the paleness of thy thoughtful cheek,
  And in the light thine ample forehead wears,
  And in thy sweetest smiles, and in thy tears,
And in thy gentle speech, a prophecy   95
  Is whispered, to subdue my fondest fears:
And through thine eyes, even in thy soul I see
A lamp of vestal fire burning internally.

12

They say that thou wert lovely from thy birth,   100
  Of glorious parents, thou aspiring Child.
I wonder not – for One then left this Earth
  Whose life was like a setting planet mild,
  Which clothed thee in the radiance undefiled
Of its departing glory; still her fame   105
  Shines on thee, through the tempests dark and wild
Which shake these latter days; and thou canst claim
The shelter, from thy Sire, of an immortal name.

13

One voice came forth from many a mighty spirit,
  Which was the echo of three thousand years;   110
And the tumultuous world stood mute to hear it,
  As some lone man who in a desert hears
  The music of his home; – unwonted fears
Fell on the pale oppressors of our race,
  And Faith, and Custom, and low-thoughted cares,   115
Like thunder-stricken dragons, for a space
Left the torn human heart, their food and dwelling-place.

14

Truth's deathless voice pauses among mankind!
  If there must be no response to my cry –
If men must rise and stamp with fury blind   120
  On his pure name who loves them, – thou and I,
  Sweet Friend! can look from our tranquillity
Like lamps into the world's tempestuous night, –
  Two tranquil stars, while clouds are passing by
Which wrap them from the foundering seaman's sight,   125
That burn from year to year with unextinguished light.

God

The thoughts which the word, God, suggests to the human mind are susceptible of as many variations as human minds themselves. The Stoic, the Platonist and the Epicurean, the Polytheist, the Dualist and the Trinitarian differ infinitely in their conceptions of its meaning. They agree only in considering it the most awful and most venerable of names, as a common term devised to express all of mystery or majesty or power which the invisible world contains. And not only has every sect distinct conceptions of the application of this name, but scarcely two individuals of the same sect, who exercise in any degree the freedom of their judgement, or yield themselves with any candour of feeling to the influencings of the visible world, find perfect coincidence of opinions to exist between them. It is interes[ting] to enquire in what acceptation Jesus Christ employed this term.

We may conceive his mind to have been predisposed on this subject to adopt the opinions of his countrymen. Every human being is indebted for a multitude of his sentiments to the religion of his early years. Jesus Christ probably studied the historians of his country with the ardour of a spirit seeking after truth. They were undoubtedly the companions of his childish years, the food and nutriment and materials of his youthful meditations. The sublime dramatic poem entitled *Job*, had familiarized his imagination with the boldest imagery afforded by the human mind and the material world. *Ecclesiastes* had diffused a seriousness and solemnity over the frame of his spirit glowing with youthful hope, and made audible to his listening heart

> The still, sad music of humanity,
> Not harsh or grating, but of ample power
> To chasten and subdue.

He had contemplated this name as having been profanely perverted to the sanctioning of the most enormous and abominable crimes. We can distinctly trace in the tissue of

his doctrines the persuasion that God is some universal
being, differing both from man and from the mind of man.
– According to Jesus Christ, God is neither the Jupiter who
sends rain upon the earth, nor the Venus through whom all
living things are produced, nor the Vulcan who presides   40
over the terrestrial element of fire, nor the Vesta that
preserves the light which is enshrined in the sun and moon
and stars. He is neither the Proteus or the Pan of the material
world. But the word God according to the acceptation of
Jesus Christ unites all the attributes which these denomina-   45
tions contain, and is the interfused and overruling Spirit of
all the energy and wisdom included within the circle of
existing things. It is important to observe that the author of
the Christian system had a conception widely differing from
the gross imaginations of the vulgar relatively to the ruling 50
Power of the Universe. He every where represents this power
as something mysteriously and illimitably pervading the
frame of things. Nor do his doctrines practically assume any
proposition which they theoretically deny. They do not
represent God as a limitless and inconceivable mystery   55
affirming at the same time his existence as a being subject to
passion and capable [   ] . . .

Blessed are the pure in heart, for they shall see God – blessed
are those who have preserved internal sanctity of soul, who
are conscious of no secret deceit, who are the same in act as   60
they are in desire, who conceal no thought, no tendencies of
thought, from their own conscience, who are faithful and
sincere witnesses before the tribunal of their own judgement
of all that passes within their mind. Such as these shall see
God. What! after death shall their awakened eyes behold   65
the King of Heaven, shall they stand in awe before the
golden throne on which he sits, and gaze upon the venerable
countenance of the paternal Monarch? Is this the reward of
the virtuous and the pure? These are the idle dreams of the
visionary or the pernicious representations of impostors   70
who have fabricated from the very materials of wisdom a
cloak for their own dwarfish and imbecile conceptions.
Jesus Christ has said no more than the most excellent
philosophers have felt and expressed – that virtue is its own
reward. It is true that such an expression as he has used was 75

prompted by the energy of genius, it was the overflowing
enthusiasm of a [   ] poet, but it is not the less literally
true, clearly repugnant to the mistaken conceptions of the
multitude. – God, it has been asserted, was contemplated by
Jesus Christ as every poet and every philosopher must have   80
contemplated that mysterious principle. He considered that
venerable word to express the overruling Spirit of the
collective energy of the moral and material world. He
affirms therefore no more than that a simple and sincere
mind is an indispensable requisite of true knowledge and   85
true happiness. He affirms that a being of pure and gentle
habits will not fail in every thought, in every object of every
thought, to be aware of benignant visitings from the invis-
ible energies by which he is surrounded. Whosoever is free
from the contamination of luxury and licence may go forth   90
to the fields and to the woods inhaling joyous renovation
from the breath of Spring, or catching from the odours and
the sounds of autumn, some diviner mood of sweetest
sadness which improves the solitary heart. Whosoever is no
deceiver or destroyer of his fellow men, no liar, no flatterer,   95
no murderer, may walk among his species, deriving from
the communion with all which they contain of beautiful or
of majestic, some intercourse with the Universal God.
Whoever has maintained with his own heart the strictest
correspondence of confidence, who dares to examine and to   100
estimate every imagination which suggests itself to his mind,
who is that which he designs to become, and only aspires to
that which the divinity of his own nature shall consider and
approve . . . he, has already seen God.

    We live and move and think, but we are not the creators   105
of our own origin and existence, we are not the arbiters of
every motion of our own complicated nature, we are not
the masters of our own imaginations and moods of mental
being. There is a power by which we are surrounded, like
the atmosphere in which some motionless lyre is suspended,   110
which visits with its breath our silent chords, at will. Our
most imperial and stupendous qualities – those on which
the majesty and power of humanity is erected – are, rela-
tively to the inferior portion of its mechanism, indeed active
and imperial; but they are the passive slaves of some   115
higher and more omnipresent Power. This power is God.

And those who have seen God, have, in the periods of their purer and more perfect nature, been harmonized by their own will, to so exquisite a consentaneity of powers, as to give forth divinest melody when the breath of universal being sweeps over their frame.

That those who are pure in heart shall see God, and that virtue is its own reward, may be considered as equivalent assertions. The former of these propositions is a metaphorical repetition of the latter. The advocates of literal interpretation have been the most efficacious enemies of those doctrines whose institutor they profess to venerate. . . .

The rule of criticism to be adopted in judging of the life, actions and words of a man who has acted any conspicuous part in the revolutions of the world should not be narrow. We ought to form a general image of his character and of his doctrines and refer to this whole the distinct portions of action and of speech by which they are diversified. It is not here asserted that no contradictions are to be admitted to have place in the system of Jesus Christ between doctrines promulgated in different states of feeling or information, or even such as are implied in the enunciation of a scheme of thought various and obscure through its immensity and depth. It is not asserted that no degree of human indignation ever hurried him beyond the limits which his calmer mood had placed to disapprobation against vice and folly. Those deviations from the history of his life are alone to be vindicated which represent his own essential character in contradiction with itself. Every human mind has, what Lord Bacon calls its *idola specus*, peculiar images which reside in the inner cave of thought. These constitute the essential and distinctive character of every human being, to which every action and every word bears intimate relation, and by which in depicturing a character the genuineness and meaning of those words and actions are to be determined.[1] Every fanatic or enemy of virtue is not at liberty to misrepresent the greatest geniuses and the most herioc defenders of all that is valuable in this mortal world. His story to gain any credit must contain some truth,

[1] Bacon<,> *Novum organum*<,> Aph<orism> 53 – *De aug<mentis> Scien<tiarum>*. Lib. V. C<ap>.4.

and that truth shall thus be a sufficient indication of his prejudice and his deceit.

With respect to the miracles which these biographers have related: I have already declined to enter into any discussion on their nature or their existence. The supposition of their 160 falsehood or their truth would modify in no degree the hues of the picture which is attempted to be delineated. To judge truly of the moral and philosophical character of Socrates it is not necessary to determine the question of the familiar Spirit which it is supposed that he believed to attend him. 165 The power of [the] human mind relatively to intercourse with or dominion over the invisible world is doubtless an interesting theme of discussion, but the connection of the instance of Jesus Christ with the established religion of the country in which I write renders it dangerous to subject 170 oneself to the imputation of introducing new gods or abolishing old ones, nor is the duty of mutual forbearance sufficiently understood to render it certain that the metaphysician and the moralist, even though he carefully sacrifice a cock to Esculapius, may not receive something analogous to 175 the bowl of hemlock for the reward of his labours.

Much, however, of what his biographers have asserted is not to be rejected merely because inferences inconsistent with the general spirit of his system are to be deduced from its admission. Jesus Christ did, what every other reformer 180 who has produced any considerable effect upon the world has done. – He accommodated his doctrines to the prepossessions of those whom he addressed. He used a language, for this view, sufficiently familiar to our comprehensions. He said – However new or strange my doctrines may appear 185 to you, they are, in fact, only the restoration and reestablishment of the original institutions, and ancient customs of your own law and religion. The constitution of your faith and policy, although perfect in their origin, have become corrupt and altered, and have fallen into decay. I 190 profess to restore them to their pristine authority and splendour. 'Think not that I am come to destroy the law and the prophets: I am not come to destroy but to fulfill. Till Heaven and Earth pass away, one jot or one tittle shall in no wise pass from the law till all be fulfilled.' – Thus, like 195 a skilful orator he secures the prejudices of his auditors, and induces them by his professions of sympathy with their feelings, to enter with a willing mind into the exposition of his own.[1] The art of persuasion differs from that of reasoning; and it is of no small moment to the success even of a true cause that the judges who are to determine on its merits should be free from those national and religious predilections which render the multitude both deaf and blind. Let not this practice be considered as an unworthy artifice. It were best for the cause of reason that mankind should acknowledge no authority but its own, but it is useful to a certain extent, that they should not consider those institutions which they have been habituated to reverence as opposing an obstacle to its admission. All reformers have been compelled to practise this misrepresentation of their own true feelings and opinions. It is deeply to be lamented that a word should ever issue from human lips which contains the minutest alloy of dissimulation or simulation, or hypocrisy or exaggeration or any thing but the precise and rigid image which is present to the mind, and which ought to dictate the expression. But the practice of entire sincerity towards other men would avail to no good end, if they were incapable of practising it towards their own minds. In fact, truth cannot be communicated until it is perceived. The interests, therefore, of truth required that an orator should so far as possible produce in his hearers that state of mind in which alone his exhortations could fairly be contemplated and examined.

Having produced this favourable disposition of mind, Jesus Christ proceeds to qualify and finally to abrogate the system of the Jewish [law]. He descants upon its insufficiency as a code of moral conduct, which it professed to be,[2] and absolutely selects the law of retaliation as an instance of the absurdity and immorality of its institutions.[3] The conclusion of the speech [   ] is in a strain of most daring and most impassioned speculation. He seems emboldened by the success of his exculpation to the multitude to declare in public the utmost singularity of his faith. He tramples upon all received opinions, on all the

---

[1] See Cicero *De Oratore.*
[2] <*Matthew* Chap. V,> verse <s> 21, 27, 31, 33.
[3] *Matt*<hew> Chap. V <, verse> 38.

cherished luxuries and superstitions of mankind. He bids 235
them cast aside the chains of custom and blind faith by
which they have been encompassed from the very cradle of
their being, and become the imitators and ministers of the
Universal God.

9   AN ADDRESS TO THE PEOPLE ON THE DEATH
OF THE PRINCESS CHARLOTTE

We Pity the Plumage, but Forget
The Dying Bird

AN
ADDRESS
TO THE PEOPLE
ON
THE DEATH OF THE PRINCESS CHARLOTTE

By
THE HERMIT OF MARLOW

I. The Princess Charlotte is dead. She no longer moves, nor
thinks, nor feels. She is as inanimate as the clay with which
she is about to mingle. It is a dreadful thing to know that
she is a putrid corpse, who but a few days since was full of
life and hope; a woman young, innocent, and beautiful,   5
snatched from the bosom of domestic peace, and leaving
that single vacancy which none can die and leave not.

II. Thus much the death of the Princess Charlotte has in
common with the death of thousands. How many women
die in childbed and leave their families of motherless chil-   10
dren and their husbands to live on, blighted by the remem-
brance of that heavy loss? How many women of active and
energetic virtues; mild, affectionate, and wise, whose life is
as a chain of happiness and union, which once being broken,
leaves those whom it bound to perish, have died, and have   15
been deplored with bitterness, which is too deep for words?

Some have perished in penury or shame, and their orphan baby has survived, a prey to the scorn and neglect of strangers. Men have watched by the bedside of their expiring wives, and have gone mad when the hideous death-rattle was heard within the throat, regardless of the rosy child sleeping in the lap of the unobservant nurse. The countenance of the physician had been read by the stare of this distracted husband, till the legible despair sunk into his heart. All this has been and is. You walk with a merry heart through the streets of this great city, and think not that such are the scenes acting all around you. You do not number in your thought the mothers who die in childbed. It is the most horrible of ruins: – In sickness, in old age, in battle, death comes as to his own home; but in the season of joy and hope, when life should succeed to life, and the assembled family expects one more, the youngest and the best beloved, that the wife, the mother – she for whom each member of the family was so dear to one another, should die! – Yet thousands of the poorest poor, whose misery is aggravated by what cannot be spoken now, suffer this. And have they no affections? Do not their hearts beat in their bosoms, and the tears gush from their eyes? Are they not human flesh and blood? Yet none weep for them – none mourn for them – none when their coffins are carried to the grave (if indeed the parish furnishes a coffin for all) turn aside and moralize upon the sadness they have left behind.

III. The Athenians did well to celebrate, with public mourning, the death of those who had guided the republic with their valour and their understanding, or illustrated it with their genius. Men do well to mourn for the dead: it proves that we love something beside ourselves; and he must have a hard heart who can see his friend depart to rottenness and dust, and speed him without emotion on his voyage to 'that bourne whence no traveller returns.' To lament for those who have benefited the state, is a habit of piety yet more favourable to the cultivation of our best affections. When Milton died it had been well that the universal English nation had been clothed in solemn black, and that the muffled bells had tolled from town to town. The French nation should have enjoined a public mourning at the deaths of Rousseau and Voltaire. We cannot truly grieve for every one who dies beyond the circle of those especially dear to us; yet in the extinction of the objects of public love and admiration, and gratitude, there is something, if we enjoy a liberal mind, which has departed from within that circle. It were well done also, that men should mourn for any public calamity which has befallen their country or the world, though it be not death. This helps to maintain that connexion between one man and another, and all men considered as a whole, which is the bond of social life. There should be public mourning when those events take place which make all good men mourn in their hearts, – the rule of foreign or domestic tyrants, the abuse of public faith, the wresting of old and venerable laws to the murder of the innocent, the established insecurity of all those, the flower of the nation, who cherish an unconquerable enthusiasm for public good. Thus, if Horne Tooke and Hardy had been convicted of high treason, it had been good that there had been not only the sorrow and the indignation which would have filled all hearts, but the external symbols of grief. When the French Republic was extinguished, the world ought to have mourned.

IV. But this appeal to the feelings of men should not be made lightly, or in any manner that tends to waste, on inadequate objects, those fertilizing streams of sympathy, which a public mourning should be the occasion of pouring forth. This solemnity should be used only to express a wide and intelligible calamity, and one which is felt to be such by those who feel for their country and for mankind; its character ought to be universal, not particular.

V. The news of the death of the Princess Charlotte, and of the execution of Brandreth, Ludlam, and Turner, arrived nearly at the same time. If beauty, youth, innocence, amiable manners, and the exercise of the domestic virtues could alone justify public sorrow when they are extinguished for ever, this interesting Lady would well deserve that exhibition. She was the last and the best of her race. But there were thousands of others equally distinguished as she, for private excellences, who have been cut off in youth and hope. The accident of her birth neither made her life more

virtuous nor her death more worthy of grief. For the public
she had done nothing either good or evil; her education had
rendered her incapable of either in a large and comprehen-
sive sense. She was born a Princess; and those who are
destined to rule mankind are dispensed with acquiring that 100
wisdom and that experience which is necessary even to rule
themselves. She was not like Lady Jane Grey, or Queen
Elizabeth, a woman of profound and various learning. She
had accomplished nothing, and aspired to nothing, and
could understand nothing respecting those great political 105
questions which involve the happiness of those over whom
she was destined to rule. Yet this should not be said in
blame, but in compassion: let us speak no evil of the dead.
Such is the misery, such the impotence of royalty. – Princes
are prevented from the cradle from becoming any thing 110
which may deserve that greatest of all rewards next to a
good conscience, public admiration and regret.

VI. The execution of Brandreth, Ludlam, and Turner, is an
event of quite a different character from the death of the
Princess Charlotte. These men were shut up in a horrible 115
dungeon, for many months, with the fear of a hideous death
and of everlasting hell thrust before their eyes; and at last
were brought to the scaffold and hung. They too had
domestic affections, and were remarkable for the exercise of
private virtues. Perhaps their low station permitted the 120
growth of those affections in a degree not consistent with a
more exalted rank. They had sons, and brothers, and sisters,
and fathers, who loved them, it should seem, more than the
Princess Charlotte could be loved by those whom the
regulations of her rank had held in perpetual estrangement 125
from her. Her husband was to her as father, mother, and
brethren. Ludlam and Turner were men of mature years,
and the affections were ripened and strengthened within
them. What these sufferers felt shall not be said. But what
must have been the long and various agony of their kindred 130
may be inferred from Edward Turner, who, when he saw
his brother dragged along upon the hurdle, shrieked horribly
and fell in a fit, and was carried away like a corpse by two
men. How fearful must have been their agony, sitting in
solitude on that day when the tempestuous voice of horror 135

from the crowd, told them that the head so dear to them was severed from the body! Yes – they listened to the maddening shriek which burst from the multitude: they heard the rush of ten thousand terror-stricken feet, the groans and the hootings which told them that the mangled 140 and distorted head was then lifted into the air. The sufferers were dead. What is death? Who dares to say that which will come after the grave?[1] Brandreth was calm, and evidently believed that the consequences of our errors were limited by that tremendous barrier. Ludlam and Turner were full of 145 fears, lest God should plunge them in everlasting fire. Mr Pickering, the clergyman, was evidently anxious that Brandreth should not by a false confidence lose the single opportunity of reconciling himself with the Ruler of the future world. None knew what death was, or could know. 150 Yet these men were presumptuously thrust into that unfathomable gulf, by other men, who knew as little and who reckoned not the present or the future sufferings of their victims. Nothing is more horrible than that man should for any cause shed the life of man. For all other calamities there 155 is a remedy or a consolation. When that Power through which we live ceases to maintain the life which it has conferred, then is grief and agony, and the burthen which must be borne: such sorrow improves the heart. But when man sheds the blood of man, revenge, and hatred, and a 160 long train of executions, and assassinations, and proscriptions is perpetuated to remotest time.

VII. Such are the particular, and some of the general considerations depending on the death of these men. But however deplorable, if it were a mere private or customary 165 grief, the public, as the public, should not mourn. But it is more than this. The events which led to the death of those unfortunate men are a public calamity. I will not impute blame to the jury who pronounced them guilty of high treason, perhaps the law requires that such should be the 170 denomination of their offence. Some restraint ought indeed to be imposed on those thoughtless men who imagine they

---

[1] 'Your death has eyes in his head – mine is not painted so.' – *Cymbeline*.

can find in violence a remedy for violence, even if their oppressors had tempted them to this occasion of their ruin. They are instruments of evil, not so guilty as the hands that 175 wielded them, but fit to inspire caution. But their death, by hanging and beheading, and the circumstances of which it is the characteristic and the consequence, constitute a calamity such as the English nation ought to mourn with an unassuageable grief.   180

VIII. Kings and their ministers have in every age been distinguished from other men by a thirst for expenditure and bloodshed. There existed in this country, until the American war, a check, sufficiently feeble and pliant indeed, to this desolating propensity. Until America proclaimed 185 itself a republic, England was perhaps the freest and most glorious nation subsisting on the surface of the earth. It was not what is to the full desirable that a nation should be, but all that it can be, when it does not govern itself. The consequences however of that fundamental defect soon 190 became evident. The government which the imperfect constitution of our representative assembly threw into the hands of a few aristocrats, improved the method of anticipating the taxes by loans, invented by the ministers of William III, until an enormous debt had been created. In the war against 195 the republic of France, this policy was followed up, until now, the *mere interest* of the public debt amounts to more than twice as much as the lavish expenditure of the public treasure, for maintaining the standing army, and the royal family, and the pensioners, and the placemen. The effect of 200 this debt is to produce such an unequal distribution of the means of living, as saps the foundation of social union and civilized life. It creates a double aristocracy, instead of one which was sufficiently burthensome before, and gives twice as many people the liberty of living in luxury and idleness, 205 on the produce of the industrious and the poor. And it does not give them this because they are more wise and meritorious than the rest, or because their leisure is spent in schemes of public good, or in those exercises of the intellect and the imagination, whose creations ennoble or adorn a 210 country. They are not like the old aristocracy men of pride and honour, *sans peur et sans tache*, but petty piddling slaves who have gained a right to the title of public creditors, either by gambling in the funds, or by subserviency to government, or some other villainous trade. They are not the 'Corinthian capital of polished society,' but the petty and creeping weeds which deface the rich tracery of its sculpture. The effect of this system is, that the day labourer gains no more now by working sixteen hours a day than he gained before by working eight. I put the thing in its simplest and most intelligible shape. The labourer, he that tills the ground and manufactures cloth, is the man who has to provide, out of what he would bring home to his wife and children, for the luxuries and comforts of those whose claims are represented by an annuity of forty-four millions a year levied upon the English nation. Before, he supported the army and the pensioners, and the royal family, and the landholders; and this is a hard necessity to which it was well that he should submit. Many and various are the mischiefs flowing from oppression, but this is the represent- ative of them all; namely, that one man is forced to labour for another in a degree not only not necessary to the support of the subsisting distinctions among mankind, but so as by the excess of the injustice to endanger the very foundations of all that is valuable in social order, and to provoke that anarchy which is at once the enemy of freedom, and the child and the chastiser of misrule. The nation, tottering on the brink of two chasms, began to be weary of a continuance of such dangers and degradations, and the miseries which are the consequence of them; the public voice loudly demanded a free representation of the people. It began to be felt that no other constituted body of men could meet the difficulties which impend. Nothing but the nation itself dares to touch the question as to whether there is any remedy or no to the annual payment of forty-four millions a year, beyond the necessary expenses of state, for ever and for ever. A nobler spirit also went abroad, and the love of liberty, and patriotism, and the self-respect attendant on those glorious emotions, revived in the bosoms of men. The government had a desperate game to play.

IX. In the manufacturing districts of England discontent and disaffection had prevailed for many years; this was the

consequence of that system of double aristocracy produced
by the causes before mentioned. The manufacturers, the
helots of luxury, are left by this system famished, without 255
affections, without health, without leisure or opportunity
for such instruction as might counteract those habits of
turbulence and dissipation, produced by the precariousness
and insecurity of poverty. Here was a ready field for any
adventurer who should wish for whatever purpose to incite 260
a few ignorant men to acts of illegal outrage. So soon as it
was plainly seen that the demands of the people for a free
representation must be conceded if some intimidation and
prejudice were not conjured up, a conspiracy of the most
horrible atrocity was laid in train. It is impossible to know 265
how far the higher members of the government are involved
in the guilt of their infernal agents. It is impossible to know
how numerous or how active they have been, or by what
false hopes they are yet inflaming the untutored multitude
to put their necks under the axe and into the halter. But 270
thus much is known, that so soon as the whole nation lifted
up its voice for parliamentary reform, spies were sent forth.
These were selected from the most worthless and infamous
of mankind, and dispersed among the multitude of famished
and illiterate labourers. It was their business if they found 275
no discontent to create it. It was their business to find
victims, no matter whether right or wrong. It was their
business to produce upon the public an impression, that if
any attempt to attain national freedom, or to diminish the
burthens of debt and taxation under which we groan, were 280
successful, the starving multitude would rush in, and con-
found all orders and distinctions, and institutions and laws,
in common ruin. The inference with which they were
required to arm the ministers was, that despotic power
ought to be eternal. To produce this salutary impression, 285
they betrayed some innocent and unsuspecting rustics into a
crime whose penalty is a hideous death. A few hungry and
ignorant manufacturers seduced by the splendid promises of
these remorseless blood-conspirators, collected together in
what is called rebellion against the state. All was prepared, 290
and the eighteen dragoons assembled in readiness, no doubt,
conducted their astonished victims to that dungeon which
they left only to be mangled by the executioner's hand. The

cruel instigators of their ruin retired to enjoy the great
revenues which they had earned by a life of villainy. The 295
public voice was overpowered by the timid and the selfish,
who threw the weight of fear into the scale of public
opinion, and parliament confided anew to the executive
government those extraordinary powers which may never
be laid down, or which may be laid down in blood, or 300
which the regularly constituted assembly of the nation must
wrest out of their hands. Our alternatives are a despotism,
a revolution, or reform.

X. On the 7th of November, Brandreth, Turner, and Ludlam
ascended the scaffold. We feel for Brandreth the less, 305
because it seems he killed a man. But recollect who insti-
gated him to the proceedings which led to murder. On the
word of a dying man, Brandreth tells us, that 'OLIVER
brought him to this' – that, '*but for* OLIVER *he would not
have been there.*' See, too, Ludlam and Turner, with their 310
sons and brothers, and sisters, how they kneel together in a
dreadful agony of prayer. Hell is before their eyes, and they
shudder and feel sick with fear, lest some unrepented or
some wilful sin should seal their doom in everlasting fire.
With that dreadful penalty before their eyes – with that 315
tremendous sanction for the truth of all he spoke, Turner
exclaimed loudly and distinctly, *while the executioner was
putting the rope round his neck*, 'THIS IS ALL OLIVER AND
THE GOVERNMENT.' What more he might have said we
know not, because the chaplain prevented any further 320
observations. Troops of horse, with keen and glittering
swords, hemmed in the multitudes collected to witness this
abominable exhibition. 'When the stroke of the axe was
heard, there was a burst of horror from the crowd.[2] The
instant the head was exhibited, there was a tremendous 325
shriek set up, and the multitude ran violently in all direc-
tions, as if under the impulse of sudden frenzy. Those who
resumed their stations, groaned and hooted.' It is a national
calamity, that we endure men to rule over us, who sanction
for whatever ends a conspiracy which is to arrive at its 330

[2] These expressions are taken from *The Examiner*, Sunday, Nov. 9th.

purpose through such a frightful pouring forth of human blood and agony. But when that purpose is to trample upon our rights and liberties for ever, to present to us the alternatives of anarchy and oppression, and triumph when the astonished nation accepts the latter at their hands, to 335 maintain a vast standing army, and add, year by year to a public debt, which, already, they know, cannot be discharged; and which, when the delusion that supports it fails, will produce as much misery and confusion through all classes of society as it has continued to produce of famine 340 and degradation to the undefended poor; to imprison and calumniate those who may offend them, at will; when this, if not the purpose, is the effect of that conspiracy, how ought we not to mourn?

XI. Mourn then People of England. Clothe yourselves in 345 solemn black. Let the bells be tolled. Think of mortality and change. Shroud yourselves in solitude and the gloom of sacred sorrow. Spare no symbol of universal grief. Weep – mourn – lament. Fill the great City – fill the boundless fields, with lamentation and the echo of groans. A beautiful 350 Princess is dead: – she who should have been the Queen of her beloved nation, and whose posterity should have ruled it for ever. She loved the domestic affections, and cherished arts which adorn, and valour which defends. She was amiable and would have become wise, but she was young, 355 and in the flower of youth the despoiler came. LIBERTY is dead. Slave! I charge thee disturb not the depth and solemnity of our grief by any meaner sorrow. If One has died who was like her that should have ruled over this land, like Liberty, young, innocent, and lovely, know that the power 360 through which that one perished was God, and that it was a private grief. But *man* has murdered Liberty, and whilst the life was ebbing from its wound, there descended on the heads and on the hearts of every human thing, the sympathy of an universal blast and curse. Fetters heavier than iron 365 weigh upon us, because they bind our souls. We move about in a dungeon more pestilential than damp and narrow walls, because the earth is its floor and the heavens are its roof. Let us follow the corpse of British Liberty slowly and reverentially to its tomb: and if some glorious Phantom 370 should appear, and make its throne of broken swords and sceptres and royal crowns trampled in the dust, let us say that the Spirit of Liberty has arisen from its grave and left all that was gross and mortal there, and kneel down and worship it as our Queen.

375

10   ON FRANKENSTEIN; OR, THE MODERN PROMETHEUS

The novel of *Frankenstein, or the Modern Prometheus*, is undoubtedly, as a mere story, one of the most original and complete productions of the age. We debate with ourselves in wonder as we read it, what could have been the series of thoughts, what could have been the peculiar experiences that awakened them, which conducted in the author's mind to the astonishing combination of motives and incidents and the startling catastrophe which compose this tale. There are perhaps some points of subordinate importance which prove that it is the Author's first attempt. But in this judgement, which requires a very nice discrimination, we may be mistaken. For it is conducted throughout with a firm and steady hand. The interest gradually accumulates, and advances towards the conclusion with the accelerated rapidity of a rock rolled down a mountain. We are held breathless with suspense and sympathy, and the heaping up of incident on incident, and the working of passion out of passion. We cry 'hold, hold, enough' – but there is yet something to come, and, like the victim whose history it relates, we think we can bear no more, and yet more is to be borne. Pelion is heaped on Ossa, and Ossa on Olympus. We climb Alp after Alp, until the horizon is seen, blank, vacant and limitless, and the head turns giddy, and the ground seems to fail under the feet.

This Novel thus rests its claim on being a source of powerful and profound emotion. The elementary feelings of the human mind are exposed to view, and those who are accustomed to reason deeply on their origin and tendency, will perhaps be the only persons who can sympathize to the full extent in the interest of the actions which are their

result. But, founded on Nature as they are, there is perhaps
no reader who can endure any thing beside a new love-
story, who will not feel a responsive string touched in his
inmost soul. The sentiments are so affectionate and so
innocent, the characters of the subordinate agents in this   35
strange drama are clothed in the light of such a mild and
gentle mind. – The pictures of domestic manners are every
where of the most simple and attaching character. The
pathos is irresistible and deep. Nor are the crimes and
malevolence of the single Being, though indeed withering   40
and tremendous, the offspring of any unaccountable pro-
pensity to evil, but flow inevitably from certain causes fully
adequate to their production. They are the children, as it
were, of Necessity and Human Nature. In this the direct
moral of the book consists; and it is perhaps the most   45
important, and of the most universal application, of any
moral that can be enforced by example. Treat a person ill,
and he will become wicked. Requite affection with scorn; –
let one being be selected, for whatever cause, as the refuse
of his kind – divide him, a social being, from society, and   50
you impose upon him the irresistible obligations – malevol-
ence and selfishness. It is thus that, too often in society,
those who are best qualified to be its benefactors and its
ornaments are branded by some accident with scorn, and
changed, by neglect and solitude of heart, into a scourge   55
and a curse.

The Being in *Frankenstein* is, no doubt, a tremendous
creature. It was impossible that he should not have received
among men that treatment which led to the consequences of
his being a social nature. He was an abortion and an   60
anomaly, and though his mind was such as its first
impressions formed it, affectionate and full of moral sensi-
bility, yet the circumstances of his existence were so mon-
strous and uncommon, that when the consequences of them
became developed in action, his original goodness was   65
gradually turned into the fuel of an inextinguishable misan-
thropy and revenge. The scene between the Being and the
blind De Lacey in the cottage is one of the most profound
and extraordinary instances of pathos that we ever recollect.
It is impossible to read this dialogue, and indeed many other   70
situations of a somewhat similar character, without feeling

the heart suspend its pulsations with wonder, and the tears stream down the cheeks! The encounter and argument between Frankenstein and the Being on the sea of ice almost approaches in effect to the expostulations of Caleb Williams with Falkland. It reminds us indeed somewhat of the style and character of that admirable writer, to whom the Author has dedicated his work, and whose productions he seems to have studied. There is only one instance, however, in which we detect the least approach to imitation, and that is, the conduct of the incident of Frankenstein's landing and trial in Ireland. – The general character of the tale indeed resembles nothing that ever preceded it. After the death of Elizabeth, the story, like a stream which grows at once more rapid and profound as it proceeds, assumes an irresistible solemnity, and the magnificent energy and swiftness as of a tempest.

The churchyard scene, in which Frankenstein visits the tombs of his family, his quitting Geneva and his journey through Tartary to the shores of the Frozen Ocean, resembles at once the terrible reanimation of a corpse, and the supernatural career of a spirit. The scene in the cabin of Walton's ship, the more than mortal enthusiasm and grandeur of the Being's speech over the dead body of his victim, is an exhibition of intellectual and imaginative power, which we think the reader will acknowledge has seldom been surpassed.

11   *From* SPECULATIONS ON METAPHYSICS: [ON A SCIENCE OF MIND]

If it were possible that a person should give a faithful history of his being from the earliest epochs of his recollection, a picture would be presented such as the world has never contemplated before. A mirror would be held up to all men in which they might behold their own recollections, and in dim perspective their shadowy hopes and fears, – all that they dare not, or that daring and desiring, they could not expose to the open light of day. – But thought can with

difficulty visit the intricate and winding chambers which it
inhabits. It is like a river whose rapid and perpetual stream   10
flows outwards; – like one in dread who speeds through the
recesses of some haunted pile and dares not look behind.
The caverns of the mind are obscure and shadowy, or
pervaded with a lustre, beautifully bright indeed, but shining
not beyond their portals. If it were possible to be where we   15
have been, vitally and indeed – if at the moment of our
presence there we could define the results of our experience
– if the passage from sensation to reflection – from a state
of passive to voluntary contemplation were not so dizzying
and so tumultuous – this attempt would be less difficult. –   20

12   OZYMANDIAS

I met a traveller from an antique land
Who said: 'Two vast and trunkless legs of stone
Stand in the desert. Near them, on the sand,
Half sunk, a shattered visage lies, whose frown,
And wrinkled lip, and sneer of cold command,   5
Tell that its sculptor well those passions read
Which yet survive, stamped on these lifeless things,
The hand that mocked them and the heart that fed;
And on the pedestal these words appear:
"My name is Ozymandias, king of kings: 10
Look on my works, ye Mighty, and despair!"
Nothing beside remains. Round the decay
Of that colossal wreck, boundless and bare
The lone and level sands stretch far away.'

13 STANZAS WRITTEN IN DEJECTION –
DECEMBER 1818, NEAR NAPLES

The Sun is warm, the sky is clear,
The waves are dancing fast and bright,
Blue isles and snowy mountains wear
The purple noon's transparent might,
The breath of the moist earth is light   5
Around its unexpanded buds;
Like many a voice of one delight
The winds, the birds, the Ocean-floods;
The City's voice itself is soft, like Solitude's.

I see the Deep's untrampled floor   10
With green and purple seaweeds strown,
I see the waves upon the shore
Like light dissolved in star-showers, thrown;
I sit upon the sands alone;
The lightning of the noontide Ocean   15
Is flashing round me, and a tone
Arises from its measured motion,
How sweet! did any heart now share in my emotion.

Alas, I have nor hope nor health,
Nor peace within nor calm around,   20
Nor that content surpassing wealth
The sage in meditation found,
And walked with inward glory crowned;
Nor fame nor power nor love nor leisure –
Others I see whom these surround,   25
Smiling they live and call life pleasure:
To me that cup has been dealt in another measure.

Yet now despair itself is mild,
Even as the winds and waters are;
I could lie down like a tired child
And weep away the life of care   30
Which I have borne and yet must bear,
Till Death like Sleep might steal on me,
And I might feel in the warm air

My cheek grow cold, and hear the Sea   35
Breathe o'er my dying brain its last monotony.

Some might lament that I were cold,
As I, when this sweet day is gone,
Which my lost heart, too soon grown old,
Insults with this untimely moan –   40
They might lament, – for I am one
Whom men love not, and yet regret;
Unlike this day, which, when the Sun
Shall on its stainless glory set,
Will linger, though enjoyed, like joy in memory yet.

14   THE TWO SPIRITS: AN ALLEGORY

First Spirit
O thou, who plumed with strong desire
Would float above the Earth – beware!
A shadow tracks thy flight of fire –
     Night is coming!
Bright are the regions of the air,   5
And when winds and beams [   ]
It were delight to wander there –
     Night is coming!

Second Spirit
The deathless stars are bright above;
If I should cross the shade of night   10
Within my heart is the lamp of love,
     And that is day!
And the moon will smile with gentle light
On my golden plumes where'er they move;
The meteors will linger around my flight,   15
     And make night day.

First Spirit
But if the whirlwinds of darkness waken
Hail and lightning and stormy rain –
See, the bounds of the air are shaken –

    Night is coming!   20
And swift the clouds of the hurricane
Yon declining sun have overtaken,
The clash of the hail sweeps o'er the plain –
    Night is coming!

Second Spirit
    I see the glare and I hear the sound –   25
I'll sail on the flood of the tempest dark
With the calm within and light around
    Which make night day;
And thou, when the gloom is deep and stark,
Look from thy dull earth slumberbound –   30
My moonlike flight thou then mayst mark
    On high, far away.

———————————

Some say there is a precipice
Where one vast pine hangs frozen to ruin
O'er piles of snow and chasms of ice   35
    Mid Alpine mountains;
And that the languid storm pursuing
That wingèd shape forever flies
Round those hoar branches, aye renewing
    Its aery fountains.   40

Some say when the nights are dry [and] clear
And the death-dews sleep on the morass,
Sweet whispers are heard by the traveller,
    Which make night day;   45
And a shape like his early love doth pass
Upborne by her wild and glittering hair,
And when he awakes on the fragrant grass
    He finds night day.

A Conversation

Preface

The meadows with fresh streams, the bees with thyme,
The goats with the green leaves of budding Spring,
Are saturated not – nor Love with tears. – *Virgil*, Ecl. X.

Count Maddalo is a Venetian nobleman of ancient family
and of great fortune, who, without mixing much in the
society of his countrymen, resides chiefly at his magnificent
palace in that city. He is a person of the most consummate
genius, and capable if he would direct his energies to such
an end, of becoming the redeemer of his degraded country.
But it is his weakness to be proud: he derives, from a
comparison of his own extraordinary mind with the dwarf-
fish intellects that surround him, an intense apprehension of
the nothingness of human life. His passions and his powers
are incomparably greater then those of other men; and,
instead of the latter having been employed in curbing the
former, they have mutually lent each other strength. His
ambition preys upon itself, for want of objects which it can
consider worthy of exertion. I say that Maddalo is proud,
because I can find no other word to express the concentered
and impatient feelings which consume him; but it is on his
own hopes and affections only that he seems to trample, for
in social life no human being can be more gentle, patient,
and unassuming than Maddalo. He is cheerful, frank, and
witty. His more serious conversation is a sort of intoxica-
tion; men are held by it as by a spell. He has travelled much;
and there is an inexpressible charm in his relation of his
adventures in different countries.

Julian is an Englishman of good family, passionately
attached to those philosophical notions which assert the
power of man over his own mind, and the immense
improvements of which, by the extinction of certain moral
superstititions, human society may be yet susceptible. With-
out concealing the evil in the world, he is for ever speculat-
ing how good may be made superior. He is a complete
infidel, and a scoffer at all things reputed holy; and Maddalo

takes a wicked pleasure in drawing out his taunts against
religion. What Maddalo thinks on these matters is not
exactly known. Julian, in spite of his heterodox opinions, is
conjectured by his friends to possess some good qualities.
How far this is possible the pious reader will determine.   40
Julian is rather serious.

    Of the Maniac I can give no information. He seems, by
his own account, to have been disappointed in love. He was
evidently a very cultivated and amiable person when in his
right senses. His story, told at length, might be like many   45
other stories of the same kind: the unconnected excla-
mations of his agony will perhaps be found a sufficient
comment for the text of every heart.

I rode one evening with Count Maddalo
Upon the bank of land which breaks the flow
Of Adria towards Venice: – a bare strand
Of hillocks, heaped from ever-shifting sand,
Matted with thistles and amphibious weeds,   5
Such as from earth's embrace the salt ooze breeds,
Is this; – an uninhabitable sea-side,
Which the lone fisher, when his nets are dried,
Abandons; and no other object breaks
The waste, but one dwarf tree and some few stakes   10
Broken and unrepaired, and the tide makes
A narrow space of level sand thereon,
Where 'twas our wont to ride while day went down.
This ride was my delight. – I love all waste
And solitary places; where we taste   15
The pleasure of believing what we see
Is boundless, as we wish our souls to be:
And such was this wide ocean, and this shore
More barren than its billows; – and yet more
Than all, with a remembered friend I love   20
To ride as then I rode; – for the winds drove
The living spray along the sunny air
Into our faces; the blue heavens were bare,
Stripped to their depths by the awakening North
And from the waves, sound like delight broke forth   25
Harmonizing with solitude, and sent
Into our hearts aërial merriment . . .

So, as we rode, we talked; and the swift thought,
Winging itself with laughter, lingered not
But flew from brain to brain, – such glee was ours –   30
Charged with light memories of remembered hours,
None slow enough for sadness; till we came
Homeward, which always makes the spirit tame.
This day had been cheerful but cold, and now
The sun was sinking, and the wind also.   35
Our talk grew somewhat serious, as may be
Talk interrupted with such raillery
As mocks itself, because it cannot scorn
The thoughts it would extinguish: – 'twas forlorn
Yet pleasing, such as once, so poets tell,   40
The devils held within the dales of Hell
Concerning God, freewill and destiny:
Of all that earth has been or yet may be,
All that vain men imagine or believe,
Or hope can paint or suffering may achieve,   45
We descanted, and I (for ever still
Is it not wise to make the best of ill?)
Argued against despondency, but pride
Made my companion take the darker side.
The sense that he was greater than his kind   50
Had struck, methinks, his eagle spirit blind
By gazing on its own exceeding light.
– Meanwhile the sun paused ere it should alight,
Over the horizon of the mountains; – Oh,
How beautiful is sunset, when the glow   55
Of Heaven descends upon a land like thee,
Thou Paradise of exiles, Italy!
Thy mountains, seas and vineyards and the towers
Of cities they encircle! – it was ours
To stand on thee, beholding it; and then   60
Just where we had dismounted, the Count's men
Were waiting for us with the gondola. –
As those who pause on some delightful way
Though bent on pleasant pilgrimage, we stood
Looking upon the evening and the flood   65
Which lay between the city and the shore
Paved with the image of the sky . . . the hoar
And aery Alps towards the North appeared

Through mist, an heaven-sustaining bulwark reared
Between the East and West; and half the sky 70
Was roofed with clouds of rich emblazonry
Dark purple at the zenith, which still grew
Down the steep West into a wondrous hue
Brighter than burning gold, even to the rent
Where the swift sun yet paused in his descent 75
Among the many-folded hills: they were
Those famous Euganean hills, which bear
As seen from Lido through the harbour piles
The likeness of a clump of peakèd isles –
And then – as if the Earth and Sea had been 80
Dissolved into one lake of fire, were seen
Those mountains towering as from waves of flame
Around the vaporous sun, from which there came
The inmost purple spirit of light, and made
Their very peaks transparent. 'Ere it fade,' 85
Said my companion, 'I will show you soon
A better station' – so, o'er the lagoon
We glided, and from that funereal bark
I leaned, and saw the city, and could mark
How from their many isles in evening's gleam 90
Its temples and its palaces did seem
Like fabrics of enchantment piled to Heaven.
I was about to speak, when – 'We are even
Now at the point I meant,' said Maddalo,
And bade the gondolieri cease to row. 95
'Look, Julian, on the west, and listen well
If you hear not a deep and heavy bell.'
I looked, and saw between us and the sun
A building on an island; such a one
As age to age might add, for uses vile, 100
A windowless, deformed and dreary pile,
And on the top an open tower, where hung
A bell, which in the radiance swayed and swung –
We could just hear its hoarse and iron tongue:
The broad sun sunk behind it, and it tolled 105
In strong and black relief. – 'What we behold
Shall be the madhouse and its belfry tower,'
Said Maddalo, 'and ever at this hour
Those who may cross the water, hear that bell

Which calls the maniacs each one from his cell 110
To vespers.' – 'As much skill as need to pray
In thanks or hope for their dark lot have they
To their stern maker,' I replied. 'O ho!
You talk as in years past,' said Maddalo.
''Tis strange men change not. You were ever still 115
Among Christ's flock a perilous infidel,
A wolf for the meek lambs – if you can't swim
Beware of Providence.' I looked on him,
But the gay smile had faded in his eye:
'And such,' – he cried, 'is our mortality 120
And this must be the emblem and the sign
Of what should be eternal and divine! –
And like that black and dreary bell, the soul,
Hung in a heaven-illumined tower, must toll
Our thoughts and our desires to meet below 125
Round the rent heart and pray – as madmen do
For what? they know not, – till the night of death
As sunset that strange vision, severeth
Our memory from itself, and us from all
We sought and yet were baffled!' I recall 130
The sense of what he said, although I mar
The force of his expressions. The broad star
Of day meanwhile had sunk behind the hill
And the black bell became invisible
And the red tower looked grey, and all between 135
The churches, ships and palaces were seen
Huddled in gloom; – into the purple sea
The orange hues of heaven sunk silently.
We hardly spoke, and soon the gondola
Conveyed me to my lodging by the way. 140

The following morn was rainy, cold and dim:
Ere Maddalo arose, I called on him,
And whilst I waited with his child I played;
A lovelier toy sweet Nature never made,
A serious, subtle, wild, yet gentle being, 145
Graceful without design and unforeseeing,
With eyes – oh speak not of her eyes! – which seem
Twin mirrors of Italian Heaven, yet gleam
With such deep meaning, as we never see

But in the human countenance: with me   150
She was a special favourite: I had nursed
Her fine and feeble limbs when she came first
To this bleak world; and she yet seemed to know
On second sight her ancient playfellow,
Less changed than she was by six months or so;   155
For after her first shyness was worn out
We sate there, rolling billiard balls about.
When the Count entered – salutations past –
'The words you spoke last night might well have cast
A darkness on my spirit – if man be   160
The passive thing you say, I should not see
Much harm in the religions and old saws
(Though I may never own such leaden laws)
Which break a teachless nature to the yoke:
Mine is another faith' – thus much I spoke,   165
And noting he replied not, added: 'See
This lovely child, blithe, innocent and free;
She spends a happy time with little care
While we to such sick thoughts subjected are
As came on you last night – it is our will   170
That thus enchains us to permitted ill –
We might be otherwise – we might be all
We dream of happy, high, majestical.
Where is the love, beauty and truth we seek
But in our mind? and if we were not weak   175
Should we be less in deed than in desire?'
'Aye, if we were not weak – and we aspire
How vainly to be strong!' said Maddalo:
'You talk Utopia.' 'It remains to know,'
I then rejoined, 'and those who try may find   180
How strong the chains are which our spirit bind;
Brittle perchance as straw . . . We are assured
Much may be conquered, much may be endured
Of what degrades and crushes us. We know
That we have power over ourselves to do   185
And suffer – what, we know not till we try;
But something nobler than to live and die –
So taught those kings of old philosophy
Who reigned, before Religion made men blind;
And those who suffer with their suffering kind   190

Yet feel their faith, religion.' 'My dear friend,'
Said Maddalo, 'my judgement will not bend
To your opinion, though I think you might
Make such a system refutation-tight
As far as words go. I knew one like you   195
Who to this city came some months ago
With whom I argued in this sort, and he
Is now gone mad, – and so he answered me, –
Poor fellow! but if you would like to go
We'll visit him, and his wild talk will show   200
How vain are such aspiring theories.'
'I hope to prove the induction otherwise,
And that a want of that true theory, still
Which seeks a "soul of goodness" in things ill
Or in himself or others has thus bowed
His being – there are some by nature proud,   205
Who patient in all else demand but this:
To love and be beloved with gentleness;
And being scorned, what wonder if they die
Some living death? this is not destiny   210
But man's own wilfull ill.' As thus I spoke,
Servants announced the gondola, and we
Through the fast-falling rain and high-wrought sea
Sailed to the island where the madhouse stands.
We disembarked. The clap of tortured hands,   215
Fierce yells and howlings and lamentings keen,
And laughter where complaint had merrier been,
Moans, shrieks and curses and blaspheming prayers
Accosted us. We climbed the oozy stairs
Into an old courtyard. I heard on high,   220
Then, fragments of most touching melody
But looking up saw not the singer there –
Through the black bars in the tempestuous air
I saw, like weeds on a wrecked palace growing,
Long tangled locks flung wildly forth, and flowing,   225
Of those who on a sudden were beguiled
Into strange silence, and looked forth and smiled
Hearing sweet sounds. – Then I: 'Methinks there were
A cure of these with patience and kind care,
If music can thus move . . . but what is he   230
Whom we seek here?' 'Of his sad history

I know but this,' said Maddalo: 'he came
To Venice a dejected man, and fame
Said he was wealthy, or he had been so;
Some thought the loss of fortune wrought him woe;   235
But he was ever talking in such sort
As you do – far more sadly – he seemed hurt,
Even as a man with his peculiar wrong,
To hear but of the oppression of the strong,
Or those absurd deceits (I think with you   240
In some respects, you know) which carry through
The excellent impostors of this earth
When they outface detection – he had worth,
Poor fellow! but a humourist in his way' –
'Alas, what drove him mad?' 'I cannot say: 245
A lady came with him from France, and when
She left him and returned, he wandered then
About yon lonely isles of desert sand
Till he grew wild – he had no cash or land
Remaining, – the police had brought him here –   250
Some fancy took him and he would not bear
Removal; so I fitted up for him
Those rooms beside the sea, to please his whim,
And sent him busts and books and urns for flowers
Which had adorned his life in happier hours,   255
And instruments of music – you may guess
A stranger could do little more or less
For one so gentle and unfortunate,
And those are his sweet strains which charm the weight
From madmen's chains, and make this Hell appear   260
A heaven of sacred silence, hushed to hear.' –
'Nay, this was kind of you – he had no claim,
As the world says' – 'None – but the very same
Which I on all mankind were I as he
Fallen to such deep reverse; – his melody   265
Is interrupted now – we hear the din
Of madmen, shriek on shriek again begin;
Let us now visit him; after this strain
He ever communes with himself again,
And sees nor hears not any.' Having said   270
These words we called the keeper, and he led
To an apartment opening on the sea –

There the poor wretch was sitting mournfully
Near a piano, his pale fingers twined
One with the other, and the ooze and wind   275
Rushed through an open casement, and did sway
His hair, and starred it with the brackish spray;
His head was leaning on a music book,
And he was muttering, and his lean limbs shook;
His lips were pressed against a folded leaf   280
In hue too beautiful for health, and grief
Smiled in their motions as they lay apart –
As one who wrought from his own fervid heart
The eloquence of passion, soon he raised
His sad meek face and eyes lustrous and glazed   285
And spoke – sometimes as one who wrote and thought
His words might move some heart that heeded not
If sent to distant lands: and then as one
Reproaching deeds never to be undone
With wondering self-compassion; then his speech   290
Was lost in grief, and then his words came each
Unmodulated, cold, expressionless;
But that from one jarred accent you might guess
It was despair made them so uniform:
And all the while the loud and gusty storm   295
Hissed through the window, and we stood behind
Stealing his accents from the envious wind
Unseen. I yet remember what he said
Distinctly: such impression his words made.

      'Month after month,' he cried, 'to bear this load   300
And as a jade urged by the whip and goad
To drag life on, which like a heavy chain
Lengthens behind with many a link of pain! –
And not to speak my grief – o not to dare
To give a human voice to my despair   305
But live and move, and wretched thing! smile on
As if I never went aside to groan
And wear this mask of falsehood even to those
Who are most dear – not for my own repose –
Alas, no scorn or pain or hate could be   310
So heavy as that falsehood is to me –
But that I cannot bear more altered faces

Than needs must be, more changed and cold embraces,
More misery, disappointment and mistrust
To own me for their father . . . Would the dust   315
Were covered in upon my body now!
That the life ceased to toil within my brow!
And then these thoughts would at the least be fled;
Let us not fear such pain can vex the dead.

'What Power delights to torture us? I know   320
That to myself I do not wholly owe
What now I suffer, though in part I may.
Alas, none strewed sweet flowers upon the way
Where wandering heedlessly, I met pale Pain,
My shadow, which will leave me not again –   325
If I have erred, there was no joy in error,
But pain and insult and unrest and terror;
I have not as some do, bought penitence
With pleasure, and a dark yet sweet offence,
For then, – if love and tenderness and truth   330
Had overlived hope's momentary youth,
My creed should have redeemed me from repenting;
But loathèd scorn and outrage unrelenting
Met love excited by far other seeming
Until the end was gained . . . as one from dreaming   335
Of sweetest peace, I woke, and found my state
Such as it is. –

                    'O thou, my spirit's mate
Who, for thou art compassionate and wise,
Wouldst pity me from thy most gentle eyes
If this sad writing thou shouldst ever see –   340
My secret groans must be unheard by thee,
Thou wouldst weep tears bitter as blood to know
Thy lost friend's incommunicable woe.

'Ye few by whom my nature has been weighed
In friendship, let me not that name degrade
By placing on your hearts the secret load   345
Which crushes mine to dust. There is one road
To peace and that is truth, which follow ye!
Love sometimes leads astray to misery.

Yet think not though subdued – and I may well   350
Say that I am subdued – that the full Hell
Within me would infect the untainted breast
Of sacred nature with its own unrest;
As some perverted beings think to find
In scorn or hate a medicine for the mind   355
Which scorn or hate have wounded – o how vain!
The dagger heals not but may rend again . . .
Believe that I am ever still the same
In creed as in resolve, and what may tame
My heart, must leave the understanding free   360
Or all would sink in this keen agony –
Nor dream that I will join the vulgar cry,
Or with my silence sanction tyranny,
Or seek a moment's shelter from my pain
In any madness which the world calls gain,   365
Ambition or revenge or thoughts as stern
As those which make me what I am, or turn
To avarice or misanthropy or lust . . .
Heap on me soon, o grave, thy welcome dust!
Till then the dungeon may demand its prey,   370
And Poverty and Shame may meet and say –
Halting beside me on the public way –
"That love-devoted youth is ours – let's sit
Beside him – he may live some six months yet."
Or the red scaffold, as our country bends,   375
May ask some willing victim, or ye friends
May fall under some sorrow which this heart
Or hand may share or vanquish or avert;
I am prepared: in truth with no proud joy
To do or suffer aught, as when a boy   380
I did devote to justice and to love
My nature, worthless now! . . .

                              'I must remove
A veil from my pent mind. 'Tis torn aside!
O, pallid as Death's dedicated bride,
Thou mockery which art sitting by my side,   385
Am I not wan like thee? at the grave's call
I haste, invited to thy wedding-ball
To greet the ghastly paramour, for whom

Thou hast deserted me . . . and made the tomb
Thy bridal bed . . . But I beside your feet   390
Will lie and watch ye from my winding sheet –
Thus . . . wide awake, though dead . . . yet stay, o stay!
Go not so soon – I know not what I say –
Hear but my reasons . . . I am mad, I fear,
My fancy is o'erwrought . . . thou art not here . . .   395
Pale art thou, 'tis most true . . . but thou art gone,
Thy work is finished . . . I am left alone! –

. . . .

  'Nay, was it I who wooed thee to this breast
Which, like a serpent, thou envenomest
As in repayment of the warmth it lent?   400
Didst thou not seek me for thine own content?
Did not thy love awaken mine? I thought
That thou wert she who said, "You kiss me not
Ever, I fear you do not love me now" –
In truth I loved even to my overthrow   405
Her, who would fain forget these words: but they
Cling to her mind, and cannot pass away.

. . . .

  'You say that I am proud – that when I speak
My lip is tortured with the wrongs which break
The spirit it expresses . . . Never one   410
Humbled himself before, as I have done!
Even the instinctive worm on which we tread
Turns, though it wound not – then with prostrate head
Sinks in the dust and writhes like me – and dies?
No: wears a living death of agonies!   415
As the slow shadows of the pointed grass
Mark the eternal periods, his pangs pass
Slow, ever-moving, – making moments be
As mine seem – each an immortality!

. . . .

  'That you had never seen me – never heard   420
My voice, and more than all had ne'er endured
The deep pollution of my loathed embrace –
That your eyes ne'er had lied love in my face –
That, like some maniac monk, I had torn out
The nerves of manhood by their bleeding root   425
With mine own quivering fingers, so that ne'er

Our hearts had for a moment mingled there
To disunite in horror – these were not
With thee, like some suppressed and hideous thought
Which flits athwart our musings, but can find   430
No rest within a pure and gentle mind ...
Thou sealedst them with many a bare broad word,
And cearedst my memory o'er them, – for I heard
And can forget not ... they were ministered
One after one, those curses. Mix them up   435
Like self-destroying poisons in one cup,
And they will make one blessing which thou ne'er
Didst imprecate for, on me, – death.
. . . .

                                    'It were
A cruel punishment for one most cruel,
If such can love, to make that love the fuel   440
Of the mind's hell; hate, scorn, remorse, despair:
But *me* – whose heart a stranger's tear might wear
As water-drops the sandy fountain-stone,
Who loved and pitied all things, and could moan
For woes which others hear not, and could see   445
The absent with the glance of fantasy,
And with the poor and trampled sit and weep,
Following the captive to his dungeon deep;
Me – who am as a nerve o'er which do creep
The else unfelt oppressions of this earth   450
And was to thee the flame upon thy hearth
When all beside was cold – that thou on me
Shouldst rain these plagues of blistering agony –
Such curses are from lips once eloquent
With love's too partial praise – let none relent   455
Who intend deeds too dreadful for a name
Henceforth, if an example for the same
They seek ... for thou on me lookedst so, and so –
And didst speak thus ... and thus ... I live to show
How much men bear and die not!   460
. . . .

                                'Thou wilt tell
With the grimace of hate how horrible
It was to meet my love when thine grew less;
Thou wilt admire how I could e'er address

Such features to love's work . . . this taunt, though true,
(For indeed nature nor in form nor hue   465
Bestowed on me her choicest workmanship)
Shall not be thy defence . . . for since thy lip
Met mine first, years long past, since thine eye kindled
With soft fire under mine, I have not dwindled
Nor changed in mind or body, or in aught   470
But as love changes what it loveth not
After long years and many trials.

                                        'How vain
Are words! I thought never to speak again,
Not even in secret, – not to my own heart –
But from my lips the unwilling accents start   475
And from my pen the words flow as I write,
Dazzling my eyes with scalding tears . . . my sight
Is dim to see that charactered in vain
On this unfeeling leaf which burns the brain
And eats into it . . . blotting all things fair   480
And wise and good which time had written there.

'Those who inflict must suffer, for they see
The work of their own hearts and this must be
Our chastisement or recompense – O child!
I would that thine were like to be more mild   485
For both our wretched sakes . . . for thine the most
Who feelest already all that thou hast lost
Without the power to wish it thine again;
And as slow years pass, a funereal train
Each with the ghost of some lost hope or friend   490
Following it like its shadow, wilt thou bend
No thought on my dead memory?
.   .   .   .

                                        'Alas, love,
Fear me not . . . against thee I would not move
A finger in despite. Do I not live
That thou mayst have less bitter cause to grieve?   495
I give thee tears for scorn and love for hate;
And that thy lot may be less desolate
Than his on whom thou tramplest, I refrain
From that sweet sleep which medicines all pain.

Then, when thou speakest of me, never say   500
"He could forgive not." Here I cast away
All human passions, all revenge, all pride;
I think, speak, act no ill; I do but hide
Under these words like embers, every spark
Of that which has consumed me – quick and dark   505
The grave is yawning . . . as its roof shall cover
My limbs with dust and worms under and over
So let Oblivion hide this grief . . . the air
Closes upon my accents, as despair
Upon my heart – let death upon despair!'   510

   He ceased, and overcome leant back awhile,
Then rising, with a melancholy smile
Went to a sofa, and lay down, and slept
A heavy sleep, and in his dreams he wept   515
And muttered some familiar name, and we
Wept without shame in his society.
I think I never was impressed so much;
The man who were not, must have lacked a touch
Of human nature . . . then we lingered not,
Although our argument was quite forgot,   520
But calling the attendants, went to dine
At Maddalo's; yet neither cheer nor wine
Could give us spirits, for we talked of him
And nothing else, till daylight made stars dim;
And we agreed his was some dreadful ill   525
Wrought on him boldly, yet unspeakable,
By a dear friend; some deadly change in love
Of one vowed deeply which he dreamed not of;
For whose sake he, it seemed, had fixed a blot
Of falsehood on his mind which flourished not   530
But in the light of all-beholding truth;
And having stamped this canker on his youth
She had abandoned him – and how much more
Might be his woe, we guessed not – he had store
Of friends and fortune once, as we could guess   535
From his nice habits and his gentleness;
These were now lost . . . it were a grief indeed
If he had changed one unsustaining reed
For all that such a man might else adorn.

The colours of his mind seemed yet unworn;   540
For the wild language of his grief was high,
Such as in measure were called poetry;
And I remember one remark which then
Maddalo made. He said: 'Most wretched men
Are cradled into poetry by wrong,   545
They learn in suffering what they teach in song.'

   If I had been an unconnected man
I, from this moment, should have formed some plan
Never to leave sweet Venice, – for to me
It was delight to ride by the lone sea;   550
And then, the town is silent – one may write
Or read in gondolas by day or night,
Having the little brazen lamp alight,
Unseen, uninterrupted; books are there,
Pictures, and casts from all those statues fair   555
Which were twin-born with poetry, and all
We seek in towns, with little to recall
Regrets for the green country. I might sit
In Maddalo's great palace, and his wit
And subtle talk would cheer the winter night   560
And make me know myself, and the firelight
Would flash upon our faces, till the day
Might dawn and make me wonder at my stay:
But I had friends in London too: the chief
Attraction here, was that I sought relief   565
From the deep tenderness that maniac wrought
Within me – 'twas perhaps an idle thought,
But I imagined that if day by day
I watched him, and but seldom went away,
And studied all the beatings of his heart   570
With zeal, as men study some stubborn art
For their own good, and could by patience find
An entrance to the caverns of his mind,
I might reclaim him from his dark estate:
In friendships I had been most fortunate –   575
Yet never saw I one whom I would call
More willingly my friend; and this was all
Accomplished not; such dreams of baseless good
Oft come and go in crowds or solitude

And leave no trace – but what I now designed   580
Made for long years impression on my mind.
The following morning urged by my affairs
I left bright Venice.

           After many years
And many changes I returned; the name
Of Venice, and its aspect, was the same;   585
But Maddalo was travelling far away
Among the mountains of Armenia.
His dog was dead. His child had now become
A woman; such as it has been my doom
To meet with few, – a wonder of this earth   590
Where there is little of transcendent worth, –
Like one of Shakespeare's women: kindly she
And with a manner beyond courtesy
Received her father's friend; and when I asked
Of the lorn maniac, she her memory tasked   595
And told as she had heard the mournful tale:
'That the poor sufferer's health began to fail
Two years from my departure, but that then
The lady who had left him, came again.
Her mien had been imperious, but she now   600
Looked meek – perhaps remorse had brought her low.
Her coming made him better, and they stayed
Together at my father's – for I played
As I remember with the lady's shawl –   605
I might be six years old – but after all
She left him'. . . . 'Why, her heart must have been tough:
How did it end?' 'And was not this enough?
They met – they parted' – 'Child, is there no more?'
'Something within that interval which bore
The stamp of *why* they parted, *how* they met; –   610
Yet if thine agèd eyes disdain to wet
Those wrinkled cheeks with youth's remembered tears,
Ask me no more, but let the silent years
Be closed and ceared over their memory
As yon mute marble where their corpses lie.'   615
I urged and questioned still, she told me how
All happened – but the cold world shall not know.

What is love? – Ask him who lives what is life; ask him who adores what is God.

I know not the internal constitution of other men, or even of thine whom I now address. I see that in some external attributes they resemble me, but when misled by that appearance I have thought to appeal to something in common and unburthen my inmost soul to them, I have found my language misunderstood like one in a distant and savage land. The more opportunities they have afforded me for experience, the wider has appeared the interval between us, and to a greater distance have the points of sympathy been withdrawn. With a spirit ill fitted to sustain such proof, trembling and feeble through its tenderness, I have every where sought and have found only repulse and disappointment.

Thou demandest what is Love. It is that powerful attraction towards all that we conceive or fear or hope beyond ourselves when we find within our own thoughts the chasm of an insufficient void and seek to awaken in all things that are, a community with what we experience within ourselves. If we reason, we would be understood; if we imagine, we would that the airy children of our brain were born anew within another's; if we feel, we would that another's nerves should vibrate to our own, that the beams of their eyes should kindle at once and mix and melt into our own, that lips of motionless ice should not reply to lips quivering and burning with the heart's best blood. This is Love. This is the bond and the sanction which connects not only man with man, but with every thing which exists. We are born into the world and there is something within us which from the instant that we live and move thirsts after its likeness. It is probably in correspondence with this law that the infant drains milk from the bosom of its mother. This propensity develops itself with the development of our nature. We dimly see within our intellectual nature a miniature as it were of our entire self, yet deprived of all that we condemn or despise, the ideal prototype of every thing excellent or lovely that we are capable of conceiving as belonging to the nature of man. Not only the portrait of our external being, but an assemblage of the minutest particulars of which our nature is composed:[1] a mirror whose surface reflects only the forms of purity and brightness: a soul within our soul that describes a circle around its proper Paradise which pain and sorrow and evil dare not overleap. To this we eagerly refer all sensations, thirsting that they should resemble or correspond with it. The discovery of its antitype: the meeting with an understanding capable of clearly estimating the deductions of our own, an imagination which should enter into and seize upon the subtle and delicate peculiarities which we have delighted to cherish and unfold in secret, with a frame whose nerves, like the chords of two exquisite lyres strung to the accompaniment of one delightful voice, vibrate with the vibrations of our own; and of a combination of all these in such proportion as the type within demands: this is the invisible and unattainable point to which Love tends; and to attain which it urges forth the powers of man to arrest the faintest shadow of that without the possession of which there is no rest or respite to the heart over which it rules. Hence in solitude, or in that deserted state, when we are surrounded by human beings and yet they sympathise not with us, we love the flowers, the grass and the waters and the sky. In the motion of the very leaves of spring in the blue air there is then found a secret correspondence with our heart. There is eloquence in the tongueless wind and a melody in the flowing of brooks and the rustling of the reeds beside them which by their inconceivable relation to something within the soul awaken the spirits to a dance of breathless rapture, and bring tears of mysterious tenderness to the eyes like the enthusiasm of patriotic success or the voice of one beloved singing to you alone. Sterne says that if he were in a desert he would love some cypress ... So soon as this want or power is dead, man becomes the living sepulchre of himself, and what yet survives is the mere husk of what once he was.

[1] These words inefficient and metaphorical ... most words so. No help –

A LYRICAL DRAMA IN FOUR ACTS

AUDISNE HAEC, AMPHIARAE, SUB TERRAM ABDITE?

Preface

The Greek tragic writers, in selecting as their subject any portion of their national history or mythology, employed in their treatment of it a certain arbitrary discretion. They by no means conceived themselves bound to adhere to the common interpretation or to imitate in story as in title their rivals and predecessors. Such a system would have amounted to a resignation of those claims to preference over their competitors which incited the composition. The Agamemnonian story was exhibited on the Athenian theatre with as many variations as dramas.

I have presumed to employ a similar licence. The *Prometheus Unbound* of Aeschylus supposed the reconciliation of Jupiter with his victim as the price of the disclosure of the danger threatened to his empire by the consummation of his marriage with Thetis. Thetis, according to this view of the subject, was given in marriage to Peleus, and Prometheus, by the permission of Jupiter, delivered from his captivity by Hercules. Had I framed my story on this model, I should have done no more than have attempted to restore the lost drama of Aeschylus; an ambition which, if my preference to this mode of treating the subject had incited me to cherish, the recollection of the high comparison such an attempt would challenge might well abate. But, in truth, I was averse from a catastrophe so feeble as that of reconciling the Champion with the Oppressor of mankind. The moral interest of the fable, which is so powerfully sustained by the sufferings and endurance of Prometheus, would be annihilated if we could conceive of him as unsaying his high language and quailing before his successful and perfidious adversary. The only imaginary being resembling in any degree Prometheus, is Satan; and Prometheus is, in my judgement, a more poetical character than Satan, because, in addition to courage, and majesty, and firm and patient opposition to omnipotent force, he is susceptible of being

described as exempt from the taints of ambition, envy, 35
revenge, and a desire for personal aggrandisement, which,
in the Hero of *Paradise Lost*, interfere with the interest. The
character of Satan engenders in the mind a pernicious
casuistry which leads us to weigh his faults with his wrongs,
and to excuse the former because the latter exceed all 40
measure. In the minds of those who consider that magnifi-
cent fiction with a religious feeling it engenders something
worse. But Prometheus is, as it were, the type of the highest
perfection of moral and intellectual nature, impelled by the
purest and the truest motives to the best and noblest ends. 45

This Poem was chiefly written upon the mountainous
ruins of the Baths of Caracalla, among the flowery glades,
and thickets of odoriferous blossoming trees, which are
extended in ever-winding labyrinths upon its immense plat-
forms and dizzy arches suspended in the air. The bright 50
blue sky of Rome, and the effect of the vigorous awakening
spring in that divine climate, and the new life with which it
drenches the spirits even to intoxication, were the inspira-
tion of this drama.

The imagery which I have employed will be found, in 55
many instances, to have been drawn from the operations of
the human mind, or from those external actions by which
they are expressed. This is unusual in modern poetry,
although Dante and Shakespeare are full of instances of the
same kind: Dante indeed more than any other poet, and 60
with greater success. But the Greek poets, as writers to
whom no resource of awakening the sympathy of their
contemporaries was unknown, were in the habitual use of
this power; and it is the study of their works (since a higher
merit would probably be denied me) to which I am willing 65
that my readers should impute this singularity.

One word is due in candour to the degree in which the
study of contemporary writings may have tinged my com-
position, for such has been a topic of censure with regard to
poems far more popular, and indeed more deservedly pop- 70
ular, than mine. It is impossible that any one who inhabits
the same age with such writers as those who stand in the
foremost ranks of our own, can conscientiously assure
himself that his language and tone of thought may not have
been modified by the study of the productions of those 75

extraordinary intellects. It is true that, not the spirit of their
genius, but the forms in which it has manifested itself, are
due less to the peculiarities of their own minds than to the
peculiarity of the moral and intellectual condition of the
minds among which they have been produced. Thus a 80
number of writers possess the form, whilst they want the
spirit of those whom, it is alleged, they imitate; because the
former is the endowment of the age in which they live, and
the latter must be the uncommunicated lightning of their
own mind. 85

The peculiar style of intense and comprehensive imagery
which distinguishes the modern literature of England, has
not been, as a general power, the product of the imitation
of any particular writer. The mass of capabilities remains at
every period materially the same; the circumstances which 90
awaken it to action perpetually change. If England were
divided into forty republics, each equal in population and
extent to Athens, there is no reason to suppose but that,
under institutions not more perfect than those of Athens,
each would produce philosophers and poets equal to those 95
who (if we except Shakespeare) have never been surpassed.
We owe the great writers of the golden age of our literature
to that fervid awakening of the public mind which shook to
dust the oldest and most oppressive form of the Christian
religion. We owe Milton to the progress and development 100
of the same spirit: the sacred Milton was, let it ever be
remembered, a republican, and a bold inquirer into morals
and religion. The great writers of our own age are, we have
reason to suppose, the companions and forerunners of some
unimagined change in our social condition or the opinions 105
which cement it. The cloud of mind is discharging its
collected lightning, and the equilibrium between institutions
and opinions is now restoring, or is about to be restored.

As to imitation, poetry is a mimetic art. It creates, but it
creates by combination and representation. Poetical abstrac- 110
tions are beautiful and new, not because the portions of
which they are composed had no previous existence in the
mind of man or in nature, but because the whole produced
by their combination has some intelligible and beautiful
analogy with those sources of emotion and thought, and 115
with the contemporary condition of them: one great poet is

a masterpiece of nature which another not only ought to study but must study. He might as wisely and as easily determine that his mind should no longer be the mirror of all that is lovely in the visible universe, as exclude from his contemplation the beautiful which exists in the writings of a great contemporary. The pretence of doing it would be a presumption in any but the greatest: the effect, even in him, would be strained, unnatural, and ineffectual. A poet is the combined product of such external influences as excite and sustain these powers; he is not one, but both. Every man's mind is, in this respect, modified by all the objects of nature and art; by every word and every suggestion which he ever admitted to act upon his consciousness; it is the mirror upon which all forms are reflected, and in which they compose one form. Poets, not otherwise than philosophers, painters, sculptors, and musicians, are, in one sense, the creators, and, in another, the creations, of their age. From this subjection the loftiest do not escape. There is a similarity between Homer and Hesiod, between Aeschylus and Euripides, between Virgil and Horace, between Dante and Petrarch, between Shakespeare and Fletcher, between Dryden and Pope; each has a generic resemblance under which their specific distinctions are arranged. If this similarity be the result of imitation, I am willing to confess that I have imitated.

Let this opportunity be conceded to me of acknowledging that I have, what a Scotch philosopher characteristically terms, 'a passion for reforming the world': what passion incited him to write and publish his book, he omits to explain. For my part I had rather be damned with Plato and Lord Bacon, than go to Heaven with Paley and Malthus. But it is a mistake to suppose that I dedicate my poetical compositions solely to the direct enforcement of reform, or that I consider them in any degree as containing a reasoned system on the theory of human life. Didactic poetry is my abhorrence; nothing can be equally well expressed in prose that is not tedious and supererogatory in verse. My purpose has hitherto been simply to familiarize the highly refined imagination of the more select classes of poetical readers with beautiful idealisms of moral excellence; aware that until the mind can love, and admire, and trust, and hope, and endure, reasoned principles of moral conduct are seeds cast upon the highway of life which the unconscious passenger tramples into dust, although they would bear the 160 harvest of his happiness. Should I live to accomplish what I purpose, that is, produce a systematical history of what appear to me to be the genuine elements of human society, let not the advocates of injustice and superstition flatter themselves that I should take Aeschylus rather than Plato as 165 my model.

The having spoken of myself with unaffected freedom will need little apology with the candid; and let the uncandid consider that they injure me less than their own hearts and minds by misrepresentation. Whatever talents a person may 170 possess to amuse and instruct others, be they ever so inconsiderable, he is yet bound to exert them: if his attempts be ineffectual, let the punishment of an unaccomplished purpose have been sufficient; let none trouble themselves to heap the dust of oblivion upon his efforts; the pile they raise 175 will betray his grave which might otherwise have been unknown.

ACT I   Scene i

SCENE: a ravine of icy rocks in the Indian Causasus. PRO-METHEUS is discovered bound to the precipice. PANTHEA and IONE are seated at his feet. Time, night. During the scene, morning slowly breaks.

Prometheus.   Monarch of Gods and Daemons, and all Spirits
But One, who throng those bright and rolling worlds
Which thou and I alone of living things
Behold with sleepless eyes! regard this Earth
Made multitudinous with thy slaves, whom thou   5
Requitest for knee-worship, prayer and praise,
And toil, and hecatombs of broken hearts,
With fear and self-contempt and barren hope;
Whilst me, who am thy foe, eyeless in hate,
Hast thou made reign and triumph, to thy scorn,   10
O'er mine own misery and thy vain revenge.
Three thousand years of sleep-unsheltered hours,
And moments aye divided by keen pangs

Till they seemed years, torture and solitude,
Scorn and despair, – these are mine empire: 15
More glorious far than that which thou surveyest
From thine unenvied throne, O Mighty God!
Almighty, had I deigned to share the shame
Of thine ill tyranny, and hung not here
Nailed to this wall of eagle-baffling mountain,   20
Black, wintry, dead, unmeasured; without herb,
Insect, or beast, or shape or sound of life.
Ah me! alas, pain, pain ever, forever!

No change, no pause, no hope! Yet I endure.
I ask the Earth, have not the mountains felt?   25
I ask yon Heaven – the all-beholding Sun,
Has it not seen? the Sea, in storm or calm
Heaven's ever-changing Shadow, spread below,
Have its deaf waves not heard my agony?
Ah me! alas, pain, pain ever, forever!   30

The crawling glaciers pierce me with the spears
Of their moon-freezing crystals; the bright chains
Eat with their burning cold into my bones.
Heaven's wingèd hound, polluting from thy lips
His beak in poison not his own, tears up   35
My heart; and shapeless sights come wandering by,
The ghastly people of the realm of dream,
Mocking me: and the Earthquake-fiends are charged
To wrench the rivets from my quivering wounds
When the rocks split and close again behind;   40
While from their loud abysses howling throng
The genii of the storm, urging the rage
Of whirlwind, and afflict me with keen hail.
And yet to me welcome is day and night,
Whether one breaks the hoar frost of the morn,   45
Or starry, dim, and slow, the other climbs
The leaden-coloured east; for then they lead
Their wingless, crawling Hours, one among whom
– As some dark Priest hales the reluctant victim –
Shall drag thee, cruel King, to kiss the blood   50
From these pale feet, which then might trample thee
If they disdained not such a prostrate slave.

Disdain? Ah no! I pity thee. What ruin
Will hunt thee undefended through wide Heaven!
How will thy soul, cloven to its depth with terror,   55
Gape like a Hell within! I speak in grief,
Not exultation, for I hate no more,
As then ere misery made me wise. The Curse
Once breathed on thee I would recall. Ye mountains,
Whose many-voicèd Echoes, through the mist   60
Of cataracts, flung the thunder of that spell;
Ye icy Springs, stagnant with wrinkling frost,
Which vibrated to hear me and then crept
Shuddering through India; thou serenest Air,
Through which the Sun walks burning without beams;   65
And ye swift Whirlwinds, who on poisèd wings
Hung mute and moveless o'er yon hushed abyss,
As thunder louder than your own made rock
The orbèd world – if then my words had power,
Though I am changed so that aught evil wish   70
Is dead within; although no memory be
Of what is hate – let them not lose it now!
What was that curse? for ye all heard me speak.

First Voice   (from the Mountains)
   Thrice three hundred thousand years
      O'er the Earthquake's couch we stood: 75
   Oft, as men convulsed with fears,
      We trembled in our multitude.

Second Voice   (from the Springs)
   Thunderbolts had parched our water,
      We had been stained with bitter blood,
   And had run mute, mid shrieks of slaughter,   80
      Through a city and a solitude.

Third Voice   (from the Air)
   I had clothed, since Earth uprose,
      Its wastes in colours not their own;
   And oft had my serene repose
      Been cloven by many a rending groan.   85

Fourth Voice   (from the Whirlwinds)
　　We had soared beneath these mountains
　　　　Unresting ages; nor had thunder,
　　Nor yon volcano's flaming fountains,
　　　　Nor any power above or under
　　　　Ever made us mute with wonder.   90

First Voice.
　　But never bowed our snowy crest
　　As at the voice of thine unrest.

Second Voice.
　　Never such a sound before
　　To the Indian waves we bore.
　　A pilot asleep on the howling sea   95
　　Leaped up from the deck in agony
　　And heard, and cried, 'Ah, woe is me!'
　　And died as mad as the wild waves be.

Third Voice.
　　By such dread words from Earth to Heaven
　　My still realm was never riven: 100
　　When its wound was closed, there stood
　　Darkness o'er the day like blood.

Fourth Voice.
　　And we shrank back: for dreams of ruin
　　To frozen caves our flight pursuing
　　Made us keep silence – thus – and thus –   105
　　Though silence is as hell to us.

The Earth.   The tongueless Caverns of the craggy hills
　　Cried, 'Misery!' then the hollow Heaven replied,
　　'Misery!' and the Ocean's purple waves,
　　Climbing the land, howled to the lashing winds,   110
　　And the pale nations heard it, – 'Misery!'
Prometheus.   I hear a sound of voices – not the voice
　　Which I gave forth. Mother, thy sons and thou
　　Scorn him, without whose all-enduring will
　　Beneath the fierce omnipotence of Jove,   115
　　Both they and thou had vanished like thin mist

Unrolled on the morning wind. Know ye not me,
The Titan? he who made his agony
The barrier to your else all-conquering foe?
O rock-embosomed lawns, and snow-fed streams,   120
Now seen athwart frore vapours, deep below,
Through whose o'ershadowing woods I wandered once
With Asia, drinking life from her loved eyes,
Why scorns the spirit which informs ye, now
To commune with me? me alone, who checked –   125
As one who checks a fiend-drawn charioteer –
The falsehood and the force of Him who reigns
Supreme, and with the groans of pining slaves
Fills your dim glens and liquid wildernesses?
Why answer ye not, still? Brethren!
The Earth.   They dare not.   130
Prometheus.   Who dares? for I would hear that curse
    again . . .
Ha, what an awful whisper rises up!
'Tis scarce like sound: it tingles through the frame
As lightning tingles, hovering ere it strike.
Speak, Spirit! from thine inorganic voice   135
I only know that thou are moving near
And love. How cursed I him?
The Earth.   How canst thou hear,
Who knowest not the language of the dead?
Prometheus.   Thou art a living spirit; speak as they.
The Earth.   I dare not speak like life, lest Heaven's fell
    King   140
Should hear, and link me to some wheel of pain
More torturing than the one whereon I roll.
Subtle thou art and good; and though the Gods
Hear not this voice, yet thou art more than God
Being wise and kind: earnestly hearken now.   145
Prometheus.   Obscurely through my brain, like shadows
    dim,
Sweep awful thoughts, rapid and thick, I feel
Faint, like one mingled in entwining love;
Yet 'tis not pleasure.
The Earth.   No, thou canst not hear:
Thou are immortal, and this tongue is known   150
Only to those who die . . .

Prometheus.   And what art thou,
   O melancholy Voice?
The Earth.   I am the Earth,
   Thy mother; she within whose stony veins,   155
   To the last fibre of the loftiest tree
   Whose thin leaves trembled in the frozen air,
   Joy ran, as blood within a living frame,
   When thou didst from her bosom like a cloud
   Of glory, arise – a spirit of keen joy!
   And at thy voice her pining sons uplifted
   Their prostrate brows from the polluting dust,   160
   And our almighty Tyrant with fierce dread
   Grew pale – until his thunder chained thee here.
   Then – see those million worlds which burn and roll
   Around us: their inhabitants beheld
   My spherèd light wane in wide Heaven; the sea   165
   Was lifted by strange tempest, and new fire
   From earthquake-rifted mountains of bright snow
   Shook its portentous hair beneath Heaven's frown;
   Lightning and Inundation vexed the plains;
   Blue thistles bloomed in cities; foodless toads   170
   Within voluptuous chambers panting crawled;
   When Plague had fallen on man and beast and
        worm,
   And Famine, – and black blight on herb and tree;
   And in the corn, and vines, and meadow-grass
   Teemed ineradicable poisonous weeds   175
   Draining their growth, for my wan breast was dry
   With grief; and the thin air, my breath, was stained
   With the contagion of a mother's hate
   Breathed on her child's destroyer – aye, I heard
   Thy curse, the which, if thou rememberest not,   180
   Yet my innumerable seas and streams,
   Mountains, and caves, and winds, and yon wide air,
   And the inarticulate people of the dead,
   Preserve, a treasured spell. We meditate
   In secret joy and hope those dreadful words,   185
   But dare not speak them.
Prometheus.   Venerable Mother!
   All else who live and suffer take from thee
   Some comfort; flowers, and fruits, and happy sounds,

And love, though fleeting; these may not be mine.
But mine own words, I pray, deny me not.   190
The Earth.   They shall be told. Ere Babylon was dust,
  The Magus Zoroaster, my dead child,
  Met his own image walking in the garden.
  That apparition, sole of men, he saw.
  For know, there are two worlds of life and death: 195
  One that which thou beholdest; but the other
  Is underneath the grave, where do inhabit
  The shadows of all forms that think and live
  Till death unite them and they part no more;
  Dreams and the light imaginings of men,   200
  And all that faith creates or love desires,
  Terrible, strange, sublime and beauteous shapes.
  There thou art, and dost hang, a writhing shade
  Mid whirlwind-peopled mountains; all the Gods
  Are there, and all the Powers of nameless worlds,   205
  Vast, sceptred Phantoms; heroes, men and beasts;
  And Demogorgon, a tremendous Gloom;
  And he, the Supreme Tyrant, on his throne
  Of burning gold. Son, one of these shall utter
  The curse which all remember. Call at will   210
  Thine own ghost, or the ghost of Jupiter,
  Hades, or Typhon, or what mightier Gods
  From all-prolific Evil since thy ruin
  Have sprung, and trampled on my prostrate sons.
  Ask, and they must reply: so the revenge   215
  Of the Supreme may sweep through vacant shades,
  As rainy wind through the abandoned gate
  Of a fallen palace.
Prometheus.   Mother, let not aught
  Of that which may be evil, pass again
  My lips, or those of aught resembling me.   220
  Phantasm of Jupiter, arise, appear!

Ione.
  My wings are folded o'er mine ears:
    My wings are crossed over mine eyes:
  Yet through their silver shade appears,
    And through their lulling plumes arise,   225
  A Shape, a throng of sounds;

    May it be no ill to thee,
  O thou of many wounds!
Near whom, for our sweet sister's sake,
Ever thus we watch and wake.   230

Panthea.
  The sound is of whirlwind underground,
    Earthquake, and fire, and mountains cloven;
  The Shape is awful like the sound,
    Clothed in dark purple, star-inwoven.
  A sceptre of pale gold   235
    To stay steps proud, o'er the slow cloud
  His veinèd hand doth hold.
Cruel he looks, but calm and strong,
Like one who does, not suffers wrong.
Phantasm of Jupiter.   Why have the secret
      powers of this strange world   240
  Driven me, a frail and empty phantom, hither
  On direst storms? What unaccustomed sounds
  Are hovering on my lips, unlike the voice
  With which our pallid race hold ghastly talk
  In darkness? And, proud Sufferer, who are thou?   245
Prometheus.   Tremendous Image, as thou art must be
  He whom thou shadowest forth. I am his foe,
  The Titan. Speak the words which I would hear,
  Although no thought inform thine empty voice.
The Earth.   Listen! And though your echoes must be
      mute,   250
  Grey mountains, and old woods, and haunted springs,
  Prophetic caves, and isle-surrounding streams,
  Rejoice to hear what yet ye cannot speak.
Phantasm.   A spirit seizes me and speaks within:
  It tears me as fire tears a thunder-cloud.   255
Panthea.   See, how he lifts his mighty looks, the Heaven
  Darkens above.
Ione.   He speaks! O shelter me!
Prometheus.   I see the curse on gestures proud and
      cold,
  And looks of firm defiance, and calm hate,
  And such despair as mocks itself with smiles,   260
  Written as on a scroll . . . yet speak – O speak!

Phantasm.

   Fiend, I defy thee! with a calm, fixed mind,
     All that thou canst inflict I bid thee do;
   Foul Tyrant both of Gods and Humankind,
     One only being shall thou not subdue.   265
   Rain then thy plagues upon me here,
   Ghastly disease, and frenzying fear;
   And let alternate frost and fire
   Eat into me, and be thine ire
Lightning, and cutting hail, and legioned forms   270
Of furies, driving by upon the wounding storms.

   Aye, do thy worst. Thou art omnipotent.
     O'er all things but thyself I gave thee power,
   And my own will. Be thy swift mischiefs sent
     To blast mankind, from yon aetherial tower.   275
   Let thy malignant spirit move
   Its darkness over those I love:
   On me and mine I imprecate
   The utmost torture of thy hate;
And thus devote to sleepless agony   280
This undeclining head while thou must reign on high.

   But thou who are the God and Lord – O thou
     Who fillest with thy soul this world of woe,
   To whom all things of Earth and Heaven do bow
     In fear and worship – all-prevailing foe!   285
   I curse thee! let a sufferer's curse
   Clasp thee, his torturer, like remorse,
   'Till thine Infinity shall be
   A robe of envenomed agony,
And thine Omnipotence a crown of pain   290
To cling like burning gold round thy dissolving brain.

   Heap on thy soul, by virtue of this Curse,
     Ill deeds, then be thou damned, beholding good –
   Both infinite as is the Universe,
     And thou, and thy self-torturing solitude.   295
   An awful image of calm power
   Though now thou sittest, let the hour
   Come, when thou must appear to be

That which thou art internally,
And after many a false and fruitless crime   300
Scorn track thy lagging fall through boundless space and
     time.

Prometheus.   Were these my words, O Parent?
The Earth.   They were thine.
Prometheus.   It doth repent me: words are quick and vain;
  Grief for awhile is blind, and so was mine.   305
  I wish no living thing to suffer pain.

The Earth.
  Misery, O misery to me,
  That Jove at length should vanquish thee.
  Wail, howl aloud, Land and Sea;
  The Earth's rent heart shall answer ye.
  Howl, Spirits of the living and the dead;   310
  Your refuge, your defence lies fallen and vanquishèd.

First Echo.
  Lies fallen and vanquishèd!

Second Echo.
  Fallen and vanquishèd!

Ione.
  Fear not: 'tis but some passing spasm;
    The Titan is unvanquished still.   315
  But see, where through the azure chasm
    Of yon forked and snowy hill
  Trampling the slant winds on high
    With golden-sandalled feet, that glow
  Under plumes of purple dye,   320
  Like rose-ensanguined ivory,
    A Shape comes now,
  Stretching on high from his right hand
  A serpent-cinctured wand.

Panthea.
  'Tis Jove's world-wandering herald, Mercury.   325

Ione.
     And who are those with hydra tresses
         And iron wings that climb the wind,
     Whom the frowning God represses
         Like vapours steaming up behind,
     Clanging loud, an endless crowd –   330

Panthea.
     These are Jove's tempest-walking hounds,
         Whom he gluts with groans and blood,
     When charioted on sulphurous cloud
         He bursts Heaven's bounds.

Ione.
     Are they now led from the thin dead,   335
         On new pangs to be fed?

Panthea.   The Titan looks as ever, firm, not proud.
First Fury.   Ha! I scent life!
Second Fury.   Let me but look into his eyes!
Third Fury.   The hope of torturing him smells like a heap
     Of corpses to a death-bird after battle.   340
First Fury.   Darest thou delay, O Herald! take cheer,
         Hounds
     Of Hell – what if the Son of Maia soon
     Should make us food and sport? who can please long
     The Omnipotent?

Mercury.   Back to your towers of iron, .
     And gnash beside the streams of fire and wail   345
     Your foodless teeth! . . . Geryon, arise! and Gorgon,
     Chimaera, and thou Sphinx, subtlest of fiends,
     Who ministered to Thebes Heaven's poisoned wine –
     Unnatural love, and more unnatural hate:
     These shall perform your task.
First Fury.   O mercy! mercy!   350
     We die with our desire – drive us not back!
Mercury.   Crouch then in silence.
                         Awful Sufferer,
     To thee unwillingly, most unwillingly
     I come, by the great Father's will driven down

To execute a doom of new revenge.   355
Alas! I pity thee, and hate myself
That I can do no more: aye from thy sight
Returning, for a season, Heaven seems Hell,
So thy worn form pursues me night and day,
Smiling reproach. Wise art thou, firm and good,   360
But vainly wouldst stand forth alone in strife
Against the Omnipotent; as yon clear lamps
That measure and divide the weary years
From which there is no refuge, long have taught
And long must teach. Even now thy Torturer arms   365
With the strange might of unimagined pains
The powers who scheme slow agonies in Hell,
And my commission is to lead them here,
Or what more subtle, foul, or savage fiends
People the abyss, and leave them to their task.   370
Be it not so! . . . there is a secret known
To thee and to none else of living things,
Which may transfer the sceptre of wide Heaven,
The fear of which perplexes the Supreme:
Clothe it in words, and bid it clasp his throne   375
In intercession; bend thy soul in prayer,
And like a suppliant in some gorgeous fane
Let the will kneel within thy haughty heart:
For benefits and meek submission tame
The fiercest and the mightiest.
Prometheus.   Evil minds   380
Change good to their own nature. I gave all
He has; and in return he chains me here
Years, ages, night and day: whether the Sun
Split my parched skin, or in the moony night
The crystal-wingèd snow cling round my hair –   385
Whilst my belovèd race is trampled down
By his thought-executing ministers.
Such is the tyrant's recompense – 'tis just:
He who is evil can receive no good;
And for a world bestowed, or a friend lost,   390
He can feel hate, fear, shame – not gratitude:
He but requites me for his own misdeed.
Kindness to such is keen reproach, which breaks
With bitter stings the light sleep of Revenge.

Submission, thou dost know, I cannot try: 395
For what submission but that fatal word,
The death-seal of mankind's captivity,
Like the Sicilian's hair-suspended sword
Which trembles o'er his crown, would he accept,
Or could I yield? – Which yet I will not yield.   400
Let others flatter Crime, where it sits throned
In brief Omnipotence; secure are they:
For Justice, when triumphant, will weep down
Pity, not punishment, on her own wrongs,
Too much avenged by those who err. I wait,   405
Enduring thus, the retributive hour
Which since we spake is even nearer now –
But hark, the hell-hounds clamour: fear delay:
Behold! Heaven lowers under thy Father's frown.

Mercury.   O that we might be spared: I to inflict   410
And thou to suffer! Once more answer me:
Thou knowest not the period of Jove's power?

Prometheus.   I know but this, that it must come.

Mercury.   Alas,
Thou canst not count thy years to come of pain?

Prometheus.   They last while Jove must reign: nor more,
         nor less
Do I desire or fear.   415

Mercury.   Yet pause, and plunge
Into Eternity, where recorded time,
Even all that we imagine, age on age,
Seems but a point, and the reluctant mind
Flags wearily in its unending flight,   420
Till it sink, dizzy, blind, lost, shelterless;
Perchance it has not numbered the slow years
Which thou must spend in torture, unreprieved.

Prometheus.   Perchance no thought can count them – yet
         they pass.

Mercury.   If thou might'st dwell among the Gods the while,
Lapped in voluptuous joy?

Prometheus.   I would not quit
This bleak ravine, these unrepentant pains.

Mercury.   Alas! I wonder at, yet pity thee.

Prometheus.   Pity the self-despising slaves of Heaven,
Not me, within whose mind sits peace serene,   430

As light in the sun, throned . . . How vain is talk!
Call up the fiends.
Ione.   O sister, look! White fire
Has cloven to the roots yon huge snow-loaded cedar;
How fearfully God's thunder howls behind!
Mercury.   I must obey his words and thine – alas!   435
Most heavily remorse hangs at my heart!
Panthea.   See where the child of Heaven with wingèd feet
Runs down the slanted sunlight of the dawn.
Ione.   Dear sister, close thy plumes over thine eyes
Lest thou behold and die – they come, they come   440
Blackening the birth of day with countless wings,
And hollow underneath, like death.
First Fury.   Prometheus!
Second Fury.   Immortal Titan!
Third Fury.   Champion of Heaven's slaves!
Prometheus.   He whom some dreadful voice invokes is here,
Prometheus, the chained Titan. Horrible forms,   445
What and who are ye? Never yet there came
Phantasms so foul through monster-teeming Hell
From the all-miscreative brain of Jove;
Whilst I behold such execrable shapes
Methinks I grow like what I contemplate,   450
And laugh and stare in loathsome sympathy.
First Fury.   We are the ministers of pain and fear,
And disappointment, and mistrust, and hate,
And clinging crime; and as lean dogs pursue
Through wood and lake some struck and sobbing fawn,   455
We track all things that weep, and bleed, and live,
When the great King betrays them to our will.
Prometheus.   O many fearful natures in one name,
I know ye; and these lakes and echoes know
The darkness and the clangour of your wings.   460
But why more hideous than your loathèd selves
Gather ye up in legions from the deep?
Second Fury.   We knew not that: Sisters, rejoice, rejoice!
Prometheus.   Can aught exult in its deformity?
Second Fury.   The beauty of delight makes lovers glad,   465
Gazing on one another: so are we.
As from the rose which the pale priestess kneels
To gather for her festal crown of flowers

The aerial crimson falls, flushing her cheek,
So from our victim's destined agony   470
The shade which is our form invests us round,
Else are we shapeless as our mother Night.
Prometheus.   I laugh your power, and his who sent you here,
To lowest scorn. Pour forth the cup of pain.
First Fury.   Thou thinkest we will rend thee bone from
        bone,   475
And nerve from nerve, working like fire within?
Prometheus.   Pain is my element, as hate is thine;
Ye rend me now: I care not.
Second Fury.   Dost imagine
We will but laugh into thy lidless eyes?
Prometheus.   I weigh not what ye do, but what ye suffer,   480
Being evil. Cruel was the Power which called
You, or aught else so wretched, into light.
Third Fury.   Thou think'st we will live through thee,
        one by one,
Like animal life, and though we can obscure not
The soul which burns within, that we will dwell   485
Beside it, like a vain loud multitude
Vexing the self-content of wisest men;
That we will be dread thought beneath thy brain,
And foul desire round thine astonished heart,
And blood within thy labyrinthine veins   490
Crawling like agony?
Prometheus.   Why, ye are thus now;
Yet am I king over myself, and rule
The torturing and conflicting throngs within,
As Jove rules you when Hell grows mutinous.

Chorus of Furies.
From the ends of the Earth, from the ends of the Earth,   495
Where the night has its grave and the morning its birth,
        Come, come, come!
O ye who shake hills with the scream of your mirth
When cities sink howling in ruin; and ye
Who with wingless footsteps trample the Sea,   500
And close upon Shipwreck and Famine's track
Sit chattering with joy on the foodless wreck:
        Come, come, come!

Leave the bed, low, cold and red,
Strewed beneath a nation dead;   505
Leave the hatred, as in ashes
    Fire is left for future burning –
It will burst in bloodier flashes
    When ye stir it, soon returning;
Leave the self-contempt implanted   510
In young spirits sense-enchanted,
    Misery's yet unkindled fuel;
Leave Hell's secrets half-unchanted
    To the maniac dreamer: cruel
More than ye can be with hate   515
    Is he with fear.
            Come, come, come!
We are steaming up from Hell's wide gate,
    And we burthen the blasts of the atmosphere,
    But vainly we toil till ye come here.   520
Ione.   Sister, I hear the thunder of new wings.
Panthea.   These solid mountains quiver with the sound
    Even as the tremulous air: their shadows make
    The space within my plumes more black than night.

First Fury.
    Your call was as a wingèd car   525
    Driven on whirlwinds fast and far;
    It rapt us from red gulfs of war.

Second Fury.
    From wide cities, famine-wasted;

Third Fury.
    Groans half-heard, and blood untasted;

Fourth Fury.
    Kingly conclaves stern and cold,   530
    Where blood with gold is bought and sold;

Fifth Fury.
    From the furnace, white and hot,
    In which –

A Fury.
    Speak not – whisper not:
  I know all that ye would tell,
  But to speak might break the spell   535
  Which must bend the Invincible,
    The stern of thought;
  He yet defies the deepest power of Hell.

Fury.
  Tear the veil!

Another Fury.
  It is torn!

Chorus.
    The pale stars of the morn
  Shine on a misery dire to be borne.   540
  Dost thou faint, mighty Titan? We laugh thee to scorn.
  Dost thou boast the clear knowledge thou waken'dst for
    man?
  Then was kindled within him a thirst which outran
  Those perishing waters: a thirst of fierce fever,
  Hope, love, doubt, desire – which consume him for ever. 545
    One came forth of gentle worth
    Smiling on the sanguine earth;
    His words outlived him, like a swift poison
      Withering up truth, peace, and pity.
    Look! where round the wide horizon   550
      Many a million-peopled city
    Vomits smoke in the bright air.
    Hark that outcry of despair!
    'Tis his mild and gentle ghost
      Wailing for the faith he kindled: 555
    Look again, the flames almost
      To a glow-worm's lamp have dwindled:
    The survivors round the embers
      Gather in dread.
        Joy, joy, joy!   560
  Past ages crowd on thee, but each one remembers;
  And the future is dark, and the present is spread
  Like a pillow of thorns for thy slumberless head.

Semichorus I.
　　Drops of bloody agony flow
　　From his white and quivering brow.　　　565
　　Grant a little respite now –
　　See, a disenchanted nation
　　Springs like day from desolation;
　　To Truth its state is dedicate,
　　And Freedom leads it forth, her mate;　　570
　　A legioned band of linkèd brothers
　　Whom Love calls children –

Semichorus II.
　　　　'Tis another's –
　　See how kindred murder kin!
　　'Tis the vintage-time for Death and Sin;
　　Blood, like new wine, bubbles within,　　575
　　　　Till Despair smothers
　　The struggling World – which slaves and tyrants win.
　　　　　　[*All the* Furies *vanish, except one.*

Ione.　　Hark, sister! what a low yet dreadful groan
　　Quite unsuppressed is tearing up the heart
　　Of the good Titan, as storms tear the deep,　　580
　　And beasts hear the sea moan in inland caves.
　　Darest thou observe how the fiends torture him?
Panthea.　　Alas! I looked forth twice, but will no more.
Ione.　　What didst thou see?
Panthea.　　A woeful sight: a youth
　　With patient looks nailed to a crucifix.　　585
Ione.　　What next?
Panthea.　　The Heaven around, the Earth below
　　Was peopled with thick shapes of human death,
　　All horrible, and wrought by human hands,
　　Though some appeared the work of human hearts,
　　For men were slowly killed by frowns and smiles:　　590
　　And other sights too foul to speak and live
　　Were wandering by. Let us not tempt worse fear
　　By looking forth: those groans are grief enough.
Fury.　　Behold an emblem: those who do endure
　　Deep wrongs for man, and scorn, and chains, but heap　　595
　　Thousandfold torment on themselves and him.

Prometheus.   Remit the anguish of that lighted stare;
 Close those wan lips; let that thorn-wounded brow
 Stream not with blood – it mingles with thy tears!
 Fix, fix those tortured orbs in peace and death,   600
 So thy sick throes shake not that crucifix,
 So those pale fingers play not with thy gore.
 O, horrible! Thy name I will not speak;
 It hath become a curse. I see, I see
 The wise, the mild, the lofty, and the just,   605
 Whom thy slaves hate for being like to thee,
 Some hunted by foul lies from their heart's home,
 An early-chosen, late-lamented home,
 As hooded ounces cling to the driven hind;
 Some linked to corpses in unwholesome cells;   610
 Some – hear I not the multitude laugh loud? –
 Impaled in lingering fire; and mighty realms
 Float by my feet like sea-uprooted isles,
 Whose sons are kneaded down in common blood
 By the red light of their own burning homes.   615
Fury.   Blood thou canst see, and fire; and canst hear
   groans;
 Worse things, unheard, unseen, remain behind.
Prometheus.   Worse?
Fury.   In each human heart terror survives
 The ravin it has gorged: the loftiest fear
 All that they would disdain to think were true: 620
 Hypocrisy and custom make their minds
 The fanes of many a worship, now outworn.
 They dare not devise good for man's estate,
 And yet they know not that they do not dare.
 The good want power, but to weep barren tears.   625
 The powerful goodness want: worse need for them.
 The wise want love; and those who love want wisdom;
 And all best things are thus confused to ill.
 Many are strong and rich, – and would be just –
 But live among their suffering fellow men   630
 As if none felt: they know not what they do.
Prometheus.   Thy words are like a cloud of wingèd snakes;
 And yet I pity those they torture not.
Fury.   Thou pitiest them? I speak no more!
               [*Vanishes.*

Prometheus.   Ah woe!
  Ah woe! Alas! pain, pain ever, for ever!   635
  I close my tearless eyes, but see more clear
  Thy works within my woe-illumèd mind,
  Thou subtle tyrant! . . . Peace is in the grave.
  The grave hides all things beautiful and good:
  I am a God and cannot find it there,   640
  Nor would I seek it: for, though dread revenge,
  This is defeat, fierce King, not victory!
  The sights with which thou torturest gird my soul
  With new endurance, till the hour arrives
  When they shall be no types of things which are.   645
Panthea.   Alas! what sawest thou?
Prometheus.   There are two woes:
  To speak, and to behold; thou spare me one.
  Names are there, Nature's sacred watchwords – they
  Were borne aloft in bright emblazonry;
  The nations thronged around, and cried aloud,   650
  As with one voice, 'Truth, Liberty, and Love!'
  Suddenly fierce confusion fell from Heaven
  Among them: there was strife, deceit, and fear;
  Tyrants rushed in, and did divide the spoil.
  This was the shadow of the truth I saw.   655
The Earth.   I felt thy torture, Son, with such mixed
      joy
  As pain and virtue give. To cheer thy state
  I bid ascend those subtle and fair spirits
  Whose homes are the dim caves of human thought,
  And who inhabit, as birds wing the wind,   660
  Its world-surrounding aether; they behold
  Beyond that twilight realm, as in a glass,
  The future: may they speak comfort to thee!
Panthea.   Look, sister, where a troop of spirits gather,
  Like flocks of clouds in spring's delightful weather,   665
  Thronging in the blue air!
Ione.   And see! more come,
  Like fountain-vapours when the winds are dumb,
  That climb up the ravine in scattered lines.
  And, hark! is it the music of the pines?
  Is it the lake? is it the waterfall?   670
Panthea.   'Tis something sadder, sweeter far than all.

Chorus of Spirits.
    From unremembered ages we
    Gentle guides and guardians be
    Of Heaven-oppressed mortality;
    And we breathe, and sicken not,   675
    The atmosphere of human thought:
    Be it dim, and dank, and grey,
    Like a storm-extinguished day,
    Travelled o'er by dying gleams;
        Be it bright as all between   680
    Cloudless skies and windless streams,
        Silent, liquid, and serene –
    As the birds within the wind,
        As the fish within the wave,
    As the thoughts of man's own mind   685
        Float through all above the grave,
    We make there our liquid lair,
    Voyaging cloudlike and unpent
    Through the boundless element –
    Thence we bear the prophecy   690
    Which begins and ends in thee!

Ione.   More yet come, one by one: the air around them
    Looks radiant as the air around a star.

First Spirit.
    On a battle-trumpet's blast
    I fled hither, fast, fast, fast,   695
    Mid the darkness upward cast –
    From the dust of creeds outworn,
    From the tyrant's banner torn,
    Gathering round me, onward borne,
    There was mingled many a cry –   700
    'Freedom! Hope! Death! Victory!'
    Till they faded through the sky;
    And one sound, above, around,
    One sound beneath, around, above,
    Was moving; 'twas the soul of love;   705
    'Twas the hope, the prophecy,
    Which begins and ends in thee.

Second Spirit.
    A rainbow's arch stood on the sea,
    Which rocked beneath, immoveably;
    And the triumphant Storm did flee,   710
    Like a conqueror, swift and proud,
    Between, with many a captive cloud,
    A shapeless, dark and rapid crowd,
    Each by lightning riven in half –
    I heard the thunder hoarsely laugh –   715
    Mighty fleets were strewn like chaff
    And spread beneath a hell of death
    O'er the white waters. I alit
    On a great ship lightning-split,
    And speeded hither on the sigh   720
    Of one who gave an enemy
    His plank – then plunged aside to die.

Third Spirit.
    I sate beside a Sage's bed,
    And the lamp was burning red
    Near the book where he had fed,   725
    When a Dream with plumes of flame
    To his pillow hovering came,
    And I knew it was the same
    Which had kindled long ago
    Pity, eloquence, and woe;   730
    And the world awhile below
    Wore the shade its lustre made.
    It has borne me here as fleet
    As Desire's lightning feet:
    I must ride it back ere morrow,   735
    Or the sage will wake in sorrow.

Fourth Spirit.
    On a Poet's lips I slept
    Dreaming like a love-adept
    In the sound his breathing kept;
    Nor seeks nor finds he mortal blisses,   740
    But feeds on the aërial kisses
    Of shapes that haunt thought's wildernesses.
    He will watch from dawn to gloom

The lake-reflected sun illume
The yellow bees i' the ivy-bloom, 745
Nor heed nor see, what things they be;
But from these create he can
Forms more real than living man,
Nurslings of immortality!
One of these awakened me, 750
And I sped to succour thee.

Ione.
Behold'st thou not two shapes from the east and west
Come, as two doves to one belovèd nest,
Twin nurslings of the all-sustaining air,
On swift still wings glide down the atmosphere? 755
And hark! their sweet, sad voices; 'tis despair
Mingled with love and then dissolved in sound.

Panthea.
Canst thou speak, sister? all my words are drowned.

Ione.   Their beauty gives me voice. See how they float
On their sustaining wings of skiey grain, 760
Orange and azure deepening into gold:
Their soft smiles light the air like a star's fire.

Chorus of Spirits.
Hast thou beheld the form of Love?

Fifth Spirit.
        As over wide dominions
I sped, like some swift cloud that wings the wide air's
    wildernesses,
That planet-crested Shape swept by on lightning-braided
    pinions, 765
Scattering the liquid joy of life from his ambrosial tresses:
His footsteps paved the world with light – but as I passed
    'twas fading,
And hollow Ruin yawned behind: great sages bound in
    madness,
And headless patriots, and pale youths who perished,
    unupbraiding,

Gleamed in the night I wandered o'er – till thou, O
   King of sadness,   770
Turned by thy smile the worst I saw to recollected
   gladness.

Sixth Spirit.
  Ah, sister! Desolation is a delicate thing:
  It walks not on the earth, it floats not on the air,
  But treads with lulling footstep, and fans with silent wing
  The tender hopes which in their hearts the best and gentlest
     bear;   775
  Who, soothed to false repose by the fanning plumes above,
  And the music-stirring motions of its soft and busy feet,
  Dream visions of aërial joy, and call the monster Love,
  And wake, and find the shadow Pain – as he whom now
     we greet.

Chorus.
  Though Ruin now Love's shadow be,   780
  Following him destroyingly
    On Death's white and wingèd steed,
  Which the fleetest cannot flee –
    Trampling down both flower and weed,
  Man and beast, and foul and fair,   785
  Like a tempest through the air;
  Thou shalt quell this Horseman grim,
  Woundless though in heart or limb.

Prometheus.   Spirits! how know ye this shall be?

Chorus.
  In the atmosphere we breathe –   790
  As buds grow red when snow-storms flee
    From spring gathering up beneath,
  Whose mild winds shake the elder brake,
  And the wandering herdsmen know
  That the white-thorn soon will blow –   795
  Wisdom, Justice, Love, and Peace,
  When they struggle to increase,
    Are to us as soft winds be

To shepherd boys – the prophecy
Which begins and ends in thee.   800

Ione.   Where are the Spirits fled?

Panthea.
          Only a sense
Remains of them, like the omnipotence
Of music, when the inspired voice and lute
Languish, ere yet the responses are mute
Which through the deep and labyrinthine soul,   805
Like echoes through long caverns, wind and roll.

Prometheus.   How fair these air-born shapes! and yet I feel
Most vain all hope but love; and thou art far,
Asia! who, when my being overflowed,
Wert like a golden chalice to bright wine   810
Which else had sunk into the thirsty dust.
All things are still: alas! how heavily
This quiet morning weighs upon my heart;
Though I should dream, I could even sleep with grief
If slumber were denied not. I would fain   815
Be what it is my destiny to be,
The saviour and the strength of suffering man,
Or sink into the original gulf of things . . .
There is no agony, and no solace left;
Earth can console, Heaven can torment no more.   820
Panthea.   Hast thou forgotten one who watches thee
The cold dark night, and never sleeps but when
The shadow of thy spirit falls on her?
Prometheus.   I said all hope was vain but love: thou lovest.
Panthea.   Deeply in truth; but the eastern star looks white, 825
And Asia waits in that far Indian vale,
The scene of her sad exile – rugged once
And desolate and frozen, like this ravine;
But now invested with fair flowers and herbs,
And haunted by sweet airs and sounds, which flow   830
Among the woods and waters, from the aether
Of her transforming presence – which would fade
If it were mingled not with thine. Farewell!

ACT II   Scene iv

The Cave of Demogorgon. ASIA and PANTHEA.

Panthea.   What veilèd form sits on that ebon throne?
Asia.   The veil has fallen . . .
Panthea.   I see a mighty Darkness
  Filling the seat of power; and rays of gloom
  Dart round, as light from the meridian sun,
  Ungazed upon and shapeless – neither limb,   5
  Nor form, nor outline; yet we feel it is
  A living Spirit.
Demogorgon.   Ask what thou wouldst know.
Asia.   What canst thou tell?
Demogorgon.   All things thou dar'st demand.
Asia.   Who made the living world?
Demogorgon.   God.
Asia.   Who made all
  That it contains – thought, passion, reason, will,   10
  Imagination?
Demogorgon.   God: Almighty God.
Asia.   Who made that sense which, when the winds of
      spring
  In rarest visitation, or the voice
  Of one belovèd heard in youth alone,
  Fills the faint eyes with falling tears which dim   15
  The radiant looks of unbewailing flowers,
  And leaves this peopled earth a solitude
  When it returns no more?
Demogorgon.   Merciful God.
Asia.   And who made terror, madeness, crime, remorse,
  Which from the links of the great chain of things   20
  To every thought within the mind of man
  Sway and drag heavily, and each one reels
  Under the load towards the pit of death;
  Abandoned hope, and love that turns to hate;
  And self-contempt, bitterer to drink than blood;   25
  Pain, whose unheeded and familiar speech
  Is howling, and keen shrieks, day after day;
  And Hell, or the sharp fear of Hell?
Demogorgon.   He reigns.

Asia. Utter his name: a world pining in pain
  Asks but his name: curses shall drag him down. 30
Demogorgon. He reigns.
Asia. I feel, I know it: who?
Demogorgon. He reigns.
Asia. Who reigns? There was the Heaven and Earth at first,
  And Light and Love; then Saturn, from whose throne
  Time fell, an envious shadow; such the state
  Of the earth's primal spirits beneath his sway 35
  As the calm joy of flowers and living leaves
  Before the wind or sun has withered them
  And semivital worms; but he refused
  The birthrights of their being, knowledge, power,
  The skill which wields the elements, the thought 40
  Which pierces this dim universe like light,
  Self-empire, and the majesty of love;
  For thirst of which they fainted. Then Prometheus
  Gave wisdom, which is strength, to Jupiter,
  And with this law alone, 'Let man be free,' 45
  Clothed him with the dominion of wide Heaven.
  To know nor faith, nor love, nor law, to be
  Omnipotent but friendless is to reign;
  And Jove now reigned; for on the race of man
  First famine, and then toil, and then disease, 50
  Strife, wounds, and ghastly death unseen before,
  Fell; and the unseasonable seasons drove
  With alternating shafts of frost and fire,
  Their shelterless, pale tribes to mountain caves;
  And in their desert hearts fierce wants he sent, 55
  And mad disquietudes, and shadows idle
  Of unreal good, which levied mutual war,
  So ruining the lair wherein they raged.
  Prometheus saw, and waked the legioned hopes
  Which sleep within folded Elysian flowers, 60
  Nepenthe, Moly, Amaranth, fadeless blooms,
  That they might hide with thin and rainbow wings
  The shape of Death; and Love he sent to bind
  The disunited tendrils of that vine
  Which bears the wine of life, the human heart; 65
  And he tamed fire which, like some beast of chase,
  Most terrible, but lovely, played beneath

The frown of man; and tortured to his will
Iron and gold, the slaves and signs of power,
And gems and poisons, and all subtlest forms   70
Hidden beneath the mountains and the waves.
He gave man speech, and speech created thought,
Which is the measure of the universe;
And Science struck the thrones of Earth and Heaven,
Which shook, but fell not; and the harmonious mind   75
Poured itself forth in all-prophetic song;
And music lifted up the listening spirit
Until it walked, exempt from mortal care,
Godlike, o'er the clear billows of sweet sound;
And human hands first mimicked and then mocked,   80
With moulded limbs more lovely than its own,
The human form, till marble grew divine;
And mothers, gazing, drank the love men see
Reflected in their race – behold, and perish.
He told the hidden power of herbs and springs,   85
And Disease drank and slept. Death grew like sleep.
He taught the implicated orbits woven
Of the wide-wandering stars; and how the Sun
Changes his lair, and by what secret spell
The pale Moon is transformed, when her broad eye   90
Gazes not on the interlunar sea.
He taught to rule, as life directs the limbs,
The tempest-wingèd chariots of the Ocean,
And the Celt knew the Indian. Cities then
Were built, and through their snow-like columns flowed   95
The warm winds, and the azure aether shone,
And the blue sea and shadowy hills were seen . . .
Such the alleviations of his state
Prometheus gave to man – for which he hangs
Withering in destined pain: but who rains down   100
Evil, the immedicable plague, which, while
Man looks on his creation like a God
And sees that it is glorious, drives him on,
The wreck of his own will, the scorn of Earth,
The outcast, the abandoned, the alone?   105
Not Jove: while yet his frown shook heaven, aye
    when
His adversary from adamantine chains

Cursed him, he trembled like a slave. Declare
Who is his master? Is he too a slave?
Demogorgon.   All spirits are enslaved which serve things
    evil: 110
Thou knowest if Jupiter be such or no.
Asia.   Whom called'st thou God?
Demogorgon.   I spoke but as ye speak,
For Jove is the supreme of living things.
Asia.   Who is the master of the slave?
Demogorgon.   If the abysm
Could vomit forth its secrets: – but a voice   115
Is wanting, the deep truth is imageless;
For what would it avail to bid thee gaze
On the revolving world? what to bid speak
Fate, Time, Occasion, Chance and Change? To these
All things are subject but eternal Love.   120
Asia.   So much I asked before, and my heart gave
The response thou hast given; and of such truths
Each to itself must be the oracle. –
One more demand; and do thou answer me
As my own soul would answer, did it know   125
That which I ask. Prometheus shall arise
Henceforth the Sun of this rejoicing world:
When will the destined hour arrive?
Demogorgon.   Behold!
Asia.   The rocks are cloven, and through the purple night
I see cars drawn by rainbow-wingèd steeds   130
Which trample the dim winds: in each there stands
A wild-eyed charioteer, urging their flight.
Some look behind, as fiends pursued them there,
And yet I see no shapes but the keen stars;
Others, with burning eyes, lean forth, and drink   135
With eager lips the wind of their own speed,
As if the thing they loved fled on before,
And now, even now, they clasped it. Their bright locks
Stream like a comet's flashing hair: they all
Sweep onward.
Demogorgon.   These are the immortal Hours,   140
Of whom thou didst demand. One waits for thee.
Asia.   A spirit with a dreadful countenance
Checks its dark chariot by the craggy gulf.

Unlike thy brethren, ghastly charioteer,
What art thou? Whither wouldst thou bear me? Speak!   145
Spirit.   I am the shadow of a destiny
  More dread than is my aspect: ere yon planet
  Has set, the Darkness which ascends with me
  Shall wrap in lasting night Heaven's kingless throne.
Asia.   What meanest thou?
Panthea.   That terrible shadow floats   150
  Up from its throne, as may the lurid smoke
  Of earthquake-ruined cities o'er the sea.
  Lo! it ascends the car . . . the coursers fly
  Terrified: watch its path among the stars
  Blackening the night!
Asia.   Thus I am answered: strange!   155
Panthea.   See, near the verge, another chariot stays;
  An ivory shell inlaid with crimson fire,
  Which comes and goes within its sculptured rim
  Of delicate strange tracery; the young spirit
  That guides it has the dove-like eyes of hope;   160
  How its soft smiles attract the soul! as light
  Lures wingèd insects through the lampless air.

Spirit.
  My coursers are fed with the lightning,
    They drink of the whirlwind's stream,
  And when the red morning is bright'ning   165
    They bathe in the fresh sunbeam;
      They have strength for their swiftness, I deem:
  Then ascend with me, daughter of Ocean.
  I desire: and their speed makes night kindle;
    I fear: they outstrip the Typhoon;   170
  Ere the cloud piled on Atlas can dwindle
    We encircle the earth and the moon:
    We shall rest from long labours at noon:
  Then ascend with me, daughter of Ocean.

ACT III   Scene iv

*A Forest. In the Background a Cave. PROMETHEUS, ASIA,
PANTHEA, IONE and the SPIRIT OF THE EARTH.*

Ione.   Sister, it is not earthly . . . how it glides
  Under the leaves! how on its head there burns
  A light like a green star, whose emerald beams
  Are twined with its fair hair! how, as it moves,
  The splendour drops in flakes upon the grass!   5
  Knowest thou it?
Panthea.   It is the delicate spirit
  That guides the earth through heaven. From afar
  The populous constellations call that light
  The loveliest of the planets; and sometimes
  It floats along the spray of the salt sea,   10
  Or makes its chariot of a foggy cloud,
  Or walks through fields or cities while men sleep,
  Or o'er the mountain tops, or down the rivers,
  Or through the green waste wilderness, as now,
  Wondering at all it sees. Before Jove reigned   15
  It loved our sister Asia, and it came
  Each leisure hour to drink the liquid light
  Out of her eyes, for which it said it thirsted
  As one bit by a dipsas; and with her
  It made its childish confidence, and told her   20
  All it had known or seen, for it saw much,
  Yet idly reasoned what it saw; and called her –
  For whence it sprung it knew not, nor do I –
  'Mother, dear mother'.
The Spirit of the Earth (running to ASIA*).* Mother, dearest
      mother!
  May I then talk with thee as I was wont?   25
  May I then hide my eyes in thy soft arms
  After thy looks have made them tired of joy?
  May I then play beside thee the long noons
  When work is none in the bright silent air?
Asia.   I love thee, gentlest being, and henceforth   30
  Can cherish thee unenvied: speak, I pray:
  Thy simple talk once solaced, now delights.

Spirit of the Earth.   Mother, I am grown wiser, though a
        child
    Cannot be wise like thee, within this day,
    And happier too, happier and wiser both.   35
    Thou knowest that toads, and snakes and loathly worms,
    And venomous and malicious beasts and boughs
    That bore ill berries in the woods, were ever
    An hindrance to my walks o'er the green world:
    And that, among the haunts of humankind,   40
    Hard-featured men, or with proud, angry looks,
    Or cold, staid gait, or false and hollow smiles,
    Or the dull sneer of self-loved ignorance,
    Or other such foul masks, with which ill thoughts
    Hide that fair being whom we spirits call man;   45
    And women too, ugliest of all things evil, –
    Though fair, even in a world where thou art fair,
    When good and kind, free and sincere like thee, –
    When false or frowning made me sick at heart
    To pass them, though they slept, and I unseen.   50
    Well – my path lately lay through a great city
    Into the woody hills surrounding it.
    A sentinel was sleeping at the gate:
    When there was heard a sound, so loud, it shook
    The towers amid the moonlight, yet more sweet   55
    Than any voice but thine, sweetest of all;
    A long, long sound, as it would never end:
    And all the inhabitants leapt suddenly
    Out of their rest, and gathered in the streets,
    Looking in wonder up to Heaven, while yet   60
    The music pealed along. I hid myself
    Within a fountain in the public square
    Where I lay like the reflex of the moon
    Seen in a wave under green leaves; and soon
    Those ugly human shapes and visages   65
    Of which I spoke as having wrought me pain,
    Passed floating through the air, and fading still
    Into the winds that scattered them; and those
    From whom they passed seemed mild and lovely forms
    After some foul disguise had fallen – and all   70
    Were somewhat changed – and after brief surprise
    And greetings of delighted wonder, all

Went to their sleep again – and when the dawn
Came, wouldst thou think that toads, and snakes and efts,
Could e'er be beautiful? – yet so they were, 75
And that with little change of shape or hue:
All things had put their evil nature off:
I cannot tell my joy, when o'er a lake
Upon a drooping bough with nightshade twined,
I saw two azure halcyons clinging downward 80
And thinning one bright bunch of amber berries,
With quick long beaks, and in the deep there lay
Those lovely forms imaged as in a sky. –
So, with my thoughts full of these happy changes,
We meet again, the happiest change of all. 85

Asia. And never will we part, till thy chaste sister
Who guides the frozen and inconstant moon
Will look on thy more warm and equal light
Till her heart thaw like flakes of April snow
And love thee.

Spirit of the Earth. What, as Asia loves Prometheus? 90

Asia. Peace, wanton – thou art yet not old enough.
Think ye, by gazing on each other's eyes
To multiply your lovely selves, and fill
With spherèd fires the interlunar air?

Spirit of the Earth. Nay, mother, while my sister trims
her lamp 95
'Tis hard I should go darkling.

Asia. Listen! look!

[*The* SPIRIT OF THE HOUR *enters.*]

Prometheus. We feel what thou hast heard and seen –
yet speak.

Spirit of the Hour. Soon as the sound had ceased
whose thunder filled
The abysses of the sky and the wide earth,
There was a change . . . the impalpable thin air 100
And the all-circling sunlight were transformed
As if the sense of love dissolved in them
Had folded itself round the spherèd world.
My vision then grew clear, and I could see
Into the mysteries of the universe. 105
Dizzy as with delight I floated down,
Winnowing the lightsome air with languid plumes,

My coursers sought their birthplace in the sun
Where they henceforth will live exempt from toil,
Pasturing flowers of vegetable fire –   110
And where my moonlike car will stand within
A temple, gazed upon by Phidian forms
Of thee, and Asia, and the Earth, and me
And you fair nymphs looking the love we feel,
In memory of the tidings it has borne,   115
Beneath a dome fretted with graven flowers,
Poised on twelve columns of resplendent stone
And open to the bright and liquid sky.
Yoked to it by an amphisbaenic snake
The likeness of those wingèd steeds will mock   120
The flight from which they find repose. – Alas,
Whither has wandered now my partial tongue
When all remains untold which ye would hear! –
As I have said, I floated to the earth:
It was, as it is still, the pain of bliss   125
To move, to breathe, to be; I wandering went
Among the haunts and dwellings of mankind,
And first was disappointed not to see
Such mighty change as I had felt within
Expressed in outward things; but soon I looked,   130
And behold, thrones were kingless, and men walked
One with the other even as spirits do,
None fawned, none trampled; hate, disdain or fear,
Self-love or self-contempt, on human brows
No more inscribed, as o'er the gate of hell,   135
'All hope abandon ye who enter here';
None frowned, none trembled, none with eager fear
Gazed on another's eye of cold command
Until the subject of a tyrant's will
Became, worse fate, the abject of his own   140
Which spurred him, like an outspent horse, to death.
None wrought his lips in truth-entangling lines
Which smiled the lie his tongue disdained to speak;
None with firm sneer trod out in his own heart
The sparks of love and hope till there remained   145
Those bitter ashes, a soul self-consumed,
And the wretch crept a vampire among men,
Infecting all with his own hideous ill.

None talked that common, false, cold, hollow talk
Which makes the heart deny the *yes* it breathes,   150
Yet question that unmeant hypocrisy
With such a self-mistrust as has no name.
And women, too, frank, beautiful and kind
As the free heaven which rains fresh light and dew
On the wide earth, passed; gentle radiant forms,   155
From custom's evil taint exempt and pure;
Speaking the wisdom once they could not think,
Looking emotions once they feared to feel,
And changed to all which once they dared not be,
Yet being now, made earth like heaven – nor pride,   160
Nor jealousy, nor envy, nor ill shame,
The bitterest of those drops of treasured gall,
Spoilt the sweet taste of the nepenthe, love.

Thrones, altars, judgement-seats and prisons; wherein
And beside which, by wretched men were borne   165
Sceptres, tiaras, swords and chains, and tomes
Of reasoned wrong, glozed on by ignorance,
Were like those monstrous and barbaric shapes,
The ghosts of a no-more-remembered fame,
Which from their unworn obelisks look forth   170
In triumph o'er the palaces and tombs
Of those who were their conquerors, mouldering round.
These imaged to the pride of kings and priests
A dark yet mighty faith, a power as wide
As is the world it wasted, and are now   175
But an astonishment; even so the tools
And emblems of its last captivity,
Amid the dwellings of the peopled earth
Stand, not o'erthrown, but unregarded now.
And those foul shapes, abhorred by God and man –   180
Which under many a name and many a form
Strange, savage, ghastly, dark and execrable,
Were Jupiter, the tyrant of the world;
And which the nations, panic-stricken, served
With blood, and hearts broken by long hope, and love   185
Dragged to his altars soiled and garlandless,
And slain amid men's unreclaiming tears,
Flattering the thing they feared, which fear was hate –

Frown, mouldering fast, o'er their abandoned shrines.
The painted veil, by those who were, called life,   190
Which mimicked, as with colours idly spread,
All men believed or hoped, is torn aside –
The loathsome mask has fallen, the man remains
Sceptreless, free, uncircumscribed – but man:
Equal, unclassed, tribeless and nationless,   195
Exempt from awe, worship, degree, – the king
Over himself; just, gentle, wise – but man:
Passionless? no – yet free from guilt or pain,
Which were, for his will made or suffered them,
Nor yet exempt, though ruling them like slaves,   200
From chance, and death and mutability,
The clogs of that which else might oversoar
The loftiest star of unascended heaven,
Pinnacled dim in the intense inane.

From   ACT IV

Demogorgon.
   This is the Day, which down the void abysm
   At the Earth-born's spell yawns for Heaven's despotism,
      And Conquest is dragged captive through the deep;
   Love, from its awful throne of patient power
   In the wise heart, from the last giddy hour   5
      Of dread endurance, from the slippery, steep,
   And narrow verge of crag-like agony, springs
   And folds over the world its healing wings.

   Gentleness, Virtue, Wisdom, and Endurance, –
   These are the seals of that most firm assurance   10
      Which bars the pit over Destruction's strength;
   And if, with infirm hand, Eternity,
   Mother of many acts and hours, should free
      The serpent that would clasp her with his length, –
   These are the spells by which to re-assume   15
   An empire o'er the disentangled Doom.

   To suffer woes which Hope thinks infinite;
   To forgive wrongs darker than Death or Night;

    To defy Power, which seems omnipotent;
To love, and bear; to hope, till Hope creates   20
From its own wreck the thing it contemplates;
    Neither to change, nor falter, nor repent:
This, like thy glory, Titan, is to be
Good, great and joyous, beautiful and free;
This is alone Life, Joy, Empire, and Victory.   25

18   *From* PREFACE TO *THE CENCI*

This story of the Cenci is indeed eminently fearful and
monstrous: any thing like a dry exhibition of it on the stage
would be insupportable. The person who would treat such
a subject must increase the ideal, and diminish the actual
horror of the events, so that the pleasure which arises from   5
the poetry which exists in these tempestuous sufferings and
crimes may mitigate the pain of the contemplation of the
moral deformity from which they spring. There must also
be nothing attempted to make the exhibition subservient to
what is vulgarly termed a moral purpose. The highest moral   10
purpose aimed at in the highest species of the drama, is the
teaching the human heart, through its sympathies and
antipathies, the knowledge of itself; in proportion to the
possession of which knowledge, every human being is wise,
just, sincere, tolerant and kind. If dogmas can do more, it is   15
well: but a drama is no fit place for the enforcement of
them. Undoubtedly, no person can be truly dishonoured by
the act of another; and the fit return to make to the most
enormous injuries is kindness and forbearance, and a reso-
lution to convert the injurer from his dark passions by peace   20
and love. Revenge, retaliation, atonement, are pernicious
mistakes. If Beatrice had thought in this manner she would
have been wiser and better; but she would never have been
a tragic character: the few whom such an exhibition would
have interested, could never have been sufficiently interested   25
for a dramatic purpose, from the want of finding sympathy
in their interest among the mass who surround them. It is
in the restless and anatomizing casuistry with which men
seek the justification of Beatrice, yet feel that she has done

what needs justification; it is in the superstitious horror   30
with which they contemplate alike her wrongs and their
revenge; that the dramatic character of what she did and
suffered, consists.

I have endeavoured as nearly as possible to represent the
characters as they probably were, and have sought to avoid   35
the error of making them actuated by my own conceptions
of right or wrong, false or true, thus under a thin veil
converting names and actions of the sixteenth century into
cold impersonations of my own mind. They are represented
as Catholics, and as Catholics deeply tinged with religion.   40
To a Protestant apprehension there will appear something
unnatural in the earnest and perpetual sentiment of the
relations between God and man which pervade the tragedy
of the Cenci. It will especially be startled at the combination
of an undoubting persuasion of the truth of the popular   45
religion with a cool and determined perseverance in enor-
mous guilt. But religion in Italy is not, as in Protestant
countries, a cloak to be worn on particular days; or a
passport which those who do not wish to be railed at carry
with them to exhibit; or a gloomy passion for penetrating   50
the impenetrable mysteries of our being, which terrifies its
possessor at the darkness of the abyss to the brink of which
it has conducted him. Religion coexists, as it were, in the
mind of an Italian Catholic with a faith in that of which all
men have the most certain knowledge. It is interwoven with   55
the whole fabric of life. It is adoration, faith, submission,
penitence, blind admiration; not a rule for moral conduct.
It has no necessary connection with any one virtue. The most
atrocious villain may be rigidly devout, and without any
shock to established faith, confess himself to be so. Religion   60
pervades intensely the whole frame of society, and is accord-
ing to the temper of the mind which it inhabits, a passion, a
persuasion, an excuse, a refuge; never a check. Cenci himself
built a chapel in the court of his Palace, and dedicated it to
St Thomas the Apostle, and established masses for the peace   65
of his soul. Thus in the first scene of the fourth act Lucretia's
design in exposing herself to the consequences of an expos-
tulation with Cenci after having administered the opiate,
was to induce him by a feigned tale to confess himself before
death; this being esteemed by Catholics as essential to   70

salvation; and she only relinquishes her purpose when she perceives that her perseverance would expose Beatrice to new outrages.

I have avoided with great care in writing this play the introduction of what is commonly called mere poetry, and I imagine there will scarcely be found a detached simile or a single isolated description, unless Beatrice's description of the chasm appointed for her father's murder should be judged to be of that nature.

In a dramatic composition the imagery and the passion should interpenetrate one another, the former being reserved simply for the full development and illustration of the latter. Imagination is as the immortal God which should assume flesh for the redemption of mortal passion. It is thus that the most remote and the most familiar imagery may alike be fit for dramatic purposes when employed in the illustration of strong feeling, which raises what is low, and levels to the apprehension that which is lofty, casting over all the shadow of its own greatness. In other respects I have written more carelessly; that is, without an over-fastidious and learned choice of words. In this respect I entirely agree with those modern critics who assert that in order to move men to true sympathy we must use the familiar language of men. And that our great ancestors the ancient English poets are the writers, a study of whom might incite us to do that for our own age which they have done for theirs. But it must be the real language of men in general and not that of any particular class to whose society the writer happens to belong. So much for what I have attempted; I need not be assured that success is a very different matter; particularly for one whose attention has but newly been awakened to the study of dramatic literature.

WRITTEN ON THE OCCASION OF THE
MASSACRE AT MANCHESTER

As I lay asleep in Italy
There came a voice from over the Sea,
And with great power it forth led me
To walk in the Visions of Poesy.

I met Murder on the way –   5
He had a mask like Castlereagh,
Very smooth he looked, yet grim;
Seven bloodhounds followed him:

All were fat; and well they might
Be in admirable plight,   10
For one by one, and two by two,
He tossed them human hearts to chew
Which from his wide cloak he drew.

Next came Fraud, and he had on,
Like Eldon, an erminèd gown;   15
His big tears, for he wept well,
Turned to mill-stones as they fell,

And the little children who
Round his feet played to and fro,
Thinking every tear a gem,   20
Had their brains knocked out by them.

Clothed with the Bible, as with light,
And the shadows of the night,
Like Sidmouth next, Hypocrisy
On a crocodile rode by.   25

And many more Destructions played
In this ghastly masquerade,
All disguised, even to the eyes,
Like Bishops, lawyers, peers or spies.

Last came Anarchy: he rode   30
On a white horse, splashed with blood;
He was pale even to the lips,
Like Death in the Apocalypse.

And he wore a kingly crown;
And in his grasp a sceptre shone;   35
On his brow this mark I saw –
'I AM GOD AND KING AND LAW.'

With a pace stately and fast,
Over English land he passed,
Trampling to a mire of blood   40
The adoring multitude.

And a mighty troop around,
With their trampling shook the ground,
Waving each a bloody sword,
For the service of their Lord;   45

And with glorious triumph, they
Rode through England proud and gay,
Drunk as with intoxication
Of the wine of desolation.

O'er fields and towns, from sea to sea,   50
Passed that Pageant swift and free,
Tearing up and trampling down
Till they came to London town;

And each dweller, panic-stricken,
Felt his heart with terror sicken   55
Hearing the tempestuous cry
Of the triumph of Anarchy.

For with pomp to meet him came
Clothed in arms like blood and flame
The hired Murderers, who did sing   60
'Thou art God and Law and King.

'We have waited weak and lone
For thy coming, Mighty One!
Our purses are empty, our swords are cold,
Give us glory and blood and gold.'   65

Lawyers and priests, a motley crowd,
To the Earth their pale brows bowed,
Like a bad prayer not overloud
Whispering – 'Thou art Law and God.'

Then all cried with one accord   70
'Thou art King and God and Lord;
Anarchy, to Thee we bow,
Be Thy name made holy now!'

And Anarchy, the Skeleton,
Bowed and grinned to every one,   75
As well as if his education
Had cost ten millions to the Nation.

For he knew the Palaces
Of our Kings were rightly his;
His the sceptre, crown and globe,   80
And the gold-inwoven robe.

So he sent his slaves before
To seize upon the Bank and Tower,
And was proceeding with intent
To meet his pensioned Parliament   85

When One fled past, a Maniac maid,
And her name was Hope, she said:
But she looked more like Despair,
And she cried out in the air –

'My father Time is weak and grey   90
With waiting for a better day –
See how idiot-like he stands
Fumbling with his palsied hands!

He has had child after child
And the dust of death is piled   95
Over every one but me –
Misery, o Misery!'

Then she lay down in the street
Right before the horses' feet,
Expecting with a patient eye   100
Murder, Fraud and Anarchy,

When between her and her foes
A mist, a light, an image rose,
Small at first, and weak and frail
Like the vapour of a vale,   105

Till as clouds grow on the blast
Like tower-crowned giants striding fast,
And glare with lightnings as they fly
And speak in thunder to the sky,

It grew – a Shape arrayed in mail   110
Brighter than the viper's scale,
And upborne on wings whose grain
Was as the light of sunny rain.

On its helm seen far away
A planet, like the Morning's lay;   115
And those plumes its light rained through
Like a shower of crimson dew;

With step as soft as wind it passed
O'er the heads of men – so fast
That they knew the presence there   120
And looked – but all was empty air.

As flowers beneath May's footstep waken,
As stars from Night's loose hair are shaken,
As waves arise when loud winds call,
Thoughts sprung where'er that step did fall.   125

And the prostrate multitude
Looked – and ankle-deep in blood
Hope, that maiden most serene,
Was walking with a quiet mien,

And Anarchy, the ghastly birth,   130
Lay dead earth upon the earth –
The Horse of Death tameless as wind
Fled, and with his hoofs did grind
To dust the murderers thronged behind.

A rushing light of clouds and splendour,   135
A sense awakening and yet tender
Was heard and felt – and at its close
These words of joy and fear arose

As if their own indignant Earth
Which gave the Sons of England birth   140
Had felt their blood upon her brow,
And shuddering with a mother's throe

Had turned every drop of blood
By which her face had been bedewed
To an accent unwithstood –   145
As if her heart cried out aloud:

'Men of England, Heirs of Glory,
Heroes of unwritten Story,
Nurslings of one mighty Mother,
Hopes of her and one another,   150

'Rise like Lions after slumber
In unvanquishable number,
Shake your chains to Earth like dew
Which in sleep had fallen on you –
Ye are many – they are few.   155

'What is Freedom? – ye can tell
That which slavery is, too well –
For its very name has grown
To an echo of your own.

''Tis to work and have such pay   160
As just keeps life from day to day
In your limbs, as in a cell
For the tyrants' use to dwell,

'So that ye for them are made
Loom and plough and sword and spade,   165
With or without your own will bent
To their defence and nourishment;

''Tis to see your children weak
With their mothers pine and peak
When the winter winds are bleak –   170
They are dying whilst I speak;

''Tis to hunger for such diet
As the rich man in his riot
Casts to the fat dogs that lie
Surfeiting beneath his eye;   175

''Tis to let the Ghost of Gold
Take from Toil a thousandfold
More than e'er its substance could
In the tyrannies of old –

'Paper coin, that forgery   180
Of the title deeds, which ye
Hold to something from the worth
Of the inheritance of Earth;

''Tis to be a slave in soul
And to hold no strong control   185
Over your own will, but be
All that others make of ye;

'And at length when ye complain
With a murmur weak and vain,
'Tis to see the tyrants' crew   190
Ride over your wives and you –
Blood is on the grass like dew.

'Then it is to feel revenge
Fiercely thirsting to exchange
Blood for blood, and wrong for wrong –   195
Do not thus when ye are strong.

'Birds find rest, in narrow nest
When weary of their wingèd quest,
Beasts find fare, in woody lair
When storm and snow are in the air;   200

'Horses, oxen, have a home
When from daily toil they come;
Household dogs, when the wind roars
Find a home within warm doors;

'Asses, swine, have litter spread   205
And with fitting food are fed;
All things have a home but one –
Thou, o Englishman, hast none!

'This is slavery – savage men
Or wild beasts within a den   210
Would endure not as ye do –
But such ills they never knew.

'What art thou, Freedom? o, could slaves
Answer from their living graves
This demand, tyrants would flee   215
Like a dream's dim imagery.

'Thou art not as imposters say
A Shadow soon to pass away,
A Superstition, and a name
Echoing from the cave of Fame: 220

'For the labourer thou art bread
And a comely table spread,
From his daily labour come,
In a neat and happy home;

'Thou art clothes and fire and food   225
For the trampled multitude –
No – in countries that are free
Such starvation cannot be
As in England now we see.

'To the rich thou art a check –   230
When his foot is on the neck
Of his victim, thou dost make
That he treads upon a snake.

'Thou art Justice – ne'er for gold
May thy righteous laws be sold   235
As laws are in England – thou
Shieldst alike both high and low.

'Thou art Wisdom – Freemen never
Dream that God will damn forever
All who think those things untrue   240
Of which Priests make such ado.

'Thou art Peace – never by thee
Would blood and treasure wasted be
As tyrants wasted them, when all
Leagued to quench thy flame in Gaul.   245

'What if English toil and blood
Was poured forth even as a flood?
It availed, o Liberty,
To dim, but not extinguish thee.

'Thou art Love – the rich have kissed   250
Thy feet, and like him following Christ
Give their substance to the free
And through the rough world follow thee,

'Or turn their wealth to arms, and make
War for thy belovèd sake   255
On wealth and war and fraud – whence they
Drew the power which is their prey.

'Science, Poetry and Thought
Are thy lamps; they make the lot
Of the dwellers in a cot   260
Such, they curse their Maker not.

'Spirit, Patience, Gentleness,
All that can adorn and bless
Art thou . . . let deeds not words express
Thine exceeding loveliness –   265

'Let a great Assembly be
Of the fearless and the free
On some spot of English ground
Where the plains stretch wide around.

'Let the blue sky overhead,   270
The green earth on which ye tread,
All that must eternal be
Witness the Solemnity.

'From the corners uttermost
Of the bounds of English coast,   275
From every hut, village and town
Where those who live and suffer, moan
For others' misery or their own –

'From the workhouse and the prison
Where pale as corpses newly risen   280
Women, children, young and old
Groan for pain and weep for cold –

'From the haunts of daily life
Where is waged the daily strife
With common wants and common cares   285
Which sows the human heart with tares –

'Lastly from the palaces
Where the murmur of distress
Echoes, like the distant sound
Of a wind alive around   290

'Those prison-halls of wealth and fashion
Where some few feel such compassion
For those who groan and toil and wail
As must make their brethren pale,

'Ye who suffer woes untold   295
Or to feel or to behold
Your lost country bought and sold
With a price of blood and gold –

'Let a vast Assembly be,
And with great solemnity   300
Declare with measured words that ye
Are, as God has made ye, free –

'Be your strong and simple words
Keen to wound as sharpened swords,
And wide as targes let them be   305
With their shade to cover ye.

'Let the tyrants pour around
With a quick and startling sound
Like the loosening of a sea
Troops of armed emblazonry.   310

'Let the charged artillery drive
Till the dead air seems alive
With the clash of clanging wheels
And the tramp of horses' heels.

'Let the fixèd bayonet   315
Gleam with sharp desire to wet
Its bright point in English blood –
Looking keen, as one for food.

'Let the horsemen's scimitars
Wheel and flash like sphereless stars   320
Thirsting to eclipse their burning
In a sea of death and mourning.

'Stand ye calm and resolute
Like a forest close and mute
With folded arms and looks which are   325
Weapons of unvanquished war,

'And let Panic who outspeeds
The career of armed steeds
Pass, a disregarded shade,
Through your phalanx undismayed.   330

'Let the Laws of your own land,
Good or ill, between ye stand
Hand to hand and foot to foot,
Arbiters of the dispute,

'The old laws of England – they   335
Whose reverend heads with age are grey,
Children of a wiser day,
And whose solemn voice must be
Thine own echo – Liberty!

'On those who first should violate   340
Such sacred heralds in their state
Rest the blood that must ensue . . .
And it will not rest on you.

'And if then the tyrants dare,
Let them ride among you there,   345
Slash and stab and maim and hew –
What they like, that let them do.

'With folded arms, and steady eyes,
And little fear, and less surprise,
Look upon them as they slay   350
Till their rage has died away.

'Then they will return with shame
To the place from which they came,
And the blood thus shed will speak
In hot blushes on their cheek: 355

'Every Woman in the land
Will point at them as they stand . . .
They will hardly dare to greet
Their acquaintance in the street.

'And the bold, true warriors   360
Who have hugged Danger in wars
Will turn to those who would be free,
Ashamed of such base company.

'And that slaughter, to the Nation
Shall steam up like inspiration,   365
Eloquent, oracular;
A volcano heard afar.

'And these words shall then become
Like oppression's thundered doom
Ringing through each heart and brain,   370
Heard again, again, again –

'"Rise like lions after slumber
In unvanquishable number,
Shake your chains to earth like dew
Which in sleep had fallen on you –   375
Ye are many – they are few"'.

I

O wild West Wind, thou breath of Autumn's being,
Thou, from whose unseen presence the leaves dead
Are driven, like ghosts from an enchanter fleeing,

Yellow, and black, and pale, and hectic red,
Pestilence-stricken multitudes: O thou,   5
Who chariotest to their dark wintry bed

The wingèd seeds, where they lie cold and low,
Each like a corpse within its grave, until
Thine azure sister of the Spring shall blow

Her clarion o'er the dreaming earth, and fill   10
(Driving sweet buds like flocks to feed in air)
With living hues and odours plain and hill:

Wild Spirit, which art moving everywhere;
Destroyer and Preserver; hear, O hear!

2

Thou on whose stream, 'mid the steep sky's commotion,   15

Loose clouds like Earth's decaying leaves are shed,
Shook from the tangled boughs of Heaven and Ocean,

Angels of rain and lightning: there are spread
On the blue surface of thine airy surge,
Like the bright hair uplifted from the head   20

[1] This poem was conceived and chiefly written in a wood that skirts the Arno, near Florence, and on a day when that tempestuous wind, whose temperature is at once mild and animating, was collecting the vapours which pour down the autumnal rains. They began, as I foresaw, at sunset with a violent tempest of hail and rain, attended by that magnificent thunder and lightning peculiar to the Cisalpine regions.

The phenomenon alluded to at the conclusion of the third stanza is well known to naturalists. The vegetation at the bottom of the sea, of rivers, and of lakes, sympathises with that of the land in the change of seasons, and is consequently influenced by the winds which announce it.

Of some fierce Maenad, even from the dim verge
Of the horizon to the zenith's height,
The locks of the approaching storm. Thou dirge

Of the dying year, to which this closing night
Will be the dome of a vast sepulchre   25
Vaulted with all thy congregated might

Of vapours, from whose solid atmosphere
Black rain, and fire, and hail will burst: O hear!

                            3
Thou who didst waken from his summer dreams
The blue Mediterranean, where he lay,   30
Lulled by the coil of his crystalline streams,

Beside a pumice isle in Baiae's bay,
And saw in sleep old palaces and towers
Quivering within the wave's intenser day,

All overgrown with azure moss and flowers   35
So sweet, the sense faints picturing them! Thou
For whose path the Atlantic's level powers

Cleave themselves into chasms, while far below
The sea-blooms and the oozy woods which wear
The sapless foliage of the ocean, know   40

Thy voice, and suddenly grow grey with fear,
And tremble and despoil themselves: O hear!

                            4
If I were a dead leaf thou mightest bear;
If I were a swift cloud to fly with thee;
A wave to pant beneath thy power, and share   45

The impulse of thy strength, only less free
Than thou, O Uncontrollable! If even
I were as in my boyhood, and could be

The comrade of thy wanderings over Heaven,
As then, when to outstrip thy skiey speed   50
Scarce seemed a vision; I would ne'er have striven

As thus with thee in prayer in my sore need.
Oh! lift me as a wave, a leaf, a cloud!
I fall upon the thorns of life! I bleed!

A heavy weight of hours has chained and bowed   55
One too like thee: tameless, and swift, and proud.

5

Make me thy lyre, even as the forest is:
What if my leaves are falling like its own!
The tumult of thy mighty harmonies

Will take from both a deep, autumnal tone,   60
Sweet though in sadness. Be thou, Spirit fierce,
My spirit! Be thou me, impetuous one!

Drive my dead thoughts over the universe
Like withered leaves to quicken a new birth!
And, by the incantation of this verse,   65

Scatter, as from an unextinguished hearth
Ashes and sparks, my words among mankind!
Be through my lips to unawakened Earth

The trumpet of a prophecy! O Wind,
If Winter comes, can Spring be far behind?   70

Part the third

HELL

Hell is a city much like London –
  A populous and a smoky city;
There are all sorts of people undone,
And there is little or no fun done;
  Small justice shown, and still less pity.   5

There is a Castle, and a Canning,
  A Cobbett, and a Castlereagh;
All sorts of caitiff corpses planning
All sorts of cozening for trepanning
  Corpses less corrupt than they.   10

There is a ***, who has lost
  His wits, or sold them, none knows which;
He walks about a double ghost,
And though as thin as Fraud almost –
  Ever grows more grim and rich.   15

There is a Chancery Court; a King;
  A manufacturing mob; a set
Of thieves who by themselves are sent
Similar thieves to represent;
  An army; and a public debt –   20

Which last is a scheme of Paper money,
  And means – being interpreted –
'Bees, keep your wax – give us the honey,
And we will plant while skies are sunny,
  Flowers, which in winter serve instead.'   25

There is great talk of Revolution –
  And a great chance of Despotism –
German soldiers – camps – confusion –

Tumults – lotteries – rage – delusion –
  Gin – suicide – and methodism.   30

Taxes too, on wine and bread,
  And meat, and beer, and tea, and cheese,
From which those patriots pure are fed
Who gorge before they reel to bed
  The tenfold essence of all these.   35

There are mincing women, mewing
  (Like cats, who *amant miserè*),
Of their own virtue, and pursuing
Their gentler sisters to that ruin,
  Without which – what were chastity?   40

Lawyers – judges – old hobnobbers
  Are there – bailiffs – chancellors –
Bishops – great and little robbers –
Rhymesters – pamphleteers – stock-jobbers –
  Men of glory in the wars, –   45

Things whose trade is, over ladies
  To lean, and flirt, and stare, and simper,
Till all that is divine in woman
Grows cruel, courteous, smooth, inhuman,
  Crucified 'twixt a smile and whimper.   50

Thrusting, toiling, wailing, moiling,
  Frowning, preaching – such a riot!
Each with never-ceasing labour,
Whilst he thinks he cheats his neighbour,
  Cheating his own heart of quiet.   55

And all these meet at levees; –
  Dinners convivial and political; –
Suppers of epic poets; – teas,
Where small talk dies in agonies; –
  Breakfasts professional and critical; –   60

Lunches and snacks so aldermanic
  That one would furnish forth ten dinners,

Where reigns a Cretan-tonguèd panic
Lest news Russ, Dutch, or Alemannic
   Should make some losers, and some winners; –   65

At conversazioni – balls –
   Conventicles – and drawing-rooms –
Courts of law – committees – calls
Of a morning – clubs – book-stalls –
   Churches – masquerades – and tombs.   70

And this is Hell – and in this smother
   All are damnable and damned;
Each one damning, damns the other;
They are damned by one another,
   By none other are they damned.   75

'Tis a lie to say, 'God damns!'
   Where was Heaven's Attorney General
When they first gave out such flams?
Let there be an end of shams,
   They are mines of poisonous mineral.   80

Statesmen damn themselves to be
   Cursed; and lawyers damn their souls
To the auction of a fee;
Churchmen damn themselves to see
   God's sweet love in burning coals.   85

The rich are damned, beyond all cure,
   To taunt, and starve, and trample on
The weak and wretched; and the poor
Damn their broken hearts to endure
   Stripe on stripe, with groan on groan.   90

Sometimes the poor are damned indeed
   To take, – not means for being blest, –
But Cobbett's snuff, revenge; that weed
From which the worms that it doth feed
   Squeeze less than they before possessed.   95

And some few, like we know who,
    Damned – but God alone knows why –
To believe their minds are given
To make this ugly Hell a Heaven;
    In which faith they live and die.   100

Thus, as in a town plague-stricken,
    Each man be he sound or no
Must indifferently sicken;
As when day begins to thicken,
    None knows a pigeon from a crow, –   105

So good and bad, sane and mad,
    The oppressor and the oppressed;
Those who weep to see what others
Smile to inflict upon their brothers;
    Lovers, haters, worst and best;   110

All are damned – they breathe an air
    Thick, infected, joy-dispelling:
Each pursues what seems most fair,
Mining like moles through mind, and there
Scoop palace-caverns vast, where Care   115
    In thronèd state is ever dwelling.

Part the fourth
SIN

Lo, Peter in Hell's Grosvenor-square,
    A footman in the devil's service!
And the misjudging world would swear
That every man in service there   120
    To virtue would prefer vice.

But Peter, though now damned, was not
    What Peter was before damnation.
Men oftentimes prepare a lot
Which, ere it finds them, is not what   125
    Suits with their genuine station.

All things that Peter saw and felt
   Had a peculiar aspect to him;
And when they came within the belt
Of his own nature, seemed to melt,   130
   Like cloud to cloud, into him.

And so, the outward world uniting
   To that within him, he became
Considerably uninviting
To those, who meditation slighting,   135
   Were moulded in a different frame.

And he scorned them, and they scorned him;
   And he scorned all they did; and they
Did all that men of their own trim
Are wont to do to please their whim, –   140
   Drinking, lying, swearing, play.

Such were his fellow-servants; thus
   His virtue, like our own, was built
Too much on that indignant fuss
Hypocrite Pride stirs up in us   145
   To bully one another's guilt.

He had a mind which was somehow
   At once circumference and centre
Of all he might or feel or know;
Nothing went ever out, although   150
   Something did ever enter.

He had as much imagination
   As a pint-pot: – he never could
Fancy another situation,
From which to dart his contemplation,   155
   Than that wherein he stood.

Yet his was individual mind,
   And new created all he saw
In a new manner, and refined
Those new creations, and combined   160
   Them, by a master-spirit's law.

Thus – though unimaginative –
   An apprehension clear, intense,
Of his mind's work, had made alive
The things it wrought on; I believe,   165
   Wakening a sort of thought in sense.

But from the first 'twas Peter's drift
   To be a kind of moral eunuch,
He touched the hem of nature's shift,
Felt faint – and never dared uplift   170
   The closest, all-concealing tunic.

She laughed the while, with an arch smile,
   And kissed him with a sister's kiss,
And said – 'My best Diogenes,
I love you well – but, if you please,   175
   Tempt not again my deepest bliss.

'Tis you are cold – for I, not coy,
   Yield love for love, frank, warm and true;
And Burns, a Scottish peasant boy –
His errors prove it – knew my joy   180
   More, learned friend, than you.

'Bocca baciata non perde ventura
   Anzi rinnuova come fa la luna: –
So thought Boccaccio, whose sweet words might cure a
Male prude, like you, from what you now endure, a   185
   Low-tide in soul, like a stagnant laguna.'

Then Peter rubbed his eyes severe,
   And smoothed his spacious forehead down
With his broad palm: – 'twixt love and fear,
He looked, as he no doubt felt, queer;   190
   And in his dream sate down.

The Devil was no uncommon creature;
   A leaden-witted thief – just huddled
Out of the dross and scum of nature;
A toad-like lump of limb and feature,   195
   With mind, and heart, and fancy muddled.

He was that heavy, dull, cold thing
  The Spirit of Evil well may be:
A drone too base to have a sting;
Who gluts, and grimes his lazy wing,   200
  And calls lust, luxury.

Now he was quite the kind of wight
  Round whom collect, at a fixed era,
Venison, turtle, hock and claret, –
Good cheer – and those who come to share it –   205
  And best East India madeira!

It was his fancy to invite
  Men of science, wit and learning,
Who came to lend each other light: –
He proudly thought that his gold's might   210
  Had set those spirits burning.

And men of learning, science, wit,
  Considered him as you and I
Think of some rotten tree, and sit
Lounging and dining under it,   215
  Exposed to the wide sky.

And all the while, with loose fat smile
  The willing wretch sat winking there,
Believing 'twas his power that made
That jovial scene – and that all paid   220
  Homage to his unnoticed chair.

Though to be sure this place was Hell;
  He was the Devil – and all they –
What though the claret circled well,
And wit, like ocean, rose and fell? –   225
  Were damned eternally.

Part the fifth
GRACE

Among the guests who often stayed
　　Till the Devil's petits-soupers,
A man there came, fair as a maid,
And Peter noted what he said,　　　　　　　　　　　230
　　Standing behind his master's chair.

He was a mighty poet – and
　　A subtle-souled psychologist;
All things he seemed to understand,
Of old or new – of sea or land –　　　　　　　　　235
　　But his own mind – which was a mist.

This was a man who might have turned
　　Hell into Heaven – and so in gladness
A Heaven unto himself have earned;
But he in shadows undiscerned　　　　　　　　　240
　　Trusted, – and damned himself to madness.

He spoke of Poetry, and how
　　'Divine it was – a light – a love –
A spirit which like wind doth blow
As it listeth, to and fro;　　　　　　　　　　　245
　　A dew rained down from God above;

'A Power which comes and goes like dream,
　　And which none can ever trace –
Heaven's light on Earth – Truth's brightest beam.'
And when he ceased there lay the gleam　　　250
　　Of those words upon his face.

Now Peter when he heard such talk
　　Would, heedless of a broken pate
Stand like a man asleep, or baulk
Some wishing guest of knife or fork,　　　　　255
　　Or drop and break his master's plate.

At night he oft would start and wake
　Like a lover, and began
In a wild measure songs to make
On moor, and glen, and rocky lake,   260
　And on the heart of man; –

And on the universal sky; –
　And the wide earth's bosom green; –
And the sweet, strange mystery
Of what beyond these things may lie,   265
　And yet remain unseen.

For in his thought he visited
　The spots in which, ere dead and damned,
He his wayward life had led;
Yet knew not whence the thoughts were fed,   270
　Which thus his fancy crammed.

And these obscure rememberances
　Stirred such harmony in Peter,
That, whensoever he should please,
He could speak of rocks and trees   275
　In poetic metre.

For though it was without a sense
　Of memory, yet he remembered well
Many a ditch and quick-set fence;
Of lakes he had intelligence,   280
　He knew something of heath, and fell.

He had also dim recollections
　Of pedlars tramping on their rounds;
Milk-pans and pails; and odd collections
Of saws and proverbs; and reflections   285
　Old parsons make in burying-grounds.

But Peter's verse was clear, and came
　Announcing from the frozen hearth
Of a cold age, that none might tame
The soul of that diviner flame   290
　It augured to the Earth:

Like gentle rains, on the dry plains,
  Making that green which late was grey,
Or like the sudden moon, that stains
Some gloomy chamber's window panes   295
  With a broad light like day.

For language was in Peter's hand,
  Like clay, while he was yet a potter;
And he made songs for all the land,
Sweet both to feel and understand,   300
  As pipkins late to mountain cotter.

And Mr – , the bookseller,
  Gave twenty pounds for some; – then scorning
A footman's yellow coat to wear,
Peter, too proud of heart, I fear,   305
  Instantly gave the Devil warning.

Whereat the Devil took offence,
  And swore in his soul a great oath then,
'That for his damned impertinence,
He'd bring him to a proper sense   310
  Of what was due to gentlemen!'

22   *From* [NOTES ON SCULPTURE]

Bacchus and Ampelus

Less beautiful than that in the royal collection of Naples
and yet infinitely lovely. The figures are walking as it were
with a sauntering and idle pace, and talking to each other
as they walk, and this is expressed in the motions of their
delicate and flowing forms. One arm of Bacchus rests with   5
its entire weight on the shoulder of Ampelus, and the other,
the fingers being gently curved as with the burning spirit
which animates their flexible joints, is gracefully thrown
forward corresponding with the advance of the opposite
leg. He has sandals and buskins clasped with two serpents'   10
heads, and his leg is cinctured with their skins. He is

crowned with vine leaves laden with their crude fruit, and
the crisp leaves fall as with the inertness of a lithe and faded
leaf over his rich and massy down-hanging hair, which
gracefully divided on his forehead falls on each side his neck   15
and curls upon his breast. Ampelus with a young lion or
lynx's skin over his shoulder holds a cup in his right hand,
and with his left half-encircles the waist of Bacchus, as you
may have seen (yet how seldom from their dissevering and
tyrannical institutions do you see) a younger and an elder   20
boy at school walking in some remote grassy spot of their
play-ground with that tender friendship towards each other
which has so much of love. – The countenance of Bacchus
is sublimely sweet and lovely, taking a shade of gentle and
playful tenderness from the arch looks of Ampelus, whose   25
cheerful face turned towards him, expresses the suggestions
of some droll and merry device. It has a divine and super-
natural beauty, as one who walks through the world
untouched by its corrupting cares; it looks like one who
unconsciously yet with delight confers pleasure and peace.   30
The flowing fullness and roundness of the breast and belly,
whose lines fading into each other, are continued with a
gentle motion as it were to the utmost extremity of his
limbs. Like some fine strain of harmony which flows round
the soul and enfolds it, and leaves it in the soft astonishment   35
of a satisfaction, like the pleasure of love with one whom
we most love, which having taken away desire, leaves
pleasure, sweet pleasure. The countenance of the Ampelus
is in every respect boyish and inferior; it has a rugged and
unreproved appearance; that of Bacchus expresses an imper-   40
turbable and godlike self-possession – he seems in the
enjoyment of a calm delight that nothing can destroy. His is
immortal beauty.

CHORUS OF SPIRITS

First Spirit.
   Palace-roof of cloudless nights!
   Paradise of golden lights!
     Deep, immeasurable, vast,
   Which art now, and which wert then;
     Of the present and the past,   5
   Of the eternal where and when,
     Presence-chamber, temple, home,
     Ever-canopying dome
     Of acts and ages yet to come!

   Glorious shapes have life in thee –   10
   Earth, and all Earth's company,
     Living globes which ever throng
   Thy deep chasms and wildernesses;
     And green worlds that glide along;
   And swift stars with flashing tresses;   15
     And icy moons most cold and bright,
     And mighty suns, beyond the night,
     Atoms of intensest light!

   Even thy name is as a God,
   Heaven! for thou art the abode   20
     Of that Power which is the glass
   Wherein man his nature sees; –
     Generations as they pass
   Worship thee with bended knees.
     Their unremaining Gods and they   25
     Like a river roll away:
     Thou remainest such – alway!

Second Spirit.
   Thou art but the mind's first chamber,
   Round which its young fancies clamber,
     Like weak insects in a cave   30
   Lighted up by stalactites;
     But the portal of the grave,

Where a world of new delights
   Will make thy best glories seem
   But a dim and noonday gleam   35
From the shadow of a dream!

Third Spirit.
  Peace! the Abyss is wreathed with scorn
At your presumption, atom-born!
   What is Heaven? and what are ye
Who its brief expanse inherit?   40
   What are the suns and spheres which flee
With the instinct of that spirit
    Of which ye are but a part?
    Drops which Nature's mighty heart
    Drives through thinnest veins. Depart!   45

What is Heaven? a globe of dew,
Filling in the morning new
   Some eyed flower whose young leaves waken
On an unimagined world.
    Constellated suns unshaken,   50
Orbits measureless, are furled
    In that frail and fading sphere,
    With ten millions gathered there
    To tremble, gleam, and disappear!

24 ENGLAND IN 1819

An old, mad, blind, despised and dying King;
Princes, the dregs of their dull race, who flow
Through public scorn, – mud from a muddy spring;
Rulers who neither see nor feel nor know,
But leechlike to their fainting Country cling   5
Till they drop, blind in blood, without a blow;
A people starved and stabbed on the untilled field;
An army whom liberticide and prey
Makes as a two-edged sword to all who wield;
Golden and sanguine laws which tempt and slay;   10
Religion Christless, Godless, a book sealed;

> A senate, Time's worst statute, unrepealed, –
> Are graves from which a glorious Phantom may
> Burst, to illumine our tempestuous day.

25   *From* A PHILOSOPHICAL VIEW OF REFORM

The consequence of this transaction [i.e. the modern scheme of public credit] has been the establishment of a new aristocracy, which has its basis in fraud, as the old one has its basis in force. The hereditary land-owners in England derived their title from royal grants; they are fiefs bestowed   5
by conquerors, or church-lands, or they have been bought by bankers and merchants from those persons. Now bankers and merchants are persons whose ... Since usage has consecrated the distortion of the word aristocracy from its primitive meaning, let me be allowed to employ the word in   10
that ordinary sense which signifies that class of persons who possess a right to the produce of the labour of others, without dedicating to the common service any labour in return. – This class of persons, whose existence is a prodigious anomaly in the social system, has ever constituted an   15
inseparable portion of it, and there has never been an approach in practice towards any plan of political society modelled on equal justice, at least in the complicated mechanism of modern life. Mankind seem to acquiesce, as in a necessary condition of the imbecility of their own will   20
and reason, in the existence of an aristocracy. With reference too to this imbecility, it has doubtless been the instrument of great social advantage, although the advantage would have been greater which might have been produced according to the forms of a just distribution of the goods and evils   25
of life. The object therefore of all enlightened legislation, and administration, is to enclose within the narrowest practicable limits this order of drones. The effect of the financial impostures of the modern rulers of England has been to increase the numbers of the drones. Instead of one   30
aristocracy, the condition [to] which, in the present state of human affairs, the friends of justice and liberty are willing to subscribe as to an inevitable evil, they have supplied us

with two aristocracies. The one, consisting [of] the great land proprietors and merchants, who receive and interchange the produce of this country with the produce of other countries; in this, because all other great communities have as yet acquiesced in it, we acquiesce. Connected with the members of [it] is a certain generosity and refinement of manners and opinion, which, although neither philosophy nor virtue, has been that acknowledged substitute for them, which at least is a religion which makes respected those venerable names. The other is an aristocracy of attornies and excisemen, and directors, and government pensioners, usurers, stock jobbers, country bankers, with their dependents and descendants. These are a set of pelting wretches in whose employment there is nothing to exercise, even to their distortion, the more majestic faculties of the soul. Though at the bottom it is all trick, there is something magnificent in the chivalrous disdain of infamy connected with a gentleman. There is something to which – until you see through the base falsehood upon which all inequality is founded – it is difficult for the imagination to refuse its respect, in the faithful and direct dealings of the substantial merchant. As usual, the first persons deceived are those who are the instruments of the fraud, and the merchant and the country gentleman may be excused for believing that their existence is connected with the permanence of the best practicable forms of social order. But in the habits and lives of this new aristocracy created out of an increase [in] the public calamities, and whose existence must be determined by their termination, there is nothing to qualify our disapprobation. They eat and drink and sleep, and in the intervals of those actions being performed with most ridiculous ceremony and accompaniments, they cringe and lie. They poison the literature of the age in which they live, by requiring either the antitype of their own mediocrity in books, or such stupid and distorted and inharmonious idealisms as alone have the power to stir their torpid imaginations. Their hopes and fears are of the narrowest description. Their domestic affections are feeble and they have no others. They think of any commerce with their species but as a means, never as an end, and as a means to the basest forms of personal advantage.

Two years ago it might still have been possible to have   75
commenced a system of gradual reform. The people were
then insulted, tempted and betrayed, and the petitions of a
million of men rejected with disdain. Now they are more
miserable, more hopeless, more impatient of their misery.
Above all, they have become more universally aware of the   80
true sources of their misery. It is possible that the period of
conciliation is past, and that after having played with the
confidence and cheated the expectations of the people, their
passions will be too little under discipline to allow them to
wait the slow, gradual and certain operation of such a   85
Reform, as we can imagine the constituted authorities to
concede.

Upon the issue of this question depends the species of
reform which a philosophical mind should regard with
approbation. If Reform shall be begun by the existing   90
Government, let us be contented with a limited beginning,
with any whatsoever opening; let the rotten boroughs be
disfranchised, and their rights transferred to the unrepre-
sented cities and districts of the Nation; it is no matter how
slow, gradual and cautious be the change; we shall demand   95
more and more with firmness and moderation, never antici-
pating but never deferring the moment of successful oppo-
sition, so that the people may become habituated [to]
exercising the functions of sovereignty, in proportion as
they acquire the possession of it. If reform could begin from   100
within the Houses of Parliament, as constituted at present;
it appears to me that what is called moderate reform, that is
a suffrage, whose qualification should be, the possession of
a certain small property; and triennial parliaments, would
be principles – a system in which for the sake of obtaining   105
without bloodshed or confusion, ulterior improvements of
a more important character, all reformers ought to
acquiesce. Not that such are first principles, or that they
would produce a system of perfect social institutions or one
approaching to [it]. But nothing is more idle than to reject a   110
limited benefit because we cannot without great sacrifices
obtain an unlimited one. We might thus reject a Represent-
ative Republic, if it were attainable, on the plea that the
imagination of man can conceive of something more abso-
lutely perfect. Towards whatsoever we regard as perfect,   115

undoubtedly it is no less our duty than it is our nature to
press forward; this is the generous enthusiasm, which
accomplishes not indeed the consummation after which it
aspires, but one which approaches it in a degree far nearer,
than if the whole powers had not been developed by a   120
delusion. – It is in politics rather than in religion that faith
is meritorious. –

If the Houses of Parliament obstinately and perpetually
refuse to concede any reform to the people, my vote is for
universal suffrage, and equal representation. It is asked,   125
how shall this be accomplished, in defiance of and in
opposition to the constituted authorities of the Nation, they
who possess whether with or without its consent the com-
mand of a standing army and of a legion of spies and police
officers, and hold all the strings of that complicated mech-   130
anism with which the hopes and fears of men are moved
like puppets? They would disperse any assembly really
chosen by the people, they would shoot and hew down any
multitude without regard to sex or age, as the Jews did the
Canaanites, which might be collected in its defence; they   135
would calumniate, imprison, starve, ruin and expatriate
every person who wrote or acted, or thought, or might be
suspected to think against them; misery and extermination
would fill the country from one end to another . . . ? . . .

The true patriot will endeavour to enlighten and to unite   140
the nation and animate it with enthusiasm and confidence.
For this purpose he will be indefatigable in promulgating
political truth. He will endeavour to rally round one stan-
dard the divided friends of liberty, and make them forget
the subordinate objects with regard to which they differ, by   145
appealing to that respecting which they are all agreed. He
will promote such open confederations among men of
principle and spirit as may tend to make their intentions
and their efforts converge to a common centre. He will
discourage all secret associations, which have a tendency,   150
by making national will develop itself in a partial and
premature manner, to cause tumult and confusion. He will
urge the necessity of exciting the people frequently to
exercise their right of assembling, in such limited numbers
as that all present may be actual parties to the proceedings   155
of the day. Lastly, if circumstances had collected a more

considerable number as at Manchester on the memorable
16th of August, if the tyrants command their troops to fire
upon them or cut them down unless they disperse, he will
exhort them peaceably to risk the danger, and to expect   160
without resistance, the onset of the cavalry, and wait with
folded arms the event of the fire of the artillery and receive
with unshrinking bosoms the bayonets of charging bat-
talions. Men are every day persuaded to incur greater perils
for a less manifest advantage. And this, not because active   165
resistance is not justifiable when all other means shall have
failed, but because in this instance temperance and courage
would produce greater advantages than the most decisive
victory. . . .

The true patriot will be foremost to publish the boldest   170
truths in the most fearless manner, yet without the slightest
tincture of personal malignity. He would encourage all
others to the same efforts and assist them to the utmost of
his power with the resources both of his intellect and
fortune. He would call upon them to despise imprisonment   175
and persecution, and lose no opportunity of bringing public
opinions and the power of the tyrants into circumstances of
perpetual contest and opposition. – . . .

The reasoners who <incline to> the opinion that, it is not
sufficient that the innovators should produce a majority in   180
the nation, but that we ought to expect such an unanimity
as would preclude any thing amounting to a serious dispute,
are prompted to this view of the question by the dread of
anarchy and massacre. Infinite and inestimable calamities
belong to oppression; but the most fatal of them all is that   185
mine of unexploded <mischief> which it has practised
beneath the foundation of society and with which, 'perni-
cious to one touch' it threatens to involve the ruin of the
entire building together with its own. But delay merely
renders these mischiefs more tremendous, not the less inevi-   190
table. For the utmost may now be the crisis if the social
disease is rendered thus periodical, chronic and incurable.

The savage brutality of the populace is proportioned to
the arbitrary character of the government, and tumults and
insurrections soon, as in Constantinople, become consistent   195
with the permanence of the causing evil, of which they
might have been the critical determination.

The public opinion in England first ought to [be] excited to action, and the durability of those forms within which the oppressors intrench themselves brought perpetually to the test of its operation. No law or institution can last if this opinion be distinctly pronounced against it. For this purpose government ought to be defied, in cases of questionable result, to prosecute for political libel. All questions relating to the jurisdiction of magistrates and courts of law respecting which any doubt could be raised ought to be agitated with indefatigable pertinacity. Some two or three of the popular leaders have shown the best spirit in this regard; they only want system and co-operation. The taxgatherer ought to be compelled in every practicable instance to distrain, whilst the right to impose taxes, as was the case in the beginning of the resistance to the tyranny of Charles I, is formally contested by an overwhelming multitude of defendants before the courts of common law. Confound the subtlety of lawyers with the subtlety of the law. All of the nation would thus be excited to develop itself, and to declare whether it acquiesced in the existing forms of government. – The manner in which all questions of this nature might be decided would develop the occasions, and afford a prognostic as to the success, of more decisive measures. Simultaneously with this active and vigilant system of opposition, means ought to be taken of solemnly conveying the sense of large bodies, and various denominations of the people in a manner the most explicit to the existing depositaries of power. Petitions, but couched in the actual language of the petitioners, and emanating from distinct assemblies, ought to load the tables of the House of Commons. The poets, philosophers and artists ought to remonstrate, and the memorials entitled their petitions might show the diversit[y] [of] conviction they entertain of the inevitable connection between national prosperity, and the freedom of the imagination and the cultivation of scientific truth, and the profound development of moral and metaphysical enquiry. Suppose these memorials to be severally written by Godwin and Hazlitt and Bentham and Hunt, they would be worthy of the age and of the cause; these, radiant and irresistible like the meridian Sun would strike all but the eagles who dared to gaze upon its beams, with blindness and confusion.

These appeals of solemn and emphatic argument from those
who have already a predestined existence among posterity, 240
would appall the enemies of mankind by their echoes from
every corner of the world in which the majestic literature of
England is cultivated; it would be like a voice from beyond
the dead of those who will live in the memories of men,
when they must be forgotten; it would be Eternity warning 245
Time.

Let us hope that at this stage of the progress of Reform,
the oppressors would feel their impotence, and reluctantly
and imperfectly concede some limited portion of the Rights
of the people; and disgorge some morsels of their undigested 250
prey. In this case, the people ought to be exhorted by every
thing ultimately dear to them to pause until by the exercise
of those rights which they have regained they become fitted
to demand more. It is better that we gain what we demand
by a process of negotiation which would occupy twenty 255
years, than that by communicating a sudden shock to the
interest of those who are the depositaries or dependents of
power we should incur the calamity which their revenge
might inflict upon us by giving the signal of civil war. – If,
after all, they consider the chance of personal ruin, and the 260
infamy of figuring on the page of history as the promoters
of civil war preferable to resigning any portion how small
soever of their usurped authority, we are to recollect that
we possess a right beyond remonstrance. It has been
acknowledged by the most approved writers on the English 265
constitution (which is in this instance merely declaratory of
the superior decisions of eternal justice) that we possess a
right of resistance. The claim of the reigning family is
founded upon a memorable exertion of this solemnly
recorded right.   270

The last resort of resistance is undoubtedly insurrection.
– The right of insurrection is derived from the employment
of armed force to counteract the will of the nation. Let the
government disband the standing army, and the purpose of
resistance would be sufficiently fulfilled by the incessant 275
agitation of the points of dispute before the courts of
common law, and by an unwarlike display of the irresistible
numbers and union of the people.

Nothing can exceed the grandeur and the energy of the character of the Devil as expressed in *Paradise Lost*. He is a Devil very different from the popular personification of evil malignity and it is a mistake to suppose that he was intended for an idealism of implacable hate, cunning, and refinement of device to inflict the utmost anguish on an enemy; these, which are venial in a slave are not to be forgiven in a tyrant; these, which are redeemed by much that ennobles in one subdued, are marked by all that dishonours his conquest in the victor.

Milton's devil as a moral being is as far superior to his God, as one who perseveres in some purpose which he has conceived to be excellent, in spite of adversity and torture; is to one who in the cold security of undoubted triumph inflicts the most horrible revenge upon his enemy, – not from any mistaken notion of bringing him to repent of a perseverance in enmity, but with the open and alleged design of exasperating him to deserve new torments.

Milton so far violated all that part of the popular creed which is susceptible of being preached and defended in argument, as to allege no superiority in moral virtue to his God over his Devil. He mingled as it were the elements of human nature, as colours upon a single pallet, and arranged them in the composition of his great picture, according to the laws of epic truth, that is, according to the laws of that principle by which a series of actions of intelligent and ethical beings, developed in rhythmical language are calculated to excite the sympathy and antipathy of succeeding generations of mankind. The writer who would have attributed majesty and beauty to the character of victorious and vindictive omnipotence, must have been contented with the character of a good Christian – he never could have been a great epic poet. It is difficult to determine in a country where the most enormous sanctions of opinion and law are attached to a direct avowal of certain speculative notions whether Milton was a Christian or not at the period of the composition of *Paradise Lost*. Is it possible that Socrates seriously believed that Æsculapius would be propitiated by

the offering of a cock? Thus much is certain, that Milton
gives the Devil all imaginable advantage; and the arguments   40
with which he exposes the injustice and impotent weak-
ness of his adversary are such as had they been printed,
distinct from the shelter of any dramatic order, would have
been answered by the most conclusive of syllogisms –
persecution.   45

As it is, *Paradise Lost* has conferred on the whole modern
mythology a systematic form; when the immeasurable and
unceasing mutability of time shall have added one more
superstition to those which have already arisen and decayed
upon the earth, commentators and critics will be learnedly   50
employed on elucidating the religion of ancestral Europe,
only not utterly forgotten, because it will have participated
in the eternity of genius. – As to the Devil – he owes every
thing to Milton. Dante and Tasso present us with a very
gross idea of him. Milton divested him of a sting and hoofs   55
and horns; clothed him with the sublime grandeur of a
graceful but tremendous Spirit – and <restored him to the
society.> . . .

The Devil is Διάβολος, an Accuser. In this character he
presented himself among the other Sons of God before His   60
father's throne to request to be allowed to tempt Job, by
tormenting him, so that God might damn him. God it seems
had some special reason for patronizing Job; and one does
not well see why he spared him at last. The expostulations
of Job with God are of most daring character; it is certain   65
he would not bear them from a Christian. If God were a
refined critic – which from his inspiration of Ezechiel would
never have been suspected – one might imagine that the
profuse and sublime strain of poetry not to be surpassed by
ancient literature had found favour [with him]. In this view,   70
he is at once the informer, the Attorney General, and the
jailor of the celestial tribunal. It is not good policy, or at
least cannot be considered as a constitutional practice, to
unite these characters. The Devil must have a great interest
to exert himself to procure a sentence of guilty from the   75
judge; for I suppose there will be no jury at the resurrection
– at least if there is, it will be so overawed by the bench and
the counsel for the Crown, as to ensure whatever verdict the
court shall please to recommend. No doubt, that as an

incentive to his exertions half goes to the informer. What an   80
army of spies and informers all Hell must afford under the
direction of that active magistrate the Devil! How many
plots and conspiracies!

If the Devil takes but half the pleasure in tormenting a
sinner which God does, who took the trouble to create   85
them, and then to invent a system of casuistry by which he
might excuse himself for devoting them to eternal torment,
this reward must be considerable. Conceive how the enjoy-
ment of half of the advantages to be derived from their ruin,
whether in person or property, must irritate the activity of a   90
delator. Tiberius or Bonaparte or Lord Castlereagh never
affixed any reward to the disclosure or the creation of
conspiracies, equal to that which God's Government has
attached to the exertions of the Devil to tempt, betray and
accuse unfortunate man. – These two considerable person-   95
ages are supposed to have entered into a sort of partnership,
in which the weaker has consented to bear all the odium of
their common actions, and allow the stronger to talk of
himself as a very honourable person, on condition of having
a participation in what is the especial delight of both of   100
them – burning men to all eternity. The dirty work is done
by the Devil, in the same manner as some starving wretch
will hire himself out to a King or a minister with a
stipulation that he shall have some portion of the public
spoil as an instrument to betray a certain number of other   105
starving wretches into circumstances of capital punishment,
when they may think it convenient to edify the rest by
hanging up a few of those whose murmurs are too loud. –

It is far from inexplicable that earthly tyrants should
employ these kind of agents – or that God should have done   110
so with regard to the Devil and his angels – or that any
depositary of power should take these measures with respect
to those by whom he fears lest that power should be wrested
from him. But to tempt mankind to incur everlasting
damnation must, on the part of God, and even on the part   115
of the Devil, arise from that very disinterested love of
tormenting and annoying which is seldom observed on earth
except among old maids, eunuchs and priests. The thing
that comes nearest to it is a troop of idle dirty boys baiting
a cat. Cooks skinning eels and boiling lobsters alive and   120

bleeding calves and whipping pigs to death, naturalists anatomizing dogs alive (a dog has as good a right and a better excuse for anatomizing a naturalist) are nothing compared to God and the Devil judging, damning and then tormenting the soul of a miserable sinner. It is pretended 125 that God dislikes it; but this is mere shamefacedness and coquetting, for he has every thing his own way and he need not damn unless he likes. The Devil has a better excuse, for as he was entirely made by God he can have no tendency or disposition the seeds of which were not originally planted 130 by his creator; and as every thing else was made by God, those seeds can only have developed themselves in the precise degree and manner determined by the impulses arising from the agency of the rest of his creation. It would be as unfair to complain of the Devil for acting ill, as of a 135 watch for going badly; the defects are to be imputed as much to God in the former case as to the watchmaker in the latter. – There is also another view of the subject, suggested by mythological writers, which strongly recommends the Devil to our sympathy and compassion, though it is less 140 consistent with the theory of God's omnipotence than that already stated. – The Devil, it is said, before his fall as an Angel of the highest rank and the most splendid accomplishments placed his peculiar delight in doing good. But the inflexible grandeur of his spirit mailed by the consciousness 145 of the purest and loftiest designs was so secure from the assault of any gross or common torments, that God was considerably puzzled to invent what he considered an adequate punishment for his rebellion; he exhausted all the varieties of smothering and burning and freezing and cruelly 150 dilacerating his external frame and the Devil laughed at the impotent revenge of his conqueror. At last the benevolent and amiable disposition which distinguished his adversary furnished God with the true method of executing an enduring and a terrible vengeance. He turned his good into evil 155 and by virtue of his omnipotence inspired him with such impulses as in spite of his better nature irresistibly determined him to act what he most abhorred and to be a minister of those iniquitous schemes, of which he was the chief and the original victim. He is forever tortured with 160 compassion and affection for those whom he betrays and ruins; he is racked by a vain abhorrence for the desolation of which he is the instrument; he is like a man compelled by a tyrant to set fire to his own possessions, and to appear as the witness against and the accuser of his dearest friends 165 and most intimate connections; and then to be their executioner and to inflict the most subtle and protracted torments upon them and to grin with a delight in their agonies. A man, were he deprived of all other refuge, might hold his breath and die – but God is represented as 170 omnipotent and the Devil as eternal. Milton has expressed this view of the subject with the sublimest pathos.

27   LINES TO A CRITIC

1
Honey from silk-worms who can gather,
   Or silk from the yellow bee?
The grass may grow in winter weather
   As soon as hate in me.

2
Hate men who cant, and men who pray,   5
   And men who rail, like thee;
An equal passion to repay
   They are not coy – like me – .

3
Or seek some slave of power and gold,
   To be thy dear heart's mate –   10
Thy love will move that bigot cold
   Sooner than me, thy hate.

4
A passion like the one I prove
   Cannot divided be;
I hate thy want of truth and love –   15
   How should I then hate thee?

I bring fresh showers for the thirsting flowers,
    From the seas and the streams;
I bear light shade for the leaves when laid
    In their noon-day dreams.
From my wings are shaken the dews that waken 5
    The sweet buds every one,
When rocked to rest on their mother's breast,
    As she dances about the sun.
I wield the flail of the lashing hail,
    And whiten the green plains under, 10
And then again I dissolve it in rain,
    And laugh as I pass in thunder.

I sift the snow on the mountains below,
    And their great pines groan aghast;
And all the night 'tis my pillow white, 15
    While I sleep in the arms of the blast.
Sublime on the towers of my skiey bowers,
    Lightning my pilot sits,
In a cavern under is fettered the thunder,
    It struggles and howls at fits; 20
Over earth and ocean, with gentle motion,
    This pilot is guiding me,
Lured by the love of the genii that move
    In the depths of the purple sea;
Over the rills, and the crags, and the hills, 25
    Over the lakes and the plains,
Wherever he dream, under mountain or stream,
    The Spirit he loves remains;
And I all the while bask in Heaven's blue smile,
    Whilst he is dissolving in rains. 30

The sanguine sunrise, with his meteor eyes,
    And his burning plumes outspread,
Leaps on the back of my sailing rack,
    When the morning star shines dead;
As on the jag of a mountain crag 35
    Which an earthquake rocks and swings,

An eagle alit one moment may sit
    In the light of its golden wings;
And when sunset may breathe, from the lit sea beneath,
    Its ardours of rest and of love,   40
And the crimson pall of eve may fall
    From the depths of Heaven above,
With wings folded I rest, on mine aery nest,
    As still as a brooding dove.

That orbèd maiden with white fire laden,   45
    Whom mortals call the moon,
Glides glimmering o'er my fleece-like floor,
    By the midnight breezes strewn;
And wherever the beat of her unseen feet,
    Which only the angels hear,   50
May have broken the woof of my tent's thin roof,
    The stars peep behind her, and peer;
And I laugh to see them whirl and flee
    Like a swarm of golden bees,
When I widen the rent in my wind-built tent,   55
    Till the calm rivers, lakes, and seas,
Like strips of the sky fallen through me on high,
    Are each paved with the moon and these.

I bind the sun's throne with a burning zone,
    And the moon's with a girdle of pearl;   60
The volcanoes are dim, and the stars reel and swim,
    When the whirlwinds my banner unfurl.
From cape to cape, with a bridge-like shape,
    Over a torrent sea,
Sunbeam-proof, I hang like a roof –   65
    The mountains its columns be.
The triumphal arch through which I march
    With hurricane, fire, and snow,
When the powers of the air are chained to my chair,
    Is the million-coloured bow;   70
The sphere-fire above its soft colours wove,
    While the moist earth was laughing below.

I am the daughter of Earth and Water,
    And the nursling of the sky;

I pass through the pores of the oceans and shores;   75
    I change, but I cannot die –
For after the rain, when never a stain
    The pavilion of Heaven is bare,
And the winds and sunbeams, with their convex gleams,
    Build up the blue dome of air,   80
I silently laugh at my own cenotaph,
    And out of the caverns of rain,
Like a child from the womb, like a ghost from the tomb,
    I arise and unbuild it again.

29   THE SENSITIVE-PLANT

PART FIRST

A Sensitive-plant in a garden grew,
And the young winds fed it with silver dew,
And it opened its fan-like leaves to the light
And closed them beneath the kisses of night.

And the Spring arose on the garden fair   5
Like the Spirit of love felt every where;
And each flower and herb on Earth's dark breast
Rose from the dreams of its wintry rest.

But none ever trembled and panted with bliss
In the garden, the field or the wilderness,   10
Like a doe in the noontide with love's sweet want
As the companionless Sensitive-plant.

The snowdrop and then the violet
Arose from the ground with warm rain wet,
And their breath was mixed with fresh odour, sent   15
From the turf, like the voice and the instrument.

Then the pied wind-flowers and the tulip tall,
And narcissi, the fairest among them all,
Who gaze on their eyes in the stream's recess
Till they die of their own dear loveliness;   20

And the Naiad-like lily of the vale
Whom youth makes so fair and passion so pale
That the light of its tremulous bells is seen
Through their pavilions of tender green;

And the hyacinth purple, and white, and blue,   25
Which flung from its bells a sweet peal anew
Of music so delicate, soft and intense,
It was felt like an odour within the sense;

And the rose like a nymph to the bath addressed,
Which unveiled the depth of her glowing breast,   30
Till, fold after fold, to the fainting air
The soul of her beauty and love lay bare:

And the wand-like lily, which lifted up,
As a Maenad, its moonlight-coloured cup
Till the fiery star, which is its eye,   35
Gazed through clear dew on the tender sky;

And the jessamine faint, and the sweet tuberose,
The sweetest flower for scent that blows;
And all rare blossoms from every clime
Grew in that garden in perfect prime.   40

And on the stream whose inconstant bosom
Was prankt under boughs of embowering blossom
With golden and green light, slanting through
Their heaven of many a tangled hue,

Broad water-lilies lay tremulously,   45
And starry river-buds glimmered by,
And around them the soft stream did glide and dance
With a motion of sweet sound and radiance.

And the sinuous paths of lawn and of moss,
Which led through the garden along and across –   50
Some open at once to the sun and the breeze,
Some lost among bowers of blossoming trees –

Were all paved with daisies and delicate bells
As fair as the fabulous asphodels,
And flowrets which drooping as day drooped too   55
Fell into pavilions, white, purple and blue,
To roof the glow-worm from the evening dew.

And from this undefiled Paradise
The flowers, as an infant's awakening eyes
Smile on its mother, whose singing sweet   60
Can first lull, and at last must awaken it,

When Heaven's blithe winds had unfolded them,
As mine-lamps enkindle a hidden gem,
Shone smiling to Heaven; and every one
Shared joy in the light of the gentle sun,   65

For each one was interpenetrated
With the light and the odour its neighbour shed,
Like young lovers, whom youth and love make dear
Wrapped and filled by their mutual atmosphere.

But the Sensitive-plant which could give small fruit   70
Of the love which it felt from the leaf to the root,
Received more than all – it loved more than ever,
Where none wanted but it, could belong to the giver.

For the Sensitive-plant has no bright flower;
Radiance and odour are not its dower –   75
It loves – even like Love – its deep heart is full –
It desires what it has not – the beautiful!

The light winds which from unsustaining wings
Shed the music of many murmurings;
The beams which dart from many a star   80
Of the flowers whose hues they bear afar;

The plumèd insects swift and free
Like golden boats on a sunny sea,
Laden with light and odour, which pass
Over the gleam of the living grass;   85

The unseen clouds of the dew which lie
Like fire in the flowers till the Sun rides high,
Then wander like spirits among the spheres,
Each cloud faint with the fragrance it bears;

The quivering vapours of dim noontide   90
Which like a sea o'er the warm earth glide,
In which every sound, and odour, and beam
Move, as reeds in a single stream;

Each, and all, like ministering angels were
For the Sensitive-plant sweet joy to bear,   95
Whilst the lagging hours of the day went by
Like windless clouds o'er a tender sky.

And when evening descended from Heaven above,
And the Earth was all rest, and the Air was all love;
And delight, though less bright, was far more deep,   100
And the day's veil fell from the world of sleep,

And the beasts, and the birds, and the insects were drowned
In an ocean of dreams without a sound,
Whose waves never mark, though they ever impress
The light sand which paves it – Consciousness,   105

(Only overhead the sweet nightingale
Ever sang more sweet as the day might fail,
And snatches of its Elysian chant
Were mixed with the dreams of the Sensitive-plant)

The Sensitive-plant was the earliest   110
Upgathered into the bosom of rest;
A sweet child weary of its delight,
The feeblest and yet the favourite,
Cradled within the embrace of night.

PART SECOND

There was a Power in this sweet place,
An Eve in this Eden; a ruling grace
Which to the flowers did they waken or dream
Was as God is to the starry scheme:

A Lady – the wonder of her kind,   5
Whose form was upborne by a lovely mind
Which, dilating, had moulded her mien and motion,
Like a sea-flower unfolded beneath the Ocean –

Tended the garden from morn to even:
And the meteors of that sublunar Heaven   10
Like the lamps of the air when night walks forth
Laughed round her footsteps up from the Earth.

She had no companion of mortal race,
But her tremulous breath and her flushing face
Told, whilst the morn kissed the sleep from her eyes,   15
That her dreams were less slumber than Paradise:

As if some bright Spirit for her sweet sake
Had deserted heaven while the stars were awake,
As if yet around her he lingering were,
Though the veil of daylight concealed him from her.   20

Her step seemed to pity the grass it pressed;
You might hear by the heaving of her breast,
That the coming and going of the wind
Brought pleasure there, and left passion behind.

And wherever her aery footstep trod,   25
Her trailing hair from the grassy sod
Erased its light vestige, with shadowy sweep,
Like a sunny storm o'er the dark green deep.

I doubt not the flowers of that garden sweet
Rejoiced in the sound of her gentle feet;   30
I doubt not they felt the spirit that came
From her glowing fingers through all their frame.

She sprinkled bright water from the stream
On those that were faint with the sunny beam;
And out of the cups of the heavy flowers   35
She emptied the rain of the thunder showers.

She lifted their heads with her tender hands
And sustained them with rods and ozier bands;
If the flowers had been her own infants she
Could never have nursed them more tenderly.   40

And all killing insects and gnawing worms
And things of obscene and unlovely forms
She bore, in a basket of Indian woof,
Into the rough woods far aloof,

In a basket of grasses and wild flowers full,   45
The freshest her gentle hands could pull
For the poor banished insects, whose intent,
Although they did ill, was innocent.

But the bee, and the beam-like ephemeris
Whose path is the lightning's, and soft moths that kiss   50
The sweet lips of flowers, and harm not, did she
Make her attendant angels be.

And many an antenatal tomb
Where butterflies dream of the life to come
She left clinging round the smooth and dark   55
Edge of the odorous cedar bark.

This fairest creature from earliest spring
Thus moved through the garden ministering
All the sweet season of summertide,
And ere the first leaf looked brown – she died!   60

PART THIRD

Three days the flowers of the garden fair,
Like stars when the moon is awakened, were;
Or the waves of Baiae, ere luminous
She floats up through the smoke of Vesuvius.

And on the fourth, the Sensitive-plant   5
Felt the sound of the funeral chant
And the steps of the bearers heavy and slow,
And the sobs of the mourners deep and low;

The weary sound and the heavy breath
And the silent motions of passing death,   10
And the smell, cold, oppressive and dank,
Sent through the pores of the coffin plank.

The dark grass and the flowers among the grass
Were bright with tears as the crowd did pass;
From their sighs the wind caught a mournful tone,   15
And sate in the pines and gave groan for groan.

The garden once fair became cold and foul
Like the corpse of her who had been its soul,
Which at first was lovely as if in sleep,
Then slowly changed, till it grew a heap   20
To make men tremble who never weep.

Swift summer into the autumn flowed,
And frost in the mist of the morning rode
Though the noonday sun looked clear and bright,
Mocking the spoil of the secret night.   25

The rose leaves like flakes of crimson snow
Paved the turf and the moss below:
The lilies were drooping, and white, and wan,
Like the head and the skin of a dying man.

And Indian plants, of scent and hue   30
The sweetest that ever were fed on dew;
Leaf by leaf, day after day,
Were massed into the common clay.

And the leaves, brown, yellow, and grey, and red,
And white, with the whiteness of what is dead,   35
Like troops of ghosts on the dry wind passed –
Their whistling noise made the birds aghast.

And the gusty winds waked the wingèd seeds
Out of their birthplace of ugly weeds,
Till they clung round many a sweet flower's stem   40
Which rotted into the earth with them.

The water blooms under the rivulet
Fell from the stalks on which they were set;
And the eddies drove them here and there
As the winds did those of the upper air.   45

Then the rain came down, and the broken stalks
Were bent and tangled across the walks;
And the leafless network of parasite bowers
Massed into ruin; and all sweet flowers.

Between the time of the wind and the snow   50
All loathliest weeds began to grow,
Whose coarse leaves were splashed with many a speck,
Like the water-snake's belly and the toad's back.

And thistles, and nettles, and darnels rank,
And the dock, and henbane; and hemlock dank,   55
Stretched out its long and hollow shank
And stifled the air, till the dead wind stank.

And plants, at whose names the verse feels loath,
Filled the place with a monstrous undergrowth,
Prickly, and pulpous, and blistering, and blue,   60
Livid, and starred with a lurid dew.

And agarics and fungi with mildew and mould
Started like mists from the wet ground cold;
Pale, fleshy, – as if the decaying dead
With a spirit of growth had been animated!   65

Their moss rotted off them, flake by flake,
Till the thick stalk stuck like a murderer's stake,
Where rags of loose flesh yet tremble on high,
Infecting the winds that wander by.

Spawn, weeds and filth, a leprous scum,   70
Made the running rivulet thick and dumb,
And at its outlet flags huge as stakes
Dammed it up with roots knotted like water-snakes.

And hour by hour, when the air was still,
The vapours arose which have strength to kill;   75
At morn they were seen, at noon they were felt,
At night they were darkness no star could melt.

And unctuous meteors from spray to spray
Crept and flitted in broad noonday
Unseen; every branch on which they alit   80
By a venomous blight was burned and bit.

The Sensitive-plant like one forbid
Wept, and the tears, within each lid
Of its folded leaves which together grew,
Were changed to a blight of frozen glue.   85

For the leaves soon fell, and the branches soon
By the heavy axe of the blast were hewn;
The sap shrank to the root through every pore
As blood to a heart that will beat no more.

For Winter came – the wind was his whip –   90
One choppy finger was on his lip;
He had torn the cataracts from the hills
And they clanked at his girdle like manacles;

His breath was a chain which without a sound
The earth, and the air, and the water bound;   95
He came, fiercely driven, in his Chariot-throne
By the tenfold blasts of the Arctic zone.

Then the weeds which were forms of living death
Fled from the frost to the Earth beneath.
Their decay and sudden flight from frost   100
Was but like the vanishing of a ghost!

And under the roots of the Sensitive-plant
The moles and the dormice died for want.
The birds dropped stiff from the frozen air
And were caught in the branches naked and bare.   105

First there came down a thawing rain
And its dull drops froze on the boughs again;
Then there steamed up a freezing dew
Which to the drops of the thaw-rain grew;

And a northern whirlwind, wandering about   110
Like a wolf that had smelt a dead child out,
Shook the boughs thus laden and heavy and stiff
And snapped them off with his rigid griff.

When Winter had gone and Spring came back
The Sensitive-plant was a leafless wreck;   115
But the mandrakes and toadstools and docks and darnels
Rose like the dead from their ruined charnels.

CONCLUSION

Whether the Sensitive-plant, or that
Which within its boughs like a Spirit sat
Ere its outward form had known decay,
Now felt this change, – I cannot say.

Whether that Lady's gentle mind,   5
No longer with the form combined
Which scattered love – as stars do light,
Found sadness, where it left delight,

I dare not guess; but in this life
Of error, ignorance and strife –   10
Where nothing is – but all things seem,
And we, the shadows of the dream,

It is a modest creed, and yet
Pleasant if one considers it,
To own that death itself must be,   15
Like all the rest, – a mockery.

That Garden sweet, that Lady fair,
And all sweet shapes and odours there,
In truth have never passed away –
'Tis we, 'tis ours, are changed – not they.   20

For love, and beauty, and delight
There is no death nor change: their might
Exceeds our organs – which endure
No light – being themselves obscure.

30   MEN OF ENGLAND: A SONG

1
MEN of England, wherefore plough
For the lords who lay ye low?
Wherefore weave with toil and care
The rich robes your tyrants wear?

2
Wherefore feed and clothe and save   5
From the cradle to the grave,
Those ungrateful drones who would
Drain your sweat – nay, drink your blood?

3
Wherefore, Bees of England, forge
Many a weapon, chain and scourge,   10
That these stingless drones may spoil
The forced produce of your toil?

4
Have ye leisure, comfort, calm,
Shelter, food, love's gentle balm?
Or what is it ye buy so dear   15
With your pain and with your fear?

5
The seed ye sow, another reaps;
The wealth ye find, another keeps;

The robes ye weave, another wears;
The arms ye forge, another bears.   20

6

Sow seed – but let no tyrant reap;
Find wealth – let no impostor heap;
Weave robes – let not the idle wear;
Forge arms – in your defence to bear.

7

Shrink to your cellars, holes and cells –   25
In halls ye deck another dwells.
Why shake the chains ye wrought, [then] see
The steel ye tempered glance on ye.

8

With plough and spade and hoe and loom
Trace your grave and build your tomb,   30
And weave your winding-sheet – till fair
England be your sepulchre.

31   TO THE LORD CHANCELLOR

1.   Thy country's curse is on thee, darkest crest
         Of that foul, knotted, many-headed Worm
     Which rends our Mother's bosom – Priestly Pest!
         Masked Resurrection of a buried Form!

2.   Thy country's curse is on thee – Justice sold,   5
         Truth trampled, Nature's landmarks overthrown,
     And heaps of fraud-accumulated gold
         Plead, loud as thunder, at Destruction's throne.

3.   And, whilst that sure slow Angel which aye stands
         Watching the beck of Mutability   10
     Delays to execute her high commands
         And, though a nation weeps, spares thine and thee,

4. O let a father's curse be on thy soul,
      And let a daughter's hope be on thy tomb;
    Be both, on thy grey head, a leaden cowl   15
      To weigh thee down to thy approaching doom!

5. I curse thee – by a parent's outraged love,
      By hopes long cherished and too lately lost,
    By gentle feelings thou couldst never prove,
      By griefs which thy stern nature never crossed –   20

6.   By those infantine smiles of happy light
      Which were a fire within a stranger's hearth,
    Quenched even when kindled . . . in untimely night
      Hiding the promise of a lovely birth –

7. By those unpractised accents of young speech   25
      Which he who is a father thought to frame
    To gentlest lore, such as the wisest teach –
      Thou strike the lyre of mind! – oh, grief and shame! –

8. By all the happy see in children's growth –
      That undeveloped flower of budding years –   30
    Sweetness and sadness interwoven both,
      Source of the sweetest hopes and saddest fears –

9. By all the days, under a hireling's care,
      Of dull constraint, and bitter heaviness –
    O wretched ye, if ever any were –   35
      Sadder than orphans . . . yet not fatherless –

10. By the false cant which on their innocent lips
      Must hang like poison on an opening bloom;
    By the dark creeds which cover with eclipse
      Their pathway from the cradle to the tomb –   40

11. By thy impious Hell, and all its terror;
      By all the grief, the madness, and the guilt
    Of thine impostures, which must be their error –
      That sand on which thy crumbling Power is built –

12. By thy complicity with lust and hate –   45
    Thy thirst for tears – thy hunger after gold –
By the ready frauds which ever on thee wait –
    The servile arts in which thou hast grown old –

13. By thy most killing sneer, and by thy smile –
    By all the snares and nets of thy black den;   50
And – for thou canst outweep the crocodile –
    By thy false tears – those millstones braining men –

14. By all the hate which checks a father's love –
    By all the scorn which kills a father's care –
By those most impious hands which dared remove   55
    Nature's high bounds – by thee – and by despair –

15. Yes, the despair which bids a father groan,
    And cry, 'My children are no longer mine –
The blood within those veins may be mine own
    But, Tyrant, their polluted soul is thine!' –   60

16. I curse thee, though I hate thee not. – O Slave!
    If thou couldst quench that earth-consuming Hell
Of which thou art a daemon, on thy grave
    This curse should be a blessing. – Fare thee well!

32   AN EXHORTATION

Chameleons feed on light and air:
    Poets' food is love and fame:
If in this wide world of care
    Poets could but find the same
With as little toil as they,   5
    Would they ever change their hue
    As the light chameleons do,
      Suiting it to every ray
      Twenty times a day?

Poets are on this cold earth   10
    As chameleons might be,

Hidden from their early birth
  In a cave beneath the sea;
Where light is, chameleons change:
  Where love is not, Poets do: 15
  Fame is love disguised – if few
    Find either, never think it strange
    That Poets range.

Yet dare not stain with wealth or power
  A Poet's free and heavenly mind: 20
If bright chameleons should devour
  Any food but beams and wind,
They would grow as earthly soon
  As their brother lizards are. –
Children of a sunnier star,   25
  Spirits from beyond the moon,
  O, refuse the boon!

33   ODE TO LIBERTY

Yet, Freedom, yet, thy banner torn but flying,
Streams like a thunder-storm against the wind.
                           Byron

I

A glorious people vibrated again
  The lightning of the nations: Liberty,
From heart to heart, from tower to tower, o'er Spain,
  Scattering contagious fire into the sky,
Gleamed. My soul spurned the chains of its dismay,   5
    And in the rapid plumes of song
    Clothed itself, sublime and strong;
As a young eagle soars the morning clouds among,
  Hovering in verse o'er its accustomed prey;
    Till from its station in the Heaven of fame   10
  The Spirit's whirlwind rapt it, and the ray
    Of the remotest sphere of living flame
Which paves the void was from behind it flung,

As foam from a ship's swiftness, when there came
A voice out of the deep: I will record the same.   15

2

The Sun and the serenest Moon sprang forth:
The burning stars of the abyss were hurled
Into the depths of Heaven. The daedal Earth,
That island in the ocean of the world,
Hung in its cloud of all-sustaining air;   20
But this divinest universe
Was yet a chaos and a curse,
For thou wert not: but, Power from worst producing
worse,
The spirit of the beasts was kindled there,
And of the birds, and of the watery forms,   25
And there was war among them, and despair
Within them, raging without truce or terms:
The bosom of their violated nurse
Groaned, for beasts warred on beasts, and worms on
worms,
And men on men; each heart was as a hell of storms.   30

3

Man, the imperial shape, then multiplied
His generations under the pavilion
Of the Sun's throne: palace and pyramid,
Temple and prison, to many a swarming million
Were as to mountain-wolves their ruggèd caves.   35
This human living multitude
Was savage, cunning, blind, and rude,
For thou wert not; but o'er the populous solitude,
Like one fierce cloud over a waste of waves,
Hung Tyranny; beneath, sate deified   40
The Sister-Pest, congregator of slaves;
Into the shadow of her pinions wide
Anarchs and priests, who feed on gold and blood
Till with the stain their inmost souls are dyed,
Drove the astonished herds of men from every side.   45

4

The nodding promontories, and blue isles,
And cloud-like mountains, and dividuous waves

Of Greece, basked glorious in the open smiles
   Of favouring Heaven: from their enchanted caves
Prophetic echoes flung dim melody   50
      On the unapprehensive wild.
      The vine, the corn, the olive mild,
Grew savage yet, to human use unreconciled;
   And, like unfolded flowers beneath the sea,
     Like the man's thought dark in the infant's brain,   55
Like aught that is which wraps what is to be,
   Art's deathless dreams lay veiled by many a vein
Of Parian stone; and, yet a speechless child,
   Verse murmured, and Philosophy did strain
   Her lidless eyes for thee; when o'er the Aegean main   60

5

Athens arose: a city such as Vision
   Builds from the purple crags and silver towers
Of battlemented cloud, as in derision
   Of kingliest masonry: the ocean-floors
Pave it; the evening sky pavilions it;   65
      Its portals are inhabited
      By thunder-zonèd winds, each head
Within its cloudy wings with sunfire garlanded; –
   A divine work! Athens, diviner yet,
     Gleamed with its crest of columns, on the will   70
Of man, as on a mount of diamond, set;
     For thou wert, and thine all-creative skill
Peopled, with forms that mock the eternal dead
   In marble immortality, that hill
   Which was thine earliest throne and latest oracle.   75

6

Within the surface of Time's fleeting river
   Its wrinkled image lies, as then it lay,
Immoveably unquiet, and for ever
   It trembles, but it cannot pass away!
The voices of its bards and sages thunder   80
      With an earth-awakening blast
      Through the caverns of the past;
(Religion veils her eyes; Oppression shrinks aghast;)
   A wingèd sound of joy, and love, and wonder,

Which soars where Expectation never flew,   85
    Rending the veil of space and time asunder!
        One ocean feeds the clouds, and streams, and dew;
One sun illumines Heaven; one Spirit vast
    With life and love makes chaos ever new,
    As Athens doth the world with thy delight renew.   90

7

Then Rome was – and from thy deep bosom, fairest,
    Like a wolf-cub from a Cadmaean Maenad,[1]
She drew the milk of greatness, though thy dearest
    From that Elysian food was yet unweanèd;
And many a deed of terrible uprightness   95
        By thy sweet love was sanctified;
        And in thy smile, and by thy side,
Saintly Camillus lived, and firm Attilius died.
    But when tears stained thy robe of vestal whiteness,
        And gold profaned thy Capitolian throne,   100
    Thou didst desert, with spirit-wingèd lightness,
        The senate of the tyrants: they sunk prone,
Slaves of one tyrant: Palatinus sighed
    Faint echoes of Ionian song; that tone
    Thou didst delay to hear, lamenting to disown.   105

8

From what Hyrcanian glen or frozen hill,
    Or piny promontory of the Arctic main,
Or utmost islet inaccessible,
    Didst thou lament the ruin of thy reign,
Teaching the woods and waves, and desert rocks,   110
        And every Naiad's ice-cold urn,
        To talk in echoes sad and stern,
Of that sublimest lore which man had dared unlearn?
    For neither didst thou watch the wizard flocks
        Of the Scald's dreams, nor haunt the Druid's
            sleep.   115
    What if the tears rained through thy scattered locks
        Were quickly dried? for thou didst groan, not weep,
When from its sea of death, to kill and burn,

---

[1] See the *Bacchae* of Euripides.

The Galilean serpent forth did creep,
And made thy world an undistinguishable heap.   120

9

A thousand years the Earth cried, 'Where art thou?'
    And then the shadow of thy coming fell
On Saxon Alfred's olive-cinctured brow:
    And many a warrior-peopled citadel,
Like rocks which fire lifts out of the flat deep,   125
        Arose in sacred Italy,
        Frowning o'er the tempestuous sea
Of kings, and priests, and slaves, in tower-crowned
    majesty;
    That multitudinous anarchy did sweep
        And burst around their walls, like idle foam,   130
    Whilst from the human spirit's deepest deep
        Strange melody with love and awe struck dumb
Dissonant arms; and Art, which cannot die,
    With divine wand traced on our earthly home
Fit imagery to pave Heaven's everlasting dome.   135

10

Thou huntress swifter than the Moon! thou terror
    Of the world's wolves! thou bearer of the quiver,
Whose sunlike shafts pierce tempest-wingèd Error,
    As light may pierce the clouds when they dissever
In the calm regions of the orient day!   140
        Luther caught thy wakening glance –
        Like lightning, from his leaden lance
Reflected, it dissolved the visions of the trance
    In which, as in a tomb, the nations lay;
        And England's prophets hailed thee as their queen, 145
    In songs whose music cannot pass away,
        Though it must flow forever: not unseen
Before the spirit-sighted countenance
    Of Milton didst thou pass, from the sad scene
    Beyond whose night he saw, with a dejected mien.   150

11

The eager Hours and unreluctant Years
    As on a dawn-illumined mountain stood,

Trampling to silence their loud hopes and fears,
  Darkening each other with their multitude,
And cried aloud, 'Liberty!' Indignation   155
    Answered Pity from her cave;
    Death grew pale within the grave,
And Desolation howled to the Destroyer, 'Save!'
  When, like Heaven's Sun girt by the exhalation
    Of its own glorious light, thou didst arise,   160
  Chasing thy foes from nation unto nation
    Like shadows: as if day had cloven the skies
At dreaming midnight o'er the western wave,
  Men started, staggering with a glad surprise,
  Under the lightnings of thine unfamiliar eyes.   165

12

Thou Heaven of earth! what spells could pall thee then
  In ominous eclipse? A thousand years
Bred from the slime of deep Oppression's den
  Dyed all thy liquid light with blood and tears,
Till thy sweet stars could weep the stain away;   170
    How like Bacchanals of blood
    Round France, the ghastly vintage, stood
Destruction's sceptred slaves, and Folly's mitred brood!
  When one, like them, but mightier far than they,
    The Anarch of thine own bewildered powers,   175
  Rose: armies mingled in obscure array,
    Like clouds with clouds, darkening the sacred
      bowers
Of serene Heaven. He, by the past pursued,
  Rests with those dead but unforgotten Hours,
  Whose ghosts scare victor kings in their ancestral
    towers.   180

13

England yet sleeps; was she not called of old?
  Spain calls her now, as with its thrilling thunder
Vesuvius wakens Etna, and the cold
  Snow-crags by its reply are cloven in sunder:
O'er the lit waves every Aeolian isle   185
    From Pithecusa to Pelorus
    Howls, and leaps, and glares in chorus:

They cry, 'Be dim, ye lamps of heaven suspended o'er
    us.'
    Her chains are threads of gold, – she need but smile
      And they dissolve; but Spain's were links of
        steel,   190
    Till bit to dust by Virtue's keenest file.
      Twins of a single destiny! appeal
To the eternal years enthroned before us
    In the dim West: impress, as from a seal,
    All ye have thought and done! Time cannot
      dare conceal.   195

14

Tomb of Arminius! render up thy dead
    Till, like a standard from a watch-tower's staff,
His soul may stream over the tyrant's head;
    Thy victory shall be his epitaph,
Wild Bacchanal of truth's mysterious wine;   200
      King-deluded Germany,
        His dead spirit lives in thee.
Why do we fear or hope? thou art already free!
    And thou, lost Paradise of this divine
      And glorious world! thou flowery wilderness!   205
    Thou island of eternity! thou shrine
      Where Desolation, clothed with loveliness,
Worships the thing thou wert! O Italy,
    Gather thy blood into thy heart: repress
      The beasts who make their dens thy sacred palaces. 210

15

O that the free would stamp the impious name
    Of KING into the dust! or write it there,
So that this blot upon the page of fame
    Were as a serpent's path, which the light air
Erases, and the flat sands close behind!   215
      Ye the oracle have heard:
        Lift the victory-flashing sword,
And cut the snaky knots of this foul gordian word,
    Which, weak itself as stubble, yet can bind
      Into a mass, irrefragably firm,   220
    The axes and the rods which awe mankind;

The sound has poison in it, 'tis the sperm
Of what makes life foul, cankerous, and abhorred;
   Disdain not thou, at thine appointed term,
   To set thine armèd heel on this reluctant worm.   225

16

O that the wise from their bright minds would kindle
   Such lamps within the dome of this dim world,
That the pale name of PRIEST might shrink and
      dwindle
   Into the hell from which it first was hurled,
A scoff of impious pride from fiends impure;   230
      Till human thoughts might kneel alone,
      Each before the judgement-throne
Of its own aweless soul, or of the Power unknown!
   O that the words which make the thoughts obscure
     From which they spring, as clouds of
       glimmering dew   235
From a white lake blot Heaven's blue portraiture,
   Were stripped of their thin masks and various hue
And frowns and smiles and splendours not their own,
   Till in the nakedness of false and true
   They stand before their Lord, each to receive its due. 240

17

He who taught man to vanquish whatsoever
   Can be between the cradle and the grave
Crowned him the King of Life: O vain endeavour! –
   If on his own high will, a willing slave,
He has enthroned the oppression and the oppressor.   245
      What if Earth can clothe and feed
      Amplest millions at their need,
And power in thought be as the tree within the seed?
   Or what if Art, an ardent intercessor,
     Diving on fiery wings to Nature's throne,   250
   Checks the great Mother stooping to caress her,
     And cries: 'Give me, thy child, dominion
Over all height and depth'? – if Life can breed
   New wants, and Wealth from those who toil and
      groan
   Rend, of thy gifts and hers, a thousandfold for one. 255

18

Come thou! but lead out of the inmost cave
  Of man's deep spirit, as the morning-star
Beckons the Sun from the Eoan wave,
  Wisdom. I hear the pennons of her car
Self-moving, like cloud charioted by flame;   260
      Comes she not, and come ye not,
      Rulers of eternal thought,
To judge, with solemn truth, life's ill-apportioned lot?
  Blind Love, and equal Justice, and the Fame
    Of what has been, the Hope of what will be?   265
  O Liberty! if such could be thy name
    Wert thou disjoined from these, or they from thee:
  If thine or theirs were treasures to be bought
  By blood or tears, have not the wise and free
Wept tears, and blood like tears? – The solemn
    harmony   270

19

Paused, and the Spirit of that mighty singing
  To its abyss was suddenly withdrawn;
Then, as a wild swan, when sublimely winging
  Its path athwart the thunder-smoke of dawn,
Sinks headlong through the aerial golden light   275
      On the heavy-sounding plain,
      When the bolt has pierced its brain;
As summer clouds dissolve, unburthened of their rain;
  As a far taper fades with fading night,
    As a brief insect dies with dying day, –   280
  My song, its pinions disarrayed of might,
    Drooped; o'er it closed the echoes far away
Of the great voice which did its flight sustain,
  As waves which lately paved his watery way
  Hiss round a drowner's head in their tempestuous
    play.   285

Rarely, rarely, comest thou,
   Spirit of Delight!
Wherefore hast thou left me now
   Many a day and night?
Many a weary night and day 5
'Tis since thou art fled away.

How shall ever one like me
   Win thee back again?
With the joyous and the free
   Thou wilt scoff at pain. 10
Spirit false! thou hast forgot
All but those who need thee not.

As a lizard with the shade
   Of a trembling leaf,
Thou with sorrow art dismayed; 15
   Even the sighs of grief
Reproach thee, that thou art not near,
And reproach thou wilt not hear.

Let me set my mournful ditty
   To a merry measure; 20
Thou wilt never come for pity,
   Thou wilt come for pleasure;
Pity then will cut away
Those cruel wings, and thou wilt stay.

I love all that thou lovest, 25
   Spirit of Delight!
The fresh Earth in new leaves dressed,
   And the starry night;
Autumn evening, and the morn
When the golden mists are born. 30

I love snow, and all the forms
   Of the radiant frost;
I love waves and winds and storms –

Every thing almost
   Which is Nature's, and may be   35
Untainted by man's misery.

I love tranquil solitude,
   And such society
As is quiet, wise and good;
   Between thee and me   40
   What difference? – but thou dost possess
The things I seek, not love them less.

I love Love – though he has wings,
   And like light can flee –
But above all other things,
   Spirit, I love thee –   45
Thou art Love and Life! O come,
Make once more my heart thy home.

35   TO A SKY-LARK

Hail to thee, blithe Spirit!
   Bird thou never wert,
That from Heaven, or near it,
   Pourest thy full heart
In profuse strains of unpremeditated art.   5

Higher still and higher
   From the earth thou springest
Like a cloud of fire;
   The blue deep thou wingest,
And singing still dost soar, and soaring ever singest. 10

In the golden lightning
   Of the sunken Sun,
O'er which clouds are bright'ning,
   Thou dost float and run;
Like an unbodied joy whose race is just begun.   15

The pale purple even
  Melts around thy flight;
Like a star of Heaven
  In the broad day-light
Thou art unseen, – but yet I hear thy shrill delight,   20

  Keen as are the arrows
    Of that silver sphere
  Whose intense lamp narrows
    In the white dawn clear,
Until we hardly see – we feel that it is there.   25

  All the earth and air
    With thy voice is loud,
  As when night is bare
    From one lonely cloud
The moon rains out her beams, and Heaven is overflowed.   30

  What thou art we know not;
    What is most like thee?
  From rainbow clouds there flow not
    Drops so bright to see,
As from thy presence showers a rain of melody.   35

  Like a Poet hidden
    In the light of thought,
  Singing hymns unbidden
    Till the world is wrought
To sympathy with hopes and fears it heeded not: 40

  Like a high-born maiden
    In a palace tower,
  Soothing her love-laden
    Soul in secret hour
With music sweet as love, which overflows her bower: 45

  Like a glow-worm golden
    In a dell of dew,
  Scattering unbeholden
    Its aërial hue

Among the flowers and grass which screen it from the
      view: 50

    Like a rose embowered
      In its own green leaves,
    By warm winds deflowered,
      Till the scent it gives
Makes faint with too much sweet those heavy-wingèd
      thieves: 55

    Sound of vernal showers
      On the twinkling grass,
    Rain-awakened flowers,
      All that ever was
Joyous and clear and fresh, thy music doth surpass.   60

    Teach us, Sprite or Bird,
      What sweet thoughts are thine;
    I have never heard
      Praise of love or wine
That panted forth a flood of rapture so divine: 65

    Chorus Hymenaeal
      Or triumphal chaunt
    Matched with thine, would be all
      But an empty vaunt,
A thing wherein we feel there is some hidden want.   70

    What objects are the fountains
      Of thy happy strain?
    What fields or waves or mountains?
      What shapes of sky or plain?
What love of thine own kind? what ignorance of pain?   75

    With thy clear keen joyance
      Languor cannot be –
    Shadow of annoyance
      Never came near thee:
Thou lovest – but ne'er knew love's sad satiety.   80

    Waking or asleep,
      Thou of death must deem

Things more true and deep
   Than we mortals dream
Or how could thy notes flow in such a crystal stream?   85

We look before and after
   And pine for what is not:
Our sincerest laughter
   With some pain is fraught;
Our sweetest songs are those that tell of saddest thought.   90

Yet if we could scorn
   Hate and pride and fear;
If we were things born
   Not to shed a tear,
I know not how thy joy we ever should come near.   95

Better than all measures
   Of delightful sound –
Better than all treasures
   That in books are found –
Thy skill to poet were, thou scorner of the ground!   100

Teach me half the gladness
   That thy brain must know,
Such harmonious madness
   From my lips would flow,
The world should listen then – as I am listening now.   105

36   LETTER TO MARIA GISBORNE

The spider spreads her webs, whether she be
In poet's tower, cellar or barn or tree;
The silk worm in the dark green mulberry leaves
His winding sheet and cradle ever weaves;
So I, a thing whom moralists call worm,   5
Sit spinning still round this decaying form
From the fine threads of rare and subtle thought –
No net of words in garish colours wrought
To catch the idle buzzers of the day –

But a soft cell where, when that fades away,   10
Memory may clothe in wings my living name
And feed it with the asphodels of Fame,
Which in those hearts that must remember me
Grow, making love an immortality.

Whoever should behold me now, I wist,   15
Would think I were a mighty mechanist,
Bent with sublime Archimedean art
To breathe a soul into the iron heart
Of some machine portentous, or strange gin,
Which, by the force of figured spells, might win   20
Its way over the sea, and sport therein;
For round the walls are hung dread engines, such
As Vulcan never wrought for Jove to clutch
Ixion or the Titans; – or the quick
Wit of that Man of God, St Dominic,   25
To convince Atheist, Turk or heretic
Or those in philanthropic council met
Who thought to pay some interest for the debt
They owed to Jesus Christ for their salvation,
By giving a faint foretaste of damnation   30
To Shakespeare, Sidney, Spenser – and the rest
Who made our land an island of the blest,
When lamplike Spain, who now relumes her fire
On Freedom's hearth, grew dim with empire –
With thumbscrews, wheels, with tooth and spike and
    jag,   35
Which fishers found under the utmost crag
Of Cornwall, and the storm-encompassed isles
Where to the sky the rude sea rarely smiles
Unless in treacherous wrath, as on the morn
When the exulting elements, in scorn,   40
Satiated with destroyed destruction, lay
Sleeping in beauty on their mangled prey,
As Panthers sleep; – and other strange dread
Magical forms the brick floor overspread –
Proteus transformed to metal did not make   45
More figures or more strange, nor did he take
Such shapes of unintelligible brass,
Or heap himself in such a horrid mass

Of tin and iron not to be understood,
And forms of unimaginable wood 50
To puzzle Tubal Cain and all his brood:
Great screws, and cones, and wheels, and groovèd blocks,
The elements of what will stand the shocks
Of wave and wind and time. – Upon the table
More knacks and quips there be than I am able 55
To catalogize in this verse of mine: –
A pretty bowl of wood, not full of wine
But quicksilver, that dew which the gnomes drink
When at their subterranean toil they swink,
Pledging the daemons of the earthquake, who 60
Reply to them in lava, cry halloo!
And call out to the cities o'er their head –
Roofs, towers, and shrines, the dying and the dead,
Crash through the chinks of earth – and then all quaff
Another rouse, and hold their ribs and laugh. 65
This quicksilver no gnome has drunk – within
The walnut bowl it lies, veinèd and thin,
In colour like the wake of light that stains
The Tuscan deep, when from the moist moon rains
The inmost shower of its white fire – the breeze 70
Is still – blue Heaven smiles over the pale Seas.
And in this bowl of quicksilver – for I
Yield to the impulse of an infancy
Outlasting manhood – I have made to float
A rude idealism of a paper boat: 75
A hollow screw with cogs – Henry will know
The thing I mean, and laugh at me, if so
He fears not I should do more mischief – next
Lie bills and calculations much perplexed,
With steam boats, frigates and machinery quaint 80
Traced over them in blue and yellow paint.
Then comes a range of mathematical
Instruments, for plans nautical and statical;
A heap of rosin, a queer broken glass 85
With ink in it, a china cup that was
What it will never be again, I think,
A thing from which sweet lips were wont to drink
The liquor doctors rail at – and which I
Will quaff in spite of them – and when we die

We'll toss up who died first of drinking tea,   90
And cry out, 'Heads or tails?' where'er we be.
Near that a dusty paint box, some odd hooks,
A half-burnt match, an ivory block, three books
Where conic sections, spherics, logarithms,
To great Laplace from Saunderson and Sims   95
Lie heaped in their harmonious disarray
Of figures – disentangle them who may.
Baron de Tott's memoirs beside them lie,
And some odd volumes of old chemistry.
Near those a most inexplicable tin thing   100
With lead in the middle – I'm conjecturing
How to make Henry understand – but, no –
I'll leave, as Spenser says, with many mo,
This secret in the pregnant womb of time,
Too vast a matter for so weak a rhyme.   105

And here like some weird Archimage sit I,
Plotting dark spells and devilish enginery,
The self-impelling steam wheels of the mind
Which pump up oaths from clergymen, and grind
The gentle spirit of our meek reviews   110
Into a powdery foam of salt abuse –
Ruffling the dull wave of their self-content.
I sit, and smile or sigh, as is my bent,
But not for them – Libeccio rushes round   115
With an inconstant and an idle sound,
I heed him more than them – the thundersmoke
Is gathering on the mountains, like a cloak
Folded athwart their shoulders broad and bare;
The ripe corn under the undulating air
Undulates like an ocean, – and the vines   120
Are trembling wide in all their trellised lines –
The murmur of the awakening sea doth fill
The empty pauses of the blast – the hill
Looks hoary through the white electric rain –
And from the glens beyond, in sullen strain   125
The interrupted thunder howls – above
One chasm of Heaven smiles, like the eye of Love,
On the unquiet world – while such things are,
How could one worth your friendship heed this war

Of worms? the shriek of the world's carrion jays,   130
Their censure, or their wonder, or their praise?

You are not here . . . the quaint witch Memory sees
In vacant chairs your absent images,
And points where once you sate, and now should be
But are not – I demand if ever we   135
Shall meet as then we met – and she replies,
Veiling in awe her second-sighted eyes,
'I know the past alone – but summon home
My sister Hope, – she speaks of all to come'.
But I, an old diviner, who know well   140
Every false verse of that sweet oracle,
Turned to the sad enchantress once again,
And sought a respite from my gentle pain
In citing every passage o'er and o'er
Of our communion – how on the sea shore   145
We watched the Ocean and the sky together
Under the roof of blue Italian weather;
How I ran home through last year's thunderstorm
And felt the transverse lightning linger warm
Upon my cheek – and how we often made   150
Feasts for each other, where good will outweighed
The frugal luxury of our country cheer,
As well it might, were it less firm and clear
Than ours must ever be – and how we spun
A shroud of talk to hide us from the Sun   155
Of this familiar life, which seems to be
But is not – or is but quaint mockery
Of all we would believe; or sadly blame
The jarring and inexplicable frame
Of this wrong world; – and then anatomize   160
The purposes and thoughts of men whose eyes
Were closed in distant years – or widely guess
The issue of the earth's great business
When we shall be, as we no longer are –
Like babbling gossips safe, who hear the war   165
Of winds, and sigh, but tremble not – or how
You listened to some interrupted flow
Of visionary rhyme, in joy and pain
Struck from the inmost fountains of my brain

With little skill perhaps – or how we sought   170
Those deepest wells of passion and of thought
Wrought by wise poets in the waste of years,
Staining their sacred waters with our tears,
Quenching a thirst ever to be renewed; –
Or how I, wisest lady! then indued   175
The language of a land which now is free
And winged with thoughts of truth and majesty
Flits round the tyrant's sceptre like a cloud
And bursts the peopled prisons – cries aloud,
'My name is Legion!' – that majestic tongue   180
Which Calderón over the desert flung
Of ages and of nations, and which found
An echo in our hearts, and with the sound
Startled Oblivion – thou wert then to me
As is a nurse when inarticulately   185
A child would talk as its grown parents do.
If living winds the rapid clouds pursue,
If hawks chase doves through the aetherial way,
Huntsmen the innocent deer, and beasts their prey,
Why should not we rouse with the Spirit's blast   190
Out of the forest of the pathless past
These recollected pleasures?

                              You are now
In London, that great sea whose ebb and flow
At once is deaf and loud, and on the shore
Vomits its wrecks, and still howls on for more.   195
Yet in its depth what treasures! You will see
That which was Godwin, – greater none than he
Though fallen – and fallen on evil times – to stand
Among the spirits of our age and land
Before the dread Tribunal of *to come*   200
The foremost ... while Rebuke cowers, pale and
   dumb.
You will see Coleridge, he who sits obscure
In the exceeding lustre, and the pure
Intense irradiation of a mind
Which, with its own internal lightning blind,   205
Flags wearily through darkness and despair –
A cloud-encircled meteor of the air,

A hooded eagle among blinking owls. –
You will see Hunt, one of those happy souls
Who are the salt of the earth – and without whom   210
This world would smell like what it is, a tomb;
Who is, what others seem – his room no doubt
Is still adorned with many a cast from Shout,
With graceful flowers, tastefully placed about,
And coronals of bay from ribbons hung,   215
And brighter wreaths in neat disorder flung,
The gifts of the most learn'd among some dozens
Of female friends, sisters-in-law and cousins.
And there is he with his eternal puns
Which beat the dullest brain for smiles, like duns   220
Thundering for money at a poet's door.
Alas, it is no use to say 'I'm poor!'
Or oft in graver mood, when he will look
Things wiser than were ever read in book
Except in Shakespeare's wisest tenderness. –   225
You will see Hogg – and I cannot express
His virtues though I know that they are great,
Because he locks, then barricades, the gate
Within which they inhabit – of his wit
And wisdom, you'll cry out when you are bit.   230
He is a pearl within an oyster shell,
One of the richest of the deep. And there
Is English Peacock with his mountain fair,
Turned into a Flamingo, that shy bird
That gleams in the Indian air. Have you not heard   235
When a man marries, dies or turns Hindoo,
His best friends hear no more of him? – but you
Will see him and will like him too, I hope,
With the milk-white Snowdonian antelope
Matched with this cameleopard – his fine wit   240
Makes such a wound, the knife is lost in it,
A strain too learnèd for a shallow age,
Too wise for selfish bigots – let his page
Which charms the chosen spirits of the time
Fold itself up for the serener clime   245
Of years to come, and find its recompense
In that just expectation. – Wit and sense,
Virtue and human knowledge, all that might

Make this dull world a business of delight,
Are all combined in Horace Smith. – And these,   250
With some exceptions which I need not tease
Your patience by descanting on – are all
You and I know in London. –

                    I recall
My thoughts, and bid you look upon the night.
As water does a sponge, so the moonlight   255
Fills the void, hollow, universal air –
What see you? – unpavilioned heaven is fair
Whether the moon, into her chamber gone,
Leaves midnight to the golden stars, or wan
Climbs with diminished beams the azure steep,   260
Or whether clouds sail o'er the inverse deep
Piloted by the many-wandering blast,
And the rare stars rush through them dim and fast. –
All this is beautiful in every land –
But what see you beside? – a shabby stand   265
Of hackney coaches, a brick house, or wall
Fencing some lordly court, white with the scrawl
Of our unhappy politics, or worse –
A wretched woman reeling by, whose curse
Mixed with the watchman's, partner of her trade,   270
You must accept in place of serenade –
Or yellow-haired Pollonia murmuring
To Henry some unutterable thing. –
I see a chaos of green leaves and fruit
Built round dark caverns, even to the root   275
Of the living stems that feed them – in whose bowers
There sleep in their dark dew the folded flowers;
Beyond, the surface of the unsickled corn
Trembles not in the slumbering air, and borne
In circles quaint, and ever-changing dance,   280
Like wingèd stars the fire-flies flash and glance
Pale in the open moonshine, but each one
Under the dark trees seems a little sun,
A meteor tamed, a fixed star gone astray
From the silver regions of the milky way; –   285
Afar the contadino's song is heard,
Rude, but made sweet by distance – and a bird

Which cannot be the nightingale, and yet
I know none else that sings so sweet as it
At this late hour – and then all is still –   290
Now, Italy or London – which you will!

   Next winter you must pass with me. I'll have
My house by that time turned into a grave
Of dead despondence and low-thoughted care
And all the dreams which our tormentors are.   295
O, that Hunt, Hogg, Peacock and Smith were there,
With every thing belonging to them fair!
We will have books – Spanish, Italian, Greek –
And ask one week to make another week
As like his father as I'm unlike mine –   300
Which is not his fault, as you may divine.
Though we eat little flesh and drink no wine,
Yet let's be merry! we'll have tea and toast,
Custards for supper, and an endless host
Of syllabubs and jellies and mince-pies   305
And other such lady-like luxuries –
Feasting on which, we will philosophize!
And we'll have fires out of the Grand Duke's wood
To thaw the six weeks' winter in our blood.
And then we'll talk – what shall we talk about?   310
O, there are themes enough for many a bout
Of thought-entangled descant; – as to nerves,
With cones and parallelograms and curves
I've sworn to strangle them if once they dare
To bother me – when you are with me there,   315
And they shall never more sip laudanum
From Helicon or Himeros; – well, come,
And in despite of God and of the devil
We'll make our friendly philosophic revel
Outlast the leafless time – till buds and flowers   320
Warn the obscure inevitable hours
Sweet meeting by sad parting to renew –
'Tomorrow to fresh woods and pastures new'.

Song of Apollo

The sleepless Hours who watch me as I lie
   Curtained with star-enwoven tapestries
From the broad moonlight of the open sky,
   Fanning the busy dreams from my dim eyes, –
Waken me when their mother, the grey Dawn,   5
Tells them that dreams and that the moon is gone.

Then I arise; and climbing Heaven's blue dome,
   I walk over the mountains and the waves,
Leaving my robe upon the ocean foam;
   My footsteps pave the clouds with fire; the caves   10
Are filled with my bright presence, and the air
Leaves the green Earth to my embraces bare.

The sunbeams are my shafts with which I kill
   Deceit, that loves the night and fears the day;
All men who do, or even imagine ill   15
   Fly me; and from the glory of my ray
Good minds and open actions take new might,
Until diminished by the reign of night.

I feed the clouds, the rainbows and the flowers
   With their aetherial colours; the moon's globe   20
And the pure stars in their eternal bowers
   Are cinctured with my power as with a robe;
Whatever lamps on Earth or Heaven may shine
Are portions of one spirit; which is mine.

I stand at noon upon the peak of Heaven;   25
   Then with unwilling steps, I linger down
Into the clouds of the Atlantic even;
   For grief that I depart they weep and frown –
What look is more delightful, than the smile
With which I soothe them from the Western isle?   30

I am the eye with which the Universe
   Beholds itself, and knows it is divine;

All harmony of instrument and verse,
　All prophecy and medicine are mine,
All light of art or nature; – to my song   35
Victory and praise, in its own right, belong.

Song of Pan

From the forests and highlands
　We come, we come,
From the river-girt islands
　Where loud waves were dumb,
　　Listening my sweet pipings.   5
　　　The wind in the reeds and the rushes,
　　　The bees on the bells of thyme,
　　　The birds in the myrtle bushes,
　　　The cicadae above in the lime,
　　　　And the lizards below in the grass,   10
Were silent as even old Tmolus was,
　　　Listening my sweet pipings.

Liquid Peneus was flowing,
　And all dark Tempe lay
In Pelion's shadow, outgrowing   15
　The light of the dying day,
　　Speeded with my sweet pipings.
　　　The sileni and sylvans and fauns
　　　And the nymphs of the woods and the waves
　　　To the edge of the moist river-lawns   20
　　　And the brink of the dewy caves,
　　　　And all that did then attend and follow
Were as silent for love, as you now, Apollo,
　　　For envy of my sweet pipings.

I sang of the dancing stars,   25
　I sang of the dædal Earth,
And of Heaven, and the giant wars,
　And Love and Death and Birth;
　　And then I changed my pipings,
　　　Singing how, down the vales of Mænalus   30
　　　I pursued a maiden and clasped a reed.
　　　Gods and men, we are all deluded thus! –

It breaks on our bosom and then we bleed.
They wept as I think both ye now would,
If envy or age had not frozen your blood,   35
At the sorrow of my sweet pipings.

38   SONNET TO THE REPUBLIC OF BENEVENTO

Nor happiness, nor majesty, nor fame,
Nor peace nor strength, nor skill in arms or arts,
Shepherd those herds whom Tyranny makes tame:
Verse echoes not one beating of their hearts;
History is but the shadow of their shame;   5
Art veils her glass, or from the pageant starts
As to oblivion their blind millions fleet,
Staining that Heaven with obscene imagery
Of their own likeness. – What are numbers, knit
By force or custom? Man, who man would be,   10
Must rule the empire of himself; in it
Must be supreme, establishing his throne
On vanquished will; quelling the anarchy
Of hopes and fears; being himself alone.

39   TO THE MOON

Art thou pale for weariness
Of climbing Heaven, and gazing on the earth,
Wandering companionless
Among the stars that have a different birth, –
And ever changing, like a joyless eye   5
That finds no object worth its constancy?

Verses addressed to the noble and unfortunate lady

EMILIA V——

NOW IMPRISONED IN THE CONVENT OF——

L'anima amante si slancia fuori del creato, e si crea nell'infinito un Mondo tutto per essa, diverso assai da questo oscuro e pauroso baratro.

Her own words

ADVERTISEMENT

The writer of the following lines died at Florence, as he was preparing for a voyage to one of the wildest of the Sporades, which he had bought, and where he had fitted up the ruins of an old building, and where it was his hope to have realised a scheme of life, suited perhaps to that happier and better world of which he is now an inhabitant, but hardly practicable in this. His life was singular; less on account of the romantic vicissitudes which diversified it, than the ideal tinge which it received from his own character and feelings. The present poem, like the *Vita nuova* of Dante, is sufficiently intelligible to a certain class of readers without a matter-of-fact history of the circumstances to which it relates; and to a certain other class it must ever remain incomprehensible, from a defect of a common organ of perception for the ideas of which it treats. Not but that, *gran vergogna sarebbe a colui, che rimasse cosa sotto veste di figura, o di colore rettorico: e domandato non sapesse denudare le sue parole da cotal veste, in guisa che avessero verace intendimento.*

The present poem appears to have been intended by the writer as the dedication to some longer one. The stanza on the opposite page is almost a literal translation from Dante's famous *canzone*

Voi, ch'intendendo, il terzo ciel movete, &c.

The presumptuous application of the concluding lines to his own composition will raise a smile at the expense of my unfortunate friend: be it a smile not of contempt, but pity.

My Song, I fear that thou wilt find but few
Who fitly shall conceive thy reasoning,
Of such hard matter dost thou entertain;
Whence, if by misadventure, chance should bring
Thee to base company (as chance may do),   5
Quite unaware of what thou dost contain,
I prithee, comfort thy sweet self again,
My last delight! tell them that they are dull,
And bid them own that thou art beautiful.

EPIPSYCHIDION

Sweet Spirit! Sister of that orphan one,
Whose empire is the name thou weepest on,
In my heart's temple I suspend to thee
These votive wreaths of withered memory.

Poor captive bird! who, from thy narrow cage,   5
Pourest such music, that it might assuage
The rugged hearts of those who prisoned thee,
Were they not deaf to all sweet melody;
This song shall be thy rose: its petals pale
Are dead, indeed, my adored Nightingale!   10
But soft and fragrant is the faded blossom,
And it has no thorn left to wound thy bosom.

High, spirit-wingèd Heart! who dost for ever
Beat thine unfeeling bars with vain endeavour,
Till those bright plumes of thought, in which arrayed   15
It over-soared this low and worldly shade,
Lie shattered; and thy panting, wounded breast
Stains with dear blood its unmaternal nest!
I weep vain tears: blood would less bitter be,
Yet poured forth gladlier, could it profit thee.   20

Seraph of Heaven! too gentle to be human,
Veiling beneath that radiant form of Woman
All that is insupportable in thee
Of light, and love, and immortality!
Sweet Benediction in the eternal Curse!   25
Veiled Glory of this lampless Universe!

Thou Moon beyond the clouds! Thou living Form
Among the Dead! Thou Star above the Storm!
Thou Wonder, and thou Beauty, and thou Terror!
Thou Harmony of Nature's art! Thou Mirror   30
In whom, as in the splendour of the Sun,
All shapes look glorious which thou gazest on!
Ay, even the dim words which obscure thee now
Flash, lightning-like, with unaccustomed glow;
I pray thee that thou blot from this sad song   35
All of its much mortality and wrong
With those clear drops, which start like sacred dew
From the twin lights thy sweet soul darkens through,
Weeping, till sorrow becomes ecstacy:
Then smile on it, so that it may not die.   40

   I never thought before my death to see
Youth's vision thus made perfect. Emily,
I love thee; though the world by no thin name
Will hide that love, from its unvalued shame.
Would we two had been twins of the same mother!   45
Or, that the name my heart lent to another
Could be a sister's bond for her and thee,
Blending two beams of one eternity!
Yet were one lawful and the other true,
These names, though dear, could paint not, as is due,   50
How beyond refuge I am thine. Ah me!
I am not thine: I am a part of *thee*.

   Sweet Lamp! my moth-like Muse has burnt its wings;
Or, like a dying swan who soars and sings,
Young Love should teach Time, in his own grey style,   55
All that thou art. Art thou not void of guile,
A lovely soul formed to be blest and bless?
A well of sealed and secret happiness,
Whose waters like blithe light and music are,
Vanquishing dissonance and gloom? A Star   60
Which moves not in the moving Heavens, alone?
A smile amid dark frowns? a gentle tone
Amid rude voices? a belovèd light?
A Solitude, a Refuge, a Delight?
A lute, which those whom love has taught to play   65

Make music on, to soothe the roughest day
And lull fond grief asleep? a buried treasure?
A cradle of young thoughts of wingless pleasure?
A violet-shrouded grave of Woe? – I measure
The world of fancies, seeking one like thee,   70
And find – alas! mine own infirmity.

   She met me, Stranger, upon life's rough way,
And lured me towards sweet Death; as Night by Day,
Winter by Spring, or Sorrow by swift Hope,
Let into light, life, peace. An antelope,   75
In the suspended impulse of its lightness,
Were less ethereally light: the brightness
Of her divinest presence trembles through
Her limbs, as underneath a cloud of dew
Embodied in the windless Heaven of June   80
Amid the splendour-wingèd stars, the Moon
Burns, inextinguishably beautiful:
And from her lips, as from a hyacinth full
Of honey-dew, a liquid murmur drops,
Killing the sense with passion; sweet as stops   85
Of planetary music heard in trance.
In her mild lights the starry spirits dance,
The sun-beams of those wells which ever leap
Under the lightnings of the soul – too deep
For the brief fathom-line of thought or sense.   90
The glory of her being, issuing thence,
Stains the dead, blank, cold air with a warm shade
Of unentangled intermixture, made
By Love, of light and motion: one intense
Diffusion, one serene Omnipresence,   95
Whose flowing outlines mingle in their flowing,
Around her cheeks and utmost fingers glowing
With the unintermitted blood, which there
Quivers, (as in a fleece of snow-like air
The crimson pulse of living morning quiver,)   100
Continuously prolonged, and ending never,
Till they are lost, and in that Beauty furled
Which penetrates and clasps and fills the world;
Scarce visible from extreme loveliness.
Warm fragrance seems to fall from her light dress,   105

And her loose hair; and where some heavy tress
The air of her own speed has disentwined,
The sweetness seems to satiate the faint wind;
And in the soul a wild odour is felt,
Beyond the sense, like fiery dews that melt   110
Into the bosom of a frozen bud. –
See where she stands! a mortal shape indued
With love and life and light and deity,
And motion which may change but cannot die;
An image of some bright Eternity;   115
A shadow of some golden dream; a Splendour
Leaving the third sphere pilotless; a tender
Reflection of the eternal Moon of Love
Under whose motions life's dull billows move;
A Metaphor of Spring and Youth and Morning;   120
A Vision like incarnate April, warning,
With smiles and tears, Frost the Anatomy
Into his summer grave.

                    Ah, woe is me!
What have I dared? where am I lifted? how
Shall I descend, and perish not? I know   125
That Love makes all things equal: I have heard
By mine own heart this joyous truth averred:
The spirit of the worm beneath the sod
In love and worship, blends itself with God.

    Spouse! Sister! Angel! Pilot of the Fate   130
Whose course has been so starless! O too late
Belovèd! O too soon adored, by me!
For in the fields of immortality
My spirit should at first have worshipped thine,
A divine presence in a place divine;   135
Or should have moved beside it on this earth,
A shadow of that substance, from its birth;
But not as now: – I love thee; yes, I feel
That on the fountain of my heart a seal
Is set, to keep its waters pure and bright   140
For thee, since in those *tears* thou hast delight.
We – are we not formed, as notes of music are,
For one another, though dissimilar;

Such difference without discord, as can make
Those sweetest sounds in which all spirits shake   145
As trembling leaves in a continuous air?

   Thy wisdom speaks in me, and bids me dare
Beacon the rocks on which high hearts are wrecked.
I never was attached to that great sect   150
Whose doctrine is, that each one should select
Out of the crowd a mistress or a friend,
And all the rest, though fair and wise, commend
To cold oblivion, though it is in the code
Of modern morals, and the beaten road   155
Which those poor slaves with weary footsteps tread,
Who travel to their home among the dead
By the broad highway of the world, and so
With one chained friend, perhaps a jealous foe,
The dreariest and the longest journey go.   160

   True Love in this differs from gold and clay,
That to divide is not to take away.
Love is like understanding, that grows bright,
Gazing on many truths; 'tis like thy light,
Imagination! which from earth and sky,   165
And from the depths of human fantasy,
As from a thousand prisms and mirrors, fills
The Universe with glorious beams, and kills
Error, the worm, with many a sun-like arrow
Of its reverberated lightning. Narrow
The heart that loves, the brain that contemplates,   170
The life that wears, the spirit that creates
One object, and one form, and builds thereby
A sepulchre for its eternity.

   Mind from its object differs most in this:
Evil from good; misery from happiness;   175
The baser from the nobler; the impure
And frail, from what is clear and must endure.
If you divide suffering and dross, you may
Diminish till it is consumed away;
If you divide pleasure and love and thought,   180
Each part exceeds the whole; and we know not

How much, while any yet remains unshared,
Of pleasure may be gained, of sorrow spared:
This truth is that deep well, whence sages draw
The unenvied light of hope; the eternal law   185
By which those live, to whom this world of life
Is as a garden ravaged, and whose strife
Tills for the promise of a later birth
The wilderness of this Elysian earth.

   There was a Being whom my spirit oft   190
Met on its visioned wanderings, far aloft,
In the clear golden prime of my youth's dawn,
Upon the fairy isles of sunny lawn,
Amid the enchanted mountains, and the caves
Of divine sleep, and on the air-like waves   195
Of wonder-level dream, whose tremulous floor
Paved her light steps; – on an imagined shore,
Under the grey beak of some promontory
She met me, robed in such exceeding glory
That I beheld her not. In solitudes   200
Her voice came to me through the whispering woods,
And from the fountains, and the odours deep
Of flowers, which, like lips murmuring in their sleep
Of the sweet kisses which had lulled them there,
Breathed but of *her* to the enamoured air;   205
And from the breezes whether low or loud,
And from the rain of every passing cloud,
And from the singing of the summer-birds,
And from all sounds, all silence. In the words
Of antique verse and high romance, – in form   210
Sound, colour – in whatever checks that Storm
Which with the shattered present chokes the past;
And in that best philosophy, whose taste
Makes this cold common hell, our life, a doom
As glorious as a fiery martyrdom;   215
Her Spirit was the harmony of truth. –

   Then, from the caverns of my dreamy youth
I sprang, as one sandalled with plumes of fire,
And towards the loadstar of my one desire,
I flitted, like a dizzy moth, whose flight   220

Is as a dead leaf's in the owlet light,
When it would seek in Hesper's setting sphere
A radiant death, a fiery sepulchre,
As if it were a lamp of earthly flame. –
But She, whom prayers or tears then could not tame,   225
Passed like a God throned on a wingèd planet,
Whose burning plumes to tenfold swiftness fan it,
Into the dreary cone of our life's shade;
And as a man with mighty loss dismayed,
I would have followed, though the grave between   230
Yawned like a gulf whose spectres are unseen:
When a voice said: – 'O Thou of hearts the weakest,
'The phantom is beside thee whom thou seekest.'
Then I – 'Where?' – the world's echo answered 'Where!'
And in that silence, and in my despair,   235
I questioned every tongueless wind that flew
Over my tower of mourning, if it knew
Whither 'twas fled, this soul out of my soul;
And murmured names and spells which have control
Over the sightless tyrants of our fate;   240
But neither prayer nor verse could dissipate
The night which closed on her; nor uncreate
That world within this Chaos, mine and me,
Of which she was the veiled Divinity,
The world I say of thoughts that worshipped her: 245
And therefore I went forth, with hope and fear
And every gentle passion sick to death,
Feeding my course with expectation's breath,
Into the wintry forest of our life;
And struggling through its error with vain strife,   250
And stumbling in my weakness and my haste,
And half-bewildered by new forms, I passed
Seeking among those untaught foresters
If I could find one form resembling hers,
In which she might have masked herself from me.   255
There, – One, whose voice was venomed melody,
Sate by a well, under blue night-shade bowers;
The breath of her false mouth was like faint flowers,
Her touch was as electric poison, – flame
Out of her looks into my vitals came,   260
And from her living cheeks and bosom flew

A killing air, which pierced like honey-dew
Into the core of my green heart, and lay
Upon its leaves; until, as hair grown grey
O'er a young brow, they hid its unblown prime   265
With ruins of unseasonable time.

    In many mortal forms I rashly sought
The shadow of that idol of my thought.
And some were fair – but beauty dies away:
Others were wise – but honeyed words betray: 270
And One was true – oh! why not true to me?
Then, as a hunted deer that could not flee,
I turned upon my thoughts, and stood at bay,
Wounded and weak and panting; the cold day
Trembled, for pity of my strife and pain;   275
When, like a noon-day dawn, there shone again
Deliverance. One stood on my path who seemed
As like the glorious shape which I had dreamed,
As is the Moon, whose changes ever run
Into themselves, to the eternal Sun;   280
The cold chaste Moon, the Queen of Heaven's bright isles,
Who makes all beautiful on which she smiles;
That wandering shrine of soft yet icy flame
Which ever is transformed, yet still the same,
And warms not but illumines. Young and fair   285
As the descended Spirit of that sphere,
She hid me, as the Moon may hide the night
From its own darkness, until all was bright
Between the Heaven and Earth of my calm mind,
And, as a cloud charioted by the wind,   290
She led me to a cave in that wild place,
And sate beside me, with her downward face
Illumining my slumbers, like the Moon
Waxing and waning o'er Endymion.
And I was laid asleep, spirit and limb,   295
And all my being became bright or dim
As the Moon's image in a summer sea,
According as she smiled or frowned on me;
And there I lay, within a chaste cold bed:
Alas, I then was nor alive nor dead: –   300
For at her silver voice came Death and Life,

Unmindful each of their accustomed strife,
Masked like twin babes, a sister and a brother,
The wandering hopes of one abandoned mother,
And through the cavern without wings they flew,   305
And cried 'Away, he is not of our crew.'
I wept, and though it be a dream, I weep.

     What storms then shook the ocean of my sleep,
Blotting that Moon, whose pale and waning lips
Then shrank as in the sickness of eclipse; –   310
And how my soul was as a lampless sea,
And who was then its Tempest; and when She,
The Planet of that hour, was quenched, what frost
Crept o'er those waters, till from coast to coast
The moving billows of my being fell   315
Into a death of ice, immoveable; –
And then – what earthquakes made it gape and split,
The white Moon smiling all the while on it,
These words conceal: – if not, each word would be
The key of staunchless tears. Weep not for me!   320

     At length, into the obscure Forest came
The Vision I had sought through grief and shame.
Athwart that wintry wilderness of thorns
Flashed from her motion splendour like the Morn's,
And from her presence life was radiated   325
Through the grey earth and branches bare and dead;
So that her way was paved, and roofed above
With flowers as soft as thoughts of budding love;
And music from her respiration spread
Like light, – all other sounds were penetrated   330
By the small, still, sweet spirit of that sound,
So that the savage winds hung mute around;
And odours warm and fresh fell from her hair
Dissolving the dull cold in the frore air:
Soft as an Incarnation of the Sun,   335
When light is changed to love, this glorious One
Floated into the cavern where I lay,
And called my Spirit, and the dreaming clay
Was lifted by the thing that dreamed below
As smoke by fire, and in her beauty's glow   340

I stood, and felt the dawn of my long night
Was penetrating me with living light:
I knew it was the Vision veiled from me
So many years – that it was Emily.

 Twin Spheres of light who rule this passive Earth,   345
This world of love, this *me*; and into birth
Awaken all its fruits and flowers, and dart
Magnetic might into its central heart;
And lift its billows and its mists, and guide
By everlasting laws, each wind and tide   350
To its fit cloud, and its appointed cave;
And lull its storms, each in the craggy grave
Which was its cradle, luring to faint bowers
The armies of the rainbow-wingèd showers;
And, as those married lights, which from the towers   355
Of Heaven look forth and fold the wandering globe
In liquid sleep and splendour, as a robe;
And all their many-mingled influence blend,
If equal, yet unlike, to one sweet end; –
So ye, bright regents, with alternate sway   360
Govern my sphere of being, night and day!
Thou, not disdaining even a borrowed might;
Thou, not eclipsing a remoter light;
And, through the shadow of the seasons three,
From Spring to Autumn's sere maturity,   365
Light it into the Winter of the tomb,
Where it may ripen to a brighter bloom.
Thou too, O Comet beautiful and fierce,
Who drew the heart of this frail Universe
Towards thine own; till, wrecked in that convulsion,   370
Alternating attraction and repulsion,
Thine went astray and that was rent in twain;
Oh, float into our azure heaven again!
Be there love's folding-star at thy return;
The living Sun will feed thee from its urn   375
Of golden fire; the Moon will veil her horn
In thy last smiles; adoring Even and Morn
Will worship thee with incense of calm breath
And lights and shadows; as the star of Death
And Birth is worshipped by those sisters wild   380

Called Hope and Fear – upon the heart are piled
Their offerings, – of this sacrifice divine
A World shall be the altar.

Lady mine,
Scorn not these flowers of thought, the fading birth
Which from its heart of hearts that plant puts forth   385
Whose fruit, made perfect by thy sunny eyes,
Will be as of the trees of Paradise.

The day is come, and thou wilt fly with me.
To whatsoe'er of dull mortality
Is mine, remain a vestal sister still;   390
To the intense, the deep, the imperishable,
Not mine but me, henceforth be thou united
Even as a bride, delighting and delighted.
The hour is come: – the destined Star has risen
Which shall descend upon a vacant prison.   395
The walls are high, the gates are strong, thick set
The sentinels – but true love never yet
Was thus constrained: it overleaps all fence:
Like lightning, with invisible violence
Piercing its continents; like Heaven's free breath,   400
Which he who grasps can hold not; liker Death,
Who rides upon a thought, and makes his way
Through temple, tower, and palace, and the array
Of arms: more strength has Love than he or they;
For it can burst his charnel, and make free   405
The limbs in chains, the heart in agony,
The soul in dust and chaos.

Emily,
A ship is floating in the harbour now,
A wind is hovering o'er the mountain's brow;
There is a path on the sea's azure floor,   410
No keel has ever ploughed that path before;
The halcyons brood around the foamless isles;
The treacherous Ocean has forsworn its wiles;
The merry mariners are bold and free:
Say, my heart's sister, wilt thou sail with me?   415
Our bark is as an albatross, whose nest

Is a far Eden of the purple East;
And we between her wings will sit, while Night
And Day, and Storm, and Calm, pursue their flight,
Our ministers, along the boundless Sea,   420
Treading each other's heels, unheededly.
It is an isle under Ionian skies,
Beautiful as a wreck of Paradise,
And, for the harbours are not safe and good,
This land would have remained a solitude   425
But for some pastoral people native there,
Who from the Elysian, clear, and golden air
Draw the last spirit of the age of gold,
Simple and spirited; innocent and bold.
The blue Aegean girds this chosen home,   430
With ever-changing sound and light and foam
Kissing the sifted sands, and caverns hoar;
And all the winds wandering along the shore
Undulate with the undulating tide:
There are thick woods where sylvan forms abide;   435
And many a fountain, rivulet, and pond,
As clear as elemental diamond,
Or serene morning air; and far beyond,
The mossy tracks made by the goats and deer
(Which the rough shepherd treads but once a year,)   440
Pierce into glades, caverns, and bowers, and halls
Built round with ivy, which the waterfalls
Illumining, with sound that never fails
Accompany the noon-day nightingales;
And all the place is peopled with sweet airs;   445
The light clear element which the isle wears
Is heavy with the scent of lemon-flowers,
Which floats like mist laden with unseen showers,
And falls upon the eye-lids like faint sleep;
And from the moss violets and jonquils peep,   450
And dart their arrowy odour through the brain
Till you might faint with that delicious pain;
And every motion, odour, beam, and tone,
With that deep music is in unison,
Which is a soul within the soul – they seem   455
Like echoes of an antenatal dream. –
It is an isle 'twixt Heaven, Air, Earth, and Sea

Cradled, and hung in clear tranquillity;
Bright as that wandering Eden Lucifer,
Washed by the soft blue Oceans of young air.   460
It is a favoured place. Famine or Blight,
Pestilence, War and Earthquake, never light
Upon its mountain-peaks; blind vultures, they
Sail onward far upon their fatal way:
The wingèd storms, chaunting their thunder-psalm   465
To other lands, leave azure chasms of calm
Over this isle or weep themselves in dew,
From which its fields and woods ever renew
Their green and golden immortality.
And from the sea there rise, and from the sky   470
There fall, clear exhalations, soft and bright,
Veil after veil, each hiding some delight,
Which Sun or Moon or zephyr draw aside,
Till the isle's beauty, like a naked bride
Glowing at once with love and loveliness,   475
Blushes and trembles at its own excess:
Yet, like a buried lamp, a Soul no less
Burns in the heart of this delicious isle,
An atom of th'Eternal, whose own smile
Unfolds itself, and may be felt not seen   480
O'er the grey rocks, blue waves, and forests green,
Filling their bare and void interstices. –
But the chief marvel of the wilderness
Is a lone dwelling, built by whom or how
None of the rustic island-people know: 485
'Tis not a tower of strength, though with its height
It overtops the woods; but, for delight,
Some wise and tender Ocean-King, ere crime
Had been invented, in the world's young prime,
Reared it, a wonder of that simple time,   490
An envy of the isles, a pleasure-house
Made sacred to his sister and his spouse.
It scarce seems now a wreck of human art,
But as it were Titanic; in the heart
Of Earth having assumed its form, then grown   495
Out of the mountain, from the living stone,
Lifting itself in caverns light and high:
For all the antique and learnèd imagery

Has been erased, and in the place of it
The ivy and the wild-vine interknit   500
The volumes of their many-twining stems;
Parasite flowers illume with dewy gems
The lampless halls, and when they fade, the sky
Peeps through their winter-woof of tracery
With Moon-light patches, or star atoms keen,   505
Or fragments of the day's intense serene, –
Working mosaic on their Parian floors.
And, day and night, aloof, from the high towers
And terraces, the Earth and Ocean seem
To sleep in one another's arms, and dream   510
Of waves, flowers, clouds, woods, rocks, and all that we
Read in their smiles, and call reality.

   This isle and house are mine, and I have vowed
Thee to be lady of the solitude. –
And I have fitted up some chambers there   515
Looking towards the golden Eastern air,
And level with the living winds, which flow
Like waves above the living waves below. –
I have sent books and music there, and all
Those instruments with which high spirits call   520
The future from its cradle, and the past
Out of its grave, and make the present last
In thoughts and joys which sleep, but cannot die,
Folded within their own eternity.
Our simple life wants little, and true taste   525
Hires not the pale drudge Luxury, to waste
The scene it would adorn, and therefore still,
Nature, with all her children, haunts the hill.
The ring-dove, in the embowering ivy, yet
Keeps up her love-lament, and the owls flit   530
Round the evening tower, and the young stars glance
Between the quick bats in their twilight dance;
The spotted deer bask in the fresh moonlight
Before our gate, and the slow, silent night
Is measured by the pants of their calm sleep.   535
Be this our home in life, and when years heap
Their withered hours, like leaves, on our decay,
Let us become the over-hanging day,

The living soul of this Elysian isle,
Conscious, inseparable, one. Meanwhile　　　　　　　540
We two will rise, and sit, and walk together,
Under the roof of blue Ionian weather,
And wander in the meadows, or ascend
The mossy mountains, where the blue heavens bend
With lightest winds, to touch their paramour;　　　　545
Or linger, where the pebble-paven shore,
Under the quick, faint kisses of the sea
Trembles and sparkles as with ecstasy, –
Possessing and possessed by all that is
Within that calm circumference of bliss,　　　　　　550
And by each other, till to love and live
Be one: – or, at the noontide hour, arrive
Where some old cavern hoar seems yet to keep
The moonlight of the expired night asleep,
Through which the awakened day can never peep;　　555
A veil for our seclusion, close as Night's,
Where secure sleep may kill thine innocent lights;
Sleep, the fresh dew of languid love, the rain
Whose drops quench kisses till they burn again.
And we will talk, until thought's melody　　　　　　560
Become too sweet for utterance, and it die
In words, to live again in looks, which dart
With thrilling tone into the voiceless heart,
Harmonizing silence without a sound.
Our breath shall intermix, our bosoms bound,　　　565
And our veins beat together; and our lips
With other eloquence than words, eclipse
The soul that burns between them and the wells
Which boil under our being's inmost cells,
The fountains of our deepest life, shall be　　　　　570
Confused in passion's golden purity,
As mountain-springs under the morning Sun.
We shall become the same, we shall be one
Spirit within two frames, oh! wherefore two?
One passion in twin-hearts, which grows and grew,　575
Till, like two meteors of expanding flame,
Those spheres instinct with it become the same,
Touch, mingle, are transfigured; ever still
Burning, yet ever inconsumable:

In one another's substance finding food,   580
Like flames too pure and light and unimbued
To nourish their bright lives with baser prey,
Which point to Heaven and cannot pass away:
One hope within two wills, one will beneath
Two overshadowing minds, one life, one death,   585
One Heaven, one Hell, one immortality,
And one annihilation. Woe is me!
The wingèd words on which my soul would pierce
Into the height of love's rare Universe,
Are chains of lead around its flight of fire. –   590
I pant, I sink, I tremble, I expire!

   Weak Verses, go, kneel at your Sovereign's feet,
And say: – 'We are the masters of thy slave;
'What wouldest thou with us and ours and thine?'
Then call your sisters from Oblivion's cave,   595
All singing loud: 'Love's very pain is sweet,
But its reward is in the world divine
Which, if not here, it builds beyond the grave.'
So shall ye live when I am there. Then haste
Over the hearts of men, until ye meet   600
Marina, Vanna, Primus, and the rest,
And bid them love each other and be blest:
And leave the troop which errs, and which reproves,
And come and be my guest, – for I am Love's.

41   A DEFENCE OF POETRY

According to one mode of regarding those two classes of
mental action, which are called Reason and Imagination,
the former may be considered as mind contemplating the
relations borne by one thought to another, however pro-
duced; and the latter as mind acting upon those thoughts so   5
as to colour them with its own light, and composing from
them as from elements, other thoughts, each containing
within itself the principle of its own integrity. The one is the
τὸ ποιειν or the principle of synthesis, and has for its objects
those forms which are common to universal nature and   10

existence itself; the other is the τὸ λογιζειν or principle of analysis, and its action regards the relations of things, simply as relations; considering thoughts, not in their integral unity, but as the algebraical representations which conduct to certain general results. Reason is the enumeration of quantities already known; Imagination the perception of the value of those quantities, both separately and as a whole. Reason respects the differences, and Imagination the similitudes of things. Reason is to Imagination as the instrument to the agent, as the body to the spirit, as the shadow to the substance.

Poetry, in a general sense, may be defined to be 'the expression of the Imagination': and poetry is connate with the origin of man. Man is an instrument over which a series of external and internal impressions are driven, like the alternations of an ever-changing wind over an Aeolian lyre; which move it, by their motion, to ever-changing melody. But there is a principle within the human being and perhaps within all sentient beings, which acts otherwise than in the lyre, and produces not melody alone, but harmony, by an internal adjustment of the sounds or motions thus excited to the impressions which excite them. It is as if the lyre could accommodate its chords to the motions of that which strikes them, in a determined proportion of sound; even as the musician can accommodate his voice to the sound of the lyre. A child at play by itself will express its delight by its voice and motions; and every inflection of tone and every gesture will bear exact relation to a corresponding antitype in the pleasurable impressions which awakened it; it will be the reflected image of that impression; and as the lyre trembles and sounds after the wind has died away, so the child seeks, by prolonging in its voice and motions the duration of the effect, to prolong also a consciousness of the cause. In relation to the objects which delight a child, these expressions are, what Poetry is to higher objects. The savage (for the savage is to ages what the child is to years) expresses the emotions produced in him by surrounding objects in a similar manner; and language and gesture together with plastic or pictorial imitation, become the image of the combined effect of those objects and of his apprehension of them. Man in society, with all his passions and his pleasures, next becomes the object of the passions and pleasures of man; an additional class of emotions produces an augmented treasure of expressions; and language, gesture, and the imitative arts become at once the representation and the medium, the pencil and the picture, the chisel and the statue, the chord and the harmony. The social sympathies, or those laws from which as from its elements society results, begin to develop themselves from the moment that two human beings coexist; the future is contained within the present as the plant within the seed; and equality, diversity, unity, contrast, mutual dependence, become the principles alone capable of affording the motives according to which the will of a social being is determined to action, inasmuch as he is social; and constitute pleasure in sensation, virtue in sentiment, beauty in art, truth in reasoning, and love in the intercourse of kind. Hence men, even in the infancy of society, observe a certain order in their words and actions, distinct from that of the objects and the impressions represented by them, all expression being subject to the laws of that from which it proceeds. But let us dismiss those more general considerations which might involve an enquiry into the principles of society itself, and restrict our view to the manner in which the imagination is expressed upon its forms.

In the youth of the world, men dance and sing and imitate natural objects, observing in these actions, as in all others, a certain rhythm or order. And, although all men observe a similar, they observe not the same order, in the motions of the dance, in the melody of the song, in the combinations of language, in the series of their imitations of natural objects. For there is a certain order or rhythm belonging to each of these classes of mimetic representation, from which the hearer and the spectator receive an intenser and a purer pleasure than from any other: the sense of an approximation to this order has been called taste, by modern writers. Every man, in the infancy of art, observes an order which approximates more or less closely to that from which this highest delight results: but the diversity is not sufficiently marked, as that its gradations should be sensible, except in those instances where the predominance of this faculty of approximation to the beautiful (for so we may be permitted to name the relation between this highest pleasure and its cause) is very great. Those in whom it exists in excess are poets, in the most universal sense of the word; and the pleasure resulting from the manner in which they express the influence of society or nature upon their own minds, communicates itself to others, and gathers a sort of reduplication from that community. Their language is vitally metaphorical; that is, it marks the before unapprehended relations of things, and perpetuates their apprehension, until the words which represent them become through time signs for portions or classes of thoughts, instead of pictures of integral thoughts; and then, if no new poets should arise to create afresh the associations which have been thus disorganized, language will be dead to all the nobler purposes of human intercourse. These similitudes or relations are finely said by Lord Bacon to be 'the same footsteps of nature impressed upon the various subjects of the world'[1] – and he considers the faculty which perceives them as the storehouse of axioms common to all knowledge. In the infancy of society every author is necessarily a poet, because language itself is poetry; and to be a poet is to apprehend the true and the beautiful, in a word the good which exists in the relation, subsisting, first between existence and perception, and secondly between perception and expression. Every original language near to its source is in itself the chaos of a cyclic poem: the copiousness of lexicography and the distinctions of grammar are the works of a later age, and are merely the catalogue and the form of the creations of Poetry.

But Poets, or those who imagine and express this indestructible order, are not only the authors of language and of music, of the dance and architecture and statuary and painting; they are the institutors of laws and the founders of civil society and the inventors of the arts of life and the teachers, who draw into a certain propinquity with the beautiful and the true that partial apprehension of the agencies of the invisible world which is called religion. Hence all original religions are allegorical, or susceptible of allegory, and like Janus have a double face of false and true. Poets, according to the circumstances of the age and nation

---

[1] *The Advancement of Learning*, Book I, chapter iii.

in which they appeared, were called in the earlier epochs of
the world legislators or prophets: a poet essentially com-
prises and unites both these characters. For he not only
beholds intensely the present as it is, and discovers those 135
laws according to which present things ought to be ordered,
but he beholds the future in the present, and his thoughts
are the germs of the flower and the fruit of latest time. Not
that I assert poets to be prophets in the gross sense of the
word, or that they can foretell the form as surely as they 140
foreknow the spirit of events: such is the pretence of
superstition which would make poetry an attribute of
prophecy, rather than prophecy an attribute of poetry. A
Poet participates in the eternal, the infinite and the one; as
far as relates to his conceptions, time and place and number 145
are not. The grammatical forms which express the moods
of time, and the difference of persons and the distinction of
place are convertible with respect to the highest poetry
without injuring it as poetry, and the choruses of Aeschylus,
and the Book of Job, and Dante's *Paradise* would afford 150
more than any other writings examples of this fact, if the
limits of this essay did not forbid citation. The creations of
sculpture, painting and music are illustrations still more
decisive.

Language, colour, form and religious and civil habits of 155
action are all the instruments and the materials of poetry;
they may all be called poetry by that figure of speech which
considers the effect as a synonym of the cause. But poetry in
a more restricted sense expresses those arrangements of
language, and especially metrical language, which are cre- 160
ated by that imperial faculty whose throne is curtained
within the invisible nature of man. And this springs from
the nature itself of language, which is a more direct represen-
tation of the actions and passions of our internal being, and
is susceptible of more various and delicate combinations 165
than colour, form or motion, and is more plastic and
obedient to the control of that faculty of which it is the
creation. For language is arbitrarily produced by the Imagin-
ation and has relation to thoughts alone; but all other
materials, instruments and conditions of art have relations 170
among each other, which limit and interpose between
conception and expression. The former is as a mirror which

reflects, the latter as a cloud which enfeebles, the light of which both are mediums of communication. Hence the fame of sculptors, painters and musicians, although the intrinsic 175 powers of the great masters of these arts, may yield in no degree to that of those who have employed language as the hieroglyphic of their thoughts, has never equalled that of poets in the restricted sense of the term; as two performers of equal skill will produce unequal effects from a guitar and 180 a harp. The fame of legislators and founders of religions, so long as their institutions last, alone seems to exceed that of poets in the restricted sense: but it can scarcely be a question whether, if we deduct the celebrity which their flattery of the gross opinions of the vulgar usually conciliates, together 185 with that which belonged to them in their higher character of poets, any excess will remain.

We have thus circumscribed the word Poetry within the limits of that art which is the most familiar and the most perfect expression of the faculty itself. It is necessary how- 190 ever to make the circle still narrower, and to determine the distinction between measured and unmeasured language; for the popular division into prose and verse, is inadmissible in accurate philosophy.

Sounds as well as thoughts have relation both between 195 each other and towards that which they represent; and a perception of the order of those relations has always been found connected with a perception of the order of the relations of thoughts. Hence the language of poets has ever affected a certain uniform and harmonious recurrence of 200 sound, without which it were not poetry, and which is scarcely less indispensable to the communication of its influence, than the words themselves without reference to that peculiar order. Hence the vanity of translation; it were as wise to cast a violet into a crucible that you might 205 discover the formal principle of its colour and odour, as seek to transfuse from one language into another the creations of a poet. The plant must spring again from its seed or it will bear no flower – and this is the burthen of the curse of Babel.   210

An observation of the regular mode of the recurrence of this harmony in the language of poetical minds, together with its relation to music, produced metre, or a certain

system of traditional forms of harmony and language. Yet
it is by no means essential that a poet should accommodate 215
his language to this traditional form, so that the harmony
which is its spirit, be observed. The practice is indeed
convenient and popular and to be preferred, especially in
such composition as includes much action: but every great
Poet must inevitably innovate upon the example of his 220
predecessors in the exact structure of his peculiar versifica-
tion. The distinction between poets and prose-writers is a
vulgar error. The distinction between philosophers and
poets has been anticipated. Plato was essentially a poet –
the truth and splendour of his imagery and the melody of 225
his language [are] the most intense that it is possible to
conceive: he rejected the measure of the epic, dramatic and
lyrical forms, because he sought to kindle a harmony in
thoughts divested of shape and action, and he forbore to
invent any regular plan of rhythm which would include, 230
under determinate forms, the varied pauses of his style.
Cicero sought to imitate the cadence of his periods but with
little success. Lord Bacon was a poet.[2] His language has a
sweet and majestic rhythm, which satisfies the sense, no less
than the almost superhuman wisdom of his philosophy 235
satisfies the intellect; it is a strain which distends, and then
bursts the circumference of the reader's mind, and pours
itself forth together with it into the universal element with
which it has perpetual sympathy. – All the authors of
revolutions in opinion are not only necessarily poets as they 240
are inventors, nor even as their words unveil the permanent
analogy of things by images which participate in the life of
truth; but as their periods are harmonious and rhythmical
and contain in themselves the elements of verse, being the
echo of the eternal music. Nor are those supreme poets, who 245
have employed traditional forms of rhythm on account of
the form and action of their subjects, less capable of
perceiving and teaching the truth of things, than those who
have omitted that form. Shakespeare, Dante and Milton (to
confine ourselves to modern writers) are philosophers of the 250
very loftiest power.

A Poem is the very image of life expressed in its eternal

[2] See the *Filum Labyrinthi*, and the *Essay on Death* particularly.

truth. There is this difference between a story and a poem, that a story is a catalogue of detached facts, which have no other bond of connection than time, place, circumstance, cause and effect; the other is the creation of actions according to the unchangeable forms of human nature, as existing in the mind of the creator, which is itself the image of all other minds. The one is partial, and applies only to a definite period of time, and a certain combination of events which can never again recur; the other is universal, and contains within itself the germ of a relation to whatever motives or actions have place in the possible varieties of human nature. Time, which destroys the beauty and the use of the story of particular facts, stripped of the poetry which should invest them, augments that of Poetry; and for ever develops new and wonderful applications of the eternal truth which it contains. Hence epitomes have been called the moths of just history; they eat out the poetry of it. The story of particular facts is as a mirror which obscures and distorts that which should be beautiful; Poetry is a mirror which makes beautiful that which is distorted.

The parts of a composition may be poetical, without the composition as a whole being a poem. A single sentence may be considered as a whole though it may be found in the midst of a series of unassimilated portions; a single word, even, may be a spark of inextinguishable thought. And thus all the great historians, Herodotus, Plutarch, Livy, were poets; and although the plan of these writers, especially that of Livy, constrained them from developing this faculty in its highest degree, they made copious and ample amends for their subjection, by filling all the interstices of their subjects with living images.

Having determined what is poetry, and who are poets, let us proceed to estimate its effects upon society.

Poetry is ever accompanied with pleasure: all spirits on which it falls, open themselves to receive the wisdom which is mingled with its delight. In the infancy of the world neither poets themselves nor their auditors are fully aware of the excellence of poetry: for it acts in a divine and unapprehended manner, beyond and above consciousness: and it is reserved for future generations to contemplate and measure the mighty cause and effect in all the strength

and splendour of their union. Even in modern times, no
living poet ever arrived at the fullness of his fame; the jury 295
which sits in judgement upon a poet, belonging as he does
to all time, must be composed of his peers: it must be
impanelled by Time from the selectest of the wise of many
generations.

A Poet is a nightingale who sits in darkness, and sings to 300
cheer its own solitude with sweet sounds; his auditors are as
men entranced by the melody of an unseen musician, who
feel that they are moved and softened, yet know not whence
or why. The poems of Homer and his contemporaries were
the delight of infant Greece; they were the 305
elements of that social system which is the column upon
which all succeeding civilization has reposed. Homer
embodied the ideal perfection of his age in human character;
nor can we doubt that those who read his verses were
awakened to an ambition of becoming like to Achilles, 310
Hector and Ulysses: the truth and beauty of friendship,
patriotism and perserving devotion to an object, were
unveiled to their depths in these immortal creations: the
sentiments of the auditors must have been refined and
enlarged by a sympathy with such great and lovely imper- 315
sonations, until from admiring they imitated, and from
imitation they identified themselves with the objects of their
admiration. Nor let it be objected that these characters are
remote from moral perfection, and that they can by no
means be considered as edifying patterns for general imita- 320
tion. Every epoch under names more or less specious has
deified its peculiar errors; Revenge is the naked Idol of the
worship of a semi-barbarous age; and self-deceit is the veiled
Image of unknown evil before which luxury and satiety lie
prostrate. But a poet considers the vices of his 325
contemporaries as the temporary dress in which his cre-
ations must be arrayed, and which cover without concealing
the eternal proportions of their beauty. An epic or dramatic
personage is understood to wear them around his soul, as
he may the ancient armour or the modern uniform around 330
his body; whilst it is easy to conceive a dress more graceful
than either. The beauty of the internal nature cannot be so
far concealed by its accidental vesture, but that the spirit of
its form shall communicate itself to the very disguise, and

indicate the shape it hides from the manner in which it is 335
worn. A majestic form and graceful motions will express
themselves through the most barbarous and tasteless cos-
tume. Few poets of the highest class have chosen to exhibit
the beauty of their conceptions in its naked truth and
splendour; and it is doubtful whether the alloy of costume, 340
habit etc., be not necessary to temper this planetary music
for mortal ears.

The whole objection however of the immorality of poetry
rests upon a misconception of the manner in which poetry
acts to produce the moral improvement of man. Ethical 345
science arranges the elements which poetry has created, and
propounds schemes and proposes examples of civil and
domestic life: nor is it for want of admirable doctrines that
men hate, and despise, and censure, and deceive, and
subjugate one another. But Poetry acts in another and a 350
diviner manner. It awakens and enlarges the mind itself by
rendering it the receptacle of a thousand unapprehended
combinations of thought. Poetry lifts the veil from the
hidden beauty of the world; it makes familiar objects be as
if they were not familiar; it reproduces all that it represents, 355
and the impersonations clothed in its Elysian light stand
thenceforward in the minds of those who have once contem-
plated them, as memorials of that gentle and exalted content
which extends itself over all thoughts and actions with
which it coexists. The great secret of morals is Love; or a 360
going out of our own nature, and an identification of
ourselves with the beautiful which exists in thought, action
or person, not our own. A man to be greatly good, must
imagine intensely and comprehensively; he must put himself
in the place of another and of many others; the pains and 365
pleasures of his species must become his own. The great
instrument of moral good is the imagination: and poetry
administers to the effect by acting upon the cause. Poetry
enlarges the circumference of the imagination by replenish-
ing it with thoughts of ever new delight, which have the 370
power of attracting and assimilating to their own nature all
other thoughts, and which form new intervals and interstices
whose void for ever craves fresh food. Poetry strengthens
the faculty which is the organ of the moral nature of man,
in the same manner as exercise strengthens a limb. A poet, 375

therefore, would do ill to embody his own conceptions of right and wrong, which are usually those of his place and time, in his poetical creations, which participate in neither. By this assumption of the inferior office of interpreting the effect, in which perhaps after all he might acquit himself but imperfectly, he would resign a glory in a participation in the cause. There was little danger that Homer or any of the eternal Poets, should have so far misunderstood themselves as to have abdicated this throne of their widest dominion. Those in whom the poetical faculty, though great is less intense, as Euripides, Lucan, Tasso, Spenser, have frequently affected a moral aim; and the effect of their poetry is diminished in exact proportion to the degree in which they compel us to advert to this purpose.

Homer and the cyclic poets were followed at a certain interval by the dramatic and lyrical Poets of Athens, who flourished contemporaneously with all that is most perfect in the kindred expressions of the poetical faculty; architecture, painting, music, the dance, sculpture, philosophy, and we may add, the forms of civil life. For although the scheme of Athenian society was deformed by many imperfections which the poetry existing in Chivalry and Christianity has erased from the habits and institutions of modern Europe; yet never at any other period has so much energy, beauty and virtue been developed; never was blind strength and stubborn form so disciplined and rendered subject to the will of man, or that will less repugnant to the dictates of the beautiful and the true, as during the century which preceded the death of Socrates. Of no other epoch in the history of our species have we records and fragments stamped so visibly with the image of the divinity in man. But it is Poetry alone, in form, in action or in language, which has rendered this epoch memorable above all others, and the storehouse of examples to everlasting time. For written poetry existed at that epoch simultaneously with the other arts, and it is an idle enquiry to demand which gave and which received the light, which all as from a common focus have scattered over the darkest periods of succeeding time. We know no more of cause and effect than a constant conjunction of events: Poetry is ever found to coexist with whatever other arts contribute to the happiness and perfection of man. I appeal to

what has already been established to distinguish between
the cause and the effect.

It was at the period here adverted to, that the Drama had
its birth; and however a succeeding writer may have 420
equalled or surpassed those few great specimens of the
Athenian drama which have been preserved to us, it is
indisputable that the art itself never was understood or
practised according to the true philosophy of it, as at
Athens. For the Athenians employed language and action, 425
music, painting, the dance, and religious institution to
produce a common effect in the representation of the highest
idealisms of passion and of power; each division in the art
was made perfect in its kind by artists of the most consum-
mate skill, and was disciplined into a beautiful proportion 430
and unity one towards the other. On the modern stage a
few only of the elements capable of expressing the image of
the poet's conception are employed at once. We have
tragedy without music and dancing; and music and dancing
without the highest impersonation of which they are the fit 435
accompaniment, and both without religion and solemnity;
religious institution has indeed been usually banished from
the stage. Our system of divesting the actor's face of a mask,
on which the many expressions appropriated to his dramatic
character might be moulded into one permanent and 440
unchanging expression, is favourable only to a partial and
inharmonious effect; it is fit for nothing but a monologue,
where all the attention may be directed to some great master
of ideal mimicry. The modern practice of blending comedy
with tragedy, though liable to great abuse in point of 445
practice, is undoubtedly an extension of the dramatic circle,
but the comedy should be as in *King Lear*, universal, ideal
and sublime. It is perhaps the intervention of this principle
which determines the balance in favour of *King Lear* against
the *Oedipus Tyrannus* or the *Agamemnon* or, if you will, 450
the trilogies with which they are connected; unless the
intense power of the choral poetry, especially that of the
latter, should be considered as restoring the equilibrium.
King Lear, if it can sustain this comparison, may be judged
to be the most perfect specimen of the dramatic art existing 455
in the world; in spite of the narrow conditions to which the
poet was subjected by the ignorance of the philosophy of

the Drama which has prevailed in modern Europe. Calderón
in his religious *autos* has attempted to fulfil some of the
high conditions of dramatic representation neglected by 460
Shakespeare; such as the establishing a relation between the
drama and religion, and the accommodating them to music
and dancing; but he omits the observation of conditions still
more important, and more is lost than gained by a substitu-
tion of the rigidly-defined and ever-repeated idealisms of a 465
distorted superstition for the living impersonations of the
truth of human passion.

But we digress. – The Author of the *Four Ages of Poetry*
has prudently omitted to dispute on the effect of the Drama
upon life and manners. For, if I know the knight by the 470
devise of his shield, I have only to inscribe *Philoctetes* or
Agamemnon or *Othello* upon mine to put to flight the Giant
Sophisms which have enchanted him, as the mirror of
intolerable light, though on the arm of one of the weakest
of the Paladins, could blind and scatter whole armies of 475
necromancers and pagans. The connection of scenic exhi-
bitions with the improvement or corruption of the manners
of men, has been universally recognized: in other words, the
presence or absence of poetry in its most perfect and
universal form, has been found to be connected with good 480
and evil in conduct or habit. The corruption which has been
imputed to the drama as an effect begins, when the poetry
employed in its constitution, ends; I appeal to the history of
manners whether the periods of the growth of the one and
the decline of the other have not corresponded with an 485
exactness equal to any other example of moral cause and
effect.

The drama at Athens or wheresoever else it may have
approached to its perfection, ever coexisted with the moral
and intellectual greatness of the age. The tragedies of the 490
Athenian poets are as mirrors in which the spectator beholds
himself, under a thin disguise of circumstance, stripped of
all but that ideal perfection and energy which every one
feels to be the internal type of all that he loves, admires and
would become. The imagination is enlarged by a sympathy 495
with pains and passions so mighty that they distend in their
conception the capacity of that by which they are conceived;
the good affections are strengthened by pity, indignation,

terror and sorrow; and an exalted calm is prolonged from
the satiety of this high exercise of them into the tumult of 500
familiar life; even crime is disarmed of half its horror and
all its contagion by being represented as the fatal conse-
quence of the unfathomable agencies of nature; error is thus
divested of its wilfulness; men can no longer cherish it as
the creature of their choice. In a drama of the highest order 505
there is little food for censure or hatred: it teaches rather
self-knowledge and self-respect. Neither the eye or the mind
can see itself unless reflected upon that which it resembles.
The drama, so long as it continues to express poetry, is as a
prismatic and many-sided mirror, which collects the bright- 510
est rays of human nature and divides and reproduces them
from the simplicity of these elementary forms; and touches
them with majesty and beauty, and multiplies all that it
reflects, and endows it with the power of propagating its
like wherever it may fall.   515

But in periods of the decay of social life, the drama
sympathizes with that decay. Tragedy becomes a cold
imitation of the form of the great masterpieces of antiquity,
divested of all harmonious accompaniment of the kindred
arts; and often the very form misunderstood: or a weak 520
attempt to teach certain doctrines, which the writer consid-
ers as moral truths; and which are usually no more than
specious flatteries of some gross vice or weakness with
which the author in common with his auditors are infected.
Hence what has been called the classical and the domestic 525
drama. Addison's *Cato* is a specimen of the one, and would
it were not superfluous to cite examples of the other! To
such purposes poetry cannot be made subservient. Poetry is
a sword of lightning ever unsheathed, which consumes the
scabbard that would contain it. And thus we observe that 530
all dramatic writings of this nature are unimaginative in a
singular degree; they affect sentiment and passion which
divested of imagination are other names for caprice and
appetite. The period in our own history of the grossest
degradation of the drama is the reign of Charles II when all 535
forms in which poetry had been accustomed to be expressed
became hymns to the triumph of kingly power over liberty
and virtue. Milton stood alone illuminating an age unwor-
thy of him. At such periods the calculating principle per-

vades all the forms of dramatic exhibition, and poetry ceases 540
to be expressed upon them. Comedy loses its ideal univer-
sality: wit succeeds to humour; we laugh from self-compla-
cency and triumph instead of pleasure; malignity, sarcasm
and contempt succeed to sympathetic merriment; we hardly
laugh, but we smile. Obscenity, which is ever blasphemy 545
against the divine beauty in life, becomes, from the very veil
which it assumes, more active if less disgusting: it is a
monster for which the corruption of society for ever brings
forth new food, which it devours in secret.

The Drama being that form under which a greater number 550
of modes of expression of poetry are susceptible of being
combined than any other, the connection of poetry and
social good is more observable in the drama than in
whatever other form. And it is indisputable, that the highest
perfection of human society has ever corresponded with the 555
highest dramatic excellence: and that the corruption or the
extinction of the drama in a nation where it has once
flourished is a mark of a corruption of manners, and an
extinction of the energies which sustain the soul of social
life. But, as Machiavelli says of political institution, that life 560
may be preserved and renewed, if men should arise capable
of bringing back the drama to its principles. And this is true
with respect to poetry in its most extended sense: all
language, institution and form require not only to be
produced but to be sustained: the office and character of a 565
poet participates in the divine nature as regards providence
no less than as regards creation.

Civil war, the spoils of Asia, and the fatal predominance
first of the Macedonian, and then of the Roman arms were
so many symbols of the extinction or suspension of the 570
creative faculty in Greece. The bucolic writers who found
patronage under the lettered tyrants of Sicily and Egypt
were the latest representatives of its most glorious reign.
Their poetry is intensely melodious; like the odour of the
tuberose it overcomes and sickens the spirit with excess of 575
sweetness; whilst the poetry of the preceding age was as a
meadow-gale of June which mingles the fragrance of all the
flowers of the field and adds a quickening and harmonizing
spirit of its own which endows the sense with a power of
sustaining its extreme delight. The bucolic and erotic deli- 580

cacy in written poetry is correlative with that softness in
statuary, music, and the kindred arts, and even in manners
and institutions which distinguished the epoch to which we
now refer. Nor is it the poetical faculty itself, or any mis-
application of it, to which this want of harmony is to be 585
imputed. An equal sensibility to the influence of the senses
and the affections is to be found in the writings of Homer
and Sophocles: the former especially has clothed sensual and
pathetic images with irresistible attractions. Their superior-
ity over these succeeding writers consists in the presence of 590
those thoughts which belong to the inner faculties of our
nature, not in the absence of those which are connected
with the external: their incomparable perfection consists in
a harmony of the union of all. It is not what the erotic poets
have, but what they have not, in which their imperfection 595
consists. It is not inasmuch as they were Poets, but inasmuch
as they were not Poets, that they can be considered with any
plausibility as connected with the corruption of their age.
Had that corruption availed so as to extinguish in them the
sensibility to pleasure, passion and natural scenery, which is 600
imputed to them as an imperfection, the last triumph of evil
would have been achieved. For the end of social corruption
is to destroy all sensibility to pleasure; and therefore it is
corruption. It begins at the imagination and the intellect as
at the core, and distributes itself thence as a paralyzing 605
venom, through the affections into the very appetites, until
all become a torpid mass in which sense hardly survives. At
the approach of such a period, Poetry ever addresses itself
to those faculties which are the last to be destroyed, and its
voice is heard, like the footsteps of Astraea departing from 610
the world. Poetry ever communicates all the pleasure which
men are capable of receiving: it is ever still the light of life;
the source of whatever of beautiful or generous or true can
have place in an evil time. It will readily be confessed that
those among the luxurious citizens of Syracuse and Alex- 615
andria who were delighted with the poems of Theocritus,
were less cold, cruel and sensual than the remnant of their
tribe. But Corruption must utterly have destroyed the fabric
of human society, before Poetry can ever cease. The sacred
links of that chain have never been entirely disjoined, which 620
descending through the minds of many men is attached to

those great minds whence as from a magnet the invisible effluence is sent forth which at once connects, animates and sustains the life of all. It is the faculty which contains within itself the seeds at once of its own and of social renovation. 625 And let us not circumscribe the effects of the bucolic and erotic poetry within the limits of the sensibility of those to whom it was addressed. They may have perceived the beauty of these immortal compositions, simply as fragments and isolated portions: those who are more finely organized, or 630 born in a happier age, may recognize them as episodes of that great poem, which all poets, like the co-operating thoughts of one great mind, have built up since the beginning of the world.

The same revolutions within a narrower sphere had place 635 in ancient Rome: but the actions and forms of its social life never seem to have been perfectly saturated with the poetical element. The Romans appear to have considered the Greeks as the selectest treasuries of the selectest forms of manners and of nature and to have abstained from creating in 640 measured language, sculpture, music or architecture, any thing which might bear a particular relation to their own condition whilst it should bear a general one to the universal constitution of the world. But we judge from partial evidence, and we judge perhaps partially. Ennius, Varro, 645 Pacuvius and Accius, all great poets, have been lost. Lucretius is in the highest, and Virgil in a very high sense, a creator. The chosen delicacy of the expressions of the latter are as a mist of light which conceal from us the intense and exceeding truth of his conceptions of nature. Livy is instinct 650 with poetry. Yet Horace, Catullus, Ovid, and generally the other great writers of the Virgilian age, saw man and nature in the mirror of Greece. The institutions also and the religion of Rome were less poetical than those of Greece, as the shadow is less vivid than the substance. Hence Poetry in 655 Rome seemed to follow rather than accompany the perfection of political and domestic society. The true Poetry of Rome lived in its institutions, for whatever of beautiful, true and majestic they contained could have sprung only from the faculty which creates the order in which they consist. 660 The life of Camillus; the death of Regulus; the expectation of the senators in their godlike state of the victorious Gauls;

the refusal of the Republic to make peace with Hannibal
after the battle of Cannae, were not the consequences of a
refined calculation of the probable personal advantage to 665
result from such a rhythm and order in the shows of life, to
those who were at once the poets and the actors of these
immortal dramas. The imagination beholding the beauty of
this order, created it out of itself according to its own idea:
the consequence was empire, and the reward everliving 670
fame. These things are not the less poetry, *quia carent vate
sacro*. They are the episodes of that cyclic poem written by
Time upon the memories of men. The Past, like an inspired
rhapsodist, fills the theatre of everlasting generations with
its harmony.   675

At length the ancient system of religion and manners had
fulfilled the circle of its revolutions. And the world would
have fallen into utter anarchy and darkness but that there
were found poets among the authors of the Christian and
Chivalric systems of manners and religion, who created 680
forms of opinion and action never before conceived; which,
copied into the imaginations of men, became as generals to
the bewildered armies of their thoughts. It is foreign to the
present purpose to touch upon the evil produced by these
systems: except that we protest, on the ground of the 685
principles already established, that no portion of it can be
attributed to the poetry they contain.

It is probable that the poetry of Moses, Job, David,
Solomon and Isaiah had produced a great effect upon the
mind of Jesus and his disciples. The scattered fragments 690
preserved to us by the biographers of this extraordinary
person are all instinct with the most vivid poetry. But his
doctrines seem to have been quickly distorted. At a certain
period after the prevalence of a system of opinions founded
upon those promulgated by him, the three forms into which 695
Plato had distributed the faculties of mind underwent a sort
of apotheosis, and became the object of the worship of the
civilized world. Here it is to be confessed that 'Light seems
to thicken', and

>   the crow makes wing to the rooky wood,   700
>   Good things of day begin to droop and drowse,
>   And night's black agents to their preys do rouse.

But mark how beautiful an order has sprung from the dust and blood of this fierce chaos! how the World, as from a resurrection, balancing itself on the golden wings of knowl- 705 edge and of hope, has reassumed its yet unwearied flight into the Heaven of time! Listen to the music, unheard by outward ears, which is as a ceaseless and invisible wind nourishing its everlasting course with strength and swiftness.

The poetry in the doctrines of Jesus Christ, and the 710 mythology and institutions of the Celtic conquerors of the Roman Empire, out-lived the darkness and the convulsions connected with their growth and victory, and blended themselves into a new fabric of manners and opinion. It is an error to impute the ignorance of the dark ages to the 715 Christian doctrines or the predominance of the Celtic nations. Whatever of evil their agencies may have contained sprung from the extinction of the poetical principle, con- nected with the progress of despotism and superstition. Men, from causes too intricate to be here discussed, had 720 become insensible and selfish: their own will had become feeble, and yet they were its slaves, and thence the slaves of the will of others; lust, fear, avarice, cruelty and fraud characterised a race amongst whom no one was to be found capable of *creating* in form, language or institution. The 725 moral anomalies of such a state of society are not justly to be charged upon any class of events immediately connected with them, and those events are most entitled to our approbation which could dissolve it most expeditiously. It is unfortunate for those who cannot distinguish words from 730 thoughts that many of these anomalies have been incorpo- rated into our popular religion.

It was not until the eleventh century that the effects of the poetry of the Christian and the Chivalric systems began to manifest themselves. The principle of equality had been 735 discovered and applied by Plato in his *Republic*, as the theoretical rule of the mode in which the materials of pleasure and of power produced by the common skill and labour of human beings ought to be distributed among them. The limitations of this rule were asserted by him to 740 be determined only by the sensibility of each, or the utility to result to all. Plato, following the doctrines of Timaeus and Pythagoras, taught also a moral and intellectual system

of doctrine comprehending at once the past, the present and
the future condition of man. Jesus Christ divulged the sacred 745
and eternal truths contained in these views to mankind, and
Christianity, in its abstract purity, became the exoteric
expression of the esoteric doctrines of the poetry and
wisdom of antiquity. The incorporation of the Celtic nations
with the exhausted population of the South, impressed upon 750
it the figure of the poetry existing in their mythology and
institutions. The result was a sum of the action and reaction
of all the causes included in it; for it may be assumed as a
maxim that no nation or religion can supersede any other
without incorporating into itself a portion of that which it 755
supersedes. The abolition of personal and domestic slavery,
and the emancipation of women from a great part of the
degrading restraints of antiquity were among the conse-
quences of these events.

The abolition of personal slavery is the basis of the highest 760
political hope that it can enter into the mind of man to
conceive. The freedom of women produced the poetry of
sexual love. Love became a religion, the idols of whose
worship were ever present. It was as if the statues of Apollo
and the Muses had been endowed with life and motion and 765
had walked forth among their worshippers; so that Earth
became peopled by the inhabitants of a diviner world. The
familiar appearances and proceedings of life became won-
derful and heavenly; and a paradise was created as out of
the wrecks of Eden. And as this creation itself is poetry, so 770
its creators were poets; and language was the instrument of
their art − 'Galeotto fù il libro, e chi lo scrisse'. The
Provencal trouveurs, or inventors, preceded Petrarch, whose
verses are as spells which unseal the inmost enchanted
fountains of the delight which is in the grief of Love. It is 775
impossible to feel them without becoming a portion of that
beauty which we contemplate: it were superfluous to explain
how the gentleness and the elevation of mind connected
with these sacred emotions can render men more amiable,
and generous, and wise, and lift them out of the dull vapours 780
of the little world of self. Dante understood the secret things
of love even more than Petrarch. His *Vita nuova* is an
inexhaustible fountain of purity of sentiment and language:
it is the idealized history of that period, and those intervals

of his life which were dedicated to love. His apotheosis of 785
Beatrice in Paradise and the gradations of his own love and
her loveliness, by which as by steps he feigns himself to have
ascended to the throne of the Supreme Cause, is the most
glorious imagination of modern poetry. The acutest critics
have justly reversed the judgement of the vulgar, and the 790
order of the great acts of the *Divine Drama*, in the measure
of the admiration which they accord to the *Hell*, *Purgatory*
and *Paradise*. The latter is a perpetual hymn to everlasting
love. Love, which found a worthy poet in Plato alone of all
the ancients, has been celebrated by a chorus of the greatest 795
writers of the renovated world; and the music has penetrated
the caverns of society, and its echoes still drown the
dissonance of arms and superstition. At successive intervals
Ariosto, Tasso, Shakespeare, Spenser, Calderón, Rousseau,
and the great writers of our own age, have celebrated the 800
dominion of love: planting as it were trophies in the human
mind of that sublimest victory over sensuality and force.
The true relation borne to each other by the sexes into
which human kind is distributed has become less misunder-
stood; and if the error which confounded diversity with 805
inequality of the powers of the two sexes has been partially
recognized in the opinions and institutions of modern
Europe, we owe this great benefit to the worship of which
Chivalry was the law, and poets the prophets.

The poetry of Dante may be considered as the Bridge 810
thrown over the stream of Time which unites the modern
and ancient World. The distorted notions of invisible things
which Dante and his rival Milton have idealized are merely
the mask and the mantle in which these great poets walk
through eternity enveloped and disguised. It is a difficult 815
question to determine how far they were conscious of the
distinction which must have subsisted in their minds
between their own creeds and that of the people. Dante at
least appears to wish to mark the full extent of it by placing
Ripheus whom Virgil calls *justissimus unus* in Paradise, and 820
observing a most heretical caprice in his distribution of
rewards and punishments. And Milton's poem contains
within itself a philosophical refutation of that system of
which, by a strange but natural antithesis, it has been a chief
popular support. Nothing can exceed the energy and mag- 825

nificence of the character of Satan as expressed in *Paradise Lost*. It is a mistake to suppose that he could ever have been intended for the popular personification of evil. Implacable hate, patient cunning, and a sleepless refinement of device to inflict the extremest anguish on an enemy, – these things 830 are evil; and although venial in a slave are not to be forgiven in a tyrant; although redeemed by much that ennobles his defeat in one subdued, are marked by all that dishonours his conquest in the victor. Milton's Devil as a moral being is as far superior to his God as one who perseveres in some 835 purpose which he has conceived to be excellent in spite of adversity and torture, is to one who in the cold security of undoubted triumph inflicts the most horrible revenge upon his enemy, – not from any mistaken notion of inducing him to repent of a perseverance in enmity, but with the alleged 840 design of exasperating him to deserve new torments. Milton has so far violated the popular creed (if this shall be judged to be a violation) as to have alleged no superiority of moral virtue to his God over his Devil. And this bold neglect of a direct moral purpose is the most decisive proof of the 845 supremacy of Milton's genius. He mingled as it were the elements of human nature, as colours upon a single pallet, and arranged them into the composition of his great picture according to the laws of epic truth: that is, according to the laws of that principle by which a series of actions of the 850 external universe and of intelligent and ethical beings is calculated to excite the sympathy of succeeding generations of mankind. The *Divina Commedia* and *Paradise Lost* have conferred upon modern mythology a systematic form; and when change and time shall have added one more 855 superstition to the mass of those which have arisen and decayed upon the earth, commentators will be learnedly employed in elucidating the religion and political conditions of ancestral Europe, only not utterly forgotten because it will have been stamped with the eternity of genius.   860

Homer was the first, and Dante the second epic poet: that is, the second poet the series of whose creations bore a defined and intelligible relation to the knowledge, and sentiment, and religion, of the age in which he lived, and of the ages which followed it: developing itself in correspon- 865 dence with their development. For Lucretius had limed the

wings of his swift spirit in the dregs of the sensible world:
and Virgil with a modesty that ill became his genius, had
affected the fame of an imitator even whilst he created anew
all that he copied; and none among the flock of mock-birds, 870
though their notes were sweet, Apollonius Rhodius, Quintus
Calaber Smyrnaeus, Nonnus, Lucan, Statius or Claudian
have sought even to fulfil a single condition of epic truth.
Milton was the third epic poet: for if the title of epic in its
highest sense be refused to the *Aeneid*, still less can it be 875
conceded to the *Orlando furioso*, the *Gerusalemme liberata*,
the *Lusiad* or the *Faerie Queene*.

Dante and Milton were both deeply penetrated with the
ancient religion of the civilized world; and its spirit exists in
their poetry probably in the same proportion as its forms 880
survived in the unreformed worship of modern Europe. The
one preceded and the other followed the Reformation at
almost equal intervals. Dante was the first religious
reformer, and Luther surpassed him rather in the rudeness
and acrimony than in the boldness of his censures of papal 885
usurpation. Dante was the first awakener of entranced
Europe; he created a language in itself music and persuasion
out of a chaos of inharmonious barbarisms. He was the
congregator of those great spirits who presided over the
resurrection of learning; the Lucifer of that starry flock 890
which in the thirteenth century shone forth from republican
Italy, as from a heaven, into the darkness of the benighted
world. His very words are instinct with spirit; each is as a
spark, a burning atom of inextinguishable thought – and
many yet lie covered in the ashes of their birth, and pregnant 895
with a lightning which has yet found no conductor. All high
poetry is infinite – it is as the first acorn which contained all
oaks potentially; veil after veil may be undrawn and the
inmost naked beauty of the meaning never exposed. A great
poem is a fountain forever overflowing with the waters of 900
wisdom and delight; and after one person and one age has
exhausted all of its divine effluence which their peculiar
relations enable them to share; another and yet another
succeeds, and new relations are ever developed, the source
of an unforeseen and unconceived delight. 905

The age immediately succeeding to that of Dante, Petrarch
and Boccaccio was characterized by a revival of painting,

sculpture, music and architecture. Chaucer caught the sacred inspiration, and the superstructure of English litera- ture is based upon materials of Italian invention.   910

But let us not be betrayed from a defence into a critical history of Poetry and its influence on society. Be it enough to have pointed out the effects of Poets in the large and true sense of the word upon their own and all succeeding times, and to revert to the partial instance cited as illustration of 915 an opinion the reverse of that attempted to be established in the *Four Ages of Poetry*.

But Poets have been challenged to resign the civic crown to reasoners and mechanists on another plea. It is admitted that the exercise of the imagination is more delightful, but 920 it is alleged that that of reason is more useful. Let us examine as the ground of this distinction what is here meant by Utility. Pleasure or good in a general sense, is that which the consciousness of a sensitive and intelligent being seeks, and in which when found it acquiesces. There are two kinds 925 of pleasure, one durable, universal and permanent; the other transitory and particular. Utility may either express the means of producing the former or the latter. In the former sense, whatever strengthens and purifies the affections, enlarges the imagination, and adds a spirit to sense, is 930 useful. But the meaning in which the Author of the *Four Ages of Poetry* seems to have employed the word utility is the narrower one of banishing the importunity of the wants of our animal nature, the surrounding men with security of life, the dispersing the grosser delusions of superstition, and 935 the conciliating such a degree of mutual forbearance among men as may consist with the motives of personal advantage.

Undoubtedly the promoters of Utility in this limited sense, have their appointed office in society. They follow the footsteps of poets, and copy the sketches of their creations 940 into the book of common life. They make space and give time. Their exertions are of the highest value so long as they confine their administration of the concerns of the inferior powers of our nature within the limits of what is due to the superior ones. But whilst the sceptic destroys gross 945 superstitions, let him spare to deface, as some of the French writers have defaced, the eternal truths charactered upon the imaginations of men. Whilst the mechanist abridges,

and the political economist combines, labour, let them
beware that their speculations, for want of correspondence 950
with those first principles which belong to the imagination,
do not tend, as they have in modern England, to exasperate
at once the extremes of luxury and want. They have
exemplified the saying, 'To him that hath, more shall be
given; and from him that hath not, the little that he hath 955
shall be taken away.' The rich have become richer, and the
poor have become poorer; and the vessel of the state is
driven between the Scylla and Charybdis of anarchy and
despotism. Such are the effects which must ever flow from
an unmitigated exercise of the calculating faculty.   960

It is difficult to define pleasure in its highest sense; the
definition involving a number of apparent paradoxes. For,
from an inexplicable defect of harmony in the constitution
of human nature, the pain of the inferior is frequently
connected with the pleasures of the superior portions of our 965
being. Sorrow, terror, anguish, despair itself are often the
chosen expressions of an approximation to the highest good.
Our sympathy in tragic fiction depends on this principle:
tragedy delights by affording a shadow of the pleasure
which exists in pain. This is the source also of the melan- 970
choly which is inseparable from the sweetest melody. The
pleasure that is in sorrow, is sweeter than the pleasure of
pleasure itself. And hence the saying, 'It is better to go to
the house of mourning, than to the house of mirth.' Not
that this highest species of pleasure is necessarily linked with 975
pain. The delight of love and friendship, the ecstasy of the
admiration of nature, the joy of the perception and still
more of the creation of poetry is often wholly unalloyed.

The production and assurance of pleasure in this highest
sense is the true Utility. Those who produce and preserve 980
this pleasure are Poets or poetical philosophers.

The exertions of Locke, Hume, Gibbon, Voltaire,
Rousseau[3] and their disciples, in favour of oppressed and
deluded humanity are entitled to the gratitude of mankind.
Yet it is easy to calculate the degree of moral and intellectual 985

---

[3] I follow the classification adopted by the author of the *Four Ages of Poetry*.
But Rousseau was essentially a poet. The others, even Voltaire, were mere
reasoners.

improvement which the world would have exhibited, had
they never lived. A little more nonsense would have been
talked for a century or two; and perhaps a few more men,
women and children burnt as heretics. We might not at this
moment have been congratulating each other on the aboli- 990
ton of the Inquisition in Spain. But it exceeds all imagination
to conceive what would have been the moral condition of
the world if neither Dante, Petrarch, Boccaccio, Chaucer,
Shakespeare, Calderón, Lord Bacon, nor Milton had ever
existed; if Raphael and Michelangelo had never been born; 995
if the Hebrew poetry had never been translated; if a revival
of the study of Greek literature had never taken place; if no
monuments of ancient sculpture had been handed down to
us; and if the poetry of the religion of the ancient world had
been extinguished together with its belief. The human mind 1000
could never, except by the intervention of these excitements,
have been awakened to the invention of those grosser
sciences, and that application of analytical reasoning to the
aberrations of society, which it is now attempted to exalt
over the direct expression of the inventive and creative 1005
faculty itself.

We have more moral, political and historical wisdom
than we know how to reduce into practice: we have more
scientific and economical knowledge than can be accommo-
dated to the just distribution of the produce which it 1010
multiplies. The poetry in these systems of thought is con-
cealed by the accumulation of facts and calculating pro-
cesses. There is no want of knowledge respecting what is
wisest and best in morals, government and political econ-
omy, or at least what is wiser and better than what men 1015
now practise and endure. But we 'let *I dare not* wait upon *I
would*, like the poor cat i' the adage'. We want the creative
faculty to imagine that which we know; we want the
generous impulse to act that which we imagine; we want
the poetry of life: our calculations have outrun conception; 1020
we have eaten more than we can digest. The cultivation of
those sciences which have enlarged the limits of the empire
of man over the external world, has, for want of the poetical
faculty, proportionally circumscribed those of the internal
world, and man, having enslaved the elements, remains 1025
himself a slave. To what but a cultivation of the mechanical

arts in a degree disproportioned to the presence of the creative faculty which is the basis of all knowledge is to be attributed the abuse of all invention for abridging and combining labour, to the exasperation of the inequality of mankind? From what other cause has it arisen that the discoveries which should have lightened, have added a weight to the curse imposed on Adam? Poetry, and the principle of Self, of which money is the visible incarnation, are the God and the Mammon of the world. 1030 1035

The functions of the poetical faculty are twofold: by one it creates new materials of knowledge and power and pleasure; by the other it engenders in the mind a desire to reproduce and arrange them according to a certain rhythm and order, which may be called the beautiful and the good. 1040 The cultivation of poetry is never more to be desired than at periods when, from an excess of the selfish and calculating principle, the accumulation of the materials of external life exceed the quantity of the power of assimilating them to the internal laws of human nature. The body has then become 1045 too unwieldy for that which animates it.

Poetry is indeed something divine. It is at once the centre and circumference of knowledge; it is that which comprehends all science, and that to which all science must be referred. It is at the same time the root and the blossom of 1050 all other systems of thought; it is that from which all spring, and that which adorns all; and that which if blighted denies the fruit and the seed, and withholds from the barren world the nourishment and the succession of the scions of the tree of life. It is the perfect and consummate surface and bloom 1055 of things; it is as the odour and the colour of the rose to the texture of the elements which compose it, as the form and splendour of unfaded beauty to the secrets of anatomy and corruption. What were Virtue, Love, Patriotism, Friendship, – what were the scenery of this beautiful Universe which we 1060 inhabit, what were our consolations on this side of the grave, and what were our aspirations beyond it, if Poetry did not ascend to bring light and fire from those eternal regions where the owl-winged faculty of calculation dare not ever soar? Poetry is not like reasoning, a power to be 1065 exerted according to the determination of the will. A man cannot say, 'I will compose poetry'. The greatest poet even cannot say it: for the mind in creation is as a fading coal which some invisible influence, like an inconstant wind, awakens to transitory brightness: this power arises from 1070 within, like the colour of a flower which fades and changes as it is developed, and the conscious portions of our nature are unprophetic either of its approach or its departure. Could this influence be durable in its original purity and force, it is impossible to predict the greatness of the results: 1075 but when composition begins, inspiration is already on the decline, and the most glorious poetry that has ever been communicated to the world, is probably a feeble shadow of the original conceptions of the Poet. I appeal to the greatest poets of the present day, whether it be not an error to assert 1080 that the finest passages of poetry are produced by labour and study. The toil and the delay recommended by critics can be justly interpreted to mean no more than a careful observation of the inspired moments, and an artificial connection of the spaces between their suggestions by the 1085 intertexture of conventional expressions; a necessity only imposed by a limitedness of the poetical faculty itself. For Milton conceived the *Paradise Lost* as a whole before he executed it in portions. We have his own authority also for the muse having 'dictated' to him 'the unpremeditated song'; 1090 and let this be an answer to those who would allege the fifty-six various readings of the first line of the *Orlando furioso*. Compositions so produced are to poetry what mosaic is to painting. This instinct and intuition of the poetical faculty is still more observable in the plastic and 1095 pictorial arts: a great statue or picture grows under the power of the artist as a child in the mother's womb, and the very mind which directs the hands in formation is incapable of accounting to itself for the origin, the gradations, or the media of the process. 1100

Poetry is the record of the happiest and best moments of the happiest and best minds. We are aware of evanescent visitations of thought and feeling sometimes associated with place or person, sometimes regarding our own mind alone, and always arising unforeseen and departing unbidden, but 1105 elevating and delightful beyond all expression: so that even in the desire and the regret they leave there cannot but be pleasure, participating as it does in the nature of its object.

It is as it were the interpenetration of a diviner nature through our own, but its footsteps are like those of a wind 1110 over the sea, which the coming calm erases, and whose traces remain only upon the wrinkled sand which paves it. These and corresponding conditions of being are experienced principally by those of the most delicate sensibility and the most enlarged imagination; and the state of mind 1115 produced by them is at war with every base desire. The enthusiasm of virtue, love, patriotism and friendship is essentially linked with such emotions; and whilst they last self appears as what it is, an atom to an Universe. Poets are not only subject to these experiences as spirits of the most 1120 refined organization, but they can colour all that they combine with the evanescent hues of this ethereal world; a word, a trait in the representation of a scene or a passion will touch the enchanted chord, and reanimate, in those who have ever experienced these emotions, the sleeping, the 1125 cold, the buried image of the past. Poetry thus makes immortal all that is best and most beautiful in the world; it arrests the vanishing apparitions which haunt the interlunations of life, and veiling them in language or in form sends them forth among mankind bearing sweet news of kindred 1130 joy to those with whom their sisters abide – abide, because there is no portal of expression from the caverns of the spirit which they inhabit into the universe of things. Poetry redeems from decay the visitations of the divinity in Man.

Poetry turns all things to loveliness: it exalts the beauty 1135 of that which is most beautiful, and it adds beauty to that which is most deformed: it marries exultation and horror, grief and pleasure, eternity and change: it subdues to union under its light yoke all irreconcilable things. It transmutes all that it touches, and every form moving within the 1140 radiance of its presence is changed by wondrous sympathy to an incarnation of the spirit which it breathes: its secret alchemy turns to potable gold the poisonous waters which flow from death through life: it strips the veil of familiarity from the world, and lays bare the naked and sleeping beauty 1145 which is the spirit of its forms.

All things exist as they are perceived; at least in relation to the percipient – 'The mind is its own place, and of itself / Can make a Heaven of Hell, a Hell of Heaven.' But Poetry

defeats the curse which binds us to be subjected to the 1150
accident of surrounding impressions; and whether it spreads
its own figured curtain or withdraws life's dark veil from
before the scene of things, it equally creates for us a being
within our being. It makes us the inhabitants of a world to
which the familiar world is as a Chaos. It reproduces the 1155
common Universe of which we are portions and percipients,
and it purges from our inward sight the film of familiarity
which obscures from us the wonder of our being. It compels
us to feel that which we perceive, and to imagine that which
we know. It creates anew the universe after it has been 1160
annihilated in our minds by the recurrence of impressions
blunted by re-iteration. It justifies that bold and true word
of Tasso: *Non merita nome di creatore se non Iddio ed il
Poeta.*

A Poet, as he is the author to others of the highest 1165
wisdom, pleasure, virtue and glory, so he ought personally
to be the happiest, the best, the wisest and the most
illustrious of men. As to his glory, let Time be challenged to
declare whether the fame of any other institutor of human
life be comparable to that of a poet. That he is the wisest, 1170
the happiest and the best, inasmuch as he is a poet, is equally
incontrovertible: the greatest Poets have been men of the
most spotless virtue, of the most consummate prudence,
and, if we would look into the interior of their lives, the
most fortunate of men: and the exceptions, as they regard 1175
those who possessed the poetic faculty in a high yet inferior
degree, will be found on consideration to confine rather
than destroy the rule. Let us for a moment stoop to the
arbitration of popular breath, and usurping and uniting in
our own persons the incompatible characters of accuser, 1180
witness, judge and executioner, let us decide without trial,
testimony or form that certain motives of those who are
'there sitting where we dare not soar' are reprehensible. Let
us assume that Homer was a drunkard, that Virgil was a
flatterer, that Horace was a coward, that Tasso was a 1185
madman, that Lord Bacon was a peculator, that Raphael
was a libertine, that Spenser was a poet-laureate. It is
inconsistent with this division of our subject to cite living
poets, but Posterity has done ample justice to the great
names now referred to. Their errors have been weighed and 1190

found to have been dust in the balance, if their sins 'were as scarlet, they are now white as snow': they have been washed in the blood of the mediator and the redeemer Time. Observe in what a ludicrous chaos the imputations of real and of fictitious crime have been confused in the contemporary calumnies against poetry and poets; consider how little is as it appears, or appears as it is; look to your own motives, and judge not, lest ye be judged.

Poetry, as has been said, differs in this respect from logic that it is not subject to the control of the active powers of the mind, and that its birth and recurrence have no necessary connection with consciousness or will. It is presumptuous to determine that these are the necessary conditions of all mental causation when mental effects are experienced insusceptible of being referred to them. The frequent recurrence of the poetical power, it is obvious to suppose, may produce in the mind an habit of order and harmony correlative with its own nature and with its effects upon other minds. But in the intervals of inspiration, and they may be frequent without being durable, a Poet becomes a man and is abandoned to the sudden reflux of the influences under which others habitually live. But as he is more delicately organized than other men, and sensible to pain and pleasure both his own and that of others in a degree unknown to them, he will avoid the one and pursue the other with an ardour proportioned to this difference. And he renders himself obnoxious to calumny, when he neglects to observe the circumstances under which these objects of universal pursuit and flight have disguised themselves in one another's garments. – But there is nothing necessarily evil in this error. And thus cruelty, envy, revenge, avarice, and the passions purely evil, have never formed any portion of the popular imputations on the lives of poets.

I have thought it most favourable to the cause of truth to set down these remarks according to the order in which they were suggested to my mind by a consideration of the subject itself, instead of following that of the treatise which excited me to make them public. Thus although devoid of the formality of a polemical reply, if the views which they contain be just, they will be found to involve a refutation of the *Four Ages of Poetry*, so far at least as regards the first division of the subject. I can readily conjecture what should have moved the gall of the learned and intelligent Author of that paper; I confess myself like him unwilling to be stunned by the *Theseids* of the hoarse Codri of the day: Bavius and 1235 Maevius undoubtedly are, as they ever were, insufferable persons. But it belongs to a philosophical critic to distinguish rather than confound.

The first part of these remarks has related to Poetry in its elements and principles; and it has been shown, as well as 1240 the narrow limits assigned them would permit, that what is called Poetry in a restricted sense has a common source with all other forms of order and of beauty according to which the materials of human life are susceptible of being arranged; and which is Poetry in an universal sense.   1245

The second part will have for its object an application of these principles to the present state of the cultivation of Poetry, and a defence of the attempt to idealize the modern forms of manners and opinion, and compel them into a subordination to the imaginative and creative faculty. For 1250 the literature of England, an energetic development of which has ever preceded or accompanied a great and free development of the national will, has arisen as it were from a new birth. In spite of the low-thoughted envy which would undervalue contemporary merit, our own will be a memor- 1255 able age in intellectual achievements, and we live among such philosophers and poets as surpass beyond comparison any who have appeared since the last national struggle for civil and religious liberty. The most unfailing herald, companion and follower of the awakening of a great people to 1260 work a beneficial change in opinion or institution, is Poetry. At such periods there is an accumulation of the power of communicating and receiving intense and impassioned conceptions respecting man and nature. The persons in whom this power resides, may often as far as regards many 1265 portions of their nature, have little apparent correspondence with that spirit of good of which they are the ministers. But even whilst they deny and abjure, they are yet compelled to serve, the Power which is seated on the throne of their own soul. It is impossible to read the compositions of the most 1270 celebrated writers of the present day without being startled with the electric life which burns within their words. They

measure the circumference and sound the depths of human
nature with a comprehensive and all-penetrating spirit. And
they are themselves perhaps the most sincerely astonished at 1275
its manifestations, for it is less their spirit than the spirit of
the age. Poets are the hierophants of an unapprehended
inspiration, the mirrors of the gigantic shadows which
futurity casts upon the present, the words which express
what they understand not, the trumpets which sing to battle 1280
and feel not what they inspire: the influence which is moved
not but moves. Poets are the unacknowledged legislators of
the world.

42   ADONAIS

An Elegy on the death of John Keats, author of Endymion,
Hyperion, etc.

> Ἀστὴρ πρὶν μὲν ἔλαμπες ἐνὶ ζωοῖσιν Ἑῷος.
> νῦν δὲ θανὼν λάμπεις Ἕσπερος ἐν φθιμένοις.
>
> *Plato*

Preface

> Φάρμακον ἦλθε, Βίων, ποτὶ σὸν στόμα, φάρμακον εἶδες.
> πῶς τευ τοῖς χείλεσσι ποτέδραμε, κοὐκ ἐγλυκάνθη;
> τίς δὲ βροτὸς τοσσοῦτον ἀνάμερος, ἢ κεράσαι τοι,
> ἢ δοῦναι λαλέοντι τὸ φάρμακον; ἔκφυγεν ᾠδάν.
>
> *Moschus, Epitaph. Bion*

It is my intention to subjoin to the London edition of this
poem a criticism upon the claims of its lamented object
to be classed among the writers of the highest genius who
have adorned our age. My known repugnance to the narrow
principles of taste on which several of his earlier composi-   5
tions were modelled proves at least that I am an impartial
judge. I consider the fragment of *Hyperion* as second to
nothing that was ever produced by a writer of the same
years.
    John Keats died at Rome of a consumption, in his twenty-   10
fourth year, on the [twenty-third] of [February] 1821; and

was buried in the romantic and lonely cemetery of the
Protestants in that city, under the pyramid which is the
tomb of Cestius, and the massy walls and towers, now
mouldering and desolate, which formed the circuit of   15
ancient Rome. The cemetery is an open space among the
ruins, covered in winter with violets and daisies. It might
make one in love with death, to think that one should be
buried in so sweet a place.

The genius of the lamented person to whose memory I   20
have dedicated these unworthy verses was not less delicate
and fragile than it was beautiful; and where cankerworms
abound, what wonder if its young flower was blighted in the
bud? The savage criticism on his *Endymion*, which appeared
in the *Quarterly Review*, produced the most violent effect   25
on his susceptible mind; the agitation thus originated ended
in the rupture of a blood-vessel in the lungs; a rapid
consumption ensued, and the succeeding acknowledgements
from more candid critics of the true greatness of his powers
were ineffectual to heal the wound thus wantonly inflicted.   30

It may be well said that these wretched men know not
what they do. They scatter their insults and their slanders
without heed as to whether the poisoned shaft lights on a
heart made callous by many blows or one like Keats's
composed of more penetrable stuff. One of their associates   35
is, to my knowledge, a most base and unprincipled calum-
niator. As to *Endymion*, was it a poem, whatever might be
its defects, to be treated contemptuously by those who had
celebrated, with various degrees of complacency and pane-
gyric, *Paris*, and *Woman*, and a *Syrian Tale*, and Mrs   40
Lefanu, and Mr Barrett, and Mr Howard Payne, and a long
list of the illustrious obscure? Are these the men who in
their venal good nature presumed to draw a parallel between
the Rev Mr Milman and Lord Byron? What gnat did they
strain at here, after having swallowed all those camels?   45
Against what woman taken in adultery dares the foremost
of these literary prostitutes to cast his opprobrious stone?
Miserable man! you, one of the meanest, have wantonly
defaced one of the noblest specimens of the workmanship
of God. Nor shall it be your excuse, that, murderer as you   50
are, you have spoken daggers, but used none.

The circumstances of the closing scene of poor Keats's life

were not made known to me until the *Elegy* was ready for
the press. I am given to understand that the wound which
his sensitive spirit had received from the criticism of *Endy-*   55
mion was exasperated by the bitter sense of unrequited
benefits; the poor fellow seems to have been hooted from
the stage of life, no less by those on whom he had wasted
the promise of his genius, than those on whom he had
lavished his fortune and his care. He was accompanied to   60
Rome, and attended in his last illness by Mr Severn, a young
artist of the highest promise, who, I have been informed,
'almost risked his own life, and sacrificed every prospect to
unwearied attendance upon his dying friend.' Had I known
these circumstances before the completion of my poem, I   65
should have been tempted to add my feeble tribute of
applause to the more solid recompense which the virtuous
man finds in the recollection of his own motives. Mr Severn
can dispense with a reward from 'such stuff as dreams are
made of.' His conduct is a golden augury of the success of   70
his future career – may the unextinguished Spirit of his
illustrious friend animate the creations of his pencil, and
plead against Oblivion for his name!

Adonais

I

I weep for Adonais – he is dead!
O, weep for Adonais! though our tears
Thaw not the frost which binds so dear a head!
And thou, sad Hour, selected from all years
To mourn our loss, rouse thy obscure compeers,   5
And teach them thine own sorrow, say: with me
Died Adonais; till the Future dares
Forget the Past, his fate and fame shall be
An echo and a light unto eternity!

2

Where wert thou, mighty Mother, when he lay,   10
When thy Son lay, pierced by the shaft which flies
In darkness? where was lorn Urania
When Adonais died? With veilèd eyes,
Mid listening Echoes, in her Paradise

She sate, while one, with soft enamoured breath,   15
Rekindled all the fading melodies
With which, like flowers that mock the corse
    beneath,
He had adorned and hid the coming bulk of death.

3

O, weep for Adonais – he is dead!
Wake, melancholy Mother, wake and weep!   20
Yet wherefore? Quench within their burning bed
Thy fiery tears, and let thy loud heart keep
Like his, a mute and uncomplaining sleep;
For he is gone, where all things wise and fair
Descend; – oh, dream not that the amorous Deep   25
Will yet restore him to the vital air;
Death feeds on his mute voice, and laughs at our
    despair.

4

Most musical of mourners, weep again!
Lament anew, Urania! – He died,
Who was the Sire of an immortal strain,   30
Blind, old, and lonely, when his country's pride
The priest, the slave, and the liberticide
Trampled and mocked with many a loathèd rite
Of lust and blood; he went, unterrified,
Into the gulf of death; but his clear Sprite   35
Yet reigns o'er earth; the third among the sons of
    light.

5

Most musical of mourners, weep anew!
Not all to that bright station dared to climb;
And happier they their happiness who knew,
Whose tapers yet burn through that night of time   40
In which suns perished; others more sublime,
Struck by the envious wrath of man or God,
Have sunk, extinct in their refulgent prime;
And some yet live, treading the thorny road
Which leads, through toil and hate, to Fame's serene
    abode.   45

6

But now, thy youngest, dearest one, has perished –
The nursling of thy widowhood, who grew,
Like a pale flower by some sad maiden cherished,
And fed with true love tears, instead of dew;
Most musical of mourners, weep anew!   50
Thy extreme hope, the loveliest and the last,
The bloom, whose petals nipped before they blew
Died on the promise of the fruit, is waste;
The broken lily lies – the storm is overpast.

7

To that high Capital, where kingly Death   55
Keeps his pale court in beauty and decay,
He came; and bought, with price of purest breath,
A grave among the eternal. – Come away!
Haste, while the vault of blue Italian day
Is yet his fitting charnel-roof! while still   60
He lies, as if in dewy sleep he lay;
Awake him not! surely he takes his fill
Of deep and liquid rest, forgetful of all ill.

8

He will awake no more, oh, never more! –
Within the twilight chamber spreads apace   65
The shadow of white Death, and at the door
Invisible Corruption waits to trace
His extreme way to her dim dwelling-place;
The eternal Hunger sits, but pity and awe
Soothe her pale rage, nor dares she to deface   70
So fair a prey, till darkness, and the law
Of change, shall o'er his sleep the mortal curtain draw.

9

O, weep for Adonais! – The quick Dreams,
The passion-wingèd Ministers of thought,
Who were his flocks, whom near the living streams   75
Of his young spirit he fed, and whom he taught
The love which was its music, wander not, –
Wander no more, from kindling brain to brain,
But droop there, whence they sprung; and mourn their lot

Round the cold heart, where, after their sweet pain, 80
They ne'er will gather strength, or find a home again.

10

And one with trembling hands clasps his cold head,
And fans him with her moonlight wings, and cries,
'Our love, our hope, our sorrow, is not dead;
See, on the silken fringe of his faint eyes, 85
Like dew upon a sleeping flower, there lies
A tear some Dream has loosened from his brain.'
Lost Angel of a ruined Paradise!
She knew not 'twas her own; as with no stain
She faded, like a cloud which had outwept its rain. 90

11

One from a lucid urn of starry dew
Washed his light limbs as if embalming them;
Another clipped her profuse locks, and threw
The wreath upon him, like an anadem,
Which frozen tears instead of pearls begem; 95
Another in her wilful grief would break
Her bow and wingèd reeds, as if to stem
A greater loss with one which was more weak;
And dull the barbèd fire against his frozen cheek.

12

Another Splendour on his mouth alit, 100
That mouth, whence it was wont to draw the breath
Which gave it strength to pierce the guarded wit,
And pass into the panting heart beneath
With lightning and with music: the damp death
Quenched its caress upon his icy lips; 105
And, as a dying meteor stains a wreath
Of moonlight vapour, which the cold night clips,
It flushed through his pale limbs, and passed to its eclipse.

13

And others came . . . Desires and Adorations,
Wingèd Persuasions and veiled Destinies, 110
Splendours, and Glooms, and glimmering Incarnations
Of hopes and fears, and twilight Fantasies;

And Sorrow, with her family of Sighs,
And Pleasure, blind with tears, led by the gleam
Of her own dying smile instead of eyes,   115
Came in slow pomp; – the moving pomp might seem
Like pageantry of mist on an autumnal stream.

14

All he had loved, and moulded into thought,
From shape, and hue, and odour, and sweet sound,
Lamented Adonais. Morning sought   120
Her eastern watch-tower, and her hair unbound,
Wet with the tears which should adorn the ground,
Dimmed the aërial eyes that kindle day;
Afar the melancholy thunder moaned,
Pale Ocean in unquiet slumber lay,   125
And the wild winds flew round, sobbing in their dismay.

15

Lost Echo sits amid the voiceless mountains,
And feeds her grief with his remembered lay,
And will no more reply to winds or fountains,
Or amorous birds perched on the young green spray,   130
Or herdsman's horn, or bell at closing day,
Since she can mimic not his lips, more dear
Than those for whose disdain she pined away
Into a shadow of all sounds: – a drear
Murmur, between their songs, is all the woodmen
    hear.   135

16

Grief made the young Spring wild, and she threw
    down
Her kindling buds, as if she Autumn were,
Or they dead leaves; since her delight is flown,
For whom should she have waked the sullen year?
To Phoebus was not Hyacinth so dear   140
Nor to himself Narcissus, as to both
Thou, Adonais: wan they stand and sere
Amid the faint companions of their youth,
With dew all turned to tears; odour, to sighing ruth.

17

Thy spirit's sister, the lorn nightingale   145
Mourns not her mate with such melodious pain;
Not so the eagle, who like thee could scale
Heaven, and could nourish in the sun's domain
Her mighty youth with morning, doth complain,
Soaring and screaming round her empty nest,   150
As Albion wails for thee: the curse of Cain
Light on his head who pierced thy innocent breast,
And scared the angel soul that was its earthly guest!

18

Ah, woe is me! Winter is come and gone,
But grief returns with the revolving year;   155
The airs and streams renew their joyous tone;
The ants, the bees, the swallows reappear;
Fresh leaves and flowers deck the dead Season's bier;
The amorous birds now pair in every brake,
And build their mossy homes in field and brere;   160
And the green lizard, and the golden snake,
Like unimprisoned flames, out of their trance awake.

19

Through wood and stream and field and hill and Ocean
A quickening life from the Earth's heart has burst
As it has ever done, with change and motion,   165
From the great morning of the world when first
God dawned on Chaos; in its stream immersed,
The lamps of Heaven flash with a softer light;
All baser things pant with life's sacred thirst;
Diffuse themselves; and spend in love's delight   170
The beauty and the joy of their renewèd might.

20

The leprous corpse touched by this spirit tender
Exhales itself in flowers of gentle breath;
Like incarnations of the stars, when splendour
Is changed to fragrance, they illumine death   175
And mock the merry worm that wakes beneath;
Nought we know, dies. Shall that alone which knows
Be as a sword consumed before the sheath

By sightless lightning? – the intense atom glows
A moment, then is quenched in a most cold repose.   180

21

Alas! that all we loved of him should be,
But for our grief, as if it had not been,
And grief itself be mortal! Woe is me!
Whence are we, and why are we? of what scene
The actors or spectators? Great and mean   185
Meet massed in death, who lends what life must borrow.
As long as skies are blue, and fields are green,
Evening must usher night, night urge the morrow,
Month follow month with woe, and year wake year
   to sorrow.

22

He will awake no more, oh, never more!   190
'Wake thou,' cried Misery, 'childless Mother, rise
Out of they sleep, and slake, in thy heart's core,
A wound more fierce than his with tears and sighs.'
And all the Dreams that watched Urania's eyes,
And all the Echoes whom their sister's song   195
Had held in holy silence, cried: 'Arise!'
Swift as a Thought by the snake Memory stung,
From her ambrosial rest the fading Splendour sprung.

23

She rose like an autumnal Night, that springs
Out of the East, and follows wild and drear   200
The golden Day, which, on eternal wings,
Even as a ghost abandoning a bier,
Has left the Earth a corpse. Sorrow and fear
So struck, so roused, so rapt Urania;
So saddened round her like an atmosphere   205
Of stormy mist; so swept her on her way
Even to the mournful place where Adonais lay.

24

Out of her secret Paradise she sped,
Through camps and cities rough with stone, and steel,
And human hearts, which to her aery tread   210

Yielding not, wounded the invisible
Palms of her tender feet where'er they fell:
And barbèd tongues, and thoughts more sharp than they,
Rent the soft Form they never could repel,
Whose sacred blood, like the young tears of May,   215
Paved with eternal flowers that undeserving way.

25

In the death-chamber for a moment Death,
Shamed by the presence of that living Might,
Blushed to annihilation, and the breath
Revisited those lips, and life's pale light   220
Flashed through those limbs, so late her dear delight.
'Leave me not wild and drear and comfortless,
As silent lightning leaves the starless night!
Leave me not!' cried Urania: her distress
Roused Death: Death rose and smiled, and met   225
    her vain caress.

26

'Stay yet awhile! speak to me once again;
Kiss me, so long but as a kiss may live;
And in my heartless breast and burning brain
That word, that kiss, shall all thoughts else survive,
With food of saddest memory kept alive,   230
Now thou art dead, as if it were a part
Of thee, my Adonais! I would give
All that I am to be as thou now art!
But I am chained to Time, and cannot thence depart!

27

'Oh gentle child, beautiful as thou wert,   235
Why didst thou leave the trodden paths of men
Too soon, and with weak hands though mighty heart
Dare the unpastured dragon in his den?
Defenceless as thou wert, oh where was then
Wisdom the mirrored shield, or scorn the spear?   240
Or hadst thou waited the full cycle, when
Thy spirit should have filled its crescent sphere,
The monsters of life's waste had fled from thee like deer.

28

'The herded wolves, bold only to pursue;
The obscene ravens, clamorous o'er the dead;   245
The vultures to the conqueror's banner true
Who feed where Desolation first has fed,
And whose wings rain contagion; – how they fled,
When like Apollo, from his golden bow,
The Pythian of the age one arrow sped   250
And smiled! – The spoilers tempt no second blow,
They fawn on the proud feet that spurn them lying low.

29

'The sun comes forth, and many reptiles spawn;
He sets, and each ephemeral insect then
Is gathered into death without a dawn,   255
And the immortal stars awake again;
So is it in the world of living men:
A godlike mind soars forth, in its delight
Making earth bare and veiling heaven, and when
It sinks, the swarms that dimmed or shared its light   260
Leave to its kindred lamps the spirit's awful night.'

30

Thus ceased she: and the mountain shepherds came,
Their garlands sere, their magic mantles rent;
The Pilgrim of Eternity, whose fame
Over his living head like Heaven is bent,   265
An early but enduring monument,
Came, veiling all the lightnings of his song
In sorrow; from her wilds Ierne sent
The sweetest lyrist of her saddest wrong,
And love taught grief to fall like music from his tongue. 270

31

Midst others of less note, came one frail Form,
A phantom among men; companionless
As the last cloud of an expiring storm
Whose thunder is its knell; he, as I guess,
Had gazed on Nature's naked loveliness,   275
Actaeon-like, and now he fled astray
With feeble steps o'er the world's wilderness,

And his own thoughts, along that rugged way,
Pursued, like raging hounds, their father and their prey.

32

A pardlike Spirit beautiful and swift –   280
A Love in desolation masked; – a Power
Girt round with weakness; – it can scarce uplift
The weight of the superincumbent hour;
It is a dying lamp, a falling shower,
A breaking billow; – even whilst we speak   285
Is it not broken? On the withering flower
The killing sun smiles brightly: on a cheek
The life can burn in blood, even while the heart may break.

33

His head was bound with pansies overblown,
And faded violets, white, and pied, and blue;   290
And a light spear topped with a cypress cone,
Round whose rude shaft dark ivy tresses grew
Yet dripping with the forest's noonday dew,
Vibrated, as the ever-beating heart
Shook the weak hand that grasped it; of that crew   295
He came the last, neglected and apart;
A herd-abandoned deer struck by the hunter's dart.

34

All stood aloof, and at his partial moan
Smiled through their tears; well knew that gentle band
Who in another's fate now wept his own –   300
As in the accents of an unknown land
He sung new sorrow; sad Urania scanned
The Stranger's mien, and murmured: 'Who art thou?'
He answered not, but with a sudden hand
Made bare his branded and ensanguined brow,   305
Which was like Cain's or Christ's – Oh! that it should be
    so!

35

What softer voice is hushed over the dead?
Athwart what brow is that dark mantle thrown?
What form leans sadly o'er the white death-bed,

In mockery of monumental stone, 310
The heavy heart heaving without a moan?
If it be He, who gentlest of the wise,
Taught, soothed, loved, honoured the departed one,
Let me not vex, with inharmonious sighs,
The silence of that heart's accepted sacrifice. 315

36

Our Adonais has drunk poison – oh!
What deaf and viperous murderer could crown
Life's early cup with such a draught of woe?
The nameless worm would now itself disown:
It felt, yet could escape, the magic tone 320
Whose prelude held all envy, hate, and wrong,
But what was howling in one breast alone,
Silent with expectation of the song,
Whose master's hand is cold, whose silver lyre unstrung.

37

Live thou, whose infamy is not thy fame! 325
Live! fear no heavier chastisement from me,
Thou noteless blot on a remembered name!
But be thyself, and know thyself to be!
And ever at thy season be thou free
To spill the venom when thy fangs o'erflow: 330
Remorse and Self-contempt shall cling to thee;
Hot Shame shall burn upon thy secret brow,
And like a beaten hound tremble thou shalt – as now.

38

Nor let us weep that our delight is fled
Far from these carrion kites that scream below; 335
He wakes or sleeps with the enduring dead;
Thou canst not soar where he is sitting now. –
Dust to the dust! but the pure spirit shall flow
Back to the burning fountain whence it came,
A portion of the Eternal, which must glow 340
Through time and change, unquenchably the same,
Whilst thy cold embers choke the sordid hearth of
shame.

39

Peace, peace! he is not dead, he doth not sleep –
He hath awakened from the dream of life –
'Tis we, who lost in stormy visions, keep   345
With phantoms an unprofitable strife,
And in mad trance, strike with our spirit's knife
Invulnerable nothings. – *We* decay
Like corpses in a charnel; fear and grief
Convulse us and consume us day by day,   350
And cold hopes swarm like worms within our living
     clay.

40

He has outsoared the shadow of our night;
Envy and calumny and hate and pain,
And that unrest which men miscall delight,
Can touch him not and torture not again;   355
From the contagion of the world's slow stain
He is secure, and now can never mourn
A heart grown cold, a head grown grey in vain;
Nor, when the spirit's self has ceased to burn,
With sparkless ashes load an unlamented urn.   360

41

He lives, he wakes – 'tis Death is dead, not he;
Mourn not for Adonais. – Thou young Dawn
Turn all thy dew to splendour, for from thee
The spirit thou lamentest is not gone;
Ye caverns and ye forests, cease to moan!   365
Cease ye faint flowers and fountains, and thou Air
Which like a mourning veil thy scarf hadst thrown
O'er the abandoned Earth, now leave it bare
Even to the joyous stars which smile on its despair!

42

He is made one with Nature: there is heard   370
His voice in all her music, from the moan
Of thunder, to the song of night's sweet bird;
He is a presence to be felt and known
In darkness and in light, from herb and stone,
Spreading itself where'er that Power may move   375

Which has withdrawn his being to its own;
Which wields the world with never wearied love,
Sustains it from beneath, and kindles it above.

43

He is a portion of the loveliness
Which once he made more lovely: he doth bear   380
His part, while the one Spirit's plastic stress
Sweeps through the dull dense world, compelling there
All new successions to the forms they wear;
Torturing th'unwilling dross that checks its flight
To its own likeness, as each mass may bear;   385
And bursting in its beauty and its might
From trees and beasts and men into the Heavens'
    light.

44

The splendours of the firmament of time
May be eclipsed, but are extinguished not;
Like stars to their appointed height they climb,   390
And death is a low mist which cannot blot
The brightness it may veil. When lofty thought
Lifts a young heart above its mortal lair,
And love and life contend in it, for what
Shall be its earthly doom, the dead live there   395
And move like winds of light on dark and stormy air.

45

The inheritors of unfulfilled renown
Rose from their thrones, built beyond mortal thought,
Far in the Unapparent. Chatterton
Rose pale, his solemn agony had not   400
Yet faded from him; Sidney as he fought
And as he fell and as he lived and loved
Sublimely mild, a Spirit without spot,
Arose; and Lucan, by his death approved:
Oblivion as they rose shrank like a thing reproved.   405

46

And many more, whose names on Earth are dark,
But whose transmitted effluence cannot die

So long as fire outlives the parent spark,
Rose, robed in dazzling immortality.
'Thou art become as one of us,' they cry,   410
'It was for thee yon kingless sphere has long
Swung blind in unascended majesty,
Silent alone amid an Heaven of Song.
Assume thy wingèd throne, thou Vesper of our throng!'

47

Who mourns for Adonais? oh, come forth   415
Fond wretch! and know thyself and him aright,
Clasp with thy panting soul the pendulous Earth;
As from a centre, dart thy spirit's light
Beyond all worlds, until its spacious might
Satiate the void circumference: then shrink   420
Even to a point within our day and night;
And keep thy heart light lest it make thee sink
When hope has kindled hope, and lured thee to the
   brink;

48

Or go to Rome, which is the sepulchre,
O, not of him, but of our joy: 'tis nought   425
That ages, empires, and religions there
Lie buried in the ravage they have wrought;
For such as he can lend, – they borrow not
Glory from those who made the world their prey;
And he is gathered to the kings of thought   430
Who waged contention with their time's decay,
And of the past are all that cannot pass away.

49

Go thou to Rome, – at once the Paradise,
The grave, the city, and the wilderness;
And where its wrecks like shattered mountains rise,   435
And flowering weeds, and fragrant copses dress
The bones of Desolation's nakedness
Pass, till the Spirit of the spot shall lead
Thy footsteps to a slope of green access
Where, like an infant's smile, over the dead,   440
A light of laughing flowers along the grass is spread.

50

And grey walls moulder round, on which dull Time
Feeds, like slow fire upon a hoary brand:
And one keen pyramid with wedge sublime,
Pavilioning the dust of him who planned   445
This refuge for his memory, doth stand
Like flame transformed to marble; and beneath,
A field is spread, on which a newer band
Have pitched in Heaven's smile their camp of death,
Welcoming him we lose with scarce extinguished
    breath.   450

51

Here pause: these graves are all too young as yet
To have outgrown the sorrow which consigned
Its charge to each; and if the seal is set,
Here, on one fountain of a mourning mind,
Break it not thou! too surely shalt thou find   455
Thine own well full, if thou returnest home,
Of tears and gall. From the world's bitter wind
Seek shelter in the shadow of the tomb.
What Adonais is, why fear we to become?

52

The One remains, the many change and pass;   460
Heaven's light forever shines, Earth's shadows fly;
Life, like a dome of many-coloured glass,
Stains the white radiance of Eternity,
Until Death tramples it to fragments. – Die,
If thou wouldst be with that which thou dost seek!   465
Follow where all is fled! – Rome's azure sky,
Flowers, ruins, statues, music, words, are weak
The glory they transfuse with fitting truth to speak.

53

Why linger, why turn back, why shrink, my Heart?
Thy hopes are gone before: from all things here   470
They have departed; thou shouldst now depart!
A light is passed from the revolving year,
And man, and woman; and what still is dear

Attracts to crush, repels to make thee wither.
The soft sky smiles, – the low wind whispers near: 475
'Tis Adonais calls! oh, hasten thither,
No more let Life divide what Death can join together.

54

That Light whose smiles kindles the Universe,
That Beauty in which all things work and move,
That Benediction which the eclipsing Curse   480
Of birth can quench not, that sustaining Love
Which through the web of being blindly wove
By man and beast and earth and air and sea,
Burns bright or dim, as each are mirrors of
The fire for which all thirst, now beams on me,   485
Consuming the last clouds of cold mortality.

55

The breath whose might I have invoked in song
Descends on me; my spirit's bark is driven
Far from the shore, far from the trembling throng
Whose sails were never to the tempest given;   490
The massy earth and spherèd skies are riven!
I am borne darkly, fearfully, afar;
Whilst burning through the inmost veil of Heaven,
The soul of Adonais, like a star,
Beacons from the abode where the Eternal are.   495

43   LINES WRITTEN ON HEARING THE NEWS OF
THE DEATH OF NAPOLEON

What! alive and so bold, o Earth?
    Art thou not overbold?
    What! leapest thou forth as of old
In the light of thy morning mirth,
The last of the flock of the starry fold?   5
Ha! leapest thou forth as of old?
Are not the limbs still when the ghost is fled,
And canst thou move, Napoleon being dead?

How! is not thy quick heart cold?
  What spark is alive on thy hearth?   10
How! is not *his* death-knell knolled?
  And livest *thou* still, Mother Earth?
Thou wert warming thy fingers old
O'er the embers covered and cold
Of that most fiery spirit, when it fled –   15
What, Mother, do you laugh now he is dead?

'Who has known me of old,' replied Earth,
  'Or who has my story told?
  It is thou who art overbold.'
And the lightning of scorn laughed forth   20
As she sung, 'To my bosom I fold
All my sons when their knell is knolled,
And so with living motion all are fed,
And the quick spring like weeds out of the dead.

'Still alive and still bold,' shouted Earth,   25
  'I grow bolder and still more bold.
  The dead fill me ten thousandfold
Fuller of speed, and splendour, and mirth.
I was cloudy, and sullen, and cold,
Like a frozen chaos uprolled,   30
Till by the spirit of the mighty dead
My heart grew warm. I feed on whom I fed.

'Aye, alive and still bold,' muttered Earth.
  'Napoleon's fierce spirit rolled,
  In terror and blood and gold,   35
A torrent of ruin to death from his birth.
Leave the millions who follow to mould
The metal before it be cold;
And weave into his shame, which like the dead
Shrouds me, the hopes that from his glory fled.'   40

'Do you not hear the aziola cry?
Methinks she must be nigh – '
  Said Mary as we sate
In dusk, ere stars were lit or candles brought –
  And I who thought   5
This Aziola was some tedious woman
Asked, 'Who is Aziola?' – how elate
I felt to know that it was nothing human,
No mockery of myself to fear or hate!
  And Mary saw my soul,   10
And laughed and said – 'Disquiet yourself not,
  'Tis nothing but a little downy owl.'

Sad aziola, many an eventide
  Thy music I had heard
By wood and stream, meadow and mountainside,   15
And fields and marshes wide,
Such as nor voice, nor lute, nor wind, nor bird
  The soul ever stirred –
Unlike and far sweeter than them all.
Sad aziola, from that moment I   20
Loved thee and thy sad cry.

45 *From* HELLAS

The apathy of the rulers of the civilized world to the
astonishing circumstance of the descendants of that nation
to which they owe their civilization rising as it were from
the ashes of their ruin is something perfectly inexplicable to
a mere specatator of the shows of this mortal scene. We are 5
all Greeks – our laws, our literature, our religion, our arts
have their root in Greece. But for Greece, Rome, the
instructor, the conqueror, or the metropolis of our ancestors
would have spread no illumination with her arms, and we
might still have been savages, and idolators; or, what is 10
worse, might have arrived at such a stagnant and miserable
state of social institution as China and Japan possess.

The human form and the human mind attained to a perfection in Greece which has impressed its image on those faultless productions whose very fragments are the despair of modern art, and has propagated impulses which cannot cease, through a thousand channels of manifest or imperceptible operation to ennoble and delight mankind until the extinction of the race.

The modern Greek is the descendant of those glorious beings whom the imagination almost refuses to figure to itself as belonging to our Kind, and he inherits much of their sensibility, their rapidity of conception, their enthusiasm, and their courage. If in many instances he is degraded, by moral and political slavery to the practice of the basest vices it engenders, and that below the level of ordinary degradation; let us reflect that the corruption of the best produces the worst, and that habits which subsist only in relation to a peculiar state of social institution may be expected to cease so soon as that relation is dissolved. In fact, the Greeks, since the admirable novel of *Anastasius* could have been a faithful picture of their manners, have undergone most important changes; the flower of their Youth, returning to their Country from the universities of Italy, Germany and France have communicated to their fellow citizens the latest results of that social perfection of which their ancestors were the original source. The university of Chios contained before the breaking out of the Revolution eight hundred students, and among them several Germans and Americans. The munificence and energy of many of the Greek princes and merchants, directed to the renovation of their country with a spirit and a wisdom which has few examples, is above all praise.

The English permit their own oppressors to act according to their natural sympathy with the Turkish tyrant, and to brand upon their name the indelible blot of an alliance with the enemies of domestic happiness, of Christianity and civilization.

Russia desires to possess not to liberate Greece, and is contented to see the Turks, its natural enemies, and the Greeks, its intended slaves, enfeeble each other until one or both fall into its net. The wise and generous policy of England would have consisted in establishing the indepen-

dence of Greece, and in maintaining it both against Russia
and the Turk; – but when was the oppressor generous or   55
just?

Should the English people ever become free they will
reflect upon the part which those who presume to represent
their will, have played in the great drama of the revival of
liberty, with feelings which it would become them to   60
anticipate. This is the age of the war of the oppressed
against the oppressors, and every one of those ringleaders
of the privileged gangs of murderers and swindlers, called
Sovereigns, look to each other for aid against the common
enemy and suspend their mutual jealousies in the presence   65
of a mightier fear. Of this holy alliance all the despots of the
earth are virtual members. But a new race has arisen
throughout Europe, nursed in the abhorrence of the opin-
ions which are its chains, and she will continue to produce
fresh generations to accomplish that destiny which tyrants   70
foresee and dread.

The Spanish peninsula is already free. France is tranquil
in the enjoyment of a partial exemption from the abuses
which its unnatural and feeble government are vainly
attempting to revive. The seed of blood and misery has been   75
sown in Italy and a more vigorous race is arising to go forth
to the harvest. The world waits only the news of a revolution
of Germany to see the Tyrants who have pinnacled them-
selves on its supineness precipitated into the ruin from
which they shall never arise. Well do these destroyers of   80
mankind know their enemy when they impute the insurrec-
tion in Greece to the same spirit before which they tremble
throughout the rest of Europe, and that enemy well knows
the power and the cunning of its opponents, and watches
the moment of their approaching weakness and inevitable   85
division to wrest the bloody sceptres from their grasp.

Two Choruses

I

Worlds on worlds are rolling ever
   From creation to decay,
Like the bubbles on a river
   Sparkling, bursting, borne away.

But *they* are still immortal   5
Who, through Birth's orient portal
And Death's dark chasm hurrying to and fro,
Clothe their unceasing flight
In the brief dust and light
Gathered around their chariots as they go;   10
New shapes they still may weave,
New gods, new laws receive,
Bright or dim are they as the robes they last
On Death's bare ribs had cast.

A Power from the unknown God,   15
A Promethean conqueror, came;
Like a triumphal path he trod
The thorns of death and shame.
A mortal shape to him
Was like the vapour dim   20
Which the orient planet animates with light;
Hell, Sin, and Slavery came
Like bloodhounds mild and tame,
Nor preyed, until their Lord had taken flight;
The moon of Mahomet   25
Arose, and it shall set
While blazoned as on Heaven's immortal noon
The cross leads generations on.

Swift as the radiant shapes of sleep
From one whose dreams are Paradise   30
Fly, when the fond wretch wakes to weep
And Day peers forth with her blank eyes,
So fleet, so faint, so fair,
The Powers of earth and air
Fled from the folding-star of Bethlehem: 35
Apollo, Pan, and Love,
And even Olympian Jove
Grew weak, for killing Truth had glared on them;
Our hills and seas and streams,
Dispeopled of their dreams,   40
Their waters turned to blood, their dew to tears,
Wailed for the golden years.

II

The world's great age begins anew,
    The golden years return,
The earth doth like a snake renew
    Her winter weeds outworn;
Heaven smiles, and faiths and empires gleam   5
Like wrecks of a dissolving dream.

A brighter Hellas rears its mountains
    From waves serener far,
A new Peneus rolls his fountains
    Against the morning-star;   10
Where fairer Tempes bloom, there sleep
Young Cyclads on a sunnier deep.

A loftier Argo cleaves the main
    Fraught with a later prize;
Another Orpheus sings again,   15
    And loves, and weeps, and dies;
A new Ulysses leaves once more
Calypso for his native shore.

O, write no more the tale of Troy,
    If earth Death's scroll must be!   20
Nor mix with Laian rage the joy
    Which dawns upon the free;
Although a subtler Sphinx renew
Riddles of death Thebes never knew.

Another Athens shall arise,   25
    And to remoter time
Bequeath, like sunset to the skies,
    The splendour of its prime;
And leave, if nought so bright may live,
All earth can take or Heaven can give.   30

Saturn and Love their long repose
    Shall burst, more bright and good
Than all who fell, than One who rose,
    Than many unsubdued;

Not gold, not blood, their altar dowers,   35
But votive tears and symbol flowers.

 O cease! must hate and death return?
  Cease! must men kill and die?
 Cease! drain not to its dregs the urn
  Of bitter prophecy.   40
The world is weary of the past,
O might it die or rest at last!

46 THE FLOWER THAT SMILES TODAY

 The flower that smiles today
  Tomorrow dies;
 All that we wish to stay
  Tempts and then flies;
 What is this world's delight?   5
 Lightning, that mocks the night,
  Brief even as bright. –

 Virtue, how frail it is! –
  Friendship, how rare! –   10
 Love, how it sells poor bliss
  For proud despair!
 But these, though soon they fall,
 Survive their joy, and all
  Which ours we call. –

 Whilst skies are blue and bright,   15
  Whilst flowers are gay,
 Whilst eyes that change ere night
  Make glad the day;
 Whilst yet the calm hours creep,
 Dream thou – and from thy sleep   20
  Then wake to weep.

Swiftly walk o'er the western wave,
    Spirit of Night!
Out of the misty eastern cave
Where, all the long and lone daylight
Thou wovest dreams of joy and fear,   5
Which make thee terrible and dear,
    Swift be thy flight!

Wrap thy form in a mantle grey,
    Star-inwrought!
Blind with thine hair the eyes of Day,   10
Kiss her until she be wearied out –
Then wander o'er city and sea and land,
Touching all with thine opiate wand –
    Come, long-sought!

When I arose and saw the dawn   15
    I sighed for thee;
When light rode high, and the dew was gone,
And noon lay heavy on flower and tree,
And the weary Day turned to his rest,
Lingering like an unloved guest,   20
    I sighed for thee.

Thy brother Death came, and cried,
    'Wouldst thou me?'
Thy sweet child Sleep, the filmy-eyed,
Murmured like a noontide bee,   25
'Shall I nestle near thy side?
Wouldst thou me?' and I replied,
    'No, not thee!'

Death will come when thou art dead,
    Soon, too soon –   30
    Sleep will come when thou art fled;
Of neither would I ask the boon
I ask of thee, belovèd Night –

Swift be thine approaching flight,
   Come soon, soon! 35

48   ROSE LEAVES, WHEN THE ROSE IS DEAD

Rose leaves, when the rose is dead,
Are heaped for the beloved's bed,
And so thy thoughts, when thou art gone,
Love itself shall slumber on.

Music, when soft voices die, 5
Vibrates in the memory, –
Odours, when sweet violets sicken,
Live within the sense they quicken.

49   O WORLD, O LIFE, O TIME

O World, O Life, O Time,
  On whose last steps I climb,
Trembling at that where I had stood before –
  When will return the glory of your prime?
    No more, O never more! 5

Out of the day and night
  A joy has taken flight –
Fresh spring and summer [   ] and winter hoar
  Move my faint heart with grief, but with delight
    No more, O never more! 10

When passion's trance is overpast,
If tenderness and truth could last
Or live, whilst all wild feelings keep
Some mortal slumber, dark and deep,
I should not weep, I should not weep!   5

It were enough to feel, to see
Thy soft eyes gazing tenderly,
And dream the rest – and burn and be
The secret food of fires unseen,
Could thou but be what thou hast been.   10

After the slumber of the year
The woodland violets reappear;
All things revive in field or grove
And sky and sea, but two, which move
And form all others – life and love.   15

51   ONE WORD IS TOO OFTEN PROFANED

1

One word is too often profaned
    For me to profane it,
One feeling too falsely disdained
    For thee to disdain it;
One hope is too like despair   5
    For prudence to smother,
And pity from thee more dear
    Than that from another.

2

I can give not what men call love;
    But wilt thou accept not   10
The worship the heart lifts above
    And the Heavens reject not, –
The desire of the moth for the star,

Of the night for the morrow,
The devotion to something afar   15
From the sphere of our sorrow?

52   TO EDWARD WILLIAMS

1

The serpent is shut out from Paradise –
The wounded deer must seek the herb no more
In which its heart's cure lies –
The widowed dove must cease to haunt a bower
Like that from which its mate, with feignèd sighs,   5
Fled in the April hour –
I too, must seldom seek again
Near happy friends a mitigated pain.

2

Of hatred I am proud, – with scorn content;
Indifference, which once hurt me, is now grown   10
Itself indifferent.
But, not to speak of love, Pity alone
Can break a spirit already more than bent.
The miserable one
Turns the mind's poison into food: 15
Its medicine is tears, – its evil, good.

3

Therefore, if now I see you seldomer,
Dear friends, dear *friend*, know that I only fly
Your looks, because they stir
Griefs that should sleep, and hopes that cannot die.   20
The very comfort which they minister
I scarce can bear; yet I
(So deeply is the arrow gone)
Should quickly perish if it were withdrawn.

4

When I return to my cold home, you ask   25
Why I am not as I have lately been?

You spoil me for the task
Of acting a forced part in life's dull scene, –
Of wearing on my brow the idle mask
Of author, great or mean,   30
In the world's carnival. I sought
Peace thus, and but in you I found it not.

5

Full half an hour today I tried my lot
With various flowers, and every one still said,
'She loves me, loves me not.'   35
And if this meant a Vision long since fled –
If it meant Fortune, Fame, or Peace of thought –
If it meant – (but I dread
To speak what you may know too well) –
Still there was truth in the sad oracle.   40

6

The crane o'er seas and forests seeks her home.
No bird so wild but has its quiet nest
When it no more would roam.
The sleepless billows on the Ocean's breast
Break like a bursting heart, and die in foam   45
And thus, at length, find rest.
Doubtless there is a place of peace
Where *my* weak heart and all its throbs will cease.

7

I asked her yesterday if she believed
That I had resolution, – one who *had*   50
Would ne'er have thus relieved
His heart with words, but what his judgement bade
Would do, and leave the scorner unrelieved. –
These verses were too sad
To send to you, but that I know,   55
Happy yourself, you feel another's woe.

53   TO JANE: THE RECOLLECTION
Feb. 2, 1822

Now the last day of many days,
All beautiful and bright as thou,
The loveliest and the last, is dead.
Rise Memory, and write its praise!
Up to thy wonted work! come, trace   5
The epitaph of glory fled;
For now the Earth has changed its face,
A frown is on the Heaven's brow.

1
We wandered to the pine forest
    That skirts the ocean foam;   10
The lighest wind was in its nest,
    The Tempest in its home;
The whispering waves were half asleep,
    The clouds were gone to play,
And on the bosom of the deep   15
    The smile of Heaven lay;
It seemed as if the hour were one
    Sent from beyond the skies,
Which scattered from above the sun
    A light of Paradise.   20

2
We paused amid the pines that stood
    The giants of the waste,
Tortured by storms to shapes as rude
    As serpents interlaced,
And soothed by every azure breath   25
    That under Heaven is blown
To harmonies and hues beneath,
    As tender as its own;
Now all the tree-tops lay asleep
    Like green waves on the sea,   30
As still as in the silent deep
    The Ocean woods may be.

3

How calm it was! the silence there
 By such a chain was bound
That even the busy woodpecker   35
 Made stiller with her sound
The inviolable quietness;
 The breath of peace we drew
With its soft motion made not less
 The calm that round us grew. –   40
There seemed from the remotest seat
 Of the white mountain-waste,
To the soft flower beneath our feet
 A magic circle traced,
A spirit interfused around,   45
 A thrilling silent life,
To momentary peace it bound
 Our mortal nature's strife; –
And still I felt the centre of
 The magic circle there   50
Was one fair form that filled with love
 The lifeless atmosphere.

4

We paused beside the pools that lie
 Under the forest bough –
Each seemed as 'twere, a little sky   55
 Gulfed in a world below,
A firmament of purple light
 Which in the dark earth lay
More boundless than the depth of night
 And purer than the day,   60
In which the lovely forests grew
 As in the upper air,
More perfect, both in shape and hue,
 Than any spreading there;
There lay the glade, the neighbouring lawn,   65
 And through the dark green wood
The white sun twinkling like the dawn
 Out of a speckled cloud.

5

Sweet views, which in our world above
   Can never well be seen,   70
Were imaged in the water's love
   Of that fair forest green;
And all was interfused beneath
   With an Elysian glow,
An atmosphere without a breath,   75
   A softer day below –
Like one beloved, the scene had lent
   To the dark water's breast,
Its every leaf and lineament
   With more than truth exprest;   80
Until an envious wind crept by,
   Like an unwelcome thought
Which from the mind's too faithful eye
   Blots one dear image out. –
Though thou art ever fair and kind   85
   And forests ever green,
Less oft is peace in S[helley]'s mind
   Than calm in water seen.

54 *From* GOETHE'S FAUST:
PROLOGUE IN HEAVEN

The Lord *and the* Host *of* Heaven: to them Mephistopheles.
Enter three Archangels.

Raphael.
The Sun makes music as of old
   Amid the rival spheres of Heaven,
On its predestined circle rolled
   With thunder speed: the Angels even
Draw strength from glazing on its glance,   5
   Though none its meaning fathom may; –
The world's unwithered countenance
   Is bright as at Creation's day.

Gabriel.
And swift and swift, with rapid lightness,

The adornèd Earth spins silently,   10
Alternating Elysian brightness
   With deep and dreadful night; the sea
Foams in broad billows from its deep
   Up to the rocks, and rocks and Ocean,
Onward, with spheres which never sleep,   15
   Are hurried in eternal motion.

Michael.
And tempests in contention roar
   From land to sea, from sea to land;
And, raging, weave a chain of power,
   Which girds the earth, as with a band. –   20
A flashing desolation there,
   Flames before the thunder's way;
But thy servants, Lord, revere
   The gentle changes of thy day.

Chorus of the Three.
The Angels draw strength from thy glance,   25
   Though no one comprehend thee may; –
Thy world's unwithered countenance
   Is bright as on Creation's day.

Enter Mephistopheles.
Mephistopheles.   As thou, O Lord, once more art kind
      enough   30
   To interest thyself in our affairs,
And ask, 'How goes it with you there below?'
And as indulgently at other times
Thou tookedst not my visits in ill part,
Thou seest me here once more among thy household.
Though I should scandalize this company,   35
You will excuse me if I do not talk
In the high style which they think fashionable;
My pathos certainly would make you laugh too,
Had you not long since given over laughing.
Nothing know I to say of suns and worlds;   40
I observe only how men plague themselves; –
The little God o'the world keeps the same stamp,
As wonderful as on Creation's day. –

A little better would he live, hadst thou
Not given him a glimpse of Heaven's light   45
Which he calls reason, and employs it only
To live more beastlily than any beast.
With reverence of your Lordship be it spoken,
He's like one of those long-legged grasshoppers,
Who flits and jumps about, and sings for ever   50
The same old song i' the grass. There let him lie,
Burying his nose in every heap of dung.
The Lord.   Have you no more to say? Do you come here
   Always to scold and cavil and complain?
   Seems nothing ever right to you on Earth?   55
Mephistopheles.   No, Lord; I find all there, as ever, bad
    at heart.
   Even I am sorry for man's days of sorrow;
   I could myself almost give up the pleasure
   Of plaguing the poor things.
The Lord.   Knowest thou Faust?   60
Mephistopheles.   The Doctor?
The Lord.   Ay; my servant Faust.
Mephistopheles.   In truth,
   He serves you in a fashion quite his own;
   And the fool's meat and drink are not of earth.
   His aspirations bear him on so far
   That he is half aware of his own folly;   65
   For he demands from Heaven its fairest star
   And from the earth the highest joy it bears,
   Yet all things far and all things near are vain
   To calm the deep emotions of his breast.
The Lord.   Though he now serves me in a cloud of error,   70
   I will soon lead him forth to the clear day.
   When trees look green, full well the gardener knows
   That fruits and blooms will deck the coming year.
Mephistopheles.   What will you bet? – now, I am sure
    of winning . . .
   Only, observe you give me full permission   75
   To lead him softly on my path.
The Lord.   As long
   As he shall live upon the earth, so long
   Is nothing unto thee forbidden – Man
   Must err till he has ceased to struggle.

Mephistopheles.   Thanks.
  And that is all I ask; for willingly   80
  I never make acquaintance with the dead.
  The full fresh cheeks of youth are food for me,
  And if a corpse knocks, I am not at home.
  For I am like a cat – I like to play
  A little with the mouse before I eat it.   85
The Lord.   Well, well, it is permitted thee! Draw thou
  His spirit from its springs; as thou find'st power,
  Seize him and lead him on thy downward path;
  And stand ashamed when failure teaches thee
  That a good man, even in his darkest longings,   90
  Is well aware of the right way.
Mephistopheles.   Well and good.
  I am not in much doubt about my bet,
  And if I lose, then 'tis your turn to crow;
  Enjoy your triumph then with a full breast.
  Ay; dust shall he devour, and that with pleasure,   95
  Like my old paramour, the famous Snake.
The Lord.   Pray come here when it suits you; for I never
  Had much dislike for people of your sort.
  And, among all the spirits who rebelled,
  The knave was ever the least tedious to me.   100
  The active spirit of man soon sleeps, and soon
  He seeks unbroken quiet; therefore I
  Have given him the Devil for a companion,
  Who may provoke him to some sort of work,
  And must create forever. – But ye, pure   105
  Children of God, enjoy eternal beauty!
  Let that which ever operates and lives
  Clasp you within the limits of its love;
  And seize with sweet and melancholy thoughts
  The floating phantoms of its loveliness.   110
               Heaven closes, the Archangels exeunt.
Mephistopheles.   From time to time I visit the old fellow,
  And I take care to keep on good terms with him.
  Civil enough is this same God Almighty,
  To talk so freely with the Devil himself.

Ariel to Miranda; – Take
This slave of music for the sake
Of him who is the slave of thee;
And teach it all the harmony,
In which thou canst, and only thou,   5
Make the delighted spirit glow,
Till joy denies itself again
And too intense is turned to pain;
For my permission and command
Of thine own prince Ferdinand   10
Poor Ariel sends this silent token
Of more than ever can be spoken;
Your guardian spirit Ariel, who
From life to life must still pursue
Your happiness, for thus alone   15
Can Ariel ever find his own;
From Prospero's enchanted cell,
As the mighty verses tell,
To the throne of Naples he
Lit you o'er the trackless sea,   20
Flitting on, your prow before,
Like a living meteor.
When you die, the silent Moon
In her interlunar swoon
Is not sadder in her cell   25
Than deserted Ariel;
When you live again on Earth
Like an unseen Star of birth
Ariel guides you o'er the sea
Of life from your nativity;   30
Many changes have been run
Since Ferdinand and you begun
Your course of love, and Ariel still
Has tracked your steps and served your will;
Now, in humbler, happier lot   35
This is all remembered not;
And now, alas! the poor sprite is
Imprisoned for some fault of his

In a body like a grave: –
From you, he only dares to crave   40
For his service and his sorrow
A smile today, a song tomorrow.
The artist who this idol wrought
To echo all harmonious thought
Felled a tree, while on the steep   45
The woods were in their winter sleep
Rocked in that repose divine
On the wind-swept Apennine;
And dreaming, some of autumn past
And some of spring approaching fast,   50
And some of April buds and showers
And some of songs in July bowers
And all of love, – and so this tree –
O that such our death may be –
Died in sleep, and felt no pain,   55
To live in happier form again,
From which, beneath Heaven's fairest star,
The artist wrought this loved guitar,
And taught it justly to reply
To all who question skilfully   60
In language gentle as thine own;
Whispering in enamoured tone
Sweet oracles of woods and dells
And summer winds in sylvan cells
For it had learnt all harmonies   65
Of the plains and of the skies,
Of the forests and the mountains,
And the many-voicèd fountains,
The clearest echoes of the hills,
The softest notes of falling rills,   70
The melodies of birds and bees,
The murmuring of summer seas,
And pattering rain and breathing dew
And airs of evening; – and it knew
That seldom heard mysterious sound,   75
Which, driven on its diurnal round
As it floats through boundless day
Our world enkindles on its way –
All this it knows, but will not tell

To those who cannot question well   80
The spirit that inhabits it:
It talks according to the wit
Of its companions; and no more
Is heard than has been felt before
By those who tempt it to betray   85
These secrets of an elder day. –
But, sweetly as its answers will
Flatter hands of perfect skill,
It keeps its highest holiest tone
For our belovèd Jane alone. –   90

56 TO JANE

The keen stars were twinkling
And the fair moon was rising among them,
    Dear Jane.
  The guitar was tinkling
But the notes were not sweet till you sung them   5
    Again. –

  As the moon's soft splendour
O'er the faint cold starlight of Heaven
    Is thrown –
  So your voice most tender   10
To the strings without soul had then given
    Its own.

  The stars will awaken,
Though the moon sleep a full hour later,
    Tonight;   15
  No leaf will be shaken
While the dews of your melody scatter
    Delight.

  Though the sound overpowers,
Sing again, with your dear voice revealing   20
    A tone
  Of some world far from ours,

Where music and moonlight and feeling
    Are one.

57 LINES WRITTEN IN THE BAY OF LERICI

Bright wanderer, fair coquette of Heaven,
To whom alone it has been given
To change and be adored for ever,
Envy not this dim world, for never
But once within its shadow grew   5
One fair as [thou], but far more true. –
She left me at the silent time
When the moon had ceased to climb
The azure dome of Heaven's steep,
And like an albatross asleep,   10
Balanced on her wings of light,
Hovered in the purple night,
Ere she sought her Ocean nest
In the chambers of the west. –
She left me, and I stayed alone   15
Thinking over every tone,
Which though now silent to the ear
The enchanted heart could hear
Like notes which die when born, but still
Haunt the echoes of the hill: 20
And feeling ever – O too much –
The soft vibrations of her touch,
As if her gentle hand even now
Lightly trembled on my brow;
And thus although she absent were   25
Memory gave me all of her
That even fancy dares to claim. –
Her presence had made weak and tame
All passions, and I lived alone
In the time which is our own;   30
The past and future were forgot
As they had been, and would be, not. –
But soon, the guardian angel gone,
The demon reassumed his throne

In my faint heart . . . I dare not speak   35
My thoughts; but thus disturbed and weak
I sate and watched the vessels glide
Along the Ocean bright and wide,
Like spirit-wingèd chariots sent
O'er some serenest element   40
To ministrations strange and far;
As if to some Elysian star
They sailed for drink to medicine
Such sweet and bitter pain as mine. –
And the wind that winged their flight   45
From the land came fresh and light,
And the scent of sleeping flowers
And the coolness of the hours
Of dew, and the sweet warmth of day
Was scattered o'er the twinkling bay;   50
And the fisher with his lamp
And spear, about the low rocks damp
Crept, and struck the fish who came
To worship the delusive flame:
Too happy, they whose pleasure sought   55
Extinguishes all sense and thought
Of the regret that pleasure [   ],
Seeking life alone, not peace.

58   THE TRIUMPH OF LIFE

Swift as a spirit hastening to his task
   Of glory and of good, the Sun sprang forth
Rejoicing in his splendour, and the mask

   Of darkness fell from the awakened Earth.
The smokeless altars of the mountain snows   5
   Flamed above crimson clouds, and at the birth

Of light, the Ocean's orison arose
   To which the birds tempered their matin lay.
All flowers in field or forest which unclose

Their trembling eyelids to the kiss of day,   10
Swinging their censers in the element,
    With orient incense lit by the new ray

Burned slow and inconsumably, and sent
    Their odorous sighs up to the smiling air,
And in the succession due, did Continent,   15

    Isle, Ocean, and all things that in them wear
The form and character of mortal mould
    Rise as the Sun their father rose, to bear

Their portion of the toil which he of old
    Took as his own and then imposed on them;   20
But I, whom thoughts which must remain untold

    Had kept as wakeful as the stars that gem
The cone of night, now they were laid asleep,
    Stretched my faint limbs beneath the hoary stem

Which an old chestnut flung athwart the steep   25
    Of a green Apennine: before me fled
The night; behind me rose the day; the Deep

    Was at my feet, and Heaven above my head;
When a strange trance over my fancy grew
    Which was not slumber, for the shade it spread   30

Was so transparent that the scene came through
    As clear as when a veil of light is drawn
O'er evening hills, they glimmer; and I knew

    That I had felt the freshness of that dawn,
Bathed in the same cold dew my brow and hair,   35
    And sate as thus upon that slope of lawn

Under the self-same bough, and heard as there
    The birds, the fountains and the Ocean hold
Sweet talk in music through the enamoured air.

    And then a Vision on my brain was rolled . . .   40

As in that trance of wondrous thought I lay
  This was the tenor of my waking dream:
Methought I sate beside a public way

   Thick strewn with summer dust, and a great stream
Of people there was hurrying to and fro   45
  Numerous as gnats upon the evening gleam,

All hastening onward, yet none seemed to know
  Whither he went, or whence he came, or why
He made one of the multitude, yet so

  Was borne amid the crowd as through the sky   50
One of the million leaves of summer's bier. –
  Old age and youth, manhood and infancy,

Mixed in one mighty torrent did appear,
  Some flying from the thing they feared and some
Seeking the object of another's fear,   55

  And others as with steps towards the tomb
Pored on the trodden worms that crawled beneath,
  And others mournfully within the gloom

Of their own shadow walked, and called it death . . .
  And some fled from it as it were a ghost,   60
Half fainting in the affliction of vain breath.

  But more, with motions which each other crossed,
Pursued or shunned the shadows the clouds threw
  Or birds within the noonday aether lost,

Upon that path where flowers never grew;   65
  And weary with vain toil and faint for thirst
Heard not the fountains whose melodious dew

  Out of their mossy cells forever burst,
Nor felt the breeze which from the forest told
  Of grassy paths, and wood lawns interspersed   70

With overarching elms and caverns cold,
   And violet banks where sweet dreams brood, but they
Pursued their serious folly as of old . . .

   And as I gazed methought that in the way
The throng grew wilder, as the woods of June   75
   When the south wind shakes the extinguished day –

And a cold glare, intenser than the noon
   But icy cold, obscured with light
The Sun as he the stars. Like the young moon

   When on the sunlit limits of the night   80
Her white shell trembles amid crimson air,
   And whilst the sleeping tempest gathers might

Doth, as a herald of its coming, bear
   The ghost of her dead mother, whose dim form
Bends in dark aether from her infant's chair,   85

   So came a chariot on the silent storm
Of its own rushing splendour, and a Shape
   So sate within as one whom years deform

Beneath a dusky hood and double cape
   Crouching within the shadow of a tomb,   90
And o'er what seemed the head, a cloud like crape

   Was bent, a dun and faint etherial gloom
Tempering the light; upon the chariot's beam
   A Janus-visaged Shadow did assume

The guidance of that wonder-wingèd team.   95
   The shapes which drew it in thick lightnings
Were lost: I heard alone on the air's soft stream

   The music of their ever-moving wings.
All the four faces of that charioteer
   Had their eyes banded . . . little profit brings   100

Speed in the van and blindness in the rear,
   Nor then avail the beams that quench the Sun,
Or that his banded eyes could pierce the sphere

   Of all that is, has been, or will be done. –
So ill was the car guided, but it passed   105
   With solemn speed majestically on . . .

The crowd gave way, and I arose aghast,
   Or seemed to rise, so mighty was the trance,
And saw like clouds upon the thunder-blast

   The million with fierce song and maniac dance   110
Raging around; such seemed the jubilee
   As when to greet some conqueror's advance

Imperial Rome poured forth her living sea
   From senate-house and prison and theatre,
When Freedom left those who upon the free   115

   Had bound a yoke which soon they stooped to bear.
Nor wanted here the true similitude
   Of a triumphal pageant, for where'er

The chariot rolled, a captive multitude
   Was driven; all those who had grown old in power   120
Or misery, – all who have their age subdued,

   By action or by suffering, and whose hour
Was drained to its last sand in weal or woe,
   So that the trunk survived both fruit and flower;

All those whose fame or infamy must grow   125
   Till the great winter lay the form and name
Of their green earth with them forever low,

   – All but the sacred few who could not tame
Their spirits to the Conqueror, but as soon
   As they had touched the world with living flame   130

Fled back like eagles to their native noon,
  Or those who put aside the diadem
Of earthly thrones or gems, till the last one

  Were there; – for they of Athens and Jerusalem
Were neither mid the mighty captives seen,   135
  Nor mid the ribald crowd that followed them

Or fled before . . . Now swift, fierce and obscene
  The wild dance maddens in the van, and those
Who lead it, fleet as shadows on the green,

  Outspeed the chariot and without repose   140
Mix with each other in tempestuous measure
  To savage music . . . Wilder as it grows,

They, tortured by the agonizing pleasure,
  Convulsed, and on the rapid whirlwinds spun
Of that fierce spirit, whose unholy leisure   145

  Was soothed by mischief since the world begun,
Throw back their heads and loose their streaming hair,
  And in their dance round her who dims the Sun

Maidens and youths fling their wild arms in air
  As their feet twinkle; they recede, and now   150
Bending within each other's atmosphere

  Kindle invisibly; and as they glow,
Like moths by light attracted and repelled,
  Oft to their bright destruction come and go,

Till – like two clouds into one vale impelled   155
  That shake the mountains when their lightnings mingle,
And die in rain, – the fiery band which held

  Their natures, snaps . . . ere the shock cease to tingle,
One falls and then another in the path
  Senseless, nor is the desolation single, –   160

Yet ere I can say *where*, the chariot hath
  Passed over them; nor other trace I find
But as of foam after the Ocean's wrath

  Is spent upon the desert shore. – Behind,
Old men, and women foully disarrayed   165
  Shake their grey hair in the insulting wind,

Limp in the dance and strain with limbs decayed
  To reach the car of light which leaves them still
Farther behind and deeper in the shade.

  But not the less with impotence of will   170
They wheel, though ghastly shadows interpose
  Round them and round each other, and fulfil

Their part and to the dust whence they arose
  Sink, and corruption veils them as they lie,
And frost in these performs what fire in those.   175

  Struck to the heart by this sad pageantry,
Half to myself I said, 'And what is this?
  Whose shape is that within the car? and why' –

I would have added – 'is all here amiss?'
  But a voice answered: 'Life' . . . I turned and knew   180
(O Heaven have mercy on such wretchedness!)

  That what I thought was an old root which grew
To strange distortion out of the hill side
  Was indeed one of that deluded crew,

And that the grass which methought hung so wide   185
  And white, was but his thin discoloured hair,
And that the holes it vainly sought to hide

  Were or had been eyes. – 'If thou canst forbear
To join the dance, which I had well forborne,'
  Said the grim Feature, of my thought aware,   190

'I will unfold that which to this deep scorn
   Led me and my companions, and relate
The progress of the pageant since the morn;

   'If thirst of knowledge doth not thus abate,
Follow it even to the night, but I   195
   Am weary' . . . Then like one who with the weight

Of his own words is staggered, wearily
   He paused, and ere he could resume, I cried,
'First who art thou?'. . . 'Before thy memory

   'I feared, loved, hated, suffered, did, and died,   200
And if the spark with which Heaven lit my spirit
   Earth had with purer nutriment supplied,

'Corruption would not now thus much inherit
   Of what was once Rousseau – nor this disguise
Stain that within which still disdains to wear it. –   205

   'If I have been extinguished, yet there rise
A thousand beacons from the spark I bore.'
   'And who are those chained to the car?' 'The wise,

'The great, the unforgotten: they who wore
   Mitres and helms and crowns, or wreaths of light,   210
Signs of thought's empire over thought; their lore

   'Taught them not this – to know themselves; their might
Could not repress the mutiny within,
   And for the morn of truth they feigned, deep night

'Caught them ere evening.' 'Who is he with chin   215
   Upon his breast, and hands crossed on his chain?'
'The child of a fierce hour; he sought to win

   'The world, and lost all it did contain
Of greatness, in its hope destroyed; and more
   Of fame and peace than Virtue's self can gain   220

'Without the opportunity which bore
   Him on its eagle's pinion to the peak
From which a thousand climbers have before

   'Fall'n as Napoleon fell.' – I felt my cheek
Alter to see the great form pass away   225
   Whose grasp had left the giant world so weak

That every pigmy kicked it as it lay –
   And much I grieved to think how power and will
In opposition rule our mortal day –

   And why God made irreconcilable   230
Good and the means of good; and for despair
   I half disdained mine eye's desire to fill

With the spent vision of the times that were
   And scarce have ceased to be . . . 'Dost thou behold,'
Said then my guide, 'those spoilers spoiled, Voltaire,   235

   'Frederick, and Kant, Catharine, and Leopold,
Each hoary anarch, demagogue and sage
   Whose name the fresh world thinks already old,

'For in the battle Life and they did wage
   She remained conqueror – I was overcome   240
By my own heart alone, which neither age

   'Nor tears nor infamy nor now the tomb
Could temper to its object.' – 'Let them pass',
   I cried,' – the world and its mysterious doom

'Is not so much more glorious than it was   245
   That I desire to worship those who drew
New figures on its false and fragile glass

   'As the old faded.' – 'Figures ever new
Rise on the bubble, paint them how you may;
   We have but thrown, as those before us threw,   250

'Our shadows on it as it passed away.
  But mark, how chained to the triumphal chair
The mighty phantoms of an elder day –

'All that is mortal of great Plato there
Expiates the joy and woe his master knew not –   255
  That star that ruled his doom was far too fair,

'And Life, where long that flower of Heaven grew not,
  Conquered the heart by love which gold or pain
Or age or sloth or slavery could subdue not;

And near [   ] walk the twain,   260
The tutor and his pupil, whom Dominion
  Followed as tame as vulture in a chain. –

'The world was darkened beneath either pinion
  Of him whom from the flock of conquerors
Fame singled as her thunderbearing minion;   265

'The other long outlived both woes and wars,
Throned in the thoughts of men, and still had kept
  The jealous keys of truth's eternal doors

'If Bacon's spirit had not leapt
  Like lightning out of darkness; he compelled   270
The Proteus shape of Nature's as it slept

'To wake and to unbar the caves that held
The treasure of the secrets of its reign. –
  See the great bards of old, who inly quelled

'The passions which they sung, as by their strain   275
  May well be known: their living melody
Tempers its own contagion to the vein

'Of those who are infected with it – I
Have suffered what I wrote, or viler pain! –

'And so my words were seeds of misery,
Even as the deeds of others.' – 'Not as theirs,'   280
   I said – he pointed to a company

In which I recognized amid the heirs
   Of Caesar's crime, from him to Constantine,
The Anarchs old whose force and murderous snares   285

   Had founded many a sceptre-bearing line
And spread the plague of blood and gold abroad,
   And Gregory and John and men divine

Who rose like shadows between Man and God
   Till that eclipse, still hanging under Heaven,   290
Was worshipped by the world o'er which they strode

   For the true Sun it quenched. – 'Their power was given
But to destroy,' replied the leader; 'I
   Am one of those who have created, even

'If it be but a world of agony.' –   295
   'Whence camest thou and whither goest thou?
How did thy course begin,' I said, 'and why?

   'Mine eyes are sick of this perpetual flow
Of people, and my heart of one sad thought. –
   Speak.' – 'Whence I came, partly I seem to know,   300

'And how and by what paths I have been brought
   To this dread pass, methinks even thou mayst guess;
Why this should be, my mind can compass not,

   'Whither the conqueror hurries me, still less.
But follow thou, and from spectator turn   305
   Actor or victim in this wretchedness,

'And what thou wouldst be taught I then may learn
   From thee. Now listen . . . In the April prime
When all the forest tips began to burn

'With kindling green, touched by the azure clime   310
Of the young year, I found myself asleep
    Under a mountain, which from unknown time

'Had yawned into a cavern high and deep,
    And from it came a gentle rivulet
Whose water like clear air in its calm sweep   315

    'Bent the soft grass and kept for ever wet
The stems of the sweet flowers, and filled the grove
    With sound which whoso hear must needs forget

'All pleasure and all pain, all hate and love,
    Which they had known before that hour of rest: 320
A sleeping mother then would dream not of

    'The only child who died upon her breast
At eventide, a king would mourn no more
    The crown of which his brow was dispossessed

'When the sun lingered o'er the Ocean floor   325
    To gild his rival's new prosperity:
Thou wouldst forget thus vainly to deplore

    'Ills, which if ills, can find no cure from thee,
The thought of which no other sleep will quell,
    Nor other music blot from memory –   330

'So sweet and deep is the oblivious spell.
    Whether my life had been before that sleep
The Heaven which I imagine, or a Hell

    'Like this harsh world in which I wake to weep,
I know not. I arose and for a space   335
    The scene of woods and waters seemed to keep,

'Though it was now broad day, a gentle trace
    Of light diviner than the common Sun
Sheds on the common Earth, but all the place

'Was filled with many sounds woven into one   340
Oblivious melody, confusing sense
   Amid the gliding waves and shadows dun;

'And as I looked, the bright omnipresence
   Of morning through the orient cavern flowed,
And the Sun's image radiantly intense   345

'Burned on the waters of the well that glowed
Like gold, and threaded all the forest maze
   With winding paths of emerald fire – there stood

'Amid the Sun, as he amid the blaze
   Of his own glory, on the vibrating   350
Floor of the fountain, paved with flashing rays,

   'A Shape all light, which with one hand did fling
Dew on the earth, as if she were the Dawn,
   Whose invisible rain forever seemed to sing

'A silver music on the mossy lawn,   355
   And still before her on the dusky grass
Iris her many-coloured scarf had drawn. –

   'In her right hand she bore a crystal glass
Mantling with bright Nepenthe; – the fierce splendour
   Fell from her as she moved under the mass   360

'Of the deep cavern, and with palms so tender
   Their tread broke not the mirror of its billow,
Glided along the river, and did bend her

   'Head under the dark boughs, till like a willow
Her fair hair swept the bosom of the stream   365
   That whispered with delight to be their pillow. –

'As one enamoured is upborne in dream
   O'er lily-paven lakes mid silver mist
To wondrous music, so this Shape might seem

'Partly to tread the waves with feet which kissed   370
The dancing foam, partly to glide along
  The airs that roughened the moist amethyst,

'Or the slant morning beams that fell among
  The trees, or the soft shadows of the trees;
And her feet ever to the ceaseless song   375

  'Of leaves and winds and waves and birds and bees
And falling drops moved in a measure new
  Yet sweet, as on the summer evening breeze

'Up from the lake a shape of golden dew
  Between two rocks, athwart the rising moon,   380
Dances i' the wind, where eagle never flew. –

  'And still her feet, no less than the sweet tune
To which they moved, seemed as they moved, to blot
  The thoughts of him who gazed on them; and soon

'All that was, seemed as if it had been not,   385
  As if the gazer's mind was strewn beneath
Her feet like embers, and she, thought by thought,

  'Trampled its fires into the dust of death,
As Day upon the threshold of the east
  Treads out the lamps of night, until the breath   390

'Of darkness reillumines even the least
  Of Heaven's living eyes – like Day she came,
Making the night a dream; and ere she ceased

  'To move, as one between desire and shame
Suspended, I said: "If, as it doth seem,   395
  Thou comest from the realm without a name

'Into this valley of perpetual dream,
  Show whence I came, and where I am, and why –
Pass not away upon the passing stream."

'"Arise and quench thy thirst," was her reply.   400
And as a shut lily, stricken by the wand
    Of dewy morning's vital alchemy,

'I rose; and, bending at her sweet command,
    Touched with faint lips the cup she raised,
And suddenly my brain became as sand   405

'Where the first wave had more than half erased
The track of deer on desert Labrador,
    Whilst the empty wolf from which they fled amazed

'Leaves his stamp visibly upon the shore
    Until the second bursts – so on my sight   410
Burst a new vision never seen before;

'And the fair Shape waned in the coming light,
As veil by veil the silent splendour drops
    From Lucifer, amid the chrysolite

'Of sunrise, ere it strike the mountain tops –   415
    And as the presence of that fairest planet,
Although unseen, is felt by one who hopes

'That his day's path may end as he began it
In that star's smile, whose light is like the scent
    Of a jonquil when evening breezes fan it,   420

'Or the soft note in which his dear lament
    The Brescian shepherd breathes, or the caress
That turned his weary slumber to content –

'So knew I in that light's severe excess
The presence of that Shape which on the stream
    Moved, as I moved along the wilderness,   425

'More dimly than a day-appearing dream,
    The ghost of a forgotten form of sleep,
A light from Heaven whose half-extinguished beam

'Through the sick day in which we wake to weep   430
Glimmers, forever sought, forever lost. –
  So did that shape its obscure tenour keep

'Beside my path, as silent as a ghost;
  But the new Vision, and its cold bright car,
With solemn speed and stunning music crossed   435

  'The forest, and as if from some dread war
Triumphantly returning, the loud million
  Fiercely extolled the fortune of her star.

'A moving arch of victory the vermilion
  And green and azure plumes of Iris had   440
Built high over her wind-winged pavilion,

  'And underneath, aetherial glory clad
The wilderness, and far before her flew
  The tempest of the splendour which forbade

'Shadow to fall from leaf or stone; – the crew   445
  Seemed in that light like atomies that dance
Within a sunbeam. – Some upon the new

  'Embroidery of flowers that did enhance
The grassy vesture of the desert, played,
  Forgetful of the chariot's swift advance;   450

'Others stood gazing till within the shade
  Of the great mountains its light left them dim. –
Others outspeeded it, and others made

  'Circles around it like the clouds that swim
Round the high moon in a bright sea of air;   455
  And more did follow, with exulting hymn,

'The chariot and the captives fettered there;
  But all like bubbles on an eddying flood
Fell into the same track at last and were

'Borne onward. – I among the multitude   460
Was swept; me sweetest flowers delayed not long,
  Me not the shadow nor the solitude,

'Me not the falling stream's Lethean song,
  Me, not the phantom of that early form
Which moved upon its motion, – but among   465

  'The thickest billows of the living storm
I plunged, and bared my bosom to the clime
  Of that cold light, whose airs too soon deform. –

'Before the chariot had begun to climb
  The opposing steep of that mysterious dell,   470
Behold a wonder worthy of the rhyme

  'Of him whom from the lowest depths of Hell
Through every Paradise and through all glory
  Love led serene, and who returned to tell

'In words of hate and awe the wondrous story   475
  How all things are transfigured, except Love;
For deaf as is a sea which wrath makes hoary

  'The world can hear not the sweet notes that move
The sphere whose light is melody to lovers –
  A wonder worthy of his rhyme: the grove   480

'Grew dense with shadows to its inmost covers,
  The earth was grey with phantoms, and the air
Was peopled with dim forms, as when there hovers

  'A flock of vampire-bats before the glare
Of the tropic sun, bringing ere evening   485
  Strange night upon some Indian isle, – thus were

'Phantoms diffused around, and some did fling
  Shadows of shadows, yet unlike themselves,
Behind them; some like eaglets on the wing

'Were lost in the white blaze; others like elves　　　490
Danced in a thousand unimagined shapes
　　Upon the sunny streams and grassy shelves;

'And others sate chattering like restless apes
　　On vulgar hands and over shoulders leapt;
Some made a cradle of the ermined capes　　　495

　　'Of kingly mantles; some upon the tiar
Of pontiffs sate like vultures; others played
　　Within the crown which girt with empire

'A baby's or an idiot's brow, and made
　　Their nests in it; the old anatomies　　　500
Sate hatching their bare brood under the shade

　　'Of demons' wings, and laughed from their dead eyes
To reassume the delegated power
　　Arrayed in which these worms did monarchize

'Who make this earth their charnel. – Others more　　　505
　　Humble, like falcons sate upon the fist
Of common men, and round their heads did soar,

　　'Or like small gnats and flies as thick as mist
On evening marshes thronged about the brow
　　Of lawyer, statesman, priest and theorist;　　　510

'And others like discoloured flakes of snow
　　On fairest bosoms and the sunniest hair
Fell, and were melted by the youthful glow

　　'Which they extinguished; for like tears, they were
A veil to those from whose faint lids they rained　　　515
　　In drops of sorrow. – I became aware

'Of whence those forms proceeded which thus stained
　　The track in which we moved; after brief space
From every form the beauty slowly waned,

'From every firmest limb and fairest face   520
The strength and freshness fell like dust, and left
   The action and the shape without the grace

'Of life; the marble brow of youth was cleft
   With care, and in the eyes where once hope shone
Desire like a lioness bereft   525

   'Of its last cub, glared ere it died; each one
Of that great crowd sent forth incessantly
   These shadows, numerous as the dead leaves blown

'In Autumn evening from a poplar tree. –
   Each, like himself and like each other were,   530
At first, but soon distorted, seemed to be

   'Obscure clouds moulded by the casual air;
And of this stuff the car's creative ray
   Wrought all the busy phantoms fluttering there

'As the Sun shapes the clouds – thus, on the way,   535
   Mask after mask fell from the countenance
And form of all, and long before the day

   'Was old, the joy which waked like Heaven's glance
The sleepers in the oblivious valley, died,
   And some grew weary of the ghastly dance   540

'And fell, as I have fallen, by the wayside,
   Those soonest from whose forms most shadows passed
And least of strength and beauty did abide.' –

   'Then, what is Life?' I said . . . the cripple cast
His eye upon the car which now had rolled   545
   Onward, as if that look must be the last,

And answered: 'Happy those for whom the fold
   Of

NOTES

Abbreviations

DMAG = *A Discourse on the Manners of the Ancient Greeks relative to the Subject of Love*; DP = *A Defence of Poetry*; HIB = *Hymn to Intellectual Beauty*; JM = *Julian and Maddalo*; L = *Letters*; LC = *Laon and Cythna*; LMG = *Letter to Maria Gisborne*; MA = *The Mask of Anarchy*; ODD = *On the Devil, and Devils*; OL = *Ode to Liberty*; OWW = *Ode to the West Wind*; PBT = *Peter Bell the Third*; PL = *Paradise Lost*; PU = *Prometheus Unbound*; PVR = *A Philosophical View of Reform*; TL = *The Triumph of Life*.

Square brackets [ ] indicate editorial intervention; angled brackets < > indicate cancellation in Shelley's manuscript.

1   Queen Mab

Written between Apr. 1812 and Feb. 1813 (the prose notes were finished later, probably by 21 May). Printed and distributed privately as *Queen Mab. A Philosophical Poem with Notes* (1813) in the form of 'A small neat Quarto on fine paper & so as to catch the aristocrats: They will not read it, but their sons & daughters may.' Shelley had been the subject of reports to the Home Office from Dublin, Holyhead and Barnstaple, where his servant was found in possession of *Declaration of Rights* and 'The Devil's Walk', and imprisoned. He knew that he was under surveillance. Although he did not attempt 'to temper my constitutional enthusiasm', he now turned to poetry because 'A Poem is safe, the iron-souled Attorney general would scarcely dare to attack "Genus Irritabile Vatum" [the irritable race of poets]'. Perhaps Shelley also directed himself towards what he later called 'the more select classes of poetical readers' partly for prudential reasons: the authorities were more likely to prosecute the author of a text which might stimulate revolutionary or heretical tendencies among the masses (cf. the attempt to control the journalism of William Cobbett through the punitive use of paper-stamp taxation). Yet when *Queen Mab* was printed Shelley did not risk open publication but preferred to circulate the poem discreetly (compare these tactics with the detailed circulation list for his

pamphlet on the death of Princess Charlotte). His caution may well
have been justified since *Queen Mab* was used as evidence against him
in 1817 when Harriet's family contested custody of his two children.
In 1821 it was sold piratically by William Clark, who was prosecuted
by the Society for the Suppression of Vice. Shelley wrote two public
disclaimers, one to his publisher and one to Leigh Hunt's *Examiner*, in
which, although he noted that *Queen Mab* was 'worthless' as a poem
and 'crude and immature' in its ideas and 'was not intended for
publication', he also recorded his protest against 'this system of
inculcating the truth of Christianity and the excellence of Monarchy
... by such unequivocal arguments as confiscation, and imprisonment,
and invective, and slander, and the insolent violation of the most sacred
ties of nature and society'. In fact, Clark's copies were passed on to the
radical bookseller Richard Carlile, whose imprisonment on a charge of
blasphemous libel for publishing Paine's *Age of Reason* Shelley himself
had contested in a long, unpublished letter to the *Examiner* in Nov.
1819. Privately, Shelley allowed himself a measure of self-mockery: the
poem had been 'written by me when very young, in the most furious
style, with long notes against Jesus Christ, & God the Father and the
King & the Bishops & marriage & the Devil knows what'. Yet even if
he rejected 'all the bad poetry in it', and even if he had modified the
cutting edge of his youthful radicalism, many of his later ideas on
politics and religion bear strong similarities to those expressed in *Queen
Mab*.

Queen Mab has rarely received fair treatment from modern editors;
the influential Oxford edition (first published in 1904 and still in print)
consigns it to the category of Juvenilia at the back of the book, where
it is printed in double columns, and its irreverent use of lower case in
connection with God (e.g. *he*, *his*) is silently replaced by more orthodox
capitals. Shelley's notes are regularly omitted from editions of his
poetry and of his prose. Admittedly, the notes are variable in quality
and sometimes congested with quotation, but without them our sense
of the complex nature of his philosophical poem and of its impact on a
reading public is seriously impoverished.

The narrative structure of the poem follows the course of history
from the past through the present to the 'secrets' of the future. Apart
from a slight encircling framework, the action is based on a series of
extended explorations of human society in which Queen Mab (a
benevolent and didactic 'fairy' who mediates between humanity and its
higher possibilities) instructs the young Ianthe in the sad realities of
history and the possibility of achieving a better future. The excerpted
passage from Book VII concentrates on religion. The book begins with
Ianthe's recollection 'I was an infant when my mother went / To see an
atheist burned'. Mab assures her that, although the name of God has
caused much misery, 'Making the earth a slaughter-house', 'there is no

god'; the claim is supported by a prose note which begins with the reservation that 'This negation must be understood solely to affect a creative Deity'. Mab then summons up the phantom of Ahasuerus, or the Wandering Jew, 'a phantasmal portraiture / Of wandering human thought' who provides a grim and ironical account of the Creation and the Incarnation. This powerfully negative translation of the biblical narrative may be informed by Shelley's hostility towards his own father and towards established Christianity, but its narrative subtlety should not be underestimated: like the received notion of God, Ahasuerus is a projection 'from the dreams / Of human error's dense and purblind faith', and his affirmation of the existence of God attests a reality which is psychological rather than philosophical. The Wandering Jew was a figure who haunted Shelley's imagination: he appears as Ahasuerus in *Hellas*, where he confronts the Emperor Mahmud with a view of time and reality which destabilizes conventional thought (bringing 'Doubt, insecurity, astonishment') as it introduces a visionary perspective. Ahasuerus' account achieves its fullest resonance when it is read in counterpoint with Shelley's Note, which distinguishes, as Ahasuerus does not, between God the Father, 'a hypocritical Demon', and Christ, 'one of those true heroes who have died in the glorious martyrdom of liberty', who 'for a vain attempt to reform the world, paid the forfeit of his life to that overbearing tyranny which has since so long desolated the universe in his name'. For a later view of Christ, see *On Christianity* and Notes. The *Spirit* in the extract is the disembodied Ianthe; the *murderer* (100) is Moses; *Many are called* (156) is an allusion to Matthew 20:16, 22:40.

Even love is sold presents a passionate case against 'the despotism of marriage', which was influenced by Godwin, Mary Wollstonecraft and, notably, *The Empire of the Nairs: or, The Rights of Woman* (1812) by Sir James Lawrence. According to Shelley, the most significant argument against marriage was the fact of 'prostitution both *legal* and *illegal*'. Prostitution was a notorious feature of London in Shelley's time – Claire Clairmont noted in her diary that Thomas Holcroft calculated a population of 100,000 prostitutes (although this must have been a gross over-estimate; it does indicate the impact of the problem). Leigh Hunt recorded that this social problem haunted Shelley: 'In a moment's notice [it] would overshadow the liveliest of his moods.' Like Blake in 'London', he perceived a close connection between the marriage laws and the phenomenon of prostitution (see *PBT*, 36–40 and note in present edition). For a much later poetic exposition of the value of free love, see *Epipsychidion*, 150–89.

Shelley includes a footnote which cites Gibbon's *Decline and Fall* to illustrate how 'the first Christian emperor made a law by which seduction was punished with death' and 'the hatred of the primitive Christian toward love and even marriage'.

45 **temporizing** adapting ourselves or conforming to the times and circumstances.
51 **votarist** one bound by a vow; a devotee.
106 **anathematizing** cursing.

Crime is madness

Shelley's vegetarianism was central to his ethical code. It was based on a respect for the rights of animals, and an abhorrence for the shedding of blood and its degrading effects on those who are complicit with such practices. The poem itself envisages vegetarianism as part of a code of equality which embraces the whole creation: 'All things are void of terror: Man has lost / His terrible prerogative, and stands / An equal amidst equals' (VIII. 225–7). As this prose extract shows, vegetarianism also carried significant implications not only for personal behaviour but for politics, economics and the conduct of public life. In this note it leads Shelley to articulate a vision of life which is utopian, agricultural, even pastoral perhaps, based on a model of economic self-sufficiency which is strongly patriotic, if not insular. Ultimately, Shelley developed a more sophisticated understanding of politics, but the utopian ideal recurs throughout his poetry and his prose writings, and his violent rejection of 'the odious and disgusting aristocracy of wealth' leaves its mark on later works such as *MA* and *PVR*. Shelley was friendly with John Frank Newton, author of *The Return to Nature; or, A Defence of the Vegetable Regimen* (1811). His reading included vegetarian and medical texts such as Joseph Ritson's *An Essay on Abstinence from Animal Food, as a Moral Duty* (1802), Thomas Trotter's *A View of the Nervous Temperament* (3rd edition, 1812) and William Lambe's *Reports on the Effects of a Peculiar Regimen on Scirrhous Tumours and Cancerous Ulcers* (1809). This note on *Queen Mab* seems to be a revised version of *A Vindication of Natural Diet*, which was probably written in 1812 and published separately, not long before *Queen Mab*, in 1813. Shelley himself adopted vegetarian practice in Mar. 1812 and maintained it for the rest of his life.

6 **sane mind** Juvenal, *Satires*, X. 356.
9 **no Utopian advantages** it is not based on an abstract and unworkable ideal.
18 **Locke** in *An Essay Concerning Human Understanding* (1690).
35–6 **auto da fé** the public burning of a heretic.
40 **Muley Ismael** Ismail Ibn Sharīf (1672–1727), second ruler of the Alawī dynasty of Morocco, notorious for his cruelty.
60 **pabulum** food, aliment, nutriment.
100 See *the untilled field* in 'England in 1819'.
138 Shelley was involved in the building of an embankment and the reclaiming of land from the sea at Tremadoc in North Wales in

1812-13. **Pratt** Samuel Jackson Pratt, *Cottage-Pictures; or, The Poor* (3rd edn, 1803).

2   To Wordsworth

Written 1814 or 1815. Published with *Alastor* (1816). Shelley had spent three months at Keswick (Nov. 1811–Jan. 1812), where he hoped to meet Wordsworth, Coleridge and Southey. In the event, he encountered only Southey, who treated him patronizingly and whom he later suspected (mistakenly) of attacking his morality in the *Quarterly Review*. Shelley never met Wordsworth but he continued to be much exercised by his poetic example and increasingly disillusioned by the conservatism of his politics. This irregular sonnet might have been occasioned by a reading of *The Excursion* (on 20 Sept. 1814 Mary Shelley recorded a joint impression – 'much disappointed. He is a slave') or of the *Poems* which were published in 1815. It engages in reproachful dialogue with the older poet by following the example of his own sonnet 'London, 1802' (where he famously invokes Milton: 'Milton, thou shouldst be living at this hour'. *Thou wert as a lone star* (7) ironically recalls Wordsworth's address to Milton: 'Thy soul was like a Star, and dwelt apart'. The opening lines refer in part to 'Ode: Intimations of Immortality' while the word *common* (5) both suggests a matrix of shared feeling and makes use of a characteristic Wordsworthian adjective (e.g. *life's common way* in 'London, 1802'). There may also be a connection with Shelley's translation of Dante's reproachful sonnet to Guido Cavalcanti, which was included in the *Alastor* volume; see especially 'I dare not now through thy degraded state / Own the delight thy strains inspire'. For Shelley's relations with Wordsworth, see also 'Verses Written on Receiving a Celandine', *Alastor* and *PBT*.

3   Alastor

Written in autumn and early winter 1815; published Feb. 1816. The title was provided by Shelley's friend, Thomas Love Peacock, who noted that the Greek word *alástor* signified 'an evil genius' and should not be interpreted as 'the name of the hero of the poem'. More precisely, Peacock's word suggests an avenging spirit, though the term seems to have emerged recently as part of a Gothic terminology for the spirit world (see 'Imps, alastors, and every other class of cacodemons' (1810) and 'The midnight mass will soon be read, / Which even the alastors dread' (1812)). The poem is deeply personal, as Mary Shelley points out, in drawing attention to a doctor's diagnosis that Shelley was dying of consumption and in suggesting that, in the death of the poet, Shelley was engaging with that 'death which he had often contemplated during the last months as certain'. Certainly, the poem's calculated exploration of the ambiguous allure of another world can be connected to Shelley's recurrent concern with the mystery of death (see the early letters or *HIB*), but it is a mistake to identify the central figure too closely with Shelley himself. More recent critics have detected resemblances to Wordsworth or to Coleridge, though such simple decoding seems as crudely unjust to the poem's richness of signification as any interpretation which is plainly autobiographical.

Other readers have detected more challenging narrative strategies. The relation between the Preface and the poem deserves special consideration, as does the relation between the narrative voice of the poem and the poet whose fate it describes. Wordsworth is strongly present at the beginning and end of the poem, causing Earl Wasserman to identify the narrator as 'Wordsworthian', while the Preface concludes with the Pedlar's lament for Margaret in *The Excursion*, in lines which might seem an ironical commentary on Wordsworth himself. The reflexive nature of the poet's love should be related to the narcissistic patterns of imagery in the poem and to Shelley's theories in *On Love*.

Preface

49 vacancy 'vacant' and 'vacancy' are significant and recurrent terms throughout the poem (see 191, 195, 201, 662). See also 'Mont Blanc', 144.

50 all else totally different.

55–7 Wordsworth, *The Excursion*, I. 500–2, slightly misquoted.

Epigraph 'Not yet did I love, yet I loved to love; I sought something to love, being in love with love' (See Augustine, *Confessions*, III, i). Shelley quoted this passage in an 'Advertisement' to 'Poems to Mary' in *The Esdaile Notebook*.

3 See 'And I could wish my days to be / Bound each to each by natural piety' (Wordsworth, 'My heart leaps up'); see also *The Excursion*, III. 216.

13–15 See *The Excursion*, II. 41–7.

17 your wonted favour see *PL*, VIII. 202.

23ff. These lines seem to touch on Shelley's own youthful practices as described by early biographers such as his friend Thomas Jefferson Hogg. The interest in alchemy was closely connected with Shelley's early concern with science but also drew on his passion for romance. This passage also suggests in part the studies of the young Victor Frankenstein.

24 charnels cemeteries; buildings or vaults where corpses or bones are deposited.

26 obstinate questionings see 'those obstinate questionings / Of sense and outward things' (Wordsworth, 'Ode: Intimations of Immortality', 144–5).

44 fane sanctuary or temple.

45–9 See Wordsworth, 'Tintern Abbey', 95–102.

49 Cf. 'man's deep and searchless heart' (*LC*, 4204); see also 298 below, 'Ode to Naples', 8, and *PU*, IV. 279.

56 The 'melancholy' cypress was traditionally associated with mourning.

69 ambient surrounding (see 'the ambient Aire', *PL*, VII. 87–9).

71 See 'How charming is divine philosophy' (Milton, *Comus*, 476).

76 alienated see *PL*, IX.9, X.378.

77 See 'the dread of something after death, / The undiscover'd country from whose bourn / No traveller returns' (*Hamlet*, III.i.77–9).

85 bitumen lakes as Reiman and Powers point out, this formulation occurs in a favourite poem of the young Shelley, Southey's *Thalaba*, VI.15. There may also be a connection with the burning lakes of *PL*, which includes the phrase 'a black bituminous gurge' (XII.41).

93 frequent crowded (a Miltonic Latinism).

94 chrysolite see *PL*, III.596.

97 green earth see 'Tintern Abbey', 106.

101 Like that of Shelley himself, the Poet's relationship with the natural world is manifested in vegetarian practice.

108 awful ruins Shelley's itinerary may owe something to his reading of *Les Ruines, ou Méditations sur les révolutions des empires* (Paris, 1791; English translation, 1792) by Constantin François Chasseboeuf, comte de Volney, in which the narrator visits the ancient monuments and ruins of Egypt, Syria, and Palmyra (the subject of a poem by Peacock, 1806) where he is instructed by a spectral figure that man is master of his own destiny. As Reiman and Powers point out, the Poet travels backwards in time. Tyre and Balbec were in Phoenicia, Memphis and Thebes in Egypt.

125–7 Cf. Wordsworth, 'I wandered lonely as a cloud', 11–15.

140–5 The Poet travels eastward through Arabia, Persia, the Desert of Karmin, over the Hindu Kush mountains (source of the rivers Indus and Oxus, and the Indian Caucasus in Act I of *PU*) and into the Vale of Kashmir in north-west India ('that far Indian vale' which is the location of Asia's exile in *PU*, II.i).

153 Cf. 'thy voice is as the tone / Of my heart's echo' ('To' ['Yet look on me'], 5–6). For a prose articulation of the reflexive nature of love, see Shelley's account in *On Love*, below.

163 numbers verses or musical periods or groups of notes.

167 symphony harmony of sound, concord, consonance.

168 ineffable cf. the more extended account in *LC*, 2605–14, where 'inexpressive speech' is replaced by the complex experience of love in which the mental and the physical 'Had found a voice'.

189 Involved enfolded, enwrapped; see 660.

210 Cf. the following fragment, which dates from 1820/1 and may be connected with *Adonais*: 'I went into the deserts of dim sleep – / That world which, like an unknown wilderness / Bounds this with its recesses wide and deep'.

272 **Chorasmian** the desert land south of the Sea of Aral and about the lower course of the Oxus.

299 **shallop** a boat, propelled by oars or by a sail, for use in shallow waters.

307 **slimy** cf. Coleridge, 'The Rime of the Ancient Mariner', 238.

322 **chafèd** angered, vexed, ruffled.

325 A characteristic Shelleyan image; in *LC* the eagle and the serpent wreathed in fight symbolically prefigure the conflicts between good and evil, and between power and its challengers, which are at the centre of the poem.

333 Cf. 'Now came still Evening on' (*PL*, iv.598).

365 **Ingulfed** swallowed up in a gulf, abyss, or whirlpool; plunged into a gulf.

417 Cf. Coleridge, 'Frost at Midnight', 1.

425 **Mocking** imitating.

426 **implicated** intertwined.

449 **swells** not cited in *OED* in this sense.

460 **depending** hanging or inclining downwards.

507 **searchless** inscrutable, impenetrable, resisting investigation (see note on 49 above).

528 **windlestrae** a dry, thin, withered stalk of grass.

531 **roots** this seems to be a mistake for 'trunks'.

546 **its precipice** headlong descent (so, Reiman and Powers, who explain that *its* refers to the stream in 540).

585 For a later version, see *OWW*, 4.

610 **sightless** either invisible or blind.

672–5 Medea created a magic potion which revivified the aged Aeson; when she spilled some on the ground, flowers and grass sprang up (Ovid, *Metamorphoses*, vii.275ff.).

677 **one living man** for the Wandering Jew, who was condemned to wander the earth until the Second Coming as a punishment for insulting Christ, see note to *Queen Mab*, p. 399.

682 **dark magician** cf. the 'desperate alchemist' (31).

705 **senseless** unfeeling.

713 Cf. Wordsworth, 'Ode: Intimations of Immortality', 204.

4 *Hymn to Intellectual Beauty*

Written late June 1816 (conceived during a voyage round Lake Geneva with Lord Byron). Published in the *Examiner* (19 Jan. 1817) and with *Rosalind and Helen* (1819). Drawing on eighteenth-century poetic traditions and especially on the alternative 'hymns' of the French Revolution, Shelley's heterodox hymn substitutes an abstract ideal for the received notion of divinity, and Love, Hope and Self-esteem for the orthodox virtues; yet its language and poetic conventions are those of religious and visionary poetry. The divine can only be adumbrated through images drawn from the sensible world and Shelley, like all religious poets, employs analogies from nature. The mysterious 'Power' to which Shelley dedicates himself is recognized through intuition, revelation and faith; it is manifested both in the beautiful forms of the natural world and in its effects on the 'human heart', but Shelley's title seems to suggest that the emotional expression of the 'heart' should ultimately lead the perceiving mind towards the concept of a higher principle which informs all experiences of the beautiful. 'Intellectual beauty' was a term whose resonances would have been familiar to many readers, including radicals, feminists and Romantic Hellenists; it was variously employed by William Godwin, Mary Wollstonecraft and other writers of the late eighteenth and early nineteenth centuries. The poem owes something to Spenser's 'An Hymne to Heavenly Beautie' and to Wordsworth's 'Ode: Intimations of Immortality'.

HIB now exists in two 'final' versions and a much-corrected draft. Version B was printed by Leigh Hunt, who had mislaid the copy sent to him by Shelley; this *Examiner* version was the basis of all texts until 1976, when a previously unknown notebook which included versions of HIB and of 'Mont Blanc' was discovered in Barclay's Bank in Pall Mall. This notebook had been entrusted to Byron's friend Scrope Davies, and its texts of HIB and 'Mont Blanc' had clearly been intended for publication. In these unusual circumstances, the rediscovered texts have a special authority since they are not discarded drafts but alternative versions. The present edition reproduces both poems exactly from the manuscripts with no editorial intervention. The line references below are to version B.

3 **This various world**   replaced such draft versions as 'All that [   ] thought' and 'All human hearts'.

21 **fear and dream**   'care & pain' (draft).

27 **name of God and ghosts and Heaven**   Shelley's correction of the less blasphemously specific 'names of Demon, Ghost, and Heaven' which was printed in the *Examiner*. The draft reads: 'names of Ghost & God & Heaven'. Cf. 'The name of God / Has fenced about all crime with holiness, / Himself the creature of his worshippers, / Whose names and attributes and passions change, / Seeva, Buddh, Foh, Jehovah, God or Lord' (*Queen Mab*, VII.26–30). See also the account in *Queen Mab* of 'three words' – God, hell and heaven (IV.208–10): 'One shape of many names ... / Its names are each a

sign which maketh holy / All power' (*LC*, 3276–80: a version of Aeschylus' *Prometheus Bound*, 210 which Shelley copied into one of his notebooks). See note on 53–4 below.

37 **Self-esteem** a proper valuation of one's own true worth (as opposed to self-contempt).

53–4 'I called on the false name with which our youth is fed / He heard me not – ' (draft). Here again Shelley's revision may have been motivated by prudence.

58 Cf. Wordsworth, 'To the Small Celandine', ll.17–18.

60 The moment of religious revelation; this ecstasy is closely allied to those of poetic inspiration and of sexual pleasure.

67 Cf. Milton, 'Il Penseroso', 87.

70 **dark slavery** subjection to poisonous names and false notions of divinity (whose consequences are social and political as much as spiritual).

83 **SPIRIT fair** 'awful Power' (draft).

84 A significant variation both on the usual injunction to fear God and keep his commandments and on Christ's 'Thou shalt love the Lord thy God with all thy heart . . . and thy neighbour as thyself'. The new emphasis is on self-knowledge and self-control as a realistic basis for charity and social concern.

5   *Verses Written on Receiving a Celandine in a Letter from England*

Written June/July 1816. Published posthumously (1925). This poem records Shelley's disillusionment with the defection of Wordsworth from the ranks of the radicals. Wordsworth accepted a Government post as Distributor of Stamps in 1813 (hence the 'impious gold' of 39), celebrated the Battle of Waterloo and invoked Carnage as 'God's daughter' (43–8). Wordsworth had addressed three poems to the lesser celandine; Shelley makes ironical use of the pattern of the third, which discovers in the celandine an emblem of the human condition involuntarily subject to the process of ageing. The poem also acknowledges the true greatness of Wordsworth, which was a positive influence on *HIB* and 'Mont Blanc' (written in July 1816) and which also influenced Canto III of *Childe Harold* (Byron recalled how Shelley 'used to dose me with Wordsworth physic even to nausea'). For a later view of Wordsworth, see *Peter Bell the Third*.

2 **blue** the celandine is, in fact, yellow.

5–6 **primrose . . . violet** cf. 'To the Small Celandine', i.4–5.

26 **familiar** closely related.

30 Like Milton after the Restoration (*PL*, VII.25–6).

47 **left**   having been left (ablative absolute construction).
53 **They ... not**   his hopes do not need his sanction nor his foes his condemnation.
56 **overlive**   survive.

6   Mont Blanc

Written July 1816, dated 23 July by Shelley (the day of the expedition rather than of the completed poem, which had been transcribed by 29 Aug.). Published in *History of a Six Weeks' Tour* (1817). For the background, see the last of 'Letters Written in Geneva' in *History*, and its fuller private version in Shelley's letter to Peacock (*L*, 1. 495–502; see Appendix 2). Shelley admitted that the sight of the mountains had created in him 'a sentiment of extatic wonder, not unallied to madness'. He claimed that 'Mont Blanc' 'was composed under the immediate impression of the deep and powerful feelings excited by the objects which it attempts to describe; and as an undisciplined overflowing of the soul, rests its claim to approbation on an attempt to imitate the untameable wildness and inaccessible solemnity from which those feelings sprang' (Preface to *History of a Six Weeks' Tour*). Shelley's susceptibility to mountain scenery is well illustrated by an entry for August 1814 in Claire Clairmont's diary which records his first reaction to the Alps: 'We were so happy—Shelley in an ecstacy and declared how great was his joy – How great is my rapture he said, I a fiery young man with my heart full of Youth, and with my Beloved at my side, I behold these lordly immeasurable Alps – They look like a second world gleaming on me, they look like dreams more than realities, they are so pure and heavenly white.' The Shelleys arrived at Pont Pellisier on 22 July; the draft is headed 'The Scene of Pellisier, at the extremity of the vale of Servoz', a perspective which is specifically retained in one of the two final versions of the poem. The first 48 lines were written in pencil, which suggests that 'Mont Blanc' may have been begun, if not completed, on the spot. Shelley's poem should be read in the context of Coleridge's 'Hymn before Sun-rise in the Vale of Chamouni' (1802; 1809) which celebrates God in his mountain creation. Coleridge exclaimed: 'Who *would* be, who *could* be an Atheist in this valley of wonders!' On 23 July Shelley described himself (in Greek) in the hotel register at Chamonix as a lover of mankind, a democrat and an atheist; this was a calculated response to the customary attitude represented by Coleridge and also by writers like the Reverend T. S. Whalley, whose 'irregular epic' *Mont Blanc* (1788) anticipated a number of Shelley's concerns and some of his imagery and language but found in the mountain a witness to Christian theology. Shelley believed that man must learn from nature not to subject himself to false and crippling

notions of divinity, which had political as well as spiritual consequences
(cf. *PU*). Consequently, the poem is centred on the relations between
the perceiving mind and the external universe. Shelley suggests that
man has imposed his own fantasies on the natural scene, whose only
moral significance is its complete detachment from the will of a creator
God.

The textual history of this poem is fascinating but complicated. There
is a much-corrected draft and two completed versions which carry
equal authority (for an explanation of the circumstances, see headnote
to *HIB*). One version (a fair-copy in Shelley's hand) was mislaid and
was not printed till 1976. This text is printed here as version A.
A second version was printed in *History* (1817). This text (which is
included here as version B) must have been reconstructed from the
draft. According to Matthews and Everest, 'the likeliest assumption is
that Shelley did himself produce a second version of "Mont Blanc" in
the autumn of 1817, sometimes forgetting choices and substitutions he
had made when copying from the draft in the previous summer, and
perhaps at times unable to read his own tangled draft'. The present
edition allows the reader the opportunity to compare the two versions.
Version A follows the fair-copy exactly with no attempt at editorial
intervention. The line numbers in the following notes are keyed to
version B.

1-11 Flowing through its ravine, the river Arve (which runs through
      Chamonix into Lake Geneva) supplies a metaphor for the rela-
      tions between subject and object; with great compression, Shelley
      begins by defining the operations of mind in terms of the natural
      scene, which is not described in its own right till 11. The draft
      includes two cancelled attempts at a first line: 'In daylight thoughts,
      bright or obscure' and 'In day the eternal stream of various
      thoughts'.

6 **half its own** because it renders and receives (see 38-40 and
   Wordsworth, 'Tintern Abbey', 107-8).

15 **awful** worthy of, or commanding, profound respect or reveren-
    tial fear; solemnly impressive, sublimely majestic / causing dread;
    terrible, dreadful, appalling.

27 **unsculptured** see Shelley's journal entry of 21 July 1816 describ-
    ing two waterfalls: 'They were no more than mountain rivulets, but
    the height from which they fell, at least 200 feet, made them assume
    a character inconsistent with the smallness of their stream. The first
    fell in two parts; - & struck first on an enormous rock resembling
    precisely some colossal Egyptian statue of a female deity. It struck
    the head of the visionary Image & gracefully dividing then fell
    in folds of foam, more like cloud than water, imitating a veil of
    the most exquisite woof' (Mary Shelley's *Journal*, 1.113). **strange**

sleep apparent immobility or silence in which 'thou [the ravine] dost lie'.

29 'And its hue wane, doth blend them all and steep / Their tumult in its own eternity' (draft).

34 **Dizzy Ravine!** On 25 July Shelley recorded that the glacier of Montanvert was 'a scene in truth of dizzying wonder'. Cf. review of *Frankenstein*, which describes the passage from sensation to reflection as 'so dizzying and so tumultuous', and whose account of the effects of reading Mary Shelley's novel invokes the mountain scenery which informed the writing of 'Mont Blanc' and of *Frankenstein* in the summer of 1816: 'We climb Alp after Alp until the horizon is seen blank, vacant, and limitless; and the head turns giddy, and the ground seems to fail under our feet.' For Shelley's particular concern with the gulfs and precipices of cerebral processes, especially self-scrutiny, and the perilous gaps of language, see headnote to 'On a Science of Mind'; see also 'We are on the verge where words abandon us, and what wonder if we grow dizzy to look down the dark abyss of how little we know' (*On Life*).

35ff. The collaborative relationship between the external world and the perceiving mind. **separate fantasy** cf. 'All was as much our own as if we had been the creators of such impressions in the minds of others, as now occupied our own' (*L*, I. 497).

43 **that** generally interpreted as the legion of wild thoughts. **thou** the ravine.

47–8 The sense is ambiguous, perhaps deliberately so. *Either* these images are derived from a Universe of Things outside the poet, perhaps from a Universal Mind – in which case the existence of the ravine in Shelley's mind depends on the permissive grace of a mysterious force; *or* they are maintained in existence by Shelley's own mind.

53 **unfurled** spread out (thus cutting off Shelley's vision) or drawn aside.

57 **very spirit fails** 'mind is faint / With aspiration' (cancelled in draft).

71–4 References to widely held theories on the volcanic origin of mountains.

76ff. There are two ways of interpreting the data of this natural scene: one leads to 'awful doubt' (77) (perhaps a belief in dark divinities such as the Ahrimanes of the Zoroastrian system or perhaps a fear that everything is merely random), while the other leads to a calm 'faith' (77) that the fierce presence of the mountain is unconnected with the designs of any divinity. Thus, the message of the mountain, if properly understood, can help to repeal those repressive systems of politics and religion ('codes of fraud and woe',81) which depend on false notions of deity. 'But for such faith' (79) is puzzling and may be the result of a mistake in copying; it has been suggested, though not very convincingly, that Shelley intended 'But' as an adverb meaning 'only'. 'But for' appears in the draft, although it originally read 'In such a faith', as does the intermediate fair copy in Shelley's hand (Version A).

79 Draft versions include: 'To such high thoughts of Nature reconciled' (cancelled).

80 Cf. 'Hymn before Sun-rise', 58–63: 'GOD! let the torrents, like a shout of nations, / Answer! and let the ice-plains echo, GOD! / GOD! sing ye meadow – streams with gladsome voice! / Ye pine-groves with your soft and soul-like sounds! / And they too have a voice, yon piles of snow, / And in their perilous fall shall thunder, GOD!' and 85, 'Earth, with her thousand voices, praises GOD'.

84 'The powers that <rule> move the world themselves are still / Remote serene and inaccessible' (draft).

86 **daedal** artful, carefully wrought.

96ff. Essentially the Epicurean doctrine expounded by Lucretius in *De rerum natura*. The natural scene can teach the attentive observer that no divinity is present in this creation; if it does exist, it dwells apart, as unconcerned as the mountain peak.

105 **city of death** for Shelley's interest in geological and catastrophic theory, see letter to Peacock in Appendix 2. **distinct** marked in a manner so as to be distinguished; decorated, adorned.

135–6 Cf. 'How silently!' ('Hymn before Sun-rise', 7).

136–7 'The glare / Of the clear sun strikes the white waste' (draft).

139 'The unpolluted dome / Of Heaven is not more silent' (draft).

142–4 The concluding emphasis is on the power of the human mind; but Shelley ends characteristically with a question rather than a statement.

7 Laon and Cythna

Written between Mar./Apr. and Sept. 1817. Published in Dec. 1817 but quickly withdrawn from circulation, strategically altered, and reissued as *The Revolt of Islam* in Jan. 1818. Shelley described his poem, which was 'in the style and for the same object as "Queen Mab"', as 'a tale illustrative of such a Revolution as might be supposed to take place in an European nation, acted upon by the opinions of what has been called (erroneously as I think) the modern philosophy, & contending with antient notions & the supposed advantage derived from them to those who support them' (*L*, 1. 557, 563–4). The Revolution of the Golden City (i.e. Constantinople) is 'the *beau idéal* as it were of the French Revolution'; that is, it explores the unfulfilled potential of the French Revolution (which for Shelley was 'the master-theme of the epoch') while acknowledging those problems which had, temporarily at least, eclipsed and frustrated its better possibilities. Like many of the Romantic poets, Shelley registered the shock of the apparent failure of the Revolution and its ideals and the subsequent career of Napoleon (see 'Feelings of a Republican . . .'); but, unlike poets of an earlier generation such as Wordsworth and Coleridge, he chose to interpret these events as part of an open-ended narrative rather than as elements in a history which had already achieved its tragic closure. Some of his more discursive ideas on this subject and its implications for those who hoped for political change in England are set out explicitly and temperately in *PVR*.

At the centre of his visionary romance Shelley placed the eponymous brother and sister Laon and Cythna. To Cythna he gave a significant role in the action of a poem whose revolutionary scope included the feminist aim of liberation from 'servitude / In which the half of humankind were mewed / Victims of lust and hate, the slaves of slaves' (985–7). In Laon he created one of those figures of the poet in which he projects an idealized version of himself.

The relation between Laon and Cythna not only looks forward to the combined force of Prometheus and Asia in *PU* but deliberately and provocatively introduces the theme of incest. In choosing to treat the subject of incestuous love between brother and sister, Shelley was touching a nerve in the national sensibility. Incest was a common element in Gothic and sentimental fiction and, according to Montagu Summers, featured in at least nineteen novels between 1765 and 1807. Writers of the Romantic period employed it not only to achieve a *frisson* or to flout convention but, paradoxically, to give metaphorical expression to a communion and a shared experience which had its own exclusive purity. Shelley was later to argue that incest was 'like many other *incorrect* things a very poetical circumstance. It may be the excess of love or hate' (*L*, II. 154). *The Cenci* explores the excess of hate; by contrast, *LC* was 'an experiment on the temper of the public mind' to ascertain whether readers could suspend their prejudices in reading of an incestuous love which, in the original version, was attributed to 'Nature's modesty'. Shelley's poem challenged the received code of his readers by reminding them that 'To the pure all things are pure!' (2596; cf. Titus 1:15), while his original Preface (reprinted here) appealed to them to transcend traditional categories of interpretation.

Shelley's publisher, Charles Ollier, judged it necessary to withdraw *Laon and Cythna*, which was eventually reissued under the title *The Revolt of Islam* minus the paragraph in the Preface which asked for a charitable interpretation of incest without naming it, and with a number of prudential changes in phrasing which involved not only relations between brother and sister but matters of religion. Shelley had tried to dissuade Ollier: 'I don't believe that if the book was quietly and regularly published the Government would touch anything of a character so refined and so remote from the conceptions of the vulgar. They would hesitate before they invaded a member of the higher circles of the republic of letters. But if they see us tremble, they will make no distinctions; they will feel their strength' (*L*, I. 579). Shelley here places his trust in the status of poetry as a medium which, because of its characteristic indirectness and because of its expense to potential readers, would probably neither reach nor influence a wider or 'more vulgar' reading public and would therefore be treated more indulgently by prosecuting authorities. For this defensive emphasis on the refinement of his audience, see the prefaces to *PU* and to *Epipsychidion* (a poem which also carries incestuous implications).

Preface

7 **tempests** the French Revolution, the Napoleonic Wars, and those disturbances and instabilities in English public life which had led in March 1817 to the suspension of Habeas Corpus.

24–5 **methodical and systematic argument** Shelley had already attempted this approach in another work which was written at Marlow, *A Proposal for Putting Reform to the Vote* (Feb. 1817). This *Proposal* might be said to relate to *LC* roughly as *PVR* would later relate to *PU*.

30–1 **narrative, not didactic** see the penultimate paragraph of the Preface to *PU*.

31–57 This summary bears a very close and intended resemblance to the pattern of the French Revolution. In that context, 'Rulers of the World' (48) can be equated with the so-called 'Holy Alliance', that is, the governments of Austria, Prussia and Russia who combined to restore the monarchy to France (see the Preface to *Hellas*, from which Shelley's attack on the Alliance was removed by his publisher).

36–7 Ecclesiastes 4:1.

56–7 **eternity of genius and virtue** a constant concern for Shelley, politically, personally and poetically. In the poem, the revolutionaries Laon and Cythna are executed but they are received into a 'mighty Senate' of the departed 'Great' and understand that 'virtue, though obscured on Earth, not less / Survives all mortal change in lasting loveliness' (4782–3).

69 **epidemic transport** contagious excitement. See De Quincey's 'On Murder Considered as One of the Fine Arts', which identifies in Shelley's account of the crowd in *LC* 4450–9 'a sublime sort of magic contagion'.

71–90 Shelley provides a detailed analysis of the French Revolution in the gradualist context of *PVR*, where he states: 'Their desire to wreak revenge to this extent, in itself a mistake, a crime, a calamity, arose from the same source as their other miseries and errors and affords an additional proof of the necessity of that long-delayed change which it accompanied and disgraced'. His attitude towards the French at the time of the Revolution and their inability to avoid violence or to effect an immediate and total self-transformation can be compared to his views on the Irish (in letters and in *An Address to the Irish People*) and on the modern Greeks (Preface to *Hellas*), and to his behaviourist reading of Frankenstein's monster.

86–114 For a more detailed account, see *PVR*. For a more positive reading of the emergent balance of his own age, see Preface to *PU*: 'The cloud . . . restored'.

91 epoch a point in time beginning a new or distinctive period.

113–14 intellect and virtue for a poetic formulation, cf. Demogorgon's final speech at the end of *PU*. For an analysis in terms of contemporary politics, see *PVR*.

115–18 An impatient desire for a better state of things led to a failure to recognize the complexity of the problems which had to be resolved. When the initial phases of the French Revolution failed to satisfy the hopes of its most optimistic supporters, they were shocked for a time into abandoning them altogether.

118–26 This moral and psychological problem had been explored by Wordsworth in books III and IV of *The Excursion* (1814), which were entitled 'Despondency' and 'Despondency Corrected'.

128–32 Drummond's *Academical Questions* (1805) was celebrated by Shelley for its 'clear and vigorous statement of the intellectual system'. The Reverend Thomas Malthus first published his theory of population in 1798; in 1803 a much-expanded version appeared as *An Essay on the Principle of Population; or, A View of its Past and Present Effects on Human Happiness; with an Inquiry into our Prospects respecting the Future Removal of the Evils which it Occasions*. Later editions were published in 1806, 1807, 1817 (the year of Shelley's Preface) and 1826. Malthus presented a statistical argument against perfectibility: 'This natural inequality of the two powers, of population, and of production in the earth, and that great law of our nature which must constantly keep their effects equal, form the great difficulty that appears to me insurmountable in the way to the perfectibility of society.' Shelley regarded such theories as, in effect, an endorsement of the *status quo*. In *PVR* Shelley indignantly opposed Malthus' theory that 'the evils of the poor arise from an excess of population' which was to be controlled by 'war, vice and misery' and by the requirement that they 'abstain from marrying under penalty of starvation'. He had already attacked Malthus' 'sophisms' in *Proposals for an Association of Philanthropists* (1812): 'Are we to be told that these [evils] are remedyless, because the earth would, in case of their remedy, be overstocked? . . . Rare sophism! How will the heartless rich hug thee to their bosoms, and lull their conscience into slumber with the opiate of thy reconciling dogmas!' Shelley's most severe attack on Malthus was reserved for the poem 'A Ballad' (also known as 'Young Parson Richards'), unfinished, unpublished till 1927 and still little known. This ballad presents a confrontation between a priest whose code is specifically Malthusian and a poor woman whose child he has fathered.

135-6   Cf. 'the slow, gradual and certain operation' of reform in *PVR*.

155-98   Shelley's account of his qualifications to be an epic poet can be compared to the more politically orientated *curriculum vitae* which he had sent to Godwin on 10 Jan. 1812 (see Appendix I). Many of the experiences invoked in this account can be traced in *History of a Six Weeks' Tour* and in Shelley's letters of summer 1816. The 'ravages of tyranny and war' were visible in post-Napoleonic France – for example, in Nogent-sur-Seine which had been 'entirely desolated by the Cossacs' and in Saint-Aubin, where the Shelleys found 'the cottages roofless, the rafters black and the walls dilapidated'.

179   Certainly Godwin and Byron, and possibly Hunt and Peacock.

180   **modern Italy**   as opposed to the literature of Ancient Rome. There is little evidence that Shelley was conversant with contemporary Italian poetry.

184   For an extended definition, see *DP*.

199-220   Similar claims are made in the Preface to *PU*, in *DP* and, more negatively, in *PBT*.

215   John Ford (1586–after 1639), author of eighteen plays, including *'Tis Pity She's a Whore*.

221-34   The nine-line Spenserian stanza concludes with an alexandrine, that is, a line of twelve syllables or six feet, as opposed to the standard five of the other lines. Examples of the misplaced alexandrine occur at 1652 and 3788, both of which remained unrevised in *The Revolt of Islam*. The full title of the poem concludes: 'In the Stanza of Spenser'. Shelley may well have been influenced by the example of *Childe Harold*, the third canto of which he had read in manuscript and delivered to John Murray. He asked himself: 'Is this an imitation of Ld. Byron's poem? – it is certainly written in the same metre' (notebook). Perhaps his account of 'the common influence' of the age was partly conditioned by an anxious recognition of this debt to Byron.

242-3   Longinus (? first century AD), author of *On the Sublime*, and Nicholas Boileau (1636–1711), translator of the *Ars poetica* of Horace and author of *Art poétique* (1674), both codified and analysed the works of their creative predecessors.

249-51   See 'murderer as you are' (Preface to *Adonais*).

253 The major reviewing periodicals printed their critiques anonymously (see *Adonais*, 319, 327).

265ff. Throughout his career Shelley was regularly concerned with the question of judgement, whether individual, judicial, moral or literary-critical. Prose works such as *Letter to Lord Ellenborough* (1812), the legal deposition set out in *Declaration in Chancery* (1817), the public letter to the *Examiner* on Richard Carlile (1819) and *ODD* (1820), are all concerned with the grounds and validity of legal judgement, while the fragment known as *A System of Government by Juries* proposes a political use for the jury system. *DP* resonantly asserts the ultimate judgement of posterity against the 'arbitration of popular breath' and the 'continuing calumnies against poetry and poets'.

271 **De rerum natura** which exercised a strong influence on the young Shelley.

324 Shelley makes a similar disclaimer in the Preface to *Frankenstein*.

324ff. The final paragraph was omitted when *Laon and Cythna* was re-issued as *The Revolt of Islam*.

Dedication

3 Shelley playfully engages with the model of Spenserian romance, whose influence permeates the poem as a whole. This line also lightly conceals a private allusion to Shelley's role-playing as the 'Elfin Knight' (the manuscript of *HIB* was initialled E. K., as was Shelley's review of Godwin's *Mandeville*). In the draft William Godwin is a 'champion' for 'the oppressed'. The line may also refer to Shelley's pseudonym Victor in the early collection *Original Poetry* by Victor and Cazire (1810).

5–9 See note to Preface (pp. 56–7).

10–17 Mary Shelley remembered in her Note: 'the poem was written in his boat, as it floated under the beech-groves of Bisham [near Marlow on the Thames], or during wanderings in the neighbouring country, which is distinguished for particular beauty'.

19 The manuscript reads 'By <youths> childhoods silver winged visions <nurst>'; see 'By solemn vision, and bright silver dream, / His infancy was nurtured' (*Alastor*, 67–8).

19–27 As the Preface declares, Shelley's purpose in writing *LC* was to 'startle the reader from the trance of ordinary life' and so create through the reading experience an equivalent to his own visionary awakening. Between 1804 and 1810 Shelley was at Eton College, where, according to one account, he was known as 'Mad Shelley' and 'surrounded, hooted, baited like a maddened bull' (Mary Shelley produced an idealized account of this in *Lodore* (1835)). Such images of alienation can be exaggerated (see, for example, Shelley's own recollections in 'The Boat on the Serchio') and it is also perilous to decode so self-conscious a poetic text into biographical simplifications; yet it might be remembered that conditions in public schools in Shelley's day were often harsh and that on occasion mutinies did take place. Shelley originally wrote: 'the harsh rude voices <of the> from the school <mates> <room> as they pass'.

28–36 For an account of a similar moment of intuition which also bears the traces of 'conversion' or 'religious experience', see *HIB*. This vocational commitment is Shelley's version of the Spenserian knight's dedication to the cause of his lady. 'I feared not those who ruled, nor did I hate / Mine equals, but was lone, untameable / Like some wild beast that cannot find its mate / A solitary gazelle / Which in the desert wilderness doth dwell / Secure in its own swiftness' (unused passage in draft).

37–40 Cf. the more comprehensive and circumstantially autobiographical account of Shelley's poetic education in the Preface. The draft shows that he originally intended to include a more extended and self-pitying portrait: 'Mine equals shunned a boy so sad & wild / And those who ruled me, found untameable / The spirit of a meek & gentle child; / Nor with a bitter scorn of wrong I smiled / When hoary men or youths of strength mature / Struck me with fruitless blows; thus undefiled / <By awe or by submission, inly pure>'.

41–2 Cf. Blake's 'mental fight' in *Jerusalem*. Line 41 originally began 'Wove linked thought' (see 'Man, O, not Men! a chain of linkèd thought!', *PU*, IV.394).

46ff. This allegorized version of his love-life looks forward to *Epipsychidion*. The draft seems to refer to biographical specificities which are kept at a distance: 'One whom I found was dear but false to me / the other's heart was like a heart of stone / which crushed & withered <mine>'. The published version has achieved a safer, less revealing, perspective in which the specific 'One' has become the generalized 'one not false to me'.

56–63 The 16-year-old Mary Godwin boldly took the initiative in declaring her love for the married Shelley at her mother's grave in Old St Pancras Churchyard. For the tyranny of custom, see 86, 115.

69–71 See 'Stanzas Written in Dejection', 21–3.

76 See 'had learned to breathe the atmosphere of scorn' (*LC*, 981).

77 **two ... babes** William (born 24 Jan. 1816; died 7 June 1819) and Clara Everina (born 2 Sept. 1817; died 24 Sept. 1818).

84–90 In a letter of 11 Dec. 1817 Shelley told Godwin: 'I felt the precariousness of my life, and I engaged in this task [of writing the poem], resolved to leave some record of myself. Much of what the volume contains was written with the same feeling – as real, though not so prophetic – as the communications of a dying man.' Amphion was an archetypal poet in Greek myth who magically constructed the walls of Thebes through the creative power of his playing on the lyre (see *Hellas*, 1006). 'Truth's' (87) is anticipated in a draft of line 22 which remembers 'the day & hour / . . . when Truth first came upon me'.

100–8   Mary Wollstonecraft Godwin (1759–97), pioneering feminist and author of *Vindication of the Rights of Woman*, had died after giving birth to her daughter Mary in 1797; her memory and her influence had played an important part in the early stages of the relationship between Mary and Shelley (see note to 56–63). William Godwin (1756–1836), novelist, political theorist and philosophical anarchist, who had married Mary Wollstonecraft in 1797, was a major influence on the development of Shelley's early intellectual life; his *Political Justice* caused Shelley to 'truly *think* & *feel*' and showed him that he had 'duties to perform' (see Appendix 1). The fame of Mary Godwin's parents is discussed in Shelley's review of *Mandeville*, published in Dec. 1817. Both were celebrated in Europe. Godwin's reputation had suffered temporarily in England because of his 'daring to announce the true foundation of morals' and his refusal to gratify the rich and the powerful, but he was 'destined to inherit lasting renown': 'Godwin has been to the present age in moral philosophy what Wordsworth is in poetry.'

109–18   The draft of 109 reads 'A voice went forth from that unshaken Spirit', identified by Shelley as 'The author of an enquiry concerning Political Justice & its influence on Morals & Happiness'. For voices, see 'Mont Blanc', 76ff.; for the impact of truth, *PU*, II.iii.36–42. *Truth* is a term with strong Godwinian resonances: see 'Sound reasoning and truth, when adequately communicated, must always be victorious over error: Sound reasoning and truth are capable of being so communicated: Truth is omnipotent' (*Political Justice*, I, 5).

124–6   Cf. *Adonais*, 494–5; 'unextinguished' is a recurrent Shelleyan adjective (cf. 'unextinguished hearth', *OWW*, 67, and 'unextinguished fire', *PU*, III.i.5).

8   On Christianity

Written late 1817. Published posthumously (1859). Shelley's concern with religious questions can be traced through the whole of his poetic career; it provides a recurrent focus for the early letters and for a number of prose works, including *The Necessity of Atheism* (1811), some of the notes to *Queen Mab* (1813), *A Refutation of Deism* (1814; reprinted 1815) and *On the Devil, and Devils* (written 1819/20), while it also constitutes a significant context for many of the political essays. *Queen Mab* presents an extraordinary image of Christ as one who taught 'justice, truth, and peace, / In semblance', a vindictive deceiver who smiled with 'godlike malice'. Yet Shelley seems to have been susceptible to an alternative interpretation and from an early stage he began to make some distinction between Christ and Christianity as it had manifested itself historically. In 1812 and 1813 he prepared a small book of *Biblical Extracts*, never published and now apparently lost: 'I have often thought that the moral sayings of Jesus Christ might be very useful if selected from the mystery and immorality which surrounds them.' This was intended for a wide public, unlike *A Refutation* which was written in a subtle and ironical mode and dedicated *sunetoisin* (to the initiated) because of the risk of legal prosecution. *On Christianity* should not be confused with this missing book, but much of it is, in fact, commentary on the sayings of Christ and a demonstration both of the metaphorical nature of parts of the text and of its immediate ethical and political relevance. Shelley's Christ is not the Son of God but an extraordinary individual, the product of a specific historical situation whose teaching was also urgently relevant to an England balanced between anarchy and despotism after the Napoleonic wars. Christ bore some similarity to Socrates and to Rousseau; he was a subtle public speaker, who knew how to address an audience which was not yet ready to receive the full force of his message; he was a poet whose imagination had been stimulated by the Old Testament; above all, he was a courageous opponent of the *status quo*, the 'enemy of oppression and of falsehood', and 'the advocate of equal justice'. Shelley's Christ was a radical and a 'great Reformer' (*PVR*); if his doctrines were acted upon, 'no political or religious institution could subsist a moment' since 'Every man would be his own magistrate and priest. Doctrines of reform were never carried to so great a length as by Jesus Christ. The *Republic* of Plato and the *Political Justice* of Godwin are probable and practical systems in the comparison.' It was this approach to a reading of Christ that caused Shelley to comment 'Jacobinism' in his notes on Luke 1:52 and 'Magnificent Jacobinism' on 6:20–6.

1–3ff.   For the name of God, see note to *HIB*, 27.

13   **influencings**   see 'Mont Blanc', 38, and Southey, *The Curse of Kehama*, xv.3.x ('Though all other things / Were subject to the starry influencings').

30–2   Wordsworth, 'Tintern Abbey', 91–3, slightly misquoted.

43   The elusive, shape-changing, self-transforming Proteus was identified with the principle of matter; Pan (literally the Greek for *whole*) was the animating spirit of the natural world, 'universal Pan' in *The Witch of Atlas*, 113.

56–7   For God subject to passion, see *LC*, 3235–52.

58   **see God**   Shelley provides his own gloss (or interpretation) of Matthew 5:8.

71–2   Cf. *Macbeth*, V.ii.22.

89ff. Shelley's ideal conforms to his own conception of the liberating and purifying potential of vegetarianism (see note from *Queen Mab*); it is probably also influenced by Rousseau ('perhaps the philosopher among the moderns, who in the structure of his feelings and understanding resembles most nearly the mysterious Sage of Judaea').

93–4 sweetest sadness cf. *OWW*, 60–1 (this passage also includes the image of the lyre).

109–16 For a similar passage using the image of the Aeolian lyre, see *DP*, 40ff.

119 consentaneity accord, agreement.

158ff. Shelley's attitude to miracles was characteristically sceptical. The *daimon* or familiar spirit of Socrates is referred to in Plato's *Apology*. According to Shelley, Socrates claimed that 'A supernatural force has sway over the greatest things in all human undertakings.'

174–6 In the *Phaedo* (118a) Socrates makes arrangements for a cock to be sacrificed to Aesculapius shortly before he dies from the effects of hemlock; this seems to suggest that he wishes to propitiate some supernatural force. Shelley's 'the country in which I write' probably indicates that this essay was written when he was still living in England. Cf. the account in *ODD* of Milton and the restrictions on publication (pp. 185–6).

192–5 Matthew 5:17 (with changes).

199 Shelley's note refers to Cicero, *De oratore* (see especially 2.42ff.).

228 Shelley's note refers to Matthew 5:21, 27, 31, 33.

229 Shelley's note refers to Matthew 5:38.

9 *An Address to the People on the Death of the Princess Charlotte*

Written 11–12 Nov. 1817. Like *A Proposal for Putting Reform to the Vote*, this pamphlet was issued under the name of 'The Hermit of Marlow'. In Mar. 1817 Shelley had settled at Marlow, where he made practical attempts to relieve the distress of local laceworkers. The role of 'Hermit' was partly an invocation of the world of Spenserian romance which had also generated the pseudonym of 'Elfin Knight'. A hermit would have the advantage of that kind of disinterested point of perspective which Shelley attributes to the semi-autobiographical figure of Athanase: 'His soul had wedded Wisdom, and her dower / Is love and justice, clothed in which he sate / Apart from men, as in a lonely tower / Pitying the tumult of their dark estate'. A hermit plays a significant part in the action of *LC* (which Shelley also composed at Marlow in the spring and summer of 1817), where his writings help to bring about a change of consciousness which the eponymous hero and heroine translate into the dimension of politics.

Shelley's essay is concerned with the coincidence of two causes of public mourning – the death, in childbirth, of the daughter of the Prince

Regent, and the hanging and quartering on the following day of Jeremiah Brandreth, Isaac Ludlam and William Turner, three working men who were convicted as leaders of the 'Derbyshire Insurrection'. The death of the princess, which occasioned public mourning and later featured in numerous poems and tributes, including a passage in Byron's *Childe Harold*, occurred in the course of nature. The execution of the Pentridge Three was much more problematic, since the conspiracy was notoriously instigated and led by an *agent provocateur* known as 'Oliver'. Their deaths were not in the course of nature and should have been the cause of public lamentation since what was at stake was not the unprovoked death of an amiable princess but the death of liberty. Shelley's plea for national grieving probably owes something to Plato's *Menexenus*, part of which he translated, but is also centrally indebted to the radical press, notably to the report of the execution in Hunt's *Examiner*. Shelley was deeply impressed by these events: the name 'Oliver' features in one of his notes to Luke's Gospel (late 1819), and the system of informers and *agents provocateurs* is indicted in 'England in 1819' and explored at length in the context of biblical politics in *ODD* (see pp. 186-8 above). The pamphlet was written after a discussion with Hunt, Godwin and Shelley's publisher, Ollier, who is said to have printed twenty copies, though none are now known to be extant and our only source is a reprint of 1843. The *Address* invokes the 'People of England', and much of its language is accordingly direct. The epigraph is taken from a passage in Thomas Paine's *The Rights of Man* in which he criticized and controverted Edmund Burke's description of Marie Antoinette at Versailles in his *Reflections on the Revolution in France*.

16 **too deep for words** cf. 'too deep for tears' (last line of Wordsworth, 'Ode: Intimations of Immortality').

49-50 *Hamlet*, III.1.79-80 (misquoted).

72-6 In 1794 a number of leaders of the reform movement were indicted on a charge of treason. Among them were John Horne Tooke (1736-1812), philologist and founder of the Constitutional Society, and Thomas Hardy (1752-1832), founder of the London Correspondence Society. After a celebrated trial, and an intervention by William Godwin, who wrote *Cursory Strictures* in their defence, they were acquitted.

151-62ff. Shelley advanced similar arguments at greater length in *On the Punishment of Death* (probably intended for *PVR*), where he argued against capital punishment and paid particular attention to its effect on spectators and to the encoding of revenge in the penal system. He claimed that 'those nations in which the penal code has been particularly mild have been distinguished from all others by the rarity of crime'.

203ff. Shelley's analysis of the double aristocracy is expounded at greater length in chapter 2 of *PVR* (see pp. 178–80 above). Cf. 'The odious and disgusting aristocracy of wealth is built upon the ruins of all that is good in chivalry or republicanism; and luxury is the forerunner of a barbarism scarce capable of cure' (*Queen Mab*, note to VIII.211–12; see p. 13 above).

212 'Without fear and without stain'; a chivalric ideal (*tache* is more usually *reproche* (reproach)).

214 **funds** the stock of the national debt, considered as a mode of investment.

236 **anarchy** here used in a more conventional and conservative sense than in *MA*. Shelley's economic analysis provides the foundation for *MA*, 156ff. The 'two chasms' are the alternatives of 'anarchy and oppression' (or despotism). The 'public voice' here refers to claims for constitutional reform; it should be compared to the voices of *MA* and to the public reform meeting which occasioned 'Peterloo'.

254 **manufacturers** factory workers, those who work with their hands.

255 **helots** slaves, serfs.

267 **infernal agents** Shelley's language seems to look forward to the argument of *ODD*, where the Devil himself is a government informer.

272 **forth** a quotation from Luke 20:20, a passage which Shelley annotated ironically in 1819: 'Oliver an improvement on this'.

286ff. Shelley perhaps underestimates the private circumstances of the three ringleaders.

312ff. Here Shelley seems to be accommodating himself to the expectations of his audience; cf. *On Christianity*, p. 180ff.

345ff. Cf. the direct appeal to 'Men of England' in *MA* and in 'Men of England: A Song'.

370–5 **glorious Phantom** see 'England in 1819' and *MA*, 110ff. For the celebration of Liberty as Queen, see 'A New National Anthem', which adapts the words and rhythm of the National Anthem to recognize and resurrect 'from England's grave' the virtues of Liberty, 'Her murdered Queen'. Like the conclusion of his essay, Shelley's alternative anthem seems to pick up a radical tradition which can be found, for example, in Joseph Mather's 'God Save Great Thomas Paine' (no. 522 in Roger Lonsdale, ed., *The New Oxford Book of Eighteenth-Century Verse*).

10   On Frankenstein; or, The Modern Prometheus

Probably written in early 1818; published posthumously (1832). Shelley could have written this review at any time after May 1817, when *Frankenstein* was completed, but it is likely that his laudatory account was connected with the publication of the book early in 1818. Shelley had a sophisticated sense of audience and was often prepared to take special steps (including the use of personal or assumed names) in order to promote interest in his own work. In this case, the anonymous author was Mary Shelley, but Shelley himself had been closely involved with the text at various stages and had made many interventions in the interests of style, accuracy, thematic continuity and narrative sequence (estimated by Anne Mellor at five or six changes per manuscript page where evidence is available). He had heavily revised the concluding pages, and contributed the original Preface (to which this review is a complement) in the persona of the author. The effect of Shelley's contributions and suggested revisions is highly controversial; editors such as James Rieger and E. B. Murray interpret his role as positive, but some feminist readers, notably Mellor, detect an influence which, while constructive in details, sometimes contradicted the implications of Mary Shelley's original, frequently translated it into a prose style which was 'stilted, ornate, putatively Ciceronian [i.e. Latinate]', and generally imposed on it the signs of his philosophy and the weight of his own patriarchal authority. By consenting to this, 'Mary Shelley has substituted Percy Shelley's style for her own' and 'enveloped her novel in a protective covering of borrowed speech'.

Mellor reads Shelley's review in the light of this interpretation of his larger role. Shelley is 'both promoting Mary and protecting her from possible adverse criticism' and his review 'is thus an act of appropriation as well as of tribute'. This reading does not properly acknowledge either the constant generosity of Shelley's praise for a work that 'resembles nothing that ever preceded it' or the strategies of Shelley's other reviews and of his self-promotions, which may appear to concede minor weaknesses or limitations while arguing for larger achievements. On the other hand, it demonstrates that *Frankenstein* is, at least, a particularly rich example of the complex politics and psychology of intertextuality which also marks other works by Percy and by Mary Shelley (such as that cluster of texts centred on the figure of Matilda) but which still remains largely unexplored.

One of Anne Mellor's central claims is that Percy Shelley did not or could not accept Mary's critique of the moral errors of Victor Frankenstein and consistently interpreted him sympathetically. This tendency to misread left its mark on some of his verbal suggestions for the text and, notably, on his review, where he identifies Frankenstein himself as a 'victim'. Such an interpretation of Shelley may have been animated by the belief that, in its criticism of the visionary scientist who is afflicted by moral myopia, Mary Godwin Shelley was engaging both with her father's trust in the omnipotence of truth and with her future husband's faith in the transforming power of science. Yet, if Shelley 'misreads' *Frankenstein*, his reading concentrates not on Victor but on the monster. In spite of 'victim', Shelley's review suggests less an exoneration of Victor than an attempt to understand those factors which lead to alienation. His reading is best understood when taken in the context of his accounts of the social conditioning of oppressed peoples such as the Irish, the modern Greeks and the French (see especially the Prefaces to *LC* and to *Hellas*).

8 **catastrophe** dénouement: the change or revolution which produces the conclusion or final event of a drama or narrative.

18 Cf. *Macbeth*, I.v.55.

21 **Pelion ... Ossa** add greatness to greatness (the underlying reference is to two giants in Greek mythology who piled mountains on top of each other in an attempt to scale the heavens and overthrow the divine order).

31 **result** As in his review of Godwin's *Mandeville* ('a wind which tears up the deepest waters of the ocean of mind'), Shelley acknowledges the destabilizing effects of fiction through images which suggest the natural sublime. He is also concerned to distinguish this kind of philosophical and imaginative narrative from the Gothic novel. See his Preface to *Frankenstein*, where he invokes 'the truth of the elementary principles of human nature' and cites the examples of Homer, Shakespeare and Milton. See also: 'I have chosen a story of human passion in its most universal character ... appealing ... to the common sympathies of the human breast' (Preface to *LC*, which owes a debt to the Advertisement to *Lyrical Ballads*).

56 **a curse** Shelley's interpretation of the psychology of the 'Being' (a term derived from the novel, where he is also 'monster', 'daemon' and 'fiend') and of his terms of reference is informed by his own experience of alienation (see 'scorn' in the dedicatory verses to *LC*).

60 **abortion** this word, which has helped to fuel much critical interpretation, was one of Shelley's own contributions to the text of the novel.

76 Shelley's reference to Falkland in Godwin's *Caleb Williams* hints that his attitude to *Frankenstein* may have been more complex than is often conceded. He observed that Godwin 'with that sublime casuistry which is the parent of toleration and forbearance, persuades us personally to love [Falkland], while his actions must forever remain the theme of our astonishment and abhorrence'. This 'casuistry' suggests possible connections with Satan and Beatrice Cenci (see Prefaces to *PU* and *The Cenci*, and notes).

11 [On a Science of Mind]

This title is not Shelley's own but is used here for ease of reference. Written ?1817. Printed posthumously (1839/40) as part of *Speculations on Metaphysics*, into which it has been integrated by most editors.

Shelley states: 'We are intuitively conscious of our own existence and of that connection in the train of our successive ideas which we term our identity.' The 'science of mind' has the advantage over other sciences that 'Every student may refer to the testimonials which he bears within himself to ascertain the authorities upon which any assertion rests'. If we are to distinguish the differences between individuals, we must visit the 'deepest abyss of this vast and multitudinous cavern'. The imagery of the cavern recurs notably in *On Christianity*, where Shelley claims: 'Every human being has what Lord Bacon calls its *idola specus* [images of the cave; *Novum organum*, 1.42], peculiar images which reside in the inner cave of thought. These constitute the essential and distinctive character of every human being, to which every action and every word bears intimate relation.' On one occasion at least, Shelley attempted to consult the testimonials within himself by analysing his dreams. This brief investigation includes an account of the phenomenon of *déja vu* on a walk near Oxford, when he encountered the sight of a windmill among plashy meadows enclosed by stone walls. His analysis was left unfinished, with the explanation: 'Here I was obliged to leave off, overcome by thrilling horror.' Mary Shelley (who printed this strange fragment as part of *Speculations on Morals*) appended an editorial note: 'I remember well his coming to me from writing it, pale and agitated, to seek refuge from the fearful emotions it excited.' She added that his 'nervous temperament was wound up by the delicacy of his health to an intense degree of sensibility'. Shelley's reaction may throw some light on the phrase 'so dizzying and so tumultuous' in *On a Science of Mind*; both can be compared to his account of the effect of *Frankenstein* on a reader when 'the head turns giddy, and the ground seems to fail under our feet'. The vertiginous threat may be connected with Shelley's recurrent anxiety when faced with the stirrings of autobiographical impulse, and with a distrust of excessive sensibility (whose symptoms and sometimes fatal pattern had been analysed by Thomas Trotter in *A View of the Nervous Temperament*). For the dangers of self-anatomizing, see also *The Cenci*, II.ii.108-14 and the Preface, which identifies in Protestant practice 'a gloomy passion for penetrating the impenetrable mysteries of our being, which terrifies its possessor at the darkness of the abyss to the brink of which it has conducted him'. For a poetic exploration of individual mind, see *Alastor*. For a fascinating, if speculative, reconstruction of Shelley's Oxford experience, see Crook and Guiton, *Shelley's Venomed Melody*, pp. 56ff.

12   *Ozymandias*

Written late 1817. Published in the *Examiner* (11 Jan. 1818) under the name *Glirastes* (dormouse, or dormouse as preacher). Ozymandias is the Greek name for the Pharaoh Ramses II, who reigned from 1279 to

1213, carried out extensive building projects and erected many colossal statues, and was widely regarded as a model king. Shelley's poem should not be subjected to any simple decoding but it is worth noting that Oriental contexts were frequently invested with an English application and that Thomas Paine had referred to George III as a 'hardened, sullen tempered Pharaoh' (*Common Sense*). 'Ozymandias' was written in contest with Horace Smith (see note to *LMG*, 247), whose sonnet on the same subject was printed in the *Examiner* on 1 Feb. 1818 (see Appendix 3).

1 **a traveller** conceivably Walter Coulson, editor of *The Traveller*, who visited the Shelleys in late 1817, a reference to Robert Pococke's *A Description of the East* (1743), which portrays several statues of Ramses and of Memnon in various stages of disintegration. The poem is deliberately unspecific and flexible in its use of facts.

3 'desert . . . / Near' (Shelley's holograph).

4–5 Statues of Ozymandias, in accord with the tradition of the pharaohs, are serene, untroubled and youthful. Shelley's version carries the outward signs of those emotions which control the tyrant.

6–8 The passions depicted in the statue survive both the sculptor's hand and the heart of the pharaoh who gave them life. **mocked** imitated (perhaps with a hint of silent irony).

10–11 This inscription is usually traced back to Diodorus Siculus; in fact, it was an historical commonplace.

13 *Stanzas written in Dejection, near Naples*

Written Dec. 1818. Published posthumously (1824). In a letter of the same month Shelley recorded that he had 'depression enough of spirits & not good health'; the main causes were the death of his daughter in September and the subsequent estrangement from Mary – but dejection was a recurrent condition with the Romantic poets.

4 orig. 'The purple atmosphere of light': the colour is recorded by Shelley in his letters and by Turner in his water-colours.

10–11 See: 'We set off an hour after sunrise one radiant morning in a little boat, there was not a cloud in the sky nor a wave upon the sea which was so translucent that you could see the hollow caverns clothed with the glaucous sea-moss, & the leaves & branches of those delicate weeds that pave the unequal bottom of the water' (*L*, II.61).

22 **the sage** possibly Socrates or Diogenes (since 23 was originally 'Who lived alone and called it pleasure').

22–3 **crowned** Shelley's philosophical anarchism characteristically expresses itself in the translation of power from outward institutions to the autonomy of the individual. The linguistic structure of *PU* is partly based on this shift of control from the tyrannical Jupiter towards a new system of responsibility in which man is 'the king / Over himself' (III.iv.196–7).

14   The Two Spirits: An Allegory

Written ?late 1818. Published posthumously (1824). The two Spirits may be associated respectively with pessimistic and optimistic philosophies. The Second Spirit is dedicated to hope, love and infinite possibility; the First is cautious, limited and sceptical. This dialogue represents a characteristic feature of Shelley's intellectual word, the perpetual balancing of hypothesis against hypothesis, the guarded approach to the ultimately unknowable truth. The narrator's conclusion (33–48) devotes one stanza to each pole of the dialectic, though it is probably significant that the final words are on the side of hope rather than despair. The setting of these stanzas should be compared to those of 'Mont Blanc' and *PU*, the dialectical method to that of *JM*.

10 **shade of night**   the conical shadow cast by the earth in space.

15   Julian and Maddalo

Begun probably in Sept. 1818 and finished by 15 Aug. 1819, when it was sent to Hunt for anonymous publication. Published posthumously (1824). The poem had its origins in a meeting and conversation between Shelley and Byron at Venice on 23 Aug. 1818 described in a letter to Mary, part of which is now missing. The poets rode on the Lido, discussed Byron's 'wounded feelings' and Shelley's affairs, including the custody hearing in Chancery, and talked about literary matters, including Canto IV of *Childe Harold*. Julian is based on Shelley, Maddalo on Byron, and Maddalo's child on Allegra, Byron's daughter by Claire Clairmont, who had been sent to Venice in April, and concern for whose future was the reason for Shelley's visit. The name 'Maddalo' (accented on the first syllable) was derived from a courtier in Tasso's circle, while 'Julian', the 'complete infidel', may have been suggested by the proximity of the Julian Alps and may carry a trace of Julian the Apostate. 'Julian' was also the central figure in an unfinished poem by Byron. The madman 'is also in some degree a painting from nature, but, with respect to time and place, ideal'. It has been suggested that he was based on Torquato Tasso (1544–95), author of *Gerusalemme liberata*, whose dungeon at Ferrara Shelley visited in November and whose predicament inspired him to begin a fragmentary play (Goethe's *Torquato Tasso* had appeared in 1790, and Byron's *Lament of Tasso* in July 1817; see also *Childe Harold*, IV.35–9). Shelley was much possessed by his contact with the records of the 'hopeless persecution' of 'unoffending genius'. Other interpretations discover connections between the madman and Shelley himself, whose recent marital disagreements may well be alluded to covertly in the enigmatic monologue (cf. 'Stanzas Written in Dejection' and the curious beginning of 'Lines Written among the Euganean Hills'). Manuscript evidence indicates that the poem was structured so as to frame the soliloquy; there is reason to believe that parts of the soliloquy which draw on Shelley's own discontents may have been added to the poem at a late stage, perhaps even after the death of William in June 1819 (Matthews, Reiman, Jones). Yet this is largely irrelevant to an understanding of the poem since Shelley deliberately avoids specificity. Indeed, although there is a sense in which the poem can be seen as an argument between the authors of two very different poems on the subject of Prometheus (Byron's short poem had been written in 1816 and Shelley began *PU* at Este in September), there is also a sense in which Shelley is arguing against himself. The easy narrative flow is rudely interrupted by the maniac's soliloquy which, like the rest of the poem, is written in couplets, but which is deliberately fragmented so as to produce an effect of discontinuity and discord. *JM* is strongly influenced by Shelley's interest in the tradition of the dialogue (which Tasso himself had practised). The soliloquy might seem to tilt the balance towards the pessimism of Maddalo but the poem remains challengingly open-ended.

Shelley instructed his publisher not to print *JM* with *PU*, because 'It is an attempt in a different style, in which I am not yet sure of myself, a *sermo pedestris* [prosaic] way of treating human nature quite opposed to the idealism of that drama.' He told Leigh Hunt: 'I have employed a certain familiar style of language to express the actual way in which people talk with each other whom education and a certain refinement of sentiment have placed above the use of vulgar idioms' (vulgarity, he added, was not confined to any particular class). It was Shelley's intention to match *JM* with three other poems set in Rome, Florence and Naples, 'but the subjects of which will be all drawn from dreadful or beautiful realities, as that of this was' (*L*, ii.164).

Preface

1–27   Shelley's private view of Byron was less tactful. See his critique of Canto IV of *Childe Harold*, which he regarded as the product of Byronic self-contempt rather than misanthropy: 'The spirit in which it is written is, if insane, the most wicked & mischievous insanity that ever was given forth. It is a kind of obstinate & selfwilled folly in which he hardens himself. I remonstrated with him in vain on the tone of mind from which such a view of things alone arises ... [He] is heartily & deeply discontented with himself, & contemplating in the distorted mirror of his own thoughts, the nature & the destiny of man, what can he behold but objects of contempt & despair? But that he is a great poet, I think the address to Ocean [*Childe Harold*, IV.1603ff.] proves' (*L*, II. 58).

19 concentered Byron's Prometheus, who is more selfish and less hopeful than Shelley's, finds on his defiant resistance his own 'concentred recompense'.

48 text of every heart cf. 'the inscription on his heart', 'Even love is sold', p. 10 above.

15-16 we . . . / . . . we altered from 'you' in draft in both cases.

51 eagle spirit according to legend, the eagle can look directly at the sun without being blinded. Byron is too narrowly concerned with self and, like Coleridge in *LMG*, is blinded by his own 'internal lightning'.

57 Shelley quoted this bittersweet paradox in a letter to Thomas Medwin of 17 Jan. 1820, where he defined Italy as 'The Paradise of exiles – the retreat of Pariahs'; see also *L*, II. 174.

60 thee Italy. 'To stand beneath the dome' (draft).

87 station a point at which one stands or may stand to obtain a view (first usage in this sense dated 1822 by *OED*).

88 'The gondolas themselves are things of a most romantic & picturesque appearance; I can only compare them to moths of which a coffin might have been the chrysalis. They are hung with black, & painted black, & carpeted with grey . . .' (*L*, II.42).

92 Cf. *The Tempest*, IV.i.151.

96 'Look Yorick' (draft). Here Maddalo identifies Julian with the narrator of Sterne's *A Sentimental Journey*. The implication may have been that Julian was a sentimental traveller too easily responsive to the impulses of the heart. This clue is also suggestive because the structure of Sterne's prose with its network of dashes might provide a model for Shelley's 'unconnected exclamations'.

117 Shelley could not swim, as Byron would have known since they were together in a boat during a storm on Lake Geneva in 1816.

143 'And whilst I waited, romped in the saloon' (draft).

170-6 The basic premise of *PU*, where regenerated man emerges 'free from guilt or pain, / Which were for his will made or suffered them' (III.iv.198-9). See also *OL*, 241-5.

173 The punctuation is intended (similar constructions are common in Shelley). The sense is: 'We might be as happy, high, majestical as in our wildest dreams'.

188 those . . . philosophy the Greek philosophers, who dispassionately analysed the great problems of existence before the Christian Church inhibited philosophical and theological speculation.

204 Cf. 'there is some soul of goodness in things evil, / Would men observingly distil it out' (*Henry V*, IV.i.3-4).

214 San Servolo (or San Servilio) is an island with a Benedictine monastery which in 1725 became an asylum for 'maniacs of noble family or comfortable circumstances' under the care of the Hospital Fathers of St John of God. A hospital and church (still standing) were built between 1734 and 1759. In 1797, under Napoleonic influence, class distinctions were abolished. Théophile Gautier provides a description at a later date (*Voyage en Italie* (1852)).

238 **peculiar**   personal, relating exclusively to himself. Cf. 449–50.

244 **humourist**   a man subject to humours; fantastical, whimsical.

320   See the interrogation in *PU*, II.iv.

354–7   Another premise which is central to *PU*.

433 **cearedst**   sealed, shut up (like a corpse in a coffin). Cf. 614; *Adonais*, 453–5. **my memory**   the memory of me.

471   He has been changed not by his own inconstancy but by her reluctance to love him in return.

516 **in his society**   in company with him.

536 **nice**   refined. **gentleness**   although the Maniac *is* an inoffensive creature, gentleness here specifically implies the behaviour of a gentleman.

574   Cf. 'His soul had wedded Wisdom, and her dower / Is love and justice, clothed in which he sate / Apart from men, as in a lonely tower, / Pitying the tumult of their dark estate' ('Athanase', 31–4).

587 **Armenia**   Byron had been studying Armenian in 1817–18. 'Among the mountain tribes of India' (draft).

16   On Love

Written July 1818, probably between 20 and 25 July. This essay seems to have been composed directly after Shelley had finished his translation of Plato's *Symposium*; it must have been directly inspired by his work as translator, as was his *A Discourse on the Manners of the Ancient Greeks Relative to the Subject of Love*. The discourse was intended to explain the Greek practice of homosexual love, which features centrally in the *Symposium* (which Shelley called '*Erotikos*, or a Discussion upon Love'). Shelley tried to 'induce the reader to cast off the cloak of his self-flattering prejudices' and, before passing judgement on the Greeks, to acknowledge the limitations of British *mores*, which hypocritically tolerated a widespread and notorious system of prostitution. Though Shelley himself was susceptible to male beauty and celebrated sentimental friendships among men (see 'Bacchus and Ampelus'), he found fault with Greek homosexuality not least because it marginalized women: 'This invidious distinction of humankind as a class of beings [of] intellectual nature into two sexes is a remnant of savage barbarism which we have less excuse than they for not having totally abolished.' Unlike *A Discourse*, *On Love* ignores social and historical factors and concentrates on the psychological. Its account of the stages of love owes much to the *Symposium* and especially to Agathon's speech, while its combination of philosophical definition and analysis with impassioned and poetic prose can be compared to Shelley's own account of Plato's achievement in the Preface to his translation: 'Plato exhibits the rare union of close and subtle logic, with the Pythian enthusiasm of poetry, melted by the splendour and harmony of his periods into one irresistible stream of musical impressions, which hurry the persuasions onward as in a breathless career. His language is that of an immortal spirit rather than a man.' Shelley's reference to Sterne suggests that his prose may also owe debts to the language of feeling as developed in the novel of sensibility (not only by Sterne, who is cited in the draft of *JM*, but also by Rousseau). His account of the psychology of love looks back to *Alastor* (Preface and 149–91) and forward to *Epipsychidion*.

1 **airy children** cf. *PU*, I. 741–2.
2 **soul within our soul** cf. *Epipsychidion*, 238.
3 **overleap** cf. Satan's entry into Paradise (*PL*.,iv.181).
4 **antitype** that which is shadowed forth or represented by the 'type' or symbol.
5 **lyres** for other examples of the Aeolian lyre, see *Alastor*, 42–9, *On Christianity* (pp. 109–21 above) and *OWW*, (p. 57).
6 **the voice of one singing** for the effects of singing on the hearer, see 'To Constantia', and *PU*, II.ii.25ff. and II.v.72ff. and 'To Jane'. For music and love, see *Alastor*, 153–72.
7 **Sterne** 'was I in a desert, I would find out wherewith in it to call forth my affections – If I could not do better, I would fasten them upon some sweet myrtle, or seek some melancholy cypress to connect myself to – ' ('In the Street: Calais' in *A Sentimental Journey*, ed. Ian Jack (London, 1968), p. 28.

17 *Prometheus Unbound*

Written autumn 1818 (Act I), spring 1819 (Acts II and III), autumn 1819 (Act IV). Published 1820. Shelley's play takes as its starting point the *Prometheus Bound* of Aeschylus but, in spite of incidental debts, is a highly original and independent creation. The first act of Shelley's play comes closest to Aeschylus: it focuses on Prometheus, the benefactor of mankind and founder of human civilization, who has stolen fire from heaven, for which offence he has been nailed to a rock in the Caucasus and tortured physically and mentally. Aeschylus' play was part of a trilogy of which the other plays have not survived; however, we do know that in the final play Prometheus came to terms with Jupiter. Shelley could not accept such a compromise and provided his own version, since Aeschylus had 'left the tale untold', that is, had failed to realize the best potential of his subject. In Shelley's version, heroic resistance is not sufficient; Prometheus is fortified by the love of Asia, who is the central figure of Act II. *PU* is a response to the grim political realities of the years between the failure of the French Revolution and the passing of the Reform Bill; like its predecessor, *LC*, it is a deliberate 'experiment on the temper of the public mind as to how far a thirst for a happier condition of moral and political society survives ... the tempests which have shaken the age in which we live.' Shelley's shrewd and carefully argued pamphlet *A Philosophical View of Reform* shows that he was well aware of 'the difficult and unbending realities of actual life'; the 'beautiful idealism' of his play was dictated by the needs of the situation and by his artistic conscience. Shelley's great achievement was to translate politics into moral and psychological terms; while his play obviously deals with the external world of politics and public events, there is a sense in which it can be regarded as taking place in the mind of Prometheus. Jupiter, for example, is a typical tyrant but he is also a projection of the darker forces within Prometheus himself. When Prometheus has achieved a proper moral and psychological equilibrium, Jupiter disappears. Shelley's choice of the term 'lyrical drama' is significant. Stuart Curran notes: 'in the Romantic period lyrical drama is a term applicable to any serious dramatic effort containing music, from opera to choral drama. Though no music was intended to accompany the drama, music imagery is a significant element throughout, and the generic subtitle likewise accentuates and justifies the large number and variety of lyrical intrusions in the work.' Shelley first wrote *PU* as a three-act play which was largely completed in April 1819 but which he continued to revise and expand. In October he instructed his publisher to print this version although (as Neil Fraistat has demonstrated) he had clearly begun work on what was to become the fourth act. As Fraistat argues, 'the composition of *PU* was a much more fluid, continuous, and revisionary process than we have yet recognized'.

Epigraph

'Do you hear these things, Amphiaraus, hidden under the earth?' (a line from *Epigoni*, a lost play by Aeschylus quoted by Cicero). Amphiaraus was a seer who became an oracular god; the context of the story concerns attitudes towards suffering. Here the question is directed towards Aeschylus.

Preface

15 The secret was that Zeus would eventually be overthrown by a child produced by his own union with Thetis. Shelley makes ironical

use of this element of the plot when the fall of Jupiter is activated by Demogorgon, who says, 'I am thy child'.

24   catastrophe: see note to *On Frankenstein*, 8.

31   Satan   Shelley's interpretation of the character of Satan was further developed in *ODD* and in *DP* (see texts and notes below). Shelley's sympathetic reading can be compared to that of Blake in *The Marriage of Heaven and Hell.*   **casuistry:**   the analytic reasoning of the casuist, that part of ethics which resolves cases of conscience, applying the general rules of religion and morality to particular instances in which 'circumstances alter cases', or in which there appears to be a conflict of duties. See also Shelley's response to Beatrice in the Preface to *The Cenci* and to Falkland in *On Frankenstein*, 76.

47   Caracalla   Shelley's particular susceptibility to Roman ruins also surfaces in the unfinished story *The Colosseum*.

61–6   For the Greek poets, see Preface to *The Cenci*, 77–9.

67ff.   Manuscript evidence shows that paragraphs 5 to 9 of the Preface were written later than the first four which were intended for the three-act version of *PU*. Shelley's emphasis on a spirit of the age which accounts for an unwilled similarity between contemporaries was stimulated by a review of *LC* in the *Quarterly* for April 1819 which accused him of imitating Wordsworth while failing to notice that Shelley had anticipated such criticism in the Preface to *LC*. Shelley did not see this review till 15 October. The same review seems to have inspired, or helped to inspire, *PBT* which addresses itself to the question of influence in a verse-form which deliberately imitates Wordsworth, while criticizing his practice and resisting the contagion of his example.

86ff.   Cf. the account of the connection between literature and social change in *PVR* and later in *DP*.

131–3   Cf. 'Shakespeare and Lord Bacon and the great writers of the age of Elizabeth and James the First were at once the effects of this new spirit in men's minds, and the causes of its more complete development' (*PVR*, which was written shortly after Shelley completed the Preface to *PU*).

143   Scotch philosopher: Robert Forsyth in *The Principles of Moral Science* (1805). Shelley is partly in dialogue with Peacock who used Forsyth's phrase to define an element in the character of Scythrop Glowry, a satirical but not unfriendly version of Shelley in *Nightmare Abbey* (1818). For the original passages in Peacock and Forsyth, see Appendix 4.

147   William Paley, author of *The Principles of Moral and Political Philosophy* (1785) and Thomas Robert Malthus, author of *An Essay on the Principle of Population* (1798, with several revisions and expansions; see Preface to *LC*, note 13). Paley and Malthus are named as supporters of systems which endorse and confirm the status quo. Cf. 'I would rather be wrong, by God, with Plato than be correct with those men' (Cicero on the Pythagoreans, *Tusculan Disputations*, 1.xvii.39).

158–61 This appears to be a version of the Parable of the Sower (e.g. Luke 8:5–15).

162 systematical history PVR is an indication of Shelley's taste for historical surveys. Presumably, Plato is mentioned here as the author of *The Republic*.

Act I. Stage directions **Indian Caucasus** Indian is Shelley's addition, because the Hindu Kush mountains were thought to have been the cradle of civilization. **morning slowly breaks** the setting is similiar to the bleak Alpine world of 'Mont Blanc'. As the revolutionary day dawns gradually, man's environment is reclaimed from the snows and ice and becomes a paradise on earth.

1 Daemons spirits intermediary between man and God.

2 One Prometheus (or possibly Demogorgon).

6–8 Jupiter is here associated with the vindictive God of Christianity who rules over men's hearts and minds by a system of rewards and punishments based on expectation of an afterlife. **hecatombs** large sacrifices. **self-contempt** a failure to acknowledge one's own true human dignity.

9 eyeless in hate the syntax is ambiguous – rightly so, since when Prometheus responds to Jupiter with hatred they become identified.

59 recall remember *and* revoke. Prometheus chooses to undergo a process of psychotherapy whereby he can relive the past and then cast out hatred.

65 burning without beams 'Beyond our atmosphere the sun would appear a rayless orb of fire in the midst of a black concave' (note to *Queen Mab*).

83 Colour is not inherent in objects but is a property of light.

121 frore frozen.

124 informs gives characteristic life and shape.

135 inorganic associated with mortality and therefore incomprehensible to an immortal, like Prometheus.

137 And love almost certainly means 'And lovest'.

141 wheel of pain the earth's axis, oblique until man achieves his harmonious paradise; here suggesting the wheel on which Ixion was tortured in Hades.

192 Zoroaster Persian sage (magus) whose religious philosophy posited a world divided between the powers of light and darkness. Much of the mythological framework and symbolism of *PU* has Zoroastrian associations (see Curran). To meet one's double is traditionally a sign of impending death: no such incident has been discovered in the life of Zoroaster himself but the strange spiritual manifestation is close to his philosophy, which posited the existence of Fravashis or daemonic forces similar to guardian spirits.

207 Demogorgon a crucial figure in this play. Notoriously hard to define, he seems to represent the 'voiceless and invisible Consequence' (Aeschylus), an amoral force which links cause with effect.

212 Hades lord of the underworld. **Typhon** a monster.

216 shades the ghosts who people the underworld.

229ff. sweet sister's Ione and Panthea are the sisters of Asia, inter-mediaries between her and Prometheus.

262ff. It is important to remember that these are the words of Prometheus spoken by the phantasm of Jupiter. What is involved is more than a dramatic irony: in his hating mood, Prometheus is identified with Jupiter.

273–4 Man imposes tyrannies on himself, and may revoke them.

289 Like the poisoned tunic given to Hercules by Nessus' wife.

292–3 Like Satan in *PL* (II. 210–11).

306–11 The Earth has failed to recognize that the true victory is to abstain from perpetuating the cycle of violence.

345 Probably a word-play on Phlegethon and Cocytus, two streams in Hades (though Shelley's punctuation is ambiguous).

347–9 After delivering Thebes from the Sphinx, Oedipus unwittingly married his mother and cursed his sons, so that they killed one another.

371 a secret that if Jupiter has a son by Thetis, he will be greater than his father. This is a crucial factor in the Greek original. In Shelley, Jupiter is brought down by other means, though Demogor-gon, who activates his fall, could be seen as the inevitable offspring of his actions.

377 fane temple.

387 thought-executing servants who execute his commands, though there may be implications of efficiency and of ruthlessness, repressing truth 'in Heaven-defying minds'. The word is derived from the storm scene in *King Lear*, whose 'sulphurous and thought-executing fires' (III.ii.4) may provide a context of lightning and thunderbolt for the words of Prometheus.

398–9 Damocles was compelled to dine under a sword suspended by a single hair to illustrate the insecurity of kingly power.

479 lidless unclosed, never sleeping.

492–4 The tyranny of Jupiter is replaced by a properly constituted internal monarchy; Shelley never argues for anarchy or total freedom from controls. Cf. 'Sonnet to the Republic of Benevento'.

530–1 Dealings at summit conferences such as the Congress of Vienna (1814–15).

539 'The Furies having mingled in a strange dance divide, and in the background is seen a plain covered with burning cities' (stage direction in manuscript).

546–63 The wars of religion are a sad perversion of the humane and benevolent doctrines of Christ, with whom Prometheus is associated (563).

567–77 The French Revolution, from its hopeful beginnings to the Terror and the consequent despair in the possibilities of democracy.

567 **disenchanted** delivered from evil spells (cf. Coleridge: 'when to whelm the disenchanted nation, / Like fiends embattled by a wizard's wand, / The Monarchs marched in evil day', 'France: An Ode', 28–30).

609 **hooded ounces** hunting leopards, hooded before they are unleashed.

618–31 The point of this temptation is that it is a true report. However, the condition is not necessarily permanent; there is still hope because Prometheus can rise above apathy and despair. **ravin** prey, spoil. **they do** the words of Christ, asking forgiveness for his persecutors; here used insidiously as an argument for despair.

658–61 The spirits rise like angels from within individual human minds and help to create a climate of opinion, a spirit of the age (cf. Preface). The first four present visions of hope, the fifth is transitional, and the sixth suggests those misgivings and relapses into melancholy which can waylay even the optimistic.

737–51 The Poet of 'beautiful idealisms' transcends the specific realities of the everyday world (as in 'To a Sky-lark'). This is the highest kind of poetry; the yellow bees have their place, too, in poems such as *JM*.

765–6 Love (associated with the illuminating power of electricity) has the crest of Venus on his helmet.

772–9 Based on a passage in Plato's *Symposium* (195) which describes how Love 'dwells within, and treads on the softest of existing things'. The Platonic source should not disguise the fact that the sudden disillusionment is generally characteristic of Romantic psychology and can also be related in some ways to the trauma caused by the unexpected trajectory of the French Revolution. 'Desolation' can be compared to 'dismay' (*OL*, 5) and to 'visions of despair' (*LC*, 3). For a later example, see the sudden switch of mood at the end of *Hellas*.

Act II Scene IV This act has concentrated on Asia, who is a crucial complement to the patient heroism of Prometheus. Beginning from a vale in the Indian Caucasus, she is drawn by a series of dreams, echoes and spirit-voices towards a 'Pinnacle of Rock among Mountains', where, with her sister Panthea, she finds herself in 'the realm / Of Demogorgon, and the mighty portal, / Like a volcano's meteor-breathing chasm, / Whence the oracular vapour is hurled up'. They then proceed 'Through the grey, void Abysm, / Down, down!' towards the crater of what appears to be a volcano from which, at the appropriate moment, Demogorgon will erupt and overthrow Jupiter. The location is traditional to the oracular earth-spirit; the visit to the underworld is a recurring feature of epic poetry. Much of this scene and the rest of the act is informed by Shelley's own direct experience of volcanic landscape on his visit to Vesuvius in Dec. 1818.

2–7 As Carl Grabo pointed out, this passage makes use of the discovery in 1800 of infra-red rays. Geoffrey Matthews goes much further when he claims that 'Demogorgon is, in fact, realised in terms of molten magma, the obscure and terrible volcanic agent hidden in the depths of the earth'. Demogorgon, who is first mentioned as a 'tremendous Gloom' (I.207; see note), is presented paradoxically and in language which makes recurrent use of negatives. Shelley draws on Milton's account of the shapelessness of Death (PL, II.666–70) and the 'darkness visible' of hell, but there may also be a suggestion of Milton's God, 'Dark with excessive bright' (III.380). This darkness is awful and challenging to the observer but it is also charged with positive potential. The ambivalence of Demogorgon and his underground context should not be underestimated. Among other things, he may be associated with the untested force of the unrepresented multitude, which might express itself in terms of violence but is derived from fundamental rights which eventually must be asserted. Such political interpretations draw strength from the possible Peacockian etymology Demos + gorgon = the people as gorgon (or monster) and perhaps from the fact, noted by E. P. Thompson, that there was a short-lived radical paper called the Gorgon. When Asia is on her journey towards Demogorgon's cave, she hears echoes which tell her 'In the world unknown / Sleeps a voice unspoken'. This must be connected with the 'voice to be accomplished' of the conch which sounds at the end of Act III. After the interview with Demogorgon, the act concludes with a celebration of the beauty of Asia, who has been transfigured by events, and a final love-duet.

19ff. The image is based on the sight of about 300 fettered criminals hoeing the weeds in St Peter's Square (L, II. 93–4). See Introduction, p. xxvii.

32ff. Based, with significant differences, on Prometheus Bound, 196–254 and 442–506.

33–4 Saturn presided over the Golden Age but, since he can also be identified with Time, this state of happiness is far from permanent. Shelley had little time for Golden Ages or noble savages because 'uncivilized man is the most pernicious and miserable of beings'.

52 unseasonable because in the Golden Age there had been perpetual spring.

61 Homeric tranquillizer; antidote to Circe's potions; unfading flower.

78–9 Man's divinity is emphasized by his Christ-like ability to walk on the water.

80 **mocked**   created a superior version of (cf. I.747–8).

95ff.   See Shelley's description of Pompeii (Appendix 5).

123 The context is specifically oracular; see the lines quoted in headnote to this scene.

126ff.   Now that Asia has acknowledged the power of Love, the destined hour has come. The two Spirits represent two aspects of the revolutionary change which is about to take place: the necessary harshness involved in the fall of Jupiter and the hope of a more radiant future.

150ff.   These lines describe a volcanic explosion.

157 **ivory shell**   Asia's chariot associates her with Venus.

Act III Scene IV   Jupiter, who has misread the situation till the last, has fallen after a bloodless encounter with Demogorgon, who arrives in the Car of the Hour with unmistakable suggestions of seismic activity, 'The Earthquake of his chariot thundering up / Olympus'. When asked to identify himself, he replies: 'Eternity – demand no direr name.' After a pastoral interlude with Ocean and Apollo, Prometheus is liberated by Hercules and then invites Asia and her sisters to retire with him to a cave, 'Where we will sit and tell of time and change / As the world ebbs and flows, ourselves unchanged'. The reader is reminded that, precisely because Prometheus is 'the type of the highest perfection of moral and intellectual nature', he is not subject to the limitations of mortality. He is both a culture-hero, the founder of human civilization, and an example of that self-empire to which humanity can aspire. The concluding scene of this act (originally of the whole play) is largely devoted to reports on the regenerated world, external effects described by the Spirit of the Earth, internal by the Spirit of the Hour.

19 **dipsas**   a legendary snake, mentioned by Lucan and Milton, whose bite excited a raging thirst.

51 **a great city**   Here, as in *LC*, Shelley places the climactic act of political transformation in civic space. The location is generalized, but a number of significant details are derived from Rome, where most of Act III was written.

54ff.   **a sound**   From Scene iii we know that this sound was produced by the Spirit of the Hour, from a 'mystic' and 'many-folded' shell given to Asia by Proteus, who breathed 'within it / A voice to be accomplished' (cf. 'Mont Blanc', 80). The instructions of Prometheus to the Spirit represent a further harmonizing of revolutionary potential: the 'mighty music ... shall be / As thunder mingled with clear echoes'. Cf. the trumpet of the resurrection in *OWW*.

63 reflex reflected image.

79-83 The nightshade is no longer poisonous, and the halcyons, who are traditionally associated with calm weather, have turned vegetarian.

94 interlunar between the old moon and the new, therefore dark.

100-5 'In the general regeneration the earth's atmosphere ceases to act as a prism, thus no longer distorting sunlight into varied colours and a glare that hides realities' (Reiman / Powers).

107 Winnowing beating, flapping.

110 Pasturing feeding on.

112 Phidian like those created by Phidias, the most famous sculptor of classical Athens, responsible for designing the sculptures of the Parthenon, including the Elgin Marbles, which Shelley saw in London. For Shelley's celebration of the humanistic achievement of Greek sculpture, see Preface to *Hellas*.

115-21 These descriptions are informed by Shelley's observation of the antiquities of Rome, specifically of the Pantheon and the Sala della Biga in the Vatican Museum, where he could have seen a chariot yoked by an 'amphisbaenic snake' (119); the legendary amphisbaena (mentioned by Lucan and Milton) has a head at either end and can therefore move in either direction.

136 Dante, *Inferno*, III.9.

140 abject outcast, degraded person.

163 nepenthe a drug or potion, which brings forgetfulness of pain or grief.

164-72 The relics of the *ancien régime* or old system, which has now been superseded, are as irrelevant and obsolete as the inexplicable shapes on Egyptian obelisks erected in the setting of an alien city. Reiman suggests that the 'shapes' are hieroglyphs which (unlike the legend on the statue of Ozymandias) had yet to be decoded in Shelley's day, but 'look forth / In triumph' may indicate representations of pharaohs or of divinities. Undoubtedly, these lines were inspired by the sight of obelisks at the centre of Rome. In *A Classical Tour through Italy*, 3rd edn (1815), John Chetwoode Eustace recorded that ten obelisks were still standing in contemporary Rome but his interpretation was exactly the opposite to Shelley's ironical vision: 'We cannot but look upon them as so many acknowledgements of homage, so many testimonials of submission to the mistress of the Universe.' **glozed on** commented on, glossed, explained.

176 astonishment This term is recurrently used in the Bible (eight times in Jeremiah) to suggest that frame of mind which will harshly acknowledge the fate of a fallen city. Given this context, it should perhaps be noted that *captivity* also carries strong Biblical resonances.

180-3 those foul shapes evil takes on many forms, all of which are at odds with 'the overruling Spirit of the collective energy of the moral and material world' ('God'). See note to *HIB*, 27.

185–7 Some editors refer to executions for adultery, but Shelley was probably thinking of the sacrifice of Iphigenia by her father Agamemnon; Lucretius had described the scene vividly, concluding with the bitter cry 'Tantum religio potuit suadere malorum' [To such a pitch of evil could religion prompt] (*De rerum natura*, 1.80–101). **unreclaiming** unprotesting and, by their passivity, failing to assist in the reclamation of the earth from its present barrenness (Shelley had helped to reclaim land from the sea at Tremadoc in Wales).

190   **the painted veil** those ephemeral illusions which, like the curtain in a theatre, interpose between man and reality. Cf. 'Sonnet' ('Lift not the painted veil, which those who live').

200–4 Shelley's regenerated man is still subject to certain limitations (this realism should be compared to the Utopian visions of Godwin and Condorcet). By a continuous effort of will, man may transcend guilt or pain, though he is not exempt from them. **intense** probably means very blue (cf. *OWW*, 34), though with a suggestion of eager aspiration. **inane** empty space (as in Lucretius and Milton). Originally, the play concluded with this speech by the Spirit of the Hour. However, Shelley's fair copy here includes the name *Prometheus*, which suggests that at one point he may have considered allocating a final word to Prometheus, who had also been granted the first word.

Act IV Shelley originally intended to finish the play after Act III. The last act was written late in 1819 and represents a cosmic celebration which is indebted to Shelley's encounter with opera and ballet. Many of the words and images (e.g. 'fire', 'chains', 'adamantine', 'unmeasured', 'unimagined') which had previously signified the confines and penalties of man's imprisonment under Jupiter are now repossessed and redeployed so as to express their positive potential.

18   Preface to 'The Cenci'

Written May–Aug. 1819; printed in Leghorn and published anonymously in London in spring 1820. Shelley's play was based on an account of the history of the Cenci family which Mary had copied from manuscript in May 1818 and which he intended to prefix to his text. This story (summarized in the Preface) produced 'national and universal interest' in Rome, where it had achieved a status as part of a national mythology which Shelley compared to the stories of King Lear and Oedipus before Shakespeare and Sophocles translated them into dramatic form. Shelley was further inspired both by the brooding presence of the Cenci Palace and by Guido Reni's portrait of Beatrice Cenci (which, ironically, seems to have influenced Amelia Curran's notoriously effeminate portrait of himself). He claimed that the story 'would be as a light to make apparent some of the most dark and secret caverns of the human heart' (see 'On a Science of Mind'); the moral and imaginative challenge to the dramatist was to explore the motivation of one who, unlike the heroically patient Prometheus, could not 'forgive wrongs darker than Death or Night' and was provoked into understandable but tragic retaliation. *The Cenci* was composed after Shelley had written Acts II and III of *PU* and before he wrote the final act; by selecting a 'sad reality', it allows Shelley to explore some of the darker potentialities of the resistance to tyranny which were generically impossible within the beautiful idealism of *PU*. Shelley's investigation of violence in *The Cenci* meshes suggestively with his reactions to the news from England in the late summer of 1819 and to poems such as *MA*. In a letter of 6 Sept. he responds to the news of Peterloo in the words of Beatrice: 'Something must be done / What, yet I know not' (III.i.86–7).

Shelley intended *The Cenci* for the London stage and arranged for Peacock to offer it to Covent Garden. He hoped that Beatrice would be played by the Irish actress Eliza O'Neill ('God forbid that I shd. see her play it – it wd. tear my nerves to pieces') and the Count by Edmund Kean. He recognized the danger of treating the subject of incest but argued that, 'like many other *incorrect* things', it was 'a very poetical circumstance' and noted that *Oedipus Tyrannus* was performed 'on the fastidious French stage'. His own treatment of the subject draws strength from the unspeakability of the crime, conditioned not only by the circumstances of contemporary theatre but by Beatrice's refusal to speak a language which is shared by her father, the court and the church and validated by the self-justifying mechanisms of patriarchal authority. In spite of Shelley's precautions, his play was not performed till 1886 when the Shelley Society staged it privately; professional performances in Paris (1891), Coburg, Moscow and Prague all preceded the first London production in 1922.

10–13   Cf. the final sentence of the Preface to *JM* and the objectives formulated in 'On a Science of Mind'.

17–22   Shelley's Prometheus resists this temptation to revenge (see the comparison with Satan in the Preface to *PU*).

28   **casuistry**   cf. Preface to *PU* on the 'pernicious casuistry' involved in weighing Satan's wrongs against his faults (a paragraph probably written between Apr. and Sept. 1819).

50–3   Cf. Orsino's speech in II.ii.108–14.

66–71   Cf. IV.11.12–15, and *Hamlet*, III.iii.80–96.

77–9   III.i.243–65; this is an example of the imagery of mind which Shelley specifies in the Preface to *PU*, where he acknowledges a specific debt not to the Spanish playwright but to the Greek dramatists. A draft passage cites a line from 'the Greek Shakespeare',

Sophocles (translated as 'Coming to many ways in the wanderings of careful thought') and comments: 'What a picture does this line suggest of the mind as a wilderness of intricate paths, wide as the universe which is here made its symbol, a world within a world which he, who seeks some [rarer] knowledge with respect to what he ought to do, searches throughout, as he would search the external universe for some valued thing which was hidden from him upon its surface'.

80ff. Shelley's practical objectives were conditioned primarily by his desire to achieve an appropriate diction for the stage 'with a certain view to popularity'. He told Medwin that his 'chief endeavour was to produce a delineation of passions which I had never participated in, in chaste language, & according to the rules of enlightened art' (*L*, II,189). This rather neoclassical emphasis on impersonality should not obscure Shelley's obvious debts in the formulation of his concepts to the Preface to *Lyrical Ballads*. For the 'familiar style', see also Shelley's account of the diction of *JM* in a letter of 15 Aug. 1819 (*L*, II. 108; see p. 369 above).

For a more extended use of the language of religion to express the operations of the imagination, see *DP*; see also *On Christianity*, which anticipates both these examples in its interpretation of religious metaphor. The raising of the low and the levelling of the lofty suggests Hazlitt's account of Wordsworth's revolutionary Muse in *The Spirit of the Age*. Behind both passages lies the biblical redistribution of power (e.g. 'He hath put down the mighty from their seats, and exalted them of low degree' (Luke 1:52), identified by Shelley as 'Jacobinism').

19   The Mask of Anarchy

Written Sept. 1819 and sent for publication in the *Examiner* on the 23rd. Published posthumously (1832). On 16 Aug. 1819 Henry Hunt was addressing a crowd of 60,000 working people in Manchester on the subject of parliamentary reform, when the yeomanry attempted to arrest him. In the ensuing confusion, they were joined by a detachment of regular cavalry, who charged the crowd: the toll was fifteen dead and 500 injured (both approximate figures). Because it took place on St Peter's Fields this unhappy incident became known as 'Peterloo' (with ironical reference to Wellington's success on another field). Shelley developed the parallel in a draft passage for *PBT*: 'You've killed British the French, / And made a sweet stench / Of corpses, at Water & Peter-loo / <Sidmouth> is gratified / <Canning> is satisfied / Gratify Walter & Pater too'. Shelley first heard the news when he read the issues of the *Examiner* for 22 and 29 Aug.: 'These are, as it were, the distant thunders of the terrible storm which is approaching. The tyrants here, as in the French Revolution, have first shed blood. May their execrable lessons not be learnt with equal docility!' Here Shelley adumbrates the doctrine of passive resistance which is central to his poem: it is essential that the reformers should not become involved in the fruitless cycle of violence but that they can see 'in the frank & spirited union of the advocates for Liberty, an asylum against every form in which oppression can be brought to bear against them'. The claims of pacifism were not easily met: many readers of the poem have been troubled by its darker undertones. Certainly, Shelley was greatly exercised by the implications of Peterloo, and its violent impress is palpable in *PVR* and in his public letter to the *Examiner* in defence of Richard Carlile (written at the beginning of November but not published) which gives a less restrained account than that in *MA*: 'we hear that a troop of the enraged master manufacturers are let loose with sharpened swords upon a multitude of their starving dependents & in spite of the remonstrances of the regular troops that they ride over them & massacre without distinction of sex or age, & cut off women's breasts & dash the heads of infants against the stones' (*L*, II. 136). The 'Mask' of the title refers to the allegorical pageant, the masquerade which gives the poem its basic shape; it also suggests the impostures and deceits of authority (in the first of his *Examiner* articles Leigh Hunt had referred to 'the Men in the Brazen Masks of power' while Shelley himself described the monarchy as 'merely the mask' of the power of the rich). 'Anarchy' suggests that despotic power is allied to chaos rather than to true authority. Characteristically, Shelley inverts the language of those alarmists and defenders of the *status quo* who resisted reform on the grounds that anything short of unanimity would result in 'anarchy and massacre' (*PVR*). Likewise, the masque itself, 'the celebration in pageant or in drama of the harmony and order of a king-centred society, is reversed and exposed as the expression of an ethic that is socially divisive, anarchic' (Cronin). Hunt had made a similar point in his leader of 22 Aug.: 'Can any thing, in fact, on the face of the transaction, afford a more revolting specimen of impatient, violent, arbitrary feeling on the part of the retainers of Government? Or one more foolish as well as violent? For they talk of the revolutionary tendencies of the Reformers; but how can revolutionary tendencies be more excited than by government's lawlessly drawing the sword, and being the first to shed blood systematically?' (See note on 331 below.) This poem is 'of the exoteric species' and was specifically intended for the *Examiner*; Leigh Hunt, who had suffered enough for his frankness, preferred not to publish it till after the Reform Bill had been passed. As Richard Cronin notes, 'The reader . . . ought to be aware both of the voice of the balladeer, and of Shelley manipulating that voice.' For examples of a 'popular' ballad, see Appendix 6.

1–4 Shelley is following the conventions of visionary poetry. Cf. the opening of *TL*.

6 **Castlereagh** Robert Stewart, Viscount Castlereagh (1769–1822), Foreign Secretary since 1812, Leader of the Commons, associated by radicals with war and oppression, particularly in Ireland and in the Napoleonic wars, but also at home; his extreme unpopularity was later to excite cheering in the streets during his funeral procession.

8 **Seven bloodhounds** 'the seven states (Austria, Bourbon France, Portugal, Prussia, Russia, Spain, Sweden) which, with England, agreed in 1815 to postpone indefinitely the abolition of the slave trade' (Matthews).

15 The Lord Chancellor in his robes (ermine was a symbol of purity). Eldon was famous for weeping in public (he could 'outweep the crocodile') yet such displays were proved meaningless by his judgements in Chancery where, far from suffering the little children to come unto him, he outraged human feeling by separating them from their parents. In 1817 he had refused Shelley the custody of his two children by Harriet (see notes on 'To the Lord Chancellor'). For millstones and children, see Luke 17:2.

24 **Sidmouth** Home Secretary, who raised large sums of money to build churches for the industrial poor, whom he repressed through the activities of the police and a complex network of spies, informers and *agents provocateurs*.

29 **spies** see note to 24 and to 'England in 1819', 10, and headnotes to *Address to the People* and *ODD*.

30–3 'And I looked, and behold a pale horse; and his name that sat on him was Death, and Hell followed with him. And power was given unto them over the fourth part of the earth, to kill with sword, and with hunger, and with the beasts of the earth' (Revelation 6:8).

49 For the psychological effects of desolation, see *PU*, I.772–9.

81–2 In 1817 Habeas Corpus had been suspended on suspicion of a plot to seize the Bank of England and the Tower of London. Here, that seizure of the focal points of power is carried out by government itself.

88 Hope and Despair can be hard to distinguish. One of the temptations facing reformers after the apparent failure of the French Revolution was to surrender their ideals; like Prometheus they had to learn 'To hope, till hope creates / From its own wreck the thing it contemplates'.

90 **Time** In the course of history many hopes of political reform have been frustrated; short of bloody conflict, one is still left. Shelley concretizes his vision of history forever aspiring towards something better in the figure of one of the oppressed poor.

97 Cf. Wordsworth, 'The Thorn', 65–6.

110 **a Shape** This has been identified both as Liberty and as Public

Enlightenment (Hunt), but Shelley deliberately avoids specificity. The Shape is associated with a snake (in Shelley the principle of good resisting evil) and with Venus (the planet of love). It bears obvious similarities to the glorious phantom in 'England in 1819'.

145   accent   speech, utterance.

148   unwritten   in the characteristic Shelleyan sense of a story which is yet to be written and whose potential is therefore unfulfilled; perhaps, also, with an implication that the poor and the underprivileged had previously been excluded from the annals of history (unlike the 'storied dead' of Thomas Gray's 'Elegy').

176ff.   the Ghost of Gold   paper money (Banknotina in *Swellfoot the Tyrant*). See 'The rich no longer being able to rule by force, have invented this scheme that they may rule by fraud' (*PVR*). Cf. *PBT*, 166-71.

180ff.   A paper currency might eventually force the people (i) to lose control of their own will and (ii) to indulge the desire to fight back – two serious infringements of Shelley's ethical ideals.

197-208   'The foxes have holes, and the birds of the air have nests; but the Son of man hath not where to lay his head' (Matthew 8:20).

220   Fame   Rumour.

225   clothes and fire and food   cf. 'But there is something else "dear and valuable", which has nothing to do with such super-abundance; and that is, "meat, clothes, and fire" [Pope, *Epistles to Several Persons*, 3.82]. These are dear and valuable to the poor; and Reform is dear and valuble to them, in proportion as they think it will help to restore them' (Hunt, *Examiner*, 22 Aug.).

239   damn for ever   in a free and enlightened community nobody would believe in the myth of eternal damnation. Shelley considered that religion was 'intimately connected with politics' and that by threatening punishment after death it diverted and frustrated attempts to alter the political *status quo*.

245   Britain, Austria, Prussia, Holland, Spain and Sardinia formed a coalition against revolutionary France in 1793.

250-1   perhaps like Mary Magdalen, as a sign of repentance and submission (Luke 7:45).   **like him following Christ**   Zacchaeus (Luke 19:1-10).

257-8   The sources of the power and privilege which was once theirs but which they now seek to eliminate.

266   a great Assembly   as at Peterloo and the other great meetings held by the reformers; Shelley may have had in mind also the Assemblies held in the early days of the French Revolution.

305   targes   shields.

319-20   scimitars   short, curved, single-edged swords, used among Orientals, especially Turks and Persians. The detail suggests an analogy between the tactics of the authorities at Peterloo and the tyrannical force of the Ottoman Empire (cf. the central metaphor of *LC*). On 1 Dec. 1819 *The Black Dwarf* printed a poem on Peterloo which shows how the model of Greek resistance to Turkish hegemony was powerfully present to the English radical imagination: this poem identifies the crowd as 'each helpless Greek' and addresses the cavalry as 'ye English Janizaries of the *north*'. **sphereless stars** 'stars shooting from their spheres, i.e. meteors' (Matthews). *OED* identifies this as the first usage of *sphereless*.

330 **phalanx** a compact body of people massed or ranged in order or, more generally, a group banded together for a common purpose. Cf. 'Let them [the oppressors] be instructed to know their impotence; & let those who are exposed to their rage, who occupy the vanguard of the phalanx of their opponents see in the frank & spirited union of the advocates for Liberty, an asylum against every form in which oppression can be brought to bear against them' (L, II. 148).

331ff. **the Laws** Hunt refers frequently to Magna Carta and the Bill of Rights. See 'Are not the Ministers themselves the most notorious of these violators of the constitution? ... Is not justice continually delayed in the most scandalous manner, contrarily to the provisions of Magna Carta? Is not a standing army illegally kept up in time of peace, contrary to the provisions of the Bill of Rights?' (*Examiner*, 25 July). The radical perspective is well illustrated by a passage in *The Black Dwarf* (21 Apr. 1819): 'The old genius of the country, arising from the tombs of our ancestors, points to the cause of their freedom as the best and only means of recovering our own!' (247).

334 '... the soldier is a man and an Englishman. This unexpected reception would probably throw him back upon a recollection of the true nature of the measures of which he was made the instrument and the enemy might be converted into the ally'.

344–63 Shelley discusses the merits of passive resistance in *PVR* (1819). It is the best course 'not because active resistance is not justifiable when all other means shall have failed, but because in this instance temperance and courage would produce greater advantages than the most decisive victory'. Regular soldiers (as opposed to the militia engaged at Peterloo) might thus be brought to reflect on the realities of their situation and to ally themselves with their fellow-countrymen.

364 For the volcano as an image of revolutionary change, see *PU*. **oracular** traditionally, oracles were thought to be inspired by the inhalation of volcanic vapours (see *PU*, II.iii.3–10).

369 **thundered** cf. 'they fear the thousands and thousands whose voices are getting up like the wind in so many quarters of the country, and whose rising, though not for revolution, is "As the sound / Of thunder heard remote" [*PL*, II.476–7]. And no doubt this is a fearful consideration for the truly lawless' (Hunt, *Examiner*, 25 July).

20   *Ode to the West Wind*

Written late Oct. 1819. Published with *PU* (1820). This ode brings together nature, politics and Shelley's private life in a richly complex fusion which transcends all three. The drafts show Shelley distancing himself from details which were specifically personal: instead, he plays the role of the prophetic poet, an Isaiah looking forward to a regenerated society. Although the poem has the structure of a hymn and celebrates a numinous force, Shelley's most compelling concern is political and he looks to nature for confirmation that out of seeming death can come new life. Formally, the ode is highly inventive: each stanza is a sonnet built out of four groups of *terza rima* and a concluding couplet. The rhyme scheme is particularly appropriate to Shelley's theme of resurrection and potentiality since the middle line of each tercet generates the first rhyme of the next group of three lines. In 1819 *terza rima* was highly unusual in English poetry. Shelley had already employed it in 'Athanase' and he would use it again in a number of uncompleted poems, most notably in *TL*.

4   **hectic** feverish.
5–6   **pestilence-stricken** Like his older contemporaries Blake and Coleridge, Shelley's apocalyptic imagination encouraged him to interpret social phenomena in terms which were essentially biblical. Plague features significantly in *LC*, where it was partly influenced by the example of John Wilson's *The City of the Plague* (1816). See *PBT*, 100–16 in this edition and note. The simile which compares falling leaves to the souls of men has a long lineage in epic, including Homer (cited by Shelley in a note to *Queen Mab*) and Milton, who combines an Italian context with suggestions of romance ('His legions, angel forms, who lay entranced / Thick as autumnal leaves that strew the brooks / In Vallombrosa', *PL*, 1.301–3).
9   **azure sister** the gentle west wind of spring, usually masculine (Zephyrus or Favonius).
10   There are suggestions here of the Resurrection which are taken up again at the end of the poem. Cf. 'for the trumpet shall sound, and the dead shall be raised incorruptible, and we shall be changed' (I Corinthians 15:52).
15–18   Fractocumulus or scud, 'clouds running beside thunderstorms, which can be seen discharging water into the sea but which themselves are composed of water evaporated from the sea' (Ludlam): these 'opposing streams of liquid and of vapour' suggest the 'tangled boughs'.
20–3   **locks** not to be confused with the loose clouds, these are 'the equally high but dense plume of fibrous cloud which reaches far ahead of the towering cloud columns at the heart of a thunderstorm'

(Ludlam). These clouds of ragged texture 'almost lean forward, so that they can readily be imagined to be fleeing from the storm centre, "like ghosts from an enchanter"'. **Maenads** female followers of Bacchus, usually in a frenzy. Shelley's description may have been influenced by a relief depicting four Maenads, which he saw at Florence: 'The tremendous spirit of superstition aided by drunkenness and producing something beyond insanity seems to have caught them in its whirlwinds and to bear them over the earth as the rapid volutions of a tempest bear the ever-changing trunk of a waterspout, as the torrent of a mountain river whirls the leaves in its full eddies. Their hair loose and floating seems caught in the tempest of their own tumultuous motion, their heads are thrown back leaning with a strange inanity upon their necks, and looking up to Heaven, while they totter and stumble even in the energy of their tempestuous dance.'

25 **dome** Matthews notes the resemblance of the weather conditions to the phenomena which accompany volcanic eruptions, and claims that the dome ' – a favourite word of Humboldt's for the cones of the Cordillera – has its strong volcanic overtones as well as its share of starlight'.

29–42 The Mediterranean phenomenon known to meteorologists as 'the autumn break', which accompanies the fall of the barometer in late October and marks the sudden onset of winter. For the underwater sights on the Shelleys' boat-trip to Baiae, see note on 'Stanzas Written in Dejection', 10–11. This experience was reworked in August 1820 in 'Ode to Naples', 23ff. See also 'as dead leaves wake / Under the wave, in flowers and herbs which make / Those green depths beautiful when skies are blue' (*LC*, 2284–6).

32 In Dec. 1818 Shelley took a boat trip in the Bay of Baiae and observed 'the ruins of its antique grandeur standing like rocks in the transparent sea under our boat'. Baiae had been a fashionable resort with the Romans; Eustace's popular guidebook recorded that 'Baiae, indeed, was not only the seat of voluptuousness, but sometimes also the theatre of cruelty'.

34 **intenser day** of a deeper blue than the sky.

42 **despoil** strip (of their leaves).

51 **striven** perhaps as Jacob wrestled with the angel.

54 Here Shelley despairs not only as a private individual but as a prophetic poet who is a vehicle of the spirit of inspiration. Cf. the Psalms. See also 'The thorns which I have reaped are of the tree / I planted, – they have torn me, – and I bleed' (Byron, *Childe Harold*, IV.88).

56 **tameless** cf. 'untameable' (*LC* draft, note to 28). Cf. Shelley's self portrait (unused passages from *LC* on p. 358 above; notes to 28–36, 37–40).

57ff. Cf. *LC*, 83–90, and *On Christianity*, 109–21. **new birth** the Shelleys were awaiting the birth of a new child – Percy Florence was eventually born on 12 Nov. (Clara had died on 24 Sept. 1818 and William on 7 June 1819). This coded private meaning is absorbed in the larger contexts of public life and of literary achievement which are invoked in the first chapter of *PVR*, which was written shortly after *OWW*. See 'The literature of England, an energetic development of which has ever followed or preceded a great and free development of the national will, has arisen, as it were, from a new birth.' The whole passage, with its trumpet and its forward-looking faith in the agency of poetry, can be closely related to the conclusion of the ode. For the potentiality of poetry, see *DP*, 614ff., 893–905. See also a cancelled draft passage in *TL*, which refers to 'the new birth of this new tide of time' (i.e. France and Europe during the period of the Revolution and its aftermath).

63   dead thoughts his unsuccessful poems (notably *LC*), which had not fulfilled their true social function. Shelley had received the *Quarterly* on 15 Oct. and was animated to expand the Preface to *PU* as a direct response (see headnote).

69   trumpet see note on 10 above. Cf. also the trumpet at the end of *DP* (which originally appeared in the first chapter of *PVR*) and the transforming 'sound' of *PU*, III.iv.54.

70 'If Winter comes Spring lags not far behind' (draft). The political implications are important (a similar metaphor was used, for example, by Thomas Paine at the conclusion of *The Rights of Man* and by Shelley himself in *Proposals for an Association* (1812). Shelley hoped that the new birth would not involve violence. In one of his notebooks he wrote: 'the spring rebels not against winter but it succeeds it – the dawn rebels not against night but it disperses it.'

21   Peter Bell the Third

Written late Oct. 1819 and sent to Hunt on 2 Nov. for publication. Published posthumously (1839). Shelley was inspired by two reviews in the *Examiner*: Keats's review of *Peter Bell: A Lyrical Ballad* by John Hamilton Reynolds (a spoof and parody of Wordsworth's *Peter Bell*, whose appearance it antedated by a week), and Hunt's review of Wordsworth's poem. Reynolds's poem appeared on 15 Apr., Wordsworth's poem on 22 Apr., Keats's review on 25 Apr., and Hunt's review of Wordsworth on 2 May. It is not clear whether Shelley read Wordsworth's *Peter Bell* or Reynolds's pre-emptive parody ('the antenatal Peter, / Wrapped in weeds of the same metre'); it is possible that he absorbed all the evidence he needed from his reading in June of the two reviews, both of which included quotations. *PBT* (so named because it was now the third poem in a sequence) itself registers the significance of reviews in its analysis of the London literary world, particularly in Part Six ('Damnation'; not included in the present selection) which begins, '"O that mine enemy had written / A book!" – cried Job'. This emphasis, together with the mock-scholarship of the footnotes and the prophetic linking of the collapse of moral and social values to a corruption and failure of literary imagination, indicates that Shelley's poem is a direct descendant of Pope's *Dunciad*. Like *The Dunciad*, which ends with a cosmic yawn, *PBT* concludes with the negative influence of Peter, 'A wide contagious atmosphere' which is equated with 'A power to infect and to infest'. Perhaps the composition of the poem was ultimately and directly triggered not by Hunt and Keats or even Wordsworth but by the *Quarterly*'s claim that Shelley had imitated Wordsworth in *LC*, a claim which he first read on 15 Oct. and which seems to have inspired parts of the Preface to *PU* (see notes) and a passage in *PVR*, and which may have left its impress on *OWW*. *PBT* specifically engages with the problem of Wordsworth as a model for his contemporaries by adapting a Wordsworthian verse-form ('weeds of the same metre') in order to explore the damaging possibilities of such literary influence and to demonstrate its own independence. Although it is mostly genial in tone, and concedes great imaginative virtues to Peter / Wordsworth, it is unmistakably a corrective and revisionary text. Wordsworth, the poet who had publicly invested in the permanent forms of nature and who had associated the city with the decline of public values in poems such as 'Written in London, September 1802' and 'London, 1802', is ironically compromised by his association with metropolitan culture. The poem recurrently suggests the instability of the city, which is manifested in its economics. This brings together the warnings of writers such as Sir Richard Phillips, who identified in London those factors which inevitably led to the decline of all great cities, and Anna Barbauld, whose controversial poem 'Eighteen Hundred and Eleven' envisaged London as a city of ruins visited by American tourists. Shelley's preface explicitly introduces this apocalyptic possibility in a passage which echoes Volney's *Les Ruines* (a book also studied by Frankenstein's monster) and Isaiah: 'when London shall be an habitation of bitterns; when St Paul's and Westminster Abbey shall stand, shapeless and nameless ruins, in the midst of an unpeopled marsh; when the piers of Waterloo Bridge shall become the nuclei of islets of reeds and osiers, and cast the jagged shadows of their broken arches on the solitary stream'. See Horace Smith's 'Ozymandias', Appendix 3).

The equation between London and Hell goes back to the seventeenth century, if not earlier, but in Shelley's case it has a particular point since it can be related to *ODD* which seems to have been written shortly after *PBT*, and in which Shelley makes explicit connections between the role of the Devil in orthodox theology and contemporary systems of law and politics. These analogies are given added force by the fact that they can be traced in part to a Shelley broadside of 1812 'The Devil's Walk', which in turn was based on Coleridge's 'The Devil's Thoughts'. Here again, there is a satisfying circularity, since *PBT* is engaged not only with Wordsworth but with the phenomenon of the 'Lake Poets'.

Shelley asked that his *Peter Bell* be published anonymously: 'My Motive in this is solely not to prejudge myself in the present moment, as I have only expended a few days on this party squib & of course taken little pains. The verses & language, I have let come as they would, & I am about to publish more serious things this winter.' Elsewhere Shelley referred to the poem as 'a joke' and 'a trifle unworthy of me seriously to acknowledge'. He had long been exercised by Wordsworth's defection from the ranks of the reformers. He continued to admire Wordsworth's great poetry but considered that the dullness of *The Excursion* and the later poetry was the direct result of Wordsworth's moral and political derelictions. This disillusionment was given comical but forceful expression in the Preface: 'Peter is a polyhedric Peter, or a Peter with many sides. He changes colours like a chameleon, and his coat like a snake. He is a Proteus of a Peter. He was at first sublime, pathetic, impressive, profound; then dull; then prosy and dull; and now dull – oh so very dull! it is an ultra-legitimate dullness.' In Shelley's fiction, Peter (Wordsworth) has been taken to hell by the Devil, who has offered him 'a situation'. Cf. 'Verses . . . on Receiving a Celandine' and 'An Exhortation'.

6–7 With an alliterative gusto reminiscent of popular verse, Shelley links four diverse characters: John Castle, informer and *agent provocateur*; George Canning, liberal Tory; William Cobbett, journalist, pamphleteer and influential radical; Viscount Castlereagh, Foreign Secretary, hated alike by radical leaders and by the people.

9 **cozening** cheating, defrauding by deceit. **trepanning** catching in a trap, luring into a course of action, swindling.

11 The name Southey is cancelled in the fair copy.

16 **Chancery Court** the court presided over by the Lord Chancellor where in 1817 Shelley was deprived of the custody of his two children by Harriet.

20–5 See headnote to *PVR*.

26–7 'These . . . are awful times. The tremendous question is now agitating, whether a military & judicial despotism is to be established by our present rulers, or some form of government less unfavourable to the real & permanent interests of all men is to arise from the conflict of passions now gathering to overturn them' (*L*, II.148).

30 **methodism** Shelley's attitude to Methodism may have been largely conditioned by Leigh Hunt who attacked *Peter Bell* as

'another didactic little horror ... founded on the bewitching principles of fear, bigotry and diseased impulse'. Hunt was unequivocal in his criticism: 'The very hope of such things as Methodism is founded in hopelessness, and that too of the very worst sort – namely, hopelessness of others, and salvation for itself.' Gin, suicide and Methodism all offer strategies of despair.

37 **amant miserè**   love miserably (that is, give voice to their love by caterwauling); pronounced with mock-gentility to rhyme with 'chastity'.

40 'What would this husk and excuse for a virtue be without its kernel prostitution, or the kernel prostitution without this husk of a virtue? I wonder the women of the town do not form an association, like the Society for the Suppression of Vice, for the support of what may be called the "King, Church, and Constitution" of their order. But this subject is almost too horrible for a joke' (Shelley's note).

41 **hobnobbers**   those who drink together, or to each other, or are on familiar terms.

44 **stockjobbers**   members of the Stock Exchange who deal in stocks on their own account; 'A low wretch who gets money by buying and selling shares in the funds' (definition of 1755). See *PVR*, p. 179 above.

56 **levees**   assemblies held by a prince or person of distinction.

63 **a Cretan-tonguèd panic**   a panic based on unreliable rumours; apprehension in relation to financial and commercial matters.

66–7 **conversazioni**   social gatherings for the discussion of the arts or for learned conversation. **conventicles**   meetings or assemblies of a clandestine, irregular or illegal character; meetings of Nonconformists or Dissenters from the Church of England for religious worship.

71–5   This stanza performs three main functions: (1) It alludes to a passage in Wordsworth's *Peter Bell* which Shelley employed as an epigraph to his own poem ('Is it a party in a parlour, / Crammed just as they on earth were crammed, / Some sipping punch – some sipping tea; / But, as you by their faces see, / All silent, and all – damned!'); (2) it is a parody of the naiveties of the Wordsworthian style. Cf. 'Not a brother owneth he, / Peter Bell he hath no brother; / His mother had no other son, / No other son e'er called her mother; / Peter Bell hath brother none' (Reynolds); (3) by its circularity, it suggests the claustrophobic and self-condemning philosophy of this underworld.

76–85   Shelley includes a note on 76 which plays on the English habit of swearing: 'This libel on our national oath, and this accusation of all our countrymen of being in the daily practice of solemnly asseverating [asserting emphatically] the most enormous falsehood, I fear deserves the notice of a more active Attorney General than that here alluded to.' Shelley claims that damnation is not a sentence passed by a divine judge but a condition resulting from a free and deliberate choice. Hell is not a place so much as a state of mind which man imposes on himself. 'In this view, he [the Devil] is at once the informer, the Attorney General, and the jailor of the celestial tribunal' (see *ODD*, 70–72 and note). **flams**   humbug, deception.

92–3   Shelley was frightened that Cobbett's demagoguery would incite the poor and the oppressed to violent revolution which would *not* lead them to the kingdom of Heaven promised to them in the Sermon on the Mount (Matthew 5). Leigh Hunt recorded that 'the poor read [Major] Cartwright and Cobbett with an anxious and pertinacious interest, commensurate with their sense of suffering' (*Examiner*, 1 Aug. 1819). Shelley invents an ode for Peter/Wordsworth which parodically transforms his 'Ode: 1815' into a celebration of the bloodshed at Peterloo (634–52 in complete text). This is accompanied by a note: 'It is curious to observe how often extremes meet. Cobbett and Peter use the same language for a different purpose: Peter is indeed a sort of metrical Cobbett. Cobbett is, however, more mischievous than Peter, because he pollutes a holy and now unconquerable cause with the principles of legitimate murder; whilst the other only makes a bad one ridiculous and odious.'

96–100   an ironical picture of Shelley the idealist. These lines sum up the whole of Shelley's poetic endeavour; cf. the faith of Julian and the sceptical response of Maddalo in *JM*, 159–211.

100–16   For the influence of the climate of opinion, see the role of the Furies and the Spirits in the First Act of *PU*. For literary contagion, see headnote to *PBT*. See also note to *OWW*, 5.

104–5   Cf. *Macbeth*, III.ii.50–1.

117   **Peter ... Square**   Wordsworth moving in polite society.

147–56   Shelley suggests a certain narrowness of perspective, an egotistical limitation in Wordsworth. The implications are best illustrated by a passage from *DP*: 'The great secret of morals is Love; or a going out of our own nature, and an identification of ourselves with the beautiful which exists in thought, action or person, not our own. A man to be greatly good, must imagine intensely and comprehensively; he must put himself in the place of another and of many others; the pains and pleasures of his species must become his own. The great instrument of moral good is the imagination: and poetry administers to the effect by acting upon the cause.'

167ff.   Cf. 'Turned to a formal puritan, / A solemn and unsexual man' (550–1 in complete text of *PBT*). This is the first usage of 'unsexual' recorded in *OED*; the second, by De Quincey, refers to Dorothy Wordsworth. Shelley's own view of poetry is more explicitly sexual: 'it strips the veil of familiarity from the world, and lays bare the naked and sleeping beauty, which is the spirit of its forms' (*DP*).

173   **a sister's kiss**   this may be an ironical allusion to Wordsworth's

relations with Dorothy. The fair copy includes these lines: 'Another – "Impious Libertine! / That commits i—t with his sister / In ruined Abbies – mighty fine / To write odes on *it*!" – I opine / <Peter had never even kissed her>'. Shelley's play with the subject of incest introduces a subject which had been injurious to his own reputation. In a note to the poem which Mary Shelley excluded in 1839 Shelley indulged himself at the expense of suspicious and censorious readers by suggesting the potentially dangerous charge of the word *it*: 'some curious persons have attempted to discover it by placing a dash between the only two letters which compose *It*'. **Diogenes** a Cynic philosopher, famous for his contempt of the flesh and of bodily comforts.

179 **Burns** in the draft of *Adonais* an unnamed figure in the procession, who presumably represents Wordsworth, is 'Clothed in the skirts of a Scotch puritan'. Burns represents a different Scottish tradition.

182–4 'Mouth for kisses was never the worse; rather, it renews as the moon does' (moral of *Decameron*, 2:7). Shelley, who approved of Boccaccio's 'more serious theories of love', remarked that the application of this lighter one 'might do some good to the common narrow-minded conceptions of love'.

228 **petits-soupers** informal suppers for a few intimate friends.

229 **a man** Coleridge.

237–41 A common criticism of Coleridge: see Peacock's portrayals of him as Flosky in *Nightmare Abbey* and as Moley Mystic of Cimmerian Hall in *Melincourt*. Cf. *LMG*, 202–8.

242ff. This rhapsodic passage is probably based both on first-hand accounts of Coleridge's conversation and on Shelley's reading of *Biographia literaria*. The poetic theory bears a close similarity to some of the most celebrated passages in *DP*.

244–5 See John 3:8.

252ff. The influence of Coleridge on Wordsworth which was partly responsible for *Lyrical Ballads*.

261 Cf. 'the human heart by which we live' ('Ode: Intimations of Immortality', 6).

275 **rocks and trees** characteristic Wordsworthian subject-matter (see especially, 'Rolled round in earth's diurnal course, / With rocks, and stones, and trees').

281 The Pedlar features prominently in *The Excursion*; the parson can be found both in 'The Brothers' and in *The Excursion*. Hunt had cited the lines on Carnage in his *Examiner* leader of 22 Aug.

301 **pipkins** earthenware pots or pans. **cotter** peasant who occupies a cottage, usually with land attached.

22 Bacchus and Ampelus

Written ?Oct.–Nov. 1819. Published posthumously in an incomplete and imperfect text (1847). Apparently, no original of this text is extant. Since the texts by Thomas Medwin and H. B. Forman both give some cause for anxiety, I have attempted to provide a speculative reconstruction of Shelley's original; in this I am greatly indebted to the pioneering example of E. B. Murray. In Oct. 1819 Shelley moved to Florence, where, as he later reported, he 'dedicated every sunny day to the study of the gallery' although in Naples he had complained that the 'bodily fatigue of standing for hours in galleries, exhausts me'. On 13 or 14 Oct. he announced that one of his chief aims in Italy was to observe in 'statuary & painting the degree in which, & the rules according to which, that ideal beauty of which we have so intense yet so obscure an apprehension is realized in external forms'. This programme of observation resulted in a series of short prose pieces including notable accounts of the *Laocöon* (which he had seen in Rome), the *Niobe* and a *Minerva* (which influenced *OWW* in its description of Maenads). Shelley's mixture of technical analysis and impassioned appreciation owes much to the work of Johann Joachim Winckelmann, whose *Histoire de l'art chez les anciens* (1764; tr. from the German 1802) he had read aloud to Mary in Naples. From Winckelmann Shelley may have derived some of his neoclassical criteria, and Winckelmann's celebration of the male body also finds its echo in the unashamed physicality of Shelley's prose. Of one male statue Shelley exclaims: 'Curse these fig leaves; why is a round tin thing more decent than a cylindrical marble one?' Though Shelley believed that the social conditions of Greece, as transmitted through art and literature, predominantly favoured the cultivation of masculine beauty, he also celebrated images of the feminine. In the *Venus Anadyomene* he records 'the tongue lying against the lower lip as in the listlessness of passive joy' and the 'pointed and pear-like bosom ever virgin' which provokes a dying fall of regretful irony: 'the virgin Mary might have this beauty, but alas!' This passing flicker of comparison holds one of the keys to Shelley's admiration for the fragmentary remains of Greek sculpture which is also given expression in *DMAG* and in the Preface to *Hellas*. Greek sculpture, and the mythology which it embodied, was a happy and liberating contrast to the work of an artist such as Michelangelo ('a kind of Titus Andronicus') whether in his *Day of Judgement* for the Sistine Chapel or in his own statue of Bacchus, which was 'the most revolting mistake of the spirit and meaning'. Shelley is particularly animated in his account of divinities who exhibit youthfulness and joy. See, for example, Mercury, whose 'countenance expresses an imperturbable and god-like self-possession; he seems in the enjoyment of delight which nothing can destroy'.

23 *Ode to Heaven*

Written Dec. 1819. Published with *PU* (1820). 'The creation – such as it was perceived by his mind – a unit in immensity, was slight and narrow, compared with the interminable forms of thought that might exist beyond, to be perceived perhaps hereafter by his own mind; or which are perceptible to other minds that fill the universe, not of space in the material sense, but of infinity in the immaterial one' (Mary Shelley). The First Spirit celebrates heaven as an objective reality, seemingly eternal; the Second Spirit ('a Remoter Voice' in manuscript) redefines heaven in subjective terms; the Third Spirit ('a louder and still remoter Voice' in manuscript) accuses the first two speakers of presumption and suggests there is no distinction between subject and object, between the individual mind and external heaven. The final lines stress both the limitations of human perception and human life (37–45) and their infinite possibilities as part of the universe (46–54). For the terms of the debate, cf. 'Mont Blanc'; for the dialectical method, cf. 'The Two Spirits'.

19–22 Man has created God in his own likeness and located him in heaven.
38 **atom-born** suggests the Epicurean theory as developed by Lucretius in *De rerum natura*; atoms are the component elements of everything that exists, including man, and the only ultimate reality.
48 **eyed** implies the perceiving powers of the mind.

24 *England in 1819*

Written late 1819 and sent to Hunt for publication. Published posthumously (1839). Cf. Burdett's Election Address on 11 Oct. 1812, published in the *Examiner*: 'an army of spies and informers ... a Phantom for a king; a degraded aristocracy; an oppressed people ... vague and sanguinary Laws ...'

1 A combination perhaps of King Lear and Gloucester (note the 'tempestuous day' as an image for the state of contemporary England). Jonathan Bate records that '*Lear* was considered too politically sensitive to be staged during the Regency years'. George III was soon to die (29 Jan. 1820) at the age of 81, sixty years after coming to the throne. He had been irremediably insane since 1811.
2 **Princes** the sons of George III, notorious for their coarse tastes, dissolute habits and ostentatious extravagance.
7 See notes to *MA*: St Peter's Fields, where the demonstrators were stabbed by the militia, might have been cultivated to save them from starvation.

8-9 Here (as in 4-6) it is implied that this oppressive system contains the seed of its own destruction.

10 A legal system based on violence ('sanguine': bloody) and on mercenary considerations ('Golden'); 'tempt and slay' refers to the government's use of *agents provocateurs* who stimulated revolution in order that it might be put down *pour encourager les autres*.

11 followed originally by 'A cloak of lies worn on Power's holiday' (cf. Fraud in *MA*, who is 'Clothed with the Bible, as with light').

12 the unreformed Parliament. The draft of 'To the Lord Chancellor' includes the cancelled line 'A senate of impostors and oppressors'.

13-14 Cf. *Address to the People* (1817), which draws a contrast between the public mourning for the young Princess Charlotte and the public failure to recognize the death of British Liberty, symbolized by the execution of the Derby rioters, who had been led on to insurrection by a government agent: 'Let us follow the corpse of British Liberty slowly and reverentially to its tomb: and if some glorious Phantom should appear and make its throne of broken swords and sceptres and royal crowns trampled in the dust, let us say that the Spirit of Liberty has arisen from its grave and left all that was gross and mortal there, and kneel down and worship it as our Queen.'

25 A Philosophical View of Reform

Written late 1819-early 1820. Published posthumously (1920), revised edition (1973). This unfinished essay is a significant expression of Shelley's political thinking at a time when he was animated to great creative fertility by the implications of public events such as Peterloo and the trial of Richard Carlile (see Chronology and headnotes to *MA*, *PBT* and *ODD*). He had already tried to influence political opinion in the direction of peaceful change in *A Proposal for Putting Reform to the Vote throughout the Kingdom*, which had been published under the name of the Hermit of Marlow in late February or early March 1817 and distributed to a carefully considered list of sympathetic readers. *A Proposal* was explicit in its indignation against the prevailing state of English politics: 'An hospital for lunatics is the only theatre where we can conceive so mournful a comedy to be exhibited as this mighty nation now exhibits.' Shelley feared the dangers of 'anarchy and despotism' if measures were not taken to 'restore the people to a sovereignty thus held in their contempt'. Two and a half years later he returned to the subject. His 'octavo on reform' was 'boldly but temperately written' and intended 'to be an instructive and readable book, appealing from the passions to the reason of men' (*L*, II. 164, 201). It was influenced by Godwin's *Political Justice*, by Clarendon's

History of the Rebellion (Shelley was later to attempt a play on the subject of Charles I), by Plato's *Republic* and by Jeremy Bentham's *Introduction to the Principles of Morals and Legislation* (1789), which it somewhat resembled as 'a kind of standard book for the philosophical reformers politically considered' although it was 'different & perhaps more systematic'. Shelley's essay includes an ambitious historical survey of political reform which scrutinizes with particular interest the shape of recent events in America and Europe effected by the reforming or revolutionary tendency under the influence of 'Time, the great innovator'. Had the essay been completed and published, it would have made a strikingly clear-headed and pragmatic contribution to what Shelley identified as 'a crisis' in the national destiny of England. A letter of 14–18 Nov. 1819 to Leigh Hunt reveals the frame of mind in which Shelley had approached his task: 'I fear that in England things will be carried violently by the rulers, and that they will not have learned to yield in time to the spirit of the age. The great thing to do is to hold the balance between popular impatience and tyrannical obstinacy; to inculcate with fervour both the right of resistance and the duty of forbearance. You know my principles incite me to take all the good I can get in politics, for ever aspiring to something more. I am one of those whom nothing will fully satisfy, but who am ready to be partially satisfied by all that is practicable' (*L*, II. 153).

The first passage extracted here concerns the social consequences of the economic system. Shelley, whose views were much influenced by William Cobbett's *Paper against Gold*, suspected and feared both the national debt and the substitution of paper money for gold and its inflationary effects, which he represented by the personification Banknotina in *Swellfoot the Tyrant* (1820). In a system where 'all great transactions of personal property' are 'managed by signs', 'A man may write on a piece of paper what he pleases' while inflation increases both the labours of the poor and the luxuries of the rich which they supply (see *MA* and 'Men of England: A Song'). Shelley's analysis reveals the strong feeling against both the city and 'the City' (as the centre of economic life) that also marks *PBT*, which was probably written only weeks before *PVR*. Here, for once, the radical Shelley also reveals some of the influence of his upbringing in an identification, however reluctant, with the supposed stabilities of 'old' money, landed wealth and a traditional aristocracy.

The second extract demonstrates the gradualism of Shelley's politics; its blend of visionary optimism, concrete reforming measures and patient practicality should be set against the more poetic idealism of *PU* and the satirical indignation of 'England in 1819'. Shelley's recurrent and anxious concern with the processes of law (see note to *LC* Preface, 265) is here directed towards extending the scope of democratic expression and resistance to injustice. Significantly, the voice of public opinion is associated with poets, philosophers and artists in a paragraph which develops some of the implications of that celebrated passage on literature and the spirit of the age which concluded the first chapter of *PVR* and which later appeared in revised form as the conclusion to *DP*. Yet, with the partial exception of Leigh Hunt, the writers who are named here are not poets but are included because of their political prose – Godwin and Bentham as theorists, and Hazlitt and Hunt primarily as political essayists. Byron's name is cancelled in the manuscript, perhaps for personal reasons but more probably because the passage shifted its emphasis in the writing. Shelley's insistence on the intellectual and imaginative distinction of his literary contemporaries, who were its creations as well as its creators, also links *PVR* to the final paragraphs of the Preface to *PU*, which were written in the autumn of 1819. In a lengthy anonymous essay on the 'Rise and Progress of Popular Disaffection' (in which Shelley's *Proposal* was one of the three works ostensibly under review) Southey cited with approval Wesley's resistance to 'those principles that naturally tend to anarchy and confusion'. The antidote was clear: 'The laws, and nothing but the laws, can preserve us from this catastrophe' (*Quarterly Review*, Jan. 1817).

75 **Two years ago** The movement for reform was countered by the suspension of Habeas Corpus from March 1817 till the end of Jan. 1818.

77 **tempted and betrayed** apparently a reference to the fate of the leaders of the Derbyshire insurrection (see *Address to the People*, and 'tempt and slay', 'England in 1819', 10). Shelley comments 'so soon as the whole nation lifted up its voice for parliamentary reform, spies were sent forth'.

135 **Canaanites** Shelley combines still vivid memories of Peterloo with the Biblical account of divinely sanctioned incursions by the Jews on neighbouring nations; see especially the account by Theosophus in *A Refutation of Deism*.

162 **folded arms** cf. *MA*, 321, 344. A fundamental solidarity between the soldiers and the English people is asserted in *MA* as it is here.

175 **imprisonment and persecution** Shelley envisaged this for himself, even when he was in Italy. See his letter in defence of Richard Carlile: 'I hope this is no blasphemy, & that I am not to be dragged home by the enmity of our political adversaries to be made a sacrifice to the superstitious fury of the ruling sect. But I am prepared both to do my duty & to abide by whatever consequences may be attached to its fulfilment' (*L*, II. 137).

187 **pernicious** *PL*, VI.520 (the passage describes the Satanic invention of gunpowder).

204 **political libel** charges of blasphemous and seditious libel had been used frequently against radical printers, publishers and writers.
211 **distrain** seize.
229 **memorials** statements of facts forming the basis of or expressed in the form of a petition.
238 **eagles** see *JM*, 50–2, and *LMG*, 202–8.

26 *On the Devil, and Devils*

Written Dec. 1819 and/or early 1820 (probably Jan.). This witty and provocative 'Lucianic' essay seems to have been directly inspired by Shelley's reading of Luke's Gospel in Nov. and Dec. 1819. 'Who the devil is the Devil?' he asked in one of his notes. His reading focused on several passages involving devils, including the 'droll story' of the Gadarene swine (Matthew 5:11–13; Luke 8:32–3), which had been dismissed by one of the speakers in *A Refutation of Deism* as 'one of those stale absurdities' which did not prove the divine origins of Christianity; this story of a miraculous intervention receives much ironical attention in this more mature essay. *ODD* includes an extended interpretation of the character of Satan and the radical theology of *PL* which builds on the recently completed Preface to *PU* and looks forward to *DP*, where much of the text is absorbed with only minor variations, but the most challenging passage is omitted. Whether Shelley would have dared to publish the full text in England, where, as Blackstone stated, Christianity was 'part of the laws', is an open question; the essay itself (though not *DP*) is explicit in its claim that Milton only avoided 'persecution' through the use of what Shelley calls 'dramatic order' (i.e. the fictional and dramatic framework of *PL*).

A particularly significant part of Shelley's essay is devoted to the politics of heaven. Shelley interprets the role of Satan as *agent provocateur*, informer and chief agent for the prosecution in terms which would have been all too familiar to his contemporaries. Some readers have identified the influence of the Cato Street Conspiracy of Feb. 1820, a plot to assassinate the Cabinet which was exposed by the evidence of a government spy called Edwards. Yet Shelley's notes on Luke reveal that his reading the Bible in terms of contemporary politics almost certainly ante-dated Cato Street and that the spies who kept Christ under observation reminded him not of Edwards but of Oliver (see note on *An Address*, 272). Shelley's interest in the system of spying also features in 'England in 1819' and in the reference to Castle (or Castles) in *PBT*.

15–18 See *PL*, 1.211–15.
37–9 'Whether we regard the mistaken principles of republicanism which distinguished that great man' (cancelled in MS).

37   In Plato's *Phaedo* (118a) Socrates arranges for a cock to be sacrificed to Aesculapius shortly before his death.

44   **conclusive**   originally 'persuasive'. **syllogisms**   arguments.

55–8   Cf. 'The Devil, I safely can aver / Has neither hoof, nor tail, not sting' (*PBT*, 76–7).

64–70   In *DP* Shelley classifies the Book of Job with the 'highest poetry'. He once considered making it the subject of a play.

71   **he**   the Devil.

71–2   Cf. 'Accuser, witness, judge, / What, all in one' (Beatrice to the judge, *The Cenci*, V.II.174–5).

83   'innocent souls must they corrupt' (cancelled in MS).

86   **casuistry**   cf. 'the restless and anatomizing casuistry' defined in the Preface to *The Cenci*, which was written only a few months before this essay, and 'pernicious casuistry' in the Preface to *PU*.

88   'His business must consist in finding out conspiracies & their sins & then provoking men to them' (cancelled in MS).

91   **delator**   informer, secret or professional accuser. **Castlereagh**   see note to *MA*, 6.

103   After 'minister': 'to be bandied about by the national hatred' (cancelled in MS).

122   **anatomizing dogs**   see 'The Grotto del Cane too we saw, because other people see it, but wd. not allow the dog[s] to be exhibited in torture for our curiosity. The poor little animals stood moving their tails in a slow & dismal manner as if perfectly resigned to their condition; a curlike emblem of voluntary servitude' (*L*, II. 78, from Naples).

137   The watchmaker was a widely used figure for a creative deity in eighteenth-century philosophy. Shelley would have encountered it in the works of William Paley (see Preface to *PU*), whose orthodox theology he was encouraged to read by his father, and he borrows it for the Deist arguments expounded by Theosophus in *A Refutation of Deism*.

155   **good into evil**   see 'all good to me is lost; / Evil be thou my good' (*PL*, IV.109–10).

170   **hold his breath**   like the assassin Marzio in *The Cenci*, V.ii.183–5. For Satan's better feelings, see 'no purposed foe / To you whom I could pity thus forlorn / Though I unpitied' (*PL*, IV.373–5).

27   Lines to a Critic

Written 1819 or 1820. Published posthumously (1824). The critic may well be Robert Southey, whom Shelley (incorrectly) believed to be the author of a highly personalized attack on his moral character in the *Quarterly Review* for Apr. 1819. Reverberations continued, and as late as June 1820 Shelley wrote to Southey to ask if he was responsible. The poem can probably be linked to 'Lines to a Reviewer' and to the fragmentary 'Satire on Satire' in which he comments: 'I will only say, / If any friend would take Southey some day, / And tell him, in a country walk alone, / Softening harsh words with friendship's gentle tone, / How incorrect his public conduct is, / And what men think of it, 'twere not amiss.' In all three poems Shelley renounces hate and turns the other cheek.

7–8   Cf. 'Of your antipathy / If I am the Narcissus, you are free / To pine into a sound with hating me' ('Lines to a Reviewer'). Narcissus was not responsive to the love of Echo; likewise, Shelley does not reciprocate the critic's hatred.

13   **prove**   feel, experience.

28   *The Cloud*

Written probably early 1820. Published with *PU* (1820). This poem is informed by Shelley's observation of cloud behaviour and by his scientific reading, but its animation is derived from the central conception of the spirit of the cloud, which personifies the tantalizingly elusive principle of life.

17–30   According to Adam Walker, 'water rises through the air, flying on the wings of electricity'. The 'pilot' is the electricity which guides the cloud; there is a mutual attraction between this positive force and the negative electricity below ('the genii', 'The Spirit he loves'), which results in thunderstorms or rain. The informing principle of the cloud remains intact even though the cloud itself may disappear. **dissolving**   can be read as both transitive and intransitive.

58   **these**   the stars.

71   **sphere-fire**   the sun.

75   **pores**   Erasmus Darwin referred to 'each nice pore of ocean, earth, and air', while Adam Walker described how rain 'sinks into the chinks and pores of the ground'. The cloud is mainly formed by 'sweat' drawn up by the sun from the sea, rivers and rivulets.

79   **convex**   'The earth's atmosphere bends a ray of sunlight into a curve ... convex to an observer in a cloud looking down' (King-Hele). The difference from the limited perspective of troubled humanity is tactfully suggested.

81–4   The empty tomb ('cenotaph') is unbuilt as the cloud fills the sky and the blue dome disappears.

29   *The Sensitive-plant*

Written March 1820. Published with *PU* (1820). The sensitive-plant is the *mimosa pudica*, whose apparent sentience provided writers of the eighteenth century and the Romantic period with a convenient image for exploring the position of man in the scheme of things and for representing the figure of the poet (see William Cowper, 'The Poet, the Oyster, and the Sensitive Plant'). Shelley scrupulously avoids the explicit equations of Cowper, even if his plant might seem to suggest a displaced self-portrait. Shelley's writing is informed by his scientific interests, represented for example by his notes taken from Davy's *Elements of Agricultural Chemistry* and given a poetical focus by his youthful appetite for Erasmus Darwin, notably *The Loves of the Plants* (1789), which later appeared in *The Botanic Garden* (1791). The poem, which was written in Pisa, looks back to *OWW* of the previous autumn, which it recalls in various words or images (e.g. 'Maenad' (1.34), 'sea-flower' (2.8), 'Baiae' (3.3), and especially 3.34-8), but which it also challenges: here the spring does not offer a gentle new birth but a grotesque parody of resurrection from which the sensitive-plant is itself excluded (3.114-17). The poet's faith in something better is severely tested and can only be rescued by a recognition that we must rise above the limits of a perception which is merely sensual towards intuitions of a higher reality. 'The Sensitive-plant' bears some similarity to the unfinished allegorical poem 'The Woodman and the Nightingale' which laments: 'The world is full of Woodmen who expel / Love's gentle Dryads from the haunts of life, / And vex the nightingales in every dell'. See also *Adonais*; and, for a later poem which pays special attention to the processes of natural growth, see 'The Zucca'.

1.12 companionless the sensitive-plant is hermaphroditic; unlike the other flowers in the garden, it is also an annual. This adjective is also used to describe Adonais (272).

1.15-16 The metaphysical precision of Shelley's imagery suggests a dimension of existence or experience appropriate to the harmony and unity of a Paradise garden before the Fall, in which the normal divisions between the senses are transcended (see especially 25-8). This synaesthesia is not primarily paradoxical but an intimation of a higher unity. Shelley's synaesthetic effects make recurrent use of musical similes and analogies; the combination of voice and instrument often provides intimations of 'some world far from ours, / Where music and moonlight and feeling / Are one' ('To Jane'; see also 'To Constantia').

1.17 wind-flowers anemones.

1.25ff. This passage introduces a number of flowers whose names have Greek mythological associations. Narcissus fell in love with the reflection of his own image; receiving no response from the supposed object of his affections, he committed suicide. Hyacinthus was killed by Zephyrus, who was jealous of Apollo's love for him. Both Narcissus and Hyacinthus were transformed into flowers after death.

The Maenads or female followers of Bacchus were beautiful but fanatical and dangerous (see note to *OWW*, 20–3). The 'fabulous asphodels' (57) were associated in legend with Elysium (108), the abode of the blessed after death. 'Naiads' (21) were freshwater nymphs.

1.38 blows blooms.

1.63 mine-lamps Sir Humphry Davy had invented the safety-lamp for miners in 1815.

1.69 atmosphere Shelley's scientific interests led him to focus recurrently on the effects of atmosphere both on individuals and society. Frequently, he uses it as a metaphor for social context (cf. 'the atmosphere of human thought', *PU*, I.676, and 'A wide contagious atmosphere', *PBT*, 735).

1.74 In a review of Peacock's *Rhododaphne* written in 1818, Shelley described as a 'profound allegory' the statement in Plato's *Symposium* that 'Love is not itself beautiful, but seeks the possession of beauty.'

2.5–8 Shelley's description bears obvious traces of his Platonic reading.

2.6 Cf. 'That superior gracefulness which is truly the expression of the mind' (Wollstonecraft, *A Vindication of the Rights of Woman*).

2.10 sublunar literally, beneath the moon and therefore terrestrial, of this earth, subject to fluctuation and impermanence. Cf. 'The City's moonlit spires and myriad lamps / Like stars in a sublunar sky did glow' (*LC*, 1725–6).

2.38 ozier made of willow.

2.47–8 The draft includes this alternative: 'whose intent / Was like ours, who do ill yet are innocent'.

2.49 ephemeris the ephemera, mayfly or dayfly, so called because it lives for only one day (see *The Witch of Atlas*, 9–16).

2.53 antenatal according to *OED*, this word, meaning 'previous to birth', was first used in English by Shelley in *PBT*, 3. For 'tomb', see 'Each like a corpse within its grave' (*OWW*, 8).

2.58 'And in this Republic of odours and hues' (draft). This line was derived from Calderón (see *LMG*, 180–4 and headnotes) whose patterns of imagery, where stars and flowers were often interchangeable, left their impress both on this poem and on *Adonais*.

3.62 agarics mushrooms with gills on the underside of the cap.

3.65–8 These lines are cancelled in Mary Shelley's fair copy. For a Gothic description of a decomposing corpse on a gibbet, see the early poem 'Zeinab and Kathema', 145–50.

3.70 Spawn mycelium (i.e. the vegetative body of fungi: a mass of branching filaments that spread through the nutrient substratum).

3.72 flags endogenous plants with long swordlike leaves; generally, reeds or rushes.

3.78 unctuous oily.

3.113 griff claw (an unusual and archaic usage).

Conc 21–4 Draft versions include: 'For love and thought there is not death' (21) and 'their light / Outlives our <feelings> visions' (22–3). Earl Wasserman explains that these lines 'must mean, not that our senses cannot *tolerate* light, but that they cannot long *continue* to experience the brilliant forms of Being which the garden manifests as Existence and that as the senses fade and die they mistakenly report that it is the sensory shapes manifested by the forms that vanish'. Cf. Shelley's account in *On Life* of his dissatisfaction with materialist philosophy: 'I was discontented with such a view of things as it afforded; man is a being of high aspirations "looking both before and after", whose "thoughts that wander through eternity", disclaim alliance with transience and decay, incapable of imaging to himself annihilation, existing but in the future and the past, being, not what he is, but what he has been, and shall be. Whatever may be his true and final destination, there is a spirit within him at enmity with nothingness and dissolution (change and extinction). This is the character of all life and being.' See also *On a Future State*.

23–4 Cf. 'Perception, I believe, is, in some degree, in all sorts of animals; though in some possibly the avenues provided by nature for the reception of sensations are so few, and the perception they are received with so obscure and dull, that it comes extremely short of the quickness and variety of sensation which is in other animals' (Locke, *An Essay Concerning Human Understanding*, in a passage directly following his discussion of sensation in vegetables).

30 Men of England: A Song

Written 1819. Published posthumously (1839). On 1 May 1820 Shelley asked Leigh Hunt if he 'knew of any bookseller who would like to publish a little volume of *popular songs* wholly political, & destined to awaken & direct the imagination of the reformers' (*L*, II. 191). This book was never completed, but Shelley did write a number of poems which seemed to meet his own criteria. These include *MA*, 'Lines Written during the Castlereagh Administration' (more correctly 'To Sidmouth and Castlereagh'), 'A New National Anthem', 'England in 1819', and 'Ballad of the Starving Mother' (later known as 'Young Parson Richards'; first published 1921, corrected version 1970); the fragments beginning 'People of England, ye who toil and groan' and 'What men gain fairly – that they should possess' may also have been associated with the projected book. The need for caution may have helped to inhibit quick publication just as it caused Shelley to displace the threateningly English application of 'An Ode to the Assertors of Liberty', which seems like *MA* to engage with the moral and political consequences of Peterloo, under the title 'An Ode written October 1819, before the Spaniards had recovered their liberty' when it appeared with *PU*. As late as 1839 Mary Shelley still preferred to conceal the original specificity of 'To Sidmouth and Castlereagh' under the less dangerous title of 'Similes of Two Political Characters of 1819'. 'Song' has much in common with *MA*, including its economic analysis, but the tone is more pessimistic and the poem is potentially more threatening than *MA*, since it is unable to suggest any remedy.

9   The central image of bees and drones draws upon a commonplace in contemporary radical discourse (it can be found, for example, in Paine and Spence) which identified the working classes with bees. Similar analyses are offered in the fragment 'People of England, ye who toil and groan' (where the people 'are like gods who give them [their oppressors] all they have / And nurse them from the cradle to the grave') and in the detailed economic analysis of *PVR* (which refers specifically to the 'order of drones').

27–8   For the shaking of chains, see *MA*, 153, 370. Shelley envisages another Peterloo or perhaps the frustration of those strategies for peaceful reform which are set out in *MA*. The text here is problematic but it is clear that Shelley sees the 'Men of England' as trapped in a vicious circle which compromises their prospects of liberty and social justice.

27   The manuscript appears to read 'when see'; Mary Shelley's version reads 'Ye see'. Shelley's line seems to suggest the self-defeating futility of certain kinds of work carried out by the labouring classes.

29–32   Cf. the ending of 'England in 1819', which makes more positive use of the chiliastic imagery of death and resurrection which featured so strongly in much radical writing of the time. Cf. also the first stanza of 'Lines Written during the Castlereagh Administration', especially 'the death-white shore / Of Albion, free no more'.

31   *To the Lord Chancellor*

Written perhaps in 1820, possibly in May/June or later. Published posthumously (1839). This poem has been dated 1819 by Mary Shelley, and 1817 by other editors, but manuscript evidence strongly suggests that it dates from a later period, where it might have been associated with a scheme to publish a volume of popular poems and with the resurgent indignation of 'A Hate-Song'. After the suicide of Harriet, Shelley was refused custody of his two children in a celebrated hearing before Lord Eldon, on the alleged grounds of immorality and atheism (*Queen Mab* was cited to show that he 'blasphemously derided the Truth of the Christian revelation'). Shelley was confirmed in the view that he was on a trial as a critic of the contemporary power-structure.

He even suspected that he might be forbidden the custody of his son by Mary. The notebook which contains *ODD* also includes the following: 'I envy death the body far less than the oppressor, the minds of those they have torn from me ... The one can only kill the body, but the other can prevent the affections.' In February 1820 Shelley had received a letter concerning financial arrangements for the maintenance of Ianthe and Charles; this may have triggered his anger. He did not publish the poem: as Mary said, it was 'not written to exhibit the pangs of distress to the public' but was 'the spontaneous outburst of a man who brooded over his wrongs and woes'. This fluent example of the flyting may have been influenced by the curse in Byron's *Manfred* (Act I), which Shelley particularly admired (*L*, II. 283).

4 Masked cf. *MA*, in which Eldon also appears. **a buried Form** the Star Chamber.

13 An unused passage in the draft emphasizes the religious founda- tions of the Chancellor's 'gloomy Power': he is addressed as 'Pallid Survivor of the priestly [   ]', deprived by Freedom of 'Thy mitre & the pastoral cross'.

19 prove feel, experience.

25 'By those sweet accents which at my command / Should have been framed to love & lore divine / Now like a lute [originally lyre] fretted by some rude hand / Uttering harsh discords – they must echoe thine' (stanza cancelled in fair copy).

28 The crux of the case was the children's education. **strike** Shelley tried *touch* then *tune*. The draft here continues with a stanza which was omitted from the fair copy: 'By thy smooth slaves who will be thy successors / And by thy fellow <ministers> who would be thee / <A senate of imposters and oppressors> / Whose words are serpents tangled cunningly'.

33ff. hireling The children were to be looked after by specially appointed guardians, who would instruct them in the religious faith which Shelley had so passionately criticized in *Queen Mab*.

41 'By all the terrors of thy fabled Hell' (draft).

43 which must be their error which will inevitably cause them to form false opinions.

51-2 Eldon was famous for weeping on the bench (cf. *MA*, 14–20).

54 'By all the hate which meets a father's love / <When Christians teach, his> children' (draft).

58 'I dare no longer call my children mine' (draft).

32 *An Exhortation*

Written Apr. 1820. Published with *PU* (1820). Shelley told Maria Gisborne this was 'a kind of excuse for Wordsworth'. For Shelley, as for Keats, the chameleon's ability to grow 'like what it looks upon' usually suggested the poetic imagination; here it may suggest the turncoat, since Peter Bell (also based on Wordsworth) 'changes colours like a chameleon, and his coat like a snake. He is a Proteus of a Peter'. The 'boon' in the final line is probably an ironic reference to Wordsworth's own lament, 'We have given our hearts away, a sordid boon' ('The world is too much with us').

33 Ode to Liberty

Written early in 1820. Published with *PU* (1820). Shelley was inspired by the rising in Spain which began on 1 Jan. and whose repercussions in Italy he was able to observe from closer range and to celebrate in the *Ode to Naples*. Although these stirrings may have seemed like an answer to his question at the end of *OWW*, Shelley's revolutionary optimism is qualified by his awareness of the difficulties involved in making the potential permanently real (cf. 'Sonnet to the Republic of Benevento'). This formal ode owes debts not only to Pindar and the tradition of prophetic poetry but to eighteenth-century poems such as Gray's 'The Progress of Poesy' and Collins's 'Ode to Liberty'. The epigraph is taken from *Childe Harold*, IV.xcviii. Shelley translated most of this ode into Italian.

1 **vibrated** emitted the electric charge of revolution whose current links nation with nation.

5–15 Many of these images are traditional to visionary or 'inspired' poetry; Shelley is deliberately adopting the conventions of the ode. Pindar compares his poetry to an eagle dropping on its prey (*Nemeans*, III.80–2), while both he and Dante use the image of the ship. The 'rapid plumes of song' recall Shelley's translation of Plato's *Ion*, where the souls of poets are 'arrayed in the plumes of rapid imagination'. The 'voice out of the deep', later 'the great voice' (283), suggests that Shelley was also placing himself in the line of the biblical prophets: in particular it recalls the 'great voice' of Revelation 16:17.

5 **dismay** see note on *PU*, I. 772.

16ff. a description of the Creation. **daedal** complex, richly adorned and carefully wrought like the work of the master-craftsman Daedalus.

20 The atmosphere of the earth which sustains human life.

22 **a chaos and a curse** key words with Shelley to describe the state of unregenerated man. In *Epipsychidion* the curse is redeemed and the chaos ordered by love, in *DP* by poetic imagination.

23 **thou** Liberty. **power ... worst** a process examined in the plays of Aeschylus.

28   **their violated nurse**   the earth.

31ff.   Cf. Asia's account of the human condition before Prometheus (*PU*, II.iv.49–58).

41   **The Sister-Pest**   religion.

43   **Anarchs**   see introductory note to *MA*.

45   **astonished**   dismayed, terrified, bewildered.

47   **dividuous**   which break up.

58   **Parian stone**   the favourite marble of the Greek sculptors.

60   **lidless**   unsleeping, unblinking, watchful.

61ff.   Although he was aware of its political and moral limitations, Shelley regarded classical Athens as the most perfect example of human civilization; 'what we are and hope to be, is derived, as it were, from the influence and inspiration of these glorious generations'. More perfect than the visionary city of cloud, Athens was a reality based on Liberty ('For thou wert') and on man's will and desire to improve his own world.

65   **pavilions**   makes a canopy for it.

69–71   The image is derived from the Acropolis, the Athenian hill ('mount') on which stood the Parthenon and other public buildings.

73   **mock**   imitate (not deride; no Yeatsian ironies are intended). **the eternal dead**   perhaps the Athenian heroes or demi-gods.

75   **latest oracle**   probably refers to the recent stirrings in Greece; 'oracle' perhaps because it conveyed the divine message of liberty to those who were prepared to consider its meaning.

76–9   Cf. *PU*, III.iii.159ff. Athens is a civilizing idea, a mental reality of continuing relevance. Shelley is here concerned with an ideal; this makes an interesting contrast with the moral realism of Wordsworth's 'Elegiac Stanzas on Peele Castle' from which 79 is derived.

80–2   'Volcanoes had always been thought to contain caves, and to generate underground winds' (Matthews).

92–3   The wolf was the emblem of Rome; in Euripides' *Bacchae* the Maenads (followers of Dionysus) give suck to fawns and wolf-cubs while under the influence of the god. **Cadmaean**   from Thebes, which was ruled by Cadmus.

93–4   In the early years of the Roman republic, Athens was still great.

98   **Camillus**   L. Furius Camillus, Roman leader who went into voluntary exile when accused of embezzling spoils but did not refuse his country's call and saved Rome from the Gauls in 387 BC. **Attilius**   M. Attilius Regulus, who commanded the Roman armies against the Carthaginians. Captured and sent to Rome on parole to negotiate a treaty, he dissuaded the senate from accepting the Carthaginian terms and voluntarily returned to Carthage, where he was tortured to death. His virtues were celebrated by Horace (*Odes*, 3.5). Cf. *DP*, 661–8.

99ff. These lines chart the gradual decline of the Republic into an empire.

103-4 The first poets of the Empire, notably Horace and Virgil, were much influenced by Greek models.

106 Hyrcanian waste and uncultivated region south of the Caspian Sea.

111 Naiad water nymph.

115 Liberty was not in evidence in the Scandinavian or Celtic countries, represented here by their most sensitive cultural and religious antennae. **Scald** Scandinavian bard.

117 groan, not weep a response of passive suffering and disgust rather than of redeeming pity; Prometheus transcends the first and achieves the second.

119 the Galilean serpent the Christian Church.

124-8 The rise of the Italian city states is related to the imagery of volcanic action; their assertion of freedom from popes and emperors is intimately connected with their great artistic achievements. Cf. 'Love . . . has been celebrated by a chorus of the greatest writers of the renovated world; and the music has penetrated the caverns of society, and its echoes still drown the dissonance of arms and superstition' (*DP*, 794-8).

139 dissever dissolve, disperse, divide.

141-4 The Reformation is here related both to the electrical charge of revolution (cf. 1-2) and to the Resurrection (cf. *OWW*). **Luther's leaden lance** 'Dante was the first religious reformer, and Luther surpassed him rather in the rudeness and acrimony than in the boldness of his censures of papal usurpation' (*DP*, 883-6).

145-7 prophets 'those mighty intellects of our own country that succeeded the Reformation, the translators of the Bible, Shakespeare, Spenser, the Dramatists of the reign of Elizabeth, and Lord Bacon' (Preface to *LC*).

148-9 Milton, 'a republican, and a bold inquirer into morals and religion' (Preface to *PU*), alone illuminated the Restoration in which all forms of poetry became 'hymns to the triumph of kingly power over liberty and virtue' (*DP*).

151-65 The period between the Restoration and the end of the eighteenth century, when hopes of liberty were fulfilled in the American War of Independence.

151 Cf. the Spirit of the Hour in *PU*.

166 Cf. 'O happy Earth! reality of Heaven!' (*Daemon of the World*, 292).

171-80 The conservative ('sceptred and mitred') powers of Europe allied themselves against the French revolutionaries. They were resisted by Napoleon, a freedom fighter who became a tyrant (175) and suffered the appropriate pangs of conscience (178-80).

181–7   The interconnection of the volcanic regions of the globe (which was first fully expounded by John Michell in 1760) provides a scientific basis for this image of a sympathetic network of revolutionary activity.

185–6   **Aeolian**   responsive to the influence of the wind (Aeolus), a precursor of earthquake. **from Pithecusa to Pelorus**   from the Bay of Naples to Sicily.

188   **Be dim**   i.e. in comparison with this new light of ours (Locock).

189–91   **Her chains**   England's. Compared to Spain with its long tradition of autocratic rule, England should have little trouble in breaking the power of the moneyed interests ('threads of gold') which control her.

192ff.   The twins are Spain and England; since they share a destiny, England will presumably follow the example of the Spanish Revolution. Both countries are called on to make their mark on history, like engraved seals which leave an impression on wax (cf. *L*, II. 276).

196   **Arminius**   the father of German independence, conqueror of the Romans in AD 9.

199   **Thy**   Germany's.

200   **mysterious**   associated with religious ritual.

204   **thou**   Italy.

218   **gordian word**   The empire of Asia was promised by an oracle to him who could untie the complicated knot made by King Gordius of Phrygia; Alexander cut it with one stroke of his sword.

221   The *fasces*, a bundle of rods with an axe in the middle, was carried before Roman magistrates as an emblem of their authority.

225   **reluctant**   struggling, offering resistance.

231–40   Shelley employs conventional religious imagery to describe the divinity in man, the 'Immortal Deity / Whose throne is in the depth of Human thought'. In 233 he displays his usual unwillingness to be dogmatic as to whether the source of human inspiration is internal or external.

234–5   For Shelley's distrust of language, see 'To a Sky-lark', *Epipsychidion* and 'These words inefficient and metaphorical . . . most words so. No help – ' (MS note to *On Love*).

243–5   Cf. the relations between Jupiter and Prometheus.

249   **intercessor**   Art plays the role traditionally allotted to the saints and to the Blessed Virgin. **Diving**   'Driving' (1820).

254–5   Wealth appropriates from the labouring classes a thousand gifts of Liberty and Nature for each one which it allows them to keep (for a detailed economic analysis, see *PVR*).

258   **Eoan**   eastern, pertaining to the dawn.

271–85   Shelley is developing the traditional motif of failing inspiration. Cf. *DP*, especially 'a Poet becomes a man and is abandoned to the sudden reflux of the influences under which others habitually live'.

34 Song

Written May 1820. Published posthumously (1824).

35 To a Sky-lark

Written summer 1820 (probably June). Published with *PU* (1820). 'It was on a beautiful summer evening, while wandering among the lanes whose myrtle hedges were the bowers of the fireflies, that we heard the carolling of the skylark' (Mary Shelley). This poem has much in common with the stanzas on poetry and music in the Homeric *Hymn to Mercury* (translated in July) and with *DP* (1821). As usual with Shelley, it carefully exploits synaesthetic effects to evoke feelings which transcend the power of ordinary words; it also acknowledges openly the inadequacy of language and of image to capture the essence of the skylark's song. The unusual stanza form has been related both to the flight of the bird and to its song, whose extended trill is reproduced in 'the delicate hesitant poise of each stanza upon its prolonged floating last line' (Kathleen Raine).

3 **or near it** as usual, Shelley qualifies his assertion.
5 **unpremeditated** cf. *PL*, IX.24.
8 **a cloud of fire** primarily, this means a cloud illuminated by the setting sun but it may also refer to the *nuée ardente* of a volcano (at Vesuvius in 1772 it 'appeared in the night tinged like clouds with the setting sun'). Cf. *PU*, I.157–8.
22 **silver sphere** Venus (the morning star) which gradually disappears with the coming of daylight (cf. *TL*, 413–20).
37 **in the light of thought** The poet's personal identity is subsumed in the radiance of inspiration.
66 **Hymeneal** for a wedding.
86 Cf. *Hamlet*, IV.iv.37.
103 **harmonious madness** 'For a poet is indeed a thing ethereally light, winged, and sacred, nor can he compose anything worth calling poetry until he becomes inspired and as it were mad; or whilst any reason remains in him' (Shelley's version of Plato's *Ion*). Plato's *Phaedrus*, which Shelley had read in May, may also have influenced both this phrase and the whole conception of the poem.

36 Letter to Maria Gisborne

Written late June 1820, posted 1 July. Published posthumously (1824). The original letter is not extant. This verse epistle, which was in the first place a private letter and which Shelley himself did not prepare for publication, was written when the Shelleys were staying at Leghorn in the house of their friends John and Maria Gisborne, who were on a visit to London. Maria had been a friend of the Godwins and had recently given Shelley lessons in Spanish; the fluent delight with which Shelley here develops his images may owe more than a little to these tutorials on Calderón. The workshop described in the poem belonged to Mrs Gisborne's son, Henry Reveley, a nautical engineer who had been engaged in designing a steamboat with Shelley's enthusiastic support (though Shelley described it as 'a sort of Asymptote which seems ever to approach & never to arrive'). The slightly archaic diction and the touches of romance help to emphasize the shared delight in literature which marked Shelley's friendship with Maria Gisborne. There is also a relaxed and recreational manner which looks forward to his translation of the Homeric *Hymn to Mercury*, which he finished on 14 July.

Shelley combines the mode of the verse letter (which he had attempted twice in 1811) and the poem of invitation. His poetic good spirits cannot disguise the fact that he is trying to 'struggle with despondency' but the poem does not reveal the extent of the problems which caused him to write to the Gisbornes on 30 June: 'What remains to me? Domestic peace and fame? You will laugh when you hear me talk of the latter; indeed it is only a shadow. The seeking of a sympathy with the unborn and the unknown is a feeble mode of allaying the love within us; and even that is beyond the grasp of so weak an aspirant as I. Domestic peace I might have ... but have not, for Mary suffers dreadfully from the state of Godwin's circumstances' (*L*, II. 206–7).

The particular intimacy of this poem allows Shelley to introduce a series of informal portraits of his friends in London. The list is of special interest and poignancy since it constitutes the nucleus of his reading public and underlines his intellectual isolation in Italy. Five of the six named here (Godwin, Hunt, Hogg, Peacock and Horace Smith) are included in a list of eight 'treasures of London' which he had sent to Ollier in September 1819 with instructions that they should receive all his books; the three who do not feature in the poem are Keats (whom the Gisbornes did meet), Thomas Moore and Byron (who, of course, was in Italy). Coleridge, who was part of the Gisborne circle but whom Shelley never met, features in the poem but not in Ollier's list. The poem bears a number of similarities to a prose letter written to the Gisbornes on 26 May (see Appendix 7).

The title of the poem seems to have been provided by Mary Shelley and there is a case for following Geoffrey Matthews and boldly re-titling it *Letter to the Gisbornes* (see note on 254 below). However, since the received title is now so well established, to replace it might cause more trouble than enlightenment. In the absence of Shelley's original letter, this version of the text tries to recapture something of the intimate flow of a verse epistle by following, as closely as possible, the punctuation and capitalization of Shelley's draft.

5 **moralists call worm** Shelley's private morality had been attacked in the *Quarterly Review*.

10 **that** this decaying form. Like a caterpillar, Shelley will emerge from the cocoon gloriously resurrected.

12 **asphodels** immortal flowers in Elysium.

17 **Archimedean** like that of Archimedes, Sicilian mathematician and inventor, one of whose works was a treatise 'On Bodies floating in Fluids'.

19 **gin** engine; mechanical contrivance or device; machine; product of ingenuity.

20 **force ... figured spells** mathematical calculations, which can tame the elements as if by magic. The phrase combines the geometrical shapes or formulae which are used to activate magic spells with the calculations of Reveley, the engineer.

23–4 **Vulcan** blacksmith and armourer to Jupiter (Zeus). **Ixion** bound to a wheel in Hades for seducing Zeus' wife. **Titans** the giant sons of Heaven and Earth who rebelled against Saturn; Shelley here fuses them with the giants whose later rebellion was suppressed by Zeus.

25 **St Dominic** founder of the Dominicans and a prominent figure in the Inquisition.

27ff. Philip II's Council authorized the Spanish Armada of 1588; their Catholic faith allowed them to presume that English Protestants were doomed to eternal damnation because they were outside the fold of the Church.

33–4 '... Ferdinand has proclaimed the Constitution of 1812 & called the Cortes – The Inquisition is abolished. The dungeons opened & the Patriots pouring out' (Mary Shelley to Maria Gisborne, 31 Mar. 1820). Shelley anticipated the event in 'An Ode to the Assertors of Liberty' (1819) and celebrated its place in the pattern of European revolutionary politics in *OL*. In *PVR* Shelley noted: 'In Spain and in the dependencies of Spain, good and evil in the forms of Despair and Tyranny are struggling foot to foot.' He paid particular attention to torture: the system was 'defended by unspeakable tortures employed not merely as punishments but as precautions; by secret death and captivity and the application to political purposes of the execrated and enormous instruments of religious cruelty'.

45 **Proteus** the old man of the sea, who could assume any shape in order to elude capture.

51 **Tubal Cain** according to Genesis (4:23) the first artificer in brass and iron.

53–4   '. . . the Boilers, & the Keel of the Boat, & the Cylinder, & all the other elements of that soul which is to guide our "Monstruo di fuego e acqua [agua]" over the sea' (L, II. 132).

55   **knacks**   ingenious contrivances, toys, quips; odd and whimsical trifles.

59   **swink**   labour, toil.

65   **rouse**   a full draught of liquor, a bumper.

75   a rough model in the form of a paper boat.

95   a famous mathematician and astronomer; the authors of textbooks on geometry and algebra.

98   **Baron de Tott**   author of the popular *Mémoires sur les Turcs et les Tartares* (1784).

103–4   **many mo**   Spenser, *Faerie Queene*, IV.i.8 (*mo*=more). 'womb of time' *Othello*, I.iii.377.

106   **Archimage**   the great enchanter in Spenser's *Faerie Queene*.

109–12   On 26 June, a day on which he also wrote to the Gisbornes in England, Shelley remonstrated with Robert Southey on the offensively personal and un-Christian spirit of the review of *The Revolt of Islam* in the *Quarterly* for Apr. 1819. The tone of this letter is strikingly different from that of the poem. **meek**   ironically recalls a Christian characteristic which was absent from most of the reviews.

114   **Libeccio**   the south-west wind. Cf. 'The Libecchio here howls like a chorus of fiends all day' (L, II. 213).

119–20   Cf. *Epipsychidion*, 434.

142   **the sad enchantress**   Memory.

154–66   Memory's catalogue of 'how' is interrupted here by a long parenthesis in which the 'shroud of talk' is the subject of the infinitives 'hide', 'blame', 'anatomize' and 'guess'.

168   **visionary rhyme**   during autumn 1819 Shelley had read *PU* to the Gisbornes.

170–4   The image is probably that of an oasis (cf. L, II. 150).

175–86   In the summer of 1819 Maria Gisborne (*wisest lady*) taught Shelley enough Spanish to read the plays of Calderón, the Spanish playwright Pedro Calderón de la Barca (1600–81), whose work included many *autos sacramentales* or religious plays. **indued**   put on, perhaps also with the sense of *learnt*. The connection between national literature and political freedom is strongly asserted in *PVR*. Shelley asks of the country which produced Calderón and Cervantes, 'what else did it, but breathe through the tumult of the despotism and superstition which invested them, the prophecy of a glorious consummation'.

180   Mark 5:9.

197–201   **Godwin**   William Godwin (1756–1836), author of *Political Justice*, once the inspiration of Shelley's utopian radicalism but now a shrivelled and cautious shadow of his former self and an importunate and impecunious father-in-law. In spite of personal animosities, Shelley still acknowledged his essential greatness, as we can tell from the implied parallel with Milton (*PL*, VII.25–6).

202–8 Shelley suggests that Coleridge is the victim of his own extraordinary abilities; he has the eagle's capacity to look directly into the sun but he has blinded himself by the dazzle of his own brilliance. Cf. *JM*, 50–2 on Maddalo/Byron. **obscure** echoes contemporary criticisms of Coleridge, not least those of Peacock.

205 'Deep, many visioned fathomless' (cancelled in original).

206 **Flags wearily** originally 'Gropes dizzily'.

209–25 Leigh Hunt (1784–1859), poet, essayist and critic; editor of the *Examiner*; good friend and courageous and perceptive reviewer of the poetry of Keats and Shelley, whose true merits he was one of the first to recognize. Cf. the description by Keats in *Sleep and Poetry*.

213 **Shout** Robert Shout, statuary with a shop in High Holborn. Hunt himself recorded that 'he has a room up stairs, full of casts from the antique, large and small, that amounts to an exhibition'.

216 **neat disorder** cf. 'sweet disorder' (Herrick, 'Delight in Dissorder').

226–30 Thomas Jefferson Hogg (1792–1862) was sent down from Oxford with Shelley for refusing to answer questions concerning *The Necessity of Atheism*. He remained a close friend, involved himself with Shelley's wives and women friends, and wrote a two-volume biography of the young Shelley which was unreliable but highly influential.

233–47 Thomas Love Peacock (1785–1866) was another close friend of Shelley and greatly influenced his taste in Greek literature. He worked at the India House ('turns Hindoo'), and had recently married a Welsh girl ('Snowdonian Antelope'). **cameleopard** giraffe.

233 Peacock was originally not 'English' but 'Indian'.

243–7 Cf. 8–14.

247–50 Horace Smith (1779–1849), stockbroker and author with his brother of *Rejected Addresses*, a witty collection of parodies. A draft stanza seems to show that Shelley had once considered including the Smith brothers in the procession of literary figures in *Adonais*.

254 **you** In Shelley's draft this was originally 'ye', which suggests that the letter may well have been intended for a plural audience, rather than simply and exclusively for Maria Gisborne.

257 **unpavilioned** not covered with a canopy of clouds.

261 **inverse deep** the sky is an inverted image of the sea.

267 'Some lordly <greenhouse> courts, white with a scrawl' (draft).

269–73 The horrible reality of London prostitution is set against two manifestations of Italian night-life which are more agreeable – the serenade, and the amorous murmurings of Apollonia, the landlord's daughter.

286 **Contadino** Italian peasant.

292ff. Cf. the invitation to Emilia at the end of *Epipsychidion*.

302 Shelley remained a vegetarian and water-drinker on principle.

305 **syllabubs** dishes made of cream and wine.

306 Originally 'These Mary will contrive'; Shelley also wrote 'The welcome sauce of the divinest smile', which indicates that he considered a metaphoric extension of the invitation to a feast.

308 **the Grand Duke** of Tuscany, in which Leghorn was situated. See: 'We live here under a nominal tyranny, administered according to the philosophic laws of Leopold, & the mild opinions which are the fashion here. Tuscany is unlike all the other Italian states, in this respect' (*L*, II. 177).

316–7 I won't need to dull my nerves with the opiate of poetic composition (Helicon is the home of the Muses) or of amorous involvement (Himeros, says Shelley, is 'a synonym of Love').

320 **friendly philosophic revel** in effect, an extended symposium.

323 The final line of Milton's 'Lycidas'.

37 *Two Songs for 'Midas'*

Written 1820 for Mary Shelley's play *Midas*. Published posthumously (1824). The sun-god Apollo and the goat-god Pan compete in a singing contest before Tmolus, the official adjudicator, who votes for Apollo, and Midas, king of Phrygia, who supports Pan – for which he is given ass's ears. The songs represent not only two kinds of poetry but the respective possibilities of supra-mortal and mortal existence.

Apollo

19–20 Colour is not inherent in things but a property of light.

21–2 Most stars obtain their energy, like the sun, by transmuting hydrogen into helium (King-Hele) but Shelley's main concern is with the sun as a symbol of light and energy.

31–2 Cf. 'Mundi oculus' (Ovid); 'Thou Sun, of this great world both eye and soul' (*PL*, v.171). This Narcissistic self-satisfaction is appropriate to the divine nature, which has no self-doubts or hesitations.

33–4 Apollo was the god of music, poetry, prophecy and medicine.

Pan

Pan is the animating spirit of the whole natural world (Pan means whole): cf. 'that universal Pan who may be a God or man' (*On Christianity*).

14 **Tempe** a valley in Thessaly; 'the poets describe it as the most delightful spot on the earth' (Lemprière).

18ff. See note to choruses from *Hellas*, 1.34.

26 **daedal** see note to *OL*, 16.

27 **giant wars** wars of the Giants against Zeus, which involved piling Pelion on Ossa.

31 The nymph Syrinx was changed by the gods into a reed of which Pan made himself a pipe; his music, unlike that of Apollo, is closely connected with his unhappiness.

34 **both ye** Apollo (affected by envy) and Tmolus (affected by age).

38 *Sonnet to the Republic of Benevento*

Probably written at the end of summer 1820 (with *Ode to Naples*). Published posthumously (1824) under title 'Political Greatness'. The sonnet was written in the context of the rising of the Carbonari against Ferdinand of Naples in 1820 (see notes to *OL*). Benevento was a small papal state situated in the midst of Neapolitan territory. In July 1820 Benevento and Ponte-Corvo 'drove out the Roman garrisons, disclaimed their allegiance to the Pope, and sent to request admission to the rights of Neapolitan citizenship and fraternity'. This request was unsuccessful. 'The principalities then fought to obtain the concession of certain privileges and reform from their own government; but the papal court insisted upon their unconditional submission, and the two cities then formed themselves into an independent republic, and took measures for the defence of their independence' (*Annual Register*). The poem suggests that political revolutions are of little value unless they are accompanied or preceded by an interior, psychological revolution.

6 **pageant** as shown in the glass (orig. 'mirror') of art.
6–7 Cf. *TL*.
8–9 staining the potential Heaven of Art with their ugly reality.
9–10 **What . . . custom** ultimately neither physical force nor habit is significant (when compared to the power of individual man).
10–14 Cf. the triumph of Prometheus over Jupiter, and *TL*, 211–13. 'He [Diogenes] said, It is in the power of each individual to level the inequality which is the topic of the complaint of mankind. Let him be aware of his own worth and the station which he really occupies in the scale of moral beings . . . Every man possesses the power in this respect to legislate for himself' (*On Christianity*).

39 *To the Moon*

Written 1820 or 1821. Published posthumously (1824). After a gap, the manuscript continues: 'Thou chosen sister of the spirit / That gazes on thee till it pities.' This suggests that Shelley may have intended to relate this symbol of alienation to a specific human context (cf. opening invocation of 'Lines Written in the Bay of Lerici').

40   *Epipsychidion*

Written after Dec. 1820; finished 16 Feb. 1821. Published anonymously (1821). The title has been interpreted variously as 'soul out of my soul', 'soul within the soul' and 'a little additional soul': all of these interpretations are based on the false assumption that there is such a thing as an *epipsyche*. It seems much more likely that the title means 'little soul song', on the analogy of *epithalamion* to which it provides a more liberated alternative. The poem charts a personal history of love, false and true, making use of an idealized framework largely derived from the first *canzone* of Dante's *Convivio* (which Shelley translated) and from his *Vita nuova*: the Song of Songs also contributes to the central conjunction of sister and bride. The climax is the appearance of Emilia (the Sun to Mary's Moon), an idealized version of Teresa Emilia Viviani, daughter of the governor of Pisa, who had been imprisoned in a convent to await the selection of a suitable husband and with whom Shelley identified intensely for a brief period after he first visited her on 3 Dec. 1820 and before he became disillusioned. Emilia and Shelley corresponded in Italian; some of the language and imagery and the emotional climate of the poem can be traced to these letters and to Emilia's essay 'Il vero amore', which is quoted in the epigraph. Shelley translated several passages of *PU* and most of *OL* into Italian for Emilia. These translations included 'Life of Life', which in its almost sacramental celebration of the feminine closely prefigures parts of *Epipsychidion*, and 'My soul is an enchanted boat', which has much in common with its climatic invitation to the voyage. The 'Italian Platonics' of Shelley's poem were also closely associated with the composition of 'Fiordispina' and 'Ginevra', narrative poems in couplets, both with Italian settings and both unfinished.

Not without good reason, Shelley was particularly sensitive to the danger that his poem would be read in terms which were crudely physical and biographical. Though it is undeniably based on biographical realities, he took pains to alchemize it and to protect it by special measures. Ollier was instructed to issue it anonymously and to print only 100 copies: 'It is to be published simply for the esoteric few; and I make its author a secret, to avoid the malignity of those who turn sweet food into poison' (*L*, II. 263). By October he was writing to Gisborne both lamenting the initial responses and exaggerating the unreality of the poem: 'The Epipsychidion is a mystery – As to real flesh & blood, you know that I do not deal in those articles, – you might as well go to a ginshop for a leg of mutton, as expect any thing human or earthly from me ... [Even the cognoscenti] are inclined to approximate me to the circle of a servant girl & her sweetheart' (*L*, II. 363). Both Shelley's capacity to achieve artistic detachment and his recurrent anxiety about malicious reviewers are illustrated by an unfinished poem which has been interpreted traditionally as draft material for *Epipsychidion* but which, as Tatsuo Tokoo has persuasively shown, was written in late 1819, a year before Shelley first met Emilia Viviani. In these lines he teases his readers: 'If any should be curious to discover / Whether to you I am a friend or lover, / Let them read Shakespeare's sonnets, taking thence / A whetstone for their dull intelligence / That tears and will not cut.' He cites the authorities of Socrates, Plato and Christ in support of the kind of ideal love which the poem celebrates, conceals the identity of the dedicatee and enjoys the prospect of the reviewers' baffled responses: 'Why, if you were a lady, it were fair / The world should know – but, as I am afraid, / The Quarterly would bait you if betrayed; / And if, as it will be sport to see them stumble / Over all sorts of scandals, hear them mumble / Their litany of curses – some guess right, / And others swear you're a Hermaphrodite . . .' Probably these responses were provoked by that review in the *Quarterly* which also left its mark on *OWW* and the Preface to *PU*. What is most significant, perhaps, is the fact that some of the most impassioned passages in *Epipsychidion*, including a draft of the opening, were first written in this context and with reference to an unidentified lady who was not Emilia.

Epigraph 'The soul that loves is hurled forth from the created world and creates in the infinite a world for itself and for itself alone, most different from this present dark and dismal pit.'

Advertisement **Sporades** two groups of Greek islands in the Aegean. **gran vergogna . . . intendimento** means 'it would be a great disgrace to him who should rhyme anything under the garb of a figure or of rhetorical colouring, if afterwards, being asked, he should not be able to denude his words of this garb, in such wise that they should have a true meaning'.

feelings 'He had framed to himself certain opinions, founded no doubt upon the truth of things, but built up to a Babel height; they fell by their own weight, and the thoughts that were his architects become unintelligible one to the other, as men upon whom confusion of tongues has fallen' (draft).

stanza i.e. the prefatory verses to *Epipsychidion*, which are Shelley's version of the concluding lines of the first canzone of Dante's *Convivio*, which prefaces Trattato II and whose first line Shelley translated as 'Ye who intelligent the Third Heaven move'. *Epipsychidion* concludes with an envoi addressed to the poem which takes its cue both from the prefatory verses and from a Dante sonnet to Cavalcanti which Shelley also translated; this conclusion is not a translation.

My Song . . . in the first edition these prefatory lines were printed on their own on a page facing the opening lines of the poem. Shelley's version of the Italian is fairly accurate except that he has added 'tell them that they are dull'.

1 **that orphan one** Shelley's presiding Spirit. **Sister** Only a week after their first meeting, Emilia asked Shelley to call her *Sorella* (sister) and announced that she would address him as her beloved *Fratello* (brother). **name** Shelley, who enjoyed name-play would have been aware that Percy was a homophone for the Italian *persi* (lost).

15 Cf. Plato's description of the souls of poets 'arrayed in the plumes of rapid imagination' (Shelley's translation of the *Ion*).

21–6 Cf. the description of Asia (*PU*, II.v.48–71).

33 The inadequacy of language is one of the poem's main themes.

38 **lights** eyes.

43–4 The world will misinterpret and disapprove of our relationship.

45 Cf. 'O that thou wert as my brother, that sucked the breast of my mother' (Song of Songs 8:1).

46 **another** his wife.

60–1 **A Star** the North Star.

85–6 **stops of planetary music** cadences of the music of the spheres, audible ('heard in trance') to those who rise above the restrictions of everyday consciousness.

89–90 Cf. 'the deep truth is imageless' (*PU*, II.iv.116).

91ff. This passage seems to combine the language of science with that of religious devotion. Diffusion is 'the spontaneous molecular mixing or inter-penetration of two fluids without chemical combination', hence the inter-mixture is 'unentangled'. Cf. 'This whiteness is produced by a successive intermixture of the colours, without their being assimilated' (Newton). **Stains** colours. **unintermitted** continuous.

100 Shelley's draft is very confused but it appears that he may have intended a plural and omitted to make the necessary changes.

117 **third sphere** the sphere of Venus or love (*il terzo ciel*).

121–2 April is made flesh, Frost is a skeleton.

145–6 Cf. 'The slow, soft stroke of a continuous wind / In which the leaves tremblingly were / All bent' (Shelley's translation of Dante, *Purgatorio*, XXVIII. 9–11).

161ff. **True Love** (ideal love) was originally 'Free Love' but Shelley abandoned this because its connotations are misleading. For the general idea, see *Purgatorio*, XV. 46–75).

185–9 This paradox represents the potential paradise which lies behind the unredeemed world.

190 The autobiographical narrative begins here. **a Being** an idealized female figure (a characteristic feature of Shelley's mental world).

199–200 Cf. Dante's Beatrice in *Paradiso* and Asia in *PU*.

211-12 **that Storm** those disturbing contemporary, or everyday, influences which separate us from our past.

221-2 **owlet light** twilight. **Hesper** the evening star (cf. 'the desire of the moth for the star').

228 **the dreary cone** the earth's shadow in space (the 'pyramid of night', *PU*, IV.444).

240 **sightless** probably 'invisible', but Destiny is also blind ('the world's eyeless charioteer'). Cf. *HIB*, 27-31.

243-5 The world of thoughts ('mine') is created out of and within the chaos of the poet himself ('me'). Cf. 'All things exist as they are perceived; at least in relation to the percipient – "The mind is its own place, and of itself can make a Heaven of Hell, a Hell of Heaven." ... It [Poetry] makes us the inhabitants of a world to which the familiar world is as a Chaos' (*DP*, 1147-55).

249 **wintry forest** an image derived from *Inferno*, I.

256-66 A reference to Shelley's cousin Harriet Grove or to a prostitute at Oxford who infected him with venereal disease. Shelley avoids specifics: both the setting and the woman's attributes suggest the traditional enchantress who offers the poet a false love.

268 **idol** image. Cf. 'Every human mind has, what Lord Bacon calls its *idola specus*, peculiar images which reside in the inner cave of thought.'

271 **One** perhaps Harriet Grove.

272-4 Cf. *Adonais*, 276-9.

277 **One** Shelley's wife, Mary Godwin (for a more flattering version of Mary's influence see the Dedication to *LC*).

294 **Endymion** a shepherd loved by the Moon (Diana).

300-6 a living death (cf. Life-in-Death in Coleridge, 'The Rime of the Ancient Mariner').

308ff. Though this could refer to later disturbances in the pattern of Shelley's married life, it probably refers to the suicide of Shelley's first wife Harriet ('She') and perhaps of Fanny Godwin, and to the subsequent seizure of his children. The Tempest may be Harriet's sister Eliza, whom Shelley held responsible for the suicide and who instituted the Chancery proceedings against him.

334 **frore** frozen, frosty.

345 **Twin Spheres** Emilia (sun) and Mary (moon).

368ff. Claire Clairmont, Mary's half-sister and the mother of Byron's daughter Allegra, who accompanied the Shelleys to Italy. She had a close relationship with Shelley emotionally as well as intellectually and there was constant friction between her and Mary. At this time she was living in Florence; 373 is, in the literal sense, an invitation to return, more generally a plea to repair the estrangement.

374 **Love's folding-star** Venus, 'The star that bids the shepherd fold [his sheep]' (Milton, *Comus*, 93).

400 **continents** those things which contain it.

408 **ship** Here the poem picks up a theme of one of Shelley's letters to Emilia in which he quotes Dante's sonnet to Cavalcanti, including the lines containing the wish that they and their community of friends might embark on a 'magic ship'.

412 **halcyons** legendary birds which charmed the winds and waves into calm, while brooding on their floating nests.

445 **peopled . . . airs** cf. *The Tempest*, III.ii.134.

454 Synaesthesia is characteristic of Shelley's attempts to convey the essence of mystical experience. Cf. 'the divinest odour . . . produces a sensation of voluptuous faintness like the combinations of sweet music' (*L*, II. 85).

456 **antenatal** previous to birth.

459 **Lucifer** Venus as morning star.

482 **their . . . interstices** space between them.

492 For sister and spouse, see Song of Songs 4:9, 10, 12; 5:1.

494 **Titanic** built by the Titans, the giant sons of Heaven and Earth.

501 **volumes** coils.

506 **serene** expanse of blue sky.

507 **Parian** made of white marble from the Greek island, Paros.

581 **unimbued** pure, unstained, not impregnated by any foreign substance.

587ff. a conventional collapse of poetic inspiration (cf. *OL*).

601 The Shelley circle is translated into Dantesque terms.

41 *A Defence of Poetry*

Written Feb.–Mar. 1821. Published posthumously (1840). Shelley's essay is both a public statement and part of a private debate, since it was directly occasioned by Thomas Love Peacock's 'The Four Ages of Poetry', which had appeared in *Ollier's Literary Miscellany* in 1820. Ollier was Shelley's publisher, while Peacock was a close friend who worked for the East India Company and was best known as a novelist, but who had started his own literary career as a poet and whose *Rhododaphne* had been greeted by Shelley as 'a poem of the most remarkable character'. With a provocative wit and a satirical eye for the failings of his poetic contemporaries, Peacock argued that the progress of civilization coincided with a gradual decline in the power of poetry and in its social value and significance. In the advanced society of early nineteenth-century England, poetry had outlived its usefulness and had become an anachronism: 'A poet in our times is a semi-barbarian in a civilized community' (see Appendix 8). The tone and the ironical strategies of Peacock's argument are elusive; yet, with whatever reservations, he struck a note which was in tune with utilitarian thinking (see, for example, Macaulay's essay of 1825, which makes a similar case).

On 15 Feb. Shelley told Peacock that he had been excited to 'a sacred rage . . . of vindicating the insulted Muses'. He had hoped 'to break a lance with you, within the lists of a magazine, in honour of my mistress Urania'; his withdrawal from this contest was unlucky for Peacock since 'first having unhorsed poetry, and the universal sense of the wisest in all ages, an easy conquest would have remained to you in me, the knight of the shield of shadow and the lance of gossamere' (*L*, II. 261). The mock-Spenserian courtesy and self-deprecation indicate that he did not desire a breach of friendship, but the discarded drafts of a letter to Ollier also reveal that he was deeply disturbed and challenged by Peacock's argument. He acknowledged Peacock's wit, spirit and learning but considered them 'the spurs of a hobby [horse]', the tokens of an act of intellectual suicide, a self-consuming paradox. Yet, even if Peacock's essay seemed to succeed in cutting its 'own throat', Shelley recognized that his arguments carried a dangerous threat and must be controverted since, although they were 'self-murdering', they were also 'parricidal': 'He would extinguish Imagination which is the Sun of life, & grope his way by the cold & uncertain & borrowed light of the Moon which he calls Reason, – stumbling over the interlunar chasm of time where she deserts us, and an owl, rather than an eagle, stare with dazzled eyes on the watery orb which is the Queen of his pale Heaven' (draft letter to Ollier; *L*, II. 271–4). As this final sentence indicates, Shelley's reply would set out to celebrate the creative powers of imagination and would enforce its claims not so much by reasoned argument as by the poetic inventiveness of its own imagery and language and the force of its own convictions.

In March he told Peacock that his own essay was taking 'a more general view of what is Poetry' than Peacock had done; in fact, Shelley's definition goes far beyond the normal confines of literary criticism and embraces not only all artists but the institutions of religion and of law and the foundations of civil society. At certain points, Shelley engages specifically with Peacock's arguments, but his essay ranges more widely and offers both a generous definition of poetry as the action of the imagination and a brief history of the relations between poetry and social and moral progress. The emphasis on social function is particularly significant in view of the fact that the famous concluding passage which celebrates poets as 'unacknowledged legislators' was taken, with variations, from the unpublished *PVR* (see p. 400 above). A powerful passage on the subversive morality of Milton was taken from its original context in *ODD* and prudentially revised. *DP* was significantly influenced by Plato's *Ion*, which Shelley had first translated in Dec. 1819 or early 1820, which he was reading and translating early in 1821, and translated fragments of which are interspersed among the drafts for *DP*. There are close connections between the presentation of poetry and the poet in *DP* and in *Adonais*.

The present text is based, with due caution, on Mary Shelley's fair copy, but a special effort has been made to reconstruct Shelley's punctuation and capitalization by consulting and following his own fair copy, and even the draft when possible. This may lead to some inconsistencies (Shelley is sometimes erratic in his capitalizing of 'Poets' and 'Poetry'), but it often seems closer to the quick of Shelley's prose than is Mary's version, which is often overpunctuated and occasionally misleading.

9–11   The Greek words signify respectively making and reasoning.

23   **connate**   born at the same time.

38   **antitype**   see Prologue to *PBT*, 16.

108   Bacon, *The Advancement of Learning, iii, 1*.

117–18   **the chaos of a cyclic poem**   the disordered formless matter which was later shaped into a cycle of mythic or heroic poetry. Cyclic poems were a series of epics written by later poets to continue or complete the Homeric narratives. **copiousness of lexicography**   the capacity of dictionaries to provide an inclusively generous catalogue of linguistic usage.

130   **Janus**   Roman god of beginnings, traditionally figured with two or four faces (see *TL*, 94).

133   Early legislators such as Solon transmitted their laws in verse form. **prophets**   the Roman *vates* signified 'Diviner Fore-Seer or Prophet' (Sidney, *An Apologie for Poetry*).

138   **germs**   seeds.

210   See Genesis 2, where the diversity of languages is presented as a divine punishment for overbearing human ambition.

222   **the distinction**   'It is not ryming and versing, that maketh Poesie. One may bee a Poet without versing, and a versifier without Poetry' (Sidney, *An Apologie*). 'Not but that many poets (and I smile because the reader will smile: – at the apparent paradox resulting from the incommensurability of popular and philosophical language) – have written in metre' (draft).

224   Shelley had expressed his admiration for the poetic attributes of Plato's prose in the Preface to his own translation of the *Symposium* (1818) (see p. 372 above).

232   **periods**   sentences.

245   **eternal music**   Shelley is perhaps making use of the concept of the music of the spheres, which goes back to classical antiquity (see p. 341).

272   **distorted**   this distinction between poetry and history can be traced back to Sidney and Aristotle and is developed in Wordsworth's Preface to *Lyrical Ballads*. *Bacon's Advancement of Learning*, II, 2, 4 is the source of Shelley's reference to *epitomes* (summaries).

278–83   Peacock had written that 'the history of Herodotus [the founder of Greek historiography] is half a poem'. Livy was the historian of ancient Rome. The draft adds: 'his description of the defeat of Asdrubal the account of the orgies of the Roman Bacchants, his description of the Vale of Tempe'.

282   **interstices**   minute openings or crevices between things.

284   The draft reads: 'Poetry is the aloe which blooms once in every age, with blossoms which are ever lovely.'

292   **generations**   here, as elsewhere, Shelley is much concerned with the process of selecting a jury (see p. 357, note to 265).

310–11   leading figures in the *Iliad* and the *Odyssey*.

322   **peculiar**   its own, specific to itself.

341   **planetary music**   the music of the spheres which accompanied the movements of the planets but which was beyond the scope of human hearing after the Fall.

356   **Elysian**   delightful, glorious, blissful, as in the Elysian Fields, which in Greek myth were the dwelling-place of the blessed after death.

36off.   For a more extended formulation, cf. *On Love*.

400   The draft reads: 'never was such joy of life felt so intensely; never were so many individuals so free to speak or think or feel as the spirit within them dictated.'

403ff.   Shelley is referring to the fifth century BC (Socrates died in 399 BC). For his celebration of the achievements of Greek civilization, see *DMAG* (1818), *Notes on Sculpture* (1819) and the Preface to *Hellas* (see p. 297). The draft reads: 'It is as if the continent of Paradise were overwhelmed and some shattered crag remained covered with asphodel [and] amaranth which bear a golden flower.'

451   **trilogies**   respectively the 'Theban Plays' (*Antigone, Oedipus Tyrannus* and *Oedipus Coloneus*) by Sophocles, linked by subject-matter but not strictly a trilogy, and the *Oresteia* (*Agamemnon, Choephoroe, Eumenides*) by Aeschylus.

458   **Calderón**   the Spanish playwright Pedro Calderón de la Barca (1600–81), whose work included many *autos sacramentales* or religious plays. Shelley regarded him as 'a kind of Shakespeare' and translated scenes from his Faustian play *El mágico prodigioso*.

471ff.   Shelley knew Peacock's fondness for plays such as the *Philoctetes* of Sophocles. Here Shelley's own fair copy reads 'Giant Sophisms', which translates the specious subtlety of Peacock's argument into those terms of romance which were so congenial to Shelley himself (see for example 'Dedication' to *LC* and 'ghosts from an enchanter fleeing' of *OWW*) and which were specifically part of his playful engagement with Peacock (see headnote). Paladins are knightly champions; necromancers are practitioners of black magic.

495ff.   Shelley's account of the psychological effects of the drama can be compared to his analyses of the emotional impact and aesthetic equilibrium of Greek statues, especially those of Niobe and of Minerva.

526   Joseph Addison's *Cato* (1713).

528-30   Cf. Byron's 'So, we'll go no more a roving', 5-6.

542   **smile**   Shelley's resistance to the inhumanity of malicious laughter is explained in the sonnet 'To Laughter' (discovered among the Scrope Davies papers in 1976), where he 'weeps without shame to see / How many broken hearts lie bare to thee'. See also 'Fragment of a Satire upon Satire', where he resists the temptation 'to make innocent ink / With stagnant truisms of trite Satire stink'.

560   Niccolò Machiavelli (1469-1527), Florentine political theorist and historian, whose works included *The Prince*, *Discourses* and *Florentine History*.

571ff.   These poets included Theocritus, Callimachus, and Bion and Moschus (both of whom Shelley partially translated).

576-7   **meadow-gale**   see Coleridge, 'The Rime of the Ancient Mariner', 457.

606   **venom**   Shelley was acutely interested in snakes, and a special concern for the effects of snake-bite seems to have been developed by his reading of the Roman poet Lucan.

610   A mythological figure who exercised a particular hold on the Renaissance imagination, Astraea was identified with the principle of justice. She was translated into the heavens when human corruption brought an end to the Golden Age.

619ff.   This image is based on a passage in Plato's *Ion*, a dialogue on poetic inspiration which Shelley himself translated (see headnote). Magnetism also played a part in Shelley's own life (see 'The Magnetic Lady').

632   Shelley's 'great poem' owes something both to the phenomenon of the Homeric cycle and to his own recurring interest in the idea of one great mind.

635   'It is like one watching a beloved friend in pain or in decay, who murmurs half articulate consolations; which are rather felt than heard' (draft).

645-52   This list begins with four early Roman writers whose work is preserved only in fragments (respectively an epic poet, a tragic poet, a scholar and agriculturalist, and another tragic poet); it concludes with the authors of *De rerum natura* (whose passionately rationalist approach to religion and science had exhilarated the younger Shelley) and of the *Aeneid*.

653   **mirror of Greece**   the poets of what is generally regarded as the 'Golden Age' of Roman literature were much indebted to Greek models, which they translated, extended, developed and sometimes

specifically challenged (as in the case of Virgil's engagement with Homer in the *Aeneid*).

661-4 For Camillus and Regulus, see *OL*, 98 and note. The Gauls entered Rome in 390 BC and found the senators posed to receive them with such dignified equanimity that they might have been statues of the gods. After the Carthaginian Hannibal heavily defeated the Romans in 216 BC, many towns switched their allegiance to him, but the Romans refused to capitulate. Shelley's primary sources for these stories of Roman heroism were probably Horace and Livy (see 278ff.).

671-2 'Because they lack a sacred poet' (Horace, *Odes*, 4.9.28).

674 rhapsodist Shelley's image is probably based on the Greek rhapsodes (professional reciters of poetry, particularly that of Homer) who featured in Plato's *Ion*. The Italian *improvvisatore* Tommaso Sgricci, whom Shelley knew in Pisa and one of whose performances he reviewed in Italian, represented a modern development of this tradition in which he improvised one-man performances based on the traditions and imagery of Greek tragedy.

682 generals see 'The Spartans in their war against the Messenians were commanded by the oracle of Delphos to apply to Athens for a general: who sent them the Poet Tyrtaeus – and his [   ]. This fired them with victory. Let us in our combat against error and oppression, listen to the [   ]. We are the Spartans and our sufferings are the Messenians and Poetry is the Apollo, and the Poets are Tyrtaeus' (cancelled and incomplete passage in associated draft).

690-92 For the influence of the Old Testament on the imagination of Christ, see *On Christianity*, 20ff. (p. 65 above).

698-702 *Macbeth*, III.ii.50-3.

709 At this point in the draft Shelley chides himself: 'But this is not argument – not illustration – an illustration ought not to precede the thing to be illustrated.'

736 In *On Christianity* Shelley had elaborated on Christ's debt as a reformer to the concepts of Plato and noted that in Plato's *Republic* 'laws should watch over the equal distribution of the external instruments of unequal power'. In Oct. 1821 he claimed that Plato's 'speculations on civil society' (in the *Republic*) were 'surely the foundations of true politics'.

747-9 Christ's teaching simplified and made publicly accessible those ideas which had only been available to a select or initiated minority. Shelley used the same terms to distinguish between those poems of his own that were addressed to the more 'select classes of poetical readers' and those that were intended for a wider public.

772 '... a Galeotto was the book, and he who wrote it' (Dante, *Inferno*, V.137). In this ambivalent tribute to the power of poetry, Francesca recalls how she and Paolo were brought together by their reading of the story of Lancelot and Guinevere. The Romance of Lancelot du Lac performed the function of go-between for its readers just as Galeotto (Galahad) had done for Lancelot and Guinevere.

773 **trouveurs** or *trouvères*, a group of French poets of the twelfth and thirteenth centuries, northern counterparts to the troubadours of Provence.

773 Francesco Petrarca (1304–74), whose 'sublime and chivalric sensibility' gave him the edge over the Greek lyric poets in Shelley's estimation. Shelley much admired the 'tender & solemn enthusiasm' of his love poetry, and his *Trionfi* provided a model for *TL*.

794–8 Shelley is thinking of Agathon's speech in the *Symposium* which had influenced his own *On Love*. **superstition** cf. 'Tasso's situation [i.e. his imprisonment] was widely different from that of any persecuted being of the present day, for from the depth of dungeons public opinion might now at length be awakened to an echo that would startle the oppressor' (*L*, II. 47).

799 Rousseau is the only prose writer in this list: he is included not for his work as political philosopher or autobiographer but primarily as the author of *La Nouvelle Héloïse* (1761), in which Shelley recognized 'the divine beauty of Rousseau's imagination'.

801 **trophies** for Shelley's sense of unceasing war in which the conditions of human life were gradually (if painfully) bettered, see his summary in *On Christianity* of the 'imperfect attempts' to achieve a system of more equal rights to property and power: 'They are so many trophies erected in the enemies' land to mark the limits of the victorious progress of truth and justice.' See also his account of those compromises between the spirit of truth and the spirit of imposture which marked the slow progress of reform: 'the maxims so strongly recorded remain as trophies of our difficult and incomplete victory, planted in the enemies' land' (*PVR*).

818–22 Dante notes the gap between popular expectation and higher reality: 'Who would believe, down in the erring world the Trojan Ripheus in this circle to be the fifth of the holy lights?' (*Paradiso*, xx.67–9). See Virgil, *Aeneid*, II.424–7 for Ripheus, 'the one man among the Trojans most just'.

822ff. This interpretation of *PL* can be compared with the Preface to *PU* and especially with the earlier extended analysis in *ODD*, much of which is here transferred into *DP* with little or no change but some of which is more dangerously outspoken (see pp. 185–6 above). For 'new torments', see *PL*, I.211–15.

866–7 'Lucretius entangled the wings of his swift spirit in atoms' (draft): Shelley is here referring to the scientific theory whose materialism provided the basis of Lucretius' attack on established religion. There may also be some reference to the legend that

Lucretius took a love-philtre and eventually committed suicide. **limed** trapped (with, or as with, birdlime).

871–2 Shelley lists in order three Greek and three Latin authors of 'secondary' epic, including two for whom he had a personal taste: Apollonius Rhodius, author of *Argonautica*, and Lucan, author of *Pharsalia*.

876–7 Sixteenth-century epics, the work of respectively Ariosto, Tasso, Camoes and Spenser.

887–8 Shelley is thinking of Dante's account in *De vulgari eloquentia* of the dialects of Italy and of the supreme vernacular which transcends them.

890–3 **Lucifer** literally 'light-bearer' and, astronomically, the planet Venus when it rises as morning-star (there is a close connection with the controlling imagery of *Adonais*). Lucifer was also identified with Satan; see Isaiah 14:12 and *PL*, V.708–9 ('His countenance, as the morning star that guides / The starry flock, allured them'), which Shelley applied to himself in *L*, II. 356. In *On the Revival of Literature* Shelley claimed that the writings of Dante and Petrarch were 'the bright luminaries which had afforded glimmerings of literary knowledge to the oldest benighted traveller toiling up the hill of fame'. Shelley's emphasis on Italian republicanism (*L*, II. 122) was influenced by his reading of Simonde de Sismondi's *Histoire des républiques italiennes du moyen âge* (1807–9).

905 'A great Poem is torches from which a thousand lamps may be enkindled' (draft). Cf. the conclusion of *OWW*.

919 **mechanists** perhaps, in this context, utilitarian pragmatists (see 948 below).

946–7 **French writers** with the notable exceptions of Montaigne and Rousseau, Shelley considered most French writers as 'weak, superficial, vain, with little imagination': here he seems to associate them with a mood of scepticism.

948 **mechanist** the machine-maker. **combines labour** 'organizes the specialization of labour' (Matthews).

954–6 Shelley's version of a statement attributed to Christ in three of the Gospels (e.g. Luke 8:18).

958–9 **Scylla and Charybdis** the two sides of the dangerous Straits of Messina, personified respectively as a monster in a cave and a monster in the form of a whirlpool, therefore polarized extremes, escape from one of which results in exposure to the other. For political usage, see James Gillray's *Britannia between Scylla and Charybdis: or – The Vessel of the Constitution steered clear of the Rock of Democracy, and the Whirlpool of Arbitrary Power* (Apr. 1793).

971–2 See 'To a Sky-lark', 90.

973-4   Ecclesiastes 7:2 (which has 'feasting' instead of Shelley's 'mirth'): the next verse states that 'Sorrow is better than laughter'.

990-1   The Spanish Inquisition had been abolished in Mar. 1820.

999   **ancient world**   Shelley lamented the wilful misinterpretation of this rich imaginative dimension: 'the Christians contrived to turn the wrecks of the Greek mythology as well as the little they understood of their philosophy to purposes of deformity and falsehood' (*ODD*). *The Witch of Atlas* and the Homeric *Hymn to Mercury*, which was partly its source and inspiration, were attempts to reanimate the 'religion of joy' (Keats's phrase) which Shelley recognized in Greek art and literature. This 'poetry of the religion' of the Greeks was identified with a set of values which challenged a number of the principles of orthodox Christianity.

1033   **curse**   the obligation to work ('In the sweat of thy face shalt thou eat bread'; Genesis 3:19).

1035   Matthew 6:24; Luke 16:13.

1068   **fading coal**   see Isaiah 6:6.

1086   **intertexture**   cf. 'the intertexture of the atmosphere' (*The Witch of Atlas*, 463).

1089-90   *PL*, IX.23-4 (cf. 'To a Sky-lark', 5, and 'unpremeditated wit', *Hymn to Mercury*, 69). *Orlando furioso* went through several editions and a complicated process of expansion and revision, but Sismondi claimed that Ariosto desired to write like an *improvvisatore* 'who, in reciting, is carried away by his subject, and contents himself with filling up his verse'.

1101-2   For another view in another context, see Maddalo in *JM*, 544-6.

1128   **interlunations**   dark periods between the old and new moon. For the passage as a whole, cf. *On Christianity* (109-21).

1148-9   *PL*, I.254-5.

1152   **figured**   patterned (see 'the figured curtain of sleep', *PU*, IV.58).

1153-4   Cf. *On Love*.

1163-4   'No-one deserves the name of creator except God and the Poet.' Shelley quoted this in *On Life* and (with slight variations) in a letter of 16 Aug. 1818 where he celebrated a speech in Plato's *Phaedrus* on poetic madness: 'Every man who lives in this age and desires to write poetry, ought, as a preservative against the false and narrow systems of criticism which every poetical empiric vents, to impress himself with this sentence, if he would be numbered among those to whom may apply this proud, though sublime, expression of Tasso' (*L*, II. 29-30).

1179   **arbitration of popular breath**   judgement of the vulgar or uninitiated. Cf. the critique of the inequity of the system of justice in *ODD* and Beatrice's articulation of a similar argument in the trial scene of *The Cenci*. The quotation is from *PL*, IV.8-9.

1190-3   Isaiah 1:18, followed by a daring redeployment of Revelation 7:14.

1198   'And in judging Poets, the interpreters & creators of all religion & philosophy, look to your own hearts, & examine if as ye are ignobler, so ye are better even than the conception which you can form of the defects of the great; & then if ye would be judged, judge' (draft). See Luke 6:37.

1210   Shelley was acutely aware of a conflict between perfection of the life and of the work. To resolve the problem he inclined towards a formulation which posited a complete separation, e.g. 'The poet & the man are two different natures: though they exist together they may be unconscious of each other' (L, II. 310).

1217   obnoxious   susceptible, vulnerable.

1235   Codrus (more correctly Cordus) was the unknown author of the *Theseid* described as *rauci* (hoarse) by Juvenal, and 'a tiresome verse-reciter' like 'Care' in 'To Jane: the Invitation', 36. Codrus, Bavius and Maevius all represent bad poetry and were all targets of Roman satirists, respectively of Juvenal, Virgil and Horace. William Gifford, later to be editor of the *Quarterly Review*, had published the *Baviad* (1791) and *Maeviad* (1795).

1253   new birth   for Shelley's desire to participate in and to promote this, see *OWW*, 64, where it is also connected with the imminent birth of his son (which took place on 12 Nov.). For Shelley's assessment of his contemporaries, see Preface to *PU* and, especially, *PVR*, which is very closely followed here by *DP* from 'the literature' to the end. The original formulation in *PVR* provided the conclusion to a chapter which traced the historical progress of reform both in England and elsewhere in the world and was directly preceded by the claim that England 'has arrived like the nations which surround it, at a crisis in its destiny'.

1259   liberty   cf. Preface to *PU*.

1269   throne   As so often, Shelley adopts the language of political and religious power to define and celebrate something which is mysteriously but intimately connected with human potential. At this point in *PVR* Shelley cancelled the following sentence: 'They are usually men, who having an intense apprehension of all other things have an intense apprehension of their own pleasure and comfort, for the sake of which they sell, or waste themselves.' After 'minister' he noted in an unfinished passage: 'In this sense, Religion may be called Poetry, though distorted from the beautiful simplicity of its truth.'

1272   electric   cf. Preface to *PU*, 106-7, and Shelley's review of Sgricci, whose words *ellettrizzava* (electrified) his audience.

1276   'Spirit of the age' and 'Spirit of the times' were both formulations whose definitions and significance were politically and philosophically contested and which could be used positively or negatively, depending on one's perspective. Among Shelley's contemporaries, Hazlitt who, like many others, identified the French Revolution as one of the primary causes of the revolution in literature and thought, defined 'the Spirit of the Age' as 'the progress of intellectual refinement, warring with our mutual infirmities' (1823). Further definitions were offered by Hazlitt again in *The Spirit of the Age* (1825), by Friedrich Schlegel in *Philosophy of Language* (1828) and by John Stuart Mill in *The Spirit of the Age* (1830). For Shelley's interpretation, see *PU* (especially Preface and I.660–806) and *PVR*, where Shelley works out his idea in a context which is more specifically political than that of *DP*. Shelley uses the formulation 'the spirit of that age' in a letter of 15 Oct. 1819, where he refers to 'the new springs of thought and feeling, which the great events of our age have exposed to view' (*L*, II. 127).

1277   **hierophants**   expounders of sacred mysteries; ministers of 'revelation'. In the *PVR* version of this passage Shelley used the word 'priests', which he may have rejected because of its association with an established church. See note on 1269 above.

1279   **futurity**   This may derive from Thomas Campbell's 'coming events cast their shadows before', 'Lochiel's Warning', first published in *Gertrude of Wyoming* (1809) and used by Byron as epigraph to 'The Prophecy of Dante' (Reiman).

1281–2   Here Shelley adopts the language of theology: see, e.g., Dante, *Paradiso*, XXIV.131–2, *che tutto il ciel move, / non moto* ('who moves all heaven, unmoved').

1282–3   **legislators**   Shelley first made this bold claim in the context of political reform (see headnote to *PVR* and note on 1253 above). Cf. Imlac in Johnson's *Rasselas*, chapter x, who proclaims that a poet should write 'as the interpreter of nature, and the legislator of mankind'.

42 Adonais

Written between mid-April and early June 1821. Published July 1821. The title is probably derived from Bion's *Lament for Adonis*, a Hellenistic elegy part of which he translated and which, with Moschus' *Lament for Bion*, provided the main structural influence for his own lament. The poem mourns the recent death of Keats, whom Shelley did not know well but whom he had invited to recuperate in his house at Pisa. Shelley assumes that Keats's demise had been accelerated by the harsh treatment received by *Endymion* in the *Quarterly Review* for Apr. 1818. This interpretation was partly based on reports from friends such as Hunt and the Gisbornes and partly on the advertisement to Keats's 1820 volume, which states that 'the reception given to [*Endymion*] . . . discouraged the author from proceeding' with *Hyperion* – a statement later repudiated by Keats as 'a lie'. Like the Preface, the elegy is in part an attack on the Tory reviewers, for whom Shelley 'dipped my pen in consuming fire'. The animus of this attack is sharpened by his personal sense of neglect and his long-standing indignation against critics like Southey. Shortly before he died, Shelley confessed to Leigh Hunt that *Adonais* had been written 'in too melancholy a spirit, but he was strongly affected during the composition with a sense of himself and what he had endured, and that it was more an elegy on himself than the subject of it'. The drafts of the Preface tend to confirm this and to show how closely he identified with Keats, who had suffered for his intimacy with Hunt, Hazlitt 'and other enemies of despotism & superstition'. As an author, Shelley himself had 'dared & invited censure': 'Persecution, contumely and calumny have been heaped upon me in profuse measure.' Fortunately, he removed the extensive element of aggrieved and self-pitying justification from the Preface, although it appears in a coded and only slightly distanced form in the poem (see 271–306, especially 'Who in another's fate now wept his own'). Shelley also omitted from the poem a passage which seems to be the beginnings of a satirical portrait of Wordsworth: 'He sometimes like a pedlar limped along / With packs upon his back, and did deform / Clothed in the skirts of a Scotch puritan'. Shelley described *Adonais* as 'a highly-wrought piece of art' and 'in spite of its mysticism ... the least imperfect of my compositions'. He originally planned to precede the poem by a critical essay on *Hyperion* to justify the claim to greatness which he had made for Keats. A curious fragmentary dialogue may be associated with this; it follows another fragment in which Shelley analyses his own characteristics under the thin disguise of 'Lionel' (a name which features in *Rosalind and Helen*).

Adonais is one of a group of poems in which Shelley engages directly with the hostility of reviewers (see 'Lines to a Critic', 'Lines to a Reviewer', 'Fragment of a Satire upon Satire' and draft of *Epipsychidion*). It can also be related to 'The Woodman and the Nightingale' and 'The Sensitive-plant', both of which give allegorical expression to the fate of the frail and the sensitive in an unfeeling world.

The title of the poem has greatly exercised interpreters. It appears to be a conflation of the Greek Adonis and *Adonai*, the Hebrew word for 'lord'. According to Earl Wasserman, 'The identity of the two names, "Adonis" and "Adonai", had been widely accepted among the mythographers and was generally drawn on to establish Adonis as the god of the season cycle, which most accepted as the basis of all myths.'

Epigraph 'Thou wert the morning-star among the living / Ere they fair light had fled; / Now, having died, thou art as Hesperus, giving / New splendour to the dead' (Shelley's translation).

Preface The Greek means: 'poison came to thy lips, Bion; poison didst thou eat. To such lips could it approach and not be sweetened? What human was so brutal as to mix the drug for thee, or give it at thy bidding? He escapes my song' (trans. A. S. F. Gow).

7 **Hyperion** Shelley had his reservations about the achievement of Keats and lamented the 'system & mannerism' of his earlier works but he conceded that the 'narrow and wretched taste' which impeded Keats's writings was dispersed by 'the energy and beauty of his powers'. He was particularly enthusiastic about *Hyperion*, 'an astonishing piece of writing which promises for him that he is destined to become one of the first writers of the age'.

12–13 **cemetery of the Protestants** Shelley's young son William had been buried there in 1819 and the unfinished elegiac poem 'To William Shelley' engages with themes which are later developed in *Adonais*. The cemetery was, in fact, the Cimetero acattolico, which was completely unfenced till 1821 and subject to malicious or drunken intrusions. Non-Catholic burials had to be performed by night, partly to protect mourners from the possible hostility of the Romans; occasionally, military protection was needed.

27 **rupture** Shelley seems to have received reports through Leigh Hunt and the Gisbornes. In Nov. 1820 he had drafted a letter to William Gifford, editor of the *Quarterly Review* protesting against its treatment of *Endymion*, though conceding the poem's 'false taste' and admitting that Keats's 'canons' were 'the very reverse of my own': his letter mentioned 'the rupture of a blood vessel in the lungs' and alerted Gifford to the achievement of *Hyperion* (L, ii. 251–3).

31 **know not** Luke 23:34 (see *PU*, I, 631).

35 **penetrable stuff** *Hamlet*, III.iv.36.

36 **calumniator** Shelley mistakenly believed that Robert Southey had been the anonymous perpetrator of one or more reviews in the *Quarterly* which had paid particular attention to his own private life. Southey does seem to have played a part in spreading rumours of a 'league of incest' in Geneva which partly fuelled these attacks.

37–42 For all its deficiencies, Shelley told Gifford, *Endymion* was 'a very remarkable production for a man of Keats's age'. The other poems mentioned are: *Paris in 1815* (1817) by George Croly, *Woman* (1810) by Eaton Stannard Barrett, and *Ildarim: A Syrian Tale* (1816) by Henry Gally Knight. John Howard Payne (1791–1852) was the author of *Brutus* and *Evadne*, both reviewed in the *Quarterly* for Jan. 1820; Alicia Lefanu (1753–1817) was the author of *The Sons of Erin* (1812); the Reverend Henry Hart Milman (1791–1868) was best known for the successful verse-drama *Fazio* (1815) and the Miltonic epic *Samor* (1818).

42–4 In the *Quarterly* for May 1820 Reginald Heber had praised

Milman's *The Fall of Jerusalem*, which he contrasted favourably with Byron's 'strange predilection for the worser part of manicheism'.

44–5 gnat ... stone Matthew 23:24; John 8:7. **daggers** *Hamlet*, III.ii.387. For 'murderer', see 'the daily murder of all genius', Preface to *LC*, 249. For the attack on reviewers, see also: 'Reviewers, with some rare exceptions are in general a most stupid & malignant race; and as a bankrupt thief turns thief taker in despair, so an unsuccessful author turns critic' (cancelled in draft).

69–70 such stuff *The Tempest*, IV.i.156–7.

3 so dear a head a classical formulation (cf. Horace's *tam cari capitis*).

5 thy obscure compeers hours which have not been selected for such prominent duties.

11–12 shaft ... darkness the anonymous review in the *Quarterly* (cf. Psalms 91:5–6).

12 Urania the Muse of poetry (invoked by Milton, *PL*, VII.1–39) and therefore the mother of Adonais/Keats. She takes over the function of the mourning Aphrodite, the lover of Adonis in the original myth.

14 Paradise park or pleasure-garden; also heaven, since Urania is a heavenly muse.

29–36 the disillusionment of 'republican' Milton, who died only eight years after the Restoration. **third among the sons of light** the third great epic poet in succession to Homer and Dante. There may be a heterodox implication here: Milton's light is not that of the New Testament but the light of prophetic poetry. He faced death not with the terror proper to a Christian who believes in hell but with a calm and self-content worthy of 'the kings of thought'. The drafts include a passage which emphasizes the iconoclastic force of Milton's lyre: 'And from his touch sweet thunder flowed, and shook / All human things built in contempt of man / And sanguine thrones and impious altars quook / Prisons and citadels'. For Milton's heterodoxy, see *ODD*, 1–45 above.

39–43 Successful minor poets have known more happiness than greater spirits whose potential was thwarted or never realized.

48–9 Cf. Keats's *Isabella*, which Shelley had seen by the end of Oct. 1820.

51 extreme last, latest.

55 that high Capital Rome.

63 liquid pure, free from harshness or discord.

69 the eternal Hunger decomposition.

73–81 Here and in later stanzas (notably 12) Shelley transforms the traditional mourning Loves into a gathering of mental presences more suitable to a poet.

94 anadem headband, chaplet, garland.

99 the barbèd fire the fire of love's arrows.

107 clips embraces.

120-3 The clouds of early morning obscured the last stars instead of falling as dew. In many societies, particularly in the East, unbound hair is a sign of mourning.

127 Echo has abandoned her usual functions.

133-4 Narcissus rejected the advances of Echo, who pined away till she was only a voice.

141-4 Hyacinth was loved by Phoebus Apollo, who killed him by accident. Narcissus fell in love with his own reflection. After death both became flowers, who now exhale sighs of compassion ('ruth') rather than sweet scents.

145-51 spirit's sister Keats had written 'Ode to a Nightingale'. **scale Heaven** in epic poems like that about the sun-god Hyperion of which Shelley wrote: 'if "Hyperion" be not grand poetry, none has been produced by our contemporaries'.

158 The spring is imaged as the funeral of the winter, like the rituals of Adonis a paradoxical mixture of joy and grief, whose ultimate implications will turn out to be positive.

159-60 brake thicket. **brere** bush or shrub.

174-6 The flowers illuminate death by their fragrance, as the stars illumine night by their splendour (light). Shelley's synaesthetic boldness is held in check by the cautious precision of his own explication.

177-9 that ... knows the mind of man. For the image in 178, cf. Byron's 'So, we'll go no more a roving'. **sightless** invisible.

185-9 Since death is our creditor, the condition on which we enjoy the beauties of nature is the inevitability of time, change, sorrow.

195 their sister the Echo who had recited Adonais's poems.

202 ghost soul, principle of life.

204-6 So in this way.

208-16 This passage owes something both to Venus' quest for Adonais and to Plato's description of the influence of love (see note to *PU*, I.772-9); here the spirit of Poetry meets with unsympathetic reactions.

219 Blushed to annihilation since a blush brings blood to the face it negates the pallor of death.

227 This detail is derived from Bion.

228 heartless disheartened, dejected.

234 I am chained to Time because she is the Muse of mortal poets.

235-43 In his immaturity, Keats departed from the paths of poetic convention before he had acquired either the mental resilience to respond appropriately to his critics or the mature achievements which could have dispersed them. The 'unpastured [i.e. unfed] dragon' may include suggestions of the *Quarterly*, but is not so narrowly specific. **the mirrored shield** like that used by Perseus to kill the Gorgon Medusa – by reflecting the image of her head, the sight of which turned observers to stone. **crescent** increasing.

249–52 Byron smote and silenced his critics with *English Bards and Scotch Reviewers* (1809) as Apollo killed the dragon Python.

253–61 The great poet reveals the truth and obscures his lesser contemporaries as the sun the stars; when he dies, those lesser figures who dimmed his work by criticism or misunderstanding, or who shared in his glory by imitation or by association, will disappear also.

262 mountain shepherds The pastoral mode is used to introduce a procession of contemporary poets.

264 Pilgrim of Eternity Byron, author of *Childe Harold's Pilgrimage* (see especially 'wanderers o'er Eternity / Whose bark drives on and on, and anchored ne'er shall be' (III.669–70), which is partly derived from *PL*, II.148 and which partly anticipates the final stanza of *Adonais*). The draft includes an analysis of Byronic satire: 'His life seemed one long carnival, one merry / Farewell to flesh . . . / He laughed, and as the arrow of laughter fell / Wounding with sweet and bitter mirth, it well / Distilled the balm from its fine point to heal / The wound it had inflicted'; cf. *LMG*, 240–1.

268–70 Thomas Moore, fashionably successful Irish poet, liberal and friend of Byron, gave voice to the sad condition of Ireland ('Ierne') in his *Irish Melodies*.

271 one frail Form Shelley himself in mythological guise.

275 Actaeon-like Actaeon saw Artemis (Diana) naked, for which he was changed into a stag and then devoured by his own dogs.

280 pardlike like the leopard, which was sacred to Dionysus.

283 superincumbent which lies or presses on him.

291–2 The *thyrsus* was a staff traditionally carried by Dionysus and his Bacchantes (cypress for mourning here replacing the original pine-cone). In Plato's *Ion*, which Shelley translated, poets are compared to the Bacchantes, who 'when possessed by the God, draw honey and milk from the rivers in which, when they come to their senses, they find nothing but simple water'.

297 Cf. Cowper's self-portrait, 'I was a stricken deer, that left the herd / Long since.'

298 partial prejudiced, for reasons explained in 300.

300–1 In *On Love* Shelley recorded that when he had assumed that he could appeal to something in common with other men 'and unburthen my inmost soul to them, I have found my language misunderstood like one in a distant and savage land'.

306 Cain's or Christ's 'The introduction of the name of *Christ* as an antithesis to *Cain* is surely anything but irreverence or sarcasm' (*L*, II. 306). This is neither a simple equation nor a blasphemous conjunction. Both Cain and Christ were outcasts but the horrible irony is that while one killed his brother, the other was the harmless benefactor of humanity.

307–15 Leigh Hunt was one of the first to recognize the promise of Keats.

316 drunk poison a detail mentioned in the second epigraph. In the course of the poem the death of Adonis is accounted for in a variety of ways.

319 nameless worm the anonymous reviewer in the *Quarterly*. In his letter of protest of 26 June 1820 to Southey, Shelley complained that he had been attacked 'by a calumniator without a name – with the cowardice, no less than the malignity, of an assassin'.

327 noteless of no note, undistinguished.

336 wakes or sleep Shelley's affirmation is qualified by a characteristic fastidiousness of definition.

337 See *PL*, IV.829, which is immediately followed by the line 'Not to know me argues yourselves unknown'. Shelley also makes use of line 829 in *DP*, in the context of poetic reputation.

338 a reference to the Burial of the Dead.

381–5 plastic stress shaping, moulding, creative principle. According to the Greek philosophers, 'God in making the world, made not the best that he, or even inferior intelligences could conceive; but . . . he moulded the reluctant and stubborn materials ready to his hand, into the nearest arrangement possible to the perfect archetype existing in his contemplation' (*ODD*).

395–6 The great minds of the past are a vital influence.

397–405 A list of poets who were cut off before maturity, like Keats. Thomas Chatterton (1752–70), who poisoned himself at 17, was an emblem of unrecognized genius to the Romantics; Sir Philip Sidney died heroically at 32; Lucan (one of Shelley's favourite Roman poets) betrayed his fellow-conspirators against Nero but committed suicide with redeeming dignity at 26.

414 Vesper Hesperus, the evening star (see Epigraph).

415–23 Learn to acknowledge the vastness of the universe and the minuteness of the individual and moderate your misgivings and fear of death.

417 pendulous suspended (in space).

439–50 'The English burying place is a green slope near the walls, under the pyramidal tomb of Cestius [a Roman tribune], & is I think the most beautiful and solemn cemetery I ever beheld. To see the sun shining on its bright grass . . . and to mark the tombs, mostly of women and young people who were buried there, one might, if one were to die, desire the sleep they seem to sleep' (*L*, II. 59–60). Shelley's young son William was buried there (440, 453–5).

463 Stains enriches by colouring (as in stained glass); but see 356.

466–8 Cf. *OL*, 234–5.

477 Perhaps a reference to the marriage service.

484 **are mirrors** more correctly 'is a mirror', but Shelley is thinking of the multiplicity of the web of being.

487–95 Images of poetic inspiration (cf. *OL* and *Epipsychidion*).

43 *Lines Written on Hearing the News of the Death of Napoleon*

Written 1821. Published with *Hellas* (1822). Napoleon died on 5 May 1821. As early as 1812 Shelley had written: 'Excepting Lord Castlereagh you could not have mentioned any character but Buonaparte whom I contemn and abhor more vehemently.' In 1815 he expressed 'Feelings of a Republican on the Fall of Bonaparte', and Napoleon featured briefly in later poems such as *OL* and *TL*. Shelley once planned to base a play on his career.

3–4 This energy is characteristic of Shelley's planets; here it has a biblical flavour (cf. 'when the morning stars sang together', Job 38:7).

8 **Napoleon** originally 'thy Napoleon'.

30 Cf. 'The mists in their eastern caves uprolled' ('Boat on the Serchio', 16).

40 **hopes … fled** originally 'fair shapes he obliterated'. Napoleon had disappointed the supporters of Liberty by assuming despotic power for himself.

44 *The Aziola*

Written 1821 (probably at the Baths of San Giuliano, near Pisa, between May and the end of October). Published posthumously (1829). Mary remembered: 'the cicale at noon-day kept up their hum; the aziola cooed in the quiet evening.' The aziola is a small owl (*assiolo*).

7–9 Shelley anticipates the answer; perhaps this would have been changed if he had lived to revise the manuscript draft.

45 *Hellas*

Written autumn 1821. Published 1822. *Hellas* (Greece) celebrates the Greek rising against the Turks of which the Shelleys first heard news from their Greek friend Prince Mavrocordato, who was to play a prominent part in its later stages. The Preface gives public expression and political application to that Hellenism which marks so much of Shelley's work in verse and prose. Shelley's admiration for the Greek achievement was neither myopic nor ill-informed. It acknowledged the limitations of ancient Greek civilization but it also celebrated an achievement which was still relevant: 'what the Greeks were was a reality not a promise. And what we are and hope to be is derived, as it

were, from the influence and inspiration of these glorious generations.'
Shelley's analysis of the modern Greeks can be compared to the less
flattering first-hand account in the verse and notes of Byron's *Childe
Harold*.

11–12 In *PVR* Shelley had allowed himself to hope that 'The Great
Monarchies of Asia cannot ... remain unshaken by the earthquake
which is shattering to dust the "mountainous strongholds" of the
tyrants of the Western world'. Yet he had also recognized the
obstacles to change. One of the strongest arguments for the necessity
of reform in England was the 'inoperative and unconscious abject-
ness' to which many had been reduced: 'they neither know nor care.
They are sinking into a resemblance with the Hindoos and the
Chinese, who were once men as they are.'

14–16 See 'The wrecks and fragments of those subtle and profound
minds, like the ruins of a fine statue, obscurely suggest to us the
grandeur and perfection of the whole' (*DMAG*).

31 'The very powerful & very entertaining novel', *Anastasius: Mem-
oirs of a Greek* by the connoisseur and art-collector Thomas Hope
was published anonymously in 1819 and read by Shelley in Aug.
1821. In his *DMAG* Shelley had referred to novels by Barthélemy
and Wieland, and regretted that no book showed the Greeks precisely
as they were for fear of 'giving outrage and violation' to contempor-
ary *mores*.

33–43 Shelley's remarks were influenced by his friendship with Prince
Alexandros Mavrokordatos (or Mavrocordato) (1791–1865), to
whom *Hellas* was dedicated. Mavrokordatos, who had formed the
centre of a circle of Greek exiles in Pisa and had exchanged lessons
in Greek and English with Mary, left in June 1821 to take part in the
Greek struggle, and eventually became prime minister of the newly
independent Greek state on four occasions.

46–8 The Greek cause brought into unlikely alliance against the
hegemony of Islam both orthodox Christians and a number who,
like Shelley, were normally antagonistic to Christianity.

56–71 Charles Ollier, Shelley's publisher, removed this paragraph
from the text of the first edition; it was not published until 1892.

61–71 Shelley is here suggesting that the shared interests of monar-
chical government extend far beyond that small group of countries
which constituted the original 'Holy Alliance' (Austria, Prussia and
Russia).

70–1 In *PU* Jupiter is ironically unaware of his own vulnerability until
just before his fall, whereas *Hellas* explores in detail the premonitions
of the Emperor Mahmud, which are brought to a focus in his encoun-
ters with the prophetic Jew Ahasuerus and with the phantom of his
predecessor, Mahomet II, who warns him: 'the Anarchs of the world

of darkness keep / A throne for thee, round which thy empire lies / Boundless and mute; and for thy subjects thou, / Like us, shalt rule the ghosts of murdered life, / The phantoms of the powers who rule thee now – / Mutinous passions, and conflicting fears, / And hopes that sate themselves on dust, and die' (879–85).

72–86 This final paragraph can be compared to *OL* and to the comprehensive survey of contemporary politics in the first chapter of *PVR*.

Taking its cue from the *Persae* of Aeschylus, *Hellas* focuses on the court of the defeated emperor at Constantinople; it is suffused by a deep melancholy and world-weariness which qualify Shelley's delight in the rebirth of Greek liberty. Both choruses are spoken by Greek women, captives at the court of Mahmud. The second chorus concludes the play on a note of prophetic doubt.

I

5 **they** living and thinking beings who 'to use a common and inadequate phrase, *clothe themselves in matter*' and whose immortality, through reincarnation, is contrasted with 'the transience of the noblest manifestations of the external world' (Shelley's note).

11–14 Shelley is conjecturing 'a progressive state of more or less exalted existence, according to the degree of perfection which every distinct intelligence may have attained' (Shelley's note).

15 **Power** Christ, who, like Prometheus, came to liberate humanity but was tortured for his good intentions.

24 Institutional Christianity became an oppressive force after the death of Christ, whose teachings it traduced.

25–8 Islam (symbolized by the crescent moon) is a later development than Christianity and will disappear first.

30 **one** like Mahmud at the beginning of the play.

34ff. Shelley is careful to record in a note that he does not endorse the Christian point of view ostensibly expressed in this chorus (e.g. the identification of Truth and Christianity). Like Milton in 'On the Morning of Christ's Nativity', whose metre he has adopted, he regrets the passing of the ancient mythology ('dreams'). 'The Sylvans and Fauns with their leader the Great Pan were most poetical personages and were connected in the imagination of the Pagans with all that could enliven and delight. They were supposed to be innocent beings not greatly different in habits from the shepherds and herdsmen of which they were the patron saints. But the Christians contrived to turn the wrecks of the Greek mythology as well as the little they understood of their philosophy to purposes of deformity and falsehood' (*ODD*).

II Shelley comments: 'The final chorus is indistinct and obscure, as the event of the living drama whose arrival it foretells'. In particular, he was afraid that the Holy Alliance would help the Turks to crush the rising. To prophesy happiness rather than wars is 'a more hazardous exercise of the faculty which bards possess or feign' yet with the authority and excuse of Isaiah and Virgil (Fourth Eclogue) he anticipates 'the possible and perhaps approaching state of society'.

4   **weeds**   garments usually associated with mourning.

9–12   For the geography, see 'Song of Pan'. **Cyclads**   a group of islands in the Aegean Sea.

13   **Argo**   ship in which Jason recovered the Golden Fleece ('prize').

17–18   Ulysses was seduced by Calypso on his way home from the Trojan War.

21–4   By solving the Sphinx's riddle, Oedipus liberated Thebes from the plague; but he also murdered his father Laius, with tragic consequences ('Unnatural love, and more unnatural hate', *PU*, I.349).

31–4   **Saturn and Love**   'among the deities of a real or imaginary state of innocence and happiness' ('The golden years'). **all who fell**   the gods of Greece, Asia, and Egypt, superseded by Christ ('One who rose') **many unsubdued**   'the monstrous objects of the idolatry of China, India, the Antarctic islands, and the native tribes of America' (Shelley's note).

35–6   This religion will not be based on blood sacrifices or on mercenary considerations.

37   **cease**   The chorus is horrified by the sudden thought of what may lie in store.

39–40   Cf. 'Yet shall some few traces of olden sin lurk behind ... a second warfare, too, shall there be, and again shall a great Achilles be sent to Troy' (Virgil, *Fourth Eclogue*, trans. H. Fairclough).

46   *The flower that smiles today*

Written 1821. Published posthumously (1824). Geoffrey Matthews has suggested that this lyric was intended for the opening of *Hellas*, where it was to be sung by a favourite slave to the sleeping Mahmud, whose empire is collapsing as he sleeps.

12   **these**   Virtue, friendship and love, like all human attributes do not disappear when they decline from their original purity but continue to exist in a debased and joyless form.

20   **thou**   probably the sleeping emperor.

47   *To Night*

Written 1821. Published posthumously (1824).

48   Rose leaves, when the rose is dead

Dated 1821 by Mary Shelley. Published posthumously (1824). This text reproduces the order of the stanzas in the manuscript draft. Mary Shelley reversed this order, and most editors have followed her. The evidence is unclear: the two stanzas are followed by several abortive lines which might represent an attempt to rewrite 3–4 or might be the beginning of a new stanza.

2   **the beloved's**   originally 'a Sultana's'.
3   **thoughts**   perhaps poetic thoughts (=poems, like the 'dead thoughts' in *OWW*). This may refer to the poetry of Emilia Viviani, since drafts of *Epipsychidion* appear in the same notebook as this fragment.

49   O World, O Life, O Time

Dated 1821 by Mary Shelley. Published posthumously (1824).

8   Shelley left a gap for an adjective to describe summer.

50   When passion's trance is overpast

Written in 1821. Published posthumously (1824).

51   One word is too often profaned

Dated 1821 by Mary Shelley. Published posthumously (1824).

52   To Edward Williams

Written 26 Jan. 1822. Published posthumously (1834). Edward Ellerker Williams and his wife Jane (to whom most of Shelley's last poems were addressed) were close friends and neighbours of the Shelleys in 1821 and 1822: at this time they lived in the same building in Pisa. Williams was an old Etonian, a retired army officer with artistic leanings; he shared Shelley's taste for boating and they went down together in the *Don Juan*. The poem was accompanied by a cautionary note: 'If any of the stanzas should please you, you may read them to Jane, but to no one else, – and yet on second thoughts I had rather you would not.' Shelley himself would not have published this poem, which refers so plainly to his growing estrangement from Mary.

1   an allusion may be intended to Shelley's nickname (see note on *Prologue in Heaven*).
16   **its evil, good**   like Satan (*PL*, IV.110).

35 The final verdict was always in the negative.
41–8 'The foxes have holes, and the birds of the air have nests; but the Son of man hath not where to lay his head' (Matthew 8:20).

53 To Jane: The Recollection

Written spring 1822, probably Feb. Published posthumously (1824, 1839). This poem and 'To Jane: The Invitation', which were originally published as one piece, are centred on a walk made on 2 Feb. 1822 by Shelley, Jane Williams, and Mary, which took them through the pine forest of the Cascine near Pisa to the sea.

83 **too faithful** cf. 'with more than truth' (80). Also perhaps a reference to Shelley's allegiance to Mary, who was on the walk and who must have been associated with the 'unwelcome thought'.

54 Prologue in Heaven

Translated from Goethe's *Faust* early 1822. Published posthumously (1824). Shelley intended this and his version of the *Walpurgisnacht* for a paper in the *Liberal*, a new journal founded by Leigh Hunt, Byron and himself. He also translated three scenes from Calderón's *El mágico prodigioso*, a play which 'evidently furnished the *germ* of Faust'. His paper would probably have explored the role of the Devil in both of these plays and might have been a sequel to his unfinished essay *ODD*. The *Prologue in Heaven* had not been translated into English before, largely because it was considered blasphemous. Even Byron, who knew it was based on the Book of Job, referred to 'the daring language of the prologue, which no one will ever venture to translate'.

7 **unwithered** Shelley's substitution for *unbegreiflich* (incomprehensible).
21 **desolation** lightning.
28 Shelley provides a literal prose translation of 'this astonishing chorus' in a footnote, because 'it is impossible to represent in another language the melody of the versification; even the volatile strength and delicacy of the ideas escape in the crucible of translation, and the reader is surprised to find a *caput mortuum*' (the worthless residue from an alchemical experiment).
96 'Muhme is literally aunt, and in the same sense as we find it employed in the old English play's Paramour' (Shelley's note). When Shelley translated this passage to Byron, Byron nicknamed him 'the snake'.
99 **who rebelled** Shelley's version of *die verneinen* (who deny), perhaps intentional since he translated the words correctly in an earlier prose version.

105 create cause trouble.
107 In Goethe this is specified as *das Werdende* (the becoming).
109–10 Cf. *HIB*.

55 With a Guitar, to Jane

Written probably Apr. 1822. Published posthumously in two parts (1832, 1833). Shelley was particularly susceptible to the female voice (see 'To Constantia'). This strengthened his attraction towards Jane Williams, who, according to Mary Shelley, had 'a very pretty voice, and a taste and ear for music which is almost miraculous'. Having failed in his plan to procure her a harp from Paris, Shelley presented Jane Williams with a Pisan guitar made by Ferdinando Bottari, which is now in the Bodleian Library. This musical context allowed Shelley to engage playfully with *The Tempest*, which left its mark on other late poems and on *Fragments of an Unfinished Drama*, which also capitalizes on the kind of role-playing that characterized the Shelley circle. In the poem, Shelley identifies himself with Ariel, the sprite or spirit who was liberated from a 'cloven pine' by his master Prospero, while Edward and Jane Williams play the young lovers Ferdinand and Miranda. Ariel/Shelley is also equated with the silent guitar whose music can only be set free by the fingers of Miranda/Jane. Shelley's poem is written in octosyllabics and bears some formal similarity to Shakespeare's Epilogue, addressed by Prospero to the audience. Like Prospero, Ariel/Shelley tactfully acknowledges his total dependence on the sympathetic and life-informing response of an audience.

6 delighted spirit see *Measure for Measure*, III.i.121.
7–8 Cf. Keats's 'Ode on Melancholy'. Shelley had received Keats's 1820 volume at the end of Oct. 1820, and his last poems occasionally show its influence.
17–22 These lines look beyond the end of the play's action when Miranda will return to the Kingdom of Naples, from where she had accompanied her father into banishment.
23ff. As a spirit, Ariel is immortal. Miranda is subject to the limitations of mortality but is recurrently reincarnated. This may be a playful version of a Platonic myth but it is also appropriate to a character in a play. These lines refer to a guardian spirit or angel (a concept familiar to Neoplatonists and to Christians) while the star of birth suggests both an astrological system and the story of the Nativity.
24 interlunar swoon monthly period, between the 'old moon' and the 'new', during which the moon is invisible; cf. 'silent as the moon . . . / Hid in her vacant interlunar cell' (Milton, *Samson Agonistes*, 87–9). According to Pliny the Elder, this was the time of

the silent moon or the interlunar day; 'silent' may therefore be interpreted, among other things, as a technical term for 'not shining'.

53ff. As Leigh Hunt suggested, Shelley may be indebted here to a poem by Catullus concerning a *phaselus* or little boat.

57 fairest star Venus, star of love.

59-61 Here and in 79-80 Shelley may be drawing on his translation of the Homeric *Hymn to Mercury*, 645-50 (e.g. 'for those endowed / With art and wisdom who interrogate / It teaches, babbling in delightful mood, / All things which make the spirit most elate').

75-8 mysterious sound earth's contribution to the music of the spheres. Cf. Shelley's account in *Epipsychidion* of the Ionian isle with its 'sweet airs' and 'deep music'; here, as in 'With a Guitar', Shelley is also influenced by the music of Prospero's island in *The Tempest*. **diurnal** happening daily.

56   *To Jane (The keen stars were twinkling)*

Written in June 1822. Published posthumously (1832; 1839). 'I sate down to write some words for an ariette which might be profane – but it was in vain to struggle with the ruling spirit, who compelled me to speak of things sacred to yours & Wilhelmeister's indulgence – I commit them to your secrecy & your mercy & will try & do better another time.' By his own admission, Shelley's ideas of music were 'gross' and he was always susceptible to feminine music-makers (see 'To Constantia, Singing'). He was particularly delighted by the talents of Jane Williams: 'Williams is captain, and we drive along this delightful bay in the evening wind, under the summer moon, until earth appears another world. Jane brings her guitar, and if the past and the future could be obliterated, the present would content me so well that I could say with Faust to the passing moment, "Remain, thou, thou art so beautiful"' (*L*, II. 435-6).

17 dew in the sense of the adjective 'liquid' (pure and clear in tone). Cf. the imagery of 'To a Sky-lark'.

57   *Lines Written in the Bay of Lerici*

Written late June 1822. Published posthumously (1862). These roughly drafted and untitled lines, which refer to Shelley's friendship with Jane Williams, occur in the manuscript of *TL*, where they follow the conclusion of 'To Jane' and an unused draft passage of *TL* which continues 281 in the present version.

1-14 The opening invocation to the moon was added at a later stage of composition but it provides an important objective correlative for the poet's feelings about his beloved. After the invocation, the moon is referred to in the third person.

10–12 Albatrosses are reputed to sleep on the wing.

21–4 Jane has hypnotic powers (see 'The Magnetic Lady to her Patient').

28–9 'Thus I was happy, if the name / Of happiness' (cancelled in draft). 'Charmed by her presence, meek & tame / The demon of my spirit lay' (cancelled in draft).

29–30 **Desire & fear** 'I thought no more of pleasures lost or sorrows' (cancelled in draft).

39–44 The ships are associated with daemons, those spirits intermediary between man and god who are the good angels of Shelley's universe. For the sea as purveyor of medicine, see 'Sonnet: On Launching some Bottles filled with Knowledge into the Bristol Channel', which begins, 'Vessels of Heavenly medicine'.

55–8 The poet reflects on a concentration of purpose which is single-mindedly committed to the pursuit of pleasure and oblivious to its fatal consequences. 'Too happy' (see 'O too much' in 21) expresses this bittersweet ambivalence (cf. 'too happy in thine happiness', Keats, 'Ode to a Nightingale', 6). The next page of the manuscript contains a fragmentary poem headed *Pleasure*, which includes these lines: 'Time is flying <by> Occasion is dying / Hope is sighing / For there is / Far more to fear / In the coming year / Then desire <can hear> / In this. / Might I say that sorrow / No mask could borrow / If today like tomorrow / Would remain / And between short & bliss / And a state such as this / Would' (fragment breaks off); see note on 'To Jane' above. These paradoxes are explored at greater length in another late lyric 'We meet not as then we parted'.

58 Shelley's intentions here are not clear. He first wrote 'Destroying life not peace', then cancelled 'Destroy' and inserted 'alone' above 'not peace', and 'Seeking' under 'Destroy'. Editors read: 'Seeking life alone not peace' (Matthews), 'Seeking life not peace' (Chernaik), 'Destroying life alone not peace' (Reiman and Powers). It is not certain whether the poem was meant to conclude with this generalized reflection.

58 The Triumph of Life

Probably written between late May and the end of June 1822. Published posthumously from very rough drafts in 1824. This was Shelley's last major poem and was left unfinished and unrevised at his death. The *Life* of the title is life seen as conqueror and destroyer of man and his ideals, a grim and relentless process which only a heroic few can honourably resist. The poem is based on Petrarch's *Trionfi*, a sequence of triumphal processions involving Love, Chastity, Death, Fame, Time and Eternity, each of which triumphs over its predecessor; there is no indication as to whether Shelley intended a similar sequence or as to how he would have resolved the unfinished action of his own *Triumph*. He was also influenced by the Arches of Titus and Constantine at Rome, which provided compelling images of 'that mixture of energy & error which is called a Triumph'; by Beaumont and Fletcher; by accounts of a masque given by the Inns of Court in honour of Charles I; and especially by the frescoes of the Campo Santo at Pisa. Another major influence was Dante: the role of guide and interpreter played by Rousseau is obviously modelled on the role played by Virgil in the *Divine Comedy*. Shelley was influenced by Rousseau's theoretical writings but reserved his greatest admiration for *La Nouvelle Héloïse* (1761). When visiting the settings of that novel in 1816 he reflected that the presences of its imaginative world 'were created indeed by one mind, but a mind so powerfully bright as to cast a shade of falsehood on the records that are called reality'. This admiration was in tension with his distaste for *Les Confessions* and for what it revealed about the character of Rousseau (see Introduction). Shelley's feelings were perhaps all the stronger because of his own struggle to liberate himself from 'the dark idolatry of self'.

3 **Rejoicing in his splendour** unlike man, the powers of nature are self-confident and unashamed to acknowledge their own splendour (cf. 'The Cloud').

5 **smokeless altars** as opposed to the altars of human religion with their offerings of sacrifice.

7 **orison** prayer.

21 **But I** the narrator is out of tune with the processes of nature; he is awake through the night and turns his back to the sunrise.

23 **cone of night** earth's shadow in space.

29 **strange trance** the prelude to a visionary poem (cf. *MA*).

30–3 Cf. *PU*, IV.211–12; a paradoxical natural phenomenon.

79–85 Cf. 'For lo! the new moon winter-bright! / And overspread with phantom light, / . . . I see the old moon in her lap, foretelling / The coming-on of rain and squally blast' (Coleridge, 'Dejection: An Ode') **its** the sleeping tempest's.

91 **cloud like crape** originally 'a widow's veil of crape'.

94 **Janus-visaged** with faces at back and front. Harold Bloom sees this Shape as 'a parody of the cherubim or guiding angels of the divine chariot in Ezekiel, Revelation, Dante, and Milton'.

103 **banded** blindfolded.

111–16 a typical triumph under the Roman Empire (cf. *OL*, 99–103).

121 **their age** probably their period in history.

126 **the great winter** the end of the world.

132 **diadem** crown.

134 **they ... Jerusalem** Socrates and Jesus, in Shelley's view the greatest figures in human history.

137ff. the dance of sexual attraction ('that fierce Spirit').

175 Impotence destroys the old ('these'), sensuality the young ('those').

190 **grim Feature** cf. *PL*, x.279.

210 **wreaths of light** a combination of the laurel wreath of the poet and the halo, here a sign of intellectual rather than spiritual achievement.

211-15 They failed to acquire self-knowledge and so were unable to achieve the necessary internal equilibrium. For the importance of psychological politics, see 'Sonnet to the Republic of Benevento'.

215-7 In *OL* Napoleon is 'The Anarch of thine own [Liberty's] bewildered powers' (175).

217-24 Napoleon presented in a characteristic posture (215-16); cf. 'Feelings of a Republican on the Fall of Bonaparte', *OL*, 174-80, 'Lines Written on Hearing the News of the Death of Napoleon'. In accord with the prevailing context of *TL* and Rousseau's own perspective, this account of the career of Napoleon concentrates on the failure of the individual and is more negative than the version in *PVR*, where Shelley concludes that 'the military project of government of the great tyrant having failed ... France is as it were regenerated'.

226-7 presumably a reference to the outcome of the Napoleonic wars and the establishment of the Holy Alliance (see headnote to *Hellas*).

235-6 two sages, Voltaire (i.e. François-Marie Arouet (1694-1778), whose incisive and capacious critical intelligence epitomized the Enlightenment and Immanuel Kant (1724-1804), author of *The Critque of Judgment* (1790); and three benevolent rulers (Frederick the Great of Prussia, Catherine the Great of Russia, Leopold II of Austria). It is likely that 'demagogue' does not refer to any of these but suggests William Pitt (prime minister during the French Revolution and when war was declared on France).

237 **anarchs** see headnote to *MA*. For the conjunction, see Shelley's description of the Arch of Titus: 'magistrates and priests and generals and philosophers dragged in chains beside his wheels'.

240-3 Unlike the others who were conquered by the temptations of the external world, Rousseau was led astray by his own better qualities: 'But from those first acts of goodness, poured out with effusions of heart, were born chains of successive engagements that I had not foreseen, and of which I could no longer shake off the yoke' (*The Reveries of a Solitary*).

243 **temper** 'model' (draft). Elsewhere in *TL* this word has positive connotations which Rousseau here seems to override.

251-2 'See all the mighty & the wise enchained / See Zoroaster,

Solomon and those / Great forms to whom Egypt & India / Owed what they were and are' (cancelled in draft). Another attempt reads: 'Or as you passed I interrupted, – thus / One who awakes within a ship would say / That the stars move; as it appears to us / So is it not, however it may be. – '

254-9 Unlike Socrates, whose restraint is recorded in the *Symposium*, Plato succumbed to sexual temptations, which involved both sexes. The 'star' (256) is probably the subject of his epigram tactfully translated by Shelley as 'To Stella' but in reality addressed to a young man.

261 **the tutor and his pupil** Aristotle and Alexander.

269-73 Bacon's inductive approach to scientific fact broke with the Aristotelian tradition and caused nature to yield up its secrets. Proteus was the old man of the sea who could assume any shape to elude capture; Bacon interpreted this myth as an allegory of nature in *The Wisdom of the Ancients*.

274-9 **the great bards** The draft shows that Shelley tried in turn the Greek philosophers Democritus and Diogenes, then specified 'Homer & his brethren'; all these names were replaced by a phrase which was more inclusive and more generalized. The artistic control of great poets provides an antidote to the potentially harmful passions which they portray; Rousseau was not sufficiently insulated from his subject-matter so he infected his readers. Shelley's complicated imagery makes use of medical analogies to suggest a contrast between the reticence and restraint of 'classical literature' and the dangerous self-projection of that more directly and vulnerably personal mode of writing initiated by Rousseau in his *Confessions* (see Introduction, pp. xvii–xviii).

281 Here the draft includes a list of destroyers who are contrasted with the 'creators': 'See <Caesar, Aurunzebe & Tamerlane>'.

283-4 the Roman emperors after the death of liberty ('Caesar's crime') to the establishment of Christianity as the state religion under Constantine.

288-92 popes and theologians who imposed on the world their own false notions of divinity (cf. *LC*, 3244ff.). Shelley associated 'the tremendous Gregory' (the Great) with the imposition of 'the opinion of the world'. 'John' may be John XXII, who made notorious use of the Inquisition. In the draft Shelley wrote 'every hierarch', which he changed to the more specific 'Gregory and John'; he also wrote 'mitre cinctured <shadow> phantoms'.

308ff. a symbolic landscape to represent Rousseau's birth into this world.

314-16 Cf. Shelley's translation from the *Purgatorio*, 25-31.

335-9 Cf. Wordsworth, 'Ode: Intimations of Immortality'.

348ff. In keeping with the enigmatic nature of the narrative, the meaning of this Shape is not clear. Although she is beautiful, she has a devastating effect on the observer which is associated with the threatening radiance of the day (382–92). She seems to have all the ambivalence of nature and of life.

357 **Iris** the rainbow.

359 **Nepenthe** a drug or potion which banishes grief or trouble.

361 **palms** soles of the feet.

392 **Heaven's living eyes** the stars.

414–18 **Lucifer** Venus as the morning star (cf. 'To a Sky-lark', 18–25). **chrysolite** yellowish green.

419–23 characteristic synaesthesia to evoke a preternatural experience.

421–2 'The favourite song, *Stanço di pascolar le pecorelle*, is a Brescian national air' (Mary Shelley).

427 **day-appearing dream** translates a phrase from Aeschylus' *Agamemnon*.

439–41 For the triumphal arch of the rainbow, cf. 'The Cloud', 67–70.

456–8 Duffy compares both the fictional Saint-Preux in Paris ('me voila tout-à-fait dans le torrent', *La Nouvelle Héloïse*) and Rousseau's use of *torrent* or *tourbillon* in his autobiographical writings.

463 **Lethean** causing forgetfulness or oblivion, like the river Lethe in the Greek underworld.

471–6 Dante in the *Divine Comedy*; the love is his for Beatrice.

479 **the sphere** Venus.

499 Possible references to Napoleon's infant son, who was declared King of Rome in 1811, and to George III whose insanity became total in the same year; but the poem weaves in and out of specificity in the manner of a dream which defies simple translation.

500 **anatomies** skeletons, withered lifeless forms.

544 The manuscript shows that Shelley substituted 'said' for 'cried'. The change is significant and shows that the poem was not intended to culminate in that climactic and despairing gesture which some readers have attempted to interpret biographically. The final lines of the poem suggest an ongoing dialogue which was interrupted not by Shelley's own ultimate negation or his failure to achieve poetic closure but by his accidental death.

APPENDIX I

Letter to William Godwin

Keswick 10 Jan. – 1812

Sir

It is not otherwise to be supposed than that I should appreci-
ate your avocations far beyond the pleasure or benefit which
can accrue to me from their sacrifize. The time however will be
small which may be mis-spent in reading this letter, and much
individual pleasure as an answer might give me, I have not the
vanity to imagine that it will be greater than the happiness
elsewhere diffused during the time which its creation will
occupy. – You complain that the generalizing character of my
letter, renders it deficient in interest; that I am not an individual
to you: Yet, intimate as I am with your character and your
writings, intimacy with *yourself* must in some degree precede
this exposure of my peculiarities: It is scarcely possible however
pure may be the morality which he has endeavoured to diffuse
but that generalization must characterize the uninvited address
of a stranger to a stranger. – I proceed to remedy the fault. – I
am the Son of a man of fortune in Sussex. – The habits of
thinking of my Father and myself never coincided. Passive
obedience was inculcated and enforced in my childhood: I was
required to love because it was *my duty* to love – it is scarcely
necessary to remark that coercion obviated its own intention. –
I was haunted with a passion for the wildest and most extrava-
gant romances: ancient books of Chemistry and Magic were
perused with an enthusiasm of wonder almost amounting to
belief. My sentiments were unrestrained by anything within me:
external impediments were numerous, and strongly applied –
their effects were merely temporary. –

From a reader I became I [a] writer of Romances; before the
age of seventeen I had published two 'St Irvyne' and 'Zastrozzi'
each of which tho quite uncharacteristic of me as now I am, yet

serve to mark the state of my mind at the period of their composition. I shall desire them to be sent to you; do not however consider this as any obligation to yourself to misapply your valuable time. – It is now a period of more than two years since first I saw your inestimable book on 'Political Justice'; it opened to my mind fresh & more extensive views, it materially influenced my character, and I rose from its perusal a wiser and a better man. – I was no longer the votary of Romance; till then I had existed in an ideal world; now I found that in this universe of ours was enough to excite the interest of the heart, enough to employ the discussions of Reason. I beheld in short that I had duties to perform. – Conceive the effect which the Political Justice would have upon a mind before jealous of its independance, and participating somewhat singularly in a peculiar susceptibility. – My age is now *nineteen*; at the period to which I allude I was at Eton. – at the period to which I allude I was at Eton. – No sooner had I formed the principles which I now profess, than I was anxious to disseminate their benefits. This was done without the slightest caution. – I was twice expelled, but recalled by the interference of my Father. I went to Oxford. – Oxonian society was insipid to me, uncongenial with my habits of thinking. – I could not descend to common life. The sublime interest of poetry, lofty and exalted atchievements, the proselytism of the world, the equalization of its inhabitants were to me the soul of my soul. – You can probably form some idea of the contrast exhibited to my character by those with whom I was surrounded. – Classical reading, and poetical writing employed me during my residence at Oxford. – In the meantime I became in the popular sense of the word 'God' an Atheist. I printed a pamphlet avowing my opinion, and it's occasion. I distributed this anonymously to men of thought and learning wishing that Reason should decide on the case at issue. It was never my intention to deny it. Mr Copelstone at Oxford among others had the pamphlet; he shewed it to the master and the fellows of University College, and *I* was sent for: I was informed that in case I denied the publication no more would be said. – I refused, and was expelled. It will be necessary in order to elucidate this part of my history to inform you that I am heir by entail to an estate of 6000£ per an. – My principles have induced me to regard the law of primogeniture an evil of primary magnitude. My father's notions of family honor are incoincident with my knowledge of public good. I will never sacrifize the latter to any consideration. – My father has ever regarded me as a blot and defilement of his honor. He wished to induce me by poverty to accept of some commission in a distant regiment, and in the interim of my absence to prosecute the pamphlet that a process of outlawry might make the estate on his death devolve to my younger brother. – These are the leading points of the history of the man before you.

Others exist, but I have thought proper to make some selection, not that it is my design to conceal or extenuate any part, but that I should by their enumeration quite outstep the bounds of modesty. – Now it is for you to judge whether by permitting me to cultivate your friendship you are exhibiting yourself more really useful than by the pursuance of those avocations of which the time spent in allowing this cultivation would deprive you. I am now earnestly pursuing studious habits. I am writing 'an inquiry into the causes of the failure of the French revolution to benefit mankind.' My Plan is that of resolving to lose no opportunity to disseminate truth and happiness. I am married to a woman whose views are similar to my own. – To you as the regulator and former of my mind I must ever look with real respect and veneration.

Your's sincerely
P. B. Shelley

NOTE Some of the details in this letter are inaccurate.

APPENDIX 2

From History of a Six Weeks' Tour *(1817)*

The following morning we proceeded from St Martin on mules to Chamouni, accompanied by two guides. We proceeded, as we had done the preceding day, along the valley of the Arve, a valley surrounded on all sides by immense mountains, whose rugged precipices are intermixed on high with dazzling snow. Their bases were still covered with the eternal forests, which perpetually grew darker and more profound as we approached the inner regions of the mountains.

On arriving at a small village, at the distance of a league from St Martin, we dismounted from our mules, and were conducted by our guides to view a cascade. We beheld an immense body of water fall two hundred and fifty feet, dashing from rock to rock, and casting a spray which formed a mist around it, in the midst of which hung a multitude of sunbows, which faded or became unspeakably vivid, as the inconstant sun shone through the clouds. When we approached near to it, the rain of the spray reached us, and our clothes were wetted by the quick-falling but minute particles of water. The cataract fell from above into a deep craggy chasm at our feet, where, changing its character to that of a mountain stream, it pursued its course towards the Arve, roaring over the rocks that impeded its progress.

As we proceeded, our route still lay through the valley, or rather, as it had now become, the vast ravine, which is at once the couch and the creation of the terrible Arve. We ascended, winding between mountains whose immensity staggers the imagination. We crossed the path of a torrent, which three days since had descended from the thawing snow, and torn the road away.

We dined at Servoz, a little village, where there are lead and copper mines, and where we saw a cabinet of natural curiosities, like those of Keswick and Bethgelert. We saw in this cabinet some chamois' horns, and the horns of an exceedingly rare animal called the bouquetin, which inhabits the deserts of snow to the south of Mont Blanc: it is an animal of the stag kind; its horns weigh at least twenty-seven English pounds. It is inconceivable how so small an animal could support so inordinate a weight. The horns are of a very peculiar conformation, being broad, massy, and pointed at the ends, and surrounded with a number of rings, which are supposed to afford an indication of its age: there were seventeen rings on the larges of these horns.

From Servoz three leagues remain to Chamouni. – Mont Blanc was before us – the Alps, with their innumerable glaciers on high all around, closing in the complicated windings of the single vale – forests inexpressibly beautiful, but majestic in their beauty – intermingled beech and pine, and oak, overshadowed our road, or receded, whilst lawns of such verdure as I have never seen before occupied these openings, and gradually became darker in their recesses. Mont Blanc was before us, but it was covered with cloud; its base, furrowed with dreadful gaps, was seen above. Pinnacles of snow intolerably bright, part of the chain connected with Mont Blanc, shone through the clouds at intervals on high. I never knew – I never imagined what mountains were before. The immensity of these aerial summits excited, when they suddenly burst upon the sight, a sentiment of extatic wonder, not unallied to madness. And remember this was all one scene, it all pressed home to our regard and our imagination. Though it embraced a vast extent of space, the snowy pyramids which shot into the bright blue sky seemed to overhang our path; the ravine, clothed with gigantic pines, and black with its depth below, so deep that the very roaring of the untameable Arve, which rolled through it, could not be heard above – all was as much our own, as if we had been the creators of such impressions in the minds of others as now occupied our own. Nature was the poet, whose harmony held our spirits more breathless than that of the divinest.

As we entered the valley of Chamouni (which in fact may be considered as a continuation of those which we have followed from Bonneville and Cluses) clouds hung upon the mountains at the distance perhaps of 6000 feet from the earth, but so as effectually to conceal not only Mont Blanc, but the other *aiguilles*, as they call them here, attached and subordinate to it. We were travelling along the valley, when suddenly we heard a sound as of the burst of smothered thunder rolling above; yet there was something earthly in the sound, that told us it could not be thunder. Our guide hastily pointed out to us a part of the mountain opposite, from whence the sound came. It was an avalanche. We saw the smoke of its path among the rocks, and continued to hear at intervals the bursting of its fall. It fell on the bed of a torrent, which it displaced, and presently we saw its tawny-coloured waters also spread themselves over the ravine, which was their couch.

We did not, as we intended, visit the *Glacier des Bossons* today, although it descends within a few minutes' walk of the road, wishing to survey it at least when unfatigued. We saw this glacier which comes close to the fertile plain, as we passed, its surface was broken into a thousand unaccountable figures: conical and pyramidical crystalizations, more than fifty feet in height, rise from its surface, and precipices of ice, of dazzling splendour, overhang the woods and meadows of the vale. This glacier winds upwards from the valley, until it joins the masses of frost from which it was produced above, winding through its own ravine like a bright belt flung over the black region of pines. There is more in all these scenes than mere magnitude of proportion: there is a majesty of outline; there is an awful grace in the very colours which invest these wonderful shapes – a charm which is peculiar to them, quite distinct even from the reality of their unutterable greatness.

24 July

Yesterday morning we went to the source of the Arveiron. It is about a league from this village; the river rolls forth impetuously from an arch of ice, and spreads itself in many streams over a vast space of the valley, ravaged and laid bare by its inundations. The glacier by which its waters are nourished, overhangs this cavern and the plain, and the forests of pine which surround it, with terrible precipices of solid ice. On the other side rises the immense glacier of Montanvert, fifty miles in extent, occupying a chasm among mountains of inconceivable height, and of forms so pointed and abrupt, that they seem to pierce the sky. From this glacier we saw as we sat on a rock, close to one of the streams of the Arveiron, masses of ice detach themselves from on high, and rush with a loud dull noise into the vale. The violence of their fall turned them into powder, which flowed

over the rocks in imitation of waterfalls, whose ravines they
usurped and filled.

In the evening I went with Ducrée, my guide, the only
tolerable person I have seen in this country, to visit the glacier
of Bossons. This glacier, like that of Montanvert, comes close to
the vale, overhanging the green meadows and the dark woods
with the dazzling whiteness of its precipices and pinnacles,
which are like spires of radiant crystal, covered with a net-work
of frosted silver. These glaciers flow perpetually into the valley;
ravaging in their slow but irresistible progress the pastures and
the forests which surround them, performing a work of desola-
tion in ages, which a river of lava might accomplish in an hour,
but far more irretrievably; for where the ice has once descended,
the hardiest plant refuses to grow; if even, as in some extraordi-
nary instances, it should recede after its progress has once
commenced. The glaciers perpetually move onward, at the rate
of a foot each day, with a motion that commences at the spot
where, on the boundaries of perpetual congelation, they are
produced by the freezing of the waters which arise from the
partial melting of the eternal snows. They drag with them from
the regions whence they derive their origin, all the ruins of the
mountain, enormous rocks, and immense accumulations of sand
and stones. These are driven onwards by the irresistible stream
of solid ice; and when they arrive at a declivity of the mountain,
sufficiently rapid, roll down, scattering ruin. I saw one of these
rocks which had descended in the spring, (winter here is the
season of silence and safety) which measured forty feet in every
direction.

The verge of a glacier, like that of Bossons, presents the most
vivid image of desolation that it is possible to conceive. No one
dares to approach it; for the enormous pinnacles of ice which
perpetually fall, are perpetually reproduced. The pines of the
forest, which bound it at one extremity, are overthrown and
shattered to a wide extent at its base. There is something
inexpressibly dreadful in the aspect of the few branchless trunks,
which, nearest to the ice rifts, still stand in the uprooted soil.
The meadows perish, overwhelmed with sand and stones.
Within this last year, these glaciers have advanced three hundred
feet into the valley. Saussure, the naturalist, says that they have
their periods of increase and decay; the people of the country
hold an opinion entirely different; but as I judge, more probable.

It is agreed by all, that the snow on the summit of Mont Blanc and the neighbouring mountains perpetually augments, and that ice, in the form of glaciers, subsists without melting in the valley of Chamouni during its transient and variable summer. If the snow which produces this glacier must augment, and the heat of the valley is no obstacle to the perpetual existence of such masses of ice as have already descended into it, the consequence is obvious; the glaciers must augment and will subsist, at least until they have overflowed this vale.

I will not pursue Buffon's sublime but gloomy theory – that this globe which we inhabit will at some future period be changed into a mass of frost by the encroachments of the polar ice, and of that produced on the most elevated points of the earth. Do you, who assert the supremacy of Ahriman, imagine him throned among these desolating snows, among these palaces of death and frost, so sculptured in this their terrible magnificence by the adamantine hand of necessity, and that he casts around him, as the first essays of his final usurpation, avalanches, torrents, rocks, and thunders, and above all these deadly glaciers, at once the proof and symbols of his reign; – add to this, the degradation of the human species – who in these regions are half deformed idiotic, and most of whom are deprived of any thing that can excite interest or admiration. This is a part of the subject more mournful and less sublime; but such as neither the poet nor the philosopher should disdain to regard.

This morning we departed, on the promise of a fine day, to visit the glacier of Montanvert. In that part where it fills a slanting valley, it is called the Sea of Ice. This valley is 950 toises, or 7600 feet above the level of the sea. We had not proceeded far before the rain began to fall, but we persisted until we had accomplished more than half of our journey, when we returned, wet through.

NOTE This is Shelley's public version of his original letter to Peacock, from which it varies in punctuation and in a number of verbal details.

APPENDIX 3

Horace Smith, 'Ozymandias'

In Egypt's sandy silence, all alone,
Stands a gigantic Leg, which far off throws
The only shadow that the Desart knows: –
'I am great OZYMANDIAS,' saith the stone,
'The King of Kings; this mighty City shows
'The wonders of my hand.' – The City's gone, –
Nought but the Leg remaining to disclose
The site of this forgotten Babylon.

We wonder, – and some Hunter may express
Wonder like ours, when thro' the wilderness,
Where London stood, holding the Wolf in chace,
He meets some fragment huge, and stops to guess
What powerful but unrecorded race
Once dwelt in that annihilated place.

NOTE   This poem was later re-titled 'On a Stupendous Leg of Granite, Discovered Standing by Itself in the Deserts of Egypt, with the Inscription Inserted Below'.

APPENDIX 4

From Thomas Love Peacock, Nightmare Abbey *(1818)*

CHAPTER II

Shortly after the disastrous termination of Scythrop's passion for Miss Emily Girouette, Mr Glowry found himself, much against his will, involved in a lawsuit, which compelled him to dance attendance on the High Court of Chancery. Scythrop was left alone at Nightmare Abbey. He was a burnt child, and dreaded the fire of female eyes. He wandered about the ample pile, or along the garden-terrace, with 'his cogitative faculties immersed in cogibundity of cogitation.' The terrace terminated at the south-western tower, which, as we have said, was ruinous and full of owls. Here would Scythrop take his evening seat, on a fallen fragment of mossy stone, with his back resting against the ruined wall, – a thick canopy of ivy, with an owl in it, over his head, – and the Sorrows of Werter in his hand. He had some taste for romance reading before he went to the university, where, we must confess, in justice to his college, he was cured of the love of reading in all its shapes; and the cure would have been radical, if disappointment in love, and total solitude, had not conspired to bring on a relapse. He began to devour romances and German tragedies, and, by the recommendation of Mr Flosky, to pore over ponderous tomes of transcendental philosophy, which reconciled him to the labour of studying them by their mystical jargon and necromantic imagery. In the congenial solitude of Nightmare Abbey, the distempered ideas of metaphysical romance and romantic metaphysics had ample time and space to germinate into a fertile crop of chimeras, which rapidly shot up into vigorous and abundant vegetation.

He now became troubled with the *passion for reforming the world*. He built many castles in the air, and peopled them with secret tribunals, and bands of illuminati, who were always the imaginary instruments of his projected regeneration of the human species. As he intended to institute a perfect republic, he invested himself with absolute sovereignty over these mystical dispensers of liberty. He slept with Horrid Mysteries under his pillow, and dreamed of venerable eleutherarchs and ghastly confederates holding midnight conventions in subterranean caves. He passed whole mornings in his study, immersed in gloomy reverie, stalking about the room in his nightcap, which he pulled over his eyes like a cowl, and folding his striped calico dressing-gown about him like the mantle of a conspirator.

'Action,' thus he soliloquised, 'is the result of opinion, and to new-model opinion would be to new-model society. Knowledge is power; it is in the hands of a few, who employ it to mislead the many, for their own selfish purposes of aggrandisement and appreciation. What if it were in the hands of a few who should employ it to lead the many? What if it were universal, and the multitude were enlightened? No. The many must be always in leading-strings; but let them have wise and honest conductors. A few to think, and many to act; that is the only basis of perfect society. So thought the ancient philosophers: they had their esoterical and exoterical doctrines. So thinks the sublime Kant, who delivers his oracles in language which none but the initiated can comprehend. Such were the views of those secret associations of illuminati, which were the terror of superstition and tyranny, and which, carefully selecting wisdom and genius from the great wilderness of society, as the bee selects honey from the flowers of the thorn and the nettle, bound all human excellence in a chain, which, if it had not been prematurely broken, would have commanded opinion, and regenerated the world.'

Scythrop proceeded to meditate on the practicability of reviving a confederation of regenerators. To get a clear view of his own ideas, and to feel the pulse of the wisdom and genius of the age, he wrote and published a treatise, in which his meanings were carefully wrapt up in the monk's hood of transcendental technology, but filled with hints of matter deep and dangerous, which he thought would set the whole nation in a ferment; and he awaited the result in awful expectation, as a miner who has fired a train awaits the explosion of a rock. However, he listened and heard nothing; for the explosion, if any ensued, was not sufficiently loud to shake a single leaf of the ivy on the towers of Nightmare Abbey; and some months afterwards he received a letter from his bookseller, informing him that only seven copies had been sold, and concluding with a polite request for the balance.

Scythrop did not despair. 'Seven copies,' he thought, 'have been sold. Seven is a mystical number, and the omen is good. Let me find the seven purchasers of my seven copies, and they shall be the seven golden candle-sticks with which I will illuminate the world.'

Scythrop had a certain portion of mechanical genius, which his romantic projects tended to develope. He constructed models of cells and recesses, sliding panels and secret passages, that would have baffled the skill of the Parisian police. He took the opportunity of his father's absence to smuggle a dumb carpenter into the Abbey, and between them they gave reality to one of these models in Scythrop's tower. Scythrop foresaw that a great leader of human regeneration would be involved in fearful dilemmas, and determined, for the benefit of mankind in general, to adopt all possible precautions for the preservation of himself.

The servants, even the women, had been tutored into silence. Profound stillness reigned throughout and around the Abbey, except when the occasional shutting of a door would peal in long reverberations through the galleries, or the heavy tread of the pensive butler would wake the hollow echoes of the hall. Scythrop stalked about like the grand inquisitor, and the servants flitted past him like familiars. In his evening meditations on the terrace, under the ivy of the ruined tower, the only sounds that came to his ear were the rustling of the wind in the ivy, the plaintive voices of the feathered choristers, the owls, the occasional striking of the Abbey clock, and the monotonous dash of the sea on its low and level shore. In the mean time, he drank Madeira, and laid deep schemes for a thorough repair of the crazy fabric of human nature.

From   Robert Forsyth, The Principles of Moral Science (*1805*)

The degree in which it [the passion for reforming the world] at last fills the whole memory and thoughts, and the vehemence to which it gradually rises, prevent his perceiving that any means are extravagant or irrational which have the appearance of tending to promote its success . . . The danger is rather increased than diminished by the circumstance, that the most intelligent, accomplished, and energetic minds, are most apt to be seized by this passion. It is even apt to increase in retirement and amidst the pursuits of science; because temporary solitude and reflection are favourable to the strong discernment of what exalts and degrades our nature . . .

In times of public contention or alarm, when this passion is most apt to be excited, it is the duty of a virtuous man to recollect often, that human affairs are wisely and beneficiently administered, but so contrived, that their amelioration is slow and progressive, and that great good is never suddenly or violently accomplished. It is also his duty to render the passion we have now described unnecessary in his own mind, by acquiring that self-command which, on every occasion, may enable him to do his duty to society, without suffering himself either to be so much inflamed by opposition, or so much blinded by attachment to particular projects or notions, as to forget that force is not reason, that the edge of the sword introduces no light into the human mind, and that the certain and immediate commission of sanguinary actions can seldom be balanced by the doubtful prospect of future good.

At the upper end, supported on an elevated platform stands the temple of Jupiter. Under the colonnade of its portico we sate & pulled out our oranges & figs & bread & apples (sorry fare you will say) & rested to eat. There was a magnificent spectacle. Above & between the multitudinous shafts of the columns, was seen the blue sea reflecting the purple heaven of noon above it, & supporting as it were on its line the dark lofty mountains of Sorrento, of a blue inexpressibly deep, & tinged towards their summits with streaks of new-fallen snow. Between was one small green island. To the right was Capua, Inarime, Prochyta and Miseno. Behind was the single summit of Vesuvius rolling forth volumes of thick white smoke whose foamlike column was sometimes darted into the clear dark sky & fell in little streaks along the wind. Between Vesuvius & the nearer mountains, as thro a chasm was seen the main line of the loftiest Apennines to the east. The day was radiant & warm. Every now & then we heard the subterranean thunder of Vesuvius; its distant deep peals seemed to shake the very air & light of day which interpenetrated our frames with the sullen & tremendous sound. This scene was what the Greeks beheld. (Pompeii you know was a Greek city.) They lived in harmony with nature, & the interstices of their incomparable columns, were portals as it were to admit the spirit of beauty which animates this glorious universe to visit those whom it inspired. If such is Pompeii, what was Athens? what scene was exhibited from its Acropolis? The Parthenon and the temples of Hercules & Theseus & the Winds? The islands of the Ægean Sea, the mountains of Argolis & the peaks of Pindus & Olympus, & the darkness of the Beotian forests interspersed? ... On each side of the road beyond the gate are built the tombs. How unlike ours! They seem not so much hiding places for that which must decay as voluptuous chamber[s] for immortal spirits. They are of marble radiantly white, & two especially beautiful are loaded with exquisite bas reliefs. On the stucco wall which incloses them are little emblematic figures of a relief exceedingly low, of dead or dying animals & little winged genii, & female forms bending in groupes in some funeral office. The higher reliefs, represent one a nautical subject & the other a bacchanalian one. Within the cell, stand the cinerary urns, sometimes one, sometimes more. It is said that paintings were found within, which are now – as has been every thing moveable in Pompeii – removed & scattered about in Royal Museums. These tombs were the most impressive things of all. The wild woods surround them on either side and along the broad stones of the paved road which divides them, you hear the late leaves of autumn shiver & rustle in the stream of the inconstant wind as it were like the step of ghosts. The radiance & magnificence of these dwellings of the dead, the white freshness of the scarcely finished marble, the impassioned or imaginative life of the figures which adorn them contrast strangely with the simplicity of the houses of those who were living when Vesuvius overwhelmed their city. I have forgotten the Amphitheatre, which is of great magnitude, tho' much inferior to the Coliseum. – I now understand why the Greeks were such great Poets, & above all I can account, it seems to me, for the harmony the unity the perfection the uniform excellence of all their works of art. They lived in a perpetual commerce with external nature and nourished themselves upon the spirit of its forms. Their theatres were all open to the mountains & the sky. Their columns that ideal type of a sacred forest with its roof of interwoven tracery admitted the light & wind, the odour & the freshness of the country penetrated the cities. Their temples were mostly upaithric; & the flying clouds the stars or the deep sky were seen above. O, but for that series of wretched wars which terminated in the Roman conquest of the world, but for the Christian religion which put a finishing stroke to the antient system; but for those changes which conducted Athens to its ruin, to what an eminence might not humanity have arrived!

Two Ballads on Peterloo

1   John Stafford, 'Peterloo'

On the Sixteenth day of August, it was held at Peterloo,
A just and lawful meeting we knew it to be true,
With flags and caps of liberty they did assemble there,
Both in peace and good order, the reformers did appear.

The stage was erected and reformers stood all round,
A space was only left between for tyrants and blood hounds,
The constables and vampires they came to rule the day,
Stand steady men, stand steady and their truncheons play'd
   away.

Your flags and caps of liberty we'll entirely take away,
We'll cut all down before us and show you tyrants play,
For we know you are unarmed, and we'll murder all we can,
Both men, women and children, in spite of 'Rights of Man'.

From Smedley cottage to the hustings, it was crowded all the
   way.
The patriots joined hand in hand, the band did sweetly play,
Not the least thoughts of murder that did commence that day,
Until that cruel action on Peterloo did sway.

The brave champion of reform, when the hustings mounted on,
He fill'd them all with joy, for to see that valiant man,
To see that gallant hero, with courage bold so fair,
He won the heart of every working-man was there.

The patriots agreed that the champion took the chair,
When he saw female reformers, he smil'd at them being there,
But before he had address'd them all, there came that hellish
   crew
To murder all poor people that were come to Peterloo.

With their glittering swords and carbines to kill unarmed men
They are worse than Algerines, when strangers meet with them
For they've murdered their own neighbours, that striv'd to fill
   their purse,
And now they're half-naked must be trampled down with horse.

They form'd themselves four deep, three times over made a
   charge,
But reformers they stood firm, so they could not play at large
Until a space was opened occupied by their own crew,
For to murder all poor people that were come to Peterloo.

From the outside to the hustings, those ruffians cut away,
I've a charge against you Mr Hunt, one of the crew did say,
I am ready now to join you, I'm just at your command,
So they took him to the New Bailey, as before it had been
   plan'd.

Some flags and caps of liberty, these ruffians did destroy,
But still a valiant female her colour she did fly,
Till she could no longer hold it, amongst that murdering crew
So she fell down amongst the rest on the plains of Peterloo.

A poor woman struggling with an infant in her arms,
One of the crew came riding up for to destroy her charms,
She said spare my little creature but that butcher cut her too,
And left her with her infant bleeding on the Plains of Peterloo.

An old woman hearing this story, and believing it was true,
She went to seek her son that was gone to Peterloo,
And as she went along the street, a ruffian she did meet.
She knew him from a child, – she had liv'd in the same street.

This old woman spoke right kindly, and she call'd him by his
   name,
I know you will not hurt me, Thomas Shelberdine, she said,
But to fulfil his orders like the rest of the same crew,
He cut her down that instant as they did at Peterloo.

So now you special constables, I'll give you all your due,
For backing those proceedings that were done at Peterloo,
Both landlords and shopkeepers, your doors I'll pass by,
If you had no swords or carabines, you made your truncheons
   fly.

So come all you brave patriots wherever that you be,
You must all unite together to gain your liberty,
And not forget those tyrants, but with justice them pursue,
And all such cruel murderers that went to Peterloo.

NOTE   John Stafford was a weaver from Ashton-under-Lyne. 'Peterloo'
was intended to be sung to 'Green upon the Cape', which may be a
variant title for 'The Plains of Waterloo'. This text is derived from Roy
Palmer, *The Sound of History: Songs and Social Comment* (Oxford
and New York, 1988).

2   The Answer to Peter-Loo

On the sixteenth day of August, eighteen hundred and nineteen,
All in the town of Manchester the REBELLY CREW were seen,
They call themselves reformers, and by Hunt the traitor true,
To attend a treason meeting on the plains of Peter-Loo.

Those hearers at their patron's call came flocking into town,
Both Male and Female radical, and many a gapeing clown,
Some came without their breakfast, which made their bellies
    rue;
But got a warm baggin on the plains of Peter-Loo.

From Stayley-Bridge they did advance with a band of music fine,
And brought a cap of liberty from Ashton-under-lyne;
There was Macclesfield and Stockport lads, and Oldham roug-
    heads too,
Came to hear the treason sermon preached by Hunt at Peter-
    Loo.

About the hour of one o'clock this champion took the chair,
Surrounded by his aid-de-camps, his orders for to hear,
And disperse them through that REBELLY MOB, which around
    his standard drew;
But they got their jackets dusted on the plains of Peter-Loo.

They hoisted up treason caps and flags, as plainly you may
    see, –
And with loud acclamations shouted Hunt and liberty;
They swore no man should spoil their plan, but well our Yeomen
    knew;

They assembled in St James's Square, and marched for Peter-
    Loo.

The Rochdale band of music, with harmony sublime,
Had placed themselves convenient to amuse Hunt's concubine;
But soon their big drum head was broke, all by our Yeomen
    true;
They dropped their instruments, and run away from Peter-Loo.

When the Yeomen did advance the mob began to fly,
Some thousands of old hats and clogs behind them there did lie;
They soon pulled down their *Treason Flags*, and numbers of
    them flew;
And Hunt they took a prisoner on the plains of Peter-Loo.

Now Hunt is taken prisoner and sent to Lancaster gaol,
With seven of his foremost men, their sorrows to bewail;
His mistress sent to the hospital her face for to renew,
For she got it closely shaven on the plains of Peter-Loo.

Success attend those warlike men, our Yeomen Volunteers,
And all their Gallant Officers who knows no dread or fears,
Likewise the *Irish Trumpeter*, that loud his trumpet blew,
And took a cap of liberty from them at Peter-Loo.

Now to conclude and make an end, here's a health to GEORGE
    our KING,
And all those Gallant Yeomanry whose praises I loudly sing;
May Magistrates and Constables with zeal their duty do;
And may they prove victorious upon every Peter-Loo.

APPENDIX 7

***

Letter to John and Maria Gisborne

Pisa, 26 May 1820

My dear friends

I write to you thus early, because I have determined to accept of your kind offer about the correction of Prometheus. The bookseller makes difficulties about sending the proofs to me, & to whom else can I so well entrust what I am so much interested in having done well, & to whom would I prefer to owe the recollection of an additional kindness done to me? I enclose you two little papers of corrections & additions; – I do not think you will find any difficulty in interpolating them into the proper places. –

Well how do [you] like London, & your journey, the Alps in their beauty & their eternity – Paris in its slight & transitory colours, & the wearisome plains of France, & the *moral* people with whom you drank tea last night? Above all, *how* are you? And of this last question believe me we are now most anxiously waiting for a reply – until which I will say nothing, nor ask anything – I rely on [your] journal, with as much security as if it were already written.

I am just returned from a visit to Leghorn Casciano, & your old fortress at St Elmo – I bought the vases you saw for about 20 sequins less than Micale asked, & had them packed up, & by the polite assistance of your friend Mr Guebhard sent them on board. I found your Giuseppe very useful in all this business – He got me tea & breakfast, & I slept in your house & departed early the next morning to Casciano. Every thing seems in excellent order at Casa Ricci – garden pigeons tables chairs & beds – As I did not find my bed sealed up, I left it as I found it. What a glorious prospect you had from the windows of St Elmo! The enormous chain of the Apennines, with its many folded ridges islanded in the misty distance of the air, the sea, so immensely distant appearing as at your feet, & the prodigious expanse of the plain of Pisa, & the dark green marshes lessened almost to a strip by the height of the blue mountains overhanging them – then the wild & unreclaimed fertility of the foreground, & the chesnut trees whose vivid foliage made a sort of resting place to the sense before it darted itself to the jagged horizon of this prospect – I was altogether delighted – I had a respite from my nervous symptoms which was compensated to me by a violent cold in the head. – There was a tradition about you at St Elmo – *An English family that lived here in the time of the French*. The Doctor too at the Bagni knew you. The House is now in a most dilapidated condition, but I suppose all that is curable –

We go to the Bagni next month – but still direct to Pisa as safest. – I shall write you the *ultimates* of my commission in my next letter. – I am undergoing a course of the Pisa baths, on which I lay no singular stress, – but they soothe. I ought to have peace of mind – leisure tranquillity; this I expect soon – Our anxiety about Godwin is very great, & any information that you can give a day or two earlier than he might, respecting any decisive event in his lawsuit would be a great relief. Your impressions about Godwin (I speak especially to Madonna mia, who had known him before) will especially interest me – You know, that although I believe he is the only sincere enemy I have in the world, that added years only add to my admiration of his intellectual powers, & even the moral resources of his character. – Of my other friends I say nothing – To see Hunt, is to like him – and there is one other recommendation which he has to you, he is my friend – . To know Hogg, (if anyone can know him) is to know something very unlike & inexpressibly superior to the great mass of men. –

Will Henry write me an adamantine letter, flowing not like the words of Sophocles with honey, but molten brass & iron, & bristling with wheels & teeth? I saw his steamboat asleep under the walls. I was afraid to waken it & ask it whether it was dreaming of him for the same reason that I w$^{d.}$ have refrained from waking Ariadne after Theseus had left her – unless I had been Bacchus. –

Affectionately & anxiously yours,

P.B.S.

From *Thomas Love Peacock*, The Four Ages of Poetry
(*1820*)

A poet in our times is a semi-barbarian in a civilized community.
He lives in the days that are past. His ideas, thoughts, feelings,
associations, are all with barbarous manners, obsolete customs,
and exploded superstitions. The march of his intellect is like
that of a crab, backward. The brighter the light diffused around
him by the progress of reason, the thicker is the darkness of
antiquated barbarism, in which he buries himself like a mole, to
throw up the barren hillocks of his Cimmerian labours. The
philosophic mental tranquillity which looks round with an equal
eye on all external things, collects a store of ideas, discriminates
their relative value, assigns to all their proper place, and from
the materials of useful knowledge thus collected, appreciated,
and arranged, forms new combinations that impress the stamp
of their power and utility on the real business of life, is
diametrically the reverse of that frame of mind which poetry
inspires, or from which poetry can emanate. The highest inspi-
rations of poetry are resolvable into three ingredients: the rant
of unregulated passion, the whining of exaggerated feeling, and
the cant of factitious sentiment: and can therefore serve only to
ripen a splendid lunatic like Alexander, a puling driveller like
Werter, or a morbid dreamer like Wordsworth. It can never
make a philosopher, nor a statesman, nor in any class of life an
useful or rational man. It cannot claim the slightest share in any
one of the comforts and utilities of life of which we have
witnessed so many and so rapid advances. But though not
useful, it may be said it is highly ornamental, and deserves to be
cultivated for the pleasure it yields. Even if this be granted, it
does not follow that a writer of poetry in the present state of
society is not a waster of his own time, and a robber of that of
others. Poetry is not one of those arts which, like painting,

require repetition and multiplication, in order to be diffused among society. There are more good poems already existing than are sufficient to employ that portion of life which any mere reader and recipient of poetical impressions should devote to them, and these having been produced in poetical times, are far superior in all the characteristics of poetry to the artificial reconstructions of a few morbid ascetics in unpoetical times. To read the promiscuous rubbish of the present time to the exclusion of the select treasures of the past, is to substitute the worse for the better variety of the same mode of enjoyment.

But in whatever degree poetry is cultivated, it must necessarily be to the neglect of some branch of useful study: and it is a lamentable spectacle to see minds, capable of better things, running to seed in the specious indolence of these empty aimless mockeries of intellectual exertion. Poetry was the mental rattle that awakened the attention of intellect in the infancy of civil society: but for the maturity of mind to make a serious business of the playthings of its childhood, is as absurd as for a full-grown man to rub his gums with coral, and cry to be charmed to sleep by the jingle of silver bells.

As to that small portion of our contemporary poetry, which is neither descriptive, nor narrative, nor dramatic, and which, for want of a better name, may be called ethical, the most distinguished portion of it, consisting merely of querulous, egotistical rhapsodies, to express the writer's high dissatisfaction with the world and every thing in it, serves only to confirm what has been said of the semi-barbarous character of poets, who from singing dithyrambics and 'Io Triumphe,' while society was savage, grow rabid, and out of their element, as it becomes polished and enlightened.

Now when we consider that it is not the thinking and studious, and scientific and philosophical part of the community, not to those whose minds are bent on the pursuit and promotion of permanently useful ends and aims, that poets must address their minstrelsy, but to that much larger portion of the reading public, whose minds are not awakened to the desire of valuable knowledge, and who are indifferent to any thing beyond being charmed, moved, excited, affected, and exalted: charmed by harmony, moved by sentiment, excited by passion, affected by pathos, and exalted by sublimity: harmony, which is language on the rack of Procrustes; sentiment, which is canting egotism in the mask of refined feeling; passion, which is the commotion of a weak and selfish mind; pathos, which is the whining of an unmanly spirit; and sublimity, which is the inflation of an empty head: when we consider that the great and permanent interests of human society become more and more the main spring of intellectual pursuit; that in proportion as they become so, the subordinacy of the ornamental to the useful will be more and more seen and acknowledged; and that therefore the progress of useful art and science, and of moral and political knowledge, will continue more and more to withdraw attention from frivolous and unconducive, to solid and conducive studies: that therefore the poetical audience will not only continually diminish in the proportion of its number to that of the rest of the reading public, but will also sink lower and lower in the comparison of intellectual acquirement: when we consider that the poet must still please his audience, and must therefore continue to sink to their level, while the rest of the community is rising above it: we may easily conceive that the day is not distant, when the degraded state of every species of poetry will be as generally recognized as that of dramatic poetry has long been: and this not from any decrease either of intellectual power, or intellectual acquisition, but because intellectual power and intellectual acquisition have turned themselves into other and better channels, and have abandoned the cultivation and the fate of poetry to the degenerate fry of modern rhymesters, and their olympic judges, the magazine critics, who continue to debate and promulgate oracles about poetry, as if it were still what it was in the Homeric age, the all-in-all of intellectual progression, and as if there were no such things in existence as mathematicians, astronomers, chemists, moralists, metaphysicians, historians, politicians, and political economists, who have built into the upper air of intelligence a pyramid, from the summit of which they see the modern Parnassus far beneath them, and, knowing how small a place it occupies in the comprehensiveness of their prospect, smile at the little ambition and the circumscribed perceptions with which the drivellers and mountebanks upon it are contending for the poetical palm and the critical chair.

SHELLEY AND HIS CRITICS

The reviews & journals they say continue to attack me, but I value neither the fame they can give, nor the fame they can take away, therefore blessed be the name of the Reviews.[1]

In his lifetime and in the years immediately following his death in 1822, Shelley's detractors and disparagers predominated over those who praised him, or appraised him impartially; but, although the picture is coloured by partial readings of him, it is parti-coloured as well as party-coloured.[2] Shelley's contemporary reviewers show in the main how he was misunderstood or misrepresented, how mistakes were made, and lies were told. Those few reviewers who tried to give Shelley fame in his own time have been vindicated in their attempt by Shelley's standing in our own time. But even the many reviewers who tried to take fame away from Shelley – in their subjection to oppositional partisanship or antipathetic prejudice—now can only add a further dimension of objectifying definition and definiteness to that fame. They provide an index of the range of arguments about Shelley that have gone on and go on being argued. They often anticipate and sometimes even pre-empt the criticism of the following century and a half. Although there are, of course, changes of focus in that criticism, many of its preoccupations are continuous or recurrent concerns, so that as much as there may be progression in that criticism, there are also regular regressions and repeated repetitions. That does not mean that there is nothing new to discover about Shelley or that old questions do not need to be answered again.[3]

The Contemporary Reviews

The earliest works of Shelley that were reviewed were the volume of verse, *Original Poetry by Victor and Cazire* (1810), and the two romances *Zastrossi* (1810) and *St Irvyne, or The Rosicrucian* (1810).

More interesting than these early reviews is a very much later review of Shelley's philosophical and political pamphlets *The Necessity of Atheism* (1811) and *Declaration of Rights* (1812): its judgement of Shelley – made, by chance, shortly before 'Shelley's death – is as a writer who seriously threatens the *ancien régime* in Britain.

For 'the first of these performances', as the reviewer observes, 'Shelley was expelled from college'; for 'posting up the second on the walls of a provincial town, his servant was imprisoned'. This unsigned review in the *Brighton Magazine* selected these two works 'as with them he commenced his literary career'.[4] Furthermore they were 'extraordinary, not as an effort of genius, but as indications of that bold and daring insubordination of mind, which led the writer, at a very early age, to trample both on human and divine authority'. From the facts of the pamphlets' effects – expulsion and arrest – some readers 'may perhaps imagine that they are remarkably effective engines of atheism and democracy', but 'they rather insult than support the bad cause to which they are devoted'. The reviewer finds justification, however, for looking at 'this extravagant freak of his boyhood' in the fact that his 'subsequent writings . . . at a matured period of his life, avowed the same sentiments, and obtruded them upon the world with an effrontery unexampled in the annals of impiety'. The reviewer denies the possibility of a rational atheism: the 'splendours of a poetical imagination' such as Shelley's 'may dazzle and delight, and they may prove a mighty engine of mischief to many who have more fancy than judgment', but 'they will never efface the impression from our minds that Atheism is an inhuman, bloody, and ferocious system . . . it wages war with Heaven, and with earth: its first object is to dethrone God; its next to destroy man'.

As Newman Ivey White suggests, the fact that the *Brighton Magazine* 'turns back ten years and devotes five pages to a 'review' of these two works 'is striking evidence that in 1822 the conservative press regarded Shelley seriously and hesitated at nothing to discredit him'.[5]

The preoccupations and procedures of this review epitomize the recurrent attempts to discredit Shelley during his lifetime and afterwards by, on the one hand, denying him his effectiveness as a thinker, and, on the other hand, indicting him for the possible effects of his philosophical and political thinking. With or without the specificity of a concern with blasphemy and sedition, the charge that Shelley is characterized by 'a strange perversion of understanding, which renders him incapable of comprehending the laws of evidence, and the principles of right and reason'[6] is perhaps the commonest charge against him: certainly, it is brought against him again and again. And, if it is conceded that Shelley may 'dazzle' the reader, the concession is usually accompanied by the annulling of Shelley's intelligence in the charge that he 'dazzled' himself.

Queen Mab (1813)

The Necessity of Atheism reappeared in a modified and expanded form as one of Shelley's 'Notes' to *Queen Mab*.[7] For more than twenty years after Shelley's death, *Queen Mab* was very much more frequently printed than any other of his works; but, during his lifetime, 'circulation of the poem was certainly minimal'.[8]

In the years immediately following its first publication, it drew little notice, with the exception of a series of letters signed 'F', reviewing it in *The Theological Inquirer, or Polemical Magazine* in 1815.[9] The reviewer declares:

> I would send you a copy to reprint in your journal; but am afraid notwithstanding the freedom, candour, and impartiality you seem to aim at, that you would be intimidated from the publication, as our press is at present too much shackled to give vent to the many important truths it contains.

The review is primarily descriptive and illustrative, quoting extensively but evasively from the poem and commenting almost exclusively on its 'sublime strain of exclamation', and its 'vivid beauties of poetry'. Occasionally, there are hints of something more substantial and disturbing: 'the records of mighty nations, fallen beneath the mad blow of the conqueror's ambition; or decayed by the consumptive influence of moral corruption'.

When he writes of Ahasuerus, the Wandering Jew, the reviewer is especially cautious and circumspect, avoiding any account of Ahasuerus' bitter speech.[10] However, when he summarizes his own procedures, he is explicit about his inexplicitness and his concern with the poetry rather than the poet's opinions:

> If, in this division of the poem, which describes the systems of the present, I have confined myself to extracts characteristic, by their power of fancy and beauty of description, of the author's ability as a poet; and have not produced those indications that he is a philosopher of the first rank, with which the volume abounds, it must be attributed to the boldness of his sentiments, which, in this country, where the freedom of the press is little more than an empty name, it would be hazardous to disseminate.

The reviewer's purpose is more radical than this might suggest: he is convinced that the effect of his selection of extracts will be such 'that the energies of resolution will be impelled with increased force to the accomplishment of that great object the complete freedom of the press in matters of public opinion'. And in his closing comments on 'the copious and elegant notes to the poem' and on the poet's distinctive propensity 'to soar to other and nobler objects than the domes of superstition and the heaven of priestly invention', it is discernibly the reviewer's design to call the attention of his readers to the poem's 'important truths'.

Further reviews of *Queen Mab* follow the 1821 printing of a pirated edition of the poem, published in London by William Clarke, who was arrested and imprisoned, not because of his piracy, but because of the poem. An unsigned review in the *London Magazine and Theatrical Inquisitor*[11] scrupulously concerns itself only 'with the poetical merits of the work':

> With the speculative tenets of the writer we shall not intermeddle. If his opinions are palpably absurd and false, they must fall by their own absurdity and falsehood; and discussion could serve no other purpose than to invest them with an importance they do not intrinsically possess.

The reviewer also 'utterly' disclaims 'the private scandal from which some critics have borrowed pungency and attraction for their disquisitions': 'we can neither conceive its connection with criticism, nor its propriety from the pen of a reviewer'. This is not a reformist subterfuge but serves a seemingly genuine attempt by the reviewer to resist the tendencies of reactionary partiality. And the reviewer neither misrepresents nor underestimates 'the poetical merits of the work':

The prominent features of Mr Shelley's poetical character are energy and depth. He has not the tenderness and delicacy of some living poets, nor the fertile and soaring imagination of others. . . . But he has an intense and overwhelming energy of manner, and if he does not present us with many original conceptions, his turn of thought, as well as his expression, is strongly indicative of original genius. We apprehend, indeed, that the peculiar charm of Shelley's writing is derived from the complete conviction which he evidently entertains of the justness and importance of all he asserts . . . He constantly communicates to his readers the impression made upon his own mind, and gives it, even in our apprehension, all the vividness and strength with which it struck his own fancy. His figures, it is true, are often disproportioned, often terrific; but they burst upon us from the canvas in all the energy of life and motion. This gives interest to his sketches, even where the colouring is coarse, and the drawing deficient in exactitude.

The reviewer admits 'that the poem possesses many of the faults of a young writer'; but, more particularly, 'a few of the affectations of that school with which the author has been classed, but from whose restrictions we trust he will soon completely emancipate himself'. This is not the usual coarse-grained attack of the Tory reviewers on the so-called 'Cockney School' of poets – that circle of young writers, including Shelley and Keats, which were gathered together and published by Leigh Hunt, editor of the radical *Examiner*, but something both more judicious and more pointed to poetic ends. The reviewer ends by sternly warning Shelley that

he will not fulfil his destiny by contracting himself within the narrow limits of a circle of friends, whose standard of literary excellence is regulated by certain conventional ideas peculiar to themselves. It is not thus that his writings will acquire that extension and permanence that alone can render them truly beneficial to mankind, and productive of immortality to their author.

Illustrative of the more usual tenor of those critics who, although ready to concede some poetic excellence to Shelley, do so only to add further to their condemnation, is the unsigned review from the *Literary Gazette and Journal of Belles Lettres*:[12]

Shelley's genius . . . is doubtless of a high order; but when we look at the purposes to which it is directed . . . our souls revolt with tenfold horror at the energy it exhibits, and we feel as if one of the darkest of the fiends had been clothed with a human body, to enable him to gratify his enmity against the human race, and as if the supernatural atrocity of his hate were only heightened by his power to do injury.

The reviewer, however, seems to have no scruples about his own power to do injury:

> it is a frightful supposition, that his own life may have been a fearful commentary upon his principles – principles, which in the balance of law and justice, happily deprived him of the superintendence of his infants, while they plunged an unfortunate wife and mother into ruin, prostitution, guilt and suicide.

Although the reviewer recognizes 'great beauty' and 'genuine poetry' in *Queen Mab*, his final hope is that the 'impious volume' 'be allowed to fall into oblivion with all its deep pollutions and horrid blasphemies'.

Wiliam Bengo Collyer's review of *Queen Mab* in an essay written after Shelley's death, 'Licentious Productions in High Life', which also attacked Byron's *Don Juan* and *Cain*,[13] indicts the poem as 'nine cantos of blasphemy and impiety, such as we never thought that any one, on the outside of bedlam, could have uttered'. Worse than the poem are its notes, which 'as far as their delicacy and morality are concerned, form, in our opinion, the most dangerous part of this wicked and dangerous book, for they are more intelligible than the poem'.

Alastor; or The Spirit of Solitude, and Other Poems (1816)

An unsigned notice in the *Monthly Review, or Literary Journal*[14] 'must candidly own that these poems are beyond our comprehension', and the reviewer observes that Shelley 'appears to be a poet "whose eye, in a fine phrenzy rolling" seeks only such objects as are "above this visible diurnal sphere"'.

He entreats Shelley 'for the sake of his reviewers as well as of his other readers (if he has any), to subjoin in his next publication . . . a glossary, and copious notes, illustrative of his allusions and explanatory of his meaning'.

An unsigned review in the *British Critic*[15] begins apparently with the same quotation from Shakespeare in mind as had come to the mind of the previous reviewer, in suggesting that if Shelley 'is not blessed with the inspiration, he may at least console himself with the madness of a poetic mind'. Having 'been often condemned to pore over much profound and prosing stupidity', the reviewer is 'therefore not a little delighted with the nonsense which mounts, which rises, which spurns the earth, and all its dull realities'.

Another unsigned review (by Josiah Conder)[16] is also intent on showing up Shelley as a writer of nonsense in his undecipherable allegory: 'All is wild and specious, untangible and incoherent as a dream.' Conder's summary account of the poem shows that he understands it distinctly enough, though he sees it as merely illustrating what it aims to exhibit:

> The poem is adapted to show the dangerous, the fatal tendency of that morbid ascendancy of the imagination over the other faculties, which incapacitates the mind for bestowing an adequate attention on the real objects of this 'work-day' life, and for discharging the relative and social duties. It exhibits the utter uselessness of imagination, when wholly undisciplined and selfishly employed for the mere purposes of intellectual luxury, without reference to those moral ends to which it was designed to be subservient.

Shelley 'has genius which might be turned to better account', 'but such heartless fictions as *Alastor*, fail in accomplishing the legitimate purposes of poetry'.

Leigh Hunt, in an essay on 'Young Poets' (Shelley, John Hamilton Reynolds, and Keats) in the *Examiner*,[17] marks the beginning of a long-sustained public praise, interpretation and defence of Shelley, which lasts throughout Shelley's life and for many years after his death. Hunt's noticing of these writers enlists them into 'a new school of poetry rising of late'. He acknowledges:

> In fact it is wrong to call it a new school, and still more so to represent it as one of innovation, its only object being to restore the same love of Nature, and of *thinking* instead of mere *talking*, which formerly rendered us real poets, and not merely versifying wits, and bead-rollers of couplets.

However, his polemical espousal of the cause of these poets, and his attachment of their cause to his own, initially did nothing to enhance their individual distinction or their reputations, and led *Blackwood's Magazine* to deride them as the 'Cockney School'.

The *Alastor* volume was the earliest of Shelley's to be reviewed by *Blackwood's Edinburgh Magazine*,[18] but the review itself is a late one, later than *Blackwood*'s reviews of both *The Revolt of Islam* and *Rosalind and Helen*. The reviewer believes that readers, 'struck by the power and splendour' of the one volume already reviewed and 'by the frequent tenderness and pathos' of the other, 'will be glad to observe some of the earliest efforts of a mind destined, in our opinion, under due discipline and self-management, to achieve great things in poetry'.

The main purpose of the review is not to comment on or criticise the poem, but to 'say a few words about the treatment which Mr Shelley has, in his poetical character, received from the public'. The particular focus of this concern is the reviewer of *The Revolt of Islam* for the *Quarterly Review*, who 'does not show himself a man of such lofty principles as to entitle him to ride the high horse in company with the author of *The Revolt of Islam*'.

On the contrary, he disqualifies himself, as 'a dunce rating a man of genius':

> If he does know that Mr Shelley is a great poet, what manner of man is he who, with such conviction, brings himself, with the utmost difficulty, to admit that there is any beauty at all in Mr Shelley's writings, and is happy to pass that admission off with an accidental and niggardly phrase of vague and valueless commendation. This is manifest and mean – glaring and gross injustice on the part of a man who comes forward as the champion of morality, truth, faith, and religion ... nor will any man who loves and honours genius, even though that genius may have occasionally suffered itself to be both stained and led astray, think but with contempt and indignation and scorn of a critic who, while he pretends to wield the weapons of honour, virtue, and truth, yet clothes himself in the armour of deceit, hypocrisy, and falsehood.

This is a fine tribute from an adherent to the party so opposed to the interests Shelley espoused: but, then, the generosity of critical estimation and a declared willingness to pardon Shelley his 'extravagance and error' and 'even more serious transgressions' involve an underestimation of the seriousness with which Shelley transgressed, and constitute an attitude characteristic of a species of apparently tolerant but actually complacent Toryism:

> There are many wicked and foolish things in Mr Shelley's creed, and we have not hitherto scrupled, nor shall we henceforth scruple to expose that wickedness and that folly. But we do not think that

he believes his own creed – at least, that he believes it fully, and to utter conviction – and we doubt not but the scales will yet all fall from his eyes.

To think that Shelley does not believe his own creed – fully, and to utter conviction – and to doubt not that one day the scales will fall from his eyes is to be blinded by prejudice to both the strength and integrity of Shelley's creed and the authority and clairvoyance of the arguments which sustained it.

The Revolt of Islam (1818)

Leigh Hunt reviewed *The Revolt of Islam* in the *Examiner* early in 1818.[19] His primary concern with the poem was to remark 'on the particular qualities of its poetry, and on the deep social interests upon which it speculates'.

In Hunt's view, Shelley's opinion 'that the world is a very beautiful one externally, but wants a good deal of mending with respect to its mind and habits', for which purpose Shelley would 'quash as many cold and selfish passions as possible, and rouse up the general element of Love, till it set our earth rolling more harmoniously' is likely to draw the charge that 'he is idly aiming at perfection'. But Hunt states that Shelley 'has no such aim', and the charge itself 'in truth, is only the first answer which egotism makes to anyone who thinks he can go beyond its own ideas of the possible'. Hunt's purpose in 'noticing these objections' is to clear obstruction away from the progress of Shelley's opinions, which

would have men, instead of worshipping tyrannies and terrors of any sort, worship goodness and gladness, diminish the vices and sorrows made by custom only, encourage the virtues and enjoyments which mutual benevolence may realize; and in short, make the best and utmost of this world, as well as hope for another.

For Hunt 'the beauties of the poem consist in depth of sentiment, in grandeur of imagery, and a versification remarkably sweet, various, and noble'; and Shelley's defects as poet are 'obscurity ... and too great a sameness and gratuitousness of image and metaphor too drawn from the elements, particularly the sea'. Hunt's sense is that the poem 'is full of humanity', but 'does not go the best way to work of appealing to it [...] through the medium of its common knowledge'; in his opinion, it 'cannot possibly become popular'. But, he has no doubt that

Shelley 'is destined to be one of the leading spirits of his age, and indeed has already fallen into his place as such'.

John Gibson Lockhart reviewed *The Revolt of Islam* in *Blackwood's Edinburgh Magazine*.[20] Voltaire, in his view, had rendered himself 'utterly and entirely contemptuous' by combining in his own person a 'pernicious system of opinion concerning man and his moral government, a superficial audacity of unbelief, an overflowing abundance of uncharitableness towards almost the whole of his race, and a disagreeable measure of assurance and self-conceit'. Shelley, in 'devoting himself to the same pernicious purposes' as 'those wretched sophists of the present day, who would fain attempt to lift the load of oppressing infamy from off the memory of Voltaire', risks being branded with 'inexpiable execration', 'but he possesses the qualities of a powerful and vigorous intellect, and therefore his fate cannot be sealed so speedily as theirs'. Although he is also of the 'Cockney School', 'the base opinions of the sect have not as yet been able entirely to obscure in him the privileges of the genius born with him'.

The poem itself 'bears unfortunately the clearest marks of the author's execrable system, but is impressed every where with the more noble and majestic footsteps of his genius'.

The 'perverted power' of the poem, and its obscurity will 'prevent *The Revolt of Islam* from ever becoming any thing like a favourite with the multitude'; but, 'having entered our general protest at the creed of the author', Lockhart is ready 'to attend to nothing but the vehicle' in which Shelley's beliefs are conveyed:

> As a philosopher, our author is weak and worthless; – our business is with him as a poet, and as such, he is strong, nervous, original, well entitled to take his place near to the great creative masters, whose works have shed its truest glory around the age wherein we live.

Lockhart then outlines the 'main drift' of the narrative, finding that 'it is in the portraying of ... intense, overmastering, unfearing, unfading love, that Mr Shelley has proved himself to be a great poet'.

Although some of the grounds for Lockhart's scrupulousness are other than literary considerations – that 'Mr Shelley, whatever his errors may have been, is a scholar, a gentleman, and a poet' suggests in its second term of praise precisely what Lockhart means by 'the privileges of the genius born with him' and why he advises Shelley that he 'has it in his power to select better companions' than Leigh Hunt and 'Johnny Keats' – Lockhart is a literary critic of precise and careful judgement.

John Taylor Coleridge's review in the *Quarterly Review*[21] of both *Laon and Cythna* and *The Revolt of Islam* is one of the most malevolent reviews that Shelley received in his lifetime, despite the deceptively moderate tone in which it is couched. Although he finds Shelley 'the least pernicious' of the sect whose doctrines he carries to greatest length, since the 'naiveté and openness in his manner of laying down the most extravagant positions . . . in some measure deprives them of their venom', he is 'sorry to say' that Shelley's intention is 'in sober earnest': 'with perfect deliberation and the steadiest perseverance he perverts all the gifts of his nature, and does all the injury, both public and private, which his faculties enable him to perpetrate'.

Coleridge observes that *The Revolt of Islam* is 'the same poem' as *Laon and Cythna* (which Shelley had withdrawn from publication) 'with a new name and a few slight alterations', in which 'he has reproduced the same poison, a little, and but a little, more cautiously disguised'. He is bound to say that the poem 'is not without beautiful passages': Shelley 'is an unsparing imitator', drawing 'largely on the rich stores' of the 'mountain poet', Wordsworth,

> to whose religious mind it must be matter, we think, of perpetual sorrow to see the philosophy which comes pure and holy from his pen, degraded and perverted, as it continually is, by this miserable crew of atheists or pantheists, who have just sense enough to abuse its terms, but neither heart nor principle to comprehend its import, or follow its application.

Coleridge suggests that, 'as in most schemes of reform, it is easier to say what is to be removed and destroyed, than what is to be put in its place':

> 'Love', he says, 'is to be the sole law which shall govern the moral world'; but Love is a wide word with many significations, and we are at a loss as to which of them he would have it bear. We are loath to understand it in its lowest sense, though we believe that as to the issue this would be the correctest mode of interpreting it; but this at least is clear, that Mr Shelley does not

mean it in its highest sense: he does not mean that love, which is a fulfilling of the law, and which walks after the commandments, for he would erase the Decalogue, and every other code of laws; not the love which is said to be of God, and which is beautifully coupled with 'joy, peace, long suffering, gentleness, goodness, faith, meekness, temperance', for he pre-eminently abhors that religion, which is built on that love and inculcates it as the essence of all duties, and its own fulfilment.

Coleridge concludes by claiming to discriminate between the man and his opinions: 'while we shew no mercy to the sin, we can regard the sinner with allowance and pity'. However, he allows only that Shelley 'has not, indeed, all that is odious and contemptible in the character' of his 'friend and leader', Leigh Hunt. And he pities him only in that his 'speculations and his disappointments' began 'in early childhood', and 'even from that period he has carried about him a soured and discontented spirit – unteachable in boyhood, unamiable in youth, querulous and unmanly in manhood, – singularly unhappy in all three'. The review ends with a final touch of malice in its hints concerning Shelley's elopement with Mary Godwin in 1814, and the suicide more than two years later of his first wife, Harriet Westbrook:

> if we might withdraw the veil of private life, and tell what we *now* know about him, it would indeed be a disgusting picture that we should exhibit, but it would be an unanswerable comment on our text; it is not easy for those who *read only*, to conceive how much low pride, how much cold selfishness, how much unmanly cruelty are consistent with the laws of this 'universal' and 'lawless love'.

Rosalind and Helen (1819) and *The Cenci* (1820)

Rosalind and Helen was reviewed by, among a few others, Leigh Hunt in the *Examiner*,[22] and John Wilson ('Christopher North') in *Blackwood's Edinburgh Magazine*.[23] *The Cenci* was more extensively reviewed than any other of Shelley's works.[24] More memorable than any of the reviews, however, and more generally remembered, is John Keats's response, in his letter to Shelley of 16 August 1820:[25]

> There is only one part of it I am judge of; the Poetry, and dramatic effect, by which many spirits now a days is considered the mammon. A modern work it is said must have a purpose, which may be the God – *an artist* must serve Mammon – he must have

'self concentration' selfishness perhaps. You I am sure will forgive me for sincerely remarking that you might curb your magnanimity and be more the artist, and 'load every rift' of your subject with ore. The thought of such discipline must fall like cold chains upon you, who perhaps never sat with your wings furl'd for six Months together. And is not this extraordina[r]y talk for the writer of *Endymion*? whose mind was like a pack of scattered cards – I am pick'd up and – sorted to a pip. My Imagination is a Monastery and I am its Monk – you must explain my metap. to yourself. I am in expectation of *Prometheus* every day.

Prometheus Unbound (1820)

The *Prometheus Unbound* volume was quite widely reviewed. In an unsigned review in the *Literary Gazette, and Journal of Belles Lettres*,[26] the reviewer presents himself as necessarily having to transgress the rule of criticism 'that none ought to attempt to criticise what they do not understand'. *Prometheus Unbound* is 'little else but absolute raving': 'inflexibly unintelligible' in its 'refractory combinations of words'. Its 'punning title-page is the soothest in the book – as no one can ever think him worth binding'. The reviewer mocks Shelley's 'opposition of words, phrases, and sentiments, so violent as to be utter nonsense', his 'contradictory terms and metaphor carried to excess', his 'bestowing *colouring* epithets on every thing he mentions' his 'talent for manufacturing "villainous compounds"', and his 'condign abhorrence of any relation between [adjectives] and substantives'. The reviewer asks, 'Did ever the walls of Bedlam display more insane stuff than this?' Here, it is not Shelley's uttering wicked and dangerous blasphemy and impiety, but his utterance in itself which is identified as evidence of his madness.

John Gibson Lockhart, in *Blackwood's Edinburgh Magazine*,[27] is altogether more serious, and, as is usual with *Blackwood's*, he feels both admiration and abhorrence:

> It would be highly absurd to deny, that this gentleman has manifested very extraordinary powers of language and imagination in his treatment of the allegory, however grossly and miserably he may have tried to pervert its purpose and meaning.

The perverted meaning and purpose of the allegory are that

> the Jupiter whose downfall has been predicted by Prometheus, means nothing more than [. . .] every system of religious belief;

and that, with the fall of this, [. . .] every system of human government also should give way and perish.

His summing-up expresses the extremity of his perplexed position:

> In short it is quite impossible that there should exist a more pestiferous mixture of blasphemy, sedition, and sensuality, than is visible in the whole structure and strain of this poem – which, nevertheless, and notwithstanding all the detestation its principles excite, must and will be considered by all that read it attentively, as abounding in poetic beauties of the highest order – as presenting many specimens not easily to be surpassed, of the moral sublime of eloquence – as overflowing with pathos, and most magnificent description. Where can be found a spectacle more worthy of sorrow than such a man performing and glorying in the performance of such things?

The conclusion of his review is a defence of *Blackwood's* critical practice and principles against the imputation that its reviewers praise Shelley

> although we dislike his principles, just because we know that he is not in a situation of life to be in any danger of suffering pecuniary inconvenience from being run down by critics; and, *vice versa*, abuse Hunt, Keats and Hazlitt, and so forth, because we know they are poor men.

The claim to be disinterestedly interested only in literary judgement is distinctly at odds with the way the claim is made:

> We should just as soon think of being wroth with vermin, independently of their coming into our apartments, as we should of having any feelings about any of these people, other than what are excited by seeing them in the shape of authors.

Despite his thinking 'the principles and purposes' of Shelley's poetry 'more undisguisedly pernicious in this volume, than even in his *Revolt of Islam*', Lockhart's final hope of Shelley is that

> ere long a lamp of genuine truth may be kindled within his 'bright mind'; and that he may walk in its light the path of the true demigods of English genius, having, like them, learned to 'fear God and honour the king'.

An unsigned review in the *London Magazine, and Monthly Critical and Dramatic Review*[28] describes *Prometheus Unbound* as 'one of the most stupendous works which the daring and vigorous spirit of modern poetry and thought has created'. It is a poem of 'gigantic outlines' and of 'innumerable sweetnesses':

> a vast wilderness of beauty, which at first seems stretching out on all sides into infinitude, yet the boundaries of which are all cast by the poet; in which the wildest paths all have a certain and noble direction; and the strangest shapes which haunt its recesses, voices of gentleness and of wisdom.

The reviewer answers Lockhart's objections to Shelley's supposed perversion of the allegory's 'meaning and purpose'. The 'deliverance of Prometheus' with the 'dethroning of Jupiter' is 'a symbol of the peaceful triumph of goodness over power; of the subjection of might to right; and the restoration of love to the full exercise of its benign and all-penetrating sympathies'. The reviewer has 'no objection' to 'the ultimate prospect exhibited by that philosophical system which Mr Shelley's piece embodies'. However, he does not simply approve Shelley's aspirations, but finds that, when Shelley 'would attempt to realize in an instant his glorious visions' and 'would treat men as though they are now the fit inhabitants of an earthly paradise', or 'when he would cast down all restraint and authority as enormous evils' and 'would leave all mankind to the guidance of passions yet unsubdued, and of desires yet unregulated', 'we must protest against his wishes as tending fearfully to retard the good which he would precipitate'.

This is the protest of the pragmatic, gradualist reformer, whose idea of what is desirable is determined by a sense of what is practicable, and who therefore is unimpressed by a more radical understanding that recognizes that a sense of what is practicable can or should be determined by an idea of what is desirable.

An unsigned review, attributed to W. S. Walker, in the *Quarterly Review*[29] supposes:

> Mr Shelley may plume himself upon writing in three different styles: one which can be generally understood; another which can be understood only by the author; and a third which is absolutely and intrinsically unintelligible.

The *Prometheus Unbound* volume 'is a most satisfactory testimonial of his proficiency in the last':

In Mr Shelley's poetry all is brilliance, vacuity and confusion. We are dazzled by the multitude of words which sound as if they denoted something very grand or splendid: fragments of images pass in crowds before us; but when the procession has gone by, and the tumult of it is over, not a trace of it remains upon the memory.

In these general propositions (and, to a lesser degree, those of the review in the *Literary Gazette, and Journal of Belles Lettres*, above) are the prototypes of much of the later criticism of Shelley's poetry that culminates in F. R. Leavis's destructive account in *Revaluation*. With its focus on the kaleidoscopic and kinetic dazzle of Shelley's words and images, and on the possibility of attaching no more than conjectural meaning to them, it single-handedly and almost single-mindedly provides the repertoire for a subsequent reception of Shelley, not as a philosophical and political poet who is dangerously subversive of established authority in government and religion because he is all too intelligible, but as a poet characterizable in his linguistic and prosodic deficiencies and in the supposed muddle-headedness that they are the index of.

There is something proto-Leavisian too in the critical procedures adopted. Passages extracted from some of Shelley's poems are subjected to an inquisitional scrutiny, in which the 'careless reader' is shown how he 'may possibly have his fancy tickled into a transient feeling of satisfaction'; but 'let any man try to ascertain what is really said, and he will immediately discover the imposition that has been practised'. Walker observes that

Metaphors and similes can scarcely be regarded as ornaments of Mr Shelley's compositions; for his poetry is in general a mere jumble of words and heterogeneous ideas, connected by slight and accidental associations, among which it is impossible to distinguish the principal object from the accessory ... Another characteristic trait of Mr Shelley's poetry is, that in his descriptions he never describes the thing directly, but transfers it to the properties of something which he conceives to resemble it by language which is to be taken partly in a metaphorical meaning, and partly in no meaning at all.

These are Shelleyan traits that will have a long run in the critical record.

Shelley's subjects are 'in general ... widely remote from every thing that is level with the comprehension, or interesting to the heart of man'; in the instance of *Prometheus Unbound* 'its basis and its materials are mere dreaming, shadowy, incoherent abstractions'. It seems 'strange that such a volume should find readers, and still more strange that it should meet with admirers', but it appears 'much more surprizing, that any man of education should write such poetry as that of *Prometheus Unbound*'. Walker suggests that the admirers of Shelley's 'poetical power' see proofs of his genius in 'the very exaggeration, copiousness of verbiage, and incoherence of ideas' which he complains of as intolerable.

Shelley's 'sins against sense and taste' are great, but 'to his long lists of demerits he has added the most flagrant offences against morality and religion'. In this addition, Walker contradicts his claim that the 'predominating characteristic' of Shelley's poetry 'is its frequent and total want of meaning', for it is Shelley's frequent and total meaning that he condemns: 'He professes to write in order to reform the world. The essence of the proposed reformation is the destruction of religion and government.' Walker feels Shelley should applaud him for 'scrutinizing the merits of works which are intended to promote so detestable a purpose':

> Of Mr Shelley himself we know nothing, and desire to know nothing. Be his private qualities what they may, his poems (and it is only with his poems that we have any concern) are at war with reason, with taste, with virtue, in short, with all that dignifies man, or that man reveres.

The claim to be exclusively concerned with the poetry reappears this century, most revealingly, in Leavis's resistance to T. S. Eliot's expressed distaste for Shelley's beliefs; but it is a claim that is compromised, as here, where the supposed discovery of a Shelley frequently deficient in localised meaning actually reveals the critic's refusal of Shelley's total meaning.

General commentary (1820–2)

Shelley was well known – or notorious – enough by 1821 to have elicited some general commentary. In an unsigned article, 'Portraits of the Metropolitan Poets, No. III, Mr Percy Byshe [sic] Shelley', in the *Honeycomb*,[30] suspicions are prompted by the mode in which *Blackwood's Magazine* has dealt with Shelley:

> The principles which he professes, and the views of things which he takes, so contrary to the principles, if they may be so called, which distinguished that magazine, would be sufficient to counter-balance in the minds of the persons who contribute to that work, the harping of an Angel's Lyre.

It is 'odd enough' that Shelley 'has been favoured with sundry high commendations' for the reviewer not to believe 'that his real poetical merits have been the cause of them':

> There is therefore undoubtedly some secret machinery of which we are not aware, some friend behind the scenes, or some working of personal interest, which thus induces that magazine for once to throw aside the trammels of party prejudice, and to do justice to a man who even advocates the French Revolution.

The general point that arises out of such suspicions poses a perennial problem for criticism:

> It would be a curious thing if the public could be made acquainted with the history of every review, and see the hidden springs of affection or hatred by which the pen of the impartial critic was moved. The empiricism of patent medicines is nothing to this quackery.

The critic feels that 'Shelley has never been duly appreciated', but that this neglect 'is, however, entirely owing to himself':

> He writes in a spirit which people do not comprehend: there is something too mystical in what he says – something too high or too deep for common comprehension. He lives in a very remote poetical world, and his feelings will scarcely bear to be shadowed out in earthly light.

However, a feature of Shelley which 'favourably distinguishes him from his more imitative and trivial companions' is that whereas they are characterizable in 'the extraordinary sameness, or even deterioration, which exists between the earliest and most recent writings', Shelley has 'a soul and fire in his poetical genius which is not so suddenly burnt out'.

Another unsigned article, 'On the Philosophy and Poetry of Shelley', in the *London Magazine and Theatrical Inquisitor*[31] celebrates the 'fruitful spawn' of the French Revolution. Shelley's 'leading principles' are admired:

> His mind revolts at intolerance and bigotry; and he believes in his devotional creed as one that deserves love as well as admiration. His moral and political principles all spring from the same source, and are founded on the same dignified contempt for bigotry and the 'sway of tyranny'.

Further, they are praised even in their extremes:

> If Shelley's opinions are carried to an extravagant excess, they are at least the excesses of a devotional mind and a generous disposition. They are the excesses of an enthusiastic spirit, soaring above the trammels of superstition, relying on its own capabilities, and asserting the rights of man as a thinking and independent being.

Shelley's 'mental visions of philosophy' (in an image that Browning would more obliquely invoke in his 'Memorabilia') 'soar with an eagle's flight to the heaven of heavens, and come back laden with the treasures of humanity'. Yet this critic, too, feels that, for all his 'attractions of mind and verse', Shelley

> can never become a popular poet. He does not sufficiently link himself with man; he is too visionary for the intellect of the generality of his readers, and is ever immersed in the clouds of religious and metaphysical speculations.

The most interesting of these more general commentaries is William Hazlitt's indictment of Shelley in his essay 'On Paradox and Commonplace' in *Table Talk* (1821–2).[32] Hazlitt, himself a radical reformer in politics, savages Shelley: his ferocity is fed by a sense that Shelley 'does not sufficiently link himself with man', and is constitutionally incapable of the steadfast commitment, in strongly held conviction and consolidating action, that is necessary to the success of his cause; on the contrary, he puts the cause in jeopardy:

> The author of the *Prometheus Unbound* ... has a fire in his eye, a fever in his blood, a maggot in his brain, a hectic flutter in his speech, which mark out the philosophic fanatic. He is sanguine-complexioned, and shrill-voiced. As is often observable in the case of religious enthusiasts, there is a slenderness of constitutional *stamina*, which renders the flesh no match for the spirit. His bending, flexible form appears to take no strong hold of things,

does not grapple with the world about him, but slides from it like a river ... The shock of accident, the weight of authority make no impression on his opinions, which retire like a feather, or rise from the encounter unhurt, through their own buoyancy. He is clogged by no dull system of realities, no earth-bound feelings, no rooted prejudices, by nothing that belongs to the mighty trunk and hard husk of nature and habit, but is drawn up by irresistible levity to the regions of mere speculation and fancy ... There is no *caput mortuum* of worn-out, thread-bare experience to serve as ballast to his mind; it is all volatile intellectual salt of tartar, that refuses to combine its evanescent, inflammable essence with any thing solid or any thing lasting. Bubbles are to him the only realities: – touch them, and they vanish. Curiosity is the only proper category of his mind, and though a man in knowledge, he is a child in feeling. Hence he puts every thing into a metaphysical crucible to judge of it himself and exhibit it to others as a subject of interesting experiment, without first making it over to the ordeal of his common sense or trying it on his heart. This faculty of speculating at random on all questions may in its overgrown and uninformed state do much mischief without intending it, like an overgrown child with the power of a man.... He strives to overturn all established creeds and systems: but this is in him an effect of constitution. He runs before the most extravagant opinions, but this is because he is held back by none of the merely mechanical checks of sympathy and habit. He tampers with all sorts of obnoxious subjects, but it is less because he is gratified with the rankness of the taint, than captivated with the intellectual phosphoric light they emit. It would seem that he wished not so much to convince or inform as to shock the public by the tenor of his productions, but I suspect he is more intent upon startling himself with his electrical experiments in morals and philosophy ... With his zeal, his talent, and his fancy, he would do more good and less harm, if he were to give up his wilder theories, and if he took less pleasure in feeling his heart flutter in unison with the panic-struck apprehensions of his readers. Persons of this class, instead of consolidating useful and acknowledged truths, and thus advancing the cause of science and virtue, are never easy but in raising doubtful and disagreeable questions, which bring the former into disgrace and discredit.

Epipsychidion (1821) and *Adonais* (1821)

Altogether different in its tonalities and emphases from Hazlitt's explosive vehemence is the disarming 'Seraphina and Her Sister Clementina's Review of *Epipsychidion*' in the *Gossip*.[33] Seraphina and her sister Clementina are reading Goldsmith's *The Deserted Village*, and Clementina has just been moved to tears by it, when a gentleman, 'who had long been an admirer of Clementina', enters with the 'Seventeenth Number' of the *Gossip*, containing a review of, and extracts from, Shelley's *Epipsychidion*:[34] '"It is poetry *intoxicated*," said Clementina. "It is poetry in *delirium*," said I.' The gentleman describe it 'as a new system of poetry', and 'the poetical currency of the day': '"Bless me!" said Clementina, "what a number of adjectives, and how strangely coupled with nouns!"' She proceeds to list these until she is 'quite out of breath'. The gentleman then provides a more extensive and inclusive description of the poetry's distinctive characteristics:

'It is a species of poetry that excites no emotion but that of wonder – we wonder what it means! It lives without the vitality of life; it has animation but no heart; it worships nature but spurns her laws; it sinks without gravity and rises without levity. Its shadows are substances, and its substances are shadows. Its odours may be felt, and its sounds may be penetrated – its frosts have the melting quality of fire, and its fire may be melted by frost. Its animate beings are inanimate things, and its local habitations have no existence. It is a system of poetry made up of adjectives, broken metaphors, and indiscriminate personifications. In this poetry everything must live, and move, and have a being, and they must live and move with intensity of action and passion, though they have their origin and their end in nothing ... There is a new omnipotence in this poetry,' said the gentleman, 'things may do impossibilities with, or without impossible powers – this is the *ne plus ultra* of poetical omnipotence.'

This characterizing of Shelley, despite its thoroughgoing and inert conventionality of taste in literary matters, has an apparent aptness of description and appositeness of judgement. Its comedy is a real provocation to readers rather more attentive and attuned to Shelley: and the criticism is more telling for not having more to say than it does – the focus on the oddities and difficulties for interpretation which the poetry produces is not discernibly compromised by any disapproval of Shelley's ideas: the 'new omnipotence' of the poetry is presented as not more than a poetical omnipotence. A good bit more fun is then had at Shelley's expense when the gentleman attempts to summarise *Epipsychidion*.

An unsigned review of *Adonais* in the *Literary Chronicle, and Weekly Review*[35] attests to 'the beauty of Mr Shelley's elegy', claiming that 'to every poetic mind' (minds clearly very different from those of the sisters and their gentleman caller) 'its transcendent merits must be apparent', and quoting in support of the claim almost the whole of the poem. Another unsigned review of *Adonais*, in the *Literary Gazette, and Journal of Belles Lettres*,[36] is merely brutish about Keats's death and brutal about Shelley's elegy:

> we regret that he did not live long enough to acquire common sense, and abjure the pestilent and perfidious gang who betrayed his weakness to the grave, and are now panegyrising his memory into contempt.

Adonais is 'altogether unconnected, interjectional, and nonsensical', containing 'horrid blasphemy' and 'empty absurdity':

> The poetry of the work is *contemptible* – a mere collection of bloated words heaped on each other without order, harmony, or meaning; the refuse of a schoolboy's common-place book, full of the vulgarisms of pastoral poetry, yellow gems and blue stars, bright Phoebus and rosy-fingered Aurora; and of this stuff is Keats's wretched Elegy compiled.

Although the focus of the literary criticism here has much in common with Clementina's, it is widened to include objections to blasphemy on the one hand and schoolboy callowness on the other. The charge of puerility will recur later in the critical record, levelled not against Shelley's 'vulgarisms of pastoral poetry', but against his 'views'.

Posthumous Poems (1824)

Hazlitt is the best of Shelley's contemporary critics, and his review of the *Posthumous Poems* in the *Edinburgh Review*[37] presents a scintillating crystallization of much of the criticism represented here – stylistic and linguistic, political and moral, admiring and dispraising. For the most part negative, the review nevertheless achieves a characterization of Shelley that is lastingly illuminating. Although Hazlitt's images of Shelley's luminosity are all meant to convey Shelley's 'trusting too implicitly to the light of his own mind', they render that light in something of its brilliance, its vibrancy and its intense powers of 'Making earth bare and veiling heaven':

Mr Shelley's style is to poetry what astrology is to natural science – a passionate dream, a straining after impossibilities, a record of fond conjectures, a confused embodying of vague abstractions, – a fever of the soul, thirsting and craving after what it cannot have, indulging its love of power and novelty at the expense of truth and nature, associating ideas by contraries, and wasting great powers by their application to unattainable objects.

Poetry, we grant, creates a world of its own; but it creates it out of existing materials. Mr Shelley is the maker of his own poetry – out of nothing. Not that he is deficient in the true sources of strength and beauty, if he had given himself fair play ... But, in him, fancy, will, caprice, predominated over and absorbed the natural influences of things; and he had no respect for any poetry that did not strain the intellect as well as fire the imagination – and was not sublimed into a high spirit of metaphysical philosophy. Instead of giving a language to thought, or lending the heart a tongue, he utters dark sayings, and deals in allegories and riddles. His Muse offers her services to clothe shadowy doubts and inscrutable difficulties in a robe of glittering words, and to turn nature into a brilliant paradox ... Where we see the dazzling beacon-lights streaming over the darkness of the abyss, we dread the quicksands and the rocks below. Mr Shelley's mind was of 'too fiery a quality' to repose (for any continuance) on the probable or the true – it soared 'beyond the visible diurnal sphere,' to the strange, the improbable, and the impossible. He mistook the nature of the poet's calling, which should be guided by involuntary, not by voluntary impulses. He shook off, as an heroic and praise-worthy act, the trammels of sense, custom, and sympathy, and became the creature of his own will. He was 'all air,' disdaining the bars and ties of mortal mould. He ransacked his brain for incongruities, and believed in whatever was incredible. Almost all is effort, almost all is extravagant, almost all is quaint, incomprehensible, and abortive, from aiming to be more than it is. Epithets are applied, because they do not fit: subjects are chosen, because they are repulsive: the colours of his style, of their gaudy, changeful, startling effect, resemble the display of fireworks in the dark, and, like them, have neither durability, nor keeping, nor discriminate form. Yet Mr Shelley, with all his faults, was a man of genius; and we lament that uncontrollable violence of temperament which gave it a forced and false direction. He has single thoughts of great depth and force, single images of rare beauty, detached passages of extreme tenderness; and, in his smaller pieces, where he has attempted little, he has done most. If some casual and interesting idea touched his feelings or struck his fancy, he expressed it in pleasing and unaffected verse: but give

him a larger subject, and time to reflect, and he was sure to get
entangled in a system. The fumes of vanity rolled volumes of
smoke, mixed with sparkles of fire, from the cloudy tabernacle of
his thought. The success of his writings is therefore in general in
the inverse ratio of the extent of his undertakings; inasmuch as his
desire to teach, his ambition to excel, as soon as it was brought
into play, encroached upon, and outstripped his powers of
execution.

   With all his faults, Mr Shelley was an honest man. His unbelief
and his presumption were parts of a disease, which was not
combined in him either with indifference to human happiness, or
contempt for human infirmities. There was neither selfishness nor
malice at the bottom of his illusions. He was sincere in all his
professions ... He followed up the letter and the spirit of his
theoretical principles in his own person, and was ready to share
both the benefit and the penalty with others. He thought and
acted logically, and was what he professed to be, a sincere lover
of truth, of nature, and of human kind. To all the rage of paradox,
he united an unaccountable candour and severity of reasoning: in
spite of an aristocratic education, he retained in his manners the
simplicity of a primitive apostle. An Epicurean in his sentiments,
he lived with the frugality and abstemiousness of an ascetick. His
fault was, that he had no deference for the opinions of others, too
little sympathy with their feelings (which he thought he had a
right to sacrifice, as well as his own, to a grand ethical experiment)
– and trusted too implicitly to the light of his own mind, and to
the warmth of his own impulses.

Two further critiques of Shelley's *Posthumous Poems* are note-
worthy: the first of these is the review by 'E. Haselfoot' (W. S.
Walker?) in *Knight's Quarterly Magazine* of Aug. 1824.[38]
Haselfoot finds *Posthumous Poems* 'a work upon which the
genuine mark of intellectual greatness is stamped' and one which
effects a fundamental shift in the expectations and principles of
literary criticism: 'We feel ourselves raised above criticism, to
that of which criticism is only the shadow; we perceive that it is
from sources like these that her rules, even where true, are
exclusively derived.' In reading Shelley's poems

   we are emancipated from the minute and narrowing restraints to
   which an habitual intercourse with petty prejudices almost insen-
   sibly subjects us; we breathe freely in the open air of enlarged
   thought; and we deem ourselves ennobled by our relation to a
   superior mind, and by a sense of our own capabilities which its
   grand conceptions awaken in us.

Haselfoot is aware that 'this expression of our sentiments will probably astonish some, and scandalise others':

> We know that public opinion (that opinion to which every one is now required to surrender the independent suggestions of his own reason and conscience, on pain of ridicule and obloquy) has doomed the name of Shelley to unmixed reprobation. We are a review-and-newspaper-ridden people; and while we contend clamorously for the right of thinking for ourselves, we yet guide ourselves unconsciously by the opinion of censors whom we know to be partial and incompetent. Shelley was a leveller in politics – this all knew; and they had been told that Shelley was an Atheist, that he was a man of flagitious character, and that his poems were nothing more than a heap of bombast and verbiage, of immorality and blasphemy ... Besides this, the extravagant lengths to which he carried his system afforded more than ordinary facilities for attack; his poetical errors, being errors of excess and not of effect, were peculiarly obnoxious to that kind of ridicule in which modern criticism delights to indulge; and, to crown all, he was the friend of Leigh Hunt and Hazlitt. Hence, the critics of one party assailed him without mercy; and as the vindication of his fame was not calculated to serve any temporary purpose, the critics of the other party forbore to defend him!

This is a generally astute review of the reviewers: just, too, in its judgement of critics of the friendly party, who forbore to defend and vindicate Shelley since they saw no immediate advantage to their cause in doing so – certainly, Hazlitt was one such, as we have seen. Leigh Hunt, as we have also seen, and will see again shortly, is a better friend and a loyal defender. Haselfoot declares: 'Our only aim ... is to impress on the reader the self-evident truth, that the intellectual as well as the moral character of Shelley's writings is to be judged of from the writings themselves.' Moreover,

> It is nothing to the purpose to say, that they must necessarily be immoral, from the nature of their subjects. Such, indeed, is the received logic – they must be so, therefore they are so: but it is a mere fallacy. It is not the subject on which an author writes, but the spirit in which he treats it, that determines the tendency of his work.

Haselfoot, it is clear, is not a mere panegyrist of Shelley, but a perspicuous and scrupulous critic; justifying his own critical posture, and offering his criticisms of Shelley with precision and a certain openness:

> We are far, indeed, from holding him forth as a moral writer *par excellence*; though his faults were, perhaps, rather of omission than commission. There is a vagueness in his system; a want of substantial foundation for his principles; there is a turbulence, and a feverish restlessness, too much removed from that calm in which wisdom loves to dwell; and there are a few pictures of passion which may be considered as too warmly wrought, sublimed as they are, and almost purified, by the atmosphere of noble thoughts and images with which they are surrounded.

However, Shelley's poems cannot be considered 'writings of the same class' as 'those works which are universally allowed to be immoral'. On the contrary:

> They inculcate truth and simplicity of heart, intellectual liberty and enlargement of thought, a passionate devotion to the graces and sublimities of nature, and, above all, a love for others, fervent, deep-seated, persevering, unlimited by place or circumstance, and patient of shame, labour, and suffering, in the glorious endeavour to promote the general welfare ... They inculcate a belief in the immutability of virtue, in the omnipotence of right intention, and in the final happiness and exaltation of human nature, to be brought about by the exertions and self-sacrifices of the good and wise ... If this is not religion, it is something not wholly unallied to it; and there are numberless passages of his works in which every worthy and generous mind may recognise, with little or no change, the echo of its own high aspirations; ennobling and consoling truths, clothed in the highest beauty of imagination.

This is high praise, although one may feel some wariness, in anticipation of some of the responses to come, of that suggestion that if Shelley is not religious he is something not wholly unallied to it. However, in so far as it is a statement that suggests the possibility of both similarity and distinction, it provides a precisely poised discrimination that remains something to hold onto in an age readier to find Shelley's beliefs not only wholly allied to religion, but wholly Christian (as Robert Browning will do).

Leigh Hunt began writing about *Posthumous Poems* in 1825, but no critique by him appeared in print until the publication of *Lord Byron and some of his Contemporaries* (London, 1828). In this critique, Hunt resists Hazlitt's criticisms of Shelley's

Posthumous Poems as 'caricature of an imaginary original'. He systematically defends Shelley against each of Hazlitt's specific charges, sifting Hazlitt's falsehoods and half-truths, to establish the realities known to him of Shelley's attitudes, conduct and sympathies as a reformer. He also offers a defence of Shelley's poetry that presents a radically different depiction of the qualities of Shelley's luminosity from Hazlitt's own view of it. Hazlitt saw Shelley's 'dazzling beacon-lights streaming over the darkness of the abyss', and dreaded 'the quicksands and the rocks below'. Leigh Hunt has no such fears:

> Mr Shelley's poetry is invested with a dazzling and subtle radiance, which blinds the common observer with light. Piercing beyond this, we discover that the characteristics of his poetical writings are an exceeding sympathy with the whole universe, material and intellectual; an ardent desire to benefit his species; an impatience with tyrannies and superstitions that hold them bound; and a regret that the power of one loving and enthusiastic individual is not proportioned to his will, nor his good reception with the world at all proportioned to his love. His poetry is either made up of all these feelings united, or is an attempt to escape from their pressure into the wildest fields of imagination. I say an attempt, – because, as we have seen, escape he does not; and it is curious to observe how he goes pouring forth his baffled affections upon every object he can think of, bringing out its beauties and pretensions by the light of a radiant fancy, and resolved to do the whole detail of the universe a sort of poetical justice, in default of being able to make his fellow-creatures attend to justice political. From this arises the fault of his poetry, which is want of massiveness, – of a proper distribution of light and shade. The whole is too full of glittering points; of images touched and illustrated alike, and brought into the same prominence. He ransacks every thing like a bee, grappling with it in the same spirit of penetration and enjoyment, till you lose sight of the field he entered upon, in following him into his subtle recesses.

There is spirited defence here; but, in conceding Shelley's default and his faults, Leigh Hunt anticipates criticisms of later in the century. His final defensive move, in its imagery, is more particular in its anticipation:

> When he is obliged to give up these peculiarities, and to identify his feelings and experience with those of other people, as in his dramatic poems, the fault no longer exists. His object remains, – that of increasing the wisdom and happiness of mankind: but he

has laid aside his wings, and added to the weight and purpose of his body: the spiritual part of him is invested with ordinary flesh and blood.

One might suppose that the wings are the wings of the before-mentioned bee, but here they seem to be the wings of some spirit, perhaps even the bee-accompanying Ariel. Leigh Hunt sees Shelley as laying aside his wings, and becoming more bodily and purposeful; Matthew Arnold later divests Shelley of his flesh and blood and sees him bodiless and baffled: 'Shelley, beautiful and ineffectual angel, beating in the void his luminous wings in vain.'[39]

Leigh Hunt's concluding move is more generally ominous as he comes to recommend Shelley finally in 'two main parts' of his 'poetical genius': 'the descriptive and the pathetic' and 'grace and lyrical sweetness'. Hunt's view is that Shelley ought to have written nothing but dramas and lyrics. This narrowing of interest partly anticipates the century's later tendency to regard Shelley, even more exclusively, as essentially a lyric poet.

The Later Nineteenth Century

Mary Shelley's edition of *Posthumous Poems of Percy Bysshe Shelley* (1824) was followed by her further editions of Shelley's poetry and prose, *The Poetical Works of Percy Bysshe Shelley* and *Essays, Letters from Abroad, Translations, by Percy Bysshe Shelley* (1839). Although she was prevented from writing a memoir of her husband by his father, Sir Timothy Shelley, her intimate biographical and interpretative notes to the *Poetical Works* offered invaluable insights into Shelley's poems and knowledge of the circumstances in which Shelley wrote them, which have made them an almost indispensable adjunct to Shelley's writings. Later, however, she declined to write Shelley's biography. Shelley's friends committed their memories of him to paper, in periodical articles and, eventually, in booklength memoirs and biographies: Thomas Medwin's *Life of Percy Bysshe Shelley* (1847), Leigh Hunt's *Autobiography* (1850), Thomas Jefferson Hogg's *The Life of Shelley* (1858) (initially an 'official' life, but finally something more like an unauthorized biography), Thomas Love Peacock's *Memoirs of Shelley* (1858–62), and Edward J. Trelawny's *Recollections of Shelley and Byron* (1858), expanded later into *Records of Shelley,*

Byron and the Author (1878). These are the main commemor-
ations of Shelley by those who knew him in his life.

What might have been the first 'scholarly' edition of Shelley's
poems was W. M. Rossetti's *The Poetical Works of Percy
Bysshe Shelley* (1870), but some of Rossetti's practices of
correction were less than scrupulous and responsible; and it was
not until the publication of Harry Buxton Forman's *The Poetical
Works of Percy Bysshe Shelley* (1876-7) and *The Works of
Percy Bysshe Shelley in Verse and Prose* (1880), which set rather
more exacting standards of editorial care and faithfulness, that
a truly and lastingly scholarly edition of Shelley's writings was
provided. W. M. Rossetti's *Memoir of Shelley* (1870), written
for his edition of the poems, was the first authoritative indepen-
dently researched biography. It was superseded by Edward
Dowden's more substantial 'authorized' *The Life of Percy
Bysshe Shelley* (1886). The Shelley Society was formed that
year.

The biographical interest in Shelley was something that also
manifested itself in fictional recreations of him in various novels
throughout the century, and in poetical and critical responses to
him that were not only to his poetry and its substance and styles,
but to his reported or supposed personality. Thomas Love
Peacock had satirized him – not altogether unsympathetically –
as Scythrop Glowry in *Nightmare Abbey* (1818);[40] Benjamin
Disraeli imagined him as Marmion Herbert in *Venetia* (1837):
although as a younger man he had been subversive in his views
on politics, morals and religion, Marmion Herbert becomes in
his gentlemanly maturity the very model of a Conservative. In
his 'social' novels, Charles Kingsley referred to Shelley, quoted
from him, and presented versions of him as various characters.
These are all ineffectual or defective idealists: Lancelot Smith
and Claude Mellot in *Yeast* (1848), Alton Locke in *Alton Locke*
(1850), Claude Mellot, again, and John Briggs, later known as
Elsley Vavasour, in *Two Years Ago* (1857). Shelley was pre-
sented altogether more admiringly, but hardly less disappoint-
ingly – an unobjectionable (no 'laxities or atheism, or anything
of that kind you know', to quote Mr Brooke) and lovable
idealist – as Will Ladislaw in George Eliot's *Middlemarch*
(1871-2). He is present rather more obliquely, if not as Sue
Bridehead in *Jude the Obscure* (1894-5), on her lips and in her
ideas. She and Jude are seen as 'Shelleyan' by Phillotson: they

remind him of Laon and Cythna. In drama, Shelley appeared as the poet Eugene Marchbanks in George Bernard Shaw's *Candida* (1895), 'so uncommon as to be almost unearthly'.

The criticism of Shelley by writers who made fictional use of him is perhaps too idiosyncratic to provide views of him that can adequately represent the Victorian Age; but Kingsley and Shaw, in their extremes of fevered moralizing and cool anatomizing, respectively, provide polarities for the period. However, much of the tenor of what Kingsley says, and a good bit of his tone (the bad bit), are the predominant ones of the century.

In Kingsley's essay *Thoughts on Shelley and Byron* (1853)[41] Shelley is seen as a man whose 'whole life was a denial of external law, and a substitution in its place of internal sentiment', 'which, in his case, as in the case of all sentimentalists, turns out to mean at last, not the sentiments of mankind in general, but the private sentiments of the writer'. In Kingsley's view '"Lawless love" is Shelley's expressed ideal of the relation of the sexes; and his justice, his benevolence, his pity are all equally lawless. "Follow your instincts" is his one moral rule.' Shelley is 'incapable of anything like inductive reasoning; unable to take cognisance of any facts but those which please his taste, or to draw any conclusion from them but such as also pleases his taste'. Kingsley, in his manly Protestantism, sees the nature of the Age as 'an effeminate one': 'a mesmerising, table-turning, spirit-rapping, spiritualising, Romanising generation, who read Shelley in secret, and delight in his bad taste, mysticism, extravagance, and vague and pompous sentimentalism', and he regards Shelley's own nature as 'utterly womanish':

> Not merely his weak points, but his strong ones, are those of a woman. Tender and pitiful as a woman; and yet, when angry, shrieking, railing, hysterical as a woman ... The nature of a woman looks out of that wild, beautiful, girlish face – the nature: but not the spirit ... The lawlessness of the man, with the sensibility of the woman ... Alas for him!

Like this portrayal, Kingsley's taste for some of Shelley's poems might be described as prejudiced or even pathological, but it is less personally so than his opinions about Shelley's so-called womanishness. It is typical of an epidemic preference of the period for Shelley as lyric poet; or, as Kingsley expresses it, for 'Shelley's nightingale notes':

For nightingale notes they truly are. In spite of all his faults – and there are few poetic faults in which he does not indulge, to their very highest power – in spite of his 'interfluous' and 'innumerous', and the rest of his bad English – in spite of bombast, horrors, maundering, sheer stuff and nonsense of all kinds, there is a plaintive natural melody about this man, such as no other English poet would have uttered, except Shakespeare in some few immortal songs.

George Bernard Shaw's 'Shaming the Devil about Shelley' (1892)[42] was occasioned by the centennial celebrations of Shelley's birth and the founding of a Shelley Library and Museum in Horsham, near Shelley's birthplace in his native Sussex. It is itself a celebration of Shelley, but mischievously so, at the expense of 'civilised and self-respecting' men or gentlemen – the 'high Tories' – of that 'so true-blue a corner of England', which had 'just distinguished itself at the General Election by a gloriously solid Conservative vote'. Shaw's Shelley is here far from the 'uncommon' and 'almost unearthly' poet of *Candida*: 'In politics Shelley was a Republican, a Leveller, a Radical of the most extreme type ... In religion, Shelley was an Atheist.' Moreover, all these 'opinions which Shelley held and sedulously propagated' are 'horrifying ... from the Sussex point of view'. Shaw asks: 'Could Sussex be reconciled to them on the ground that they were mere "views" which did not affect his conduct?' And answers 'Not a bit of it':

> Shelley was not a hot-headed or an unpractical person. All his writings, whether in prose or verse, have a peculiarly deliberate quality. His political pamphlets are unique in their freedom from all appeal to the destructive passions; there is neither anger, sarcasm, nor frivolity in them; and in this respect his poems exactly resemble his political pamphlets ... His seriousness, his anxious carefulness, are ... obvious in his writings which still expose their publishers to the possibility of a prosecution for sedition or blasphemy ... And he did not go back upon his opinions in the least as he grew older. ... Thus there is no excuse for Shelley on the ground of his youth or rashness. If he was a sinner, he was a hardened sinner and a deliberate one.

If Kingsley and Shaw are agreed that Shelley was a 'sinner', and are in accord in their disparagement of those who would make him a saint, their evocation and evaluation of that sinfulness are poles apart.

The response of poets of the period is not negligible – Shelley had his imitators, some of whom (Thomas Lovell Beddoes and James Thomson, for instance) are reputable poets in their own right, and he had his admirers and detractors – but, with the exception of Robert Browning, these encounters with Shelley did not involve a sustained critical engagement. Browning, as a critic of Shelley, is disappointing in *An Essay on Percy Bysshe Shelley* (1851),[43] where he considers the different kind and degree of need for biography in the case of poets of two contrasting poetic faculties, the 'objective' and 'subjective', who can be categorized as 'the fashioner' and 'the seer'. In the case of the latter:

> in our approach to the poetry, we necessarily approach the personality of the poet; in apprehending it we apprehend him, and certainly we cannot love it without loving him. Both for love's and for understanding's sake we desire to know him, and as readers of his poetry must be readers of his biography also.

Browning's essay was originally introductory to a collection of what were supposed to be letters by Shelley. The letters, however, were spurious; and, although Browning does not approach Shelley's personality through any of them, his approach through Shelley's poetry has its own misapprehensions: 'I shall say what I think, – had Shelley lived he would have finally ranged himself with the Christians.'

Browning's 'desire to know' Shelley is more interestingly impelled in his approach to Shelley's poetry and personality in his poems than in his essay: in the intensely subjective, partly autobiographical 'seeing' of Shelley as 'Sun-treader' in the very early 'confessional' poem *Pauline* (1833); and in the more oblique and objectifying 'fashioning' of him in the later short lyric 'Memorabilia' (1855). Both poems are tributes that contribute to the critical record.

In his essay 'Thoughts on Poetry and Its Varieties' (1833),[44] John Stuart Mill asks 'What is poetry?' In attempting to answer that large and general question, Mill attends to the difference between 'the poetry of a poet and the poetry of a cultivated but not naturally poetic mind':

> The one writer has a distinct aim, common to him with any other didactic author; he desires to convey the thought, and he conveys it clothed in the feelings which he deems most appropriate to it.

The other merely pours forth the overflow of his feelings; and all the thoughts which those feelings suggest are floated promiscuously along the stream.

Mill illustrates his distinction by comparing Wordsworth and Shelley. The 'poetry more natural to a really poetic temperament' and 'more eminently and peculiarly poetry than any other' is lyric poetry. Wordsworth is 'essentially unlyrical', Shelley the reverse of Wordsworth. Shelley's 'deplorably early death' had prevented the 'intellectual progression of which he was capable' and which 'might have made him the most perfect, as he was already the most gifted, of our poets':

> For him, voluntary mental discipline had done little: the vividness of his emotions and of his sensations had done all. He seldom follows up an idea; it starts into life, summons from the fairy-land of his inexhaustible fancy some three or four bold images, then vanishes, and straight he is off on the wings of some casual association into quite another sphere. He has scarcely yet acquired the consecutiveness of thought necessary for a long poem; his more ambitious compositions too often resemble the scattered fragments of a mirror; colours brilliant as life, single images without end, but no picture. It is only when under the overruling influence of some one state of feeling, either actually experienced or summoned up in the vividness of reality by a fervid imagination, that he writes as a great poet; unity of feeling being to him the harmonizing principle which a central idea is to minds of another class, and supplying the coherency and consistency which else would have been wanting. Thus it is in many of his smaller, and especially his lyrical poems.

Such a reading of Shelley might, to use a phrase of Mill's, 'be cited as the type, the *exemplar*' of the subsequent criticism of Shelley; except that Mill is untypical, but exemplary, in not permitting his accounting for the limitations of Shelley's poetry to determine or predetermine a predominantly negative and reductive view. The contrast with F. R. Leavis is especially instructive, for instance, in Mill's observing without stricture: 'The thoughts and imagery are suggested by the feeling, and are such as it finds unsought.' Although Mill judges that Shelley's 'exuberance of imagery, when unrepressed, as in many of his poems it is, amounts to a fault', his description of that exuberance does not diminish it or detract from it:

The susceptibility of his nervous system, which made his emotions intense, made also the impressions of his external senses deep and clear ... Never did a fancy so teem with sensuous imagery as Shelley's. Wordsworth economizes an image, and detains it until he has distilled all the poetry out of it, and it will not yield a drop more: Shelley lavishes his with a profusion which is unconscious because it is inexhaustible.

George Henry Lewes's essay 'Percy Bysshe Shelley' (1841)[45] shows him close to Shaw in his sense of Shelley as 'serious' in his political aspirations: a poet who 'does not so much preach as inspire': 'He knew that it was not what we absolutely learn and carry away with us, but what we *become*, which the poet's works effect.' In 'that turbulent period in England' after the French Revolution, 'there arose a band of poets to utter the new doctrines, such as will never pass out of literature'. Although they all 'saw that the existing state of things was corrupt', Wordsworth and Coleridge 'started back at the apparition of Liberty they had called up', while Byron and Keats lacked heroic endurance. Shelley alone:

was the poet standing completely on his truth; giving up his life to it, and eternally preaching it. Look where you will throughout his various works, you will see this gospel ever lying underneath, even under the smallest poems. It stands written there, unchangeable as the word in a firework illumination remains burning through all the varieties of fire which play around it and from out of it. One may see also from this why these other men, mirroring, as they did, the immediate restlessness and disease of the period, were more *notable* than this other man who was speaking of futurity ... The vital truth Shelley everywhere enforced, although treated as a chimera by most of his contemporaries, and indulged in as a dream by some others, has become the dominant Idea – the philosophy and faith of this age, throughout Europe – it is progression, humanity, perfectibility, civilization, democracy – call it what you will – this is the truth uttered unceasingly by Shelley, and universally received by us. It is easy to laugh at the 'doctrine of perfectibility', and by grave sneers conceive that we annihilate it; but is that imperfect outlooking of the projective sympathy with humanity truly but a dream?

Lewes was perhaps premature in his belief that Shelley's unceasingly uttered 'vital truth' had been received universally (or in Europe or even in Britain) and had become the dominant idea of his age. He is right, however, that it was easy to laugh at

Shelley's ideas, or, since gravity is the prerequisite of the Victorian literary and cultural critic, to sneer at them, or, at least not to take them seriously. That is what the age proceeded predominantly to do.

Walter Bagehot, in his essay 'Percy Bysshe Shelley' (1856),[46] is half comforted by the 'scanty' information to be had of Shelley's life, since 'we know enough to check our inferences from his writings'. Shelley 'is probably the most remarkable instance of the purely impulsive character', and 'the predominant impulse in Shelley from a very early age was "a passion for reforming mankind"'; 'the evidence of Shelley's poems confirms this impression of him'.

Shelley's temperament and 'the peculiarity of his opinions' arising from it are the result of his being 'placed in circumstances which left his eager mind quite free'. His deficiency in conscience was 'aggravated by what may be called the abstract character of his intellect':

> The tendency of his mind was rather to personify isolated qualities or impulses – equality, liberty, revenge, and so on – than create out of separate parts or passions the single conception of an entire character. This is, properly speaking, the mythological tendency.

Shelley shows this tendency even when 'not writing on topics connected with ancient mythology'. Bagehot sees this as the consequence of Shelley's accepting the questioning of 'the Scotch sceptic' David Hume, and his holding, or professing to hold, 'that there was no substantial thing, either matter or mind; but only "sensations and impressions" flying about the universe, inhering in nothing and going nowhere'. Hume's was 'a better description' of Shelley's universe 'than of most people's', for Shelley's mind

> was filled with swarms of ideas, fancies, thoughts, streaming on without his volition, without plan or order. He might be pardoned for fancying that they were all; he could not see the outward world for them; their giddy passage occupied him till he forgot himself.

Plato's description was better still: having accepted 'that the all-apparent phenomena were unreal', Shelley was ready also to accept the rest of Plato's theory 'that these passing phenomena were imperfect types and resemblances – imperfect incarnations, so to speak – of certain immovable eternal, archetypal realities'. However, what is absent in Shelley, according to Bagehot's analysis, 'is that unceasing reference to ethical consciousness and ethical religion which has for centuries placed Plato first among the preparatory preceptors of Christianity'. Similarly, Shelley's political opinions are 'the effervescence of his peculiar nature' in its wanting 'to make a *tabula rasa* of all which men have created or devised; for they seem to be constructed on a false system, for an object it does not understand'.

The works of Shelley are 'in the strictest sense "remains"'; no 'long work of perfected excellence' can be expected from a poet who died at so early an age as thirty. Shelley's success 'is in fragments; and the best of these fragments are lyrical':

> The very same isolation and suddenness of impulse which rendered him unfit for the composition of great works, rendered him peculiarly fit to pour forth on a sudden the intense essence of peculiar feeling 'in profuse strains of unpremeditated art'.

Shelley's excellence 'does not, however extend equally over the whole domain of lyric poetry'. It is more in evidence in the 'abstract' lyric than in the 'human' lyric. Shelley has nothing of a Wordsworthian sense of essential and eternal passions and feelings:

> The essential feelings he hoped to change; the eternal facts he struggled to remove. Nothing in human life to him was inevitable or fixed; he fancied he could alter it all ... Shelley describes the universe. He rushes away among the stars; this earth is an assortment of imagery, he uses it to deck some unknown planet. He scorns 'the smallest light that twinkles in the heavens'. His theme is the vast, the infinite, the immeasurable. He is not of our home, nor homely; he describes not our world, but that which is common to all worlds – the Platonic idea of a world. Where it can, his genius soars from the concrete and real into the unknown, the indefinite, and the void.

Bagehot complicates his conception of Shelley's sensibility, in describing its distinctiveness and in also distinguishing it from Keats's. Keats is the exact opposite to Shelley in the nature of his sensibility, in its 'luxurious sentiment' and 'poise on fine sensation':

The sensibility of Keats was attracted too by the spectacle of the universe; he could not keep his eye from seeing, or his ears from hearing, the glories of it. All the beautiful objects of nature reappear by name in his poetry. On the other hand, the abstract idea of beauty is for ever celebrated in Shelley; it haunted his soul. But it was independent of special things; it was the general surface of beauty which lies upon all things.

Bagehot judges that the 'high intellectual impulses which animated him are too incorporeal for human nature'. But he concludes his essay with an emphasis on those impulses, introducing thereby a change of perspective – from the viewing of their incorporeality, to the viewing of their poetic incorporation – and hence a change of perception and point of view: Bagehot's predominantly negative observation and evaluation of Shelley is overturned or reversed:

The peculiarity of his style is its intellectuality; and this strikes us the more from its contrast with his impulsiveness. He had something of this in life. Hurried away by sudden desires as he was in his choice of ends, we are struck with a certain comparative measure and adjustment in his choice of means. So in his writings: over the most intense excitement, the grandest objects, the keenest agony, the most buoyant joy, he throws an air of subtle mind. His language is minutely and acutely searching; at the dizziest height of meaning the keenness of the words is greatest. As in mania, so in his descriptions of it, the acuteness of the mind seems to survive the mind itself. It was from Plato and Sophocles, doubtless, that he gained the last perfection in preserving the accuracy of the intellect when treating of the objects of the imagination; but in its essence it was a peculiarity of his own nature. As it was the instinct of Byron to give in glaring words the gross phenomena of evident objects, so it was that of Shelley to refine the most inscrutable with the curious nicety of an attenuating metaphysician. In the wildest of ecstasies his self-anatomising intellect is equal to itself.

Richard Holt Hutton's essay, 'Shelley and his Poetry'[47] was originally written in 1871, but substantially recast after the publication of Dowden's *Life* in 1886. Shelley's life, Hutton suggests, is not the key to his poetry, for his poetry 'is in a different plane from human life of any kind'. Shelley's 'natural disposition was so exceptional, so far beyond the range of ordinary experience', that it is impossible to determine 'how far it was a twist of nature inborn, and how far voluntary wilfulness', which led Shelley into the 'strange mixture of paradoxical contrasts' that characterizes his personal conduct and poetic concerns, 'as if he had combined in his own person the spirit of a loving child and the spirit of a tricksy fiend': 'There is in Shelley at once a singularly ethereal nature, and a singularly unshrinking defiance of everything in human emotion which does not at once explain itself.' Hutton views Shelley's life – as Kingsley had done – as debased by the effects of a creed that admitted only 'the authority of impulse': 'And his own lawlessness no doubt fostered, if it did not cause, the lawlessness of others.'

In his poetry, 'the highest of his creations' are not the longer poems (here Hutton was resisting Dowden's judgement) but 'those exquisite lyrics in which his genius was most completely embodied', although *Adonais* is excepted from this generally inclusive view. In *Prometheus Unbound*, 'the parts are greater than the whole':

> On the whole, he seems to have failed in working out any complex conception, while his passion was at once more aerial and more sweet than that of any other English poet ... The unique rapture of Shelley's lyrical cry of dread, of desire, of despair, is his distinguishing feature as a poet.

There is another 'unique characteristic' of Shelley's poetry: his 'mysticism':

> Shelley's poetical mysticism is, – in the quick throb of its pulses, in the flush and glow of its hectic beauty, in the thrill of its exquisite anguish, and equally exquisite delirium of imagined bliss, – essentially and to the last the mysticism of intellectual youth. His poetry is the poetry of desire ... This is the great distinction which separates him from the other mystics of his day. Wordsworth, for instance, is always exulting in the fulness of nature; Shelley always chasing its falling stars. Wordsworth gratefully pierces the homely crust of earth to find the rich fountains of life in the Eternal Mind; Shelley follows with wistful eye the fleeting stream of beauty as it for ever escapes him into the illimitable void.

Hutton recognizes as characteristic of Shelley's mind its 'not setting a bound to what we may call spiritual *familiarities*':

> he seems almost to have revelled in breaking, in imagination, through all the boundary-walls of nature, and following the wave

of desire into the penetralia of life, both human and divine. 'Superstition' was his one great foe.

However, Shelley's intellect 'subtle as it was, had no vigorous grasp in it':

> It was swift, and infinite in fertility; but the only string by which he ever bound his thoughts firmly together was continuity of desire. There was but the faintest measure of binding strength in his thought, the faintest possible volition in it. Hence he had no enjoyment at all in reality as such.

Hutton acknowledges that 'Shelley stands in the front rank of English poets':

> But still there was something of tenuity in the essence of his genius, which is clearly connected with this liability to rapid excitation. I would rather say, that his genius resembles the water taken to a mountain top, and which, under the attenuated atmospheric pressure, boils with far less heat – or in his case what *seems* to general observers far less heat – than other men's. Under the influence of a sentiment which would at most warm the surface of the other poets' minds into a genial glow, Shelley's bubbles up from its very depths, in a sort of pale passion, and seethes with imprisoned thought ... To be aware that Shelley breathes an exceedingly rarefied atmosphere of abstract sentiment, and yet to see this rarefied air intoxicating his imagination till his pulses bound as under the spell of an ardent passion, is like hearing a flow of hot thought from the lips of a spectre, or seeing the bloodless ichor coursing furiously through its veins.

This Gothic horror that is summoned as the manifestation of Shelley's intellect or imaginatioin in its lack of 'grasp' or 'grip', and in its idealising abstraction from the realities of life, is transformed in the 'dreadful phantom of possible emptiness' which Hutton sees as the root of Shelley's restlessness: the suspicion 'that when desire fails, the objects of the heart's desire may fail with it', and 'that there is nothing substantial at the heart of the universe'.

Hutton's essay on Shelley can serve as an epitaph for the Victorian Age. It was, after all, the age that invented agnosticism, or, rather, the coinage 'agnosticism' (and Hutton was witness to Thomas Huxley's invention of it in 1869). Agnosticism is not scepticism or conviction, but reveres awful doubt by elevating it into a form of awe-ful faith that is without the desire for either knowledge or belief. Hence, the Age's fear of Shelley's 'awelessness of nature', his 'curiosity', his breaking 'into the penetralia of life, both human and divine', his following the infinitude of his desire into the 'illimitable void', and his daring to risk discovering that the void is vacancy.

The Twentieth Century

William Hazlitt, in the essay 'On Paradox and Commonplace' (*Table Talk*, 1821–2) had spoken of 'Shelley's "bending, flexible form" appearing to take no strong hold of things'. That observation is variously rephrased in the criticism of Shelley in the Victorian period. It reappears, in a coarsened and hardened form, in F. R. Leavis's chapter on Shelley in *Revaluation* (1936), as the identification of what he describes as 'a recognized essential trait of Shelley's: his weak grasp upon the actual'.[48]

Leavis's essay begins as a response and resistance to 'a critic of peculiar authority', T. S. Eliot. In his chapter, 'Shelley and Keats', in *The Use of Poetry and the Use of Criticism* (1933), Eliot describes how, having been 'intoxicated by Shelley's poetry at the age of fifteen', he found it 'almost unreadable' at the age of forty-five:[49]

> The ideas of Shelley seem to me always to be ideas of adolescence
> – as there is every reason why they should be. And an enthusiasm
> for Shelley seems to me also to be an affair of adolescence: for
> most of us, Shelley has marked an intense period before maturity,
> but for how many does Shelley remain the companion of age?

There is here a cheapening perception of Shelley's ideas, and a cheap supposition of a general singleness of response to them; and Eliot's question is a question that begs questions and does not seriously ask to be answered. Eliot acknowledges that he finds Shelley's ideas 'repellent', without specifying what those ideas are or which of them repels him. Furthermore, for Eliot, 'the difficulty of separating Shelley from his ideas' is added to by 'the biographical interest which Shelley always excited' and which 'makes it difficult to read the poetry without remembering the man'. Eliot seems implicitly to lay claim to a peculiarly immediate and inward knowledge of Shelley's life and not merely of his biography; the man remembered, moreover, seems to bear very little – or a very partial – resemblance to Shelley:

'the man was humourless, pedantic, self-centred, and sometimes almost a blackguard'. According to Eliot, Shelley, in his letters, makes 'an astonishing contrast with the attractive Keats': 'Except for an occasional flash of shrewd sense, when he is speaking of someone else and not concerned with his own affairs or with fine writing, his letters are insufferably dull.' In Shelley's poetry, one of the things most evident to Eliot is that 'Shelley seems to have had to a high degree the unusual faculty of passionate apprehension of abstract ideas'. However, Eliot does not mean by such a formultion 'that Shelley had a metaphysical or philosophical mind'; he means only that 'abstractions could excite in him strong emotion'. In Eliot, Shelley's ideas excite feelings of a negative kind: 'some of Shelley's views I positively dislike, and that hampers my enjoyment of the poem in which they occur; and others seem to me so puerile that I cannot enjoy the poems in which they occur'. This poses for Eliot the question: 'is it possible to ignore the 'ideas' of Shelley's poems, so as to be able to enjoy the poetry?' It is a question about 'the problem of Belief in the enjoyment of poetry' that occupied Eliot not only, but especially, in relation to Shelley. Eliot feels permitted to infer:

> in so far as the distaste of a person like myself for Shelley's poetry is not attributable to irrelevant prejudices or to a simple blind spot, but is due to a peculiarity in the poetry and not in the reader, that it is not the presentation of beliefs which I do not hold, or – to put the case as extremely as possible – of beliefs that excite my abhorrence, that makes the difficulty.

And he suggests the following answer to his question:

> When the doctrine, theory, belief, or 'view of life' presented in a poem is one which the mind of the reader can accept as coherent, mature, and founded on the facts of experience, it interposes no obstacle to the reader's enjoyment, whether it be one that he accept or deny, approve or deprecate. When it is one which the reader rejects as childish or feeble, it may, for a reader of a well-developed mind, set up an almost complete check.

It is an extraordinarily enclosed critical position. Eliot's supposing that his distaste for Shelley's poetry 'is not attributable to irrelevant prejudices or to a simple blind spot' leaves out one thing attributable to him: not 'irrelevant prejudices', but relevant ones. In determining the conditions for a 'view of life' which are no obstacles to a reader's enjoyment, the apparently objectifying criterion of 'coherence' is compromised by that most subjective of criteria, 'maturity'. Whose mind, moreover, is Eliot thinking of but his own, with its beliefs: coherent, mature (or at least not childish and not feeble) and founded on the facts of his particular and peculiar experience? Eliot avers: 'I can only regret that Shelley did not live to put his poetic gifts, which were certainly of the first order, at the service of more tenable beliefs – which need not have been, for my purposes, more tenable to me.' But the problem of belief cannot be denied by these means: the decision as to the tenability of a belief can only be made for oneself, out of one's own beliefs. That Shelley's beliefs excite Eliot's abhorrence clearly does make the difficulty; it clearly also makes the prejudicial deprecation and denial of their worth.

F. R. Leavis, 'in attempting a restatement of the essential critical observation', hopes that it may be possible to avoid the pitfalls of 'personal statement', and Eliot's 'question of belief or disbelief':

> if one insists on the more obvious terms of literary criticism – more strictly critical terms ... It does, in short, seem worth endeavouring to make finally plain that, when one dissents from persons who, sympathizing with Shelley's revolutionary doctrines and with his idealistic ardours and fervours – with his 'beliefs', exalt him as a poet, it is strictly the 'poetry' one is criticizing.

Leavis's endeavour here is less than convincing. His dissenting from Shelleyans who, sympathizing with Shelley's beliefs, exalt him as a poet, might have been persuasive if, without sharing those sympathies, he were nevertheless to exalt Shelley as a poet. But that is not Leavis's position: like Eliot, he neither sympathizes with the ideas nor exalts the poetry; and his 'strictly' criticizing the poetry is not quite what it claims, since it is Shelley's 'ardours and fervours' in the poems – the qualities which Leavis himself attaches to Shelley's ideals – that are the focus of his criticism. Eliot had found 'peculiarities analysable in the mode of expression' in such defects as 'the catchwords of creeds outworn, tyrants and priests, which Shelley employed with such reiteration'. Leavis, in turn, finds: 'Shelley is obnoxious to the pejorative implications of "habit": being inspired was, for him, too apt to mean surrendering to a kind of hypnotic rote of favourite images, associations, and words.' Because of these, 'it is impossible to go on reading him at any length with pleasure; the elusive imagery, the high-pitched emotions, the tone and the movement, the ardours, ecstasies, and despairs, are too much the same all through'.

The evidence of the continuity or recurrence of such strictures in the critical record attests to the reality of something problematic in Shelley's 'mode of expression'. But what is problematic may be a problem that Shelley's 'mode of expression' sought to exemplify and express. What is disturbing in Leavis's essay is the exclusivity and circularity of his argument. The supposed demonstration provided in the so-called close readings – of the second stanza of 'Ode to the West Wind', for instance – would be better described as closed reading; the processes and outcome of Leavis's scrutiny are so merely predicated on his premises. Leavis finds:

> a general tendency of the images to forget the status of the metaphor or simile that introduced them and to assume an autonomy and a right to propagate, so that we lose in confused generations and perspectives the perception or the thought that was the ostensible *raison d'être* of imagery.

This he describes as 'a recognized essential trait of Shelley's: his weak grasp upon the actual'. More recent criticism (and less recent criticism, too, if one thinks back to Bagehot) has seen in this essential trait of Shelley's not 'a weak grasp upon the actual', but a strong grasp on the epistemological and linguistic problems that describing 'the actual' poses. Thus Leavis's stricture that an image in Shelley's 'Ode' stands 'for nothing he could have pointed to in the scene before him' misses and mistakes the Shelleyan *raison d'être* of imagery. That is explained early in *A Defence of Poetry*, where Shelley writes of poets' language as 'vitally metaphorical', 'marking the before unapprehended relations of things':[50] language itself is a 'a more direct representation of the actions and passions of our internal being' and 'more plastic and obedient to the control of that faculty of which it is the creation' than any other artistic medium; for, unlike 'all other materials, instruments and conditions of art … which limit and interpose between conception and expression', language 'is arbitrarily produced by the Imagination, and has relation to thoughts alone'. The charge that Shelley's sensibility 'has no more dealings with intelligence than it can help' and that his 'poetic faculty' is one that 'demands that active intelligence shall be, as it were, switched off' is everywhere presumptive in Leavis's view of Shelley and never evinced.

Leavis quotes from George Santayana's essay 'Shelley: or the Poetic Value of Revolutionary Principles' (1913)[51] for its descriptions of Shelley as having been born a 'nature preformed', 'a spokesman [actually, in Santayana's essay, 'one of these spokesmen'] of the *a priori*', 'a dogmatic, inspired, perfect, and incorrigible creature', which Leavis sees as presenting excuses as much as explanations for Shelley's 'inability to learn from experience'. Yet he and Eliot prove, in their different but not unrelated ways, 'spokesmen of the *a priori*'.

Both Eliot and Leavis seem disabled by their, in more than one sense, closed reading of Shelley: one is struck by how very few poems they look at and seem to know. (How many of Shelley's letters had Eliot read?) For Leavis to describe 'The Mask of Anarchy' as 'little more than a marginal throw-off' will hardly do as an accurate 'placing' of that poem. It is undoubtedly a poem less marginal than 'When the lamp is shattered', which is the only poem of Shelley's which Leavis analyses at any length and in its totality. Leavis goes so far as to admit:

> It would be perverse to end without recognizing that [Shelley] achieved memorable things in modes of experience that were peculiarly congenial to the European mind in that phase of its history and are of permanent interest.

But this recognition is less than generously given, and where given – to the 'consummate expression' of 'Ode to the West Wind', or the 'poignant' but 'bewildered and bewildering' *The Triumph of Life* – it is given only to be taken back again.

Shelley is now clearly a poet who has retained his interest, despite his varying reputation, long enough for that interest to be described as 'permanent'; and it is now also clear that 'the modes of experience' that were 'peculiarly congenial' to the minds of the English critic and the Anglo-American poet-critic, were of a particular phase of the Western mind, whose 'permanent' interest is not yet secured, except perhaps as a focus for contextual analysis. Eliot and Leavis – on Shelley, at least – seem to have been more limitedly enclosed, by critical principles that are discriminatory in a merely pejorative sense, than many of their nineteenth-century precursors; their 'closedness' left a damaging legacy of prejudice against Shelley in British universities, colleges and schools, until well into the middle of this century.

What the twentieth century has seen in the study of Shelley, since that early period, are both enormous advances in, and consolidations of, the materials of study, and a tremendous extending and deepening of the understanding of Shelley in the diversely exploratory approaches to that material. This has come about through scholarship and critical commitment that, initially at least (but with some notable exceptions), has been predominantly American in origin. Foremost in those materials are, of course, the texts of Shelley's writings.[52]

Shelley and his Circle 1773–1822, vol I–IV ed. Kenneth Neil Cameron; vols V–VIII ed. Donald H. Reiman (Cambridge, Mass: Harvard University Press, 1961–70, 1973–86) collects together a broad array of invaluable source materials and contextual and critical commentary relating to Shelley; a further four volumes are projected. Under the general editorship of Donald H. Reiman, two series – *The Bodleian Shelley Manuscripts* (New York and London: Garland, 1986–), of which twenty-three volumes are planned, and *Manuscripts of the Younger Romantics* (New York and London: Garland, 1985–), of which eight volumes are devoted to Shelley – will provide readers and scholars with a comprehensive collection of textual materials.

The Life of Percy Bysshe Shelley, with an introduction by Humbert Wolfe, 2 vols (London and Toronto: Dent, 1933; New York: E. P. Dutton, 1933), conveniently collects together Hogg's *Life*, Trelawny's *Recollections* and Peacock's *Memoir*. The standard life of Shelley is Newman Ivey White's two-volume *Shelley* (New York: Albert A. Knopf, 1940). Although published more than fifty years ago, its comprehensiveness and scrupulousness make it 'definitive', despite the fact that it is not up-to-date. It can be usefully supplemented (but has not been supplanted) by Richard Holmes's *Shelley: The Pursuit* (London: Weidenfeld & Nicolson, 1974; London: Quartet Books, 1976; Harmondsworth: Penguin Books, 1987). Holmes's researches add something in terms of both information and inference to controversial episodes in Shelley's life, but the popularizing purpose which they serve is elsewhere an impulse that leads to a disappointing trivializing of Shelley's feelings and beliefs. This is despite the admirable attempt, outlined in the 'Introduction', to reorient interest in Shelley as

> a writer who moved everywhere with a sense of ulterior motive, a sense of greater design, an acute feeling for the historical moment and an overwhelming consciousness of his duty as an *artist* in the immense and fiery process of social change of which he knew himself to be a part.

Michael O'Neill's *Shelley: A Literary Life*, Macmillan Literary Lives (Basingstoke and London: Macmillan, 1989) provides a more inclusive sense of Shelley's motive and design and duty as an artist; and William St Clair's *The Godwins and the Shelleys: The Biography of a Family* (London and Boston, Mass.: Faber, 1989) offers an incisive account of the historical moment in its process of social change, and of those in the Godwin and Shelley circles who participated in that process. Kenneth Neill Cameron's 'critical biographies', *The Young Shelley: Genesis of a Radical* (London and New York: Macmillan, 1950) and *Shelley: The Golden Years* (Cambridge, Mass.: Harvard University Press, 1974), are essential introductory (and more than introductory) reading, for their contextual information and their encounters with textual cruxes and critical controversies. The first of these has been especially important in the reappraisal of Shelley as poet and political thinker.

The critical record on Shelley is now too extensive and diverse to be represented with any completeness here. At its perimeters, Shelley features in studies of other authors or of subjects other than poetry: for example, the fullest account of Shelley and Shakespeare is in Jonathan Bate's *Shakespeare and the English Romantic Imagination* (Oxford: Clarendon Press, 1989); and the most considered and convincing account of Shelley's atheism is in David Berman's *A History of Atheism in Britain: From Hobbes to Russell* (London and Sydney: Croom Helm, 1988). One of the most interesting and distinguished books on Shelley is also about Byron – Charles E. Robinson's *Shelley and Byron: The Snake and Eagle Wreathed in Fight* (Baltimore, Md, and London: Johns Hopkins University Press, 1976).

With the enormous extension of Shelley commentary and criticism, there has inevitably also been an elaboration of study, in which particular elements in, or special aspects of, Shelley's writings become the central analytic concern. On Shelley as translator, Timothy Webb's *The Violet in the Crucible: Shelley and Translation* (Oxford: Clarendon Press, 1976) is definitive. On Shelley as political thinker, the problems of definition and definitive reading abound: Paul Foot's *Red Shelley* (London: Sidgwick & Jackson, 1980; London: Bookmarks, 1984) is boldly populist and primary-coloured; Paul M. S. Dawson's *The Unacknowledged Legislator: Shelley and Politics* (Oxford: Clarendon Press, 1980) is rather more sophisticated, with a more variously and subtly hued spectrum; Gerald McNeice's *Shelley and the Revolutionary Idea* (Cambridge, Mass.: Harvard University Press, 1969) and Michael Scrivener's *Radical Shelley: The Philosophical Anarchism and Utopian Thought of Percy Bysshe Shelley* (Princeton, NJ: Princeton University Press, 1982) pursue their titles' polarized concerns; and Timothy Clark's *Embodying Revolution: The Figure of the Poet in Shelley* (Oxford: Clarendon Press, 1989) investigates the relations between the introspective poet and the political radical in Shelley. Shelley as philosophical thinker is no less controversial than Shelley as political thinker: C. E. Pulos's *The Deep Truth: A Study of Shelley's Skepticism* (Lincoln, Nebr.: University of Nebraska Press, 1954) has been seminal. Shelley's aesthetic thinking is the focus of Lloyd Abbey's *Destroyer and Preserver: Shelley's Poetic Skepticism* (Lincoln, Nebr.: University of Nebraska Press, 1979) and illuminatingly investigated in Angela Leighton's *Shelley and the Sublime: An Interpretation of the Major Poems* (Cambridge: Cambridge University Press, 1984).

A different elaboration of study from the kind illustrated above, although not always separate from it, has resulted from critical approaches to Shelley made from within the positions or positings of one theory or another, or of several, whether literary in origin or derived from disciplines other than the study of literature. Among the most influential of these approaches have been structuralist, post-structuralist and, particularly, deconstructionist readings. In what must be described (making no allowances for a required indeterminacy) as deconstructive accounts of Shelley, *The Triumph of Life* is the figured text, suffering (but not suffering from) 'disfiguration' in Paul de Man's 'Shelley Disfigured' in *Deconstruction and Criticism* (London and Henley: Routledge & Kegan Paul, 1979), and the demonstrated and self-demonstrating 'dismantled' text in J.

Hillis Miller's *The Linguistic Moment: From Wordsworth to Stevens* (Princeton, NJ: Princeton University Press, 1985).

Most of the books mentioned above are not only written by university specialists in Shelley, or specialists in literary theory, or specialists in both, but are also written for other specialists and their students in other universities. So, to conclude this section, a further list of works of criticism on Shelley seems called for: those that, whatever their critical starting-point, would be instructive reading for anyone who wants to add to his or her knowledge and understanding of Shelley. They do jnot constitute 'basic reading' because, although all are in some sense introductory and general, none is undemanding or unchallenging intellectually. All repay re-reading as well as reading.

The most accessible to the non-specialist are, listing them chronologically, Judith Chernaik's *The Lyrics of Shelley* (Cleveland, Ohio, and London: Case Western Reserve University Press, 1972); Timothy Webb's *Shelley: A Voice Not Understood* (Manchester: Manchester University Press, 1977); David Pirie's *Shelley*, Open Guides to Literature (Milton Keynes: Open University Press, 1988); and Michael O'Neill's *The Human Mind's Imaginings: Conflict and Achievement in Shelley's Poetry* (Oxford: Clarendon Press, 1988).

To these should be added Earl R. Wasserman's intellectually difficult but rewarding *Shelley: A Critical Reading* (Baltimore, Md, and London: Johns Hopkins University Press, 1971); Stuart Curran's *Shelley's Annus Mirabilis: The Maturing of an Epic Vision* (San Marino, Calif.: Huntington Library, 1975); Richard Cronin's acutely discerning and discriminating *Shelley's Poetic Thoughts* (London and Basingstoke: Macmillan, 1981); William Keach's vividly and animatedly analytic *Shelley's Style* (New York and London: Methuen, 1984), Jerrold E. Hogle's *Shelley's Process: Radical Transference and the Development of His Major Works* (New York and Oxford: Oxford University Press, 1988); and Stuart M. Sperry's *Shelley's Major Verse: The Narrative and Dramatic Poetry* (Cambridge, Mass., and London: Harvard University Press, 1988).

Two books – offering collections of articles and extracted essays on Shelley, and as such particularly useful as introductory to both Shelley and modern criticism of Shelley – are *The New Shelley: Later Twentieth-Century Views*, ed. G. Kim Blank (Basingstoke and London: Macmillan, 1991), and *Shelley*, ed.

and introd. Michael O'Neill, Longman Critical Readers (London and New York: Longman, 1993). Michael O'Neill's 'Introduction' to the latter book is a valuable survey of criticism of Shelley since Eliot and Leavis, with an incisive review of more recent and contemporary criticism. G. Kim Blank's 'Introduction' is also valuable; and its appraisal of Shelley's divining intelligence, both questioning and questing, provides a late twentieth-century view which, in its positive perception of Shelley, is inclusive and corrective of many of the negative views of the past. That Shelley's ceaselessly sceptical and speculative curiosity, in his investigations into, and interrogations of, 'the human mind's imaginings', generates unanswered – and unanswerable – questions, 'does not mean that Shelley's poetry, even with its negative epistemology, is without hope':

> It only suggests that for Shelley answers only lead to other questions ... and that, in spite of all, one must go on, pushing further, looking for answers, hoping for victory, holding faith, seeking inspiration, expressing the inexpressible, and attempting to understand ... The dimensions of Shelley's political, historical, personal and literary concerns go *beyond* his sceptical disposition as it influences his stand on language and knowledge, but more often than not those concerns are negotiated *through* that sceptical disposition. In other words, it cannot be said that Shelley dismisses language as a tool of social change or method of historical reflection or means of emotional expression ... Indeed, Shelley felt that poetry had the potential to teach real lessons, describe real moments, and inspire real action ... Shelley's desire for language to recover and make manifest the original power of conception shows at once his hope that the word can shape and shake the world, and his fear that the world cannot hear his words – it can only listen for the voice and wait for Spring.

Notes to 'Shelley and his Critics'

1. Letter 678, to Horace Smith, 25 Jan. 1822, in *The Letters of Percy Bysshe Shelley*, 2 vols (Oxford, 1964), II, 379. Also letter 683, to John Gisborne 26 Jan. 1822 (*ibid.*, II, 366): 'You know I don't think much about Rev{iews} nor of the fame they give nor of that they take away.'
2. I am indebted to three collections for the contemporary reviews of Shelley's poetry quoted in this essay: Theodore Redpath, *The Young Romantics and Critical Opinion 1807-1824* (London, 1973) (hereafter *YR*); Newman Ivey White, *The Unextinguished*

Hearth (Durham, NC, 1938; repr. New York and London, 1966) (hereafter *UH*); and *Shelley: The Critical Heritage*, ed. James E. Barcus (London, 1975) (hereafter *CH*).

3. An entertaining narrative of the history of Shelley's reception is Sylva Norman, *Flight of the Skylark: The Development of Shelley's Reputation* (Norman, Okla., and London, 1954), which covers the period 1822–99, with a brief extension into this century as the book's epilogue. Another informative history is Roland A. Duerksen, *Shelleyan Ideas in Victorian Literature*, Studies in English Literature 12 (The Hague, 1966). Also useful in relation to Shelley's early posthumous reputation is Karsten Engelberg, *The Making of the Shelley Myth: An Annotated Bibliography of Criticism of Percy Bysshe Shelley, 1822–1860* (Westport, Conn., and London, 1988); and in relation to both early and more recent criticism, Clement Dunbar, *A Bibliography of Shelley Studies, 1823–1950* (New York and Folkestone, 1976).

4. May 1822, I, 540–5 (*CH*, 56–62; *UH*, 39–44).

5. *UH*, 39.

6. *Ibid.*

7. *Queen Mab*, VII, note 13 ('There is no God').

8. *CH*, 9.

9. *CH*, 63–70; *UH*, 45–52.

10. *Queen Mab*, VII, lines 84–266.

11. Mar. 1821, III, 278–81 (*CH*, 71–3; *UH*, 53–4).

12. No. 226 (19 May 1821), 305–8 (*CH*, 74–5; *UH*, 55–6).

13. *The Investigator, or Quarterly Magazine*, 1822, V, 315–73 (*CH*, 87–94; *UH*, 98–104).

14. Apr. 1816, LXXIX, 433 (*CH*, 95; *UH*, 105).

15. May 1816, n.s. V, 545–6 (*CH*, 96–7; *UH*, 105–6).

16. *Eclectic Review*, Oct. 1816, n.s. V, 391–3 (*CH*, 97–9; *UH*, 106–8; *YR*, 327–9).

17. No. 466 (1 Dec. 1816), 761–2, and no. 473 (19 Jan. 1817), 41 (*CH*, 99–100; *UH*, 108–9).

18. Nov. 1819, VI, 148–54 (*CH*, 101–5; *UH*, 110–16).

19. No. 527 (1 Feb. 1818), 75–6; no. 530 (22 Feb. 1818), 121–2; no. 531 (1 Mar. 1818), 139–41 (*CH*, 106–14; *UH*, 117–24).

20. Jan. 1819, IV, 475–82 (*CH* 115–22; *UH*, 125–32).

21. Apr. 1819, XXI, 460–71 (*CH*, 124–35; *UH*, 133–42).

22. No. 593 (9 May 1819), 302–3 (*CH*, 144–7; *UH*, 151–3).

23. June 1819, V, 268–74 (*CH*, 152–60; *UH*, 158–64).

24. *CH*, 163–224; *UH*, 167–216.

25. *CH*, 207–8.

26. No. 190 (9 Sept. 1820), 580–2 (*CH*, 226–35; *UH*, 217–25).

27. Sept. 1820, VII, 679–87 (*CH*, 235–42; *UH*, 225–31).

28. Sept. and Oct. 1820, II, 306–8, 382–91 (*CH*, 243–8; *UH*, 231–6).

29. Oct. 1821, XXVI, 168–80 (*CH*, 254–67; *UH*, 240–50).
30. No. 9 (12 Aug. 1820), 65–72 (*CH*, 270–5).
31. Feb. 1821, II, 122–7, (*CH*, 279–82).
32. *CH*, 284–6.
33. No. 20 (14 July 1821), 153–9 (*CH*, 289–95).
34. No. 17 (23 June 1821), 129–35 (*UH*, 275–6).
35. No. 133 (1 Dec. 1821), 751–4 (*CH*, 295–7; *UH*, 285–6).
36. No. 255 (8 Dec. 1821), 772–3 (*CH*, 297–30).
37. July 1824, XI, 494–514 (*CH*, 335–45; *YR*, 388–96).
38. *YR*, 399–405.
39. Matthew Arnold, *Essays in Criticism, First and Second Series*, Everyman edn (London, 1964), 330.
40. See Appendix 4 above.
41. *The Works of Charles Kingsley*, vol. XX: *Literary and General Lectures and Essays* (London, 1880), 37–58.
42. George Bernard Shaw, *Pen Portraits and Reviews* (London, 1931), 236–46.
43. Robert Browning, *An Essay on Percy Bysshe Shelley*, ed. W. Tyas Harden (London, 1888).
44. *Collected Works of John Stuart Mill*, vol. I: *Autobiography and Literary Essays*, ed. John M. Robinson and Jack Stillinger (Toronto, Buffalo and London, 1981), 341–65.
45. *Westminster Review*, XXXV (1841), 317–22.
46. *The Collected Works of Walter Bagehot*, ed. Norman St John-Stevas, vol. I: *The Literary Essays* (London, 1965), 432–76.
47. Richard Holt Hutton, *Literary Essays*, 3rd edn (London and New York, 1888), 133–87.
48. F. R. Leavis, *Revaluation: Tradition and Development in English Poetry*, Penguin edn (Harmondsworth, 1964), 170–98.
49. T. S. Eliot, *The Use of Poetry and the Use of Criticism*, 2nd edn (London, 1964), 87–102.
50. See p. 250 above.
51. *Selected Critical Writings of George Santayana*, ed. Norman Henfrey, vol. I (Cambridge, 1968).
52. See pp. 530–31 below.
53. *The New Shelley: Later Twentieth-Century Views*, ed. G. Kim Blank (Basingstoke and London, 1991), 11.

SUGGESTIONS FOR FURTHER READING

Texts

The standard complete edition of Shelley's poetry is still the Oxford edition by Thomas Hutchinson (1904; 2nd corrected edn by Geoffrey Matthews, Oxford, 1970), but this is textually inadequate and has no annotation. The edition by Neville Rogers which was intended to replace it was abandoned after two volumes. Eventually this gap will be filled by *Shelley: The Complete Poems*, a three-volume edition for Longman Annotated English Poets, which was initiated by Geoffrey Matthews and is being completed by Kelvin Everest. The first volume, which appeared in 1990, set extremely high standards especially in textual scrupulosity and in the rich range, precision and thoughtfulness of its annotation. A full edition on different principles, *The Complete Poetry of Percy Bysshe Shelley*, edited by Donald H. Reiman and Neil Fraistat, will be published by the Johns Hopkins University Press. The most authoritative and comprehensive shorter text currently available is *Shelley's Poetry and Prose*, ed. Donald H. Reiman and Sharon B. Powers (New York, 1977). This edition, which is based on a detailed reconsideration of all the textual evidence, contains most of Shelley's best poems, the *Defence of Poetry*, two short essays, limited annotation and a generous selection of influential critical essays. Other useful editions of separate works or groups of poems are as follows: *Alastor ... Prometheus Unbound ... Adonais*, ed. Peter Butter (London, 1970; annotated edition of Shelley's collections of 1816, 1820 and of *Adonais*); *The Lyrics of Shelley*, ed. Judith Chernaik (Cleveland, Ohio, and London, 1972; pioneering text of shorter poems as appendix to sensitive critical discussions); *Shelley: Selected Poems and Prose*, ed. G. M. Matthews (Oxford, 1964; succinct and helpful notes; good text); Alasdair D. F. Macrae, *Shelley: Selected Poetry and Prose* (London, 1991).

At present there is no reliable edition of the prose, though E. B. Murray has published the first volume of *The Prose Works of Percy Bysshe Shelley* (Oxford, 1993), which has set new standards in its textual care and its approach to dating, and which for the first time brings to Shelley's prose the scholarly focus that it deserves. The second volume, which will appear under the joint editorship of E. B. Murray and Timothy Webb, is now in a relatively advanced state of preparation. For those texts which do not appear in the first volume, it is still best perhaps to make sceptical use of the 1880 edition in four volumes by H. B. Forman, though convenience often dictates a consultation of *The Complete Works of Percy Bysshe Shelley*, ed. R. Ingpen and W. E. Peck (1926–30; Julian Edition) or of *Shelley's Prose: The Trumpet of a Prophecy*, ed. David Lee Clark (corrected edn Albuquerque, NM, 1966; repr. London, 1988). Unfortunately both Forman and Ingpen–Peck tend to confine their annotation to textual matters, while Clark's interpretative annotation, though fuller, is episodic, arbitrary and unreliable. None of these earlier editions can be trusted in the matter of dating. Shelley's translations from Plato have been edited by James A. Notopoulos, *The Platonism of Shelley* (Durham, NC, 1949). The standard edition of the correspondence is *The Letters of Percy Bysshe Shelley*, ed. F. L. Jones, 2 vols (Oxford, 1964), which has proved invaluable but which will certainly need to be revised and updated in the light of recent advances in editorial technique and, specifically, in Shelley scholarship.

Biographies

The most readable biography is *Shelley: The Pursuit* (London, 1974) by Richard Holmes, which offers a strongly psychological interpretation of Shelley's life as a corrective to more sentimentalized presentations of beautiful but ineffectual angels. Holmes's biography is particularly sensitive to the spirit of place and retraces Shelley's footsteps with well-tuned antennae. In spite of its great virtues, this account requires correction and revision, especially in the light of recent scholarship; it can be usefully supplemented by Newman Ivey White, *Shelley*, 2 vols (New York, 1940). Earlier treatment can no longer be regarded as fully reliable or authoritative. No biography can now aspire to genuine and unquestioned authority until the manuscript evidence of the prose, poetry and letters has been fully assessed. Shelley's life was short in chronological terms but the materials are so rich and complex that, even when the manuscripts have been fully sifted and edited, it will be difficult if not impossible to produce a single-volume biography which could be anything other than partial and programmatically selective. Claire Tomalin's attractive *Shelley and his World* (1980; London, 1992) provides a short narrative which is well supplemented by illustrations. Robert Woof's *Shelley: An Ineffectual Angel* (Grasmere, 1992) combines Shelley's life, books and contexts in an illustrated survey based on the bicentenary exhibition at Dove Cottage. *Shelley's Guitar: A Bodleian Exhibition of Manuscripts, First Editions and Relics of Percy Bysshe Shelley*, compiled by B. C. Barker-Benfield (Oxford, 1992), concentrates on Shelley's books and manuscripts; it is beautifully illustrated, and edited with meticulous and illuminating scholarship. K. N. Cameron's *The Young Shelley: Genesis of a Radical* (New York,

1950; London, 1951) is a Marxist reading of Shelley's life up to 1814 which provides an intellectual profile rather than a conventional biographical treatment. Cameron's supplementary account, *Shelley: The Golden Years* (Cambridge, Mass., 1974) introduces a suggestive range of political contexts but is even more tenuously in touch with Shelley's development as a man rather than as a writer or political thinker. Literary lives, compressed but very useful, are provided by Donald H. Reiman, *Percy Bysshe Shelley*, rev. edn (Boston, Mass., 1990) and Michael O'Neill, *Shelley* (London and New York, 1993). Specific aspects of Shelley's life are treated by Desmond Hawkins, *Shelley's First Love* (London and Hamden, Conn., 1992) and by Nora Crook and Derek Guiton, *Shelley's Venomed Melody* (Cambridge, 1986), which is, in effect, a medical biography. William St Clair, *The Godwins and the Shelleys: The Biography of a Family* (London and Boston, 1989) provides a wider background. Biographical legend and the development of Shelley's reputation are traced in Sylva Norman, *Flight of the Skylark* (Norman, Okla., 1954).

Valuable, if sometimes distorted, contemporary records are provided by: *The Letters of Mary W. Shelley*, ed. Betty Bennett (Baltimore and London, 1980–8); *The Journals of Mary Shelley, 1814–44*, ed. Paula R. Feldman and Diana Scott-Kilvert (Oxford, 1987); *The Journals of Claire Clairmont*, ed. Marion Kingston Stocking (Cambridge, Mass., 1968); *Maria Gisborne and Edward E. Williams: Their Journals and Letters*, ed. F. L. Jones (Norman, Okla., 1951); Thomas Jefferson Hogg, *The Life of Shelley* (1858); Thomas Love Peacock, *Memoirs of Shelley* (1858–62); Edward John Trelawny, *Recollections of Shelley and Byron* (1858), collected in a two-volume edition by Humbert Wolfe (1933); Edward J. Trelawny, *Records of Shelley, Byron and the Author* (1878), ed. David Wright (Harmondsworth, 1973); Thomas Medwin, *The Life of Percy Bysshe Shelley* (1847); revised edn by H. B. Forman, 1913); Leigh Hunt, *Autobiography* (1859), ed. J. E. Morpurgo (London, 1949); annotated edition of 1850 version, with details of earlier textual strata, by Timothy Webb (forthcoming). Byron's conversations may also be consulted usefully. *Shelley and his Circle 1773–1822* is an invaluable aid. This ten-volume project, sponsored by the Pforzheimer Foundation in New York, is based on original materials and provides an exhaustive study both of the texts in question and of many matters relating to Shelley, his friends and the details of contemporary life. So far eight volumes have appeared, 1–4 (1961–70) edited by K. N. Cameron; 5–8 (1973–86) edited by D. H. Reiman.

Critical anthologies

English Romantic Poets, ed. M. H. Abrams, 2nd edn (Oxford, 1975) = ERP; *Essays on Shelley*, ed. G. Kim Blank (Liverpool, 1982) = ES;

The New Shelley: Later Twentieth-Century Views, ed. Miriam Allott (Basingstoke and London, 1991) = NS; *Percy Bysshe Shelley: Bicentenary Essays*, ed. Kelvin Everest, Essay and Studies 45 (Cambridge, 1992) = PBS; *Shelley Revalued: Essays from the Gregynog Conference*, ed. Kelvin Everest (Leicester, 1983) = SR; *Shelley*, Michael O'Neill, Longman Critical Readers (London and New York, 1993); *Shelley*, ed. George M. Ridenour, Twentieth Century Views (Englewood Cliffs, NJ, 1965) = TCV; *Percy Bysshe Shelley: Special Issue*, *Durham University Journal*, new series 54 (July, 1993) = DUJ; *Shelley: Shorter Poems and Lyrics*, ed. Patrick Swinden, Casebook (London, 1976) = CB; *Shelley*, ed. R. B. Woodings, Modern Judgements (London, 1969) = MJ. Earlier criticism is collected in *The Unextinguished Hearth*, ed. Newman I. White (Durham, NC, 1938; London, 1966). *Shelley: The Critical Heritage*, ed. James E. Barcus (London and Boston, Mass., 1975) covers much the same ground as White with less detail on the circumstances of publication and a rather arbitrary additional selection of American criticism. *The Young Romantics and Critical Opinion, 1807–1824*, ed. Theodore Redpath (London, 1973) offers a well-chosen but briefer collection. Another valuable book is R. Brimley Johnson, *Shelley – Leigh Hunt: How Friendship Made History* (London, 1928), which provides an illuminating record of Hunt's letters to and criticism of Shelley. For bibliographies, see: Karsten Engelberg, *The Making of the Shelley Myth: An Annotated Bibliography of Percy Bysshe Shelley 1822–1860* (London and Westport, Conn., 1988); Clement Dunbar, *A Bibliography of Shelley Studies: 1823–1950* (New York and London, 1976). An annual bibliography is printed in *Keats-Shelley Journal*.

Critical or general books on Shelley

Lloyd Abbey, *Destroyer and Preserver: Shelley's Poetic Skepticism* (Lincoln, Nebr., 1979); Carlos Baker, *Shelley's Major Poetry: The Fabric of a Vision* (Princeton, NJ, 1948); Ellsworth Barnard, *Shelley's Religion* (Minneapolis, Minn., 1937); Stephen C. Behrendt, *Shelley and his Audiences* (Lincoln, Nebr., and London, 1989); G. Kim Blank, *Wordsworth's Influence on Shelley: A Study of Poetic Authority* (Basingstoke and London, 1988); Nathaniel Brown, *Sexuality and Feminism in Shelley* (Cambridge, Mass., and London, 1979); Peter Butter, *Shelley's Idols of the Cave* (Edinburgh, 1954); K. N. Cameron, *Shelley: The Golden Years* (Cambridge, Mass., 1974; see *Biographies*); Judith Chernaik, *The Lyrics of Shelley* (Cleveland, Ohio, and London, 1972); Timothy Clark, *Embodying Revolution: The Figure of the Poet in Shelley* (Oxford, 1989); Richard Cronin, *Shelley's Poetic Thoughts* (London and Basingstoke, 1981); Nora Crook and Derek Guiton, *Shelley's Venomed Melody* (Cambridge, 1986); Stuart Curran, *Shelley's 'Annus Mirabilis'* (San Marino, Calif., 1975); Stuart Curran, *Shelley's*

'Cenci': Scorpions Ringed with Fire (Princeton, NJ, 1970); Mario Curreli and Anthony L. Johnson, eds, Paradise of Exiles: Shelley and Byron in Pisa (Salzburg, 1988); P. M. S. Dawson, The Unacknowledged Legislator: Shelley and Politics (Oxford, 1980); Roland A. Duerksen, Shelley's Poetry of Involvement (New York and London, 1989); David Duff, Romance and Revolution: Shelley and the Politics of a Genre (Cambridge, 1994); Edward Duffy, Rousseau in England: The Context for Shelley's Critique of the Enlightenment (Berkeley, Los Angeles and London, 1979); Paul Foot, Red Shelley (London, 1980; repr. 1984); Christine Gallant, Shelley's Ambivalence (Basingstoke and London, 1989); Barbara Charlesworth Gelpi, Shelley's Goddess: Maternity, Language, Subjectivity (New York and Oxford, 1992); Carl Grabo, A Newton among Poets (Chapel Hill, NC, 1930); Jean Hall, The Transforming Image: A Study of Shelley's Major Poetry (Urbana, Ill., and London, 1980); Terence Allan Hoagwood, Skepticism and Ideology: Shelley's Political Prose and its Philosophical Context from Bacon to Marx (Iowa City, 1988); Patricia Hodgart, A Preface to Shelley (London and New York, 1985); Jerrold E. Hogle, Shelley's Process: Radical Transference and the Development of his Major Works (New York and Oxford, 1988); A. M. D. Hughes, The Nascent Mind of Shelley (Oxford, 1971); William Keach, Shelley's Style (New York and London, 1984); Desmond King-Hele, Shelley: His Thought and Work 2nd edn (London, 1971); Angela Leighton, Shelley and the Sublime: An Interpretation of the Major Poems (Cambridge, 1984); Hélène Lemaitre, Shelley: Poète des éléments (Paris, 1962); Gerald McNiece, Shelley and the Revolutionary Idea (Cambridge, Mass., 1969); Glen O'Malley, Shelley and Synaesthesia (Chicago, Ill., 1964); Michael O'Neill, The Human Mind's Imaginings: Conflict and Achievement in Shelley's Poetry (Oxford, 1989); Jean Perrin, Les Structures de L'imaginaire shelleyen (Grenoble, 1973); David Pirie, Shelley (Milton Keynes, 1988); C. E. Pulos; The Deep Truth: A Study of Shelley's Skepticism (Lincoln, Nebr., 1954); Donald H. Reiman, Percy Bysshe Shelley, 2nd edn (New York, 1990); Neville Rogers, Shelley at Work, 2nd edn (Oxford, 1967); Bryan Shelley, Shelley and Scripture: The Interpreting Angel (Oxford, 1994); Stuart Sperry, Shelley's Major Verse: The Narrative and Dramatic Poetry (Cambridge, Mass., and London, 1988); Ronald Tetreault, The Poetry of Life: Shelley and Literary Form (Toronto, 1987); William A. Ulmer, Shelleyan Eros: the Rhetoric of Romantic Love (Princeton, NJ, 1990); Earl Wasserman, Shelley: A Critical Reading (Baltimore, Md, and London, 1971); Timothy Webb, Shelley: A Voice Not Understood (Manchester, 1977); Timothy Webb, The Violet in the Crucible: Shelley and Translation (Oxford, 1976); Alan Weinberg, Shelley's Italian Experience, (Basingstoke and London, 1991); Karen A. Weisman, Imageless Truths: Shelley's Poetic Fictions (Philadelphia, Pa, 1994); Andrew J. Welburn, Power and Self-Con-

sciousness in the Poetry of Shelley (New York, 1986); Milton Wilson, *Shelley's Later Poetry: A Study of his Prophetic Imagination* (New York, 1959); Ross G. Woodman, *The Apocalyptic Vision in the Poetry of Shelley* (Toronto, 1964).

Books including chapters or sections on Shelley

Isobel Armstrong, *Language as Living Form in Nineteenth Century Poetry* (Brighton and Totowa, NJ, 1982); Jonathan Bate, *Shakespeare and the English Romantic Imagination* (Oxford, 1989); David Berman, *A History of Atheism in Britain: from Hobbes to Russell* (London and Sydney, 1988); Harold Bloom, *Poetry and Repression: Revisionism from Blake to Stevens* (New Haven, Conn., 1976); Harold Bloom, *The Visionary Company: A Reading of English Romantic Poetry*, rev. edn (Ithaca, NY and London, 1971); Leslie Brisman, *Romantic Origins* (Ithaca, NY, and London, 1978); Frederic Burwick, *The Damnation of Newton: Goethe's Color Theory and Romantic Perception* (Berlin and New York, 1986); Marilyn Butler, *Romantics, Rebels and Reactionaries: English Literature and its Background, 1760–1830* (Oxford, 1981); John Drew, *India and the Romantic Imagination* (Delhi, 1987); Steve Ellis, *Dante and English Poetry: Shelley to T. S. Eliot* (Cambridge, 1983); Neil Fraistat, *The Poem and the Book: Interpreting Collections of Romantic Poetry* (Chapel Hill, NC, and London, 1985); Paul H. Fry, *The Poet's Calling in the English Ode* (New Haven, Conn., and London, 1980); Diane Long Hoeveler, *Romantic Androgyny: The Women Within* (University Park, Pa, and London, 1990); Carol Jacobs, *Uncontainable Romanticism: Shelley, Brontë, Kleist* (Baltimore, Md, 1989); Greg Kucich, *Keats, Shelley and Romantic Spenserianism* (University Park, Pa, 1991); Nigel Leask, *British Romantic Writers and the East: Anxieties of Empire* (Cambridge, 1992); Marjorie Levinson, *The Romantic Fragment Poem: A Critique of a Form* (Chapel Hill, NC, and London, 1986); John Lucas, *England and Englishness: Ideas of Nationhood in English Poetry, 1688–1900* (London, 1990); J. Hillis Miller, *The Linguistic Moment: From Wordsworth to Stevens* (Princeton, NJ, 1985); Lucy Newlyn, *'Paradise Lost' and the Romantic Reader* (Oxford, 1993); Ralph Pite, *The Circle of Our Vision: Dante's Presence in English Romantic Poetry* (Oxford, 1994); Balachandra Rajan, *The Form of the Unfinished: English Poetics from Spenser to Pound* (Princeton, NJ, 1985); Tilottama Rajan, *Dark Interpreter: The Discourse of Romanticism* (Ithaca, NY, and London, 1980); Tilottama Rajan, *The Supplement of Reading: Figures of Understanding in Romantic Theory and Practice* (Ithaca, NJ, and London, 1990); Donald H. Reiman, *Romantic Texts and Contexts* (Columbia, Miss., 1987); Peter M. Sacks, *The English Elegy: Studies in the Genre from Spenser to Yeats* (Baltimore, Md, 1985); James B. Twitchell, *Romantic Hori-*

zons: Aspects of the Sublime in English Poetry and Painting (Columbia, Miss., 1983).

Articles

Carlene Adamson, 'Tomorrow', *Keats-Shelley Review*, 7 (1992), 98–107; Barbara T. Allen, 'Poetry and Machinery in Shelley's "Letter to Maria Gisborne"' *Nineteenth-Century Studies*, 2 (1988), 53–61; Graham Allen, 'Transumption and/in History: Bloom, Shelley and the Figure of the Poet' (DUJ); Miriam Allott, 'The Rewriting of a Literary Genre: Shelley's *The Triumph of Life*' (ES); John Archer, 'Authority in Shelley', *Studies in Romanticism*, 26 (1987), 259–73; John Jay Baker, 'Myth, Subjectivity, and the Problem of Historical Time in Shelley's "Lines Written among the Euganean Hills"', *English Literary History*, 56 (1989), 149–72; John Ross Baker, 'Poetry and Language in Shelley's *Defence of Poetry*', *Journal of Aesthetics and Art Criticism*, 39 (1981), 437–49; B. C. Barker-Benfield, 'Hogg–Shelley Papers of 1810–12', *Bodleian Library Record*, 14 (1991), 14–29; Bernard Beatty, 'Repetition's Music: *The Triumph of Life*' (PBS); Bernard Beatty 'The Transformation of Discourse: *Epipsychidion, Adonais*, and Some Lyrics' (ES); Ronald E. Becht, 'Shelley's *Adonais*: Formal Design and the Lyric Speaker's Crisis of Imagination', *Studies in Philology*, 78 (1981), 194–210; Stephen C. Behrendt, 'Beatrice Cenci and the Tragic Myth of History', in *History and Myth: Essays on English Romantic Literature*, ed. Stephen C. Behrendt, (Detroit, Ill., 1990), 214–34; Stephen C. Behrendt, 'The Exoteric Species: The Popular Idiom in Shelley's Poetry', *Genre* (1981), 473–92; Christine Berthin, '*Prometheus Unbound*, or Discourse and its Other', *Keats-Shelley Journal*, 43 (1993), 128–41; William D. Brewer, 'Questions without Answers: The Conversational Style of *Julian and Maddalo*', *Keats–Shelley Journal*, 38 (1989), 127–44; Robert A. Brinkley, 'Documenting Revision: Shelley's Lake Geneva Diary and the Dialogue with Byron in *History of a Six Weeks' Tour*', *Keats–Shelley Journal*, 39 (1990), 66–82; Robert A. Brinkley, 'On the Composition of *Mont Blanc*: Staging a Wordsworthian Scene', *English Language Notes*, 24 (1986), 45–57; Robert A. Brinkley, 'Spaces between Words: Writing *Mont Blanc*', in *Romantic Revisions*, ed. Robert Brinkley and Keith Hanley (Cambridge, 1992), 243–67; Robert A. Brinkley, 'Writing *Mont Blanc*', *Wordsworth Circle*, 18 (1987), 108–13; Leslie Brisman, 'Mysterious Tongue: Shelley and the Language of Christianity', *Texas Studies in Language and Literature*, 23 (1981), 389–417; Susan Hawk Brisman, '"Unsaying His High Language": The Problem of Voice in *Prometheus Unbound*', *Studies in Romanticism*, 16 (1977), 51–86; Nathaniel Brown, 'The "Double Soul": Virginia Woolf, Shelley and Androgyny', *Keats–Shelley Journal*, 33 (1984), 182–204; Frederick Burwick, 'The Language of

Causality in *Prometheus Unbound*', *Keats–Shelley Journal*, 31 (1982), 136–58; Marilyn Butler, 'Myth and Mythmaking in the Shelley Circle' (SR); John Buxton, 'On Reading Shelley', in *Essays and Poems presented to Lord David Cecil*, ed. W. W. Robson (London, 1970), 109–25; Stephen Bygrave, 'Allegory, Incest and Naming Names: The Shelleys, 1816–1818', in *Shelley 1792–1822*, ed. James Hogg, Salzburg Studies in English Literature (New York, 1993), 1–14; Richard S. Caldwell, '"The Sensitive Plant" as Original Fantasy', *Studies in Romanticism*, 15 (1976), 221–52; K. N. Cameron, 'Shelley and Marx', *Wordsworth Circle*, 10 (1979), 234–9; Yvonne M. Carothers, '*Alastor*: Shelley Corrects Wordsworth', *Modern Language Quarterly*, 42 (1981), 21–47; Laura Claridge, 'The Bifurcated Female Space of Desire: Shelley's Confrontation with Language and Silence', in *Out of Bounds: Male Writers and Gender(ed) Criticism*, ed. Laura Claridge and Elizabeth Langland (Amherst, Mass., 1990), 92–109; Timothy Clark, 'Shelley's "The Coliseum" and the Sublime' (DUJ); Pamela Clemit, 'Shelley's Godwin, 1812–1817' (DUJ); Frederick S. Colwell, 'Shelley and Italian Painting', *Keats–Shelley Journal*, 29 (1980), 43–66; Frederick S. Colwell, 'Shelley on Sculpture: the Uffizi Notes', *Keats–Shelley Journal*, 28 (1979), 59–77; William Crisman, 'Psychological Realism and Narrative Manner in Shelley's *Alastor* and *The Witch of Atlas*', *Keats–Shelley Journal*, 35 (1986), 126–48; Richard Cronin, 'Shelley's Language of Dissent', *Essays in Criticism*, 27 (1977), 203–15; Richard Cronin, '*Peter Bell*, Peterloo and the Politics of Cockney Poetry' (PBS); Nora Crook, 'The Boat on the Serchio', *Keats–Shelley Review*, 7 (1992), 85–97; Martyn Crucefix, 'Wordsworth, Superstition and Shelley's *Alastor*', *Essays in Criticism*, 33 (1983), 126–47; Stuart Curran '*Adonais* in Context' (SR); Stuart Curran, 'Shelley's Pisan Pastorals', in *Paradise of Exiles: Shelley and Byron in Pisa*, ed. Mario Curreli and Anthony L. Johnson (Salzburg, 1988), 15–29; Stuart Curran, 'The Political Prometheus', *Studies in Romanticism*, 25 (1986), 429–55; Graham Daldry, 'Poetry as Question: *The Triumph of Life*', *Textual Practice*, 2 (1988), 261–75; Michael Davidson, 'Refiguring Shelley: Postmodern Recuperations of Romanticism', *Keats–Shelley Journal*, 42 (1993), 48–57; Daniel Davy, 'The Harmony of the Horoscope: A Perspective on *The Cenci*', *Journal of Dramatic Theory and Criticism*, 5 (1990), 95–113; P. M. S. Dawson, 'Byron, Shelley, and the "New School"' (SR); P. M. S. Dawson, '"King Over Himself": Shelley's Philosophical Anarchism', *Keats–Shelley Memorial Bulletin*, 30 (1979), 16–35; P. M. S. Dawson, 'Shelley and Animal Magnetism', *Keats–Shelley Review*, 1 (1986), 15–34; P. M. S. Dawson, 'Shelley and Class' (NS); P. M. S. Dawson, 'Shelley and the *Improvvisatore* Sgricci: An Unpublished Review', *Keats–Shelley Memorial Bulletin*, 32 (1981), 19–29; V. A. de Luca, 'The Style of Millennial Announcement in *Prometheus Unbound*', *Keats–Shelley Journal*, 28 (1979), 78–101; Paul de Man, 'Shelley Transfigured', in *Deconstruction and Criticism*, ed. Harold Bloom *et al.* (New York, 1979), 39–73; Joseph W. Donohue, 'Shelley's Beatrice and the Romantic Concept of Tragic Character', *Keats–Shelley Journal*, 17 (1968), 53–73; John Donovan, 'Incest in *Laon and Cythna*: Nature, Custom, Desire', *Keats–Shelley Review*, 2 (1987), 49–90; Edward Duffy, 'Where Shelley Wrote and What He Wrote For: The Example of "The Ode to the West Wind"', *Studies in Romanticism*, 23 (1984), 351–77; James C. Evans, 'Masks of the Poet: A Study of Self-Confrontation in Shelley's Poetry', *Keats–Shelley Journal*, 24 (1975), 70–88; Michael Erkelenz, 'Shelley's Draft of "Mont Blanc" and the Conflict of "Faith"', *Review of English Studies*, 40 (1989), 100–3; Kelvin Everest, 'Athanase', *Keats–Shelley Review*, 7 (1992), 62–84; Kelvin Everest, '"Mechanism of a Kind Yet Unattempted": The Dramatic Action of *Prometheus Unbound*' (DUJ); Kelvin Everest, '"Ozymandias": The Text in Time' (PBS); Kelvin Everest, 'Shelley's Doubles: An Approach to *Julian and Maddalo*' (SR); Frances Ferguson, 'Shelley's *Mont Blanc*: What the Mountain Said', in *Romanticism and Language*, ed. Arden Reed (London, 1984), 202–14; Peter Finch, 'Shelley's Laon and Cythna: The Bride Stripped Bare . . . Almost', *Keats–Shelley Review*, 3 (1988), 23–46; Newell F. Ford, 'Paradox and Irony in Shelley's Poetry', *Studies in Philology*, 57 (1960), 648–62; Newell F. Ford, 'The Wit in Shelley's Poetry', *Studies in English Literature*, 1 (1961), 1–22; Neil Fraistat, 'Poetic Quests and Questioning in Shelley's *Alastor* Collection', *Keats–Shelley Journal*, 33 (1984), 161–81; John Freeman, 'Shelley's Early Letters' (SR); John Freeman, 'Shelley's Letters to his Father', *Keats–Shelley Memorial Bulletin*, 34 (1983), 1–15; David Fuller, 'Shelley and Jesus' (DUJ); Barbara Charlesworth Gelpi, 'The Nursery Cave: Shelley and the Maternal' (NS); Elise M. Gold, '*King Lear* and Aesthetic Tyranny in Shelley's *The Cenci*, *Swellfoot the Tyrant*, and *The Witch of Atlas*', *English Language Notes*, 24 (1968), 58–70; Elise M. Gold, 'Touring the Inventions: Shelley's Prefatory Writing', *Keats–Shelley Journal*, 36 (1987), 63–87; Jane Goodall, 'Artaud's Revision of Shelley's *The Cenci*: The Text and its Double', *Comparative Drama*, 21 (1987), 115–26; Nancy Moore Goslee, 'Dispersoning Emily: Drafting as Plot in *Epipsychidion*', *Keats–Shelley Journal*, 42 (1993), 104–19; Nancy Goslee, 'Shelley at Play: A Study of Sketch and Text in his *Prometheus Unbound* Notebooks', *Huntington Library Quarterly*, 48 (1985), 211–56; Deborah A. Gutschera, 'The Drama of Reenactment in Shelley's *Revolt of Islam*', *Keats–Shelley Journal*, 35 (1986), 111–25; Jean Hall, 'Poetic Autonomy in *Peter Bell the Third* and *The Witch of Atlas*' (NS); Jean Hall, 'The Divine and the Dispassionate Selves: Shelley's *Defence* and Peacock's *The Four Ages of Poetry*', *Keats–Shelley Journal*, 41 (1992), 139–63; Jean Hall, 'The Socialized Imagination: Shelley's *The Cenci* and *Prometheus Unbound*', *Studies in Romanticism*, 23 (1984),

339–50; D. Harrington Leuker, 'Imagination versus Introspection: *The Cenci* and *Macbeth*', *Keats–Shelley Journal*, 32 (1983), 172–89; R. A. Hartley, 'The Uroboros in Shelley's Poetry', *Journal of English and Germanic Philology*, 73 (1974), 524–42; Robert Hartley, 'Shelley's Copy of Dante', *Keats–Shelley Journal*, 39 (1990), 22–9; Richard H. Haswell, 'Shelley's *The Revolt of Islam*: "The Connection of Its Parts"' *Keats–Shelley Journal*, 25 (1976), 81–102; Helen E. Haworth, '*Ode to the West Wind* and the Sonnet Form', *Keats–Shelley Journal*, 20 (1971), 71–7; Bruce Heley, 'Shelley, Peacock, and the Reading of History', *Studies in Romanticism*, 29 (1990), 439–61; Richard Hendrix, 'The Necessity of Response: How Shelley's Radical Poetry Works', *Keats–Shelley Journal*, 27 (1978), 45–69; Christopher Heppner, '*Alastor*: The Poet and the Narrator Reconsidered', *Keats–Shelley Journal*, 37 (1988), 91–109; Ellen Brown Herson, 'Oxymoron and Dante's Gates of Hell in Shelley's *Prometheus Unbound*', *Studies in Romanticism*, 29 (1990), 371–93; Frederick L. Hildebrand, '*Epipsychidion*'s Cosmic Collision: A Controlling Metaphor', *Keats–Shelley Journal*, 37 (1988), 75–90; W. H. Hildebrand, 'A Look at the Third and Fourth Spirit Songs: *Prometheus Unbound*', *Keats–Shelley Journal*, 20 (1971), 87–99; William Hildebrand, 'Self, Beauty and Horror: Shelley's Medusa Moment' (NS); William H. Hildebrand, 'Naming-Day in Asia's Vale', *Keats–Shelley Journal*, 32 (1983), 190–203; J. A. Hodgson, 'The World's Mysterious Doom: Shelley's *The Triumph of Life*', *English Literary History*, 42 (1975), 595–622; Jerrold E. Hogle, 'Metaphor and Metamorphosis in Shelley's "The Witch of Atlas"', *Studies in Romanticism*, 19 (1980), 327–53; Jerrold E. Hogle, 'Shelley as Revisionist: Power and Belief in *Mont Blanc*' (NS); Jerrold E. Hogle, 'Shelley's Fiction: The "Stream of Fate"', *Keats–Shelley Journal*, 30 (1981), 78–99; Jerrold E. Hogle, 'Shelley's Poetics: The Power as Metaphor', *Keats–Shelley Journal*, 31 (1982), 159–97; Jerrold Hogle, 'Shelley's Texts and the Premises of Criticism', *Keats–Shelley Journal*, 42 (1993), 66–79; John Holloway, Introduction to *Selected Poems of Percy Bysshe Shelley* (London, 1960) (CB); Daniel J. Hughes, 'Coherence and Collapse in Shelley', *English Literary History*, 28 (1961), 260–83; Daniel J. Hughes, 'Kindling and Dwindling: The Poetic Process in Shelley', *Keats–Shelley Journal*, 13 (1964), 13–28; Daniel J. Hughes, 'Shelley, Leonardo and the Monsters of Thought', *Criticism*, 12 (1970), 195–212; Carol Jacobs, 'On Looking at Shelley's *Medusa*', *Yale French Studies*, 69 (1985), 163–79; Anne Janowitz, 'Shelley's Monument to Ozymandias', *Philological Quarterly*, 63 (1984), 477–91; Barbara Johnson, 'Apostrophe, Animation, and Abortion', *Diacritics*, 16 (1986), 29–47; Lilla Maria Crisafulli Jones, 'Poetry and Revolution: Shelley's *Ode to Naples*' in *L'esilio romantico: forme di un conflitto*, ed. Joseph Cheyne and Lilla Maria Crisafulli (Bari, 1990), 201–16; Steven E. Jones, 'Apostasy and Exhortation: Shelley's Satirical Fragments in the Huntington Notebooks', *Huntington Library Quarterly*, 53 (1990), 41–66; Steven E. Jones, 'Shelley's Fragment of a "Satire upon Satire": A Complete Transcription of the Text with Commentary', *Keats–Shelley Journal*, 37 (1988), 136–63; Stephen E. Jones, 'Shelley's "Love, The Universe": A Fragment in Context', *Keats–Shelley Journal*, 42 (1993), 80–96; I. J. Kapstein, 'The Meaning of *Mont Blanc*' (1947 (CB); William Keach, 'Obstinate Questionings: The Immortality Ode and *Alastor*', *Wordsworth Circle*, 12 (1981), 36–44; William Keach, 'Reflexive Imagery in Shelley', *Keats–Shelley Journal*, 24 (1975), 49–69; E. H. King, 'Beattie and Shelley: The Making of the Poet', *English Studies*, 61 (1980), 338–53; Desmond King-Hele, 'Shelley and Erasmus Darwin' (SR); Mark Kipperman, 'History and Ideality: The Politics of Shelley's *Hellas*', *Studies in Romanticism*, 30 (1991), 147–68; Mark Kipperman, 'The Power of Disenchantment: Fichtean Irony and the Creative Imagination in Shelley's *Mont Blanc*' in *English and German Romanticism: Cross-Currents and Controversies*, ed. James Pipkin (Heidelberg, 1985), 183–97; Karl Kroeber, 'Experience as History: Shelley's Venice, Turner's Carthage', *English Literary History*, 41 (1974), 321–39; Edward Larrissy, 'Ahasuerus-Xerxes: *Hellas* as Allegory of Dissemination' (PBS); John J. Lavelle, 'Shelley's Pythagorean Daemons' in *The Evidence of the Imagination*, ed. Donald H. Reiman, Michael C. Jaye and Betty T. Bennett (New York, 1978), 264–84; Angela Leighton, '*Adonais*: The Voice and the Text', *Keats–Shelley Memorial Bulletin*, 31 (1980), 39–51; Angela Leighton, 'Deconstruction Criticism and Shelley's *Adonais*' (SR); Angela Leighton, 'Love, Writing and Scepticism in *Epipsychidion*' (NS); John Robert Leo, 'Criticism of Consciousness in Shelley's "A Defence of Poetry"', *Philosophy and Literature*, 2 (1978), 46–59; Lawrence S. Lockridge, 'Justice in *The Cenci*', *Wordsworth Circle*, 19 (1988), 95–8; F. H. Ludlam, 'The Meterorology of the *Ode to the West Wind*' (1972) (CB); Jerome J. McGann, 'The Secrets of an Elder Day: Shelley after *Hellas*' (1966) (MJ); Gerald McNiece, 'The Poet as Ironist in "Mont Blanc" and "Hymn to Intellectual Beauty"', *Studies in Romanticism*, 14 (1975), 311–36; Anne McWhir, 'The Light and the Knife: Ab/Using Language in *The Cenci*', *Keats–Shelley Journal*, 38 (1989), 145–61; R. R. Male and J. A. Notopoulos, 'Shelley's Copy of Diogenes Laertius', *Modern Language Review*, 54 (1959), 10–21; Geoffrey Matthews, 'A Volcano's Voice in Shelley' (1957) (TCV; MJ); Geoffrey Matthews, '"Julian and Maddalo": The Draft and the Meaning', *Studia Neophilologica*, 35 (1963), 57–84; Geoffrey Matthews, 'On Shelley's *Triumph of Life*', *Studia Neophilologica*, 34 (1962), 104–34; Geoffrey Matthews, 'Shelley's Lyrics' (1969) (CB); J. Hillis Miller, 'The Critic as Host', in *Deconstruction and Criticism*, ed. Harold Bloom *et al*. (New York, 1979), 217–53; Fred L. Milne, 'The Anima Archetype in Shelley's Poetry', *Journal of Evolutionary Psychology*, 9 (1988), 236–47; Fred

L. Milne, 'The Eclipsed Imagination in Shelley's "The Triumph of Life"', *Studies in English Literature*, 21 (1981), 681–702; Peter Mortenson, 'Image and Structure in Shelley's Longer Lyrics', *Studies in Romanticism*, 4 (1965), 104–10; E. B. Murray, '*Mont Blanc*'s Unfurled Veil', *Keats–Shelley Journal*, 18 (1969), 39–48; E. B. Murray, 'Shelley's Contribution to Mary's *Frankenstein*', *Keats–Shelley Memorial Bulletin*, 29 (1978), 50–68; Brian Nellist, 'Shelley's Narratives and *The Witch of Atlas*' (ES); Leonard N. Neufeldt, 'Poetry as Subversion: The Unbinding of Shelley's Prometheus', *Anglia*, 95 (1977), 60–86; Vincent Newey, 'Shelley and the Poets: *Alastor, Julian and Maddalo, Adonais* (DUJ); Vincent Newey, ' "Shelley's Dream of Youth": *Alastor*, "Selving" and the Psychic Realm' (PBS); Vincent Newey, 'The Shelleyan Psycho-Drama: "Julian and Maddalo"' (ES); Michael O'Neill, 'A More Hazardous Exercise: Shelley's Revolutionary Imaginings', *Yearbook of English Studies*, 19 (1989), 256–64; Michael O'Neill, ' "And All Things Seem Only One": The Shelleyan Lyric' (PBS); Michael O'Neill, ' "The Bounds of the Air Are Shaken": The Shelleyan Visionary Lyric', in *Shelley 1792–1992*, ed. James Hogg, Salzburg Studies in English Literature (New York, 1993), 1–14; Michael O'Neill, ' "The Mind Which Feeds This Verse": Self and Other Awareness in Shelley's Poetry' (DUJ); Ants Oras, 'The Multitudinous Orb: Some Miltonic Elements in Shelley', *Modern Language Quarterly*, 16 (1955), 247–57; Jean de Palacio, 'Shelley traducteur de soi-même', *Revue des sciences humaines*, 158 (1975), 223–44; Coleman Parsons, 'Shelley's Prayer to the West Wind', *Keats–Shelley Journal*, 11 (1962), 31–7; Jean Perrin, 'The Actaeon Myth in Shelley's Poetry', *Essays and Studies*, 28 (1975), 29–46; Stuart Peterfreund, 'Between Desire and Nostalgia: Intertextuality in Shelley's *Alastor* and Two Shorter Poems from the *Alastor* volume', *Romanticism Past and Present*, 9 (1985), 47–66; Stuart Peterfreund, 'Seduced by Metonymy: Figuration and Authority in *The Cenci*' (NS); Stuart Peterfreund, 'The Two Languages and the Ineffable in Shelley's Major Poems', in *Ineffability: Naming the Unnamable from Dante to Beckett*, ed. Peter S. Hawkins and Anne Howland Schotter (New York, 1983), 161–81; Thomas Pfau, 'Tropes of Desire: Figuring the 'Insufficient Void' of Self-Consciousness in Shelley's *Epipsychidion*', *Keats–Shelley Journal*, 40 (1991), 99–126; John B. Pierce, '*Mont Blanc* and *Prometheus Unbound*: Shelley's Use of the Rhetoric of Silence', *Keats–Shelley Journal*, 38 (1989), 103–26; Frederick A. Pottle, 'The Role of Asia in the Dramatic Action of *Prometheus Unbound*' (1965) (TCV); Mary Quinn, 'Shelley's "Verses on the Celandine": An Elegiac Parody of Wordsworth's Early Lyrics', *Keats–Shelley Journal*, 36 (1987), 88–109; David Quint, 'Representation and Ideology in *The Triumph of Life*', *Studies in English Literature*, 18 (1978), 639–57; Joseph Raben, 'Shelley's *Prometheus Unbound*: Why the Indian Caucasus?', *Keats–Shelley Journal*, 12 (1963), 95–106; Joseph Raben,

'Shelley the Dionysian' (SR); Tilottama Rajan, 'Deconstruction or Reconstruction: Reading Shelley's *Prometheus Unbound*', *Studies in Romanticism*, 23 (1984), 317–38; Tilottama Rajan, 'The Web of Human Things: Narrative and Identity in *Alastor*' (NS); Fred V. Randel, '*Frankenstein*, Feminism, and the Intertextuality of Mountains', *Studies in Romanticism*, 23 (1984), 515–32; Claude Rawson, 'Byron Augustan: Mutations of the Mock-Heroic in *Don Juan* and Shelley's *Peter Bell the Third*', in *Byron: Augustan and Romantic*, ed. Andrew Rutherford (Basingstoke and London, 1990), 82–116; D. H. Reiman, 'Roman Scenes in *Prometheus Unbound* III.iv', *Philological Quarterly*, 46 (1967), 69–78; D. H. Reiman, 'Shelley as Agrarian Reactionary', *Keats–Shelley Memorial Bulletin*, 30 (1979), 5–15; D. H. Reiman, 'Structure, Symbol and Theme in "Lines Written Among the Euganean Hills"', *Publications of the Modern Language Association of America*, 77 (1962), 404–13; Donald H. Reiman, 'Shelley's Manuscripts and the Web of Circumstance', in *Romantic Revisions*, ed. Robert Brinkley and Keith Hanley (Cambridge, 1992), 227–42; Donna Richardson, '"The Dark Idolatry of Self": The Dialectic Imagination in Shelley's *Revolt of Islam*', *Keats–Shelley Journal*, 40 (1991), 73–98; H. M. Richmond, 'Ozymandias and the Travellers', *Keats–Shelley Journal*, 11 (1962), 65–71; John Rieder, 'Shelley's "Mont Blanc": Landscape and the Ideology of the Sacred Text', *English Literary History*, 48 (1981), 668–98; John Rieder, 'The "One" in *Prometheus Unbound*', *Studies in English Literature*, 25 (1985), 775–800; James Rieger, 'Shelley's Paterin Beatrice', *Studies in Romanticism* (1965), repr. in *The Mutiny Within* (New York, 1967); Charles E. Robinson, 'Percy Bysshe Shelley, Charles Ollier, and William Blackwood: The Contexts of Early Nineteenth-Century Publishing' (SR); Marlon B. Ross, 'Shelley's Wayward Dream-Poem: The Apprehending Reader in *Prometheus Unbound*', *Keats–Shelley Journal*, 36 (1987), 110–33; Michael Rossington, 'Shelley and the Orient', *Keats–Shelley Review*, 6 (1991), 18–36; Merle E. Rubin, 'Shelley's Skepticism: A Detachment Beyond Despair', *Philological Quarterly*, 59 (1980), 353–73; Charles J. Rzepka, '*Julian and Maddalo* as Revisionary Conversation Poem' (NS); Peter Sacks, 'Last Clouds: A Reading of *Adonais*', *Studies in Romanticism*, 23 (1984), 379–400; Earl Schulze, 'Allegory against Allegory: "The Triumph of Life"', *Studies in Romanticism*, 27 (1988), 31–62; Michael Scrivener, 'Shelley and Radical Artisan Poetry', *Keats–Shelley Journal*, 42 (1993), 22–36; David Seed, 'Shelley's "Gothick in *St Irvyne* and After' (ES); Bouthaina Shaaban, 'Shelley in the Chartist Press', *Keats–Shelley Memorial Bulletin*, 34 (1983), 41–60; Bryan Shelley, 'The Interpreting Angel in "The Triumph of Life"', *Review of English Studies*, 39 (1988), 386–99; John F. Slater, 'Self-Concealment and Self-Revelation in Shelley's *Epipsychidion*', *Papers on Language and Literature*, 11 (1975), 279–92; Gordon Spence, 'Shelley, Lucretius, and Images of

Reality', *Australasian Universities Modern Language Association*, 70 (1988), 313–20; Stuart M. Sperry, 'Necessity and the Role of the Hero in Shelley's *Prometheus Unbound*', *Publications of the Modern Language Association of America*, 96 (1981), 242–54; Lisa M. Steinman, '"These Common Woes": Shelley and Wordsworth' (NS); David M. Stocking and Marion Kingston Stocking, 'New Shelley Letters in a John Gisborne Notebook', *Keats–Shelley Memorial Bulletin*, 31 (1980), 1–9; Patrick Story, 'Pope, Pageantry, and Shelley's *Triumph of Life*', *Keats–Shelley Journal*, 21–2 (1972–3), 145–59; Ronald Tetreault, 'Quest and Caution: Psychomachy in Shelley's *Alastor*', *English Studies in Canada*, 3 (1977), 289–306; Ronald Tetreault, 'Shelley among the Chartists', *Eighteenth-Century Studies*, 16 (1990), 279–95; Ronald Tetreault, 'Shelley at the Opera', *English Literary History*, 48 (1981), 144–71; Ronald Tetreault, 'Shelley: Style and Substance' (NS); Ann Thompson, 'Shelley and Satire's Scourge', in *Literature of the Romantic Period, 1750–1850*, ed. R. T. Davies and B. G. Beatty (Liverpool, 1976), 135–50; Norman Thurston, 'Author, Narrator, and Hero in Shelley's *Alastor*', *Studies in Romanticism*, 14 (1975), 119–31; Norman Thurston, 'The Second Language of *Prometheus Unbound*', *Philological Quarterly*, 55 (1976), 126–33; Norman Thurston, 'Shelley and the Duty of Hope', *Keats–Shelley Journal*, 26 (1977), 22–8; Tatsuo Tokoo, 'The Composition of *Epipsychidion*: Some Manuscript Evidence', *Keats–Shelley Journal*, 42 (1993), 97–103; Paul Turner, 'Shelley and Lucretius', *Review of English Studies*, 10 (1959), 269–82; James B. Twitchell, 'Shelley's Metapsychological System in Act IV of *Prometheus Unbound*', *Keats–Shelley Journal*, 24 (1975), 29–48; James B. Twitchell, 'Shelley's Use of Vampirism in *The Cenci*', *Tennessee Studies in Literature*, 24 (1979), 120–33; William A. Ulmer, 'Some Hidden Want: Aspiration in "To a Sky-lark"', *Studies in Romanticism*, 23 (1984), 242–58; William A. Ulmer, 'The Politics of Metaphor in Shelley's *Epipsychidion*', *Journal of English and Germanic Philology*, 87 (1988), 535–57; Leon Waldoff, 'The Father–Son Conflict in *Prometheus Unbound*', *Psychoanalytic Review*, 62 (1975), 75–96; Constance Walker, 'The Urn of Bitter Prophecy: Antithetical Patterns in *Hellas*', *Keats–Shelley Memorial Bulletin*, 33 (1982), 36–48; Geoffrey Ward, 'Transforming Presence: Poetic Idealism in *Prometheus Unbound* and *Epipsychidion*' (ES); Tracy Ware, 'Shelley's Platonism in *A Defence of Poetry*', *Studies in English Literature*, 23 (1983), 549–66; Earl Wasserman, 'Shelley's Last Poetics', in *From Sensibility to Romanticism*, ed. F. W. Hilles and H. Bloom (1965); J. R. Watson, 'Shelley's "Hymn to Intellectual Beauty" and the Romantic Hymn' (DUJ); Timothy Webb, '"A Noble Field": Shelley's Irish Expedition and the Lessons of the French Revolution', in *Robespierre & Co.*, ed. Nadia Minerva, 3 vols (Bologna, 1990), II, 553–76; Timothy Webb, 'Naming it: Incest and Outrage in Shelley', in *Shelley 1792–1822*, ed. James Hogg, Salzburg

Studies in English Literature (New York, 1993), 186–204; Timothy Webb, 'Religion of the Heart: Leigh Hunt's Tribute to Shelley', *Keats–Shelley Review*, 7 (1992), 1–61; Timothy Webb, 'Shelley and the Ambivalence of Laughter' (PBS); Timothy Webb, 'Shelley and the Religion of Joy', *Studies in Romanticism*, 15 (1976), 357–82; Timothy Webb, '"The Avalanche of Ages": Shelley's Defence of Atheism and *Prometheus Unbound*', *Keats–Shelley Memorial Bulletin*, 35 (1984), 1–39; Timothy Webb, 'The Unascended Heaven: Negatives in *Prometheus Unbound*' (SR); Alan Weinberg, '*Il Ricciardetto* and Shelley's *The Witch of Atlas*', *Studistica d'italiana nell' Africa australe*, 3–4 (1990–1), 32–42; Barry Weller, 'Shakespeare, Shelley, and the Binding of the Lyric', *Modern Language Notes*, 93 (1978), 912–37; Kathleen M. Wheeler, 'Kant and Romanticism', *Philosophy and Literature*, 13 (1989), 42–56; Harry White, 'Shelley's Defence of Science', *Studies in Romanticism*, 16 (1977), 319–30; S. C. Wilcox, 'Sources, Symbolism, and Unity of Shelley's *Skylark*', *Studies in Philology*, 46 (1949), 560–76; Andelys Wood, 'Shelley's Ironic Vision: *The Witch of Atlas*', *Keats–Shelley Journal*, 29 (1980), 67–82; R. B. Woodings '"A Devil of a Nut to Crack": Shelley's *Charles the First*, *Studia Neophilologica*, 40 (1968), 216–37; Ross G. Woodman, "The Androgyne in *Prometheus Unbound*', *Studies in Romanticism*, 20 (1981), 225–47; Ross G. Woodman, 'Metaphor and Allegory in *Prometheus Unbound*', (NS); Ross G. Woodman, 'Shelley's "Void Circumference": The Aesthetic of Nihilism', *English Studies in Canada*, 9 (1983), 272–93; Michael Worton, 'Speech and Silence in *The Cenci*' (ES); Curt R. Zimansky, 'Cause and Effect: A Symbolism for Shelley's Poetry', *Journal of English and Germanic Philology*, 78 (1979), 209–26.

INDEX OF TITLES

INDEX OF FIRST LINES

ACKNOWLEDGEMENTS

Texts (published and unpublished) have been checked against drafts and/or fair copies where this is possible and appropriate. My main sources are as follows: *Queen Mab* (1813); 'To Wordsworth' and *Alastor* (*Alastor* [1816]); 'Hymn to Intellectual Beauty' (British Library [Scrope Davies Deposit]/*The Examiner*, 19 January 1817, with Shelley's corrections [Houghton Library, Harvard]); 'Verses Written on Receiving a Celandine' (Mary Shelley's fair copy, Houghton Library, Harvard); 'Mont Blanc' (British Library [Scrope Davies Depost]/*History of a Six Weeks' Tour*, 1817); *Laon and Cythna* (1817), supplemented by holograph draft of Dedication, Bodleian Library, MS. Shelley adds. e.14); *On Christianity* (Bodleian Library, MS. Shelley adds. e.4); *An Address to the People on the Death of the Princess Charlotte* (1843 reprint); 'On Frankenstein' (Library of Congress, Washington); *Speculations on Metaphysics* (Bodleian Library, MS. Shelley adds. c.4); 'To the Lord Chancellor' (Shelley's fair copy, Houghton Library, Harvard, supplemented by holograph draft, Bodleian Library, MS. Shelley adds. e.9); 'Ozymandias' (*Rosalind and Helen* [1819]/*The Examiner*, 11 January 1818); 'Stanzas Written in Dejection, near Naples' (Shelley's fair copy, Bodleian Library, MS. Shelley e.5, supplemented by fair copy in Pierpont Morgan Library); 'The Two Spirits' (Shelley's holograph draft, Bodleian Library, MS. Shelley adds. e.12); *Julian and Maddalo* (Shelley's fair copy, Pierpont Morgan Library, supplemented by draft in Bodleian Library, MS. Shelley adds. e.11); *On Love* (Bodleian Library, MS. Shelley adds. e.11); *Prometheus Unbound*, 'Ode to the West Wind', 'Ode to Heaven', 'Ode to Liberty', 'The Cloud', 'The Sensitive-plant', 'An Exhortation', 'To a Sky-lark' (all from *Prometheus Unbound*, 1820, corrected against fair copies in the Bodleian and Houghton Libraries); *The Cenci* (1820); *The Mask of Anarchy* (Shelley's fair copy, British Library, supplemented by Mary Shelley's corrected fair copy, Library of Congress, Washington); *Peter Bell the Third* (Mary Shelley's fair copy, Bodleian Library, MS. Shelley adds. c.5 supplemented by her edition of 1839); 'Bacchus and Ampelus' (text of H. B. Forman in *Shelley's Works* (1880) revised in the light of a new version by E. B. Murray); 'England in 1819' (Shelley's fair copy, Bodleian Library, MS. Shelley adds. e.12); *A Philosophical View of Reform* (unfinished holograph draft, Carl and Lily Pforzheimer Foundation, *Shelley and his Circle*, Volume VI, edited by Donald H. Reiman [Harvard University Press: Cambridge, Mass., 1973]; *On the Devil, and Devils* (unfinished holograph draft, Bodleian Library, MS. Shelley adds. e.9); 'Lines to a Critic' (Shelley's fair copy, Bodleian Library, MS. Shelley adds. e.12); 'To the Lord Chancellor' and 'Men of England' (Shelley's fair copies, Houghton Library, Harvard); The Sensitive-plant (Mary Shelley's fair copy, Houghton Library, Harvard); 'Rarely, rarely, comest thou' (Shelley's fair copy, Houghton Library, Harvard); *Letter to Maria Gisborne* (John Gisborne's annotated copy of *Posthumous Poems*, supplemented by Shelley's draft, Bodleian Library, MS. Shelley adds. e.9 and Mary Shelley's fair copy, Huntington Library); Two Songs for *Midas* (Shelley's holograph draft, Bodleian Library, MS. Shelley adds. e.6); 'Sonnet to the Republic of Benevento' (Shelley's fair copy, Bodleian Library, MS. Shelley adds. e.8 supplemented by fair copy, Houghton Library, Harvard); 'To the Moon' (Shelley's unfinished holograph draft, (Bodleian Library, MS. Shelley adds. e.17); *Epipsychidion* (1821) supplemented by drafts in Bodleian Library, MS. Shelley adds. e.12; '*A Defence of Poetry*' (Mary Shelley's fair copy, Bodleian Library, MS. Shelley adds. e.6 supplemented by Shelley's partial fair copy, adds. e.20 and draft, d.1); Bodleian Library, MS. Shelley adds. e.20; 'Lines Written on Hearing the News of the Death of Napoleon (*Hellas*, 1822); 'The Aziola' (Shelley's holograph draft, Bodleian Library, MS. Shelley adds. c.4, supplemented by Mary Shelley's fair copy, Pierpont Morgan Library); Preface and two Choruses from *Hellas* (1822, supplemented by fair copy by Edward Williams, Huntington Library); 'The flower that smiles today' (Shelley's fair copy, Bodleian Library, MS. Shelley adds. e.7); 'To Night' (Shelley's fair copy, Houghton Library, Harvard); 'Rose leaves, when the rose is dead' (Shelley's unfinished holograph draft, Bodleian Library, MS. Shelley adds. e.8); 'O World, O Life, O Time' (Shelley's fair copy, Bodleian Library, MS. Shelley adds. e.18); 'When passion's trance is overpast' (Shelley's holograph draft, Bodleian Library, MS. Shelley adds. e.12); 'One word is too often profaned' (Mary Shelley's fair copy, Bodleian Library, MS. Shelley adds. d.7); 'To Edward Williams' (Shelley's fair copy, Edinburgh University Library); 'To Jane: The Recollection' (Shelley's fair copy, British Library); 'Prologue in Heaven' (Shelley's fair copy, Bodleian Library, MS. Shelley adds. c.4); 'With a Guitar to Jane' (Shelley's fair copy, Bodleian Library, MS. Shelley adds. e.3); 'The keen stars were twinkling' (Shelley's fair copy, John Rylands Library, Manchester); 'Lines Written in the Bay of Lerici' (Shelley's holograph draft, Bodleian Library, MS. Shelley adds. c.4); *The Triumph of Life* (Shelley's unfinished holograph draft, Bodleian Library, MS. Shelley adds. c.4). Letters are quoted from *The Letters of Percy Bysshe Shelley*, ed. F. L. Jones, Oxford, 1964.

I should like to acknowledge the following debts for permission to consult and quote from manuscript material: Oxford University Press and the Delegates of the Clarendon Press, Oxford for permission to quote from the *Letters of Percy Bysshe Shelley*, ed. F. L. Jones; the Houghton Library, Harvard for 'Verses Written on Receiving a Celandine' and for the fair copies reproduced in facsimile in the *Harvard Shelley Notebook*, ed. G. E. Woodberry, 1929 and in *The Harvard Shelley Poetic Manuscripts*, ed. Donald H. Reiman (New York and London, 1991); the Pierpont Morgan Library, New York for *Julian and Maddalo*, 'Stanzas Written in Dejection' and 'The Aziola'; the Henry Huntington Library, San Marino California for *Letter to Maria Gisborne* and for Edward Williams' fair copy of choruses from *Hellas*; the Library of Congress, Washington for Mary Shelley's fair copy of *The Mask of Anarchy*, and for Shelley's review of *Frankenstein*; the British Library for the Wise MS. of *The Mask of Anarchy* and for 'To Jane: The Recollection'; to the John Rylands University Library, Manchester for 'The keen stars were twinkling'; Edinburgh University Library for 'To Edward Williams'; Barclay's Bank and the British Library for 'Hymn to Intellectual Beauty' and 'Mont Blanc' Scrope Davies Deposit; the Carl and Lily Pforzheimer Foundation, *Shelley and his Circle* and Donald H. Reiman for passages from *A Philosophical View of Reform*. I would especially like to thank the Keeper of Western Manuscripts, the Bodleian Library, Oxford, for permission to consult and quote the Shelley manuscripts.

Like all students of Shelley, my work has been enormously assisted by the appearance of the Garland series devoted to the *Manuscripts of the Younger Romantics* under the inspirational general guidance of Donald H. Reiman. Within the confines of the present edition it is not possible to signal every individual debt to these volumes (or indeed to all my editorial predecessors). However, I would like to offer my warmest admiration and gratitude to the editors in question, specifically to Irving Massey, P. M. S. Dawson, E. B. Murray, Carlene A. Adamson, Tatsuo Tokoo (whose index to the Bodleian Shelley manuscripts is also invaluable), Neil Fristat, Michael Erkelenz, Nora Crook, Steven E. Jones, Michael C. Neth, Michael O'Neill, and Mary A. Quinn.

My debts to fellow-scholars and readers of Shelley are numerous. In particular, I would like to express my special gratitude to the following: E. B. Murray, my co-editor of *The Prose Works of Percy Bysshe Shelley*, whose edition of the first volume, general example and work on numerous thoughtful texts, such as that of *Notes on Sculpture* has greatly influenced my own practice; P. M. S. Dawson, my fellow-editor of MS. Shelley adds. e.9 for the Garland *Manuscripts of the Younger Romantics* whose initiative and unfailing energy was a great inspiration; Michael O'Neill, who kindly allowed me to consult his fascinating work on the manuscripts of *A Defence of Poetry*; the late Geoffrey

Matthews and Kelvin Everest, whose Longman edition of *The Poems of Shelley*, volume 1 (1989) set editorial standards to which we all aspire; all the other editors of volumes in the Garland series, whose ground-breaking work helped to disentangle so many manuscript knots and conundrums; Carlene Adamson, whose pioneering work on the methodology of recording manuscript evidence was a revelation; Timothy Burnett and Judith Chernaik, for their work on the Scrope Davies papers; W. J. McTaggart for his work on the Dedication to *Laon and Cythna*; Bruce Barker-Benfield for his invaluable and authoritative assistance in the technicalities of Shelley manuscripts; and many others, including particularly John Donovan, Nora Crook, Michael O'Neill, Stephen Cheeke and George Donaldson, all of whom have helped to illuminate my understanding of Shelley. Without the immeasurable contribution of Donald Reiman, both as editor and as the inspiration and driving force behind the Garland series, my own work would have been much the poorer. The first edition of my *Selected Poems* appeared at the same time as his influential Norton Edition of *Shelley's Poetry and Prose* (edited with Sharon B. Powers) but I have been able to profit from this example in the preparation of this revised and expanded version. This edition also owes a special debt to Cecilia Smith who has helped to prepare the text with exemplary patience and attention to detail. Finally, and once again, I would like to pay a special tribute to my wife Ruth who has tolerated Shelley and Shelley manuscripts for many years and without whose support and understanding this edition could never have been finished.

POETRY
IN EVERYMAN

A SELECTION

Silver Poets of the Sixteenth Century

EDITED BY

DOUGLAS BROOKS-DAVIES
A new edition of this famous
Everyman collection **£6.99**

Complete Poems

JOHN DONNE
The father of metaphysical verse in
this highly-acclaimed edition **£6.99**

Complete English Poems, Of Education, Areopagitica

JOHN MILTON
An excellent introduction to
Milton's poetry and prose **£6.99**

Selected Poems

JOHN DRYDEN
A poet's portrait of Restoration
England **£4.99**

Selected Poems and Prose

PERCY BYSSHE SHELLEY
'The essential Shelley' in one
volume **£3.50**

Women Romantic Poets 1780-1830: An Anthology

Hidden talent from the Romantic era
rediscovered **£5.99**

Poems in Scots and English

ROBERT BURNS
The best of Scotland's greatest lyric
poet **£4.99**

Selected Poems

D. H. LAWRENCE
A new, authoritative selection
spanning the whole of Lawrence's
literary career **£4.99**

The Poems

W. B. YEATS
Ireland's greatest lyric poet
surveyed in this ground-breaking
edition **£7.99**

EVERYMAN
EVERYMAN'S
BOOK OF
EVERGREEN
VERSE
EDITED BY
DAVID HERBERT

£5.99

ESSAYS, CRITICISM AND HISTORY
IN EVERYMAN

A SELECTION

The Embassy to Constantinople and Other Writings
LIUDPRAND OF CREMONA
An insider's view of political machinations in medieval Europe **£5.99**

Speeches and Letters
ABRAHAM LINCOLN
A key document of the American Civil War **£4.99**

Essays
FRANCIS BACON
An excellent introduction to Bacon's incisive wit and moral outlook **£3.99**

Puritanism and Liberty: Being the Army Debates (1647-49) from the Clarke Manuscripts
A fascinating revelation of Puritan minds in action **£7.99**

Biographia Literaria
SAMUEL TAYLOR COLERIDGE
A masterpiece of criticism, marrying the study of literature with philosophy **£4.99**

Essays on Literature and Art
WALTER PATER
Insights on culture and literature from a major voice of the 1890s **£3.99**

Chesterton on Dickens: Criticisms and Appreciations
A landmark in Dickens criticism, rarely surpassed **£4.99**

Essays and Poems
R. L. STEVENSON
Stevenson's hidden treasures in a new selection **£4.99**

£3.99

SHORT STORY COLLECTIONS
IN EVERYMAN

A SELECTION

The Secret Self 1:
Short Stories by Women
'A superb collection' *Guardian* **£4.99**

Selected Short Stories
and Poems
THOMAS HARDY
The best of Hardy's Wessex in a
unique selection **£4.99**

The Best of
Sherlock Holmes
ARTHUR CONAN DOYLE
All the favourite adventures in one
volume **£4.99**

Great Tales of Detection
Nineteen Stories
Chosen by Dorothy L. Sayers **£3.99**

Short Stories
KATHERINE MANSFIELD
A selection displaying the remark-
able range of Mansfield's writing
£3.99

Selected Stories
RUDYARD KIPLING
Includes stories chosen to reveal the
'other' Kipling **£4.50**

The Strange Case of
Dr Jekyll and Mr Hyde
and Other Stories
R. L. STEVENSON
An exciting selection of gripping
tales from a master of suspense **£3.99**

The Day of Silence and
Other Stories
GEORGE GISSING
Gissing's finest stories, available for
the first time in one volume **£4.99**

Selected Tales
HENRY JAMES
Stories portraying the tensions
between private life and the outside
world **£5.99**

£4.99